The Official Guide to Corel® WordPerfect® Suite for Windows® 95

About the Author...

Alan Neibauer has published over 20 popular books on computer hardware and software, including **Word for Windows 95 Made Easy** and **Access for Busy People**. A graduate of the University of Pennsylvania's Wharton School, Neibauer has taught at the high school, college, and corporate levels, and is a frequent corporate trainer for WordPerfect and Quattro Pro.

The Official Guide to Corel® WordPerfect® Suite for Windows® 95

Alan Neibauer

Osborne/**McGraw-Hill**

Berkeley New York St. Louis San Francisco
Auckland Bogotá Hamburg London
Madrid Mexico City Milan Montreal
New Delhi Panama City Paris São Paulo
Singapore Sydney Tokyo Toronto

Osborne/**McGraw-Hill**
2600 Tenth Street
Berkeley, California 94710
U.S.A.

For information on translations or book distributors outside the U.S.A., or to arrange bulk purchase discounts for sales promotions, premiums, or fundraisers, please contact Osborne/**McGraw-Hill** at the above address.

The Official Guide to Corel® WordPerfect® Suite for Windows® 95

    7890 DOC 9987

    0-07-882237-8

Publisher: Brandon A. Nordin
Acquisitions Editor: Megg Bonar
Project Editor: Judy Ziajka
Copy Editor: Gary Morris
Editorial Assistants: Heidi Poulin, Gordon Hurd
Proofreader: Linda Medoff
Indexer: David Heiret
Illustrator: Leslee Bassin
Computer Designer: Jani Beckwith
Cover Designer: TMA

Ma Chère Babbette

CONTENTS AT A GLANCE

PART I
Guide to Corel Office 7

CONTENTS

PART II

Corel WordPerfect

PART III

Corel Quattro Pro

PART IV

Corel Presentations

The Official Guide to Corel® WordPerfect® Suite for Windows® 95 is a new title in the series of books dedicated to the users of Corel software. The titles in this series give users the ability to understand the depths of the software products they have purchased. The authors, along with the staff at Corel, have spent many hours working on the accuracy and features included in this book.

This book provides an in-depth overview of Corel's Windows 95 Suite product. The Corel WordPerfect Suite presents an exciting combination of powerful products which, we believe, provide significant value for users. The products in the Suite are seamlessly integrated to allow you to design and create documents with ease, and to take advantage of the product's powerful features.

The "Official Guide to Corel products" series represents a giant step in the ability of Corel to disseminate information to our users through the help of Osborne/McGraw-Hill and the fine authors involved in the series. Congratulations to the team at Osborne who have created this excellent book.

Dr. Michael C. J. Cowpland
President & CEO
Corel Corporation

FOREWORD

I've been using and writing about WordPerfect since version 4.2 for DOS, and have enjoyed watching its evolution over the years. WordPerfect was always a remarkable program that consistently improved with each release. Writing about the entire Corel WordPerfect Suite has been no less enjoyable, thanks to the staff at both Osborne/McGraw-Hill and Corel Corporation.

I wondered how we could handle the task of covering so many powerful and integrated applications in one book during the minimal time available. I've found that almost anything can be done when caring professionals work toward the same goal—a readable and complete book that truly represents the capabilities of the software.

My thanks to everyone who worked on this project, especially acquisitions editor Megg Bonar, senior project editor Janet Walden, project editor Judy Ziajka, copy editor Gary Morris, proofreader Linda Medoff, and indexer David Heiret.

Thanks also to the Osborne production team of Marcela Hancik, Jani Beckwith, Richard Whitaker, Peter Hancik, Lance Ravella, all of whom worked marvelously on this project.

Special thanks to the staff at Corel Corporation for technically reviewing the book. Thanks to Bruce Michelsen, Deena Tripp, Daniel Maryon, Julia VanDerwerken, Deirdre Calhoun, Susan Smith, George King, Elizabeth Slaughter, Lisa Baker, Kristen Black, Rick Brough, Karen Todd, Robert Waite, Brad Sulton, and Stewart Peatross.

Working alongside of me throughout this entire project has been my wife Barbara. Not only did she help keep me on track, but she coordinated our move to a new home at the same time. She was patient when I couldn't help her pack or hunt down lost items. She was understanding when I needed her help to find files and organize paperwork. We had our first date almost 33 years from the day I am writing this, and I thank providence for the honor of knowing her.

ACKNOWLEDGMENTS

Good things are often worth waiting for, and if you've waited for the Corel WordPerfect Suite you certainly will not be disappointed. What a package! The power of Windows 95 and the versatility and integration of the Suite applications make an unbeatable combination.

Consider Corel WordPerfect. In addition to all of the capabilities that you'd expect from a world-class word processing program, it checks your spelling and adds formats as you type, helps you create professional-looking Web documents, and gives you great workgroup features.

Want more? Use Corel Quattro Pro to link worksheets to the Web, analyze information and databases, and create maps illustrating the geographic distribution of your data.

Still not enough? Design professional slide shows with Corel Presentations, and publish the shows to the Web, complete with framed pages of hypertext links. Web surfers can even download your entire presentation, with sounds, graphics, and slide transitions and animations.

If you are still not convinced, then just imagine all those features along with:

- Creating charts and diagrams with CorelFLOW

- Organizing your schedule, contacts, and information with Sidekick 95

- Taming Windows 95 with Dashboard 95

- Accessing ten thousand clipart images and graphics

- Selecting from 150 fonts

- Surfing the Net with AT&T WorldNet and Netscape Navigator

All this—and more—in one tightly integrated package. It is a lot of computing power, and you have this book to help you make sense of it all.

The Official Guide to Corel® WordPerfect® Suite for Windows® 95 covers all of the Suite's key features, with enough detail and illustrations so you'll be using the software almost as fast as you can install it. As a Corel "Official Guide," every instruction in the book has been checked and approved by the experts at Corel Corporation, and just like the Suite itself, this book packs quite a punch.

In the first three chapters you will learn to use the common elements that run through the Suite's major applications—including the Corel Address Book, file management with QuickFinder, and writing tools such as Spell Check, Thesaurus, Grammatik, and QuickCorrect. You will learn to use the Desktop Application Director (DAD) and Accessories menu to work with the Suite, and special DAD features such as QuickTasks and QuickConnect. In Chapter 3 you will learn how the Suite is integrated with the Internet, and how to connect to AT&T WorldNet using Netscape Navigator for electronic mail, joining news groups, and surfing the Web.

Chapters 4 through 13 are all about Corel WordPerfect, the powerhouse word processing program praised by millions of devoted users around the world. In Chapter 4 you will learn how to create, save, and print documents, as well as how to check your spelling as you type, insert and delete text, and change the view and magnification of text and graphics on the screen. Chapter 5 is all about editing documents, and teaches you how to perform tasks such as moving and copying text, finding and replacing text, inserting comments and bookmarks, working with multiple windows, and revising documents. Formatting characters, lines, and paragraphs is covered in Chapter 6. In Chapter 7 you will learn how to create professional-looking Web pages, complete with hyperlinks, and how to use templates and styles. Templates let you create completely formatted documents, such as newsletters, with a few clicks of the mouse.

In Chapter 8 you will learn how to format pages by changing margins and page size, set up pages for binding and printing on both sides, and print booklets, envelopes, and labels. Creating tables and working with columns are covered in Chapter 9. You will learn how to create and format tables, even adding formulas and functions to perform math, and how to create multiple-column documents.

If you want to customize Corel WordPerfect or create macros to save you from repeating keystrokes, then check out Chapter 10. There you will also learn how to create custom toolbars and menus, and how to assign key combinations to your favorite tasks.

Creating form documents is covered in Chapter 11, and you'll learn all about Corel WordPerfect's graphics features in Chapter 12, which includes sections about adding pictures and charts, formatting equations, and creating special effects with text. Finally, you will learn how to share information between applications in Chapter 13, so you won't have to retype any information to use it in another program.

Corel Quattro Pro is the focus of Chapters 14 through 20. This powerful program lets you create worksheets, graphs and maps, databases, and even slide shows. After learning what the program is all about in Chapter 14, you will learn how to create worksheets in Chapter 15, and Chapter 16 teaches you how to edit and format worksheet contents.

Chapter 17 explains how to work with blocks of information, use multiple windows, and manipulate entire notebooks. Adding maps, charts, and graphics to worksheets is discussed in Chapter 18, along with combining graphics and bullet charts into slide shows. Using the map feature, for example, you can show a map of the United States, along with major highways, illustrating the geographic distribution of your company's sales or organization's membership.

In Chapter 19 you will learn how to use sophisticated but easy tools to analyze the information in your worksheet, and in Chapter 20 you'll learn how to create macros and share information with other applications.

Corel Presentations is covered in Chapters 21 through 23. You will learn how to create slides of all types in Chapter 21, add eye-catching graphics in Chapter 22, and then build complete slide shows in Chapter 23. You'll even learn how to take your slide show on the road, and how to publish it to the Internet completed with framed pages.

Finally, Chapters 24 to 27 cover CorelFLOW 3 and the bonus applications Envoy, Sidekick 95, and Dashboard 95. CorelFLOW 3 lets you design diagrams of all types—flow charts, organization charts, family trees, network diagrams, and more. With Envoy, you can make your Corel WordPerfect Suite documents, worksheets, and slide shows available to everyone—even if they do not have the Suite applications. Sidekick 95 lets you organize and keep track of appointments, people, places, and things in one handy program, and Dashboard 95 is a spiffy interface for working with all of your programs and Windows 95 features.

Because this book is organized by Suite application, you do not have to read it from cover to cover. You should read the first three chapters to get acquainted with the Suite, but then you can jump ahead to the section or chapter you are most interested in. You can read the other sections later to learn how the remaining applications and features work, so you can take full advantage of the Suite. You'll find easy-to-follow, step-by-step instructions and clear but complete details on the features that you'll want to use.

You'll also find some helpful elements along the way:

 Look for these tips to learn how the features of the Suite applications are integrated.

 OTE: *Here you'll find some additional bits of information about the topic being discussed.*

IP: *Look here for shortcuts or special techniques.*

AUTION: *Keep an eye out for these warnings about potential problems.*

EMEMBER: *You'll find important reminders here.*

The Corel WordPerfect Suite is perfect for use in the office, home, classroom, or dorm. The more you use it, the more features you'll find, and you'll grow to love its ease and versatility. You will especially like its integration with the Internet, and the many ways that you can take advantage of the vast world of resources on the World Wide Web. In fact, once you get AT&T WorldNet up and running, drop me a line describing what you like best about the Suite. You can reach me at **alann@worldnet.att.net**, or at **alann45234** through America Online, or **70365,770** at CompuServe.

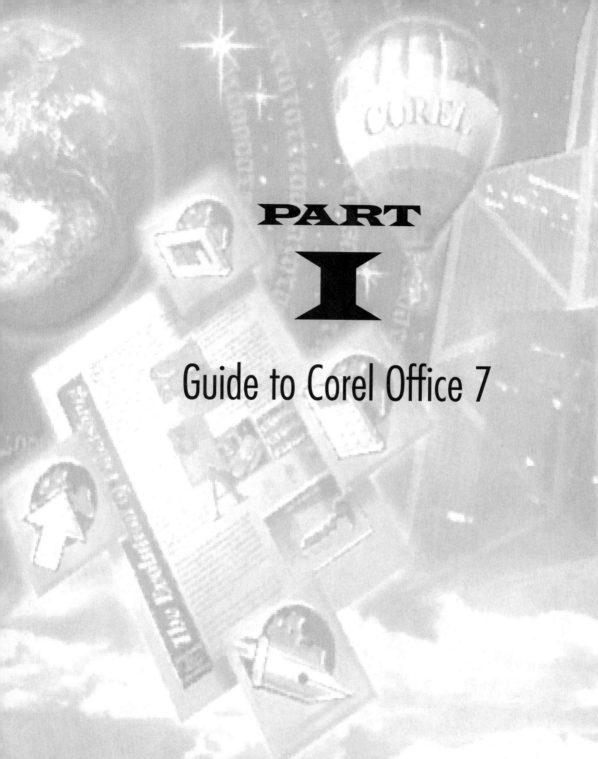

PART

I

Guide to Corel Office 7

The Corel WordPerfect Suite

Corel WordPerfect Suite 7 is a complete set of desktop applications and tools for creating, publishing, and distributing documents of all types. The applications are integrated to provide stand-alone and workgroup solutions and easy access to the Internet and online services.

Integration means convenient flow from one application to another. It also means that you can use the best features of each program to build *compound documents—* documents that can combine text, tables, charts, and graphics—without worrying about compatibility between file types and program features.

Included with the standard version of the Suite are these programs:

- Corel WordPerfect 7
- Corel Quattro Pro 7
- Corel Presentations 7
- CorelFLOW 3

- Envoy 7
- Dashboard 95
- Sidekick 95
- AT&T WorldNet

You also get a wide selection of fonts, thousands of clip-art images, and useful utilities for working with and sharing information.

Integrate IT! *Corel WordPerfect Suite applications and utilities are designed to work together. So, for example, you can easily insert a Corel Quattro Pro worksheet into a Corel Presentation slide and into a Corel WordPerfect document. You can also publish a document to Envoy by just choosing an option from an application's File menu.*

To make the Corel WordPerfect Suite easy to use, the applications are installed directly on the taskbar, and you can access them from the Start menu. Click on the Start button, and point to Corel WordPerfect Suite 7 to see the applications that you've installed and the option Accessories. Figure 1-1 shows the programs included with the Suite, as well as the accessory utilities and applets. These will be discussed later. To start a Corel WordPerfect Suite application or accessory, just click on the program name in the Start menu or use the Desktop Application Director.

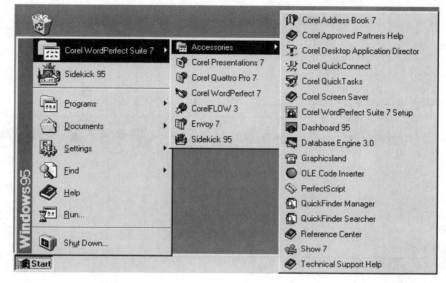

Corel
WordPerfect
Suite Start
menu and
accessories

FIGURE 1-1

Now, before looking at the individual parts of the Suite, look at the interface that binds them together.

Desktop Application Director

Buttons to start the Corel WordPerfect Suite applications and special features have been placed on the taskbar, in the *Desktop Application Director (DAD)* toolbar, as shown in Figure 1-2.

Click on the button for the program you want to run. Also on the bar are buttons to select from QuickTasks, to locate and manage files with QuickFinder, and to launch QuickConnect to browse the Web and other online services that you have installed on your system.

You can also right-click on the buttons to launch one of the features from a menu, to Exit (remove) the bar, or to display the Properties dialog box to remove specific items from the bar.

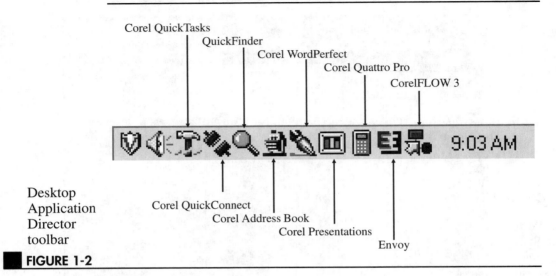

FIGURE 1-2

Corel WordPerfect Suite Accessories

In addition to the major applications and the Desktop Application Director, the Corel WordPerfect Suite includes some useful accessories. To access them, click on the Start button, point to Corel WordPerfect Suite 7, and then point on Accessories to see the menu with these items:

- *Corel Address Book* stores addresses of persons and organizations.

- *Corel Approved Partners Help* lists the names, addresses, and telephone numbers of authorized trainers and service bureaus around the world.

- *Corel Desktop Application Director* opens the DAD taskbar if it is not already displayed.

- *Corel QuickConnect* lets you go to a specific site on the Internet or other online service.

- *Corel QuickTasks* help you create a document or perform another complete Suite task.

- *Corel Screen Saver* displays a Help dialog box on how to use the Screen Saver feature from the Windows 95 Control Panel.

- *Corel WordPerfect Suite 7 Setup* lets you modify your installation by adding or deleting components.

- *Dashboard 95* runs the Dashboard application, if you installed it on your system.

- *Database Engine* is used to configure ODBC, a method for sharing information between databases and other programs.

- *Graphicsland* launches an application for transmitting files to a service bureau to create slides from Corel Presentations slide shows.

- *OLE Code Inserter* will help you insert advanced macro codes into Corel Quattro Pro and Paradox macros.

- *PerfectScript* records macros that open Corel WordPerfect Suite applications and perform tasks.

- *QuickFinder Manager* allows you to quickly search frequently used files and folders.

- *QuickFinder Searches* launches QuickFinder to locate a file or folder.

- *Reference Center* opens a dialog box to access online documentation from the Corel WordPerfect Suite CD.

- *Show 7* will run a Corel Presentations slide show without the need to open Corel Presentations.

- *Technical Support Help* explains how to get customer support.

Corel QuickTasks

QuickTasks are templates that display formatted documents or run macros that perform Corel WordPerfect Suite functions. Choosing a template from the QuickTask dialog box launches the appropriate application and opens the template. All you need to do is enter your own information. If you need to send a fax, for example, you can choose a QuickTask that will open Corel WordPerfect and display a fax cover page.

 IP: *You can also access these templates directly from their appropriate application.*

To display the QuickTasks, use either of these techniques:

■ Click on the QuickTasks button on the DAD bar.

■ Click on Start, point to Corel WordPerfect Suite 7, then Accessories, and click on Corel QuickTasks.

As you can see in Figure 1-3, the QuickTasks dialog box has eight pages of options:

■ *All* lists all of the QuickTasks from the other pages in the dialog box in alphabetic order.

■ *Correspond* includes templates for fax cover pages, letters, memos, résumés, e-mail messages, and for using the Address Book.

■ *Favorites* are the QuickTasks that you use most often.

■ *Financial* includes templates for calculating loan amortization; tracking investments; and for creating balance sheets, expense reports, income statements, purchase orders, and other useful business reports and forms.

■ *Internet* includes options to create and read a Web page, and to track your investment using a Corel Quattro Pro worksheet and a link to PCQUOTE.COM on the Internet.

■ *Organize* lets you create agendas, time sheets, calendars, organization charts, journals, and address books.

■ *Publishing* has templates for creating brochures, business cards, certificates, exams, graph paper, newsletters, pleadings, signs, press releases, reports, term papers, or simply opening a document or spreadsheet.

■ *Utilities* includes adding headers, footers, and watermarks; archiving a file; creating maps and family trees; finishing a document; performing analysis on Corel Quattro Pro data; and copying or linking information from one Corel program to another.

Double-click on the QuickTask you want to perform, or select it and click on Run.

Managing QuickTasks

As with most things in Corel WordPerfect Suite, you can customize QuickTasks to streamline your work. You can add and delete pages in the QuickTasks dialog box, called *categories,* and add and delete QuickTasks.

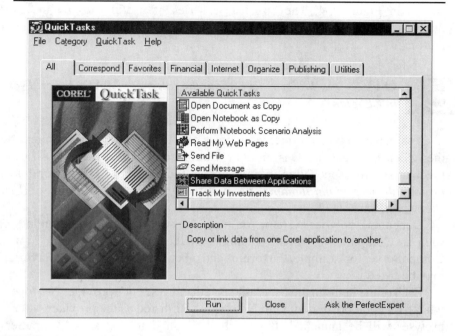

QuickTasks
dialog box

FIGURE 1-3

Use the Category menu on the QuickTasks toolbar to add, delete, and modify the names of the pages in the dialog box.

Use the QuickTasks menu to insert, delete, and modify tasks. The menu, in fact, has two options for inserting items, Add and Create. Use the Add option to insert an item that launches an application and opens a file. This is perfect for quickly opening one of your own templates and frequently used documents.

Use the Create option to record and insert a macro. You choose the Corel WordPerfect Suite application you want to write the macro in. The program will run and the record macro function will begin. When you have finished recording the macro, it is added to the QuickTask page of your choice.

Corel QuickConnect

QuickConnect is a fast way to launch yourself into cyberspace. Click on the QuickConnect button, or select it from the Accessories menu, to see the dialog box shown in Figure 1-4. The box lists a series of useful sites on the Internet—double-click on the site you want to connect to, or click on it and then on the Connect button.

OTE: *You'll learn more about the Internet and AT&T WorldNet in Chapter 3.*

You can also type an Internet address or URL in the Connect To text box, and then click Connect. URL is an abbreviation for Uniform Resource Locator, the mechanism for specifying filenames on the Internet. The general syntax is *protocol://server/path/filename*, as in http://www.wordperfect.com/product/frame_wp7.htm.

Depending on your system, you may also see sites from other online services, such as CompuServe, America Online, or the Microsoft Network. If you have CompuServe, for example, the forums and other locations from your Favorite Places may be listed.

Each of the items in the list is associated with a service provider. So, for example, when you click on an item with Netscape URL listed as the provider, your Internet browser will be launched. If you click on an item that says CompuServe, the CompuServe Information Manager will be launched.

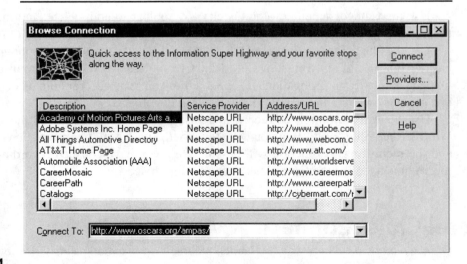

Using Quick-Connect

FIGURE 1-4

IP: *If Netscape starts but does not dial out to AT&T WorldNet, look for a shortcut on your desktop called "Shortcut to AT&T WorldNet," and double-click on it to start Dial Up Networking.*

QuickFinder

Even with the Windows Explorer, finding the correct file on your hard disk can be a problem. The Suite can help you, though, with QuickFinder. *QuickFinder* is not only available in the DAD bar, but it is integrated into most Corel WordPerfect Suite file management dialog boxes. For example, when you open or save a document using Open and Save, you have full access to the QuickFinder system.

Since QuickFinder is a common utility found in all Corel WordPerfect Suite applications, we'll discuss it in Chapter 2.

Corel Address Book

Use the *Corel Address Book* to store names, addresses, telephone numbers, e-mail addresses, and other useful information about the people you contact. You can also store information about organizations, grouping your contacts according to their company or other affiliation. The address book is fully integrated into the Corel WordPerfect Suite; you can access it directly from Corel WordPerfect when creating letters, envelopes, and labels. You should add your own information to the address book—for example, to use with Corel WordPerfect templates, so your name and address appear on fax cover pages and letters.

Here's how to use the address book:

1. Click on the Corel Address Book 7 icon in the DAD bar, or select it from the Corel WordPerfect Suite 7 Accessories menu. You can also start it from within Corel WordPerfect. The book comes with two pages, My Address and Frequent Contacts, as in Figure 1-5. You may see other pages if you've created an address book in Microsoft Exchange, and you can create additional pages or books. The Frequent Contacts page stores addresses that you contact often. When you first access an address, either from Corel WordPerfect or by dialing it, the address is copied into Frequent Contacts. The address book then keeps a count of the number of times you access the address and records the last contact date.

2. To add a person or organization to the address book, click on Add. A dialog box will appear with two choices, Person and Organization. When you add an organization, you'll be asked to enter its name, telephone number, address, fax number, and comments. You can then insert the organization's name into a person's personal record.

3. To add a person, click on Person and then on OK. You'll see the dialog box shown in Figure 1-6.

4. Enter information into the address book, and then click on OK.

As you type the first name and last names, they also appear in the display name section. The address book will use the full display name in its list, and you can access it for use with templates and other QuickTasks.

You can enter up to four telephone numbers, one for the office, home, cellular, and fax. Pull down the Phone #s list to pick the type of number, and then enter the number in the text box. You have to select one of the numbers as the default that will be listed in the address book and dialed. Display the number in the text box by selecting its type, and then click on Default.

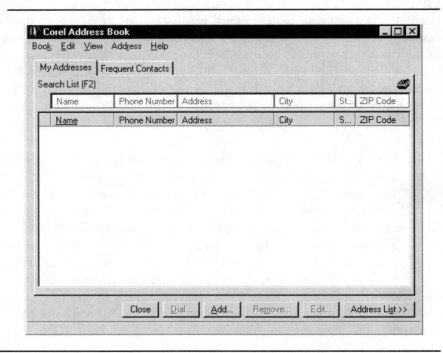

Corel
Address
Book

FIGURE 1-5

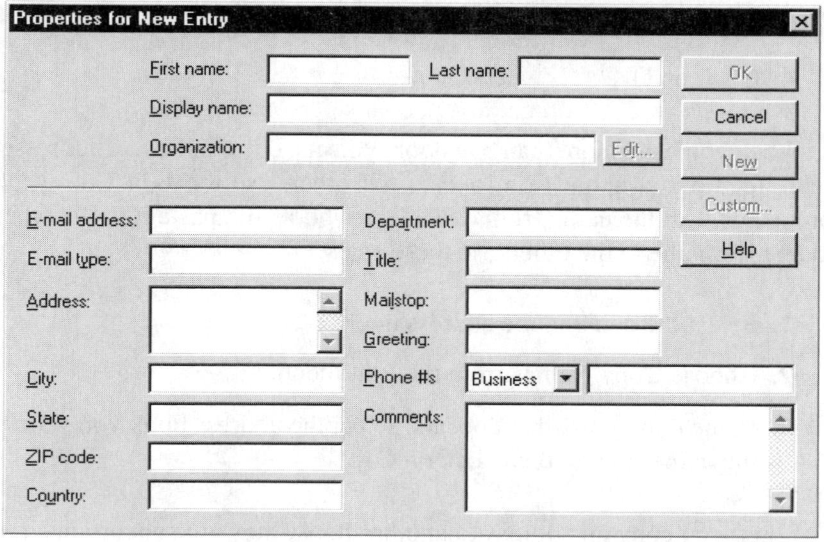

Adding a
person to
the address
book

FIGURE 1-6

When you've completed the entry, click on New to add another without having
to close the dialog box first, or click on OK. Names and organizations will be listed
in the address book, with a small icon designating organizations.

Working with Address Books

IP: *Using the buttons on the bottom of the address book, you can add,
edit, delete, and dial the phone of the selected contact.*

To create another address book, select New from the Book menu and enter a
name. A page for the book will appear in the dialog box. Click on the tab to access
it. To close an address book, click on its tab and then select Close from the Book
menu. To open the book, use the Open command.

You can also make a copy of an existing address book, using these steps:

1. Click on the Address Book tab to open it.

2. Select Save As from the File menu.

3. Type a name for the address book.

4. Click on OK.

When you have more than one book, you can copy and move addresses between them. To move a name from one to the other, use the Edit Cut and Edit Paste commands. Cut the name from one address book and paste it in the other. To copy a name from one to the other, use these steps:

1. Select the name in the address book.

2. Choose Copy Names from the Edit menu.

3. In the dialog box that appears, select the address book you want to place the names in and then click on OK.

When you copy an address to another book, they are synchronized. If you edit the listing in one book, the same changes are applied to the listing in the other. Deleting the listing from one book, however, does not remove it from the other.

The Address List button lets you create a group of individuals. You can then broadcast a message to every member of the group. Here's how:

1. Click on the Address List button. A narrow window appears to the right of the address book.

2. Double-click each name you want to add, or drag them into the address list window.

3. Click on the Save Group button.

4. In the dialog box that appears, type a group name and an optional comment, and then click on OK.

5. The group will be added to the address book, with an icon indicating that it is a group entry.

You can double-click on a name in the address list to remove it from that window.

Sorting Addresses

Your addresses appear in the same order that you entered them. When you're scanning the book to find a particular contact, however, it would be easier if the addresses were sorted in some other order, such as by name or organization. Sorting the addresses also helps you draw some conclusions about your contacts, such as how many are in a particular organization or live in the same city.

If you want to sort on a particular field, right-click on the field name or on any name, to see the QuickMenu shown here. The Sort All option sorts all of the addresses by the values in the first column, either ascending or descending. Choose to sort on the selected column to order the records by the values in the column shown.

You can also sort on a specific column, even one not displayed, by choosing Sort from the QuickMenu to see the dialog box shown in Figure 1-7. Choose the column and the order, and then click on OK. For example, use the Column Sort dialog box to sort the listing by last name, even though the column is not on the default view. An alternative is to add the column and then sort by it.

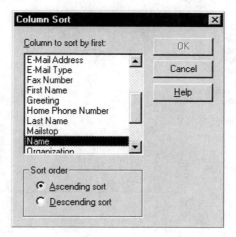

Sorting an address book

FIGURE 1-7

Changing the Address Book Display

The default display shows the most frequently used fields. You can change the order of fields, adjust the width of columns, and decide what fields are displayed, much as you can with a database or spreadsheet program.

To change the width of a column using the mouse, point to the line on its right and drag. To change the position of a column, drag its name to the left or the right.

You can make additional changes using the QuickMenu. Right-click on a column heading to see the QuickMenu that lists the names of most-often-used fields. The fields already displayed will be dimmed, so click on one of the others to display it.

For even more choices, click on More Columns in the QuickMenu to see the dialog box shown in Figure 1-8. Select the columns you want to add or remove. To change a column's width, click on it in the list and then click on the <<, smaller, larger, and >> buttons. These will be dimmed if you select more than one column. Use the move to left (up) and move to right (down) buttons to change the order of columns.

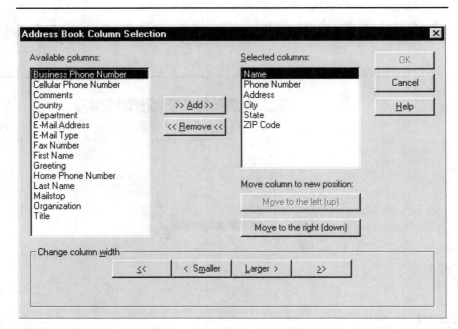

Selecting columns to display

FIGURE 1-8

Searching for Addresses

If you do not have many addresses in your book, you can locate one by scrolling the list. However, this becomes tedious as your address books grow. Rather than scrolling, you can use two techniques to locate an address—searching and filtering.

You search the address book using the search list above the first address. Here's how:

1. Click in the box representing the information you want to search for. To locate a record by the person's name, for example, click in the Name box. You can also press F2 and click on OK from the box that appears to enter the Name box, and then move to others by pressing the TAB key.

2. Type the information you are looking for.

As you enter information into the row, the address list scrolls to display a matching listing in that column. (It does not scroll until you pause typing.) For example, if you are looking for a person named George Jones, click on the Name field and type the name. The list will scroll to the first person with that name. Enter additional information on other columns to further refine your search.

Using a Filter

While searching scrolls the listing, a filter determines what addresses are shown. It filters out those addresses that don't meet the criteria that you create, displaying only those that do match.

A *filter* is a logical statement, such as "Zip Code Equals 94501." It includes a column name (Zip Code), an operator (Equals), and a condition (94501). The statement means "show only addresses that have the value 94501 in the Zip Code field." You can combine several statements in logical AND and OR operations for more exact searching, and you can even group the conditions for a precise selection.

To create a filter, follow these steps:

1. Select Define Filter from the View menu to see the dialog box shown in Figure 1-9.

2. Pull down the list in the first column, and choose the column you want to filter by.

3. Pull down the list of operators and choose from these options:

=	Equal To
!	Not Equal To
<	Less Than
<=	Less Than or Equal To
>	Greater Than
>=	Greater Than or Equal To
[ ]	Contains

4. Enter the value in the condition field.

You can include wildcards in the condition, using the asterisk to represent any number of characters and the question mark for a single character. For example, to locate all persons whose last name begins with "G," use the Equal operator and enter **G*** in the condition field. This tells the filter to locate all persons whose last name begins with the letter "G," regardless of how many characters are in the name.

To further narrow the search, pull down the list by clicking End and choose a compound operator. Select the AND operator to match persons that meet more than one condition. Use the OR operator to find persons who meet one or the other condition, but not necessarily both. There will be a separate row for each condition. Use Insert Row and Delete Row as needed to add and remove statements. For example, Figure 1-10 shows a filter that locates all persons in California, as well as those whose last name begins with the letter "G."

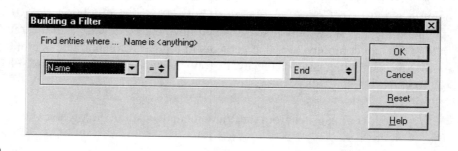

Defining a
filter

FIGURE 1-9

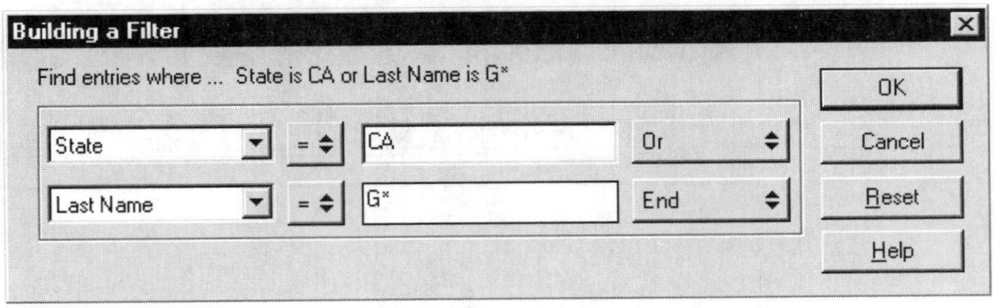

A
compound
filter

FIGURE 1-10

To delete a group, just delete the individual rows in it. Choose End to designate the last condition.

 IP: *Use Reset to remove the filter.*

When you close the dialog box, the filter will be applied, listing just those records that match the conditions. You'll see a small icon next to the Search List that shows that there is a filter and that it is enabled. To display all of the addresses without removing the filter, select Filter Enables from the View menu. The icon next to Search List changes its appearance to remind you that a filter still is defined.

To edit the filter, select Define Filter from the View menu, or click on the icon next to Search List. To remove the filter, not just disable it, click on Reset in the Define Filter dialog box.

PerfectScript

PerfectScript is a macro creation tool that you can use from the Accessories menu. Using PerfectScript, you create a macro that opens one or more Corel WordPerfect Suite applications and performs functions within them. It also gives you a common way to make a macro regardless of the application. PerfectScript does not replace the macro functions in the individual programs. Rather, it provides another layer of utility to access the applications from the DAD bar.

Creating macros from within applications is discussed in Chapters 10 and 20. To create a macro from the desktop, pull down the Accessories menu, and click on PerfectScript 7 to display the dialog box shown in Figure 1-11.

PerfectScript
dialog box

PerfectScript dialog box

Macro	Status	Location	Requestor

◼ FIGURE 1-11

To record a macro using PerfectScript, first make sure one of the Corel WordPerfect Suite applications, such as Corel WordPerfect or Corel Quattro Pro, is open. Then follow these steps:

1. Pull down the Accessories menu from the Corel WordPerfect Suite 7 option in the Start menu and click on PerfectScript 7 to start PerfectScript.

2. Open the Corel WordPerfect Suite application that you want the macro to work with.

3. Click on the PerfectScript button in the taskbar to switch to the PerfectScript dialog box, and then click on the Record button or select Record from the File menu. The Record Macro box appears.

4. Type a macro name, and then click on Record.

5. Switch to the Corel WordPerfect Suite application. The application will appear with its own record macro mode. With Corel WordPerfect, for example, you'll see its macro feature bar on the screen.

6. Record the keystrokes or menu selections that you want in the macro.

7. Click on the Stop button in the application's macro toolbar, or switch to PerfectScript and click on the Stop button.

1

The four most recent PerfectScript macros you created or edited will be listed in the PerfectScript File menu. To run the macro, pull down the File menu and click on its name. The macro will switch to or open the application and repeat the keystrokes and menu selections.

Editing and debugging macros requires knowledge of the PerfectScript macro language and a basic understanding of programming. You can see a list of all PerfectScript macro commands, for example, by clicking on the Command Reference button in the PerfectScript toolbar. You can also click on the Debug button on the toolbar to step through your macros command by command, and to look at the value of your variables. For more information on PerfectScript, search Corel WordPerfect Help and the Corel WordPerfect User's Guide in the Reference Center.

To edit macros, you must first select a macro editor. Choose Preferences from the Edit menu, and click on the Edit tab to see the PerfectScript Preferences dialog box. Enter the path and filename, choose the word processing program you want to edit the macro in, and then click on OK. You can now select Edit from the File menu, and choose a macro to edit.

Using Corel Tools
and Utilities

2

The integration of Corel WordPerfect Suite components gives us the advantage of a common set of tools. Features such as Help and Spell Check and processes such as file handling work the same way in Corel WordPerfect, Corel Quattro Pro, and Corel Presentations. Thus, once you learn the basics of these features, you don't have to retrace your steps with every application. In this chapter, you'll learn how to use these tools that are common to the three major applications.

When You Need Help

All Windows applications come with an onscreen Help system. While each Corel WordPerfect Suite application and accessory has its own help information, the interface works the same in all of them. The Corel WordPerfect Suite has even added some special features to its Help system, including Ask the PerfectExpert, Help Online, and the Show Me tab.

 IP: *Remember that you can access the Reference Center from the Accessories menu to read detailed documentation on most of the Suite applications.*

To start Help from within an application, pull down the Help menu in the menu bar to see these options:

- *Help Topics*—Get help by topic, searching for keywords, and see interactive demonstrations.

- *Ask the PerfectExpert*—Enter a keyword or phrase, or ask a question, such as "How do I print in landscape?"

- *Help Online*—Connect online to Corel via the Internet or online services such as CompuServe or America Online.

You may see some other options, depending on the application. These additional help choices will be discussed in later chapters.

Help Topics

Help Topics is perhaps the most comprehensive way to find information. The Help Topics dialog box contains up to four pages (Contents, Index, Find, and Show Me). Each page gives you a different way to search the Help database for the information you want. If you have trouble finding what you need on one page, try another.

Contents Page

The Contents page works just like a table of contents in a book. You'll see a list of major topics, each with an icon of a book. Clicking on the icon opens the book to display other topic areas, with their own book icon, or specific help topics indicated by the Help icon. Continue opening books until you see a listing for the exact information you need, and then double-click on the topic to display a Help dialog box.

In some of the Help systems you'll see Examples listed on the Contents page. Clicking on Examples displays a dialog box illustrating several samples of documents that can be created with the application. One of the samples will be selected, and an enlarged version of it appears with triangles marking parts of the document for which help is available. Click on the sample that you are interested in, and then click on a triangle to read instructions on how to create that effect.

Index Page

The Index page works like an index at the back of the book. It is an alphabetical list of the keywords in all of the Help topics. Rather than manually scroll the list, however, type the first few characters of the subject you need help with to automatically scroll the list to that part of the index. If the exact topic isn't shown, type a few more characters of the topic or scroll the list manually using the scroll bar. When you see the topic, double-click on it.

Find Page

You can also locate a help topic using the Find page. This makes available a database of all of the words in the Help system.

The first time you select Find in each application, you'll be given a choice of the type of database you want to create. Choose Minimize Database Size for a simple search of words and phrases as they appear in Help windows. Select Maximize Search Capabilities to be able to look up subjects with similar concepts. Choose

Customize Search Capabilities to specify which Help files you want to search. You can later rebuild your database to choose another option.

Once the database is created, you enter a word or phrase that you are looking for. Help displays two lists, as shown in Figure 2-1. One list shows matching words that it found in the database, and the other shows Help topics containing those words. To narrow your search, click on each of the matching words to see which topics it is found in. When you see the topic in the second list, double-click on it, or select it and then click on Display.

If you chose to maximize your search capabilities, each of the Help topics will have a check box. To locate related information, click on the check boxes for the topics you are interested in, and then click on the Find Similar button.

The number of matching topics and the Help settings appear at the bottom of the Find dialog box. The default setting is All Words, Begin, Auto, Pause. Here's what that means.

The Find page of the Help dialog box

FIGURE 2-1

- *All Words* means that the Help topic must contain all of the words that you type in any order. If you type "landscape nut," for example, no topics will be listed because none contain both words.

- *Begin* means that it will look for words that begin with the same characters that you typed.

- *Auto* means that Find will start searching for words after each of your keystrokes.

- *Pause* means that Find will wait until you pause typing before it searches.

You can change these settings by clicking on Options to see the Find Options dialog box. There you can choose to match all of the words or at least one of the words. If you selected Maximize the Search Capabilities, you can also choose to search for the words in the exact order you typed them and to display matching phrases.

The Show Words That option gives you the choice to find words that begin or end with, contain, or match those you've typed.

In the Begin Searching section, choose to start the search only after you click the Find Now button, or immediately after each keystroke, optionally waiting until you pause. The Files button lets you choose which Help files to search.

Show Me

The Show Me page of the Help system, illustrated in Figure 2-2, is a new feature. Click on one of the three options to display a list of topics available and then double-click on the demo, guide, or QuickTask you want to display.

- *Play a demo* shows in an animation how the feature works.

- *Guide me through it* takes you step by step through performing the task.

- *Do it for me* performs the task for you.

Ask the PerfectExpert

Ask the PerfectExpert, the option at the bottom of the Help dialog box, is the same option that is listed on the Help menu. Ask the PerfectExpert allows you to type a word, a phrase, or even a question, such as "How do I indent a paragraph?" You'll get a list of topics that relate to the question—just double-click on the one you want to read about.

The Show
Me page

FIGURE 2-2

Help Windows

When you select a topic, a window will appear onscreen with information about it. A typical help window is shown in the following illustration. This particular screen shows you how to create a header or footer in Corel WordPerfect. It contains a series of steps to follow and a few tips. This box also contains the Related Topics and About options that explain more about the topic. Click on one of the buttons to learn more.

You might also see words or phrases underlined with a series of dashes. These are called *jump terms or pop-up terms.* Click on the term to display a box with a definition or explanation. Click elsewhere in the Help window when you have finished.

You may also see a series of topics, each following a small square. These are additional topics that relate to the subject. Click on a topic to display its Help page.

Click on Help Topics in the Help window toolbar to return to the Help Topics dialog box. Click on Back, if it is not dimmed, to return to the previously displayed Help window. Click on Options and you'll see a menu with several choices, described here:

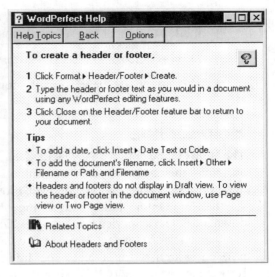

- *Annotation* lets you type a note, message, or reminder and "attach" it to the Help page. When you close the Annotation window, an icon of a paper clip will appear next to the topic. Double-click on the icon to read or edit the note.

- *Copy* places a copy of the text in the Help window in the Clipboard. You can then paste the information into a program. Only the text in the window is copied, not any graphics.

- *Print Topic* prints the contents of the Help window.

- *Font* lets you choose the size of the text in the window. Options are Small, Normal, and Large.

- *Keep Help on Top* controls how the Help window appears when you click on another window. You can choose to keep the Help window on top, displayed in the foreground, rather than moved into the background when you switch windows.

- *Use System Colors* applies the same colors that you see in the Application window to the Help system.

- *Open a file* lists the Help files that are available on your system, even if they are on the network.

- *Exit* closes the Help system.

- *Define a Bookmark* lets you mark a page in the Help system. Use it to mark a topic that you refer to often.

- *Display a Bookmark* lets you go directly to one of your defined bookmarks.

- *Version* reports the version of your Help system.

Help Online

The Help Online option on the Help menu will launch your Internet or CompuServe account—the choice is yours—to link directly into Corel Corporation's Web site. When you select this option, your web browser may start automatically, or you may see the Help Online dialog box, asking which online service you want to use. Pull down the Select a Service list, choose which service you want to use for online help, and then click on Connect. If no services are listed, click on Configure. Your system will be searched for a Netscape Internet browser and for the CompuServe Information Manager (CIM). Then it will display them in the list.

When you select CompuServe, the CIM program will start, dial up your CompuServe number, log on using your account, and move to the Corel Forum. When you select Internet, your browser will be launched, and you'll be connected to the documentation page on the Web for the application that you used to launch Help. Figure 2-3, for example, shows the online screen accessed through AT&T WorldNet when launched from Corel WordPerfect.

You can then get help or other information about Corel WordPerfect and other products, and even download a user manual. You can also find additional help demonstrations and tips and access customer support.

 IP: *If you are on the Web, visit **www.corelnet.com** for even more information on Corel Corporation.*

Quick Help

The Help system is comprehensive, but it does often require negotiating through a series of help topics to find just what you are looking for. There are several shortcuts to getting help that bypass the Help menu.

Many dialog boxes have a Help button—click on it to go directly to the Help system pages for that dialog box. If there is no Help system, press F1—the application will display a Help screen explaining that option in the box. If a dialog box is not displayed, pressing F1 shows the Help Contents page.

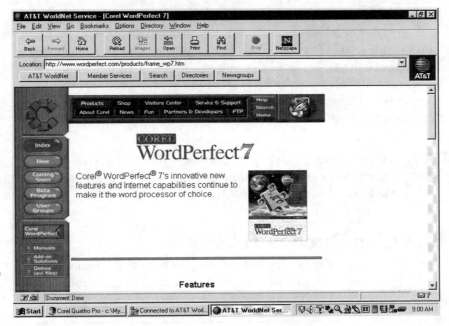

Online Help
from the
Internet

FIGURE 2-3

To find out about a specific item in a dialog box, click on the What's This? button in the box's title bar. The mouse will change to an arrow with a question mark. Point and click on the option you need help with.

You will also see a What's This? option on all QuickMenus. A QuickMenu appears when you right-click on an object. Choose the What's This? Option to read a brief description of the selected object.

Managing Files

Windows 95 offers you several ways to locate files and folders. You can use the Explorer, the Find command from the Start menu in the taskbar, or just surf through your folders starting with the My Computer icon. The Corel WordPerfect Suite incorporates its own file management capabilities directly in dialog boxes, such as Open, Insert File, and Save As, that let you access files. Through these dialog boxes, you can locate files based on their names or contents, and you can access a more powerful search engine called QuickFinder that lets you find files using search tools and logical expressions. You can also set up QuickFinder to index commonly used files and folders for even faster searches.

Figure 2-4 is an example of a file management dialog box, the Open box from Corel WordPerfect. The dialog box has a toolbar, as well as a menu bar of options. The pages of the dialog box offer you two levels of search tools. Use the Browse box to scan for files by choosing folders; to display a preview of a file; or to delete, copy, move, or rename a file. Use the QuickFinder page to search for files based on their names or contents.

 IP: *You can display the QuickFinder file management box by clicking on QuickFinder in the DAD bar, or by selecting QuickFinder Searcher from the Corel WordPerfect Suite Accessories menu.*

Browsing Through Folders

The Browse page of the dialog box lets you list files by the folder in which they are stored. First select the folder that you want to look in. The current folder being displayed

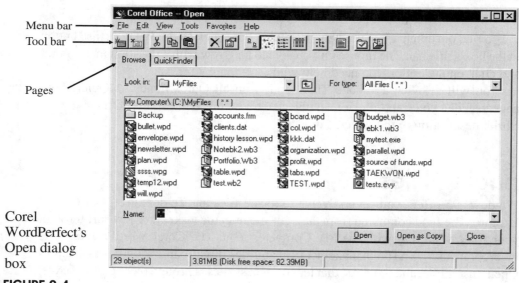

Menu bar

Tool bar

Pages

Corel WordPerfect's Open dialog box

FIGURE 2-4

appears in the Look In list. Under the list, just above the box showing the contents of the folder, is its full path—the drive and parent folders in which it is located.

To move up one level at a time, click on the Up One Level icon next to the Look In list. For example, suppose you are viewing the Template folder in the path c:\Corel\Office7\Template. The large list is displaying the folders and files within the Template folder. Here's what selecting Up One Level will display:

1st click	Office7 folder
2nd click	Corel folder
3rd click	C: drive
4th click	My Computer, including all of your drives
5th click	Desktop

Rather than clicking, however, you can just pull down the Look In list and choose the disk drive that you want to search. For example, suppose you want to find a file on drive C, but located in some entirely different path than the current folder.

1. Pull down the Look In list and click on [C:]. All of the folders in the drive will appear in the large list box, along with files on the drive's root directory.

2. In the large list box, double-click on the folder in which the file is stored. This will display all of the folders and files in that folder.

3. Continue opening folders in the same way until you see the file you are searching for.

IP: *If you know the full path and name of the file you want to locate, you can just type it in the Name box.*

Changing the Default Folder

Corel applications are set up to display a default folder when you first open a file management dialog box. This default will be used each time you start the application, unless you change it using the application's Preferences or Properties commands.

During a work session, however, the application remembers the last folder selected in the dialog box. So the next time you open the box in that session, the same folder will appear. If you do not want the application to change the folder during a session, pull down the Edit menu and deselect the Change Default Folder option.

The Favorites Folder

Chances are there are certain files and folders that you use often. Rather than search for them each time you want to access one, you can store a shortcut to it in the Favorites folder. You can then open the Favorites folder and click on the folder or file that you want to open.

To add a file to the Favorites folder, click on it in the file list, and then click on the Add to Favorites button in the toolbar. You can also pull down the Favorites menu and point to Add. You'll see two options: Add Favorite Folder and Add Favorite Item.

Selecting the first would insert a shortcut to the current folder in Favorites. Selecting the second would add a shortcut to the file. To insert the file, click on the Add Favorite Item choice. To insert the folder, click on the Add Favorite Folder choice.

IP: *You can also add a folder to Favorites by clicking on its icon in either the file list or the tree diagram, and choosing the Add Favorite Folder item.*

When you want to open the file or folder, click on the Go To/From Favorites button in the toolbar or select Go To/From Favorites in the Favorites menu. The folder will open displaying the shortcuts. Click on the folder shortcut to open the folder, or click on the document shortcut to open the document.

IP: *Select Go To/From Favorites again to return to the previous folder.*

Displaying Files

Once the correct folder is displayed, you'll need to display the files. You can do this in either the For Type list (or the As Type in the Save As dialog box), or in the Name text box.

The For Type list will offer some preset choices. Pull down the list and select All File (*.*) if you want to see every file in the folder. The other options will depend on the application you are using. In Corel WordPerfect, for example, you can choose to see templates, macros, or text files. In Corel Quattro Pro, you can select from a list of common spreadsheet program formats.

If none of the choices in the For Type list are appropriate, you can use a wildcard pattern in the Name box. Use the asterisks to represent any number of unknown characters. For example, typing **report*.*** and pressing ENTER will list only files starting with the letters *report,* and with any extension. To list just files with the DOC extension, type ***.DOC**, and press ENTER.

IP: *In the Open dialog box in Corel WordPerfect, pull down the list at the end of the Name text box to see a list of recently opened files.*

Viewing Files

By using the buttons in the toolbar and the View menu, you can select how the folders and files are displayed in the list box. All of the options display an icon along with the filename. The shape of the icon indicates its type.

- Select *Large Icons* to display each filename under a large icon that is easy to see.

- Select *Small Icons* to display each filename to the right of the icon. When there are more files than can be displayed, a vertical scroll bar will appear.

- Select *List* to display each filename to the right of the icon, but with a horizontal scroll bar to scroll left and right.

- Select *Details* to display a list with four columns—the file icon and name, its size, type, and the date it was created or last modified.

Arranging Icons and Files

By default, all items are listed in alphabetical order by name, but with all folders first, and then the files. You can change the order of the files to arrange them by their size, type, or date, as well. Pull down the View menu, point to Arrange Icons, and select the desired order. If you are displaying the files in the Details view, you can click on the column heading. Click on Type, for example, to sort the list by their type in ascending order.

IP: *Click on the heading in which the list is already sorted to change between ascending and descending order.*

In addition to the folder and file lists just described, you can display two other windows—Tree View and Preview. Here's how to use Tree View:

1. Click on Tree View to display the complete structure of your system in a list on the left, with the folder and files on the right, as shown in Figure 2-5. Unlike the Look In list, Tree View lets you expand or collapse the folder structure. A small plus sign next to a Drive or Folder icon means that it contains an additional folder.

2. Click on the plus sign to expand the drive or folder so you'll be able to see the other folders contained within it. The icon will then be marked with a minus sign—click on it to collapse the display.

3. To see the contents of a drive or folder in the list on the right, click on the Drive or Folder icon itself.

The Preview opens a viewer window in which Windows 95 will display the contents of a selected text or graphic file. You can control how the file appears using

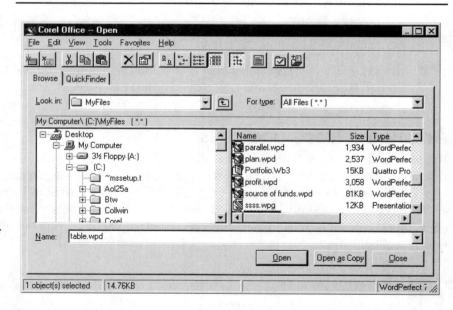

Using Tree View to display the structure of your computer folders

FIGURE 2-5

the Preview option in the View menu. Pull down the View menu, point to Preview, and then select one of these options:

- *No Preview* closes the preview window.

- *Content* displays the contents of the file in readable form.

- *Page View* displays a thumbnail display of the page.

- *Use Separate Window* displays the preview in a separate window, outside of the dialog box.

Working with Folders and Files

You can use the file management boxes not only to display and open or save files, but to delete, move, copy, and rename them as well. So you can perform many of the same functions as you can in Windows Explorer right within the Corel application.

To delete a file or folder, for example, select it in either the tree diagram or file list, and then click on the Delete button in the toolbar or press the DEL key. A dialog box will appear asking you to confirm that you want to delete the item into the Windows 95 Recycle Bin. Click on Yes or No.

To rename a folder or file, use these steps:

1. Right-click on the folder and select Rename from the QuickMenu. You can also click two separate times—not a double-click—on the name. The name will appear in reverse in a dotted box.

2. To delete the current name, press DEL or start typing a new name.

3. To edit the name, press the LEFT ARROW or RIGHT ARROW key to remove the highlight, and then proceed with the edit.

You can move or copy a file or folder to another location. When you move or copy a folder, all of the folders and files located within it move as well. To use drag and drop to move a folder, follow these steps:

1. Display the Tree View.

2. Expand the drive or folder so you can see the location where you want to insert the folder.

3. Display the icon for the folder you want to copy or move.

4. Click on the folder you want to move, and then drag it to the location in the tree diagram where you want to place it. The destination location will become highlighted.

5. To move the folder, just release the mouse. To copy the folder, hold down the CTRL key and release the mouse.

To move or copy a file, use a similar technique:

1. Display the name of the file in the list box on the right.

2. Expand the tree diagram on the left to see the drive or folder where you want to insert the file.

3. Drag the file to the drive or folder and release the mouse. Hold down CTRL as you release the mouse to copy the file.

If you prefer not to use drag and drop, you can use the QuickMenu. Follow these steps:

1. Select the folder or file you want to move.

2. Right-click on the item to display the QuickMenu.

3. Select Move to Folder or Copy to Folder, depending on what you want to do. Corel will display another Browse dialog box.

4. Select the destination location in the Browse box.

5. Click on the Move or Copy button at the bottom of the dialog box.

 IP: *You can also use the Cut, Copy, and Paste options from the Edit menu or the QuickMenu.*

Printing Files and Directory Listings

You can print a file, or a listing of a folder's contents from the file management dialog boxes. To print a file, however, it must have an extension that is associated with an application already installed on your computer. For example, the extension WPD will be associated with Corel WordPerfect, and WB3 with Corel Quattro Pro. You can print a Corel Quattro Pro worksheet directly from the file management box because Windows 95 associates the extension with the application.

- To print a file, right-click on it in the file list, and then choose Print from the QuickMenu. You can also select Print from the File menu.

- To print the contents of a folder, click on the folder, and then choose Print File List from the File menu.

QuickFinder

The Browse page will let you select what folder to display and what files to list. But if you don't know where the file is that you are looking for, you can spend a great deal of time surfing your disk. Corel WordPerfect Suite provides a faster alternative: QuickFinder.

With QuickFinder, you can locate files by their contents. For example, you could list all files that contain the phrase "budget cut" or a document that has the words "budget" and "cut" in the same paragraph. You can also index frequently used files —creating a word list that will make QuickFinder even quicker.

To start a search, click on the QuickFinder page of a file management dialog box. Use the options in the QuickFinder dialog box to locate a file based on its name and contents:

1. In the Name text box, type the filename, or type a * wildcard pattern (such as ***.DOC**).

2. Use the Look In list to choose the location that you want to search. To search your entire system, including all hard drives and floppy disks, select My Computer. Select the Include Subfolders check box to search all folders within the path.

3. Click on Find Now.

 OTE: *A dialog box may appear asking if you want to perform a pre-search to build a file index. Select Don't Pre-Search—you'll learn how to build a file index later in this chapter.*

   IP: *If you see the name of the file you are looking for in the list box while the search is proceeding, click on the Stop Find button that replaced the Find Now button.*

The files matching the name or pattern that you selected will appear in the list box using the same view that was already selected. You can change the view and manipulate the files just as you can in the Browse dialog box. In Details view, however, the box will also contain a Location list. To start a new search, click on the New Search button to clear all of the text boxes, and then enter the new filename or pattern.

You can also search for a file based on its contents. Type the text you are looking for in the Contents text box. To locate all grammatical forms of the word, select the Match Any Forms of the Word(s) check box. If you do not want to search specific files, leave the Name box empty. However, you can combine name and contents searches. For example, you can look for all files that have the .WB3 extension and contain the word "budget." Enter ***.WB3** in the Name text box and enter **Budget** in the Contents box.

Performing an Advanced Find

The Contents option in QuickFinder is useful, but it will only look for one word or phrase. For even more search options based on content, use an Advanced Find. Click on the Advanced Find button to display the dialog box shown in Figure 2-6. In this dialog box, you can specify the arrangement and location of one or more words you are looking for, and you can even look for their synonyms.

Before starting to create the search specifications, however, use the Look In list to choose the location you want to search. The Custom Search option will be dimmed unless you performed a custom installation of the Corel WordPerfect Suite and installed the Word Meanings option.

You now have to create a "search query" that specifies what you are looking for and how you want QuickFinder to search. If you just want to look for a specific word or phrase, then the query is just that word or phrase—type it in the Words box.

A query can also include three search tools to help you find specific text. It can include one or more logical operators to search for more than one word or phrase, an operator specifying the location of the words in relation to each other (the Closeness of Words option), and an operator specifying where in the document to locate the words (the Components option). You must at least specify the words you are looking for. But depending on your needs, you can have one or more of the other elements.

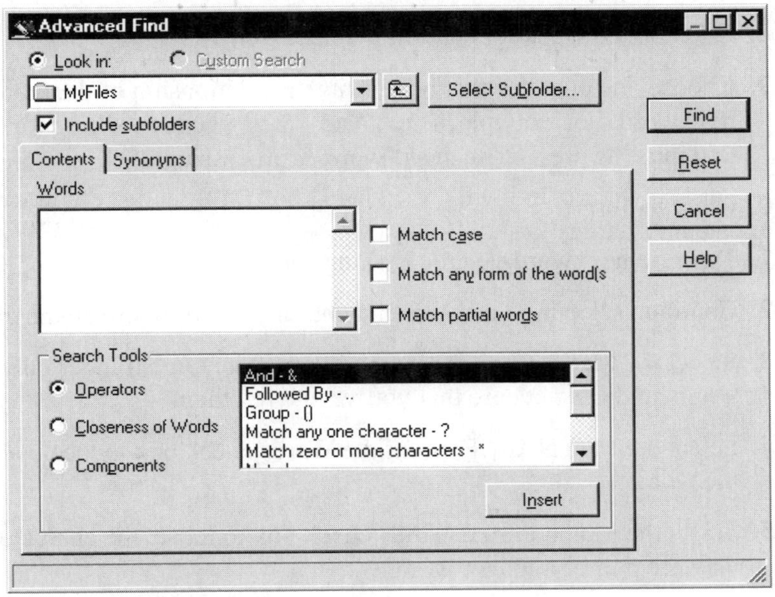

Advanced
Find dialog
box

FIGURE 2-6

Once you open the Advanced Find dialog box, build a query using all of the elements by following these steps:

1. Click on the Closeness of Words option in the Search Tools section.

2. Select one of the operators in the list—In the Entire Document, In the Text of the Document, or On the First Page.

3. Click on Insert. QuickFinder adds the operator as a code into the Words box.

4. Click on the Components option in the Search Tools section.

5. Select the operator that represents where you want the words to be located. For example, you can choose to search for words only if they are in the same paragraph, line, or sentence. There are ten choices.

6. Click on Insert.

7. Type one of the words you are searching for.

8. Click on the Operators button in the Search Tools list.

9. Choose one operator that represents the relationship of the word with the next word. For example, select And - &, if you are looking for two words that must be present, such as "word & processing."

10. Click on Insert.

11. Type the next word you are looking for.

12. Continue selecting operators and entering words to create the query.

13. Select the Match Case check box if you want QuickFinder only to locate words in the exact case that you've entered them.

14. Select the Match Any Form of the Words check box to locate all forms of the words.

15. Select the Match Partial Words check box to locate the characters even if they are part of a longer word.

If you do not want to locate synonyms for the words as well, click on Find to begin the search.

LOOKING FOR SYNONYMS   You can add to your search one or more synonyms for the words in the search query. For example, suppose you are looking for the words "love" and "war." By adding synonyms, you can extend the search for words such as "adore" and "admire," "battle" and "carnage."

If you entered a query in the Contents page, it will automatically appear in the Synonym page. If you did not enter a query in the Contents page, you can type the query or just type the word you are looking for when you open the Synonym page. If you type or change the words or query in the Synonym page, the query will also change in the Contents page.

To add synonyms, follow these steps:

1. Click on the Synonym tab of the Advanced Find dialog box. The words in your query will be listed in the Concept Net box, with synonyms for the first of the words listed to its right. Each synonym will have a check box. If you type or change the words or query in the Synonym page, click on Look Up to list the synonyms.

2. Select the check boxes for the synonyms you want to find.

3. Click on the next word, if there is one, in the Concept Net list to display its synonyms.

4. Select the check boxes for those synonyms you want to find.

5. Repeat the process for each word in the Concept Net list.

6. Click on Find.

Using QuickFinder Manager

When you perform a search for contents, QuickFinder has to look at every word in all of the files specified in the Look In box. If you are searching through many files, this may not be so quick.

To make QuickFinder quicker, you can create an *index* of the files that you search often. The index is an actual listing of every word in the files, so QuickFinder can locate contents by scanning through the index rather than the documents themselves.

Access QuickFinder Manager by using either of these techniques:

■ Click on Configure in the QuickFinder dialog box.

■ Click on QuickFinder Manager in the Corel WordPerfect Suite Accessories menu.

The QuickFinder Manager dialog box is shown in Figure 2-7. You can set up two types of indexes. A Standard Fast Search searches a single folder and all of its subfolders. A Custom Fast Search can include one or more folders, with or without their subfolders. Let's look at Standard Search first.

Creating a Standard Fast Search

If you want to create an index of the documents in a single folder, including its subfolders, display the Standard Fast Search Setup page of the QuickFinder Manager dialog box. Then create a search using these steps.

1. Click on Create to display the QuickFinder Standard Fast Search dialog box.

2. Type a name for the search.

3. Select the updating method. When you select automatic updating, QuickFinder Manager will periodically—every time period that you specify—reindex the files. This means that your searches will be more up to date, but the reindexing may occur when you are performing other tasks and may slow the system response. If you select Manual, you will have to tell QuickFinder Manager to update the index.

 **OTE:**   *To set default options for all Standard Searches, click on Preferences and make your selections from the options.*

You can now specify options to customize the index. Follow these steps:

1. Click on the Options button to display the dialog box in Figure 2-8.

2. Choose an option in the Include For Search section to determine what parts of the documents to include in the index.

3. Choose options in the Other Settings section. By default, the search includes only document files, not graphics files and program files with extensions such as EXE, COM, and DLL, and it indexes numbers as well as words.

4. Set the Search Level. Drag the slider to choose between sentence, paragraph, page, and document. This determines where word patterns must be located.

5. Choose an Extended Characters option.

6. Select where to store the index file.

7. Select where to store temporary files generated during the indexes operations.

8. Click on OK to return to the previous dialog box.

9. Click on OK to begin the indexing.

Using a Standard Search is automatic. Just open QuickFinder and perform a search that includes the folder specified. QuickFinder will automatically use the index.

If you selected to manually update the index, you should perform an update after you change the files in the folder. To do so, display the QuickFinder Manager dialog box, click in the index you want to update, and then click on the Update button. Use the Rebuild button to reindex the files from the beginning.

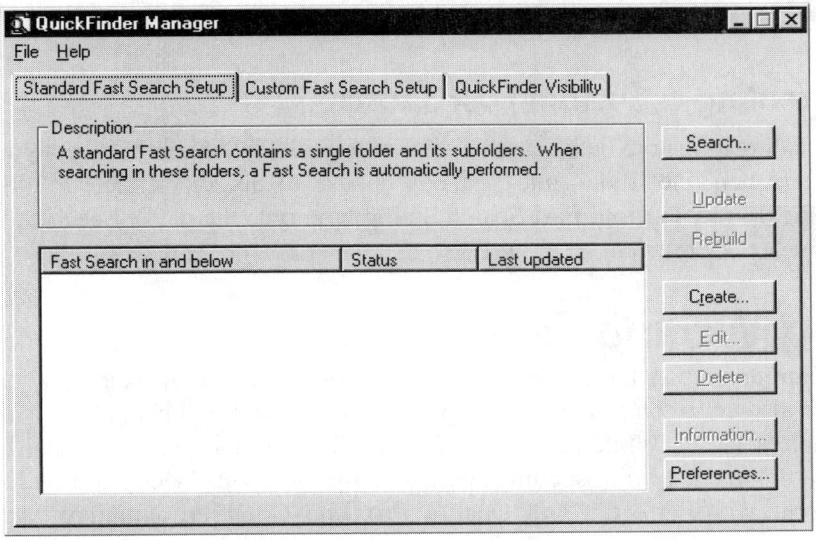

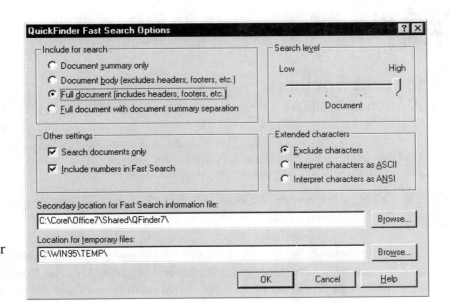

QuickFinder
Manager

FIGURE 2-7

QuickFinder
Fast Search
Options
dialog box

FIGURE 2-8

**IP:**   *Use the Edit button to change the specification of a search; click on Delete to remove a search; or click on Information to see details about the index.*

Creating a Custom Fast Search

Creating a Custom Fast Search is similar to a Standard Search, except you can select more than one folder, and you can choose to not index the subfolders. In the QuickFinder Custom Fast Search dialog box, type the path of each of the folders, or select them from the browse list, and then click on Add.

Using Writing Tools

Features such as the spell checker, thesaurus, grammar checker, and QuickCorrect are also common to the Suite applications, although not every tool is available in each program. While only Corel WordPerfect provides a special Spell As You Go feature to check your spelling automatically, the Spell Check feature can be used in Corel WordPerfect, Corel Quattro Pro, and Corel Presentations. Access these utilities from the program's Tools menu. In this section, you'll review how to use these powerful tools.

OTE: *Spell Check, Thesaurus, and Grammatik are in the same dialog box, so you can switch between them easily.*

Checking Spelling

The Spell Check feature compares every word in a document with those in a built-in word list. If a word is not found in the list, it is reported as a possible misspelling. To start the spell check, pull the Tools menu and click on Spell Check. Some applications also have a Spell Check button in the toolbar.

OTE: *In Corel Presentations, a text box must be selected to access Spell Check, Thesaurus, and Grammatik.*

Spell Check starts comparing the words in the document, the slide, or the selected cells of a worksheet with those in the dictionary. When it finds the first possible error, it displays the word and a list of alternative spellings, as shown in Figure 2-9.

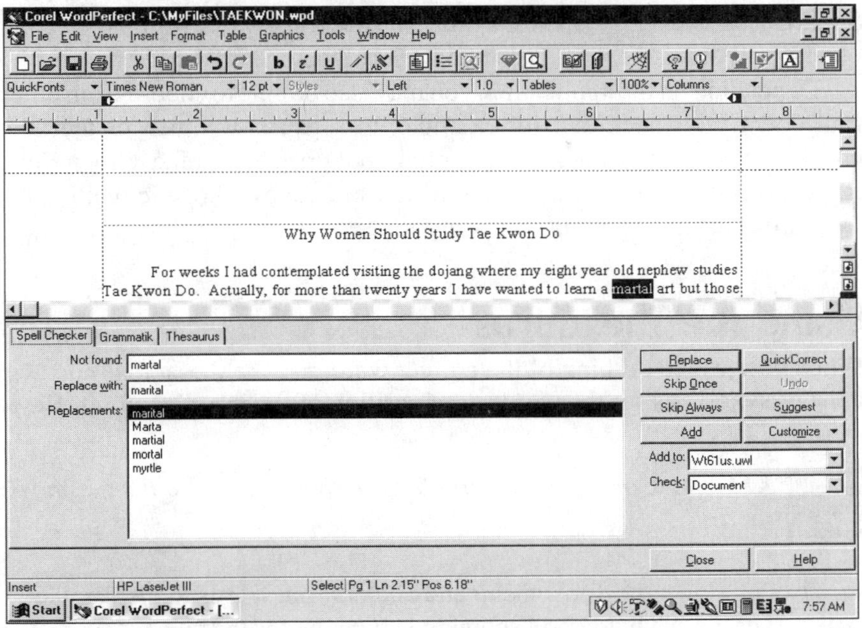

Spell Check
dialog box

FIGURE 2-9

If the Word Is Spelled Incorrectly

If the word is indeed spelled wrong, look for the correct spelling in the list. If it is
there, double-click on it to replace the misspelled word. To retype the word correctly
yourself, type the correct spelling in the Replace with text box, and then click on
Replace. If you are not sure of the correct spelling, try typing an alternate in the
Replace with text box, and then click on Suggest to look up additional words. If you
just want to skip the word and correct it later, click on Skip Once.

If the Word Is Spelled Correctly

If the word is spelled correctly but is not in the dictionary, you have several choices.
You can click on Skip Once to accept the word as it is in this instance—however,
Spell Check will stop at the same word later in the document. Click on Skip Always
to ignore the word in the remainder of the document.

You can also click on Add to insert the word into a supplemental dictionary so Spell Check does not stop at it again. To accept the word for this document but no others, pull down the Add To list and select Document Word List.

Depending on the application, you may also be able to choose from other options. Pull down the Check list, for example, to select how much of the document is checked. You can also click on the Options button to determine if Spell Check should ignore words with numbers and duplicate words, show phonetic spellings, and select what word list and spelling dictionary to use.

Using the Thesaurus

When you just can't think of the correct word, use the thesaurus. This will display a list of synonyms for the word at the position of the insertion point. Here's how:

 OTE: *Corel Quattro Pro does not have access to the thesaurus.*

1. Pull down the Tools menu and click on Thesaurus to display the Thesaurus dialog box showing synonyms for the word at the insertion point.

2. Scroll the list box to select and highlight the desired word.

3. Click on Replace.

If none of the suggested synonyms seem appropriate, double-click on one that is the best possible choice to see a second list of choices. Continue double-clicking on words to add additional lists, until you find one that you want to insert.

 IP: *To look up a synonym for another word, type it in the Replace With text box and click on Lookup.*

Checking Your Grammar

Grammatik is a program that checks your grammar, looking for words, phrases, and sentence structure that just doesn't agree with the program's grammatical rules.

OTE: *Corel Quattro Pro does not have access to Grammatik.*

2

To start the program, pull down the Tools menu and click on Grammatik. When it finds the first possible error, it displays it in a dialog box, such as the one shown in Figure 2-10, along with the following:

- A description of the problem

- A suggested correction

- The rule of grammar being violated

- The type of check being applied

If the suggested correction is acceptable, click on Replace. You can also click on Skip Once or Skip Always to leave the text as it is and to continue to the next

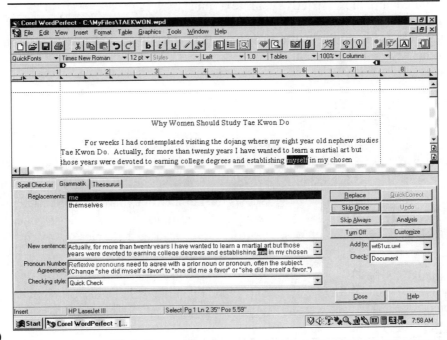

Grammatik
dialog box

FIGURE 2-10

problem. If you want to ignore the grammatical rule that is being violated for the remainder of the process, click on the Turn Off button.

You can also evaluate your writing by clicking on the Analysis button and selecting from the options shown in Table 2-1.

Customizing Grammatik

As with all Corel applications, Grammatik is set up to use certain default values. You can adjust the way Grammatik works, however, by clicking on Customize to see a menu of options. Use the Checking Styles feature, for example, to choose the range of grammatical rules that are checked during the process. You can select from ten general types of documents or sets of rules, such as formal letters or technical documents. The style you select will determine which grammatical rules are applied and how strictly your text must conform to them. You'll be given more latitude, for example, in informal letters than you will on student compositions—two other styles that are available.

Checking Styles...
Turn On Rules...
Save Rules...
User Word Lists...
Language...

✓ Auto start
Prompt before auto replacement
✓ Suggest spelling replacements
Check headers, footers, footnotes in WordPerfect

Option	Description
Parse Tree	Displays a tree diagram of the grammatical structure of your text, including the parts of speech
Parts of Speech	Displays the usage of each word under each word
Counts	Shows the number of syllables, words, sentences, paragraphs; short, long, and simple sentences; big words; and the average syllables per word, words per sentence, and sentences per paragraph
Flagged	Shows the number of each type of error detected
Readability	Shows the reading level, the use of passive voice, and the complexity of your document

Grammatik
Analysis
Options

TABLE 2-1

Streamlining Your Work with QuickCorrect and Format As You Go

It is easy to get spoiled with Corel. Not only will it check your spelling—even as you type with Corel WordPerfect—but it can correct mistakes and insert special symbols and characters as you type. This magic is performed by two special features: QuickCorrect and Format As You Go.

Using QuickCorrect

QuickCorrect can expand an abbreviation and fix your mistakes automatically as you type. In fact, QuickCorrect can correct over 125 common misspellings and typographic errors as you type. For example, if you type "adn," QuickCorrect will automatically replace it with "and." If you forget to capitalize the first letter of the sentence, QuickCorrect will do that also. It will change two spaces following a sentence to one space, and correct two irregular capitals (such as changing "WHen" to "When"). In addition, QuickCorrect will automatically make the following replacements for you:

Replace	With
(c	©
(c)	©
(r	®
--	—
1/2	½

In addition to the built-in corrections, you can add your own. Pull down the Tools menu and click on QuickCorrect to see the dialog box in Figure 2-11. The two-column list box shows QuickCorrect entries that are already defined for you. In the Replace text box, type the abbreviation that you want to use, or a word as you usually misspell it. In the With box, type the expanded word or phrase, or the correct spelling of the word. Then click on Add Entry. Your abbreviation will be added to the list, in alphabetic order. Close the dialog box. Now whenever you type the abbreviation, or misspell the word, QuickCorrect will expand or correct it for you.

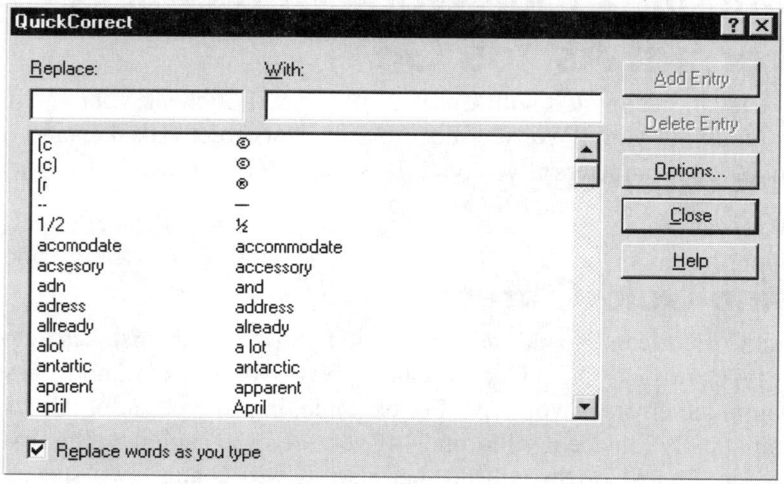

Creating
QuickCorrect
entries

FIGURE 2-11

IP: *If you select text before opening the QuickCorrect box, the text will appear in the With box—just enter the abbreviation for it.*

If you do not want QuickCorrect to replace words for you, deselect the Replace Words As You Type check box. You'll need to do this, for example, if you want to type (C) and not change it into the copyright symbol. To delete a QuickCorrect entry, select it in the list, and then click on Delete Entry.

QuickCorrect entries are not case sensitive. If you already have an abbreviation "pc," then creating one called "PC" will replace it.

Watch Your Case with QuickCorrect

When you create a QuickCorrect entry, pay attention to the case of your characters. If you enter the Replace and With text in lowercase characters, QuickCorrect will automatically insert text based on the case of the abbreviation, as shown here:

You Type	QuickCorrect Inserts
tlc	tender loving care
TLC	TENDER LOVING CARE
Tlc	Tender loving care

If you use any other combination of cases, such as "tLC," QuickCorrect will match the first letter. So "tLC" and "tlC" will both be replaced by "*t*ender loving care."

If you type the With text in all uppercase, it will always appear uppercase. If you type it with an initial capital letter, QuickCorrect will match the case of the abbreviation.

QuickCorrect Options

If you want to customize the other built-in features of QuickCorrect, click on the Options button in the QuickCorrect dialog box. (Corel Quattro Pro doesn't have the Options button.) The options that appear in the box will depend on the application you are using. From Corel WordPerfect, for example, you'll see the dialog box shown in Figure 2-12. Corel Presentations only offers the options in the top sections of the box—the Format As You Go section will not be listed.

The Sentence Corrections section determines the capitalization and spacing within a sentence. It will capitalize the first letter of a sentence, fix two initial capitals, and replace two spaces between words with one space.

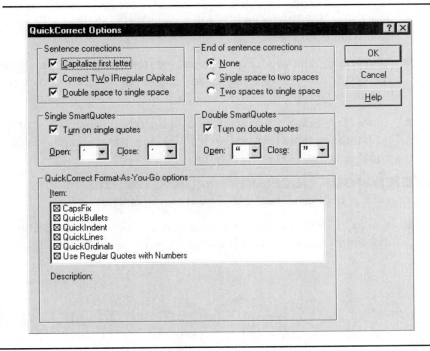

Customizing
QuickCorrect

FIGURE 2-12

The End of Sentence Corrections section determines the spacing between sentences. You can select to leave your sentences as you type them (none), or to replace a single space with two, or vice versa.

SmartQuotes are the curly types of apostrophes and quotation marks that you see in published documents. By default, QuickCorrect replaces the straight quotes that you enter from the keyboard with their curly equivalents. You can choose to turn off this feature, or select another curly quote character to insert in its place.

Format As You Go

Included as part of Corel WordPerfect's QuickCorrect feature is QuickCorrect Format As You Go. These options replace characters to format your document as you type.

- *CapsFix* corrects improper capitalization and turns off the CAPS LOCK key if you type text after accidentally turning it on.

- *QuickBullets* starts the automatic numbering or bulleted list feature. If you start a paragraph with a number or letter followed by a period and a tab, or a special character at the beginning of a line followed by an indent or tab, Corel WordPerfect will continue numbering, lettering, or bulleting the following paragraphs.

- *QuickIndent* lets you indent a paragraph from the left margin. If you press the TAB key at the beginning of any line but the first, Corel WordPerfect will indent the entire paragraph.

- *QuickLines* draws a horizontal line on the screen when you start a line with three or more hyphens, or a double line when you type three or more equal signs, and then press ENTER.

- *QuickOrdinal* replaces the characters "st," "nd," and "rd" in numbers, such as in "1st," "2nd," and "3rd," with superscripts.

- *Use Regular Quotes with Numbers* leaves plain straight quotation marks that follow numbers. This is useful when you want to indicate inches.

The Internet and AT&T WorldNet

3

The *Internet* is an informal network of computers around the world. There are thousands of companies, educational institutions, associations, and other organizations, along with millions of individuals, connected to the "Net" in one way or the other. Some individuals access the Net through their school or company, while others have individual accounts with Internet Service Providers (ISPs) or online services, such as AT&T, CompuServe, or America Online.

The *World Wide Web,* or *the Web,* as it's affectionately known, is one interface to the Net. The Web can be seen as a series of documents, all dynamically linked together so you can move from one document to another, no matter where they are actually located in the world, simply by clicking the mouse, or by typing the document's address and name.

The address of a computer on the Web is referred to as the computer's *Web site.* You don't have to worry about the geographic location of the site, just its address. As far as you are concerned, you can be connected to a site on the other side of the world or across the street with equal ease.

Integrated Internet

Internet access is integrated directly into the major applications of the Corel WordPerfect Suite. As you have already learned, you can connect to Corel Corporation from the Help Online feature, and you can click on the QuickConnect tool to go to any of your favorite sites on the Internet, as well as to CompuServe.

 The major applications in the Corel WordPerfect Suite can read and write Web documents.

The Internet is integrated into the Suite in many more ways, which you'll learn about in later chapters. Here we'll summarize some of the ways that you can take advantage of this wonderful resource.

- *Creating Web pages*—You can format and publish your own Web pages directly from Corel WordPerfect through the Internet Publisher. There is even a Web Page Expert that takes you step by step through the process of creating multiple linked pages.

- *Publishing presentations*—You can publish an entire Corel Presentations slide show on the Internet, and even add a button that readers can click to download the slide show to their computer.

- *Browsing the Web*—You can launch your Web browser from almost anywhere in the Corel WordPerfect Suite—using QuickConnect, Corel WordPerfect's Internet Publisher, or from the Help Online menu selection or toolbar button.

- *Hot links*—You can create hypertext links to Web pages and sites in your Corel WordPerfect document, Corel Quattro Pro worksheets, and Corel Presentations slides. Use the links to launch your Web browser and jump to a site. You can also use them to make documents available on your Web server by placing linked files in a public access directory.

- *Working with Web pages*—You can open HTML files—the source code for Web pages—directly into Corel WordPerfect Suite applications, and you can save your documents, spreadsheets, and presentations in HTML format.

QuickTasks

The Internet page of Corel QuickTasks offers several useful tools. The Create Web Page task, for example, launches Corel WordPerfect's Internet Publisher. Three other tasks are available, as follows.

Read My Web Pages lets you browse one or more Web pages that you want to refer to periodically, such as news pages. When you first start the QuickTask, you'll see the dialog box shown in Figure 3-1. You can add, delete, and change the order of the pages that you want to read. When you click on Next, Corel will launch your Web browser and display the first of the pages on the screen, along with a box of three buttons: Back, Next, and Cancel. Read the page, and then click on the Next button to open the next page on the list.

The Track My Investments QuickTask will let you keep track of investments, such as stocks, mutual funds, and money market funds, obtaining current pricing

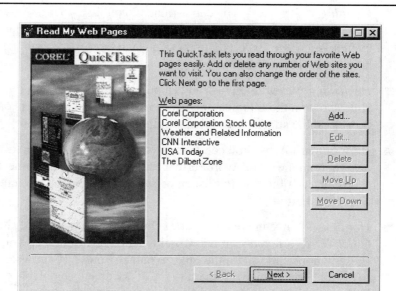

Read My
Web Pages
QuickTask

FIGURE 3-1

information through the Internet. It will create a Corel Quattro Pro worksheet to record and graph value information.

The Track My Stocks QuickTask lets you track the daily prices and volumes of your stock portfolio, recording the information in a Corel Quattro Pro worksheet.

AT&T WorldNet Service

Corel WordPerfect Suite includes all of the software you need to connect to the World Wide Web. All you have to do is install the software and sign up for an account—which may even be free!

 OTE: *If you have the Professional version of the Corel WordPerfect Suite, the Internet browser may be different than described here.*

The service is AT&T WorldNet, and the software is Netscape Navigator. Netscape Navigator is an all-purpose program that can be used to connect to any

Internet service. When you install the software using the Corel WordPerfect Suite, it is set up to access the AT&T WorldNet service. WorldNet not only connects you to the World Wide Web—the Internet's graphical interface—but it offers news, weather, sports, interviews, and other useful information. E-mail is also built in, so your Inbox will check for new mail each time you access the service.

Setting Up AT&T Service

You install the AT&T software as a separate option, not as part of the general installation of Corel WordPerfect, Corel Quattro Pro, and Corel Presentations. The software will let you register and connect to the AT&T WorldNet Service through a normal telephone line. AT&T software is not designed to access the Internet through a Local Area Network. To access the service, you should have at least 8 MB of RAM, 11 MB of free hard disk space, and a 14.4 Kbps or faster modem.

To access AT&T using Windows 95, you must use a feature called Dial-Up Networking. This software is part of your Windows 95 package, not the AT&T or Netscape Navigator packages, but the AT&T setup program will install it for you if it is not already on your system. If you did not already install Dial-Up Networking, you'll need to have your Windows 95 CD-ROM or floppies when you install AT&T.

Close all open applications, especially the Dial-Up Networking folder. Insert the Corel CD and wait until the initial screen appears. If the CD is already inserted, double-click on the My Computer icon on the Windows 95 desktop, right-click on the icon for the Corel CD, and select AutoPlay from the menu that appears. Then click on the Internet Service Setup button and follow the directions on the screen. The setup procedure installs Netscape Navigator on your system, and all of the other files and programs needed to access the Internet through AT&T WorldNet. Then it creates the group shown in Figure 3-2.

Once the software is installed, you have to register for the AT&T service. Double-click on the item labeled Double Click to Set Up Account to run the Account Setup Wizard, and then follow the directions on the screen. You'll be asked to enter your name, address, and other billing information, and then the Wizard will identify the type and speed of your modem. When all of this is done, a dialog box will appear with a button labeled Connect. Click on the button to dial AT&T and to complete the registration process.

 OTE: *If you are an AT&T long-distance customer, you may qualify for a free Internet account of five hours connect time per month.*

AT&T
group in
Windows 95
desktop

■ **FIGURE 3-2**

Connecting to the Internet

Now that you are all set up and registered, connecting to AT&T is easy. You can do so from within a Corel WordPerfect Suite application as discussed previously in this chapter, or from the Windows 95 desktop. Look for the AT&T WorldNet Service icon.

If it is on your desktop, double-click on it. Otherwise, follow these steps:

1. Click on the Start button on the taskbar.

2. Point to Programs.

3. Click on AT&T WorldNet Service.

4. Double-click on the AT&T WorldNet Service icon.

You'll see the Connect To dialog box. Make sure the information in this box is correct—it should be if you registered successfully—and then click on Connect. Your modem will dial the AT&T service, and you'll see the initial service screen in the Netscape Navigator window, shown in Figure 3-3. This is called your *home page,* because it is the initial page of the Internet that appears when you start AT&T.

   IP: *For online information on Netscape Navigator, double-click on the Netscape Navigator Handbook icon in the AT&T WorldNet Service group.*

Some Netscape Navigator Basics

Before looking at the services that are available, you should understand some of the basics of Netscape Navigator, and Web browsing in general.

Location text box　　　　　　Toolbar　　　　Status indicator

Directory buttons

AT&T home page using Netscape Navigator

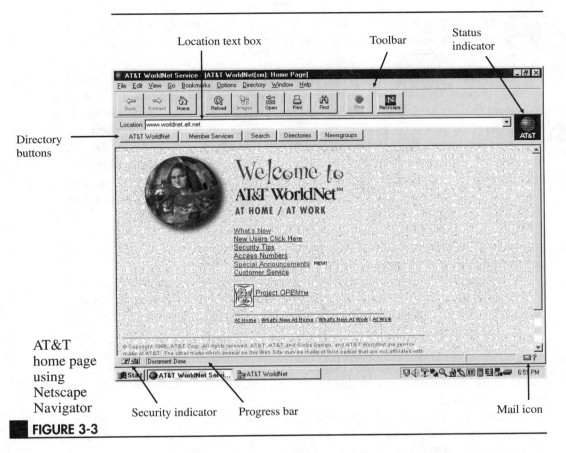

Security indicator　　Progress bar　　　　　　　Mail icon

FIGURE 3-3

It takes some time for information from the Internet to be displayed on your monitor. Sometimes text appears first with icon boxes showing where graphics will appear; then the graphics are downloaded and displayed. As the information is being transferred to your computer, the AT&T status indicator will be animated, and you'll see a message in the progress bar reporting the percentage of the information that has been transmitted, and the speed at which it is being accepted. You may also see messages that Netscape Navigator is waiting for a connection to take place—just be patient. When the entire Web page has been transmitted to your computer, the words "Document Done" will appear. Most pages will be too large to appear on the screen, so you'll see a vertical scroll bar. The information is actually both displayed and saved into a temporary file on your disk called a *cache*. The cache enables Netscape Navigator to quickly redisplay the information without having it transmitted all over again.

IP: *If you get tired of waiting and change your mind, click on the Stop button. If your previous page doesn't appear, click on Back.*

The process of moving from one place to the other on the Internet is called *navigating* or *surfing*. One way to do this is to click on *hypertext links*. These may be underlined words; text in a different color than other text, such as the words "At Home" and "At Work"; or even icons, buttons, and graphics. When you point to a hypertext link, the mouse pointer will appear like a small hand. Just click on the link to connect to another location in the same document, another document on the same computer, or another location in the world. You don't have to worry about where it takes you because you can always return to your previous location by clicking on the Back button in the toolbar.

If you return to the previous page, you'll notice that the color of the links that you've used has changed. This indicates that you have already used the link, but you can still click on it again to return to the page.

Web pages can contain several types of elements—text, links, inline images, and frames. You already know that a link lets you move to another location. A *frame* is a smaller, independent section within the window. Sometimes the contents of a frame can change automatically as you are connected to the site. A Web page may also have inline images—graphics that are dynamically linked to locations on the page and that are transmitted separately. In many instances, the text of the page will appear first so you can start reading and clicking on links right away, with the inline images being added after.

While you are using the AT&T service, you are also using the Netscape Navigator software, so you really have to learn how to operate both. AT&T is your connection to the Internet and to the other features of the WorldNet service. Netscape Navigator is the interface that you use to communicate to WorldNet and to all other sites on the Internet. Remember, while AT&T WorldNet offers information and services of its own, it is really a doorway to the entire world of the Internet. Using the features of Netscape Navigator, you can connect to any Web site, anywhere in the world.

This concept is highlighted by the two sets of buttons in the window. The toolbar, under the menu bar, is Netscape Navigator's. The Directory buttons under the box marked "Location" are AT&T's. You use the toolbar to give commands to Netscape Navigator, and the Directory buttons to navigate around the AT&T WorldNet system.

The purpose of the Toolbar buttons, shown in Table 3-1, is relatively straightforward, but the Reload button may need further clarification. The Reload button tells Netscape Navigator to redisplay the current page. If you view a page long enough, the computer that generated it may actually make changes to the page.

Button	Function
Back	Redisplays the previous Web page
Forward	Returns to the previous page after using the Back command
Home	Displays the designated home page
Reload	Redisplays the current page
Images	Loads graphic images into the page if their displays have been turned off
Open	Allows you to open a specific page
Print	Prints the displayed page
Find	Lets you locate a word or phrase in the current page
Stop	Stops the transmission of the page from AT&T WorldNet to your computer

Netscape Navigator Buttons

TABLE 3-1

When you click on Reload, Netscape Navigator determines if any changes had been made, and if so, it asks the server to transmit the entire page again. If no changes were made to the page, then Netscape Navigator reloads the image from the temporary cache file on your disk.

If you want Netscape Navigator to have the file transmitted again even if changes were not made, hold down the SHIFT key when you click on Reload.

Many Web pages are interactive. They offer forms that you can complete to send mail, or even purchase items through your credit card. In general, most of the information you send via the Net is relatively safe. However, no system is foolproof and burglar-proof. The security indicator at the bottom of the Netscape Navigator window gives you some guidance regarding the security of your transmission. Security means that the information you are sending is being encrypted so only the receiver can use it.

If the icon appears as a broken key, then the transmission is not being encrypted and is considered insecure. If the icon is an unbroken key with one tooth, it is using a medium-level encryption. Two teeth means it is using high-level encryption.

Using the QuickMenu

One other way to control Netscape Navigator is by using the QuickMenu that appears when you click the right mouse button on an object. Netscape Navigator actually calls this a pop-up menu, but it serves the same function as the QuickMenus found in Corel WordPerfect Suite applications. Here are the QuickMenu items:

- *Back* displays the previous Web page.

- *Forward* returns after you select Back or use the History list.

- *Open This Link* displays a specified page.

- *Add Bookmark for This Link* creates a bookmark of the address of the link being clicked on.

- *New Window with This Link* opens the page into another window.

- *Save This Link As* opens the linked document but saves it on your disk rather than displaying it on the screen.

- *Copy This Link Location* places the address of the link into the Clipboard.

- *Open This Image* displays a specified image on the screen.

- *Save This Image As* opens an image but saves it on the disk rather than displaying it on screen.

- *Copy This Image Location* places the address of the image into the Clipboard.

- *Load This Image* displays the image in place of the selected image icon.

- *Create Shortcut* creates a shortcut to the current Web page on the desktop—double-click on the shortcut to launch Netscape Navigator and jump to the site.

AT&T WorldNet Service

Now let's first take a look at the features of AT&T WorldNet. The Directory buttons let you use WorldNet's features:

- *AT&T WorldNet* returns to the home page.

- *Member Services* leads to help and billing information.

- *Search* lets you locate information on the Web by a keyword or phrase.

- *Directory* lets you choose from Internet and AT&T directory services.

- *Newsgroups* gives you access to newsgroup messages and mail.

The AT&T home page offers several links. Click on the At Home link on the AT&T home page for information for all members of your family. The information available, and the items in the At Home page, will vary from time to time, even daily, but a typical At Home page appears in Figure 3-4. To read an item or move to another menu of choices, click on a link of your choice. To find information about health care, for example, click on the phrase "Health & Wellness" in the index on the left of the screen. To get the latest news or weather, click on the corresponding icon on the right.

To return to the home page, click on the Home button in the Netscape Navigator icon bar, or click on the AT&T WorldNet directory button. You can also click on the Back button to return to the previous page.

A typical At Work page of WorldNet is shown in Figure 3-5. This page offers useful business, employment, and economic information, as well as links to other information services and electronic publications.

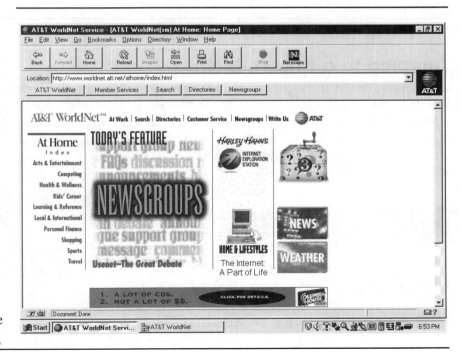

AT&T At
Home page

FIGURE 3-4

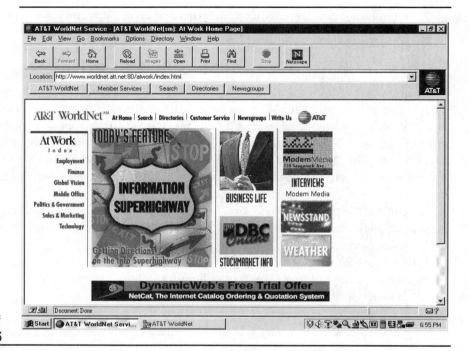

AT&T At
Work page

FIGURE 3-5

Jumping to a Known Site

You can go to a specific site if you know its address. Web pages are identified by a *Uniform Resource Locator* (*URL*) address. A URL is much like your own street address in that it tells the browser exactly where to locate the information. You'll find lists of useful or interesting addresses in magazines and newspapers, advertisements—almost anywhere these days. Type the address in the Location box at the top of the window and press ENTER.

OTE: *When you click on a link, Netscape Navigator inserts the URL into the location box and moves to it automatically.*

The syntax of the URL depends on the type of protocol it uses or its type of interface. Some of the most common are these:

■   *http* for Web pages that use HyperText Transfer Protocol

- *ftp* for transferring files through the File Transfer Protocol

- *news* for Usenet newsgroups

- *gopher* for a menu-driven interface

Following the protocol is the identifier of the computer system that contains the information. For example, the URL for WorldNet is **http://www.worldnet.att.net/**.

Use the pull-down list on the right of the location box to select from the ten most recently used sites. The list is remembered even after you close Netscape Navigator, so you can quickly return to the sites during the next session. During a session, however, you can also view a history of the locations you visited. Pull down the Window menu and click on History to see the URLs of the sites that you visited. To go back to a site, click on it in the History list and then click on the Go To button in the dialog box. Click on the Bookmark button in the History dialog box to add the site to your bookmark list.

Saving Web Pages

When you find a Web page that you are interested in, you can save it on your disk. You can even save a page before you display it, either as a formatted HTML file or as plain text. To do so, follow these steps:

1. To save the displayed page, pull down the File menu and click on Save As.

2. Pull down the Save as Type list and select either Source (*.HTM, *.HTML) or Plain text (*.TXT).

3. Type a name for the file.

4. Click on Save.

Source HTML files will contain the text and background of the page just as it appears on the Net, but without the inline graphics. You can later open it into Netscape Navigator to display it on the screen. To do so, use these steps:

1. Pull down the File menu.

2. Click on Open File.

3. Enter or select the filename.

4. Click on OK.

You can also open an HTML-formatted file directly into Corel WordPerfect and other Suite applications.

If you save the page using the Plain text option, you can open the file into any word processing program. It won't have any of the formats or graphics—just the text of the page.

 OTE: *If you are viewing a page with frames, the Save As option in the File menu will be replaced with Save Frame. Use this option to save the contents of the current frame.*

You can also save a page before you actually display it, directly from the link to it. Point to the link with the mouse and click the right mouse button to see a QuickMenu. Choose Save This Link As to jump to the link, but save it on the disk rather than display it on the screen.

Printing Web Pages

In addition to saving a Web page, you can also print it. Click on the Print button on the toolbar, or pull down the File menu and click on Print to see a dialog box, and then click on Print.

If you are displaying a page with frames, the Print option in the File menu is replaced with Print Frame.

To adjust the format of the printout, pull down the File menu and click on Page Setup to see the Page Setup dialog box. Select Options from the box, and click on OK.

 If you print the page to Envoy, you will preserve the page exactly the way it appears in the Web browser.

Searching for Information

One way to locate information is to follow the trail of links, clicking on them to move from site to site on the Internet until you find the information you are looking for. You can also search for the information using a keyword or phrase. You will be amazed at the breadth of information and services available on the Internet.

Before you go surfing around the Internet using search tools, however, keep in mind that much of the information on the Internet may not be useful, valuable, accurate, or socially acceptable. The Internet is just a ragtag network of millions of computers. No one controls, polices, or censors it—which is actually one of its greatest strengths. Searching for something on the Internet using a word or phrase may reveal a list of hundreds of locations, some of which may have very little—or even nothing—to do with the subject you had in mind.

Follow these steps to initiate a search:

1. Click on the Search button in the toolbar, or the word "Search" on the top of the At Home or At Work pages, to see the window shown in Figure 3-6.

2. Type the keywords or phrase that you want to find—such as a company name or topic. Below the Enter Keyword(s) text box is a series of icons for companies that provide directories of the Internet. They all offer similar types of service, although you may eventually find some better than others depending on your own preferences.

3. Click on the Radio button adjacent to the service you want to use, scrolling the list to see all of your choices.

4. Click on the Search button to begin the search.

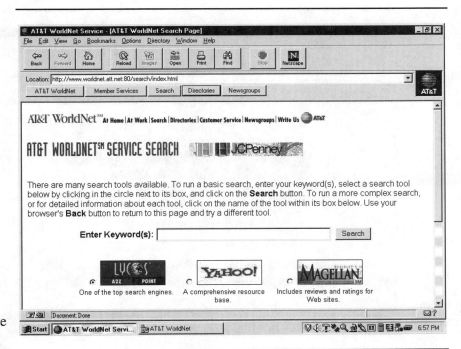

AT&T Search page

FIGURE 3-6

After a while, you'll see a screen reporting the number of matches and a list of the sites. The appearance of the screen will depend on the search directory you used. Figure 3-7, for example, shows the results of searching for "soap operas" using the Yahoo! service. In this case, Yahoo! starts the list with several categories, followed by actual sites. You can select a category and begin another search, or scroll the list looking for a location of interest. Click on the site that you are interested in, and continue surfing.

In most cases, the list will only include a first set of the locations. When you get to the end of the list, there will be a button to display additional sites.

Directories

You can go directly to one of the directory services, such as Lycos or Yahoo!, by clicking on its icon in the Search window. You can also click on the Directories button in the toolbar to see icons for all of the search companies, as well as buttons for the AT&T White Pages, AT&T 800 Directory, and AT&T WorldNet member directory. The White Pages directory will let you search for a residential or business

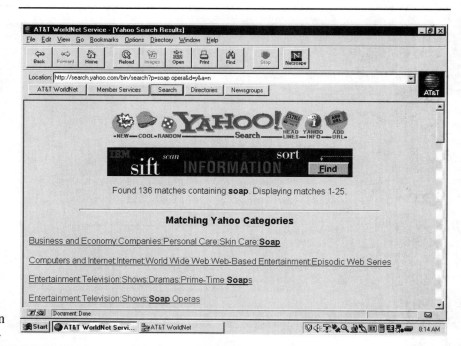

A Yahoo!
search for
soap opera
information

FIGURE 3-7

listing from the millions of entries in the telephone books throughout the country. You can search for a last name, or a name and address, in the entire country, a region, or individual state.

Using Bookmarks

Once you find an interesting site, you don't want to have to surf the Web to find it later on. You could write down the URL address that appears in the Location box. Better yet, save the address as a bookmark.

Bookmarks	Options	Directory	Window
Add Bookmark			Ctrl+D
Go to Bookmarks...			Ctrl+B
Corel WordPerfect			
Corel Corporation Home Page			
Directories			▶
Plug-Ins			▶
Ecology and Environment			▶
Computing			▶
Travel			▶
Family			▶
Weather			▶
Career			▶
Recreation and Sports			▶
The Newsstand			▶
Art and Literature			▶
Government			▶
Food			▶
Leisure			▶
Shopping			▶
Companies			▶

You use a bookmark when reading a book so you can quickly return to that same page. That's exactly how bookmarks work in Netscape Navigator. You save the URL as a bookmark so you can simply click on the bookmark name to move to that site.

If you pull down the Bookmarks menu in the Netscape Navigator toolbar, you'll see some bookmarks, along with categories of locations that AT&T has already created for you, as shown here. To move to the Corel Corporation home page, for example, just click on that item in the menu. To see some interesting sites regarding travel, point to Travel in the menu and click on a site that interests you in the submenu that appears.

You can add your own sites to the Bookmarks menu to return to them quickly. Here's how.

1. Start AT&T WorldNet and go to the page that you want to add as a bookmark.

2. Pull down the Bookmarks menu and click on Add Bookmark.

The URL of the displayed page will be added to the end of the Bookmarks menu. To later return to that site, just click on it in the menu.

 IP: *You can also create a bookmark by right-clicking on the link and selecting Add Bookmark for This Link. Choose Internet Shortcut in the QuickMenu to add a shortcut to the link on the Windows 95 desktop.*

You can edit, delete, or change the order of bookmarks in the menu by displaying the Bookmarks window. Display the window using either of these techniques:

- Select *Go To Bookmarks* from the Bookmarks menu.
- Select *Bookmarks* from the Window menu.

The Bookmarks window, shown in Figure 3-8, displays bookmarks listed in a tree diagram, much like files on your disk. To delete a bookmark, click on it in the list and choose Delete from the Edit menu.

You can also use the Edit menu to cut, copy, and paste a bookmark to another location in the tree, or you can use drag and drop—drag the bookmark to where you want it to appear.

You can also insert a bookmark without logging onto AT&T as long as you know its URL. Select Insert Bookmark from the Item menu. In the dialog box that appears, enter a bookmark name, enter its URL location and an optional description, and then click on OK.

Use the Insert Folder option from the Item menu to create a new category.

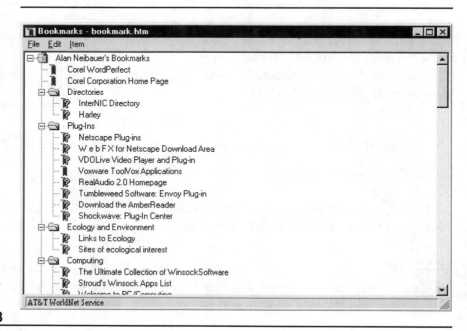

Bookmark window

FIGURE 3-8

Using the Address Book

Netscape Navigator has its own address book, separate from the Corel accessory. It doesn't store postal addresses or phone numbers—it's designed for sending e-mail and newsgroup messages. You can list names in the address book individually and in folders—groups.

When you compose a message, you can either type the recipient's address directly into the mail form, or you can select it from the address book. You can select multiple recipients, and you can even broadcast the message to everyone in a group.

To access the address book, follow these steps:

1. Pull down the Windows menu and click on Address Book to display the Address Book dialog box.

2. Pull down the Item menu and click on Add User.

3. Type a nickname for the recipient. This will let you address a message by typing an easy-to-remember nickname rather than the complete e-mail address.

4. Enter the recipient's e-mail address. Addresses are usually in the format *Name@server*, such as alincoln@logcabin.com.

5. Enter a brief description.

6. Click on OK.

You can organize persons into a group by creating a folder and then inserting addresses into the folder. The structure is similar to bookmarks and file directories. Here's how to create a folder.

1. Pull down the Item menu and click on Add List.

2. Type a name for the list and a description.

3. Click on OK.

To add an address to a mailing list, use drag and drop. Click on the name you want to add, hold down the left mouse button, and then drag the name to the folder. The name will be inserted into the folder, and it will also appear individually in its original location.

Using E-Mail

Electronic mail is built into Netscape Navigator, which is supplied by AT&T WorldNet. Look at the icon of an envelope at the lower-right corner of the window. If the icon is followed by an exclamation point, then you have mail waiting on the AT&T server. A question mark next to the icon means that something is stopping Netscape Navigator from checking your mail.

OTE: *Your AT&T e-mail address is the user name you registered with followed by @worldnet.att.net, such as alann@worldnet.att.net.*

To read or send mail, click on the icon, or pull down the Window menu and click on AT&T WorldNet Mail. The Mail window will open and the system will check for new messages. If there are messages, they will be downloaded automatically and saved in your Inbox.

IP: *To check for mail later in the sessions, click on the Get Mail toolbar button or click the Mail icon.*

The Mail window, shown in Figure 3-9, has three main parts—Mail folder, Message header list, and Message window. The tools in the window are shown in Table 3-2.

You use the Mail folder to organize your incoming and outgoing mail. You can create your own folders to store groups of messages, and Netscape Navigator can create up to four folders for you:

■ *Inbox* contains messages that you received.

■ *Outbox* contains messages that you've created but not yet sent.

■ *Sent* contains messages that you have sent.

■ *Trash* contains messages you are deleting.

To create your own folder, pull down the File menu and click on New Folder. Type a name for the folder in the box that appears, and then click on OK.

The Folder window has several columns. The Unread column will list the number of messages that you have not yet read, and the Total column shows the number of messages in each folder.

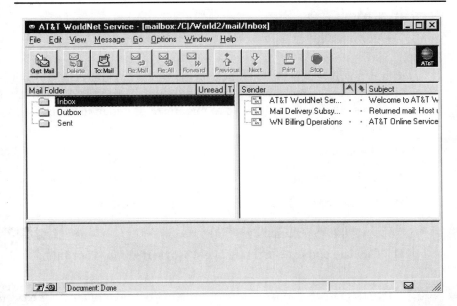

Mail
window

FIGURE 3-9

Tool	Function
Get Mail	Inserts any unread mail into your Inbox
Delete	Inserts the current messages into the Trash folder, creating the folder if necessary
To: Mail	Opens the Message Composition window to create a new message
Re: Mail	Opens the Message Composition window, with the sender's address of the current message into the To text box
Re: All	Like Re: Mail, but sends copies of the message to all those who received the original message
Forward	Opens the Message Composition window for a new message, using the current message as an attachment
Previous	Displays the previous unread message
Next	Displays the next unread message
Print	Prints the current selected message
Stop	Stops transmitting messages from AT&T

Mail
Window
Toolbar

TABLE 3-2

Reading Mail

To read mail, follow these steps:

1. If it is not already selected, click on the Inbox icon in the Mail folder. A list of your messages will appear to the right. The list is divided into five columns, although you'll have to maximize or widen the window to display them all:

   - The name of the sender

   - A Flag icon indicating if the message is classified as important

   - A Read icon indicating if you've read the message

   - The subject of the message

   - The date and time the message was inserted into your Inbox

IP: *Use drag and drop to move a message to another folder, or use the Move or Copy options from the Message menu. Click on a column title to temporarily sort the items by the Sender, Subject, or Date.*

2. Click on the message you want to read in the Message header list. Netscape Navigator will display the message in the bottom pane of the window.

3. To add the address of the message's sender to your address book, pull down the Message menu, and click on Add to Address Book.

Reading Attachments

A mail message may also include an attachment. An *attachment* is a separate document or file that was transmitted along with the message. This can be a formatted Web page or a file. The attachment either will appear as text along with the message, or you will see an icon following the message, such as this:

Attachment 2	**Type:** Application/Octet-Stream **Encoding:** Base64

If the attachment is readable, such as a text file, you can switch between displaying the text or the icon by choosing either Attachments Inline or Attachments as Links in the View menu. To download an attachment, click on the Link icon to display the Save As dialog box, enter a filename, and click on OK.

Depending on the type of file, other boxes may appear. You may see the one shown here:

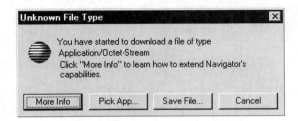

If you click on Pick App, you can select a program that will let you view the selected file. Otherwise, click on Save File. You'll have to type an extension that matches the file type, such as UUE.

Sending and Replying to Mail

Creating and sending mail is a snap. You can create mail online or offline. *Offline* means that you create the mail before actually connecting to AT&T, so you won't waste your connect time and charges.

To create a message offline, start AT&T just as you learned previously. When the Dial-Up Networking box appears, click on Cancel instead of Connect.

To send mail, follow these steps:

1. Click on the To: Mail button, or pull down the File menu and click on New Mail Message. The Message Composition window appears as in Figure 3-10.

2. Type the recipient's e-mail address in the Mail To box. If the recipient is in your address book, you can also type their nickname and press ENTER—Netscape Navigator will replace the nickname with the e-mail address. If you do not know the nickname or address, click on the Mail To button to display the address book, and then click on the recipient in the address book. Finally, click on To and then on OK.

3. Enter or select recipients for copies.

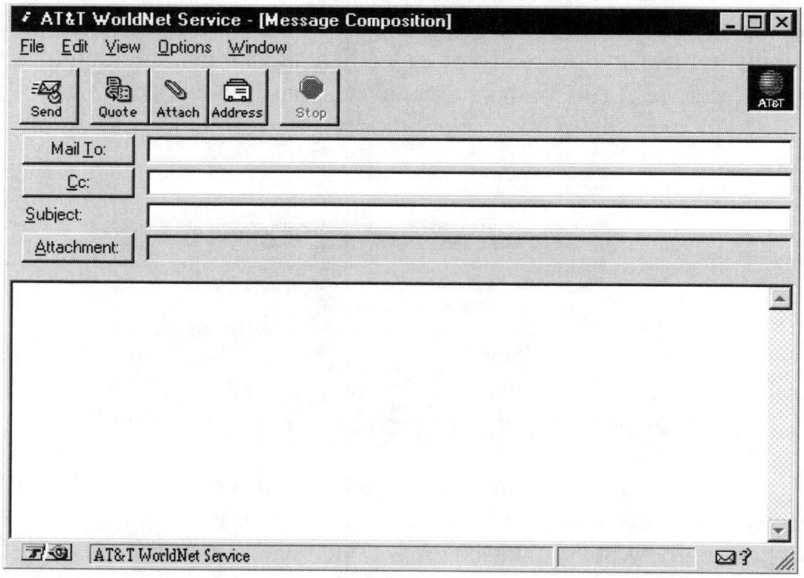

Message
Composition
window

FIGURE 3-10

4. Type a subject.

5. Click in the large text box and type your message.

6. Click on Send.

If you are offline, the mail will be added to your Outbox. The next time you go online, send the message by selecting Send Mail in Outbox from the File menu.

OTE: *If you have the address book open, start a message by clicking on the recipient's listing and then click on Choose New Mail Message from the File menu. To broadcast a message to everyone in a folder, click on the folder and then choose New Mail Message.*

Sending an Attachment

To send an attachment with your message, click on the Attachment or Attach button to see the Attachments dialog box. To attach a Web document, click on Attach

Location (URL), type the address in the box that appears, and then click on OK. To attach a file on your disk, click on Attach File, select the file, and then click on OK. You can attach any number of items to a message.

For each item, you can also choose the As Is or Convert to Plain Text option in the Attach section. Selecting As Is for a URL document, for example, will transmit the Web page fully formatted. Converting it to text will send it as ASCII text. You can also select the same options for a file on your disk.

 IP: *To send a new message with the one you are reading as an attachment, click on the Forward button.*

Replying to Mail

To reply to the message you are reading, click on the Re: Mail button. The Compose window will appear with the text of the message quoted in > characters before each line. Type your reply, and then click on Send.

If the message you received was also sent to others, click on the Re: All button to send your reply to all of the message's recipients.

 IP: *If you selected To: Mail instead of Re: Mail, click on the Quote button to insert the text of the message selected in the Mail window.*

Using Newsgroups

A *newsgroup* is a group of persons that share a common interest. Members of a newsgroup can be spread out around the world. By joining a newsgroup, you can send mail to every member of the group, and you can receive mail sent by all of the members.

Sending a message to the newsgroup is also called *posting*. It is similar to sending e-mail, except that your message will automatically be sent to every member of the group; so if there are 1000 members of the group, your message will be sent to all of them. You can also choose to send a message to a single member of the group.

**OTE:**   Usenet *is the term for the entire collection of newsgroups on the Internet.*

You read and send messages to newsgroups in the News window. To display the News window, click on the Newsgroup button in the button bar, or pull down the Window menu and click on AT&T WorldNet Newsgroups. The News window, shown in Figure 3-11, is similar to the Mail window.

The names of the newsgroups are listed in the Newsgroup pane. Messages posted by the group will be shown in the Message Header pane, and the specific message that you select to read in the Message pane.

The check mark next to the items in the Newsgroup pane means that you are subscribed to the newsgroup. This means that messages posted to the group will also be sent to you, and that you can send mail to the group. AT&T automatically subscribes you to the three groups shown in Figure 3-11. To unsubscribe, deselect the check box.

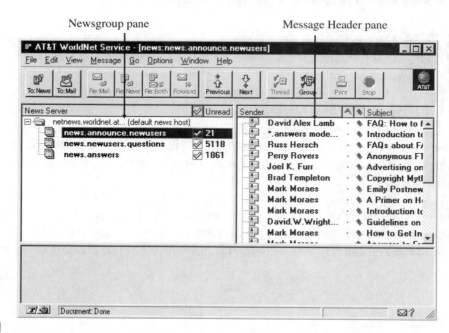

News window with unread news messages

FIGURE 3-11

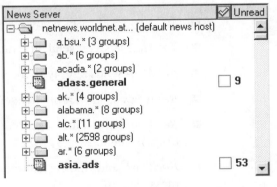

To read an item, follow these steps:

1. Click on the name of the newsgroup in the Newsgroup pane. The unread messages for the group will appear in the Message Header pane, as shown in Figure 3-11.

2. Click on the message you want to read in the Message Header pane.

3. Read the message.

By default, only messages that you have not read will be listed in the Message Header pane. If you want to reread one that you did read in the past, pull down the Options menu and click on Show All Messages. You can later select Show Only Unread Messages to return to the default setting.

If you want to list all of the newsgroups that AT&T tracks, pull down the Options menu and click on Show All Newsgroups. It will take a few minutes because the list is rather large, but all of the newsgroups will appear in the Newsgroup pane, as shown here.

Some of the groups are combined into categories around a broad general interest. These will be indicated by the Folder icon, and the number of groups in the folder appears next to its name. To see the groups in the category, double-click on the folder. A newsgroup itself will appear next to the icon of the pages. Next to each group will be the Subscribe check box, and the number of messages that you have not yet read.

 OTE: *A newsgroup name may not actually indicate its interest area. The only real way to tell the topic is to read through some of the posted messages.*

To subscribe to a group, just click in the Subscribe check box. The unread messages will then appear in the Message Header pane.

Because there are thousands of newsgroups, it is easier to see which have unread messages by listing only those that you subscribe to. To do this, pull down the Options menu and then click on either of these choices.

■ *Show Subscribed Newsgroups* lists the groups that you have subscribed to.

■ *Show Active Newsgroups* lists only the subscribed groups that contain unread messages.

AT&T keeps track of hundreds of newsgroups on its news server, but there must be thousands of other groups. To join another newsgroup, find out its URL address and then enter it in the location field of the Netscape Navigator window. You can also pull down the File menu, click on Add Newsgroup, and then type the URL in a dialog box that appears.

Newsgroup Mail

Sending newsgroup mail is similar to sending regular e-mail, with a few differences that are apparent from the different buttons in the News window. Send and reply to mail by clicking on the button for the action you want to perform to display the Message Composition window.

■ *To: News* addresses a new message to everyone in the group.

■ *To: Mail* lets you send an e-mail message to a selected recipient.

■ *Re: Mail* sends a reply to the sender of the current message.

■ *Re: News* sends a reply to everyone in the group.

■ *Re: Both* posts a message to the entire group and sends it by e-mail to the original sender.

■ *Forward* sends the current message as an attachment with a new e-mail message.

■ *Previous* displays the previous unread message.

■ *Next* displays the next unread message.

■ *Thread* marks all of the messages in the thread of the current message as read. Newsgroup messages are often grouped into threads. This is a collection of the original messages, as well as all of the replies and responses to the message.

■ *Group* marks all of the messages in the group as read.

■ *Print* prints the current selected message.

■ *Stop* stops transmitting messages from AT&T.

Customizing Netscape Navigator

When you install the AT&T software, Netscape Navigator is set up using certain default values. For example, it assigns AT&T as your home page and stores your password so you do not have to enter it when you check your mail, which is often required of Netscape Navigator users. All of the default Netscape Navigator settings are stored in a series of dialog boxes called *preferences panels.*

While you cannot change some of these settings because they are required by AT&T, you can modify most of them using the Options menu. Pull down the Options menu, and then select the preferences item you want to change:

- General Preferences

- Mail and News Preferences

- Network Preferences

- Security Preferences

Each item will display a dialog box of one or more pages. Many of these settings, especially those for Network and Security, are technical in nature, and you should not change them unless you absolutely, positively know what you are doing—or getting yourself into. Let's take a look at the General and Mail and News Preferences.

General Preferences

The General Preferences dialog box has seven pages of options. It is shown in Figure 3-12, with the Appearance page displayed. Use the pages of the dialog box to make these general changes:

- *Appearance* affects the way the Netscape Navigator window appears when you start it, including the home page and the initial window.

- *Apps* specifies the locations of some supporting Netscape Navigator applications.

- *Colors* sets the colors of links, backgrounds, and text.

- *Fonts* determines the font used to display and encode text.

- *Helpers* determines how files are treated when they are downloaded into your computer.

- *Images* controls how graphic images are displayed.

- *Language settings* are used by Netscape Navigator to tell computers what language you are using.

For many of us, the appearance options are the most useful. You can, for example, change the way that Toolbar buttons appear by selecting to display their functions as pictures (the default), as text, or both.

You can also control which AT&T window to display on startup—the Browser, Mail, or Newsgroup window. This is also where you set the home page—the first Web site that is displayed when the connection is made. By default, the home page is AT&T, but you can select to start with a blank window or enter another Web site as the initial startup page.

Use the Link Style section of the dialog box to control how links that are text in the content area appear. The setting for Follow Links determines how used links appear. When Expire After is set for 30 days, the default value, the link appears in the specified color for 30 days after you use it. After 30 days, it reverts to the default

General
Preferences

FIGURE 3-12

link color. You can change the number of days that the link appears in the specified color or select Never Expire.

Mail and News Preferences

These settings control the look of the Mail and News windows, and general ways in which these feature operate. The dialog box is similar to the one shown in Figure 3-12, but has only five pages instead of seven.

- The *Appearance* page controls the font used for text, and the font, style, size, and color of quoted text. You can also choose to use either Netscape Navigator or Windows 95 Exchange to handle mail and news functions.

- Use the *Composition* page to control the way e-mail messages are transmitted. For example, you can enter an e-mail address to automatically send copies of all of your mail and news messages, or to store all messages on a file on your disk. You can also specify whether replies should include the quoted message, and whether to use 8-bit.

- The *Servers* page determines the protocol for sending and receiving messages. Once your system is set up, about the only item you should change is the number of news messages to accept at one time. AT&T sets this at 100. You can always tell Netscape Navigator to accept the next series of messages by choosing Get More Messages from the New window File menu.

- Use the *Identity* page of the dialog box to store your name, e-mail address, an alternative reply-to address, and the name of a file storing your signature (closing) to add to the end of mail and news postings.

- The *Organization* page determines how mail and news messages are organized. You can choose to thread regular mail messages, like news messages, and how to sort mail. Use this box to determine if Netscape Navigator will ask for your password each time you check for mail.

PART II

Corel WordPerfect

Creating Documents with Corel WordPerfect

4

Corel WordPerfect is the flagship of the Corel Office suite for a very good reason. It is known around the world as an outstanding word processing program, with millions of dedicated users. Corel WordPerfect 7 is the next generation of the esteemed legacy, bringing new powerful and timesaving features to this landmark program.

Starting Corel WordPerfect

To start Corel WordPerfect, click on the Start button, point to Corel WordPerfect Suite 7, and click on Corel WordPerfect 7. You'll see the Corel WordPerfect screen shown in Figure 4-1.

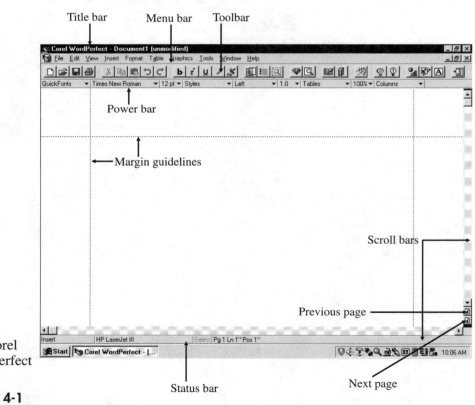

The Corel WordPerfect screen

FIGURE 4-1

At the top of the screen are the title bar, menu bar, toolbar, and power bar. Corel WordPerfect gives the name "Document1" to the first document window during the session, "Document 2" to the second, and so on. The word "unmodified" in the title bar means that you have not changed the document since it was started or opened. That word will disappear as soon as you start typing to indicate that you must save your work if you want to use it again. When you do save your document, the name you give it will appear on the title bar. The power bar has nine sections for performing common functions, such as changing the type size or centering text on the screen. Click anywhere in one of the sections to display a list of options from which you can select. You'll learn each of the functions of the toolbar and power bar throughout this book.

The blank area under the power bar is the typing area where your document will appear. The dotted lines around the typing area are the margin guidelines. They not only show you where your page margins are, but you can drag the lines to change the margins. The blinking vertical line is the insertion point where characters appear as you type. You'll also see the horizontal and vertical scroll bars. Use the vertical scroll bar to scroll lines up and down, the horizontal scroll bar to scroll right and left. At the bottom of the vertical scroll bar are the Previous Page and Next Page buttons that you can use to move from page to page through your document.

Finally, at the bottom of the screen, just above the Windows 95 Task Bar, is the status bar. This bar gives you information about your documents, as shown in Table 4-1. You'll learn later that double-clicking on a phrase in the status bar performs some related action.

What you don't yet see on the screen are four helpful, timesaving features: QuickTips, QuickMenus, QuickSpots, and QuickStatus boxes.

A QuickTip is a small box with a brief description of the function of the Toolbar, Power Bar, and Status Bar buttons that you point at with the mouse. If you're not sure what a button does, point to it and read the QuickTip, as shown here.

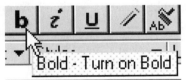

A QuickMenu is a list of items that will appear when you right-click on an object. Which menu items will show depends on where the mouse is pointing. It is usually faster to display and use the QuickMenu than it is to perform the same functions with the menu bar or toolbar, since you don't have to slide the mouse to the top of the screen. Every QuickMenu has the "What's This?" option. Click on it to read about the object you are pointing to.

A QuickSpot is a small square that appears when you move the mouse pointer over text, in a table, or over a graphic or other object. Click the left mouse button

Section	Displays
Insert	Insert means that as you type new characters within a document, existing text moves over to make room. As you work with Corel WordPerfect, other messages will appear in this section indicating that some feature is turned on, or that the insertion point is in a table, column, or other special formatted section of text.
Printer	Name of the printer being used by Corel WordPerfect.
Select	Current status of Select mode. When the word "Select" is not dimmed, you can select text by moving the insertion point with the keyboard.
Date	Current date maintained by your computer's clock.
Time	Current time maintained by your computer's clock.

Status Bar

TABLE 4-1

on the QuickSpot to display a dialog box of options. Again, the options in the dialog box depend on where the QuickSpot appears. In general, QuickSpot dialog boxes let you format the text or object where you clicked.

QuickStatus boxes will appear when you change the sizes of margins, columns, and table cells, showing their exact dimensions. As you drag the mouse, watch the QuickStatus box—release the mouse button when the dimension is what you want:

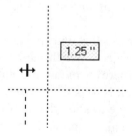

IP: *You'll also see special symbols indicating where you changed tab stops or applied certain combinations of formats and styles.*

Typing a Document

You type a document in Corel WordPerfect just as you would in any other word processing program, and almost the same as on a typewriter. The letter and number keys insert just what you see on the keys; just remember to press SHIFT or CAPSLOCK to get uppercase letters and the punctuation marks shown on the top part of the key. You can use the keypad to enter numbers, but you must first press the NUMLOCK key—otherwise you will move the insertion point.

Press the BACKSPACE key to erase your mistakes. Each time you press BACKSPACE, Corel WordPerfect deletes a character to the left of the insertion point. Indent the first line of a paragraph by pressing the TAB key, and press the ENTER key to insert a blank line or to end a paragraph. Do not press ENTER, however, when the insertion point reaches the right margin; just keep on typing. Corel WordPerfect will sense that the word you're typing will not fit on the line and it will automatically move it to the next.

When your typing reaches the bottom of the screen, just continue. The text at the top will scroll up and out of view, but it will not be deleted. You can always scroll the screen back to see it.

And don't worry about where the page ends—keep on typing. Corel WordPerfect will automatically end the page when it is full and start a new one. If you want to end a page before Corel WordPerfect does, press CTRL+ENTER.

Hard Versus Soft

When Corel WordPerfect moves the insertion point to the start of a new line, it is called a *soft return*. When it ends one page and starts another, it is called a *soft page break*. When you press ENTER to end a line, it's a *hard return*. When you press CTRL+ENTER to end a page, it's a *hard page break*.

Why bother with hard versus soft? As you insert, delete, and format text within a document, Corel WordPerfect can automatically adjust the other text on the page. If you add text to a paragraph, for example, the other text in the paragraph and on the page will move over and down to make room. If you delete text, it may move text up from the next page, always ending pages when they become full.

If you pressed ENTER to end each line at the right margin, as you do with a typewriter, then each line would be considered a separate paragraph. Text would not flow neatly to adjust to your changes. Likewise, if you press CTRL+ENTER to end a page, a new page will always start at that location, even if you delete some text from the page before.

You cannot delete a soft page break; it will adjust automatically as you work. You can delete a hard page break by pressing DEL or BACKSPACE.

 AUTION: *Never end a page by pressing ENTER until Corel WordPerfect inserts a soft page break. If you later insert or delete text, the extra blank lines will end up where you don't want them.*

Spell-As-You-Go

Corel WordPerfect automatically checks your spelling as you create your document using its new Spell-As-You-Go feature, placing a wavy red line under words it cannot find in its dictionary, as shown here:

The Three Stoges are my favorite actors. I think they are very funy.

You can leave the wavy lines where they are and correct your errors later on, or you can fix them as you work. If you know the right spelling, and the mistake was just a typo, you can press the BACKSPACE key to erase the mistake, and then type the word again.

You can also let Corel WordPerfect correct the word for you. Point to the word and click the right mouse button to see the Spell-As-You-Go QuickMenu, shown here:

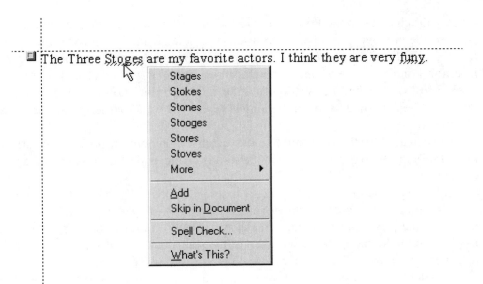

At the top of the menu are some suggested spellings. Just click on the correct word to insert it in place of your own. The word "More" means that Corel WordPerfect has found more suggested spellings than will fit on the menu—point to "More" to see these other choices.

Here are the other options on the QuickMenu:

- *Add*—Select Add if the word is spelled correctly and you want to add it to Corel WordPerfect's dictionary. The word will not be flagged with a wavy line again in any Corel WordPerfect document.

- *Skip in Document*—Choose this if you want to ignore the word only in this document. It will be flagged in other documents, however.

- *Spell Check*—Use this to start the Spell Check feature.

Inserting and Deleting Text

If you don't catch a mistake until you are past it, you don't have to press BACKSPACE to delete all of the text back to that point. Instead, move the insertion point and then make your changes to the text. To move the insertion point, move the mouse and point to the area where you want to insert or delete characters. As you move the mouse, you'll see the *shadow insertion point* move along with it. This is a gray insertion point that shows where the real insertion point will be placed when you click. Most of the time the shadow will be right with the mouse pointer, but not always. When the shadow insertion point is where you want to insert or delete, click the mouse.

You can also use the keyboard to move the insertion point by pressing the arrow keys. Press HOME to quickly move to the start of a line, and END to move to the end of the line.

Before trying to insert text, look at the first section on the left of the status bar. If it says "Insert," then you are in Insert mode. As you type, existing text will move over and down as necessary to make room. You can switch out of Insert mode by pressing the INS key, or by double-clicking on Insert in the status bar. This display will change to Typeover—now each character that you type will replace an existing one.

To delete text, press the BACKSPACE key to delete characters to the left of the insertion point, and DEL to delete characters to the right.

Scrolling the Screen

How do you move the insertion point to a place in the document that has already scrolled off the screen? The answer is *scrolling*. Scrolling means to bring into view text that has disappeared off the top or bottom, or the left or right, of the document window.

The simplest way to scroll the window is to use the arrow keys. When the insertion point is at the top line of the document window, pressing UP ARROW will scroll a new line into view—if there are any. When the insertion point is on the last line in the window, pressing DOWN ARROW will scroll a new line into view—again, if there are any.

If you have to move a great distance through a long document, however, using the arrow keys is certainly not very efficient. Instead, use the scroll bar on the left of the screen—the vertical scroll bar—to scroll up and down. Use the scroll bar at the bottom of the window—the horizontal scroll bar—to scroll left and right.

To scroll through your document line by line, just as you would by pressing the arrow key, click on the up or down triangles on the ends of the scroll bar. To scroll screen by screen, click above or below the scroll box—the box within the bar. Each time you click, Corel WordPerfect scrolls the window about the same number of lines that you can see. You can also drag the scroll box to scroll to a relative position in the document. If you drag the box to the middle of the scroll bar, Corel WordPerfect will display page five of a nine-page document, for example.

To move page by page through a document, click on the Previous Page and Next Pages buttons on the bottom of the scroll bar.

Keep in mind a very important point. Scrolling with the scroll bars and with the Previous Page and Next Page buttons does not move the insertion point, it only changes the part of the document being displayed on the screen. You'll notice that the position indicators in the status bar will not change as you scroll, so if you don't click first, the screen will scroll back to its previous location when you begin typing or press an arrow key. To insert or delete text in the displayed area, you must first click where you want to type.

To go to the start of a specific page, double-click on the position indicator on the status bar to see the Go To dialog box, shown in Figure 4-2. Type the number of the page you want to move to, and then click on OK. You can also click on Position and select the location from the list:

- Last Position

- Previous Table

- Next Table

- Top of Current Page

- Bottom of Current Page

To scroll the screen and move the insertion point with the keyboard, use these shortcuts:

Press	To Move
PGUP	Up one screen
PGDN	Down one screen
CTRL+HOME	To the start of the document
CTRL+END	To the end of the document
ALT+PGUP	To the previous page
ALT+PGDN	To the next page

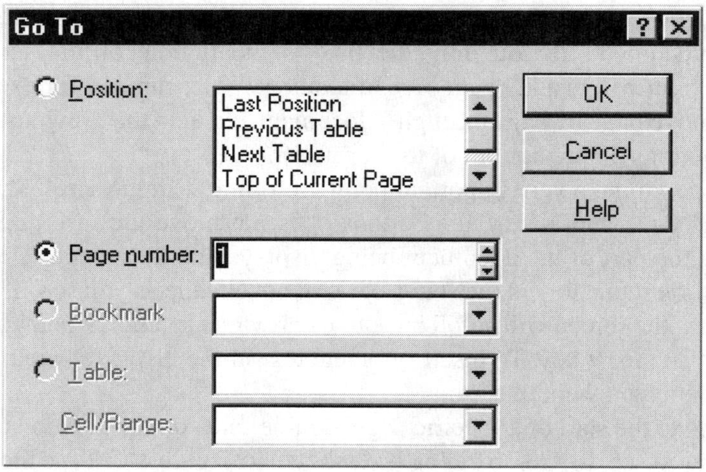

Using the
Go To box
to move
within the
document

FIGURE 4-2

Selecting Text

When you want to perform a Corel WordPerfect function on more than one character
or word at a time, you need to select them. You can select text using either the mouse
or the keyboard. Selected text appears highlighted—light letters over a dark background.
It is easy to select text with the mouse by dragging. Here's how:

1. Move the mouse so it is at one end of the text that you want to select.
   It can be at either end, in front of the first character or following the
   last character.

2. Press and hold down the left mouse button.

3. Keep the button down as you drag the mouse, until the pointer is at the
   other end of the text.

4. When you reach the end of the text, release the mouse button. The
   selected text will appear highlighted. Click the mouse to deselect the text,
   removing the highlighting.

IP: *Drag straight across the line, not up or down, unless you want to
select more than one line of text.*

Corel WordPerfect uses QuickSelect, an intelligent selection system. If you start dragging in the center of a word, the program will select the entire word when you get to the next one. If you drag to select the space before a word, Corel WordPerfect automatically selects the whole word to the right as you drag onto its first characters. Similarly, when you select the space after a word and the one following, Corel WordPerfect selects the whole word to the left as you drag onto its last character.

Something similar occurs when you drag the mouse up or down. When you drag to the line above, Corel WordPerfect automatically selects everything to the left of the original line and to the right of the new line. If you drag down to the next line, Corel WordPerfect selects everything to the right of the original and to the left of the next line.

As long as you do not release the mouse button, you can drag as much or as little text as you want. If you drag too far to the right, for example, just keep the mouse button down and drag back toward the left.

If you want to delete text quickly, select it with the mouse and then press the DEL or BACKSPACE key. You can also point to the selected text, click the right mouse button, and choose Cut or Delete from the QuickMenu that appears when you right-click on selected text.

AUTION: *Before going any further, here's a word of warning. Selected text will be deleted if you press any number, letter, punctuation key, the SPACEBAR, or the ENTER key. Corel WordPerfect uses this technique to make it easy for you to replace characters with something else. If you do not want to replace text, make certain that no text is selected before you start typing.*

Just as there are many ways to scroll the screen and move the insertion point, there are many ways to select text. Double-click to select a word, click three times to select the sentence, or click four times to select the entire paragraph.

If you double-click on a word and then delete it, Corel WordPerfect will also delete the space following the word. Corel WordPerfect figures that if you want to delete the word, you don't want to leave an extra space between the words that remain.

If you want to select a portion of text without dragging, use the SHIFT key. Place the insertion point at one end of the text, hold down the SHIFT key, and then click at the other end of the text.

Finally, you can also select text by clicking on the left margin. When you place the mouse pointer in the left margin, the pointer will be shaped like an arrow. Click the mouse once to select the sentence of text to the right of the pointer. Click twice to select the entire paragraph. If you hold down the mouse button and drag in the left margin, you will select multiple lines.

You can also select text using the Edit menu. Point to Select on the menu and choose to select the sentence, paragraph, page, or the entire document.

If you want to select text using the keyboard, remember these two important keys: F8 and SHIFT. To simulate dragging, press the F8 key, or double-click on the dimmed word "Select" in the status bar. "Select" will become bold, indicating that you are in the Select mode. Now text becomes selected as you move the insertion point using the arrow keys, other key combinations, and even by clicking the mouse. For example, if you press F8 and then RIGHT ARROW, text becomes selected as the insertion point passes over it. To get out of Select mode, press ESC.

 IP: *You can also select text using SHIFT. When you hold down SHIFT, all of the insertion point movement keystrokes also select text.*

Using Undo and Redo

It would be nice if we never made mistakes, but unfortunately, life just isn't that perfect. It is all too easy to delete characters you really want, or type characters and then change your mind about them. Because Corel WordPerfect knows we are not always perfect, it gives us a quick and easy way to correct our mistakes using the Undo and Redo commands:

Undo ⟶  ⟵ Redo

The Undo command reverses changes that you make in your document. Delete a paragraph by mistake? Use Undo to return it to the document. Type a sentence and then change your mind? Use Undo to remove it from the document. There are two ways to use Undo—from the Edit menu or from the toolbar.

 AUTION: *Not every action that you perform can be undone. For example, you cannot undo saving or printing your document.*

To reverse the change you just made to the document, pull down the Edit menu and click on Undo, or click on the Undo button in the toolbar. Corel WordPerfect

will reverse the last action you took—whether it's restoring deleted text or undoing your last typing. Corel WordPerfect "remembers" the last ten actions that you performed, even when you save and close the document. Once you undo the very last action, Corel WordPerfect will be prepared to undo the one before that; just click on Undo again or select it from the Edit menu.

Corel WordPerfect not only remembers the action that you took, it also remembers the actions that you undo. So if you undo something and then change your mind, you can *redo* it using any of these techniques:

- Pull down the Edit menu and click on Redo.
- Click on the Redo button on the toolbar.
- Pull down the Redo list in the toolbar and click on the item to redo.

Undo/Redo History

If you do make a lot of changes to your document, you can forget which action will be undone or redone when you click on the button. To see a list of your last actions, and to increase the number of actions that Corel WordPerfect remembers, choose Undo/Redo History from the Edit menu. You'll see a dialog box like the one shown in Figure 4-3.

Your last actions are listed with the most recent on top. To undo or redo the last action you took, just click on Undo or Redo. To reverse more than one action at a time, click elsewhere on the list. You cannot, however, delete a specific action other than whatever is listed on top. If you click on the third in the list, for example, Corel

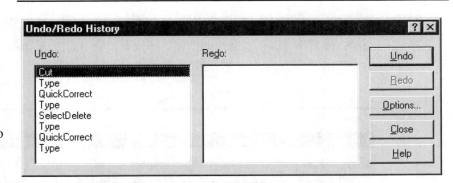

Undo/Redo
History
dialog box

FIGURE 4-3

WordPerfect will automatically select all of the actions above it as well. So to undo your last five actions, click on the fifth item in the list and then on Undo.

To change the number of items that Corel WordPerfect remembers, click on Options in the dialog box. You can tell Corel WordPerfect to remember up to 300 actions, and to remember or forget them when you close the document.

Undeleting Deleted Text

If you delete text with the BACKSPACE or DEL key, or using the Delete command from the Edit or QuickMenu, you can also restore it with the Undelete command. Undelete remembers the last three items that you deleted, regardless of how many other actions you take. To restore deleted text, choose Undelete from the Edit menu to display the dialog box shown in Figure 4-4.

The last text you deleted will reappear highlighted at the insertion point. Select Restore to restore the text at that location on the screen, or select Previous or Next to cycle between the last three deletions.

Saving a Document

You should get in the habit of saving your documents, even if you think you may not need them again. You might not find a typo or other mistake in a printed copy until a later time. If you didn't save your document, you'd have to type it all over again. To save a document, follow these steps:

1. Click on the Save button in the toolbar, or choose Save from the File menu to display the Save As dialog box.

2. Type the document name, and select the folder where you want to store it.

3. Click on Save. The word "Modified" will appear after the filename in the title bar.

Using
Undelete to
restore
deleted text

FIGURE 4-4

OTE: *By default, Corel WordPerfect saves documents with the WPD extension in the \Corel\Office7\MyFiles folder.*

When you've finished working with your document, look for the word "Unmodified" in the title bar. If it is not there, it means that you've changed the document since you last saved it, and you must save the document again. When you click on Save this time, Corel WordPerfect saves the document immediately without first opening the Save As dialog box.

IP: *Remember, use Save As from the File menu to save the document with a new name.*

In Chapter 13, you'll learn how to save your documents so you can share them with other programs.

Closing a Document

When you have finished working with your document, clear it from the screen by closing it. Click on the Close box on the right of the menu bar, or choose Close from the File menu. If you did not save your document since last changing it, a dialog box will appear asking if you want to save it now—select Yes or No.

If you are only working with one document at a time, a new blank one will appear when you close it. If you have more than one document open, closing one document will display another open document.

Printing Documents

To print your document, follow these steps:

1. Click on the Print button in the toolbar, or choose Print from the File menu to display the Print dialog box shown in Figure 4-5.

2. Choose Options from the box.

3. Click on Print.

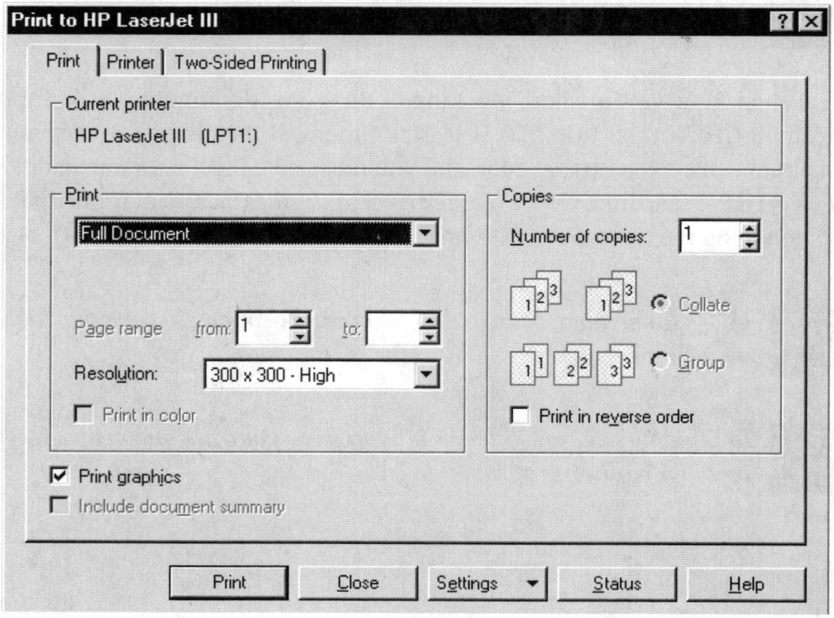

Print dialog box

FIGURE 4-5

Choose to print the entire document, the current page, a different document that's stored on your disk, or multiple pages. If you choose Multiple Pages, enter the page numbers in the From and To boxes at the Print Range option. You can automatically select to print multiple pages simply by entering numbers in the box. If you select Advanced Multiple Pages, a dialog box will appear when you click on Print. You can then enter specific pages, a range of pages, or chapters and volumes, depending on how you laid out your document. Specify the pages in the Page(s)/Label(s) text box. Use a hyphen to represent a range of pages, as in 1-6, and a comma to separate individual pages with a comma, as in 4, 6, 9. To print from one page to the end of the document, end with a hyphen, such as 10-. Begin with a hyphen to print from the first page to a specific page, as in -5.

To print more than one copy of the document, set the Number of Copies option. If your document is more than one page long, select how they are collated. Choose Collate when you want each complete set of the document to print separately. Choose Group to have multiple copies of the individual pages.

Select a resolution setting if your printer has more than one setting available. The resolution will have an effect on graphics, but not much on text.

Click on Status to see a list of the documents you printed during the current session, along with the time and date you sent them to the printer and when they began to print, as shown here.

Document	Status	Printed From	Printer	Submit Time	Begin Time
Corel Office Document	Complete	Corel WordPerf...	Envoy 7 Driver	5:05:49 PM ...	5:05:50 PM ...
Corel Office Document	Complete	Corel WordPerf...	Envoy 7 Driver	3:52:42 PM ...	3:52:43 PM ...
Corel Office Document	Complete	Corel WordPerf...	Envoy 7 Driver	3:40:30 PM ...	3:40:31 PM ...
Corel Office Document	Complete	Corel WordPerf...	Envoy 7 Driver	12:58:26 PM...	12:58:26 PM...
A:\BANK	Complete	Corel WordPerf...	HP LaserJet III	10:44:42 AM...	10:44:42 AM...
A:\FS	Complete	Corel WordPerf...	HP LaserJet III	10:44:26 AM...	10:44:27 AM...
A:\HARRY	Complete	Corel WordPerf...	HP LaserJet III	11:52:17 AM...	11:52:17 AM...
A:\harry2.doc	Complete	Corel WordPerf...	HP LaserJet III	11:50:08 AM...	11:50:08 AM...
A:\harry2.doc	Complete	Corel WordPerf...	HP LaserJet III	11:48:22 AM...	11:48:22 AM...

The option Print in Color will be dimmed if you do not have a color printer. The Include Document Summary option will be dimmed if you do not have a summary attached to the document.

 OTE: *You'll learn about the Two-Sided Printing part of this dialog box in Chapter 8.*

If your document does not print accurately, you may have the wrong printer selected. Display the Printer page of the Print dialog box, pull down the Current Printer list, and choose your printer. If your printer is not listed, click on Add Printer to start the Windows 95 Add Printer Wizard, and follow the directions on the screen.

Starting Another Document

To start a new document when you're still working with another, click on the New Blank Document button—the first button on the left side of the toolbar.

If you already have one document open, it will move to the background. You'll learn how to use multiple document windows in Chapter 5.

Quitting Corel WordPerfect

When you are finished using Corel WordPerfect, choose Exit from the File menu, or click on the Close box on the right of the Corel WordPerfect title bar. If you made any changes to the document since you last saved it, a dialog box will appear asking if you want to save the document before closing. Select Yes to save the document, No not to save it, or Cancel to remain in Corel WordPerfect.

Opening Existing Documents

To edit an existing document that is not already on the screen, you must first *open* it. When you open a document, Corel WordPerfect recalls it from the disk and displays it in a document window. Opening a document does not remove it from the disk, it just places a copy of it in your computer's memory. If you already have a document on the screen when you open another, Corel WordPerfect opens another window for the new document. The window will appear in the foreground, showing the document you just opened. The other document window will move into the background. See Chapter 5 for more information on working with multiple documents.

Because you often work on a document in more than one session, Corel WordPerfect makes it easy to reopen the last documents that you worked on. Pull down the File menu. At the bottom of the menu, Corel WordPerfect lists up to the last nine documents that you've opened or saved (see Figure 4-6). Click on the name of the document you want to open. Once a document is open, you can edit, print, or just read it.

Using the File Open Dialog Box

To open a document not listed in the File menu, you can either click on the Open tool in the toolbar or select Open from the File menu. The Open dialog box will appear. Corel WordPerfect lists files in the Corel\Office7\MyFile directory. Double-click on the document you want to open, or highlight its name and then click on Open. Use the navigation tools in the dialog box to find files in other folders and disks.

If you make changes to a document, you must save it again to record the changes to the disk. Click on the Save button in the Standard toolbar or select Save from the File menu. Corel WordPerfect will save it without displaying the Save dialog box. If you want to change its name or folder, select Save As from the File menu.

 In Chapter 13, you'll learn how to open documents created with other programs.

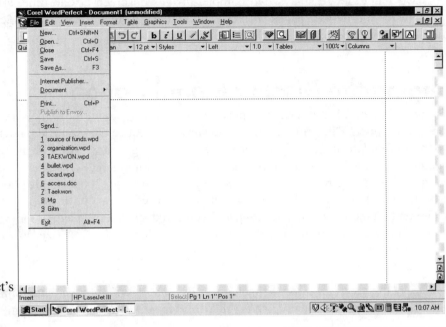

Your last nine documents listed in Corel WordPerfect's File menu

FIGURE 4-6

Changing the Document View

When you start Corel WordPerfect, it will be in Page view. This means that you'll see your document as it will appear when you print it. The margin guidelines will show the size of your margins, and you'll see headers, footers, page numbers, graphics, and other elements of your layout.

While Page view shows how your document will look when printed, it has some disadvantages, so Corel WordPerfect gives you two other views: Draft and Two Page. To change the view, pull down the View menu and choose the view you want.

In Draft view you'll see fonts, graphics, and the left and right margin guidelines, but not headers, footers, page numbers, and the top and bottom page guidelines. It lets you see more lines on the screen than Page view, while still showing most elements of your layout.

Two Page view displays two complete pages onscreen at one time, a useful preview of side-by-side pages. You can still edit and format text in Two Page view, but the text will probably be too small to read.

Changing the Display Magnification

By default, Corel WordPerfect displays your document about the same size it will be when printed. Changing to Two Page view will reduce the size of the document to two complete pages. If you are in Draft or Page view, you can adjust the magnification as you wish. If you have trouble reading small characters, you can enlarge the display. For example, set magnification at 200% to display your document at twice the printed size. You can also reduce magnification to display more text on the screen than normal, and you can display a full page or more at one time! Changing magnification does not actually change the font size, just how it appears onscreen.

IP: *You can edit and format your document no matter what magnification you select. And you can change to any view regardless of the magnification.*

There are two ways to change magnification: with the toolbar and the View menu.

To quickly see one whole page on the screen, click on the Page/Zoom Full button in the toolbar. Click on the button again to return to the previous magnification.

To select another magnification, pull down the zoom section of the power bar. You can choose 50%, 75%, 100%, 150%, 200%, Margin Width, Page Width, Full Page, and Other—to set a custom magnification. The Margin Width option sets the magnification so that the lines of text fill the width of the window. Choose Page Width so the full width of the page, including margins, fills the screen.

IP: *You can access the same options, or enter a specific magnification up to 400%, by selecting Zoom from the View menu.*

Displaying Guidelines and Toolbars

You have several ways to change what appears on the screen. If you want to see as much text as possible, you can remove the toolbar, power bar, and status bar from the screen. Here's how:

1. Pull down the View menu, and click on Toolbars/Ruler. A dialog box will appear with check boxes for the toolbar, power bar, ruler, and status bar:

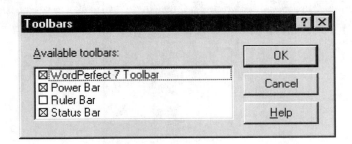

2. Deselect the items you do not want to appear.

3. Click on OK.

To remove all of the bars at one time, select Hide Bars from the View menu, and then click on OK in the dialog box that appears. WordPerfect will remove everything—the menu, scroll, ruler, power, status, and toolbars—except the Windows 95 Taskbar. Redisplay all of the bars by pressing ESC.

You can also turn on and off the guidelines. Select Guidelines from the View menu, and then select the view guidelines for tables, margins, columns, and headers and footers.

Corel WordPerfect comes with 14 different toolbars. Most contain a set of common buttons, such as Save and Print, as well as buttons for performing special functions. To display a different toolbar, point the mouse on the toolbar already on the screen, and then click the right mouse button. You'll see the QuickMenu listing the toolbars that Corel WordPerfect makes available, shown in Figure 4-7. The check marks next to a toolbar name means that the toolbar is being displayed. Click on the name of another toolbar to display—you can only display one at a time.

 IP: *To hide a toolbar, select Hide Toolbar from the QuickMenu.*

Moving a toolbar is as easy as dragging. Point the mouse to any blank area on the toolbar between or surrounding the buttons. Do not point to a button on the toolbar. Hold down the mouse button and then drag the mouse. As you drag, a gray

Selecting a
toolbar
from the
QuickMenu

FIGURE 4-7

box representing the toolbar will move along with the pointer. Release the mouse button when the box is where you want the toolbar to appear.

If you drag the toolbar somewhere above the text area, or to the bottom of the screen above the status bar, the buttons on the toolbar will appear in one row, just like the default layout. If you drag the toolbar to the far left or right of the screen, the buttons will be in one column. If you drag the toolbar into the typing area, however, the toolbar will appear as a small window, complete with a title bar and control box, as shown here:

You change the size and shape of the toolbar by dragging one of its borders, just as you can change the size and shape of any window in Windows. Click on the control box to turn off the toolbar. To turn it back on, you'll need to display the Shortcut menu and select the name of the toolbar.

The Edit and Preferences options on the Shortcut menu, by the way, let you change a button bar or create your own. With the Preference option, for example, you can choose to show icons or text on the face of buttons (or both) and change the type and size of the text.

You can also choose to use alternative menus. Right-click on the menu bar and then select the menu configuration you want: Internet Publisher Menu, WPWin 6.0a Menu, WPWin 6.1 Menu, and WPWin 7 menu. Select WPWin6.0a or WPWin 6.1 if you prefer the menus of these previous versions.

To quickly show symbols indicating spaces, carriage returns, tabs, centered text, indentations, flush right alignment, and some other formats, choose Show ¶ from the View menu. Select the options again to turn off the display.

OTE: *In Chapter 6, you will learn how to reveal all of the format codes, and in Chapter 10, you will learn how to further customize the look of Corel WordPerfect.*

Editing Documents

5

Y ou already know how to edit documents by inserting and deleting text. However, sometimes you have to make major changes, such as moving text from one location to another, or changing a word or phrase that appears several times in the document.

In this chapter, you will learn editing techniques to make your work time as efficient as possible.

Moving and Copying Text

Sometimes you type text only to discover it would be better in another location in your document. One of the great advantages of Corel WordPerfect is that you can easily move text from one place to another. You can even make a duplicate copy of text in another location. When you *move* text, you delete it from one place in your document and insert it into another location. When you *copy* text, you make a duplicate of selected text and place the copy in another location—the text in the original location is not affected.

 In Chapter 13, you will learn how to share Corel WordPerfect text with other applications.

Moving and Copying Text with Drag and Drop

Using the mouse, you can easily copy and move text using a method called *drag and drop*. This means that you drag the selected text to where you want to insert it, and then release the mouse button to drop it into place.

 OTE: *Later in this chapter you will learn how to drag and drop text between documents.*

To move text, select the text using the mouse, and then point anywhere in the selected area. Press and hold down the mouse button, and then drag the mouse to where you want to insert the text. As you drag the mouse, a small box and the insertion point will accompany the pointer:

Release the mouse button when the dotted insertion point is where you want the text to appear.

If you want to *copy* text, rather than move it, press and hold down the CTRL key while you release the mouse button. When you hold down CTRL, a plus sign will appear with the pointer, confirming that you are making a copy of the text:

OTE: *You do not have to hold down the CTRL key while you are dragging, only when you release the button.*

You can use drag and drop to move or copy text anywhere in the document, even in areas that have scrolled off the screen. When you drag the pointer past the top or bottom of the window, the screen will scroll automatically.

If you change your mind about moving the text while you are dragging, just move the pointer back to the selected text and then release the button. If you've already dropped the text and then change your mind, use the Undo command from the Edit menu, or click on the Undo button in the toolbar.

Moving and Copying Text Through the Clipboard

The *Clipboard* is an area in the computer's memory where Windows 95 temporarily stores information. You can place text into the Clipboard and later take it from the Clipboard to insert elsewhere. When you move text using the Clipboard, it's called *cut and paste*—you cut the text from one location and paste it elsewhere. When you copy text with the Clipboard, it's called *copy and paste*—you make a copy of the text and then paste it elsewhere.

To move text using cut and paste, first select the text you want to move. Then cut the text into the Clipboard by clicking on the Cut button in the toolbar. The selected text is now in the Clipboard. You can also cut text to the Clipboard by using one of these techniques:

- Select Cut from the Edit menu.

- Press CTRL+X.

- Select Cut from the QuickMenu that appears when you click the right mouse on the selected text.

Next, place the insertion point where you want to insert the text. Then paste it into the document by clicking on the Paste button. Word will insert whatever is in the Clipboard into the document. You can also paste the contents of the Clipboard using one of these techniques:

- Select Paste from the Edit menu.

- Press CTRL+V.

- Select Paste from the QuickMenu that appears when you right-click.

IP: *The Paste option will be dimmed in the Shortcut menu if no text is in the Clipboard.*

To *copy* text rather than move it, follow the same steps as above but click on the Copy button. You can also select Copy from the Edit menu, press CTRL+C, or select Copy from the QuickMenu.

Normally, Windows can store only one thing at a time in the Clipboard. So think about the consequences. If you cut some text in preparation to move it, then absentmindedly cut or copy something else, the text you want to move is erased from the Clipboard. Click on the Undo button twice to restore both cut portions of text, and then start over. If you do want to add text to what is already on the Clipboard, select the text and then choose Append from the Edit menu.

The contents of the Clipboard will remain there until you cut or copy something else, or until you exit Windows. This means that you can insert the same text over and over again in your document, as long as you do not cut or copy something else.

To insert the Clipboard contents in multiple locations, just position the insertion point and select Paste at each spot.

Inserting with Abbreviations

In Chapter 2, you learned how to use QuickCorrect to quickly insert text or expand abbreviations. QuickCorrect is useful because sometimes you find yourself writing the same word or phase over and over again. You may repeat it several times in one document, or use the same phrase in a number of documents that you write. It's not bad if you have to repeat a small word several times. But imagine having to repeat a complex scientific or medical term, or the full name of some company or government agency. Sure, you could copy the word and then paste it where you want it. But then the word would be deleted from the Clipboard if you had to cut or copy something else.

The problem with QuickCorrect, however, is that it is automatic. Suppose you create a QuickCorrect entry to replace the state abbreviation CA with California. Just imagine your chemistry teacher's response when every reference to calcium (which is abbreviated CA) in your report is printed as "California" instead. When you frequently use a word, phrase, or even a long section of text, but you do not want it to be replaced automatically, use Abbreviation instead of QuickCorrect. You can then insert a word, phrase, or entire section of text by typing the abbreviation. You could create an abbreviation for your name, for example, and then insert it by typing your initials.

You can use abbreviations to insert your name and address, for your telephone number, for standard closings, or for anything that you want to insert easily and quickly. In fact, you can have an unlimited number of abbreviations defined because Corel WordPerfect automatically saves them with the default template, a special file that is used for all new documents that you create.

To create an abbreviation, first type and select the text you want to assign to an abbreviation, and then select Abbreviation from the Edit menu. Try it now by typing your full name in a new document window. Select your name, and then choose Abbreviation from the Edit menu to display the dialog box shown in Figure 5-1.

Click on the Create button. In the box that appears, type your initials, and then click on OK. The abbreviation is added to the list. Close the dialog box.

Now whenever you want to enter the word, type the abbreviation for it and press CTRL+SHIFT+A. Corel WordPerfect will replace the abbreviation with the complete word or phrase.

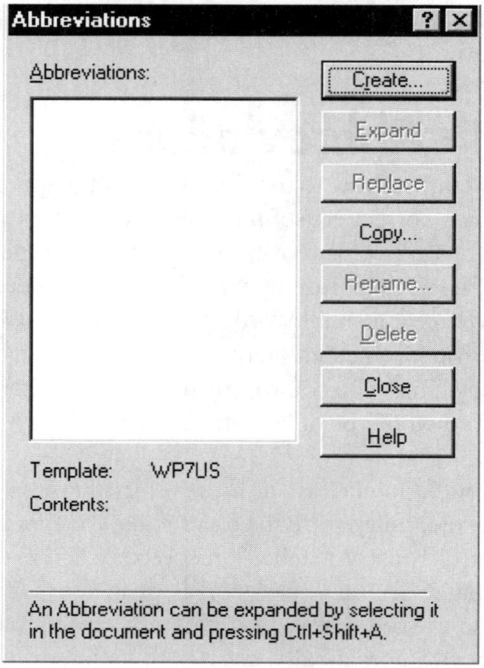

Abbreviations   ? X

Abbreviations:

Create...

Expand

Replace

Copy...

Rename...

Delete

Close

Help

Template: WP7US

Contents:

An Abbreviation can be expanded by selecting it
in the document and pressing Ctrl+Shift+A.

The
Abbreviations
dialog box

FIGURE 5-1

n OTE: *Abbreviation names are case sensitive.*

If you forget what abbreviations you used, or you want to delete one, select Abbreviations from the Insert menu. Click on it in the list, and then click on Expand.

The Replace option in the Abbreviations dialog box changes the text that an abbreviation is associated with, using the following steps:

1. Select the new text you want the abbreviation to represent.

2. Select Abbreviations from the Insert menu.

3. Click on the abbreviation you want to change, and then click on Replace.

4. Select Yes to confirm.

5. Click on Close.

To save an abbreviation to a specific template, click on the Template button when you are creating an abbreviation, and then select the template.

OTE: *Refer to Chapter 2 to refresh your memory about QuickCorrect and Format As You Go.*

Inserting the Date and Time

You probably add the date to letters, memos, and faxes. You might even add the time to faxes, logs, journals, messages, and other documents when the time of distribution or printing is important. Rather than manually typing the date or time, have Corel WordPerfect do it for you.

You can enter the date and time in two ways—as text or as a code. When you have Corel WordPerfect insert the date or time as *text*, Corel WordPerfect enters it as a series of characters, just as if you had typed it yourself. You can edit or delete individual characters, just as you can edit any text that you've typed.

When you have Corel WordPerfect insert the date and time as a *code*, however, you will *see* the date or time appear on the screen, but Corel WordPerfect has actually entered a code. The date or time will change to the current date or time whenever you open or print the document. You can't edit the date or time itself.

To insert the date or time, point to Date in the Insert menu, and then select either Date Text or Date Code.

IP: *Press CTRL+D to insert the date as text, or SHIFT+CTRL+D to insert it as code.*

Changing Date Formats

By default, Corel WordPerfect inserts the date in the format November 16, 1997. If you want to use another format, select Date Format from the Insert menu to see the dialog box shown in Figure 5-2. Choose one of the formats in the list and then click on OK. Now when you select Date Text or Date Code from the Insert menu, the date will appear in the selected format.

When you change the format, Corel WordPerfect will automatically change all dates that had been entered as a code that follow the insertion point.

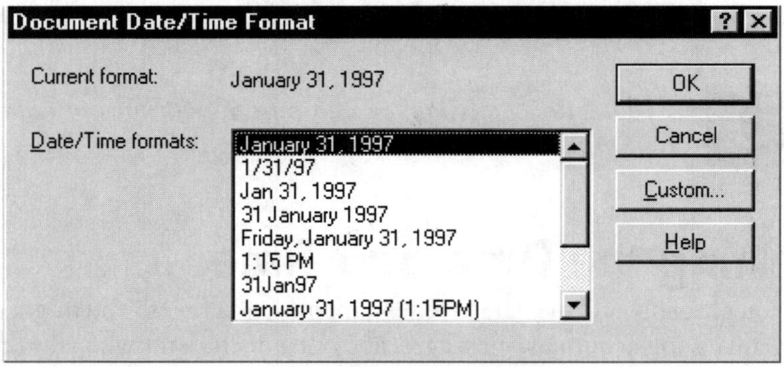

Selecting and creating date formats

FIGURE 5-2

Custom Date Formats

If none of the formats suit your tastes, you can create your own. Click on Custom in the Date Format dialog box to see the options in Figure 5-3.

The currently used format will appear in the Edit Date/Time Format text box, shown as a series of codes. A sample date in that format is displayed. To change a format, you must enter codes that represent the year, month, day, and time. All of the possible codes are shown in the list boxes in the four pages of the dialog box. Select a code from the list, and then click on Insert to add it to the Edit Date/Time Format text box.

Inserting Other Useful Objects

In addition to inserting the date, you can insert the name of the file and other items into a document. These may not be used as often as the date, but they are handy when you need them. Pull down the Insert menu and point to Other to access these options:

- *Filename* inserts the name of the current document. Nothing will appear if you have not named it yet—the default Document1 name, for example, will not be inserted.
- *Path and Filename* inserts the complete path as well as the name. The path is the location of the folder in which the document is stored, starting from the root directory of the disk drive.

- *Counter* inserts codes to consecutively number figures, tables, and other objects.

- *BarCode* inserts a POSTNET bar code. A dialog box will appear for you to enter the ZIP code.

Inserting Comments

A *comment* is an annotation, a note, reminder, or reference that you want to place in the document but not print along with it. It is a handy way to record reminders to yourself and explanations to others who may be reading or editing your document. To insert a comment, pull down the Insert menu and point to Comments to see the options Create, Edit, and Convert to Text.

 OTE: *To convert existing text into a comment, select the text, and then create the comment.*

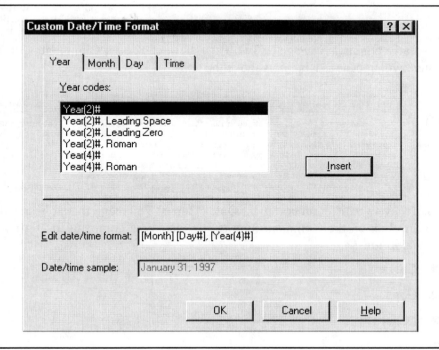

Creating your own date or time format

FIGURE 5-3

Click on Create to display the Comment window, shown in Figure 5-4. Now type the text that you want in the comment, or click on the feature bar buttons to add your initials, name, date, or time, or to move to other comments in the document. When you've finished writing the comment, click on Close in the feature bar.

 OTE: *Corel WordPerfect will only display your initials or name if they are defined as part of the Corel WordPerfect environment.*

The way a comment appears depends on your view. In Draft view, the comment will appear in a shaded text box above the paragraph where you inserted it. In Page and Two-Page views, you'll see your initials in a small box in the margin, or a Comment icon if your initials are not in the environment:

Comment initials ⟶ ARN

> For weeks I had contemplat
> Tae Kwon Do. Actually, for more t
> those years were devoted to earning
> profession of Medical Technology.
> I was really just inventing excuses fo
> weak, was a legitimate reason why I
> But one incident in particula

Comment icon ⟶

To read a comment in Page or Two-Page view, click on it with the mouse. The comment will appear as a balloon above the text.

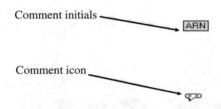

ARN

> Review the entire document for accuracy.
>
> For weeks I had contemplated visiting the dojang where my eight year old nephew studies
> Tae Kwon Do. Actually, for more than twenty years I have wanted to learn a martial art but
> those years were devoted to earning college degrees and establishing myself in my chosen
> profession of Medical Technology. In addition, I believed that "sports" did not come easy to me.
> I was really just inventing excuses for not signing up and thought that being a woman, thin and
> weak, was a legitimate reason why I could only fail in pursuing Tae Kwon Do.
> But one incident in particular happened that changed my mind. Adam, my nephew, all of

There are two different comment QuickMenus. The menu that appears when you right-click on the Comment icon or the displayed comment in Draft view has these options:

- Cut
- Copy
- Delete
- What's This?
- Edit

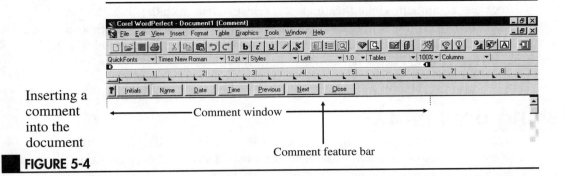

Inserting a
comment
into the
document

FIGURE 5-4

The QuickMenu that appears when you right-click on the displayed comment in Page and Two-Page view—not on the icon—has these options:

- Convert To Text
- Delete
- What's This?
- Info
- Edit

To edit a comment in its own window, double-click on it, or display the QuickMenu and click on Edit. Edit it as you wish, and then click on Close.

To print a comment, open it in the Edit window and click on the Print button in the toolbar.

To convert a comment to regular text so it appears normally in your document, use the following steps:

1. Place the insertion point after the comment.

2. Pull down the Insert menu.

3. Point to Comment.

4. Click on Convert to Text.

If you are in Page or Two-Page view, you can also click on the comment to display it, and then right-click on the displayed comment and select Convert to Text.

To delete a comment, right-click on it and select Delete from the QuickMenu.

To get the name, initials, revision color, and date the comment was created, select Info from the QuickMenu. This option only appears when you right-click on a displayed comment in Page and Two-Page views.

Setting Bookmarks

A *bookmark* marks your place in the document. Like a bookmark in a book, it allows you to quickly return to a specific location. You can add any number of bookmarks in a document, giving each a name, so you can return to a specific location later on. You can also create a QuickMark, which lets you return to a position with two clicks of the mouse, and you can set up Corel WordPerfect to automatically set a QuickMark at the last position of the insertion point when you save the document.

To create a bookmark, place the insertion point where you want the bookmark to be set. Corel WordPerfect will associate the bookmark with that location of the insertion point. If you want the bookmark to be linked to text, select the text before creating the bookmark. Then pull down the Insert menu and click on Bookmark to display the dialog box in Figure 5-5. Click on Create. In the box that appears, type a name for the bookmark and click on Close.

 OTE: *If you do not enter a name, Corel WordPerfect creates a QuickMark.*

To return to a bookmark position, select Bookmark from the Insert menu, click on the bookmark name in the list, and then click on Go To. If the bookmark is associated with selected text, click on Go To & Select. Corel WordPerfect will move to the text and select it.

You can also set one QuickMark in a document. This is a bookmark that you do not have to name. Use these steps:

1. Place the insertion point at the position you want to mark—or select text.

2. Display the Bookmark dialog box.

3. Click on Set QuickMark.

4. To return to that position, select Find QuickMark from the dialog box.

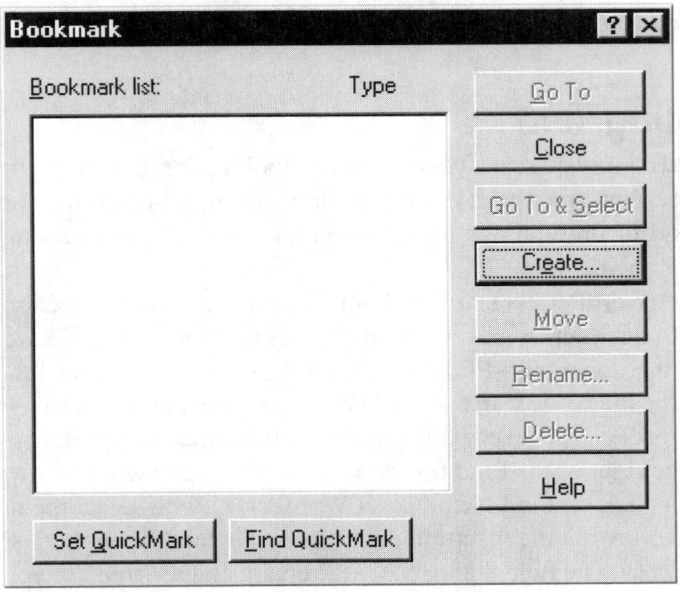

Creating a
bookmark

FIGURE 5-5

5

OTE: *See Chapter 10 to set up Corel WordPerfect to set a QuickMark for you, so you can pick up where you left off the next time you open the document.*

Other options on the dialog box let you delete, rename, and move a bookmark. Moving a bookmark associates an existing bookmark with a new location or selected text.

We'll look at inserting sounds and other items in later chapters.

Finding and Replacing Text

The Find and Replace command can be a real time-saver. Suppose you're looking for a specific reference in your document but you're not sure exactly where it is. Instead of scanning through the entire document, with a chance that you'll miss it, let Corel WordPerfect locate the text for you. The Replace part of the command can even replace text that it locates, so you can quickly correct an error in several locations, or change a word to another every place it is used.

Both the Find and the Replace functions are in the same dialog box (Figure 5-6), displayed when you select Find and Replace from the Edit menu.

Locating Text

The Find command scans your document looking for the first occurrence of the word or phrase that you specify. After it finds the word or phrase, you can repeat the command to find the next occurrence, and so on, until your entire document has been searched.

Corel WordPerfect starts looking for text at the current location of the insertion point. If you want to make sure that the entire document is searched, move to the start of the document. Pull down the Edit menu, and select Find and Replace to display the dialog box. In the Find What box, type the characters you want to locate. Corel WordPerfect saves your last ten search phrases. To select one, pull down the list on the right of the Find text box, and click on the word you want to locate.

Then click on Find Next. Corel WordPerfect will select the next occurrence of the text following the insertion point. To locate text above the insertion point, click on Find Prev. The Find dialog box will remain on the screen so you can find the next occurrence by clicking on Find Next again. If the text is not found, a dialog box appears with the message "Not Found." Select OK or press ENTER to remove the message, leaving the insertion point in its original position.

Corel WordPerfect will locate the characters you search for even if they are part of another word. Searching for the word "love," for example, will select the characters in the word "lovely." You can customize how Corel WordPerfect locates text using the Find and Replace menu bar.

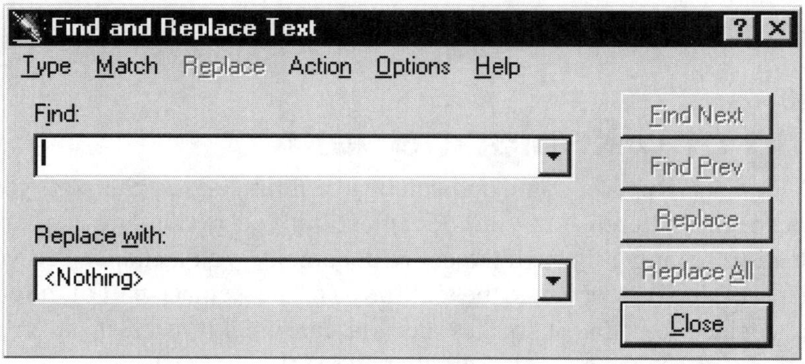

Find and
Replace
dialog box

FIGURE 5-6

The Match menu, for example, determines what is considered a match. The options are

- *Whole Word* locates just whole words that match the text you are looking for. If you are looking for "love," it will not match with "lovely."

- *Case* matches only characters in the same case. By default, searches are not case sensitive.

- *Font* lets you choose a specific font, so you can look for a word only if it is in Times Roman, for example.

- *Codes* lets you search for a formatting code, or a specific format of text. Use it, for example, to locate any text that is centered, or a specific centered word.

The Action menu determines what happens when Corel WordPerfect locates a match. The options in the menu are

- *Select Match* highlights the located text.

- *Position Before* places the insertion point before the text.

- *Position After* places the insertion point after the text.

- *Extend Selection* selects all of the text from the current location of the insertion point to the located text.

The Options menu determines the way the search operates. The options are

- *Begin Find at Top of Document* starts searching from the beginning of the document regardless of the insertion point position.

- *Wrap at Beg./End of Document* continues at the beginning of the document when Corel WordPerfect reaches the end when you did not start at the beginning. If you search using Find Prev, Corel WordPerfect will wrap to the end when it reaches the start.

- *Limit Find Within Selection* searches only the currently selected portion of text.

- *Include Headers, Footers, etc. In Find* searches for the text in headers, footers, and all document elements, even those not displayed.

■ *Limit Number of Changes* will make only a specific number of replacements that you specify, when using the Replace All command.

The Type menu determines what Corel WordPerfect looks for. The default setting is Text. You can also select Word Forms and Specific Codes. If you want to locate all forms of a word, such as "drink," "drank," and "drunk," pull down the Type option and click on Word Forms. Type one form of the verb and then click on Find Next. For example, searching for "sing" with this option selected will locate "sing," "sang," and "sung." The Specific Code option lets you search for a code that has specific settings, such as a certain indentation or margin.

Replacing Text Automatically

Making a mistake is only human, but making the same mistake more than once is downright annoying. Have you ever typed a document only to discover that you've made the same mistake several times? The Replace part of Find and Replace will search your document to find text automatically and replace it with something else. You can use it not only to correct errors but to recycle documents. Perhaps you created a sales proposal that mentions a person's name in several places. You may be able to modify the proposal for another prospect by changing just one or two words several times. You can have Corel WordPerfect scan the entire document, automatically replacing "Mr. Smith" with "Mrs. Jones." It just takes a few keystrokes.

To replace text automatically, use these steps:

1. Move the insertion point to the location where you want the replacements to begin.

2. Choose Find and Replace from the Edit menu.

3. In the Find box, enter the text that you want to replace.

4. In the Replace With box, enter the text that you want to insert. When you click in the Replace With box, the notation <Nothing> will disappear.

 AUTION: *Selecting Replace or Replace All when <Nothing> is in the Replace With box will delete the located text.*

The Replace operation will first locate the text that you want to replace, so you should select options from the menus to specify how you want the Find part of the operation to proceed. In fact, the options and the Find What text will be the same as you selected in the last Find operation. If you only want to replace the text when it appears as a whole word, for example, pull down the Match list and select Whole Word. The Match list will only be selectable when you are in the Find text box.

When you are in the Replace With text box, you can pull down the Replace list to select these options:

- *Case* toggles case-sensitive replacing on and off.

- *Font* replace with text formatted a specific way.

- *Code* lets you choose a code to insert.

Confirming Replacements

You might not want to replace every occurrence of the text in the document. For example, suppose you refer to the titles of two persons in your document. You call Mrs. Jones the President, and you refer to Mr. Smith as Vice President. After completing the letter, you learn that Mrs. Jones's correct title is Chairman. Can you use Replace All to change every occurrence of President to Chairman? Not really. If you do, you would change Mr. Smith's title to Vice Chairman.

When you do not want to replace every occurrence of the text, use the Find Next and Replace buttons. Click on Find Next to locate and select the next occurrence of the text following the insertion point. (Use Find Previous to locate text above the insertion point.) To replace the selected text, click on Replace. Corel WordPerfect will make the replacement and then automatically locate and select the next occurrence. If you want to leave the text as it is and locate the next occurrence, click on Find Next again.

Automatic Replacements

If you feel confident that you want to replace every occurrence of the text, click on the Replace All button. Corel WordPerfect will scan the document making the replacements for you. Use this option with caution. Remember, the default Find and Replace settings ignore case and locate characters even if they are part of another word. With these settings, replacing every occurrence of the text could unintentionally change parts of other words. Changing "his" to "her" would also change "history" to "hertory" and "Buddhism" to "Buddherm."

To safeguard against these types of errors, either confirm each replacement or use the Match Case and Match Whole Words options.

Finding and Replacing Formats and Codes

Sometimes you want to find information that you cannot type into the Find What box. For example, suppose you want to find a word, but only when it is in italic format. You must tell Word not only what text to locate but also its format.

 OTE: *You will learn about codes in Chapter 6.*

In the Find text box, enter the text that you want to find. Then, pull down the Match list and click on Font to display the dialog box shown in Figure 5-7. To search for text in a certain font and style, pull down the Font list and choose the font, and then select the style in the Font Style list. To search for text in a specific point size, choose the size in the Point Size list. In the Attributed section, choose any other font formats that must be applied to the text.

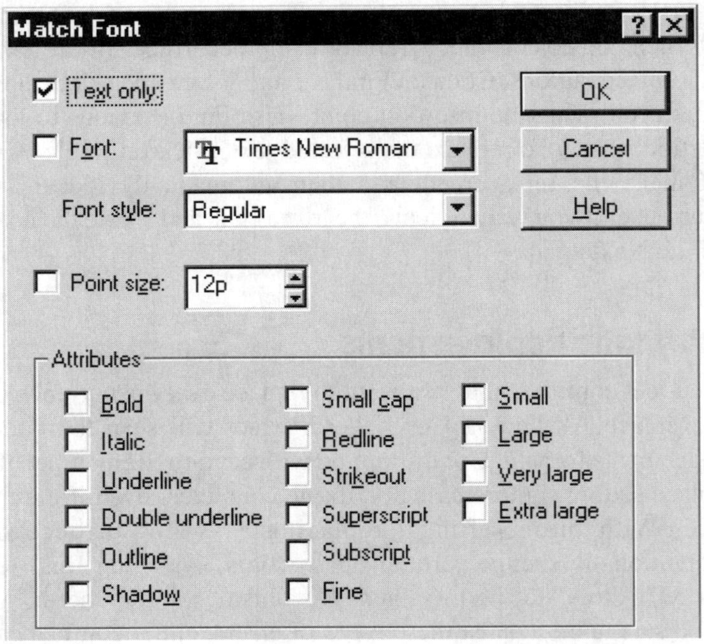

Selecting
formats and
codes to
locate

FIGURE 5-7

 **IP:**   *To later search for text without considering its format, click on Text Only.*

When you replace the text, it will appear in the same font as that replaced. To apply other formats to the replaced text, click on the Replace With box, pull down the Replace list, and click on Font. Now select the formats that you want applied to the new text. The dialog box show the formats you are locating and replacing, as follows:

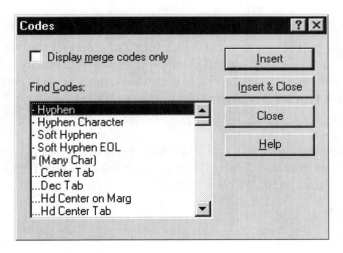

To find just a code, such as a Tab or paragraph mark, click on the Find text box, pull down the Match menu, and click on Codes to see this dialog box:

Scroll the list and choose the code that you want to locate. If you do not want to replace the code with another, click on Insert to add the code to the Find text box, and close the dialog box. If you want to replace the code with another, click on the Replace With text box. Then choose the code in the dialog box and click on Insert & Close.

 OTE: *Some codes will be dimmed when you are in the Replace With box. These are codes that cannot be inserted in place of others.*

There are other codes that have specific settings. For example, if you choose to replace a Margins code, you have to designate the margin settings. In either the Find or Replace With boxes, pull down the Type menu, and click on Specific Codes. In the box that appears, select the code you want to find or replace, then click on OK. A dialog box will appear where you can select or set the exact value.

Replacing All Word Forms

The Word Forms feature will locate and replace all forms of a word. For example, suppose you typed **He was going to walk to the store, but he already walked ten miles.** You now realize that you want the sentence to read **He was going to run to the store, but he already ran ten miles.** To make the changes, use these steps:

1. Select Find and Replace from the Edit menu.

2. Type **walk** in the Find text box.

3. Pull down the Type menu and click on Word Forms. If the word in the Find box cannot be found in Corel WordPerfect's dictionary, a warning box will appear. Click on OK to clear the warning box and enter another word or turn off Word Forms.

4. In the Replace With box, type **run**.

5. Click on Replace All. Corel WordPerfect will highlight the word "walk" in the sentence and display this dialog box asking which form of the replacement word you want to insert:

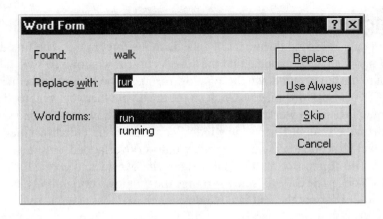

6. Click on Replace with to use the suggested "run." Corel WordPerfect will select the word "walked" and display the Word Form dialog box with the choices "run" and "ran."

7. Click on "ran" and then on Replace with.

8. Click on Close to close the Find and Replace dialog box.

 OTE: *The Use Always button in the Word Form dialog box will automatically use the same selection for all replacements. The Skip option leaves the work unchanged.*

Using Multiple Documents and Windows

Corel WordPerfect lets you have more than one document open at the same time, so you can move and copy text between documents as easily as you can within a document. For example, suppose you are on a tight deadline and you are trying to complete an important report. You realize that you need to refer to a letter that you wrote last month. With Corel WordPerfect, there's no need to rummage through your file cabinets. Just open the letter in its own window on the Corel WordPerfect screen so you can refer to it as you work on your report.

Arranging Windows on the Screen

When you open a second document, it appears in the foreground. The first document is moved into the background behind the new document window. To switch from one document to the other, pull down the Window menu. At the bottom of the menu you'll see a list of your open documents. Click on the document that you want to display.

It is much easier to work with multiple documents, however, when you can see them both on the screen. To arrange windows on the screen, pull down the Windows menu. Select Cascade to display all open windows overlapped, as shown in Figure 5-8. Select Tile Top to Bottom to display each window stacked vertically, one above the other. Choose Tile Side to Side to arrange the windows horizontally, next to each other. To edit or format the text in a window, click in it to make it active. The active window will contain scroll bars and the ruler, if it is turned on. Inactive windows do not have scrolls or rulers, and their title bars are dimmed.

When you want to display a window full screen, click on its Maximize button. To close a window, click on its Close button. The active window will be the one

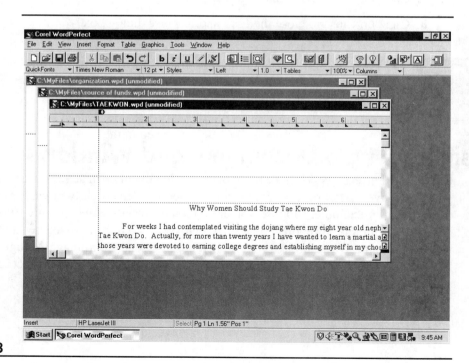

Cascaded
windows

FIGURE 5-8

affected by options you select in the menu bar and toolbar. If you click on the Print button, for example, only the document in the active window will be printed.

Moving Text Between Documents

You can move and copy text from one open document to another whether or not they are displayed at the same time. If the windows are not displayed at the same time, copy or move text using the Clipboard. If both windows are displayed, use the Clipboard or drag and drop.

To drag and drop text from one displayed window to another, select the text, point to it with the mouse, hold down the mouse button, and drag the selected text to the other window. When you release the mouse button, the window to which you dragged the text will be active. Remember to hold down the CTRL key if you want to copy the text rather than move it.

If the windows are overlapped, or stacked in the background, move or copy text using the Clipboard. Switch to the window containing the text you want to move or copy. Select the text and then click on either the Cut or the Copy button in the toolbar. Switch to the window containing the document where you want to place the text, and then click on the Paste button in the toolbar.

You can also use the Clipboard to copy or move text to a new document, or to an existing document that you have not yet opened. After you cut or copy the text to the Clipboard, click on New to start a new document, or open an existing document. Then position the insertion point and click on the Paste button.

Once you cut or copy text into the Clipboard, you can close the document that it came from. The document does not have to be open for you to paste the Clipboard contents elsewhere. If you forget what you've placed in the Clipboard, open a new document and click on Paste to display the contents of the Clipboard.

Inserting a File into a Document

Use drop and drag, or the Clipboard, to move or copy text from one document to another. You don't really even have to open a document if you want to copy all of it into another document.

To insert one entire document into the open document, place the insertion point where you want to insert the contents, and then select File from the Insert menu. Corel WordPerfect will display the Insert File dialog box, which is similar to the Open dialog box. Select the document that you want to insert, and then click on OK. Corel WordPerfect inserts the document using the page layout setting of the active document. You can now edit the inserted text, just as if it were originally part of the document.

Changing the Case of Characters

Did you type a title and then decide it would be better all uppercase? Pretty annoying, isn't it? Rather than retype everything, quickly change the case of existing characters using the Edit menu. To change the case of text, start by selecting the text, and then point to Convert Case in the Edit menu. Click on Uppercase, Lowercase, or Initial Capitals. The Initial Capitals option, by the way, changes the first letter of every word to capital except articles, prepositions, and certain other words when they do not start or end the sentence.

Repeating Actions

Sometimes you want to repeat an action a specific number of times in succession. For example, suppose you want to insert a row of 78 asterisks across the screen, or paste 10 copies of the contents of the Clipboard. The Repeat option from the Edit menu lets you repeat one action the number of times you specify. It will repeat a single keystroke, cursor movement, or a selection from the toolbar or power bar that is activated by a single click of the mouse.

When you want to repeat a keystroke, pull down the Edit menu and select Repeat to display this dialog box:

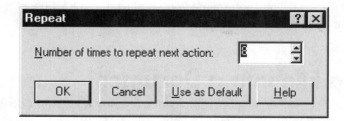

By default, your next keystroke after closing the box will be performed eight times. To repeat it a different number of times, enter the number in the text box. If you want that number to be the new default, click on the Use as Default button.

Then click on OK, and enter the keystroke or use the command that you want to repeat, such as typing an asterisk or clicking on the Paste button.

Highlighting Text

You've no doubt seen, or used, those transparent highlighting pens. When you want to mark an important word or phrase in a textbook, for example, you draw over it with a colored highlighting pen. This emphasizes the text, so you can quickly find it when scanning over the pages. You can use the Corel WordPerfect Highlight tool to do the same thing. You can even choose a color and print the highlight with the document.

To highlight text, select it and then click on the Highlight tool in the toolbar. You can also click on the Highlight tool first, before selecting text, so the mouse pointer changes to the same icon that is on the face of the button. Then drag over the text you want to highlight. When you release the mouse button, the text will be covered with the highlighting color. The Highlight function will remain on after you release the mouse button, however, so you can continue highlighting other text. This way you can scan through a document, highlighting text as you find it. To stop highlighting, click on the Highlight tool again.

 IP: *You can also turn highlighting on and off by selecting Highlight from the QuickMenu.*

Corel WordPerfect gives you several ways to remove highlighting from text. To quickly do so, click anywhere in a section of the highlighted area and click on the Highlight tool. If you want to remove the color from just part of a highlighted section, such as one word in a highlighted sentence, select the text first and then click on the Highlight tool. To remove the highlight from nonconsecutive highlighted areas, select all of the text, and then pull down the Tools menu, point to Highlight, and click on Remove Highlighting.

By default, the highlight color is yellow. To select another color, pull down the Tools menu, point to Highlight, and click on Change Color to see this dialog box:

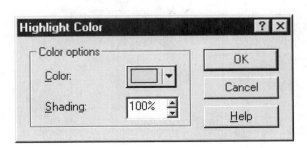

Click on the box containing the color sample to display a palette of 256 colors. Click on the color you want to use. You can also choose a shading for various degrees of the selected color. Choosing 50%, for example, prints the color in half of its intensity.

For even more choices, click on the Palette button at the bottom of the color palette to see the dialog box shown in Figure 5-9. Use this box to create custom colors by mixing red, green, and blue. If you pull down the Model list, you can also choose HLS to mix by hue, lightness, and saturation, or choose CYMK to mix cyan, yellow, magenta, and black.

IP: *You can also display this dialog box to select colors for other Corel WordPerfect formats.*

The color you choose will now be used as the default when you click on the Highlight tool—until you select another color. However, the color on the Highlight tool itself will remain yellow.

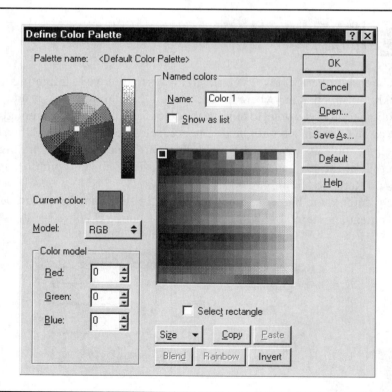

Creating
custom
highlight
colors

FIGURE 5-9

When you print your document, what you see is what you get. If you have a color printer, the highlight will print in the same color it is on the screen. If you have a monochrome printer, highlights will print in shades of gray. To hide the highlighting so it does not appear onscreen or when printed, pull down the Tools menu, point to Highlight, and click on Print/Show Highlighting. Use the same options to later redisplay the highlight.

Tracking Document Revisions

If you are working on a document with other authors, or editors, you can keep track of revisions. You'll be able to see at a glance the text that someone else added or thinks should be deleted. The changes each person makes are shown in a different color, so you can tell who made the changes. This is especially helpful when you use the Workflow feature to transmit your document across the network. You can then go through the document, quickly moving to each edited section, and accept or reject individual edits, or all that appear.

How you use this feature depends on whether you are the author or a reviewer.

Reviewing a Document

If you are reviewing a document written by someone else, pull down the File menu, point to Document, and click on Review. A dialog box will appear with two options: Author and Reviewer. Click on Reviewer to display the Reviewer pane at the top of the document, as shown in Figure 5-10.

 OTE: *If you have not yet entered your name or initials into the Corel WordPerfect environment, a dialog box will appear that gives you the opportunity.*

First, choose the color that you want your editing to appear in. Click on the Set Color button and choose a color from the palette that appears. (The palette also has a Palette button that you can click on to mix your own personal colors.) The name and colors used by other reviewers, if any, will be listed in the Other User Colors box.

Now edit the document. Text that you insert will appear in the selected color. Text that you delete will change to the color and appear with a strikeout line.

 OTE: *Click on the Show/Hide Changes button on the lower left of the Reviewer pane to temporarily remove text you deleted and show your inserted text in the normal text color.*

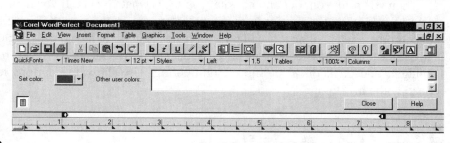

Reviewing
a document

FIGURE 5-10

When you have finished reviewing, click on the Close button in the Reviewer pane. Corel WordPerfect will display all of the text in the normal color, leaving the deleted text onscreen with the strikeout lines.

Reviewing Changes as the Author

When reviewers send back the document to you, the author, you want to review the changes and decide which ones should be made. Pull down the File menu, point to Document, then click on Review and then on Author. The Author pane will appear as shown in Figure 5-11, with the first change in the document highlighted.

Use the review buttons in the pane to look at the changes and decide which should be saved or deleted.

- *Show/Hide Changes* temporarily hides deleted text and shows all text in the normal color.

- *Next Annotation* moves to and highlights the next change.

- *Previous Annotation* moves to and highlights the previous annotation.

- *Insert Current Annotation* accepts the highlighted change, either removing deleted text or changing inserted characters into regular text.

- *Insert All Annotations* accepts all of the changes to the document.

- *Delete Current Annotation* rejects the highlighted change, replacing text that was marked for deletion, or deleting text that was added.

- *Delete All Annotations* rejects all of the changes that were made.

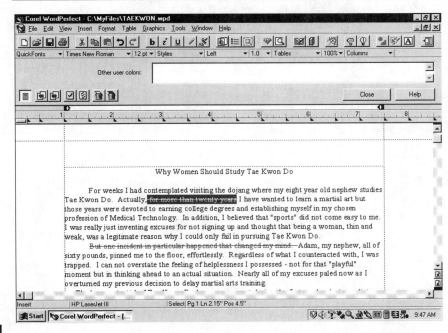

Reviewing
changes as
the author

FIGURE 5-11

 OTE: *The options in the Review pane do not affect text marked separately by the Redline or Strikeout font attributes discussed in Chapter 6.*

Formatting Text

6

When you edit a document, you change its content. When you format a document, you change its appearance. As with editing, you can format text as you type it or anytime after, so you don't have to worry about the format when you're struggling to find the right words. In this chapter you will learn how to format characters, lines, and paragraphs.

Character formatting affects the shape, size, and appearance of characters. Use these formats to make your document visually appealing and to emphasize important points. Formatting lines and paragraphs adjusts their position on the page.

Working with Corel WordPerfect Codes

Before learning how to format, you should get a basic understanding of Corel WordPerfect's codes. Every format that you apply to text, as well as noncharacter keys such as TAB and ENTER, is inserted as invisible codes into the document. The codes tell Corel WordPerfect when to turn formats on and off, insert a tab, end a paragraph, end a page, and perform every other Corel WordPerfect function. Knowing that all formats insert codes into the document will help you later understand how formats affect text.

As long as you have no problems inserting and deleting text and formatting your document, you may never have to worry about the codes. But sometimes, especially when you just can't seem to format the text the way you want, it pays to reveal the codes on the screen so you can see exactly what's happening. You may find that you accidentally pressed the wrong function key, or applied and then forgot about a format.

You reveal the codes in a separate window at the bottom of the screen. The quickest way to reveal codes is to drag one of the Reveal Codes lines, the small black rectangles at the top and bottom of the vertical scroll bar. As you drag the top line down, or the bottom line up, a bar will appear across the screen showing the size of the Reveal Codes window. When you release the mouse, you'll see a window that shows your text, as well as symbols that represent the codes, as shown in Figure 6-1.

The insertion point is seen as a red rectangle, while codes appear in boxes. Hard carriage returns (created by pressing the ENTER key) are represented by HRt, soft carriage returns (added by word wrap) are shown as SRt, tabs are Tab, and spaces are diamonds.

The Reveal
Codes
window

FIGURE 6-1

Codes that format text will surround the characters that they affect. The shape of the box indicates if it is an On code or an Off code, as you can see in these bold codes:

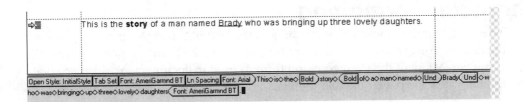

Other codes appear abbreviated when the insertion point is not immediately to their left. For example, the Tab Set code indicates that you've made a change in the tab stops. If you place the insertion point just before the code, it will be expanded to show the full tab settings:

IP: *You can also reveal codes by pressing ALT+F3, or selecting Reveal Codes from the View menu.*

If you want, you can leave the codes revealed as you continue writing. To remove the code window, drag the dividing line off the top or bottom of the screen, or select Reveal Codes from the View menu, or press ALT+F3 again.

If a code is associated with a dialog box, open the dialog box by double-clicking on the code. For example, double-clicking on a character format code, such as bold, will display the Font dialog box.

Not all codes appear at the location in the text where you applied them. A code that affects the entire page, such as changing a page size, will be placed near the start of the page, before any codes that only affect paragraphs. Corel WordPerfect will also delete duplicate or redundant codes. If you select one page size, then change your mind and choose another, Corel WordPerfect will replace the first Page Size code with the other.

You can view, delete, move, and edit codes in the Reveal Codes window. To delete a code from the document, and thus remove its format, drag it off of the Reveal Codes window. You can also delete a code by pressing DEL or BACKSPACE, as you would delete other characters.

Character Formatting

There are literally thousands of combinations of formats that you can apply to your document. You can access all of these formats using the Format command from the menu bar. Many of the most common formats used in documents are also provided as buttons on the power bar and toolbar.

Applying Bold, Italic, and Underline Formatting

Three of the most popular character formats are **bold**, *italic*, and <u>underlining</u>, by themselves or in combination. These are quick and easy to apply because buttons for them are on the toolbar.

IP: *Shortcut key combinations for the three most used character formats are CTRL+B for bold, CTRL+I for italic, and CTRL+U for underlining.*

To format text as you type it, just click on the appropriate button and then type. Try it now using the following example:

1. Type **Your bill is** and then press SPACEBAR.

2. Click on the Underline button in the toolbar and then type **seriously overdue**. Corel WordPerfect underlines the words and the spaces between them as you type.

3. Now turn off underlining by clicking on the Underline button again. This stops the formatting and changes the button so it no longer appears pressed down. This type of action is often called a *toggle*, named after a toggle switch that turns a light on and off.

 IP: *Not all toolbar buttons act as toggles.*

4. Press SPACEBAR, type **and we will be forced to take**, and then press SPACEBAR again.

5. Click first on the Bold button and then the Italic button in the toolbar. To use a combination of the formats, click on each button that you want to apply.

6. Type **legal action**, and then click on the Bold and Italic buttons again. You can click the buttons in any order.

7. Type a period and then press ENTER. Your sentence should look like the one shown here.

Your bill is <u>seriously overdue</u> and we will be forced to take *legal action*.

To format text that you've already typed, first select the text and then click on the button. You can format a single word by clicking anywhere in the word and then choosing the button from the toolbar—you do not have to select the word first.

If you format characters by mistake, or just change your mind, select the text. The formats applied will appear as depressed buttons. Click on the button representing the format you want to remove.

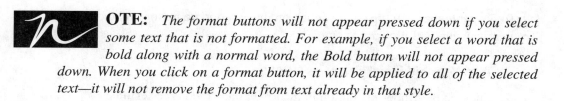

OTE: *The format buttons will not appear pressed down if you select some text that is not formatted. For example, if you select a word that is bold along with a normal word, the Bold button will not appear pressed down. When you click on a format button, it will be applied to all of the selected text—it will not remove the format from text already in that style.*

Selecting Fonts and Sizes from the Power Bar

The Formatting toolbar contains drop-down lists for selecting the font and size of characters. You can set the font and the size of text as you type it, or you can change the font and size of text—even a single character—by selecting it first. To change the font and size of a single word, however, just place the insertion point in the word before selecting the formats.

The first list on the left of the power bar is called QuickFonts. It will contain the last 20 combinations of font, size, and font attributes that you used. Each item in the QuickFonts list includes the combination of typeface, font size, and attributes. Choosing an item from the list applies all of the formats. For example, if you click on an item that says Arial 18, and that appears underlined and bold, all four attributes will be applied to selected text, or the text that you are about to type.

Use the QuickFont list to format selected text, or the word in which the insertion point is placed. QuickFonts will not affect any other text on the page.

IP: *The Font option at the bottom of the QuickFonts list will display the Font dialog box.*

The Font button on the power bar will display the font being used at the location of the insertion point. To select only another font, click on the Font button to display the fonts that are installed on your system. They are listed in alphabetical order. However, after you start using Corel WordPerfect to select fonts, you'll see several fonts at the beginning of the list, separated from the rest by a double line. These are the fonts that you've used recently. Corel WordPerfect places them first to make it easy for you to select the fonts that you use most often. To select a font, click on its name in the list and scroll the list as needed.

If you select text first, your choice will only affect that text. Otherwise, it will affect all text from the position of the insertion point to the end of the document. Its effect will end, however, when you choose another font, and it will not change text to which you already applied another font.

This is an important concept that affects many formatting commands, so make sure you understand it before going on. Let's say that you typed an entire document with the default font that Corel WordPerfect uses automatically. If you then move the insertion point to the start of the document and choose a font, all of the text in the document will change to that font.

Now suppose again that you typed an entire document in the default font. You then selected the third paragraph and chose a font from the power bar. Only that text will be affected. But now you move to the start of the document and choose a font. This time, your selection affects every paragraph except the third because it has a font already applied to it on its own.

You change the size of text using the Font Size list in the power bar. It affects text just like the Font command.

Formatting with the Font Dialog Box

The formatting options in the toolbar and power bar offer only a sampling of Corel WordPerfect's formats. For a full range of choices, display the Font dialog box shown in Figure 6-2. Display the box using any of these methods:

- Select Font from the Format menu.

- Right-click on the text window, and select Font from the QuickMenu.

- Pull down the QuickFonts list and click on Font.

- Double-click on the QuickFonts, Font, or Font Size buttons in the power bar.

- Click on the QuickSpot and then the Fonts button. You'll learn about the QuickSpot later.

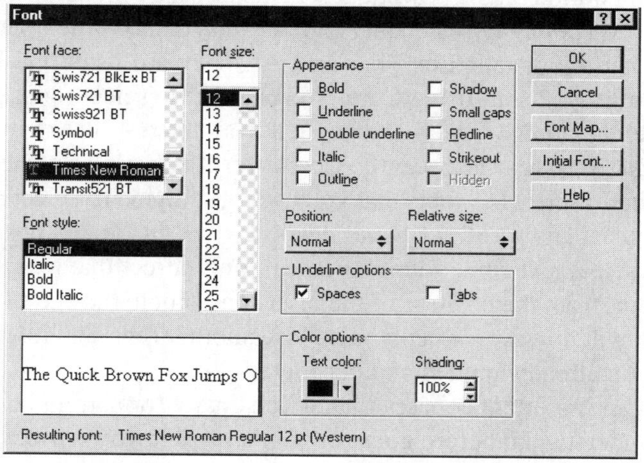

Font dialog
box

FIGURE 6-2

Make your choices from the dialog box, watching the preview panel to see their effects, and then click on OK to apply the settings to your text.

You can select a font, size, style, and appearance. When you close the dialog box, the font and size you select will be shown in the font and size boxes in the toolbar. The appearance options you select will be reflected in the look of the Bold and Italic buttons in the toolbar. If you choose the Bold appearance option, for example, the Bold button in the toolbar will appear pressed down. You can later change the font, size, and appearance using either the toolbar or the dialog box.

A font style, on the other hand, will not be reflected in the toolbar. Choosing the Bold option in the Font Style list will not press down the Bold button in the toolbar, and you won't be able to remove the style using the toolbar. This actually changes the font to a bold font, rather than applying the bold attribute. To remove the style, you must return to the Font dialog box and select Regular from the Font Style list.

Here are some other options in the dialog box:

- Select a Position option to create superscripts and subscripts.

- Choose to underline the spaces between words, the spaces inserted by pressing TAB, or just the words themselves.

- Pick a color and shading for the text. If you do not have a color printer, Corel WordPerfect will substitute an appropriate shade of gray.

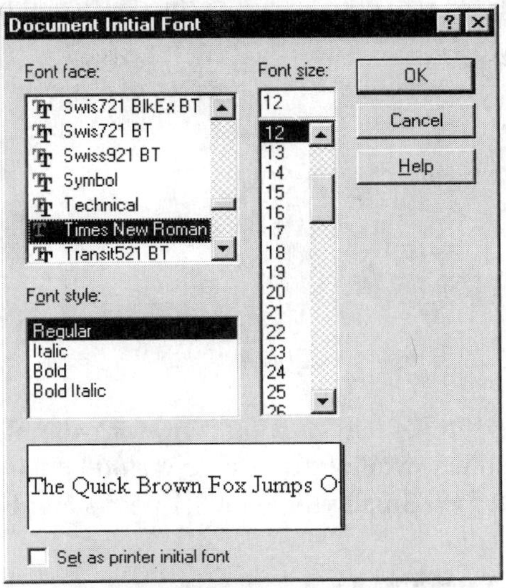

Document Initial Font

Font face:

🇹 Swis721 BlkEx BT
🇹 Swis721 BT
🇹 Swiss921 BT
🇹 Symbol
🇹 Technical
🇹 Times New Roman
🇹 Transit521 BT

Font style:

Regular
Italic
Bold
Bold Italic

Font size:

12
12
13
14
15
16
17
18
19
20
21
22
23
24
25
26

OK
Cancel
Help

The Quick Brown Fox Jumps O

☐ Set as printer initial font

Selecting an
initial font

FIGURE 6-3

You use the Initial Font button to change the default font that Corel WordPerfect uses for every new document. Click on the Initial Font button to see the dialog box shown in Figure 6-3 above. Choose a font, size, and style. If you want to change the default font for every new document created with the current printer, click on the Set As Printer Initial Font check box. Setting the Printer Initial Font will not affect existing documents you've already saved, or text in the current document formatted with font codes.

Selecting a Relative Font Size

When you choose a font size using the power bar, or the Font Size list in the Font dialog box, you are selecting a specific point size. Sometimes, however, you may want to format text in relation to the text around it. You might want a headline, for example, to be twice the size of the text in the paragraph, or a portion of legalese fine print to be half the size.

To format text in a relative size, follow these steps:

1. Select the text you want to format.

2. Open the Font dialog box.

3. Pull down the Relative Size button in the Font dialog box to see the choices Fine, Small, Normal, Large, Very Large, or Extra Large.

4. Click on OK.

Each of the relative size choices are defined as a percentage of the current font:

Option	Percentage of Current Font
Fine	60%
Small	80%
Normal	100%
Large	120%
Very Large	150%
Extra Large	200%

If you are using the default 12-point font, for example, choosing Small would format text in 9.6 points, while Extra Large would be 24 points. If you were using a 10-point text font, then Small would be 8.1 points and Extra Large 20 points.

 IP: *You can change the percentages used for relative fonts by running the macro SETATTR.WCM.*

Using Hidden Text

The Hidden Text appearance lets you enter text that you selectively either hide or reveal, print or not print. Use it to create notes to yourself that you may want to print in draft copies for your review but not on the final copy for distribution.

If the Hidden appearance option is grayed in the Font dialog box, then the display of Hidden text is turned off in the View menu. To select the Hidden option, close the dialog box and select Hidden text from the View menu.

When you select the Hidden appearance, just enter text as you would normally. When you want to hide it, so it does not appear onscreen or print with the document, select Hidden Text from the View menu. A check mark at the Hidden Text option in the menu means that hidden text will appear and print.

Using Redline and Strikeout

In Chapter 5, you learned how to add, reject, or accept reviewers' comments. Text that a reviewer inserts appears in a different color than other text, and text that is deleted appears with strikeout.

You can also mark inserted and deleted text using the redline and strikeout appearance options in the Font dialog box. Strikeout text to show that you'd like to delete it, and redline text that you'd like to add. Redline text appears in a different color than other text; strikeout text has lines through it. You have to apply these formats yourself; Corel WordPerfect will not do it for you automatically as you edit. Either select the text first and then choose the redline or strikeout appearance, or choose the format first and then type the text.

To accept or reject the changes, pull down the File menu, point to Document, and click on Remove Compare Markings for two options:

- Remove Redline Markings and Strikeout Text removes the color from redlined text and deletes the strikeout text from the document.

- Remove Strikeout Text Only deletes strikeout text but leaves the redline color on inserted text.

Using Special Characters and Symbols

Most fonts usually contain symbols and accented characters in addition to the characters shown on your keyboard. These characters and symbols are useful when you are writing scientific or technical documents, or writing in a language other than English—although an American might, for example, need to enter the £ currency symbol when writing to England. Corel WordPerfect lets you access these characters, as well as hundreds of other foreign language characters, mathematical and scientific, and graphic symbols.

These characters are collected in 15 character sets. When you want to insert an international character or symbol in your document, use this procedure:

1. Select Character from the Insert menu to see the dialog box shown in Figure 6-4.

2. Pull down the Character Set list box and select the character set. The characters in that set are displayed in the Characters box. The character sets are ASCII, Multinational, Phonetic, Box Drawing, Typographic Symbols, Iconic Symbols, Math/Scientific, Math/Scientific Extended, Greek, Hebrew, Cyrillic, Japanese, User-Defined, Arabic, and Arabic Script.

3. Click on the character that you want to insert, and then click on the Insert and Close button.

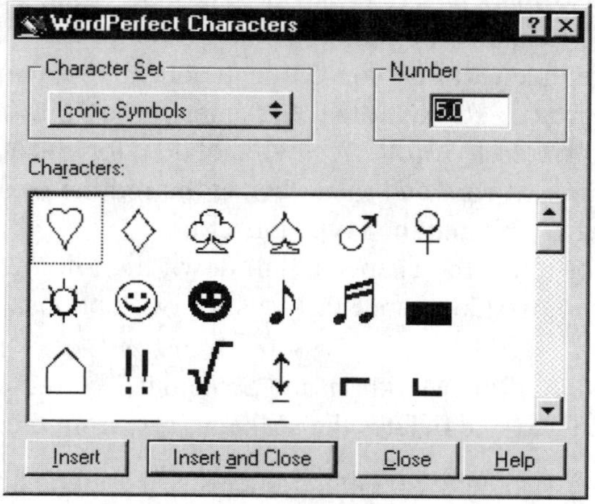

Inserting
special
characters
and symbols

FIGURE 6-4

Corel WordPerfect will insert the character at the position of the insertion point, in a size that matches the surrounding text. So if you are typing a headline in 24 points, for example, the special character will appear in 24 points. If the character is one that appears on the keyboard, Corel WordPerfect will also match the current font.

If you want to insert a number of characters, leave the dialog box on the screen and move back and forth between your document and the dialog box. Drag the dialog box out of the way, and then double-click on the character you want to insert, or choose the character and then click on Insert. Corel WordPerfect will insert the characters but leave the dialog box open so you can insert additional characters. Click in the document window to position the insertion point where you want to insert another character—even add or edit text if you want—and then click back in the dialog box when you want to insert another character.

The sets are numbered from 0 to 14, and each character is numbered within the set. You'll notice that when you click on a character, its set and character numbers appear in the Number box, such as 7,2 to represent the second character in set seven. If you know the set and number, you can enter them in the Number box yourself. When you type the character number, the set will appear in the dialog box with the character selected.

Duplicating Formats with QuickFormat

With all of the format options that Corel WordPerfect makes available, there are certainly a large number of possible combinations. If you've gone to the trouble of selecting a combination that you like for one section of text, you do not have to make the selections all over again for some other text. Just apply the same combination using QuickFormat.

When you want to copy a format, use these steps:

1. Place the insertion point in the text that uses that format.

2. Click on the QuickFormat button in the toolbar to see a dialog box with two options.

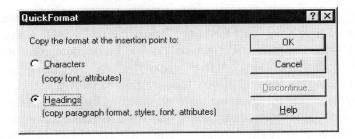

 IP: *You can also choose QuickFormat from the Format menu or from the QuickMenu.*

3. Select the Characters option in the dialog box if you only want to copy the font and character formats of the text. Select the Headings option in the dialog box if you want to copy all of the formats, including the font, line, and paragraph formats.

4. Click on OK. The shape of the mouse pointer will depend on your selection—a paintbrush if you choose characters, a paint roller if you choose headings.

5. Drag over the text that you want to apply the format to. When you release the mouse button after selecting the text, Corel WordPerfect will apply the formats. It will leave on QuickFormat, however, so you can apply the same formats to other sections of text.

6. To turn off the feature, click on the QuickFormat button again.

Formatting Lines and Paragraphs

When you want to add some style and flair to your document, apply *paragraph formats*. Paragraph formats affect the alignment of text on the page. Probably the first two paragraph formats that you'll want to learn are centering text between the margins and changing the line spacing. Again, Corel WordPerfect offers much more. As with character formats, you can format paragraphs as you type them or anytime afterward.

Introducing the Paragraph QuickSpot

When you point to a paragraph with the mouse, you'll see a small square next to the left corner of the paragraph's first line. This is the *QuickSpot*. When you click on the QuickSpot, Corel WordPerfect selects the entire paragraph and displays a QuickSpot dialog box, as shown in Figure 6-5.

As you can see, the dialog box has several drop-down lists and buttons that display dialog boxes for changing the font, inserting bullets, and saving a style. To apply a format to the selected paragraph, pull down a list and choose an option. Corel WordPerfect will apply the format but leave the dialog box onscreen so you can

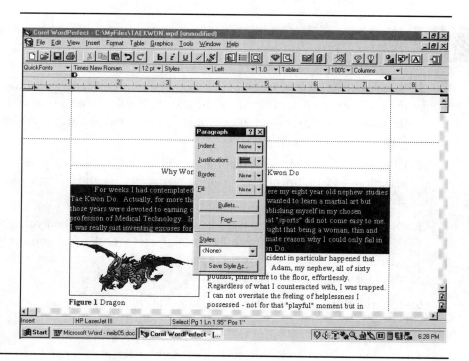

Paragraph QuickSpot dialog box

FIGURE 6-5

select other formats. To close the dialog box, click on its Close button (the box with the X in the title bar), or click on another paragraph in the document.

To format several paragraphs at the same time, select them first, and then click on the QuickSpot in front of any one. The formats you select will be applied to all of the paragraphs.

You will learn about each of the formats that you can apply, but here is a summary of their features.

- *Indent* lets you indent a paragraph from the left or both the left and right margins, create a hanging indentation, and insert a back tab that moves the insertion point into the left margin.

- *Justification* aligns text on the left, right, center, or on both the left and right margins.

- *Border* allows you to surround the paragraph with a border of your choice.

- *Fill* lets you select a background color or pattern to place behind the text.

- *Bullets* lets you insert numbers, letters, or graphic characters in front of each paragraph.

- *Font* displays the Font dialog box.

- *Styles* lets you select from predefined sets of formats.

Using the QuickMenu

You can also apply certain formats with the QuickMenu, shown here. Choose to center text, align it on the right, indent paragraphs, or return to the default table stops. To use the QuickMenu, point to the paragraph you want to format, and right-click the mouse. Then click on the format that you want to apply to the text. The options that appear in the QuickMenu depend on where you are pointing the mouse, and whether or not text is selected.

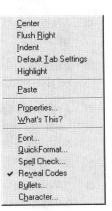

Changing Line Spacing

To change the line spacing, click on the Line Spacing button in the power bar (marked 1.0) to display its drop-down list. Then choose 1.0 (for single spacing), 1.5

(for a spacing of one and a half lines), 2.0 (for double spacing), or Other to set a specific spacing.

The line spacing command affects text in the same way as changing a font. If you select text first, the line spacing will only be applied to that text. If you did not select text, it will affect all of the text from the location of the insertion point, up to any text that has another line spacing applied to it.

To set a custom line spacing that is not listed in the power bar, choose Other from the Line Spacing button to see the Line Spacing dialog box. You can also display the dialog box by double-clicking on the Line Spacing button in the power bar, or by choosing Line from the Format menu and then clicking on Spacing. Type the line spacing or click on the up or down pointers to increment or decrement the setting in intervals of one-tenth line with each click.

Aligning Text Between the Margins

Probably the first paragraph format you'll want to use is centering. You may need to center your address on a letterhead or a title on a report. Corel WordPerfect provides six options for aligning text between the margins.

- With *Left* alignment, lines of text align evenly at the left margins, with an uneven right margin.

- *Center* alignment centers the text between the left and right margins, with uneven left and right margins.

- *Flush Right* alignment creates even right margins, with an uneven left margin.

- *Flush Right with Dot Leaders* inserts periods in the blank space to the left of right-aligned text.

- *Full* adds spaces to the lines of text, except lines ending with hard carriage returns when you pressed ENTER, so they are aligned evenly on both the left and right. This option does not affect the last line of a paragraph.

- *All* extends every line between the margins, including the last line of paragraphs, titles, and other single-line paragraphs.

You can select alignment options using the power bar and menu bar, but there are two general ways: line formatting and justification.

Line formatting affects individual lines or paragraphs. If you turn on the format and type text, the format ends when you press the ENTER key. If you place the insertion point in existing text and select a line format, only the current paragraph is affected. Text following the current paragraph will not be changed.

The *justification* commands, on the other hand, insert codes that affect all of the text starting in the paragraph where the insertion point is located—up to the first other justification code. If you are typing new text, the format remains on when you press the ENTER key. So if you use the line center command to center text, the insertion point returns to the left margin when you press ENTER. If you use the justification center command, the insertion point moves to the center of the screen when you press ENTER. You have to choose another justification command when you no longer want centered text.

 OTE: *If you select text first, both methods only affect the selected text.*

6

If you apply a justification format to text, you cannot change its format with a line formatting command. You can only change it by applying another justification. The justification commands take precedence over line formatting. If you already applied a line format to text, applying a justification format will change it. A line format command, however, will not affect justified text.

Centering Text

To center a single paragraph or selected text, select Center from the QuickMenu, or pull down the Format menu, point to Line, and click on Center. To center existing text, however, make sure you first place the insertion point *at the start of the line or paragraph.* If you start with the insertion point within the text, only text in the paragraph following the insertion will be centered.

To turn on centering for all text from the insertion point to the next justification code, or for all selected text, pull down the Align Text button in the power bar and click on Center. You can also pull down the Format menu, point to Justification, and click on Center. To turn off centering, pull down the Align Text list and choose Left, or choose Left from the Format Justification menu.

You can also center text using the QuickSpot. Click on a paragraph's QuickSpot and choose Center from the QuickSpot dialog box's Justification menu to center the paragraph.

Aligning Text on the Right

To align a single paragraph or selected text so it is flush with the right margin, select Flush Right from the QuickMenu, or pull down the Format menu, point to Line, and click on Flush Right. To align text on the right and insert periods in the blank space before the text, select Flush Right with Dot Leaders. Start with the insertion point at the start of the line to format all of the text.

To turn on flush right format for all text from the insertion point to the next justification code, or all selected text, pull down the Align Text button in the power bar and select Right. You can also pull down the Format menu, point to Justification, and click on Right.

You can also click on a paragraph's QuickSpot and select Right from the QuickSpot dialog box's Justification menu to center the paragraph.

Justifying Text

To justify text on the left and right, pull down the Align Text button in the power bar and select Full or All. You can also select Full or All from the QuickSpot dialog box Justification list. Remember, All justifies every line of text, even those ending with a hard carriage return. This can result in some strange effects by spacing out words in the last line to reach the right margin.

Enhancing Text with Borders

When you want to draw attention to a paragraph or section of text, enclose it in a border, or fill in the background with a color, shading, or pattern. It's an easy way to add a little pizzazz to a document without going all the way to graphics.

To add a border to a single paragraph, place the insertion point anywhere in it. To enhance more than one paragraph, follow these steps:

1. Select all paragraphs you want to enhance.

2. Pull down the Format menu and point to Border/Fill.

3. Click on Paragraph to see the dialog box in Figure 6-6. The box has three pages.

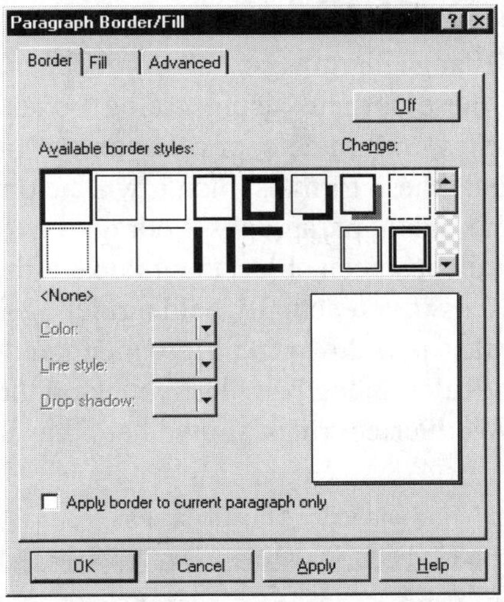

Adding a
border or
shading

FIGURE 6-6

On the Border page, you choose the color and style of lines that will surround the text. You can also choose to place the border around all of the remaining paragraphs in the document by deselecting the Apply Border To Current Paragraph Only button.

On the Fill page, you select a color or pattern to print in the background behind the text. If you select a pattern rather than a solid color, you can also choose a background and foreground color for two-tone patterns.

On the Advanced page, you customize your selected border and fill patterns. You can adjust the distance between the border lines and text, pick a drop shadow color and width, round box corners, and adjust the gradient pattern. Experiment with the options to discover how they work.

OTE: *In Chapter 8, you'll learn how to add borders around the entire page.*

If you just want to draw a line on the screen, remember the QuickLines feature of QuickCorrect Format As You Go. Type three or more hyphens or equal signs, and then press ENTER. Corel WordPerfect will draw a single or double line across the page.

Introducing the Ruler

You usually want to change margins, set tabs, or indent paragraphs specific amounts. You can set all of these formats using dialog boxes, where you can enter the measurements in inches, millimeters, or other unit of measurement. If you want to use the mouse to create these formats, then it will help if you first display the ruler. In fact, to set tabs and indent paragraphs by dragging the mouse, you must display the ruler. The ruler is an onscreen object that indicates the positions of tabs, margins, and indentations, just as if you actually held a ruler against the screen.

To display the ruler, pull down the View menu and click on Toolbars/Ruler to display the Toolbars/Ruler dialog box. Then click on the Ruler check box and click on OK. The Corel WordPerfect ruler, shown here, has three parts.

Margin and indentation indicators

Tab line   Ruled line

The middle section of the ruler is a ruled line in inches. (You can change the units of measure using the Preferences dialog box that you'll learn about in Chapter 10.) Use the ruled line to place objects in exact positions in your document.

Above the ruled line are the margin and indentation indicators, which you use to set the left and right page margins, and to indent paragraphs.

Below the ruled line is the tab line, which you use to set, delete, and change tab stops. The triangles on the tab line show the position of the default tab stops, set every half inch.

NOTE: *Because the ruler represents the spacing of your page, it will scroll as you scroll your document horizontally.*

Setting Tabs

Tab stops not only control the distance moved when you press the TAB key, but they affect how paragraphs are indented, as you will learn later in this chapter. You can use the mouse to quickly set and delete tab stops on the ruler, or you can work with tabs using a dialog box. Corel WordPerfect lets you set eight types of tab stops, as shown in Figure 6-7. The default *left* tab aligns a column along the left. Characters that you type shift normally to the right of the tab stop. A *right* tab aligns characters on the right. As you type, your text shifts toward the left of the tab stop. Use a *center* tab to center text at the tab stop. As you type, text shifts alternately to the left and to the right. Use a *decimal* tab to align a column of numbers on the decimal point. As you type, the characters shift toward the left until you type the decimal point. Decimal values then shift to the right. You can insert dot leaders with all tab types.

To set a tab, simply click in the tab line of the ruler, just below the desired position in the ruled line. To set a tab at the 1.75 inch position, for example, click here:

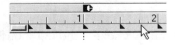

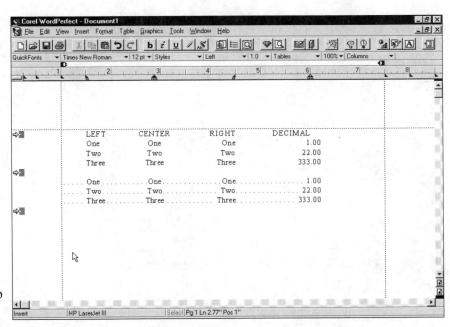

Types of tab stops

FIGURE 6-7

Left-aligned tabs are set by default. To choose another type of tab stop, right-click on the tab line to see the QuickMenu shown here.

You can also display this menu by clicking the left mouse on the button on the far left of the tab line. Click on the tab type that you want to set, with or without dot leaders. The shape of the button changes to illustrate the type of tab that you set:

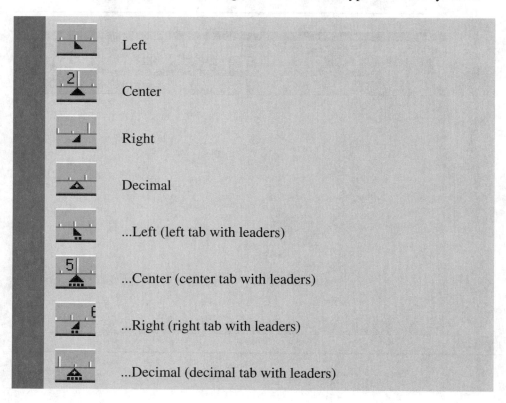

Left

Center

Right

Decimal

...Left (left tab with leaders)

...Center (center tab with leaders)

...Right (right tab with leaders)

...Decimal (decimal tab with leaders)

You can also move and delete tabs using the mouse and the ruler. To delete a tab stop, use these steps:

1. Point to its marker in the ruler.

2. Drag the mouse down into the typing area.

To move a tab stop to a different position, drag its indicator to a new position on the ruler. As you drag the tab indicator, a dotted line will appear down the screen showing where text will align. To delete all of the tab stops, right-click on the tab line and select Clear All Tabs—click on Default Tab Settings to reset to Corel WordPerfect's default tabs every half inch.

Be careful when setting, deleting, or moving tabs. If you do not have any text selected, your changes will affect all text that does not have its own tab formats. For example, suppose you type several paragraphs, pressing TAB to indent their first lines. At the end of the document, you decide you want a special paragraph indented 0.75 inches, so you drag the tab stop at the half-inch position to 0.75 on the ruler. The indentations of every other paragraph, even those above the insertion point, will adjust to that position. If you just deleted the tab stop at the half-inch position, then the indentations of the existing text will shift to the next tab on the right.

When you press TAB you are inserting a tab code into the document. The code tells Corel WordPerfect to move the insertion point to the next tab stop position on the right. If you delete the tab stop where the text was aligned, it will automatically move to the next tab stop. If you insert a tab stop prior to that position, the text will shift to that new tab stop.

To change the tab stops for just a portion of the document, select it first. This will only affect the selected text. If you later change tabs elsewhere in a document, all text except it will be affected.

Using the Tab QuickSpot

When you change the tab stops in a paragraph, Corel WordPerfect will display the Tab QuickSpot in the margin, as shown here. The QuickSpot indicates where the code was inserted that affects tab stops. If you click on the QuickSpot with the left mouse button, Corel WordPerfect will display a tab line just above the paragraph showing the tabs applied to the text:

You can use that tab line to add, delete, or change tab stops in the text. To remove the tab line from display, click elsewhere in the document.

If you select text and change the tabs, Corel WordPerfect will insert a Tab QuickSpot in the margin of the edited text, as well as at the start of the next paragraph. This shows that different tab settings apply at those locations. What happens if you change tabs within a section that has already had a different set of tabs applied?

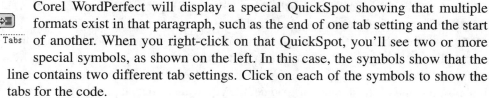

Corel WordPerfect will display a special QuickSpot showing that multiple formats exist in that paragraph, such as the end of one tab setting and the start of another. When you right-click on that QuickSpot, you'll see two or more special symbols, as shown on the left. In this case, the symbols show that the line contains two different tab settings. Click on each of the symbols to show the tabs for the code.

Setting Tabs with the Dialog Box

The Tabs dialog box, shown in Figure 6-8, gives you even greater control over tab stops, although it may not be as easy to use as clicking the mouse. To adjust tabs, right-click on the ruler and select Tab Set from the QuickMenu, or pull down the Format menu, point on Line, and click on Tab Set.

To set a tab, pull down the Type list and choose a tab type. Enter the location of the tab in the Position text box, and then click on the Set button. To delete a tab, type its location in the Position box and click on the Clear button. Click on Clear all to delete all of the tabs. If you want to restore all of Corel WordPerfect's default stops, click on Default.

The Repeat Every button lets you enter a series of evenly spaced tabs. Click on Repeat Every, and then enter the spacing in the text box. Type .75, for example, to set tabs every $\frac{3}{4}$ inch across the ruler.

You can also change the character that is used as the dot leader.

Relative Versus Absolute Tab

When you type a position setting for a tab, Corel WordPerfect sets it relative to the left margin. A tab set at 1.25, for example, will be 1.25 inches from the left margin, or 2.25 inches from the left edge of the paper using the default 1-inch margin.

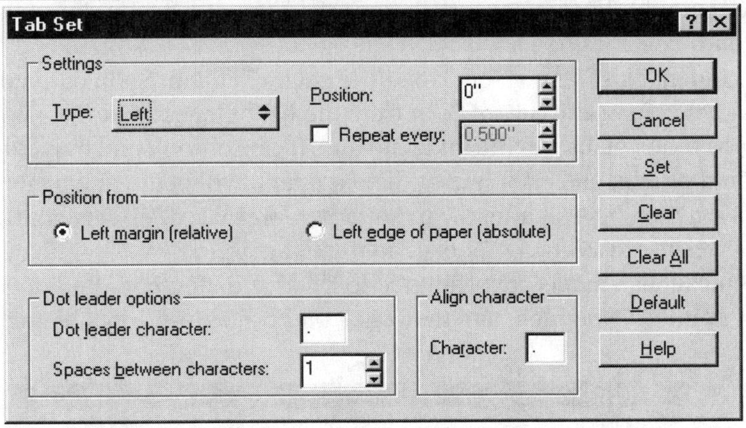

Tab Set
dialog box

FIGURE 6-8

Because the tab is relative, it will remain at that distance from the margin even if you change the left margin setting. So if you change the margin to 1.5 inches, the tab stop will still be 1.25 inches from it, but now 2.75 inches from the edge of the page.

If you want a tab stop to remain at a fixed position, regardless of the margins, click on the Left Edge Of Paper (Absolute) option in the Tab Stop dialog box. Now, changing the left margin will not affect the position of tab stops from the edge of the paper. The position of tabs will be set at a distance from the edge of the paper, rather than the margin.

Indenting Paragraphs

If you want to indent the first line of a paragraph, just press the TAB key. But you might want to indent every line of a paragraph from the left margin or from both the right and left margins. You might also want to automatically indent the first line of every paragraph to save yourself the trouble of pressing TAB. You can control paragraph indentations from the toolbar, the ruler, or the Paragraph dialog box.

OTE: *You can also indent text using the margin settings. See Chapter 8 for more information on this method.*

Corel WordPerfect gives you a variety of ways to indent text from the left. The quickest ways are to either press the F7 key or click on the Indent button on the toolbar. The Indent button only appears with screen resolutions greater than 640×480. You can also pull down the Format menu, point to Paragraph, and click on Indent.

To indent existing text, click on the Paragraph QuickSpot, pull down the Indent list, and click on Left. Select Both from the list to indent text from both margins.

Each time you use an Indent command, the insertion point moves to the next tab stop on the right, and each line of the paragraph will begin at the tab stop position. When you press ENTER after the paragraph, Corel WordPerfect ends the indentation and moves the insertion point back to the left margin.

You can also indent text from the left with a dialog box. Pull down the Format menu, point to Paragraph, and then click on Format to see this dialog box:

![Paragraph Format dialog box with First line indent, Spacing between paragraphs, Paragraph adjustments (Left margin adjustment, Right margin adjustment), and OK, Cancel, Clear All, Help buttons]

Enter the amount of left indentation in the Left Margin Adjustment box, and the amount of right indentation in the Right Margin Adjustment box. To automatically indent the first line of every paragraph, so you do not have to press TAB, enter a setting in the First Line Indent option.

To create a hanging indentation, where the first line extends to the left of the remainder of the paragraph, enter a negative number for the first line. Set the Left Margin Adjustment to where you want the remainder of the paragraph to be, and enter the negative distance for the First Line Indent. You can also set a hanging indentation by selecting Hanging Indent from the Format Paragraph list, and from the Paragraph QuickSpot dialog box.

Use the Spacing Between Paragraphs option to automatically add space between paragraphs. For example, if you want to double-space between single-spaced paragraphs, set the option at 2.

Indenting with the Ruler

You can also create indentations—from the left, from the right, for the first line, and hanging—using the ruler. To indent text from the right, drag the Right Indent Marker, which is the small triangular object at the right end of the ruler, to the position at which you want to indent the text.

To indent text from the left, use the left section of the ruler. There are actually two separate indentation controls.

First Line Indent marker

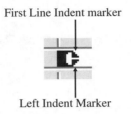

Left Indent Marker

The First Line Indent Marker controls the position of the first line of every paragraph. To indent just the first line of the paragraph, drag the top triangle on the left side of the ruler.

To indent every line of a paragraph on the left, drag the Left Indent Margin, the bottom triangle on the left of the ruler, to the right.

When you drag the Left Indent Marker, the First Line Indent marker moves also to always remain at the same relative distance. If you want to set both, set the left indentation first, and then set the first line indentation. So if you want to create a hanging indentation, first set the left indentation where you want remaining lines to appear, and then drag the First Line Indent Marker to the hanging position of the first line.

Creating Lists

Another way to enhance text is to format it as a list. A list makes it easy to read a series of related items, and helps to organize your points. There are two types of lists, bulleted and numbered. A *bulleted list* has a small graphic object, such as a circle or diamond, at the start of each paragraph. A *numbered list* looks like an outline, with numbers or letters.

You can create lists in several ways. The quickest method is to use the QuickBullet feature of QuickCorrect Format As You Go, following these steps:

1. Type an asterisk or a lowercase "o" and press TAB.

2. Type the first paragraph. When you press ENTER, Corel WordPerfect changes the asterisk to a bullet and inserts another bullet on the next line.

3. Continue typing the items for the list.

4. When you have finished, press ENTER after the final item and then press BACKSPACE to delete the bullet.

In addition to the small bullet, you can insert these other bullet characters by using these keys:

To Use This Bullet:	Start With This Character:
▸	>
◆	^
★	+
●	O
–	-

You can number lists in the same way, with QuickNumbers, using these steps:

1. Type the first number, letter, or roman numeral.

2. Type a period and press TAB.

3. Type the paragraph—Corel WordPerfect will create a hanging indentation when text wraps to the next line.

4. Press ENTER and Corel WordPerfect will insert the next highest number or letter in the series and indent the insertion point at the indented position of the line above.

To insert a single bulleted item or to add bullets to selected text, click on the Insert Bullet button on the toolbar. Corel WordPerfect will display a bullet on the screen and indent the text to the next tab position. Type the paragraph or line next to the bullet and press ENTER. Corel WordPerfect will not insert another bullet, so you have to click on the button for each line. To add bullets to existing text, select the text first and then click on the Insert Bullet button.

For more bullet and list options, use the Bullets & Numbers dialog box—either before typing the list or to format existing paragraphs. Select Bullets & Numbers from the Insert menu to display the dialog box shown in Figure 6-9. Select one of the formats in the Style list. If you did not select text first, but want to type a series of items, make sure the New Bullet or Number on Enter check box is selected.

If you are typing a numbered list, you can also enter a starting value for the first item. Otherwise, Corel WordPerfect will continue numbering where the last list in the document stopped. Enter a number even if you are using letters. For example, using the uppercase letter format (A, B...), entering 3 will start the list with C.

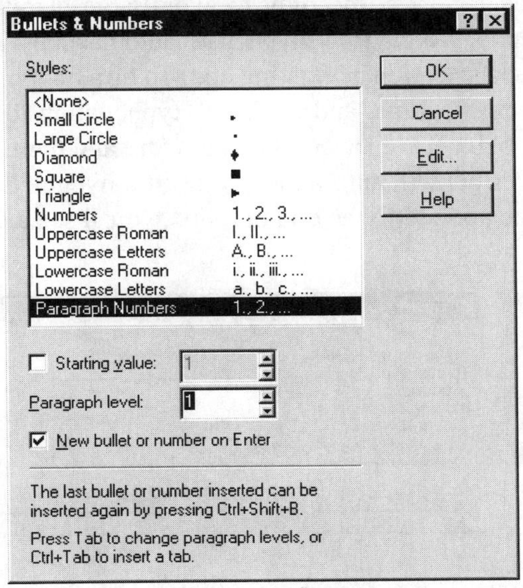

Creating
bullet and
number lists

FIGURE 6-9

The Paragraph Numbers style works like an outline. Unlike the other options, you cannot apply paragraph numbers to existing text. Instead, the number appears at the position of the insertion point in the document. You select the Paragraph Numbers to turn paragraph numbering on as you type. You can also select a starting number and a paragraph level number.

To change the paragraph number, place the insertion point to the right of the number and press TAB. This indents the paragraph and changes the number to the next lowest level number—from 2, to a, i, (1), (a), (i), 1), and a). Press SHIFT+TAB to move back to the next-highest level. If you want to actually insert a tab, without changing the level, press CTRL+TAB. Use CTRL+SHIFT+TAB for a backtab.

OTE: *The Edit button lets you create a custom bullet or list style.*

Hyphenating Text

When you justify text on both the left and right, Corel WordPerfect inserts extra space to fill out the line, but sometimes the extra space is just too obvious. You hyphenate text to reduce these extra spaces. Hyphenation will divide some words between lines, adding enough characters at the right to avoid large blank spaces between words. You can have Corel WordPerfect hyphenate automatically as you type, or you can have it hyphenate a selection of existing text. To turn on hyphenation, pull down the Format menu, point to Line, and click on Hyphenation to display the dialog box shown in Figure 6-10. Click on Hyphenation On, and then select OK.

Corel WordPerfect will automatically insert a hyphen based on certain rules. If its rules cannot be applied to the end of a line, you'll see a dialog box such as this:

Press the RIGHT ARROW or LEFT ARROW to place the hyphen where you want it to appear, and then click on the Insert Hyphen button. You can also choose to insert a space at that location or a Hyphenation SRt code—a position where Corel WordPerfect divides a word without a hyphen character.

You can always hyphenate words yourself, but don't just press the hyphen key. Pressing the hyphen key actually inserts a hyphen code that should only be used for hyphenated words such as "mother-in-law." If the word must be divided between lines, Corel WordPerfect will use one of the hyphen positions. If you later add or delete text, the hyphen may be moved to another line so it always appears between the words. If you press the hyphen to simply hyphenate a word, later editing may move the hyphen to another line, separating the word incorrectly with a hyphen character.

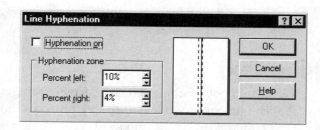

Turning on automatic hyphenation

FIGURE 6-10

If you want to hyphenate a word only when it must be divided between lines, press CTRL+SHIFT+- to enter a soft hyphen code. The hyphen will only appear when Corel WordPerfect must divide the word between lines.

If you want to hyphenate a word or other text, but do not want to divide it between lines, press CTRL+- (the CTRL and the hyphen keys together). Use this for minus signs in formulas, or for hyphens in phone numbers that you do not want divided.

Inserting Other Codes

There are other hyphenation styles available, and other special formatting codes. To access these, pull down the Format Line menu and click on Other Codes to display the Other Codes dialog box, shown in Figure 6-11. The Other Codes dialog box includes some useful features. You may not need them often, but it pays to be prepared just in case.

A *hard tab* is a tab code that moves the insertion point to the next tab stop position on the right, just like pressing the TAB key. But unlike a tab inserted with the TAB key, a hard tab will not be affected if you change the tab type. Use this type of code, for example, to set a different tab type without affecting other lines. If you set a hard center tab at two inches, for example, the tab indicator will not change, but text at that location—for that line only—will be centered. The Other Codes dialog box lets you enter hard left, right, center, and decimal hard tabs, with and without dot leaders.

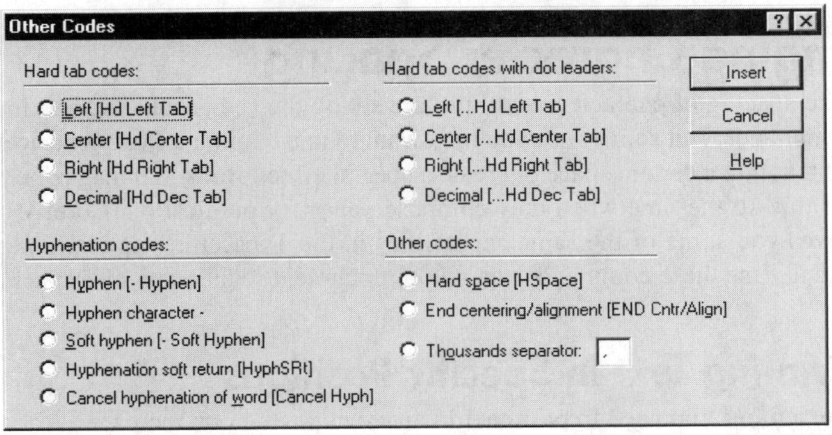

Other
Codes
dialog box

FIGURE 6-11

The dialog box also includes the Hard Space and the End Centering/Alignment codes. Use a hard space when you want to put a space between words, but do not want them ever divided between lines. Corel WordPerfect treats the hard space as a real character and will not wrap the two words at that point.

The End Centering/Alignment code stops the current centering or alignment. For example, suppose you want to type text so the first character starts at the exact center of the screen. Start by centering the insertion point with the Center command, and then select the End Centering/Alignment code from the dialog box. Your text will now move to the right as you type, rather than being centered.

The Hyphenation Codes section of the dialog box contains these five options:

- *Hyphen [- Hyphen]* will let Corel WordPerfect divide the word between lines at the hyphen position.

- *Hyphen Character* prevents Corel WordPerfect from dividing the word between lines.

- *Soft Hyphen* only displays the hyphen if the word is wrapped at that location.

- *Hyphenation Soft Return* will divide a word at that location without displaying a hyphen character.

- *Cancel Hyphenation of Word* moves the word to the next line, rather than hyphenating it.

Changing Character Spacing

The spacing of characters and lines are set by the font, font size, and line spacing commands. But sometimes you may want to make minor adjustments to spacing to fit text into a certain space or create a special effect. Book and magazine publishers do this all the time when they compose pages for publication. Corel WordPerfect gives you some of the same capabilities in the Typesetting options in the Format menu. Use these commands when your document requires precise spacing.

Printing Text in Specific Positions

Sometimes you need to print text in an exact position on the page. When filling in a preprinted form, for example, a word or phrase must appear on a line or in a box already printed on the paper. To specify an exact position, use the Advance command. It doesn't even matter where on the page you enter the code, because the text will print at the designated location regardless of where it appears on the screen.

Select Advance from the Typesetting menu to see the dialog box shown in Figure 6-12. You can set a horizontal or vertical position relative to either the current location of the insertion point or the edges of the paper. To set an exact position on the paper, set it relative to the left edge and the top edge of the page. Use positions relative to the insertion point to create custom subscripts or superscripts.

When you do set a position relative to the top of the page, Corel WordPerfect places the baseline of the text at that location so characters appear above it. This means that if you set a position two inches from the top of the page, the bottom of the text will be two inches from the top. If you want the top of the text to be two inches from the top, deselect the Text Above Position check box.

6

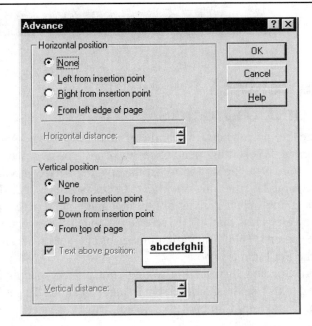

Advance
dialog box

■ **FIGURE 6-12**

Overstriking Characters

When you overstrike, you print two or more characters in the same position. Use this command to create special effects, such as slashed zeros or combinations such as shown here:

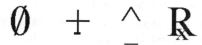

Select Overstrike from the Format Typesetting menu to see the dialog box shown here. Type the characters that you want to superimpose. To change the style or relative size of the characters, click on the left-pointing triangle at the end of the text box to select a style or size from the list. Click on OK to see the characters onscreen.

Spacing Between Words and Characters

To customize the spacing between characters and words, select Word/Letter Spacing from the Format Typesetting menu to see the dialog box shown in Figure 6-13.

Use the Word Spacing option to set the spacing between words. *Normal* is the spacing determined by the font; *Optimal* is Corel WordPerfect's default spacing. To change the spacing, select Percent of Optimal and enter a percentage of the default spacing. Use values less than 100 to reduce the spacing between words, over 100 to increase the spacing. Print a specific number of characters per inch by entering the number in the Set Pitch text box.

The Word Spacing Justification setting controls the spacing between words in fully justified text. Use the Compressed To and Expanded To settings to control the minimum and maximum amount that words can be spaced as a percentage. For

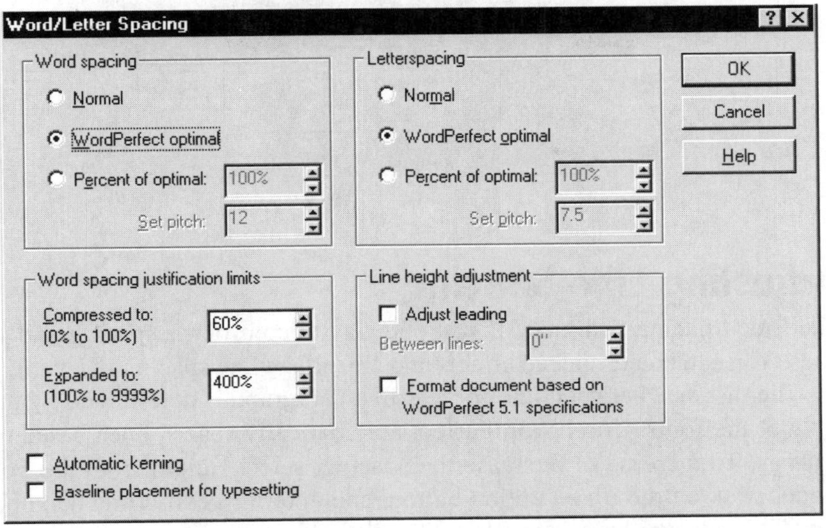

Word/Letter Spacing

Word spacing
- ○ Normal
- ◉ WordPerfect optimal
- ○ Percent of optimal: 100%
  - Set pitch: 12

Letterspacing
- ○ Normal
- ◉ WordPerfect optimal
- ○ Percent of optimal: 100%
  - Set pitch: 7.5

Word spacing justification limits
- Compressed to: 60%
  (0% to 100%)
- Expanded to: 400%
  (100% to 9999%)

Line height adjustment
- ☐ Adjust leading
  - Between lines: 0"
- ☐ Format document based on
  WordPerfect 5.1 specifications

☐ Automatic kerning
☐ Baseline placement for typesetting

OK   Cancel   Help

Customizing
space
between
characters
and words

FIGURE 6-13

example, by default, Corel WordPerfect will only reduce the spacing between words to as little as 60 percent or increase it by as much as 400 percent. If your justified text appears packed too close, increase the Compress To setting. If words appear spaced too far apart, reduce the Expanded To setting.

The Letterspacing options control the spacing between letters. Change the spacing if fonts appear too tight or too loose.

Kerning

Kerning is the process of moving together certain pairs of characters that have opposite slants, such as A and V, to create a smoother appearance with less space between them. To have Corel WordPerfect automatically kern a default set of letter combinations, check the Automatic Kerning option in the Word/Letter Spacing dialog box.

To control the spacing between two characters yourself, place the insertion point between them and select Manual Kerning from the Format Typesetting menu to see the dialog box shown next. Click on the up and down arrows at the Amount text box to adjust the space between the characters.

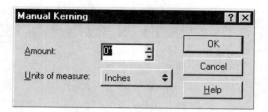

Adjusting Line Spacing

The Line Spacing command is just one way to control the spacing and position of lines. You can create special effects and customize line spacing in a variety of ways.

The distance between lines of text in a paragraph is determined by the size and style of the fonts. Corel WordPerfect automatically spaces lines based on the font settings. To increase or decrease the spacing, select Height from the Format Line menu, click on the Fixed option button, and enter a specific line height in the text box. This sets the baseline-to-baseline distance at a specific size regardless of the font size.

You can also adjust line height in the Word/Letter Spacing dialog box. Click on the Adjust Leading box in the dialog box, and then enter any extra spacing you want in points between lines in the Between Lines text box. If you enter 6p, for example, Corel WordPerfect will add an additional 6 points between lines. Enter a negative number to bring your lines closer together.

If you are using a document written with Corel WordPerfect 5.1, you can maintain the spacing set with that version by clicking on the Format Document Based on Corel WordPerfect 5.1 Specifications check box.

Setting the Baseline

The Baseline is the imaginary line on which characters sit. The position of the first baseline on the page is determined by the size of the top margin and the font. For example, if you are using a 12-point font, and the default one-inch (72-point) margin, the first baseline is 84 points from the top of the page. The position of the first baseline will affect the location of other text, such as where characters appear using Advance up and down commands.

To set a specific location for the first baseline, display the Word/Letter Spacing dialog box and click on Baseline Placement for Typesetting. This tells Corel WordPerfect to position the first baseline at the top margin, so it is in the same position on every page regardless of the font or font size being used.

Giving Printer Commands

Corel WordPerfect and Windows 95 should be able to take advantage of all of your printer's special features. If your printer has a feature that is not supported, however, you can still use it by entering printer codes. These are special commands that turn on and off printer features, such as condensed or other types of printing. Your printer's manual should include a complete list of commands.

Select Printer Command from the Format Typesetting menu to see the Printer Command dialog box. Enter the codes between angle brackets, as in <18>. The Escape character is <27>. You can also specify a file that you want downloaded to the printer.

If you have an old-fashioned daisy-wheel printer, you can also pause it to change print wheels or the ribbon color. To pause the printer, place the insertion point where you want to make the change, display the Printer Command dialog box, and click on the Pause Printer check box.

Controlling Widows and Orphans

You know that as you type, Corel WordPerfect divides your document into pages. As one page becomes full, Corel WordPerfect adds a soft page break and begins a new page. Sometimes, however, Corel WordPerfect may divide text in a way that creates widow or orphan lines. A *widow* is the first line of a paragraph that appears by itself at the bottom of a page. An *orphan* is the last line of a paragraph that appears by itself on the top of a page. With Corel WordPerfect you can avoid these situations and control how text is divided between pages.

To avoid widows and orphans, pull down the Format menu, point to Page, and select Keep Text Together. Click in the check box in the Widow/Orphan section to prevent the first and last lines of paragraphs from being divided between pages.

Widow and orphan control, however, affects just one line of a paragraph. It will not, for example, move a two-line widow to the next page, nor will it prevent a title or subtitle from appearing at the bottom of the page, with the first paragraph relating to that title starting on the next. If you want to keep a section of text on the same page—such as a title with the first paragraph in its section—select the text, display the Keep Text Together dialog box, and then click on the box in the Block Protect section. Corel WordPerfect will keep all of the selected text on the same page.

If you just want to keep a specific number of lines at the end of a paragraph together, place the insertion point in the last line of the paragraph, and display the Keep Text Together dialog box. Click on the check box in the Conditional End of Page section, and then enter the number of lines that you want to keep together in the text box.

Working with Web Pages, Styles, and Templates

7

There are many ways to make your documents look good. Formatting characters, lines, and paragraphs is just the start. If you don't want to spend a great deal of time with formatting, but still want your documents to look great, then use a few of Corel WordPerfect's special helpers. In this chapter, you'll learn three powerful ways that you can create terrific-looking documents.

Using Internet Publisher, you can create eye-catching pages for the World Wide Web without worrying about special codes and complex commands. Using templates, you can start with a completely formatted document and then just add your own text. And with styles, you can apply sets of formats with a single click of the mouse.

Creating Web Pages with Internet Publisher

If you're unaware what the Internet is, or have never heard of the World Wide Web, then you must have been living in a cave. The World Wide Web, or just "the Web" for short, is a graphic interface to the Internet, an informal network of computer systems around the world.

If you subscribe to an online service such as America OnLine, CompuServe, or Prodigy, then you have access to the Web and the Internet. You may have access to the Internet through your company's network, your school, or by any one of thousands of service providers around the world. The Web is one way that you connect to and share information across the Internet. It's now the most popular method because of its graphic capabilities, which allow you to see pictures and hear sounds as you move easily to Web sites all over the planet.

 You can also create Web pages directly from Corel Presentations and Corel Quattro Pro by saving documents in HTML format.

When you connect to a site on the Web, you are looking at a Web page. This is really just a special document that contains information, as well as hypertext links to other documents and other places on the Web. A hypertext link is a graphic or piece of text that you can click on to move to another Web location.

For a document to be used as a Web page, however, it must be written using special format codes. These codes tell the Web browser, the program that lets you contact the Web, how to display the document on the screen, and what to do when you click on a hypertext link. These formats are known as *HTML*, for HyperText Markup Language. You can create a Web document using any word processing program by typing in the HTML codes. However, trying to visualize how a Web page will appear from just looking at the codes is difficult. Since the codes must use specific formats, it is all too easy to make a mistake and get a terrible mess when you view it on the Web page screen.

Rather than type the codes, you can use Internet Publisher, which lets you create a Web page graphically, by selecting formats, styles, and page elements from the menus, the toolbar, and the power bar. You can only select Corel WordPerfect formats that have corresponding HTML codes, so your document will appear similarly to how it will look on the Web. When you are satisfied with the look of your document, Corel WordPerfect converts its codes to their HTML equivalents. Not all Web browsers support the same set of HTML codes, so Web documents may appear slightly different to some Web surfers.

 OTE: *Internet Publisher supports HTML version 2.0. You can insert codes from later versions using the Custom HTML command.*

To start Internet Publisher, pull down the File menu and click on Internet Publisher to see the dialog box shown in Figure 7-1. You have four options:

- *New Web Document* lets you design a new Web page manually or using Web Page Expert.

- *Format as Web Document* converts the current document into a Web page.

- *Publish to HTML* converts the Corel WordPerfect format codes in the document into HTML commands and saves the Web page on the disk.

- *Browse the Web* launches your Web browser.

Using the Web Page Expert

The fastest way to create a Web document is through the Web Page Expert. This is a series of dialog boxes that lead you step by step through the process. You can even

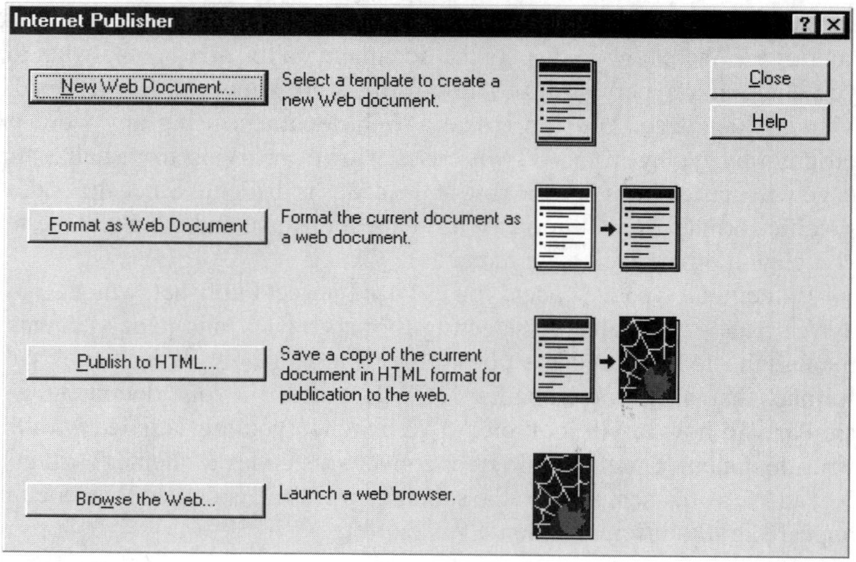

Internet
Publisher
dialog box

FIGURE 7-1

add a background graphic, as well as a menu of links that lets you move back and forth between any number of additional Web documents.

To start the Expert, click on New Web Document in the Internet Publisher window. A box will appear with two choices: <Web Page Expert> and Create a Blank Web Document. Create a Blank Web Document lets you create a document from scratch. Click on <Web Page Expert> and then on Select to start the Expert.

The Expert creates a basic Web document and displays a dialog box asking for the name of a new folder where the page should be stored. Type a new folder name—you cannot use an existing folder—and then click on the Next button to see the dialog box in the next illustration. In this dialog box, you enter name, e-mail address, and a title for the Web page, and then click on Next.

Web Page Expert

Enter a title for your web page. Also enter the name and e-mail address of the person who will maintain this web page.

Web page title:

Name:

E-mail address:

Next >

< Previous

Cancel

Tip...

The default Web page has two hypertext links. One is to a document called "My Personal Information," the other to "My Professional Information." When you click on "My Personal Information" on your Web page, for example, another document appears. In this Expert, you can create other linked pages, or delete the two default ones. If you do not want one of the default pages, select its corresponding check box. To create another page, click on Add, enter a title for the page, and then click on OK. The title will be used as the hypertext link in the home page.

When you've specified the pages, use the following steps to choose a color scheme and background wallpaper:

1. Click on Next to display a dialog box that shows 10 color schemes and 25 wallpaper backgrounds.

2. Choose a color scheme that you find pleasing to the eye.

3. Choose a wallpaper. Corel WordPerfect will display it in the background so you can see how it looks before accepting it. If you don't like it, choose another before going on.

4. When you're satisfied, click on Finished. A message will appear reminding you that only Web-compatible features will be available.

5. Click on OK to clear the message and to display your Web page, as shown in Figure 7-2.

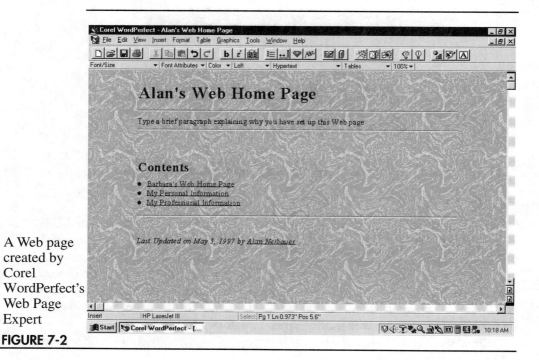

A Web page created by Corel WordPerfect's Web Page Expert

FIGURE 7-2

You can now add and format text, graphics, and sounds, and create hypertext links using the toolbar, power bar, and menus. The toolbar contains the standard first 11 buttons, as well as those shown here.

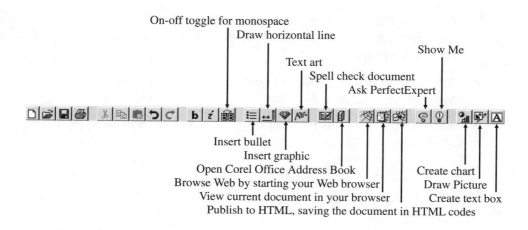

The Web power bar contains seven sections. Pull down the Font/Size list to choose a standard HTML heading, text or list format. Because only certain styles are allowed, you cannot use Corel WordPerfect's Font command to choose a specific typeface or size. The Font/Size list includes the font and size combinations that are compatible with HTML.

The Font Attributes list contains the character styles that HTML can display. In addition to the usual bold, italic, and other styles, you can select Blink, which will flash the text on and off.

Use the Color list to choose the text color, and the Align Text list to position text on the left, center, or right of the screen.

The Hypertext list allows you to set bookmarks, and to create and edit links to bookmarks in the current document, to other Web pages on your disk, and to other Web sites on the Internet. If you have hypertext links, such as "My Personal Information," move to the page by clicking on the underlined phrase. That page will have a return option to go back to the home page.

Use the Tables button to insert a table and the Zoom list to change the displayed magnification

When you have finished creating your Web page, click on the Publish to HTML button on the toolbar. Corel WordPerfect will convert its formatting codes into HTML codes and save the document with the HTML extension. You can also click on the View in Web Browser button to temporarily convert the document to HTML format and launch your Web browser so you can see how the document will appear.

7

Creating a New Web Page

You can also create a Web page from scratch, without using the Web Page Expert:

1. Start the Internet Publisher from the File menu.

2. Click on New Web Document.

3. Double-click Create a Blank Web Document. A message will appear reminding you that only Web-compatible features will be available.

4. Click on OK to clear the message and display a blank Web document.

Using an Existing Corel WordPerfect Document

If you've already created a document that you'd like to use as a Web page, open it on the screen, select Internet Publisher from the File menu, and click on Format as Web Document.

Only those formats that have HTML equivalents will be retained. These include bold, italic, underline, color, subscript, superscript, hypertext links, bullets, and numbers (but not QuickBullets). The shadow attribute will still appear onscreen but will be changed to blinking when saved in HTML formats. The redline and strikeout formats will also be retained, although some Web browsers will not display them. Footnotes are converted to endnotes and appear at the end of the document.

All other formats are deleted, such as columns, drop capitals, headers and footers, margin settings, vertical lines, and watermarks. Tabs and indentations are converted to spaces.

 IP: *If you want to change HTML codes to Corel WordPerfect formats, open the Web page in Internet Publisher, choose Internet Publisher from the File menu, and then click on Format as WP Document.*

Entering and Formatting Text

Whether or not you use Web Page Expert to create the Web page, you'll want to add your own text, headings, and other elements to your Web page. You enter and edit text in much the same way as you do in any Corel WordPerfect document. The main difference is that only HTML-compatible formats will be available from the Font/Size list or the Font dialog box. Use the styles to format selected text or text you are about to type.

The styles include the normal default text, six heading styles, and three bullet and list styles. There is also the Address style, which is typically used at the end of your Web page to give the reader your name and e-mail address, and an Indented Quotation style that indents text from both margins. The Preformatted Text style uses a monospace font that tells the browser to display it exactly as you enter it, with the same spaces and line breaks.

You use the Font/Size list, or the Insert Bullets & Numbers command, to create three types of lists.

- A *Bullet list* inserts a round bullet at the start of each line—the Web browser will determine the bullet size.

- A *Numbered list* numbers consecutive paragraphs—use the TAB key to create multiple levels.

- A *Definition list* uses no numbers or bullets, but indented paragraphs following a name or title at the left margin. With all multiple-level lists, press TAB to move to the right, SHIFT+TAB to move to the left.

Creating Web Page Titles

Corel WordPerfect displays a document's filename on the title bar, but a Web browser displays a document's title. If you do not specify a title, Corel WordPerfect will use the first heading style in the document. To create a title, select Title from the Format menu to see this dialog box:

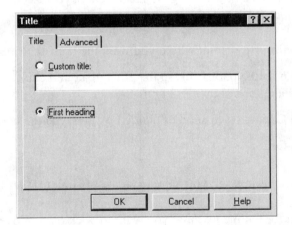

Enter the title you want to use or click on First heading to use the first heading as the title.

Creating Hypertext Links

Hypertext links are really what make the Web so powerful. They let you move from site to site—surfing the Web by clicking on keywords or graphics. There are basically three ways to use hypertext links:

- To move to another location in the same document—up or down to another paragraph or page, for example.

- To move to another HTML document on your disk. Clicking on the link will open the HTML document and display it in the browser or in Internet Publisher.

- To move to another Web site, anywhere in the world.

When you use Web Expert to create a Web page, you can create any number of additional Web documents. These documents, such as My Personal Information, are separate files on your disk. To create additional links from within the Internet Publisher, you use the hypertext command in the Internet Publisher power bar.

CREATING LINKS WITH THE DOCUMENT If you want to create a link to a location in the current Web page, you must first set a bookmark. A *bookmark* gives a name to a specific location or block of text. To go to that location, you use the name in the link.

To create a bookmark, use these steps:

1. Place the insertion point where you want the hypertext link to take you.

2. Pull down the Hypertext list in the power bar, and click on Bookmark to see the dialog box shown in Figure 7-3.

3. Click on Create to see another dialog box and type the bookmark name.

4. Click on OK.

Once the bookmark is set, you have to create the link to it, as follows:

1. Type and format the text that you want to click on to move to the bookmark. It can be before or after the bookmark, depending on if you need to jump up or down.

2. Pull down the Hypertext list in the power bar, and click on Create Link to display the Create Link dialog box shown in Figure 7-4.

3. In the bookmark text box, enter the bookmark name, or select it from the drop down list.

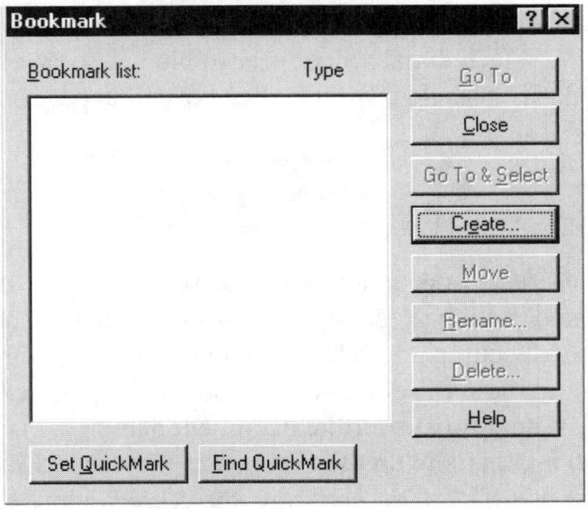

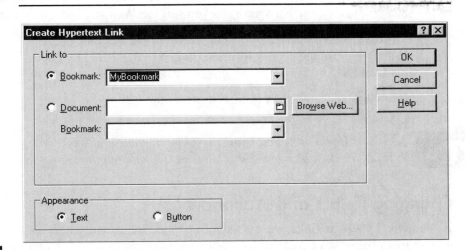

Creating a
bookmark
for a
hypertext
link

FIGURE 7-3

Creating a
hypertext
link

FIGURE 7-4

7

4. Finally, decide if you want the link to appear as text or a button. Make your choice in the Appearance section of the dialog box. If you choose Text, the selected text will appear in blue or some other color, indicating it is a link. If you select Button, the text will appear on the face of a button:

Go to description

You use the Create Link dialog box to also create links to other HTML documents on your disk, and to Web sites. To open another document as the link, enter its path and name in the Document text box, and click on the Document option button. To move to a bookmark in the document as soon as it opens, type the bookmark name in the Bookmark text box under the document name.

To jump to another site on the Web, enter the desired site's Web address in the Document text box. If you do not know the correct address, you can surf the Web to find it, using these steps:

1. Click in the Document text box.

2. Click on the Browse Web button in the toolbar to launch your Web browser. Corel WordPerfect will look for the AT&T WorldNet software or a copy of Netscape Navigator. As you surf the Web, the address of the Web page being displayed will also appear in Document text box.

3. When you find the correct location, switch to the dialog box and click on OK.

4. Exit Netscape if you have finished browsing.

 **OTE:** *If you think you know the address, enter it into the Document text box and click on Browse Web. Netscape will attempt to connect to that site.*

Changing Colors and Wallpaper

By default, hypertext links are displayed in blue. When you click on a link, it temporarily changes to a color called the Active Link color. When you return to the Web page, the link appears in what's called the Visited Link color to indicate that you've already jumped to that hypertext location. You can change the colors used for text and links, and select a wallpaper background, by selecting Text/Background Colors from the Format menu to see the dialog box shown in Figure 7-5.

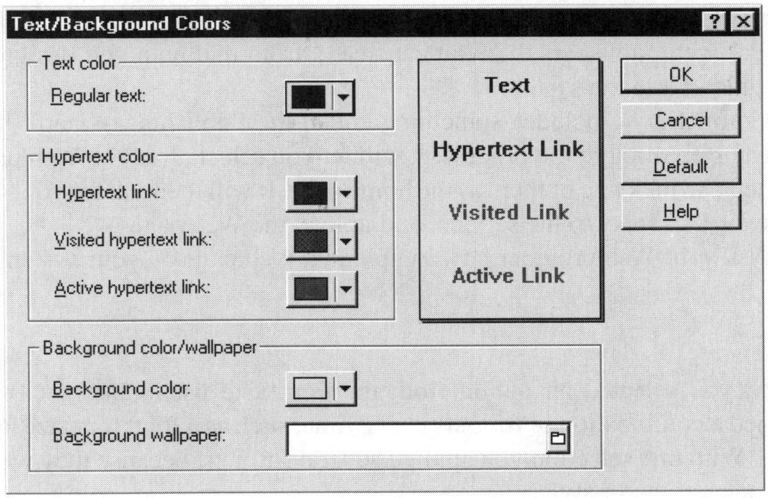

Changing
the
hypertext
colors and
wallpaper
background

FIGURE 7-5

To change the default color for text, pull down the Regular Text list and choose the color from the palette that appears. Change the colors used for default hypertext link, visited hypertext links, and active links by choosing colors from their palettes.

Filling in the background with an attractive graphic or color adds a finishing touch to a Web page. If you did not select a wallpaper with Web Page Expert, you can add a background at any time, or change the background in the Text/Background Color dialog box. Select a background color from the palette or choose a wallpaper. Clicking on the folder icon next to the Background Wallpaper text box will display a list of files with the GIF extension in the default folder where Corel WordPerfect stores wallpaper files. You can choose one of these files, or select any other GIF file that's on your system.

OTE: *You will learn in Chapter 12 how to insert graphics into your Web pages and other documents, and in Chapter 13 you will learn how to insert sound and other multimedia files.*

Uploading Web Pages

Once you have your Web page designed, you have to upload it to your system so others can see it. The exact instructions for uploading Web pages depends on your Internet service provider, or on your organization's policies.

All of the major commercial online services let you upload your own personal Web pages, although the procedures vary greatly. America OnLine, for example, has several Web publishers that you can select from that help you design a Web page and upload it to the system.

CompuServe includes something called the Publishing Wizard that leads you step by step through the process. It will let you select all of the Web pages that you created and pick one of them as the home page. It will then ask for your CompuServe password, connect to the service, and upload the Web pages.

Ask your Web provider how to upload a Web page on your system.

Styles

When you selected an option from the Font/Size list in Internet Publisher, you applied a combination of formats at one time, such as a font, font size, and character style. With one selection you applied several formats, because they were combined into one option, or style.

A *style* is just a collection of formats that you can apply to text. Remember QuickFormat? With QuickFormat you apply the formats in one paragraph of text to another paragraph. A style is a place to store the formats before you apply them. You can store many different styles and then apply them to text whenever you want.

Styles provide two benefits: consistency and flexibility. By defining a set of formats in a style, you can easily apply it to similar portions of text. Using a headline style, for example, will ensure that all headlines use the same format. It is easier than having to apply multiple formats individually.

However, one of the greatest benefits of styles is their ability to change text. If you edit a style, all of the text formatted by it will change automatically. For example, suppose you type a long document with 20 subtitles formatted the same way. If you want to change the format of the headings, you'd need to reformat each of them individually. If you used a style to format the subtitles, however, simply edit the style to the formats you want. All 20 subtitles will change immediately to the new style formats.

Corel WordPerfect comes with a set of styles ready for you to use. The styles are really provided because they are used by certain Corel WordPerfect functions, such as outlining and table of contents. To apply a Corel WordPerfect style, pull down the Styles list in the power bar and click on the style you want to apply.

Creating Styles by Example

If you decide that you want to use combinations of formats other than those provided in Corel WordPerfect's built-in styles, then create your own. You can create a style by selecting formats in a special dialog box, or by copying the formats from existing text. Copying the formats is called *style-by-example.*

The easiest way to create a style is by example, and Corel WordPerfect gives you two ways: QuickStyle and through the QuickSpot dialog box.

Here's how to use QuickStyle.

1. Format text using the options that you want to save in a style.

2. Place the insertion point in the text, pull down the style list in the power bar, and click on QuickStyle to display this dialog box:

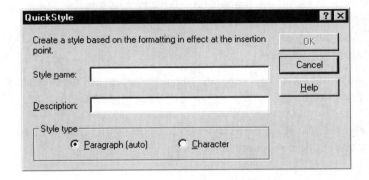

3. Type a name for the style in the Style Name text box, and enter a brief description of it in the Description box.

4. Select if you want the style to be a paragraph or character type. With a paragraph style, you can later apply it to the entire paragraph in which the insertion point is placed, without selecting the paragraph first. With a character style, you must select the text before applying the style, or apply the style and then type the text.

5. Click on OK. The name you gave the style will appear on the power bar.

6. To apply the same style to other text, pull down the style list and click on the style name.

You can also create a style with the QuickSpot dialog box. Click on the QuickSpot of the paragraph containing the formats you want to copy. At the bottom of the QuickSpot dialog box is a style list and the Save Style As button. Click on the

Save Style As box, type a name for the style in the dialog box that appears, and then click on OK.

 OTE: *You can apply a style using the style list in the QuickSpot dialog box.*

Defining Styles

Styles that you create are saved with the document. So whenever you open the document, the styles will be available in the style list of the power bar. To make your styles available for all documents, you have two options:

- Add the styles to the default template, the file Corel WordPerfect uses for all new documents.

- Save the styles in a separate file, and then recall them when you need them.

In this chapter, we'll save the styles to a separate file. You'll learn how to modify the template in the next chapter.

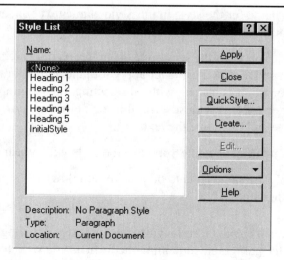

Style List
dialog box

FIGURE 7-6

To create a style, select Styles from the Format menu to see the Styles Editor dialog box in Figure 7-6. You can also display this box by double-clicking on the Style button in the power bar.

The box lists the built-in Corel WordPerfect styles. To apply a style from this list, click on it and then on the Apply button. To create a new style, click on Create to see the dialog box in Figure 7-7.

In the Style Name box, type a name up to 20 characters. This is the name that will be shown in the Style list of the power bar, so make it something that clearly identifies the styles. The name "Style1," for example, would mean nothing to you several months from now, but "ReportTitle" clearly explains why you created the style in the first place.

In the Description text box, type a brief description of the style. You will see this description when you select a style in the Style List dialog box, so use it to further clarify the style's purpose.

Next, select the style type. There are four types to choose from.

- *Paragraph paired*—A style is paired when you can turn it on and off, when the area you want to format has a beginning and an end. Create a paragraph style when you want to be able to apply it to a section of text that ends with a carriage return. You do not have to select the text first, just place the insertion point in and select the style. Corel WordPerfect will insert the Style On code at the beginning of the paragraph, and will insert the Style Off code at the carriage return. If you do not select text first, but choose the style and then type, Corel WordPerfect will turn off the style when you press ENTER.

- *Paragraph paired auto*—This is the same as a paragraph paired style with one added attraction: you can edit the style directly in the document. When you want to change the style, simply select some text that is formatted by it and change the format. The style itself will change, as well as other text formatted by it. With the paragraph paired style, you have to edit it in the Styles Editor.

- *Character paired*—Use the character style type for words or phrases that do not necessarily end with a carriage return. To use this type of style, you turn it on, type the text, and then press the RIGHT ARROW key to turn off the style. You can also apply the style to selected text.

- *Document open*—An open style does not have an end. When you apply this type of style, it stays on for the entire document, or until you override it by entering other format codes. You cannot turn it off; simply change the formats.

Styles
Editor
dialog box

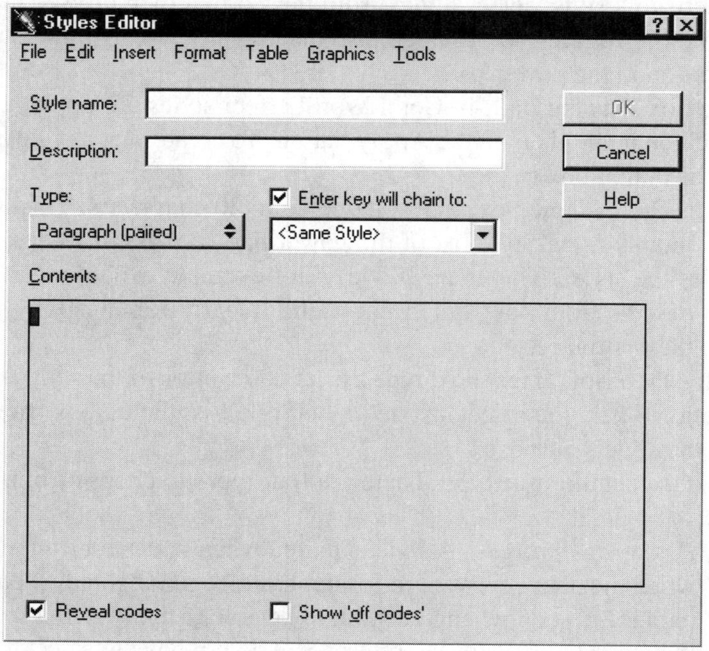

FIGURE 7-7

If you select one of the paired styles, you also can choose what happens when you press the ENTER key. This is the Enter Key Will Chain To option. With paragraph styles, for example, select <Same Style> if you want to leave the style on when you press ENTER. This way, you can turn on a style and type one or more consecutive paragraphs in the same formats. The style is actually turned off when you press ENTER but is reapplied to the next line automatically. To turn off the style, you have to use the style list.

If you want to turn off the style when you press ENTER, select None. This way you can turn on the style for a title, for example, and have it automatically turn off when you press ENTER. In addition to Same Style and None, you will be able to choose any of your own custom styles in this list, once you create some. So you can have some other styles turned on when you press ENTER.

You can also select an action on the ENTER key with character styles. Remember, to turn off a character style, you press the RIGHT ARROW key. If the Enter Key Will Chain To option is checked, and the <Same Style> is used, then pressing ENTER when a character style is on will have no effect—it will not even move to the next line.

If you want to use the ENTER key to move the insertion point to the next line and repeat the same style, clear the Enter Key Will Chain To option. To turn the style off, and move to the next line by pressing ENTER, leave Enter Key Will Chain To selected and choose <None>.

You enter the formats, and any text you want to insert, in the Contents box. Click in the Contents box, and then use the menu bar in the Styles Editor dialog box to select format options. To enter a hard return code, so your style performs a carriage return, press SHIFT+ENTER. To enter a page break, press CTRL+ENTER. To enter a tab, press CTRL+TAB.

The two other options in this dialog box are Reveal Codes and Show Off Codes. Deselecting Reveal Codes will only display text in the Contents box, not any codes. Use this option if the style contains text and you want to review it before accepting the style. By turning off the codes, you'll be better able to see and read the text.

Use the Show Off Codes option to display off codes for corresponding on codes. Normally, only the on codes are shown, such as to turn on bold or underlining. When you turn off the style, the formats in it will also be turned off. But if you want to confirm it, select this option and then apply the same format to insert the off code.

As an example, let's create several styles. We will start with a memorandum heading, a style that will include text and formats:

1. Select Styles from the Format menu, and then click on Create to display the Styles Editor.

2. Type **Memorandum** in the Name text box, and then type **Starts a Legal Memo** in the description box. This is going to be a document style because it sets the format for the entire document.

3. Pull down the Type list box and select Document (open), and then click in the Contents box.

4. We will start by selecting the legal-sized paper. Pull down the Format menu in the Styles Editor, point to Page, and click on Page Size.

5. Choose Legal in the paper size list, and then click on OK. Corel WordPerfect adds the code to select that paper size in the Contents box.

6. Pull down the Format menu and click on Font to display the Font dialog box.

7. Choose the Arial Font, size 24 points, and the Bold attribute, and then click on OK to see the codes in the Contents box.

8. Press CTRL+E to enter the center code, type **Memorandum**, the text you want to appear when you apply the style, and then press SHIFT+ENTER to enter a carriage return.

9. Display the Font dialog box again, choose New Times Roman in 12 point, and deselect the Bold attribute.

10. Click on OK.

11. Press SHIFT+ENTER two more times, then press CTRL+L for the left alignment code.

12. Select OK to accept the style and return to the Style List dialog box.

Now let's create two other paragraph styles. We'll use one to format headings, such as To, From, and Subject, and the other for a paragraph indentation format. Follow these steps.

1. Click on Create, and type **MemoHeading** in the Style Name text box.

2. Type **Memorandum** headings in the Description text box.

3. Pull down the Style list and select Character (paired). This example uses a character style so it can be turned off to allow other text to be typed on the same line using a different font.

4. Pull down the Enter Key Will Chain To list box and select <None>.

5. Click in the Contents box.

6. Pull down the Format menu and click on Font.

7. Select Arial, 14 point.

8. Select OK twice.

Now, define an indented paragraph style.

1. Select Create.

2. Type **DoubleIndent** in the Style Name box.

3. Type **Text indented on both sides** in the Description text box.

4. Pull down the Type list and select Paragraph (paired-auto).

5. Select <None> in the Enter Key Will Chain To list.

6. Click in the Contents box.

7. Select Paragraph from the Format menu and click on Format.

8. Set the left and right adjustment settings to 0.5.

9. Select OK twice.

Saving Styles

If you now save the document, the style will be saved along with it. Because you want to use the styles with other documents, however, save the styles in a separate file that can be retrieved when needed.

Still in the Style List dialog box, pull down the Options list and select Save As. Type **MemoStyles** and then click on OK. Close the Style List dialog box and then the document.

Retrieving and Using Styles

When you want to create a memo using the styles, you have to retrieve the styles from the disk, as follows:

- Pull down the Format menu and click on Styles.

- Click on Options and choose Retrieve.

- In the dialog box that appears, type **MemoStyles** and then click on OK. A message will appear asking if you want to overwrite any existing styles with those with the same name in the file you are retrieving.

- Click on Yes.

Your custom styles are now listed in the dialog box, and they will be in the Style list of the power bar. We'll use the power bar, so close the dialog box. Pull down the

Style list in the power bar and click on Memorandum. Corel WordPerfect changes the paper size and displays the memorandum heading the screen. Now let's enter the headings, as follows:

1. Pull down the Style list and click on MemoHeading.

2. Type **TO:** and then press the RIGHT ARROW key to turn off the style.

3. Press TAB twice and type the recipient's name—pick someone you know.

4. Press ENTER.

Now in the same way, complete the headings as shown here:

MEMORANDUM

TO: Joshua Schneider
FROM: Adam Chesin
SUBJECT: Budget

When you have finished, press ENTER twice. Now turn on the indented paragraph style. Pull down the Style list in the power bar and select DoubleIndent. Now type the following text and press ENTER:

> We should get together to plan the budget for next year. Let me know what day is good for you, but we should meet no latter than the 16th.

When you press ENTER, Corel WordPerfect turns off the style and returns to the default paragraph format.

You can also apply a style to existing text. To apply a paragraph style, place the insertion point anywhere in the paragraph, or select multiple paragraphs, and then choose the style from the power bar or Style List dialog box. To apply a character style, select the text first. For a document style, place the insertion point where you want the format to start.

If you created a paragraph style that does not turn off when you press ENTER, you have to turn off the style yourself. Display the Style List dialog box, and double-click on <None> in the list of styles.

Changing Styles

Styles are so powerful because they not only format text, but they can change the format as well. For example, suppose we want to change the style of the memo headings. Since they are all formatted with the same style, we just need to edit the style.

1. Pull down the Format menu and click on Styles.

2. Click on the MemoHeading style in the list and click on Edit to display the Styles Editor.

3. Click in the Contents box.

4. Press CTRL+B to insert the bold code.

5. Select OK and then click on Close to return to the document.

    All of the headings formatted with the style are now bold.

Now let's see how the paired-auto style works.

1. Select the entire indented paragraph, and click on the Italic button in the toolbar. The Double-Indent style has now been changed.

2. To confirm this, move the insertion point after the paragraph, pull down the Style list, and click on the Double-Indent style.

3. Type some text. It will be indented and italic, conforming to the changed style. If you displayed the style in the Style Editor, you would see the italic code in the Contents box.

7

Deleting a Style

To delete a style, use these steps:

1. Display the Style List dialog box, and click on the style name.

2. Pull down the Options menu and click on Delete. A dialog box will appear asking if you want to Include Codes or Leave Codes.

3. Select Leave Codes to delete the style from the list and remove the codes that it has already applied to text. This deletes the code but does not change the format of any text in the document.

4. Select Include Codes to delete the style and remove its formats from the document.

Using Templates

The document created by Web Page Expert serves as a template because it gives you a basic structure that you can edit and enhance. You can use templates of another sort to streamline your work. A template is a document that contains standard information and formats. Does your office use a standard format for faxes, memos, or letters? If so, you can create templates for them so you won't have to enter and format the standard text. Corel WordPerfect comes with a number of useful templates for common word processing tasks. But in addition to containing standard formats and text, these templates are interactive, prompting you for information to insert or taking it automatically from the Corel Office Address Book.

**IP:**   *To use a template when you first start Corel WordPerfect, click on the Create a Document Using a Template option in the Perfect Expert opening dialog box.*

To use a template for a new document, click on the New Document button in the toolbar or select New from the File menu to see the dialog box shown in the next illustration. The dialog box has two lists: on the left are categories of templates, on the right are the templates within the selected category. The Main category also includes a number of Experts, dialog boxes that take you step by step through creating a document much like Web Page Expert helps you create a Web document. To start an Expert, double-click on it and follow the dialog boxes that appear on the screen.

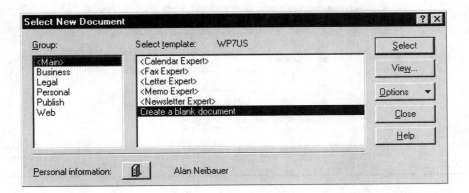

At the bottom of the dialog box is the notation "Personal Information," followed by the Address Book icon. Many templates have places for your name, address, phone number, or other information. You designate a listing from the Address Book as your personal information listing, and Corel WordPerfect uses it for templates. If the notation "No Personal Information" appears, you have not selected your name from the Address Book. To do so, click on the Address Book icon to display the book, select your name from the list, and then click on Select. If you did not yet enter your own information, click on Add and do it while the address book is open.

To use a template, first select the category in the list on the left, and then double-click on the template name on the right. If you have not yet selected an address book listing for your personal information, a message appears telling you so. Click on OK to open the address book, and select or insert your personal information.

A dialog box will now appear prompting for information that you can insert into the template, as in Figure 7-8. In most cases, you can also open the address book to select information about the recipient, such as for a fax or letter, or select or change your personal information. When you complete the dialog box and click on OK, Corel WordPerfect inserts the information into the document. You can now edit and format the text as needed. Templates are opened into new document windows, not under their filenames. So to save the document, just click on the Save button, you will not overwrite the original template file.

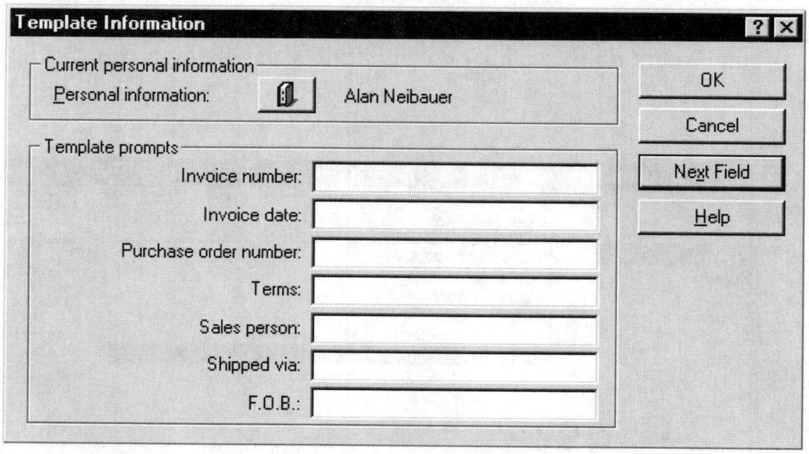

Template Information　　　?　X

Current personal information

Personal information:　　　🚪　　Alan Neibauer

Template prompts

Invoice number:

Invoice date:

Purchase order number:

Terms:

Sales person:

Shipped via:

F.O.B.:

OK

Cancel

Next Field

Help

Template
information
dialog box

FIGURE 7-8

Building a Template

Corel WordPerfect's templates are well designed, and they cover a variety of typical word processing applications, but you might have your own standard form for faxes, memos, legal notices, and any number of other documents. To ensure consistency of style, create your own templates for these documents.

Why use a template, and not just a regular document that contains the "boilerplate" text? If you open a regular document and insert information into it, clicking the Save button will replace the original file. The document will now contain more than just boilerplate text, so the next person who uses it must delete the inserted information. If you use a template, the original file will remain on disk unchanged. But in addition, using a template lets you build dialog boxes prompting for information, and even insert items directly from the address book.

Let's create a new template now.

1. Click on the New Document button or select New from the File menu.

2. Pull down the Options list in the dialog box that appears and click on New Template. Corel WordPerfect will open a special template window with its own feature bar. In this window, you enter any boilerplate text and formats that you want in every copy of the document.

3. Type and format the document shown in Figure 7-9. The empty spaces in the document will be filled in with template prompts that will be built on later.

4. When you've finished, click on the Save button to display the Save Template dialog box.

5. Type a brief description in the Description box.

6. Enter the name for the template, **Credit Notice**, in the Template Name box.

7. Select the Business group to list the template in.

8. Click on OK. Corel WordPerfect stores templates in a subfolder with the group name in the \COREL\OFFICE7\TEMPLATE folder with the WPT extension.

9. Click on Exit Template.

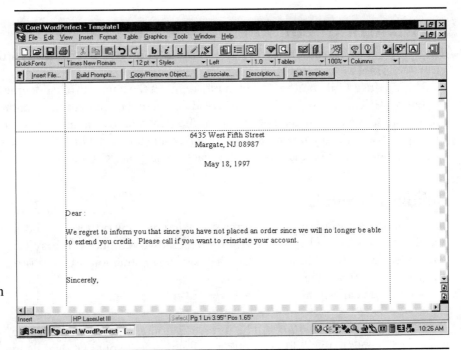

Entering information into the template

FIGURE 7-9

To use the template, select it just as you would one of Corel WordPerfect's. Click on the New Document button, select the group you added the template to, and then double-click on the template name.

Template Options

You use the Options list in the New Document dialog box to manipulate templates and groups. If you need to edit the template, for example, you have to open it again in a template window. Click on the template in the New Document dialog box, but select Edit Template from the Options list. Click on Delete in the list if you want to delete a template.

You can also use these options:

- *New Group*—to create your own category of templates
- *Delete Group*—to remove a group and any templates within it
- *Rename Group*—to change a group name

Customizing Templates

The template feature bar gives you the tools you need to further customize your templates.

Use the Insert File button, for example, to insert the contents of a document into the template. This is useful if you've already created a document that contains the boilerplate text and formats that you want the template to contain. Click on Insert File, and choose the document in the dialog box that appears. Once the document is inserted, delete any text that you do not want in the generic template.

Building Prompts

The Build Prompts button lets you create a dialog box that prompts for information, just like those provided in Corel WordPerfect's own templates. It may take a few minutes to create the dialog box, but it helps to ensure that important information is not overlooked when the template is used.

A template can actually use three types of information.

- *Personal information* will be inserted automatically from the listing you designate in the Address Book. Once you select your personal listing,

Corel WordPerfect inserts it in templates without any further prompts. You can always change the information by editing it in the Address Book, or by selecting a new Address Book listing.

■ *Prompted information* must be entered into text boxes when you use the template. The Template Information dialog box will appear with prompts and text boxes for you to enter. Use these types of prompts for information that will change with each use of the template.

■ *Address information* is retrieved from another listing in the Address Book, such as the recipient of a fax or e-mail. When you use the template, you click on the Address Book icon and select a listing from the book. Corel WordPerfect will insert information from a listing into the appropriate prompts in the dialog box, and then into the document.

As an example, add the prompts to the Credit Notice template you just created, using the following steps:

1. If the template is not on your screen, click on the New Document button, select the Business group, and then click on the Credit Notice template.

2. Pull down the Options list and click on Edit template.

3. Click on the Build Prompts button in the feature bar to display the Build Prompts dialog box shown here:

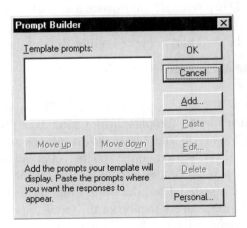

You want to enter codes that will insert the recipient's name and address from a list you select in the Address Book. Follow these steps.

1. Click on Add in the Prompt Builder dialog box to display the Add Template Prompt dialog box.

2. In the Prompt text box, type **Name of Recipient**, the prompt that you want to appear in the Template Information dialog box.

3. Pull down the Link To Address Book Field. This will display a list of fields in the Address Book.

4. Click on Name, and then on OK. When you use the template, Corel WordPerfect will insert the name from a listing you select into this prompt in the dialog box, and then into the template.

5. Click on Add in the Prompt Builder.

6. Type **Address of Recipient**.

7. Pull down the Link To Address Book Field.

8. Click on Address, and then on OK.

9. Now using the same techniques, add fields for the recipient's city, state, ZIP code, and first name.

Next, add a field to prompt for information that you need to enter into the document.

1. Click on the Add button in the Prompt Builder dialog box.

2. Type **Date of Last Order** and click on OK.

The prompts will appear in the dialog box. When you use the template, the prompts will be listed in the Template Information dialog box in the order shown in the list. Use the Move Up and Move Down buttons to reposition a prompt by selecting the prompt you want to move and then clicking on the appropriate button.

Finally, you have to add codes into the document showing where the prompted information will be inserted. Drag the Build Prompts dialog box out of the way, so you can see the inside address section of the letter. You can move back and forth between the document and the dialog box to insert codes. Then, follow these steps.

1. Place the insertion point in the second blank line under the date. If the insertion point is not at the left margin, pull down the Align Text button in the power bar and click on Left.

2. Click on Name of Recipient in the Prompt Builder box.

3. Click on the Paste button in the Prompt Builder dialog box. The prompt appears as "[Name of Recipient]" in the template.

4. Place the insertion point in the blank line under the prompt you just added.

5. Click on Address of Recipient in the Prompt Builder dialog box, and then on Paste.

6. In the same way, add the prompts for the city, state, ZIP code, recipient's first name, and the date of last order so they appear as shown on Figure 7-10. The last step is to add your name from the Personal Information listing in the Address Book.

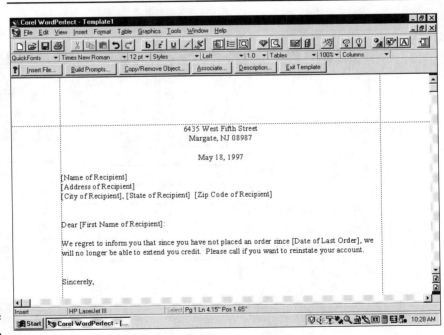

Codes for prompts in the template

FIGURE 7-10

7. Move the insertion point four lines under "Sincerely" in the document.

8. Click on Personal in the Prompt Builder dialog box to see the Personal Fields box.

9. Click on Name in the list and then on the Paste button in the dialog box. The notation "<Name>" appears in your template.

10. Click on Close to return to the Prompt Builder dialog box, and then click on OK.

When you use the new template, Corel WordPerfect will display the dialog box shown in Figure 7-11.

Click on the Address Book icon next to Recipient Information, and then double-click on the listing for the recipient. The information from that listing will appear in the appropriate sections of the dialog box. Type the date of the last order in the corresponding text box, and then click on OK. Corel WordPerfect will insert the information from the dialog box and your name from your personal listing into the document.

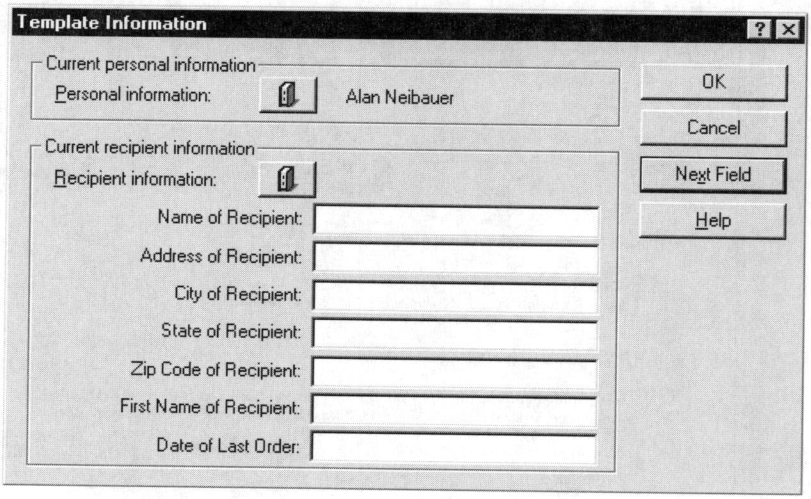

The Template Information dialog box

FIGURE 7-11

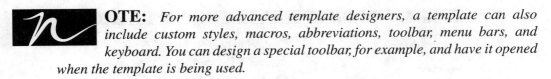

OTE: *For more advanced template designers, a template can also include custom styles, macros, abbreviations, toolbar, menu bars, and keyboard. You can design a special toolbar, for example, and have it opened when the template is being used.*

Editing the Default Template

When you start a new document that is not based on any other template, Corel WordPerfect uses the default template WP7US.WPT. This template contains all of the built-in styles used for all Corel WordPerfect features. You can edit that template to change any of Corel WordPerfect's default document settings for margins, page size, the initial font, and other formats.

To edit the template, click on the New Document button, and make certain that the Create a Blank Document option is selected in the Select Template list. Pull down the Options list and choose Edit Template.

Corel WordPerfect displays the template window and feature bar for the default template. Make any changes that you want to the default settings and then click on Save. If you change the margins and page size, for example, all new documents that use the default template will have those margins and that paper size.

If you want to revert to all of Corel WordPerfect's original default settings, delete the file WP7US.WPT in the \COREL\OFFICE7\TEMPLATE directory. Corel WordPerfect will create a new default template, with all of the factory settings, the next time it starts. To revert back to just a specific original setting, edit the template again but select the default value.

Editing Default Styles

You can also change default settings by changing styles. All of the default values are stored in styles in the default template. To change a default setting, you have to change the style in the template. You can do this from within any document, without opening the template itself.

Select Styles from the Format menu. Pull down the Options button and select Setup to display the Style Setup dialog box shown in the next illustration.

7

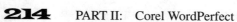

Style Setup

Display styles from
- ☑ Current document
- ☑ Default template
- ☐ Additional objects template
- ☐ System styles

Default location
- ● Current document
- ○ Default template
- ○ Additional objects template

OK
Cancel
Help

Click on the Default Template option button in the Default Location section.

Corel WordPerfect only lists a set of basic styles in the Style List box. There are actually styles for every format that can be applied by built-in Corel WordPerfect features. To see these styles, click on the System Styles in the Display section. Then click on OK. If you chose to see the System Styles, they will be listed in the Style List. To change a default setting, just edit the corresponding style. Edit the style named InitialStyle, for example, to change the default paragraph, page size, and margin formats.

To return a style to its original format, select the style in the list, pull down the Options menu, and click on Reset.

Formatting Pages

8

Page formats affect the look of the entire page, or even the entire document. They are called page formats because you do not have to select text to apply them, or because they create a different page size or layout.

Entering Measurements

When you set margins, page sizes, indentations, and other settings in Corel WordPerfect, you can type a measurement directly in a text box. Corel WordPerfect is set to use a certain unit of measurement. This means that if you just type a number in a text box, Corel WordPerfect will assume it is a certain unit. So if your system is set to use inches, when you type **2** and move to another text box, Corel WordPerfect will add the quotation marks and display it as 2".

As you will learn in Chapter 10, however, the program can be set to use other units of measurement: millimeters, centimeters, points, and 1200ths of an inch. If your system is set for millimeters, for instance, and you do not type a unit following a number, Corel WordPerfect will assume it is in millimeters and add the characters "mm" after the number.

You can always designate the unit following the number, using " or "I" for inches, "c" for centimeters, "mm" for millimeters, "p" for points, and "w" for 1200ths of an inch. If you do, however, Corel WordPerfect will always convert the amount to whatever unit your system is set for. So if your system is set to accept inches, and you type **50mm**, Corel WordPerfect will convert it to 1.97".

You can also, by the way, enter a measurement as a decimal or a fraction. If you type **5 5/8** as a page size, for example, Corel WordPerfect will convert it to 5.63".

In this and other chapters in this book, measurements will be illustrated using inches in decimal fractions. Just remember that you can use another unit of measurement as well.

Changing Margins

The top, bottom, left, and right margins determine how much text you can fit on a page. The left and right margins determine the length of the lines; the top and bottom margins determine the number of lines that fit on the page. All of the margins are set at one inch by default.

In most other word processing programs, the margins affect the entire page, if not the entire document. Corel WordPerfect is more flexible. When you change margins, Corel WordPerfect inserts a code at the beginning of the paragraph at the insertion point. The change affects only text starting at that location, up to the next margin code. This means that you can use the left margin to indent the entire page, or just individual or selected paragraphs. The margin command can serve as another way to indent text.

The advantage of using the margin command is that it is not canceled when you press ENTER, as are indentations. You can also visually see the spacing onscreen because the margin guidelines will show you the reset position, as shown in Figure 8-1. Indentations, on the other hand, only affect the current paragraph.

The quickest way to change the page margins is to use the guidelines or the margin indicators in the ruler. To use the guidelines for the top and bottom margins you must be in Page or Two-Page View; otherwise, those guidelines will not appear on the screen.

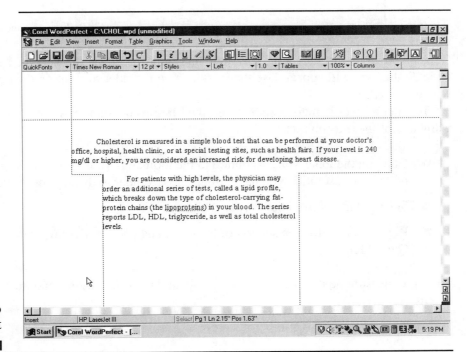

Using
margins to
indent text

FIGURE 8-1

The margin guidelines are the dotted lines around the page. If the guidelines are not displayed, use these steps:

1. Select Guidelines from the View menu.

2. Click on the Margins options in the dialog box that appears.

3. Click on OK.

When you point to a margin guideline, the mouse pointer will be shaped like a two-headed arrow. As you drag a guideline, Corel WordPerfect will display a QuickStatus box showing the margin position. Release the mouse when the margin is where you want it.

You can also set the margins using the ruler—drag the left or right margin indicators to the desired position:

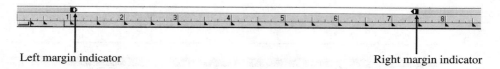

Left margin indicator   Right margin indicator

As you drag the indicator, a dotted line appears down the screen, but no QuickStatus box will appear. Use the markings on the ruler to position the margin where desired.

To enter a specific margin setting, use the Margins dialog box. Display the box using any of these techniques:

■ Click on the Page Margins button in the toolbar. If your system is in 640 × 480 resolution you have to scroll the toolbar to display this button.

■ Select Margins from the Format menu.

■ Right-click on the top section of the ruler, and choose Margins from the QuickMenu.

Enter the measurements for the left, right, top, and bottom margins, and then click on OK.

Formatting Pages for Books

Pages destined to be bound—if only in a three-ring binder—present some additional formatting opportunities. In most cases, the binding will take up some of the space on each page. In a ring-binder, for example, some space is taken up by the punched holes. This space is called the *printing offset.* You have to decide what side of the page the printing offset is located on, and the amount. How you lay out a page for binding depends on if you are printing one side or both sides of the page, but it's all done using the Two-Sided Printing Page of the Print dialog box, shown in Figure 8-2.

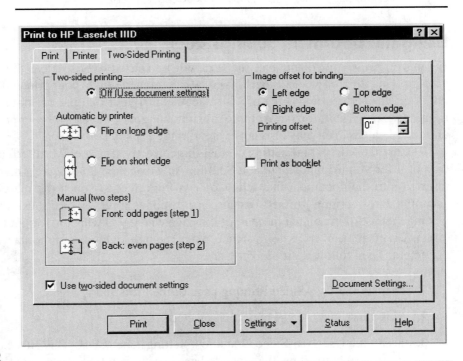

Two-Sided
Printing
dialog box

FIGURE 8-2

Binding Single-Sided Pages

To set the printing offset when you are binding one-sided pages, display the Two-Sided Printing Page of the Print dialog box. Then follow these steps:

1. Make sure the Off option button is selected in the Two-Sided Printing section of the dialog box.

2. In the Image Offset for Binding section of the dialog box, choose the edge of the paper to which you want the extra space added: Left Edge, Right Edge, Top Edge, or Bottom Edge.

3. Enter the amount of the printing offset in the text box. If you are binding pages as a booklet, for example, choose the Left Edge. If you want to turn over the pages like a flip chart, choose the Top Edge.

Using the Document Settings Code

When you print your document, the text will be shifted over to clear the offset amount. This shift, however, is performed by a command sent to your printer. It does not affect the format or spacing of your document. If your margins are not set just right, the text can shift too far over into the right margins, or even into your printer's unprintable areas. You may also not even print the ends of some lines.

Rather than worry about setting the margins correctly, let Corel WordPerfect take care of it for you using a Document Setting. A *Document Setting* is a format code inserted into the document that tells Corel WordPerfect to adjust the margins to accommodate a printing offset. Because it is a code, however, you must start by placing the insertion point at the start of the page where you want the format to take effect. To offset every page, for instance, place the insertion point at the start of the document. Then follow these steps:

1. Display the Two-Sided Printing page of the Print dialog box.

2. Make sure that the Off button is selected.

3. Select the Use Two-Sided Document Settings check box. This tells Corel WordPerfect to adjust the margins based on the printing offset in the code that you are about to enter.

4. Click on the Document Settings button to display the dialog box shown in Figure 8-3. In this dialog box you set printing options, much like you do

in the Two-Sided Printing page, but the options are inserted as a document code.

5. Make sure the Two-Sided Printing option is set to Off in this dialog box.

6. Select the edge of the page to use for binding.

7. Enter the amount of the printing offset.

8. Click on OK and then close the Print dialog box.

Because the code is inserted into the document, the printing offset will be reflected onscreen. The margins will still appear the same size as they are set, but the page size will actually appear reduced. The page size will be reduced by the amount of the printing offset.

 IP: *If you decide to turn off the printing offset, deselect the Use Two-Sided Document Settings check box.*

Duplex Printing

You can save a lot of money on paper, binding, and mailing costs by *duplex printing*—printing on both sides of the paper. The more expensive printers have this capability built in by printing on both sides of the paper at the same time. If you have

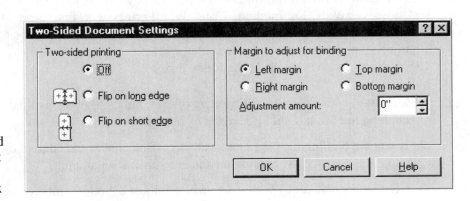

Two-Sided Document Settings dialog box

FIGURE 8-3

a duplex printer, you turn on this feature in two ways: using a printer command or a document setting.

To enter a printing command, display the Two-Sided Printing page of the Print dialog box. In the Two-Sided Printing section of the dialog box, select how you plan to turn over the pages: either Flip On Long Edge like a book, or Flip On Short Edge like a flip chart.

When you select a two-sided printing option other than Off, the choices in the Image Offset for Printing section change to Inside Edge and Outside Edge. Click on the button that indicates the side you want the printing offset on, and then enter the amount of the printing offset.

If you are not sure that your margins will accommodate the offset, use a Document Setting code to create the offset, following these steps:

1. Click on Off in the Two-Sided Printing page.

2. Select the Use Two-Sided Document Settings check box.

3. Click on the Document Settings button.

4. In the Document Settings dialog box, choose Flip on Long Edge or Flip on Short Edge, and then choose either the inside or outside edge.

5. Enter the offset.

Duplex Printing for the Rest of Us

Most of us probably do not have duplex printers; ours can only print on one side at a time. You can still print on both sides of the paper, but you have to use the two-step manual process. With this method, Corel WordPerfect will first print all the odd-numbered pages. You then reinsert the pages, and Corel WordPerfect prints the even-numbered pages on the other side of the sheets.

To use the two-step method, do the following:

1. Display the Two-Sided Printing page of the Print dialog box, and then click on the Front: Odd Pages (step 1) button.

2. If you are binding the pages and want an offset, choose the edge of the paper that you will be binding on and enter the offset amount.

3. Click on Print. Corel WordPerfect will print just the odd-numbered pages.

Now comes the critical step. You have to reinsert the same pages so they will be printed on the blank side, and so the top of the pages are in the proper position. It may take you some tries to get it just right.

4. Display the Two-Sided Printing page again, and click on the Back: Even Pages (step 2) option.

5. Click on Print to complete the document.

When you use the two-step process, you cannot enter Document Settings codes.

Changing Page Size

Corel WordPerfect's default page size is $8\frac{1}{2} \times 11$ inches. To use a different page size, such as legal paper or personal stationery, select Page in the Format menu and click on Page Size to see the dialog box shown in Figure 8-4. Pull down the Name list box to see the page sizes that Corel WordPerfect has set for your printer.

Where applicable, you'll see some page sizes in two orientations, such as Letter and Letter Landscape. In *landscape* orientation, your lines print across the wider dimension of the page, which is useful for wide tables and graphics. If it does not say "landscape," then the orientation is *portrait*, where your lines of text print across

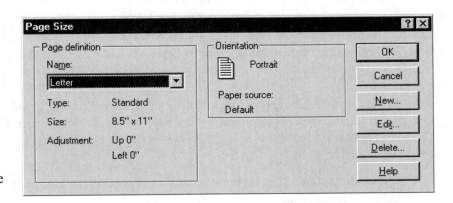

Setting page size

FIGURE 8-4

the narrow dimension of the page. Select the listing for the page size and orientation, and then click on OK.

Choosing a page size inserts a code at the beginning of the page at the insertion point. It affects every page from that point to the end of the document, or until another page size code appears. To use the same page size for an entire document, place the insertion point at the start of the document before selecting a page size.

For example, follow these steps to change to landscape orientation on $8\frac{1}{2} \times 11$-inch paper:

1. Place the insertion point at the start of the existing document, or start a new document.

2. Pull down the Format menu, point to Page, and click on Page Size.

3. Pull down the Name list and click on Letter Landscape.

4. Click on OK.

 OTE: *Changing the page size does not affect the margins. If you choose a small-sized paper, make certain the default margins are still suitable.*

Custom Page Sizes

The available Corel WordPerfect page sizes should be appropriate for most situations. If you need to use a paper size that is not already defined, you can create your own. Get a sample of the paper, and carefully measure its length and width. Decide if you want to print in portrait or landscape orientation and then follow these steps:

1. Pull down the Format menu, point to Page, and click on Page Size.

2. Click on New.

3. In the Name text box, type a descriptive name for the paper. Include the word "landscape" if you plan to set it up for landscape orientation. This isn't necessary but it serves as a reminder to help you select the correct paper size later on.

4. Choose a type from the Type list. This also is not critical, but it will also help you identify the paper later on.

5. Scroll the Size list and click on User Defined Size.

6. Enter the width of the page in the Width text box, and enter the height in the Height box.

7. To print in landscape orientation with a laser printer or inkjet printer, select Rotated in the Font section, and select Short Edge in the Paper Feed section. Otherwise, for portrait orientation, select Normal in the font section and Short Edge in the Paper Feed section.

8. Pull down the Paper Source list and choose where you feed the paper. The options in the list are determined by your printer. With laser printers, for example, you can usually choose from one or more paper trays and manual feed. Select Manual Feed if you plan to insert the sheets yourself in the manual input tray.

9. Select OK to return to the Page Size dialog box.

Your custom page size should print correctly. However, in a few rare cases, the first line of text may not print in the expected location. Something about your printer or paper may cause the first line of text to print at some location other than the top margin, or the left edge of lines to not align with the left margin. If this occurs, you have to set the Vertical and Horizontal settings in the Printing Adjustment section of the New Page Size dialog box.

If you've already created the page size, click on the page size in the Page Size dialog box, and then click on the Edit button. The setting in the Vertical option determines the distance of the first line of text from the top edge of the page. You can choose to move the first line Up or Down, and you can designate the distance to move it. So if your text always prints 1/8 inch too high, choose Up and enter .125. The Horizontal setting adjusts the distance of the left margin from the left edge of the page. Choose Left or Right, and enter the measurement to move the text.

Subdividing the Page

There are occasions when you want to print small documents, such as tickets, announcements, or envelope stuffers. These documents are usually too small to feed through your printer. One solution is to print them on a regular-sized sheet, and then cut off and throw away the waste. A more economical choice is to print several of the items on one sheet of paper, and then cut them apart.

If the paper size you want is close to some even portion of a page, such as one-half, one-quarter, or one-sixth of a sheet, then you can subdivide the page. This creates more than one logical page on the physical sheet. Corel WordPerfect will treat each logical page as a separate sheet of paper for page numbering, headers and footers, and other page elements. When you press CTRL+ENTER with a subdivided page, for example, Corel WordPerfect inserts a page break. However, Corel WordPerfect will move the insertion point to the next logical page on the sheet, and only start a new sheet when all of the logical pages have been used on the physical page.

To subdivide a page, you specify the number of rows and columns you want the page divided into. You do not have to worry about specifying their exact width and height.

To subdivide a page, select Page from the Format menu, and click on Subdivide Page to see the Subdivide Page dialog box. Specify the number of columns and rows of logical pages, and then click on OK. Your screen will appear as in Figure 8-5, with the logical page size shown. When you press CTRL+ENTER to end one logical page and start the next one, Corel WordPerfect will display a new logical page on the screen, in the position it will print on the page. You can also press ALT+PGDN or ALT+PGUP to move to the next or previous logical page.

As with changing page size, subdividing the page does not automatically change the margins. If you create a small logical page, the default one-inch margins may be too large. If you are in Page view, you'll be able to see right away the actual area in which you can enter text on the page, and whether or not you have to change the margins.

Printing Booklets

One of the best examples of using a subdivided page is printing booklets. Picture a booklet as a document with two logical pages on each side of a sheet of paper, printed in landscape orientation. You print on both sides of the page, and then fold the sheet in half for four pages on each sheet. Creating a booklet requires a landscape orientation and a subdivided page.

It also requires one other very important element, the correct order of the pages. If you just typed the pages of a four-page booklet in the order 1-2-3-4, the pages would not be in the correct order when printed. Depending on how you folded the sheet, either page 2 or 4 would be on the cover, with pages 1 and 2, or 3 and 4 on the inside. Rather than try to arrange the pages in the correct order yourself, you can turn on Corel WordPerfect's booklet printing feature. Start by selecting a page size in landscape orientation and then subdividing the page into two columns.

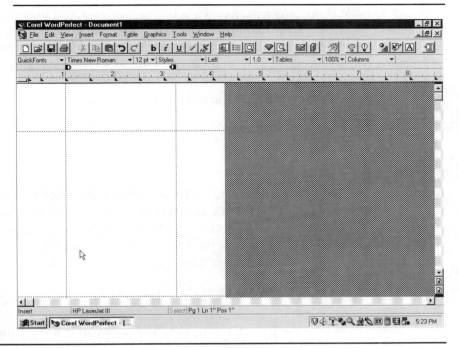

Subdivided
page

FIGURE 8-5

8

1. If you already typed the text, move the insertion point to the start of the document.

2. Select Page from the Format menu, and then click on Page Size.

3. Choose Letter (Landscape) from the list box, and click on OK.

4. Choose Page from the Format menu, and click on Subdivide Page.

5. Enter **2** for the number of columns, and then click on OK.

6. Set all of the margins to 0.5 inch to accommodate the smaller paper size.

7. Finally, turn on booklet printing. Display the Two-Sided Printing page of the Print dialog box, and click on Print as Booklet.

8. Click on Print to print the document.

Corel WordPerfect organizes the pages in the correct order, and then prints the first sides of all of the pages. It then displays a message telling you to reinsert the paper to print on the other side. Insert the pages so the blank side will be printed on, in the correct position, and then click on OK in the message box. Fold the pages in half, and you have a booklet.

If you have a duplex printer, you can print both sides at the same time using the Document Settings option.

Title Pages

A title page usually contains some text that is centered both horizontally and vertically on the page. Following the title page is the first page of the document. You could create the title page manually by pressing ENTER until the text appears to be centered. However, all of these extra carriage returns could be a problem if you later insert or delete text. So rather than enter the page manually, let Corel WordPerfect do it for you.

To center the text vertically on the page, use these steps:

1. Select Page from the Format menu, and click on Center to display the Center Pages(s) dialog box.

2. Select Current Page to center only the page at the insertion point, or Current and Subsequent Pages to center all of the pages.

3. Click on OK.

To also center the text between the left and right margins, use the line center or justification center formats.

Enclosing the Page in a Border

In Chapter 6, you learned how to use the Border/Fill command to enclose text in a border and to add a shaded background. You can also enclose the entire page in a border, and even select from decorative borders of graphic and fancy lines.

To add a page border, place the insertion point in the page, select Border/Fill from the Format menu, and then click on Page to display the dialog box shown in

Figure 8-6. There are two general types of borders, Fancy or Line. Fancy borders use graphic images and clip art, while Line borders use one or more straight lines of various thicknesses and shades.

If you select the Line type, you'll display the same options that were available for paragraph borders, but the border will surround the whole page. You can also choose to apply the border to just the current page, the default value. Deselect the Apply Border to Current Page Only check box to apply the border to all of the pages in the document.

If you select the Fancy type, you can only choose one of the available styles; no other options are available. Some of the styles are quite decorative, and many are in color if you have a color printer. When you select a style, a sample of it appears in the preview area, and the name of the file storing the graphic is shown under the list box.

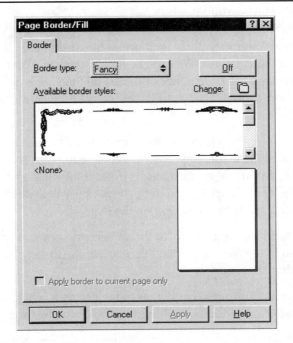

Page
Border
dialog box

FIGURE 8-6

Decorating Pages with Watermarks

A *watermark* is a graphic image or text that appears in the background of the page. It prints in a light shade of gray, so you can see it and still read the text in the foreground. Watermarks are useful to display your company logo, or even an advertising or other message, such as the word "Draft" or "Confidential."

You can have up to two watermarks on one page. Corel WordPerfect will automatically insert the watermark on all subsequent pages, but you can discontinue it when you no longer want the watermark to appear. You can also change the watermark at any time, so every page can possibly have two different watermarks.

 You can create a drawing in Corel Presentations and open it as an image to use as a Watermark in Corel WordPerfect.

Watermarks appear onscreen only in Page and Two-Page views, so change to one of these before starting these steps:

1. Choose Watermark from the Format menu. A dialog box appears where you can select either Watermark A or Watermark B, the two watermarks for the page. Choose either of these and then click on Create. Corel WordPerfect will change to Page/Zoom Full display and show the special feature bar, as in Figure 8-7.

2. If you want the watermark to be text, move the insertion point to where you want the text to appear—you'll have to press ENTER to move the insertion point down the page, or format the page as a title page. If you do use the center page option in this view, only the watermark will be affected, not the regular text on the page.

3. To use a piece of clip art for the watermark, click on the Image button in the feature bar, and then select the image file in the dialog box that appears.

4. To use an existing document as the watermark, click on the File button and choose the document file from the dialog box that appears.

5. Corel WordPerfect watermarks appear in a 25 percent shade, that is, 25 percent of the density of a solid color. To make the watermark either lighter or darker, click on the Shading button in the feature bar, and then enter a percentage.

6. Corel WordPerfect will repeat the watermark on all subsequent pages. If you want a watermark to repeat on just odd or even pages, click on the Pages button on the feature bar and choose Odd Pages, Even Pages, or Every Page from the box that appears.

7. When the watermark appears as you want it, click on Close in the feature bar. To add a second watermark to the same page, repeat the procedure but choose the other watermark option, either A or B.

To stop the watermark from appearing on a page, place the insertion point on the page, and choose Watermark from the Insert menu. Click on the watermark you want to stop, either A or B, and then click on Discontinue. To use a different watermark on the page, repeat this procedure. When you create a new watermark for a page, it replaces the one continued from a previous page.

You can use the Next and Previous buttons on the watermark feature bar to display the watermarks on other pages.

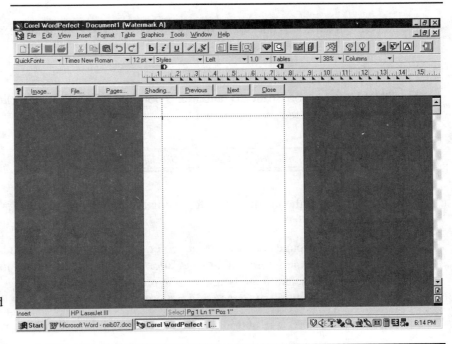

Watermark window and feature bar

FIGURE 8-7

 **IP:** *Use the Edit button in the Watermark dialog box to change the watermark.*

Using Headers and Footers

Pages of a long document can easily get separated. They can get out of order or misplaced, or one page may get stuck in the copying machine and never make it into the document at all. Headers and footers help to identify the pages of your document, as well as the document itself, and they can even create pleasing visual effects that grab and hold the reader's attention. A *header* is text or graphics that prints at the top of every page. A *footer* is text or graphics that prints at the bottom of every page. Two common uses of a header or footer are to number pages and to repeat the document's title on each page.

You create headers and footers in much the same way as a watermark. Each page can have up to two headers and two footers, and you can repeat them on every page or just odd or even pages. You can discontinue headers or footers when you want, or change headers or footers, so each page can have different ones.

To create a header or footer, follow these instructions:

1. Place the insertion point on the first page you want to contain the header or footer.

2. Choose Header/Footer from the Format menu.

3. Select Header A or Header B, and then Footer A or Footer B, and click on Create to see the feature bar shown here:

4. Enter the text of the header or footer, using the power bar, toolbar, or menus to format it.

5. To number your pages in a header or footer, place the insertion point where you want the number to appear, click on the Number button in the feature bar, and select Page Number. The number of the current page will appear onscreen, but your pages will be numbered consecutively.

6. Click on the Insert Line button to insert a horizontal line across the page.

7. As with watermarks, use the Pages button to select even pages, odd pages, or every page. If you are using two headers or two footers on the same page, however, coordinate them so they do not overlap.

8. By default, Corel WordPerfect leaves 0.167 of an inch, about one line, between the document text and the header and footer. To change the distance, click on the Distance button and enter the measurement in the box that appears.

9. Click on Close to return to the document.

Remember, you can use the Insert Date command to display the date or time in the header, or Insert Other to include the filename.

Page Numbers

You can also number pages without using a header or footer. The Page Numbers command actually gives you great flexibility in numbering, since you can choose the number style and position, and even number in chapters and volumes. You can number every page of your document consecutively, use sections to start with page 1 at the beginning of every chapter, or use roman numerals for a table of contents and index.

Select Page Numbering from the Format menu to see these options:

- *Select* lets you insert a page number on the top or bottom of the page, change the number format or starting number of a section, change the font of the page number, and create a custom number format.

- *Insert in Text* inserts the page number at the location of the insertion point in the document—it does not turn on page numbering for all pages.

- *Value/Adjust* lets you change the page number.

- *Count Pages* tells you the number of pages in the document and updates all total page counts, as in Page 1 of 10.

To number your pages, place the insertion point on the page where you want the numbers to start, and then choose Select to display the dialog box shown in Figure 8-8. Pull down the Position list box and select a position. The options are no page numbering, top left, top center, and top right; top outside alternating and top inside

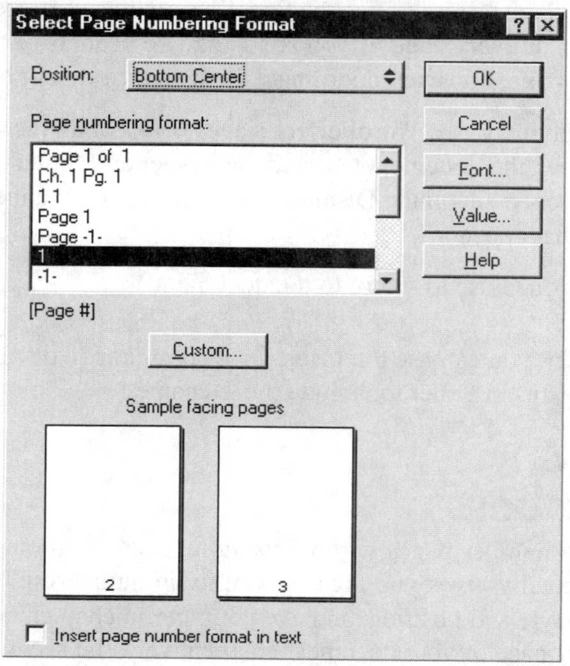

Select Page Numbering Format

Position: Bottom Center

Page numbering format:

Page 1 of 1
Ch. 1 Pg. 1
1.1
Page 1
Page -1-
1
-1-

[Page #]

Custom...

Sample facing pages

2   3

Insert page number format in text

OK
Cancel
Font...
Value...
Help

Inserting
page
numbers

FIGURE 8-8

alternating; bottom left, bottom center, and bottom right; and bottom outside
alternating and bottom inside alternating. Your choice will be reflected in the
preview area.

Next, select a format. By default, an Arabic page number will appear by itself,
but you can choose other options:

- Change to letters or roman numerals

- Include the word "Page"

- Include the total number of pages, as in Page 1 of 10

The page number will appear in the default document font. To change the font,
size, or character style, click on the Font button and make your selections from the
dialog box that appears.

You can also change the page number itself. For example, suppose you created
a long report in a number of documents. You already printed the first document, with
the pages numbered 1 through 10. Before printing the second document, you need

to change the page number of the first page to 11, so its pages will be numbered consecutively from there.

You can change the page number in two ways. If the Select Page Number Format dialog box is already open, click on the Value button to see the dialog box shown in Figure 8-9. Enter the number you want for the page in the Set Page Number box, or optionally change the chapter, volume, or secondary page numbers. You always set the number using Arabic numbers, regardless of the number format. Enter **5**, for example, if you are using roman numerals and want to number the page as V.

Once you add page numbers to a document, you can quickly change the number or the style of number. Place the insertion point where you want to make the change, select Page Numbering from the Format menu, and then click on Value/Adjust. Select the page numbering format and set the page number as desired.

 IP: *If you use page numbers, headers, and footers at the same time, make sure the numbers do not overlap.*

If you want to add your own text to a page number, then click on the Custom button in the Select Page Numbering Position dialog box. A dialog box will appear with a text box labeled "Edit custom format and text," with the code [Page #] that represents the number. Add your text, such as "Senate Report, Page [Page #]."

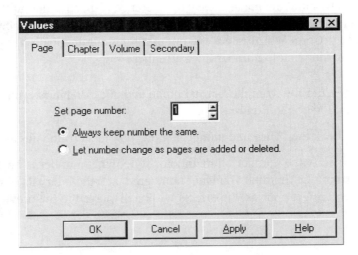

Setting the
page number

FIGURE 8-9

Suppressing Page Elements

Many documents do not include headers, footers, or page numbers on title pages or cover letters. You may also want to turn off one of these elements on a specific page of the document. If you choose the Discontinue option for a header, footer, or watermark, however, it turns the feature off for all subsequent pages as well.

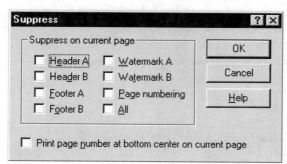

To suppress one of the elements from appearing on a page, choose Page from the Format menu, and then click on Suppress to see the dialog box shown here. Select the check boxes for the items that you do not want to appear on the current page, or click on All to suppress all of them. If your page numbering is included in a header or footer, you can suppress the header or footer but number the page anyway by checking the Print Page Number at Bottom Center on Current Page option.

Numbering Lines

Legal documents, such as contracts, pleadings, and depositions, often have line numbers down the left margin; so may printed copies of computer programs and macros. The numbers make it easy to reference a specific line in the document. If you did not have Corel WordPerfect, you could try to type the numbers yourself, but fortunately, Corel WordPerfect can number lines automatically for you.

When you want to number lines, use these steps:

1. Select Line from the Format menu and click on Numbering to see the dialog box in Figure 8-10.

2. Check the "Turn line numbering on" box to start line numbering.

3. Specify the numbering method or style, what number to begin counting from, the first line you want numbered, and the intervals of numbers. As you select options, the effects will be displayed in the preview area.

4. By default, the numbers appear 0.6 inches from the left edge of the paper. You can adjust this measurement or set a distance relative to the margin.

5. You can specify whether to restart numbering on every page, count blank lines, or insert numbers when using columns.

6. Click on the Font button to change the font, size, and style of the numbers.

7. Click on OK.

Making Text Fit

You can adjust the margins, fonts, and font size to fit text into fewer or more pages. If one or two lines of text spill over into the page, for example, you can try a slightly

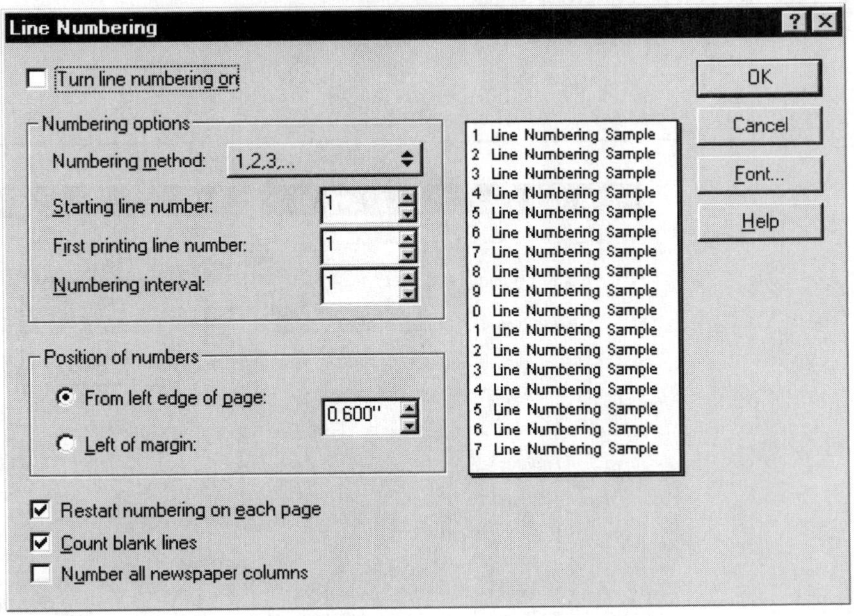

Turning
on line
numbering

FIGURE 8-10

smaller top or bottom margin for the entire document. You can also have Corel WordPerfect try to make the text fit for you. Here's how:

1. Click on the Make It Fit button in the toolbar or choose Make It Fit from the Format menu to see the dialog box shown in Figure 8-11.

2. Specify the number of pages that you want the text to fit in.

3. Select the items that Corel WordPerfect can modify to adjust the text. By default, for example, Corel WordPerfect will only change the font and line spacing. If you want Corel WordPerfect to adjust only the margins, deselect the Font and Line Spacing boxes, and select the margins that you want Corel WordPerfect to adjust.

4. Click on Make It Fit to adjust the text.

n **OTE:**   *The number of pages you set must be within 50 percent of the document's current size.*

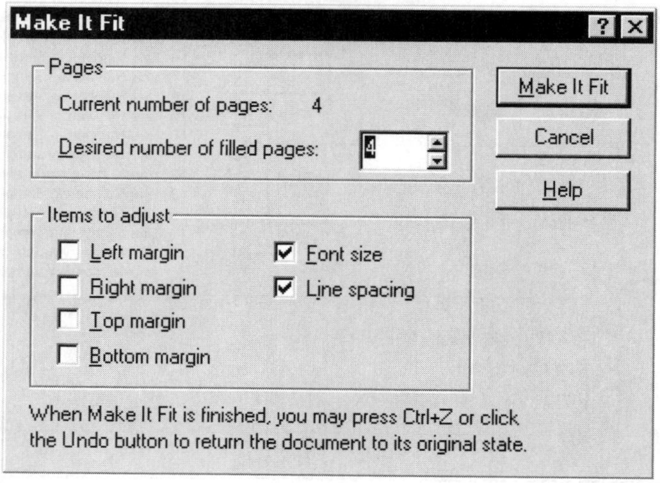

Make It Fit   ? ✕

┌─ Pages ──────────────────────────┐   ┌─────────────┐
│ Current number of pages: 4   │   │ Make It Fit │
│ <u>D</u>esired number of filled pages: [4] ▲▼ │   └─────────────┘
└──────────────────────────────────┘   ┌─────────────┐
                                           │   Cancel   │
┌─ Items to adjust ────────────────┐   └─────────────┘
│ ☐ <u>L</u>eft margin   ☑ <u>F</u>ont size   │   ┌─────────────┐
│ ☐ <u>R</u>ight margin   ☑ L<u>i</u>ne spacing │   │   <u>H</u>elp   │
│ ☐ <u>T</u>op margin   │   └─────────────┘
│ ☐ <u>B</u>ottom margin   │
└──────────────────────────────────┘

When Make It Fit is finished, you may press Ctrl+Z or click the Undo button to return the document to its original state.

Make It Fit
dialog box

FIGURE 8-11

Hypertext Links

You learned in Chapter 7 to create hypertext links for Web pages. You can use the same handy tools in any document to move quickly from one location to another. To create links, choose Hypertext/Web Links from the Tools menu to display the feature bar shown here:

Use the buttons on the bar to create, use, and customize links. When you create a link, it will appear underlined in color. Pointing to the link will change the mouse pointer to a small hand, and clicking will jump to the bookmark in the document, open a document, launch your browser and go to a Web site, or run a macro—all depending on how you defined the link.

If the insertion point is immediately to the left of a link, click on Perform to jump to its location. Click on Back to move from the location back to the link. The Previous and Next buttons move from link to link within the document. Use Create to create the link, just as you learned to do for Web pages—the Create Hypertext Link dialog box is the same. This button will appear as Delete when the insertion point is next to a link. Click on Edit to change the link closest to the insertion point. Use the Deactivate button to turn off links—it will change to Activate so you can turn them on again. Create a bookmark by clicking on the Bookmark button, and change the format of links using the Style button.

Formatting and Printing Envelopes

An envelope is just another page size, but formatting and printing envelopes can often be intimidating. Corel WordPerfect makes it easy, however, because it provides a built-in envelope feature that not only selects the correct page size but can also insert the return address, mailing address, and POSTNET bar code for you automatically.

Envelope Page Size

In order to use the envelope feature, you need to have an envelope page size defined. Chances are there is one for your printer, but check ahead of time anyway. Select

Page from the Format menu, click on Page Size, and then scroll the Name list looking for the item "Envelope #10 Landscape"—the standard business envelope for letter-sized paper.

If it is not there, create the page size as explained earlier in this chapter. Use a width of 4.13" and a height of 9.5", and then select the envelope type. If you have a laser or inkjet printer, select Rotated font orientation and Short Edge paper feed. Unless you have an envelope feeder, choose manual feed as the paper source.

Creating an Envelope

You can format and print just an envelope, or print an envelope for a letter or other document already on the screen. Here is all you have to do, for example, to create an envelope for a letter:

1. Select the recipient's address. If you just need to print a quick envelope by itself, start with a blank document screen.

2. Choose Envelope from the Format menu to display the Envelope dialog box, shown in Figure 8-12. The dialog box has two address sections, the Mailing Address and the Return Address. Each section has a place to enter an address, a Font button to change the font and font size, and an Address Book icon to select an address listing.

3. If you selected the inside address of a letter, it will automatically appear in the Mailing Address section. Otherwise, click in the section and type the address.

4. To include your return address on the envelope, enter it in the Return Address section, or click on the Address Book icon in that section and select your listing in the Corel Address Book.

 IP: *If you are using preprinted envelopes, and your name or address already appears in the Return Address section, deselect the Print Return Address check box.*

5. You may have more than one envelope page size defined for your printer, so pull down the Envelope Definitions list and check that the correct envelope size is being used.

6. To print a POSTNET bar code on your envelopes, click on Options in the Envelope dialog box to display the Envelope Options box shown in Figure 8-13.

7. Select the position for the bar code—Include and Position Above Address, or Include and Position Below Address—in the USPS Bar Code Options section.

8. Click on OK. You'll now see a text box labeled POSTNET Bar Code in the Envelope dialog box.

9. Enter the address's ZIP code in the POSTNET Bar Code box.

10. To print the envelope immediately, click on the Print Envelope button. To insert the envelope at the end of the current document, following a page break, click on Append to Doc. You can then print the letter, or envelope, or both.

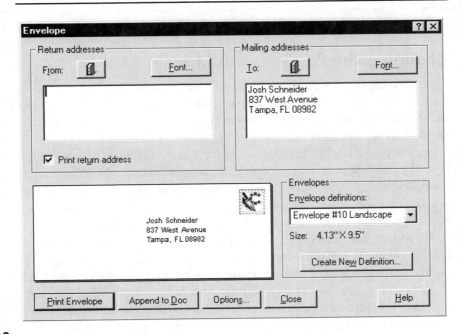

Envelope dialog box

FIGURE 8-12

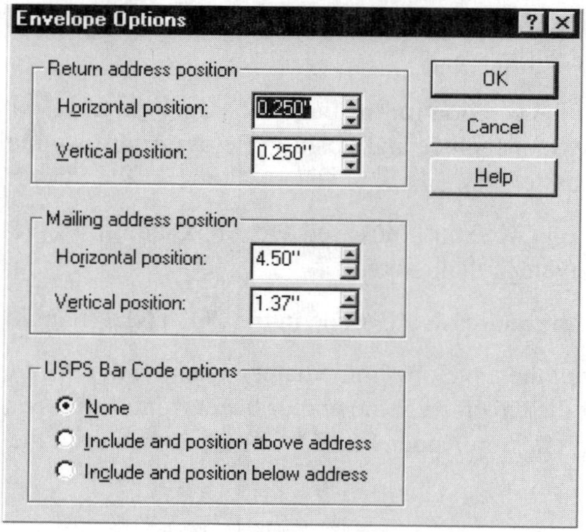

Envelope
options to
add bar
code and
change
address
position

FIGURE 8-13

Changing The Position Of Addresses

Corel WordPerfect will print the return and mailing addresses at the customary
position for the size envelope you selected. You can adjust the position if it is
incorrect, or if you just want to change it. If you already inserted the envelope into
the document, just place the insertion point in the page containing the envelope and
adjust the page margins. Either drag the margin guidelines or use the Margins dialog
box. If you included a return address, drag or set the corresponding margins. To use
the dialog box, for example, change the position of the return address by clicking in
it and then choosing Margins from the Format menu. To change the position of the
mailing address, click in it before displaying the dialog box.

If you are just creating the envelope and the Envelope dialog box is still on the
screen, change the position by clicking on Options and then adjusting the horizontal
and vertical settings in the Mailing Address Position and Return Address Position
sections. To move the mailing address further up on the envelope, for example,
decrease the Vertical Position setting in the Mailing Address Position section. To
move it more to the right, increase the Horizontal Position setting.

Formatting and Printing Labels

In many organizations, mailing addresses are printed almost exclusively on labels rather than directly on envelopes. In addition, labels can be used for any number of documents: name badges, diskette and tape identifiers, even business cards and postcards.

It is easy to format and print labels because Corel WordPerfect includes page definitions for the most popular sizes of labels made by the major label company, Avery. If you have labels from another manufacturer, you will probably find a compatible Avery number. You can also define your own label size when you cannot find a match.

IP: *You should work with labels in Page view so you can see the arrangement of labels on the page.*

To format labels, use these steps:

1. Choose Labels from the Format menu to see the dialog box shown in Figure 8-14. Corel WordPerfect classifies labels as either Laser, which come on individual sheets of paper, or Tractor-fed, continuous pages for use with dot-matrix printers. The Labels list will show all of the predefined labels, but you can click on either Laser or Tractor-fed to display just that category.

2. Scroll the Labels list and click on the label that matches yours. The specifications for the label will be shown in the Label Details section, and its layout will appear in the preview area. If none of the specifications match your labels, try another selection from the list.

3. When you find the correct label, click on Select.

OTE: *All of the label definitions are in a file called WP_WP_US.LAB. If your label vendor provides another file, click on the Change button and select the file in the dialog box that appears.*

If you are in Page view, you'll see one label on the screen. Most of the label definitions do not include margins, so you should set them yourself to avoid printing

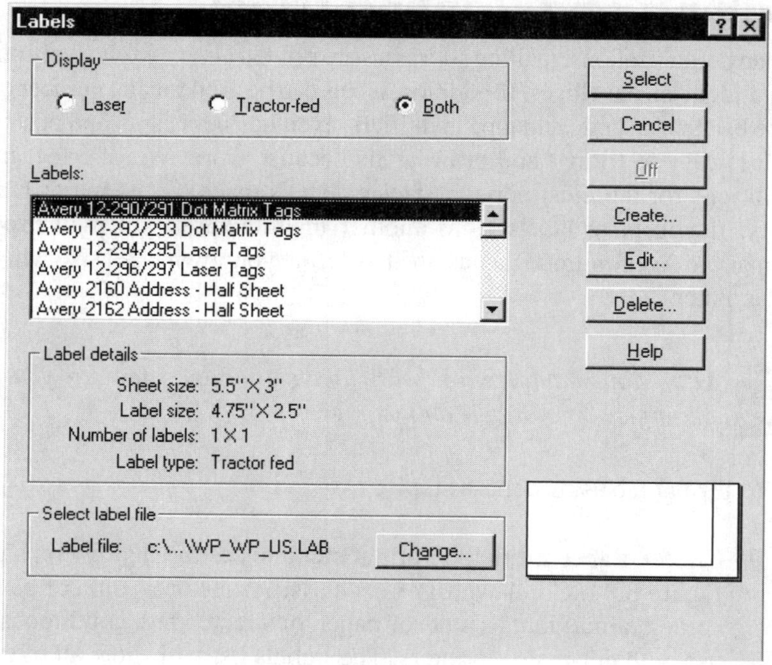

Selecting a
predefined
label format

FIGURE 8-14

in unprintable areas. Type the address or other information you want on the label, and then press CTRL+ENTER. Corel WordPerfect will display the next blank label in the same layout as they are on the page. Corel WordPerfect completes each row of labels before starting another row. In Draft view, labels always appear one below the other, separated with page break lines.

If you want to stop using the label format in the document, select Labels from the Format menu, and then click on Off in the Labels dialog box. Corel WordPerfect will add enough blank labels to fill out the current page, and then start a new page. The page will be the same size as the label carrier sheet that you turned off. If you're using a laser label that is 8.5 × 11 inches, the page size will be 8.5 × 11 inches. If you are using what's referred to as a half-size label sheet, the page size will be 4.25 × 5 inches. Change the page size to the desired size.

Defining a Label

If you cannot find an Avery label definition that matches your label stock, you can easily create your own. It will then appear in the Labels list so you can select it when needed.

To create a label, follow these steps:

1. Select Labels from the Format menu to display the Labels dialog box. If there is an Avery label close in specifications to the label you are using, select it on the list. This will serve as the starting point for your own label and you won't have to enter the elements matching the specifications. If you have a half-sheet laser label, for example, select another half-sheet label from the list. At least that way you won't have to enter the page sizes.

2. Click on the Create button to see the dialog box shown in Figure 8-15. Start by entering the Label Description. This will be the name that appears in the Labels list, so make sure it describes the label.

 IP: *Labels are listed alphabetically, so to have a particular label appear at the top, start the description with a number.*

3. Make sure the label sheet size is correct. If not, click on the Change button, which will be dimmed until you enter a description, to display the Edit Page Size dialog box.

4. Enter the sheet size and orientation, just as you did when creating a page size.

5. Click on OK.

6. Select the Label Type. This determines if the label will be listed with Laser labels, Sheet-fed labels, or both.

7. Finally, enter the measurements that describe the label. Remember, you can enter measurements in inches, points, millimeters, centimeters, or even 1200ths of an inch.

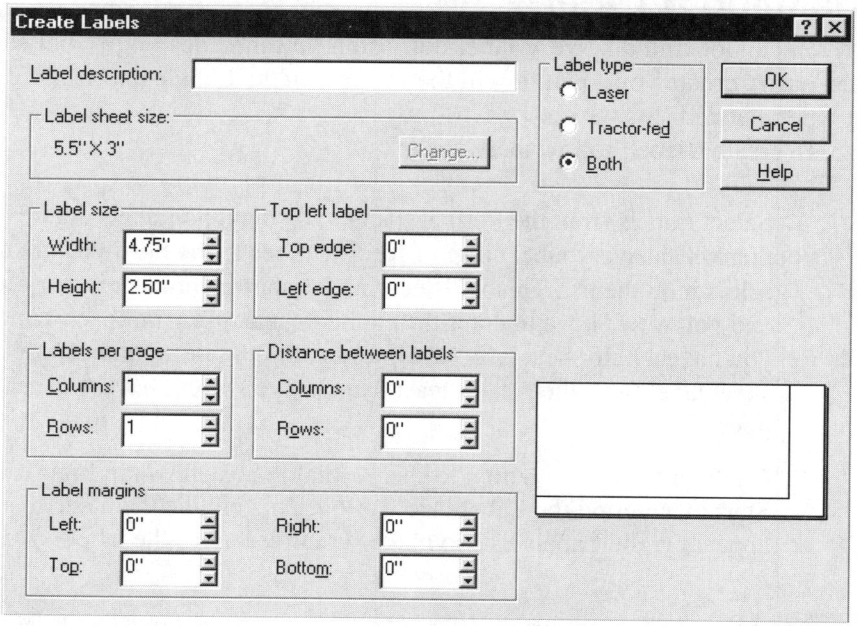

Create Labels

Label description:		Label type	
		○ Laser	OK
Label sheet size:		○ Tractor-fed	Cancel
5.5" X 3"	Change...	⊙ Both	Help

Label size
Width: 4.75"
Height: 2.50"

Top left label
Top edge: 0"
Left edge: 0"

Labels per page
Columns: 1
Rows: 1

Distance between labels
Columns: 0"
Rows: 0"

Label margins
Left: 0"   Right: 0"
Top: 0"   Bottom: 0"

Creating a
custom
label size

FIGURE 8-15

Corel WordPerfect changes the preview of the label as soon as you enter a measurement, assuming the default is inches. So if you type **5** in the width box, for example, the preview label will widen to show five inches. Once you enter **p** or **m**, the size will adjust to the actual measurement, so don't panic if your 50 millimeter labels start to appear wider than the page.

Try to be as accurate as possible with the measurements—you might even find them on the label box.

In the Label Size section, enter the width and height of the labels themselves, not including any space between labels or any margins between the labels and the edge of the carrier sheet. In the Labels Per Page section, specify the number of labels in each column and in each row. The product of those two numbers should equal the total number of labels on the page.

The Top Left Label section determines the exact position of the first label on the page. This tells Corel WordPerfect where the first line of text can be, and sets up the spacing for the remainder of the labels. If this measurement is off, then all of the labels will be off. In the Top Edge box, enter the distance from the top of the page to the top of the first label. In the Left Edge box, enter the distance from the left edge of the page to the left edge of the label.

In the Distance Between Labels section, enter any spacing between the rows and columns of labels. These are usually small measurements, so try to be precise.

The Label Margins section determines the margin areas within the label. Imagine it as the page margins for each individual label. The margins for most of Corel WordPerfect's defined labels are set at zero. If you set a margin when defining the label, however, you won't have to set the margins in the document after selecting the label.

When you've completed the specifications, click on OK. If your settings create an impossible layout, such as more labels than will fit on the page, a dialog box will appear telling you so. Click OK in the message box, and correct the problem. Once your label definition is complete, it will appear in the Labels list for you to select.

 OTE: *You can define as many custom labels as you want, giving each its own name.*

Using Tables and Columns

9

Text and numbers sometimes look best when they are neatly arranged in columns. If you want to communicate numbers, for example, format them in a table. The table format makes numbers easy to read and shows relationships and trends that cannot easily be expressed in text. To improve the appearance of text, format it in columns. Columns make newsletters look professional and can enhance almost any document.

Creating Tables

A table lets you enter text in neatly arranged rows and columns, just as you would in Corel Quattro Pro. By adding a table to your Corel WordPerfect document, you can display columns of numbers to maximize impact. You can create a table by dragging the mouse or by selecting from a dialog box.

 If you've already created a table as a Corel Quattro Pro worksheet, don't duplicate your efforts. You can share the worksheet with a Corel WordPerfect document.

Building a Table

To create the table with the mouse, use the following steps:

1. Click and hold down the mouse button on the Tables button on the power bar. A miniature grid will appear representing the rows and columns of a table.

2. Hold down the mouse button and drag down and to the right. As you drag, squares in the grid become selected and the number of rows and columns will be indicated at the top of the grid.

3. Drag the mouse until you select the number of rows and columns that you want in the table, and then release the mouse button.

Use this method to create a table with five columns and seven rows. Corel WordPerfect inserts a blank table with grid lines, and displays a special Table toolbar, as shown in Figure 9-1.

Corel
WordPerfect
Table and
Table
toolbar

FIGURE 9-1

 IP: *You can add or delete rows and columns at any time.*

The table extends from the left to the right margin, with equal-sized columns. As with a spreadsheet program, each cell in the table is referenced by its row and column numbers; for example, the upper-left cell is A1. The ruler shows the width of the cells, and the status bar shows the cell in which the insertion point is placed.

The Table toolbar contains many of the standard toolbar buttons. Following the QuickFormat button, however, the Table toolbar buttons are as follows:

- *Table SpeedFormat* lets you change the style of the entire table by selecting from predesigned formats. You can also create your own table styles.

- *Table Format* displays a dialog box for formatting cells, rows, columns, and the entire table.

- *Lines/Fill* lets you customize the lines around the table cells and add a fill or pattern to the cell background.

- *Numeric Format* controls the way numbers appear.

- *Row/Column Indicators* displays the column numbers under the ruler and the row letters in the left margin to help you identify cells.

- *Size Column to Fit* will adjust the width of a column to a specific entry, or to the widest entry in the column.

- *Formula Bar* displays an input bar and feature bar below the ruler. Use the input bar and feature bar to perform math on the cell contents.

- *QuickFill* will complete a series of entries across selected cells or copy formulas, adjusting their cell references.

- *Calculate* recalculates the resulting values of formulas.

- *Chart* creates a chart using the information in the table.

IP: *The Table toolbar will only appear when the insertion point is located in the table.*

Creating Tables Using Other Methods

The largest table you can create with the mouse is 32 columns by 45 rows. To create a table up to 64 columns and as many as 32,767 rows, select Create from the Table menu to display the dialog box you see here. Enter the number of columns and rows desired in the appropriate text boxes, and then click on OK.

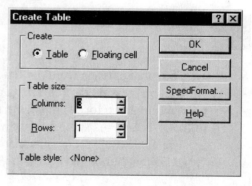

Converting Between Tables and Text

If you've already typed information in columns separated by tabs, you can automatically convert the text into a table. For example, suppose you had typed the text shown here before reading this chapter. Since the information would look better

```
Jane    President       100,000
John    Vice President        80,000
Jacob   Treasurer       50,000
```

as a table, select the text and then choose Create from the Table menu to display a dialog box asking if you want to create a table from Tabular Columns or from Parallel Columns. Since the sample table uses tabs between information in each line, click on Tabular Columns and then on OK to convert the text into a table.

Entering Information into Tables

After you create the table, you are ready to enter text into it. To enter text, place the insertion point in a cell and type. You can place the insertion point by clicking in the cell, or by pressing TAB, SHIFT+TAB, or the arrow keys. If you type more text than can fit in a cell, Corel WordPerfect will automatically wrap the text and increase the row height. It will not widen the cell automatically.

 AUTION: *Do not press* ENTER *to move out of a cell. When you press* ENTER, *the height of the current cell will increase by one line. To delete the extra line, press* BACKSPACE.

Make sure the insertion point is in the first cell in the second row, and type **Chesin**. By default, everything you type in a cell—text and numbers—is left aligned. Press the DOWN ARROW to reach the next cell in the row and then complete the table as shown here:

Chesin	67856	56435	34678	74130
Schneider	56786	67865	45126	78090
Wilson	43456	54367	76578	75432
Randolph	67544	67543	86467	56788
Total				
Average				

 IP: *Use the toolbar, power bar, and Format menu to format text in cells just as you format any text in the document.*

Selecting Cells

To format a cell, row, or column at a time, you do not necessarily have to select it first. But if you want to cut or copy an entire column or row, you must select it. To select a cell, point to its top border so the mouse appears as an up-pointing arrow, or point to the left border so the mouse appears as a left-pointing arrow.

- Click once to select the cell.

- Click twice to select the row (if you are pointing to the right) or the column (if you are pointing up).

- Click three times to select the entire table.

To select multiple cells, rows, or columns, select one first and then drag the mouse.

Saving Time with QuickFill

In many cases, a row or column of labels will be a series, such as the days of the week, months of the year, or four quarters. When you need to enter a series of incrementing values such as these, you only need to type the first of the series yourself. The QuickFill command will do the rest. Here's how to use it.

1. Enter the first of the series into its cell—type **Qtr 1** in cell B1.

2. Select the cell and drag to select the other cells in the row or column that you want to fill. In this case, drag over cells B1 to E1.

3. Click on the QuickFill button in the Table toolbar, or select QuickFill from the Table menu or QuickMenu.

Corel WordPerfect will complete the series for you, inserting Qtr 2, Qtr 3, and Qtr 4 in the other selected cells.

If Corel WordPerfect does not recognize the series, it will repeat the first value in the remaining cells. In this case, try entering the first two of the series yourself, and then selecting both and dragging across the row or down the column before using QuickFill. Corel WordPerfect will complete a series of roman numerals if you start with I, for example, but it will not enter consecutive Arabic numbers or letters based on one initial value. To number cells 1, 2, 3, 4, and so on, you must enter the first two values. To insert a series of years, enter the first two years, and then use QuickFill.

Moving and Copying Cells

All of the same techniques that you know for moving and copying text can also be applied to tables. You can move cells using drag and drop or the Clipboard.

To move or copy just the contents of a cell but not the formats applied to it, click in the cell and drag so the text within it is selected. Do not click on the cell border.

When you move or copy cells, you insert the contents and formats of the cells into another location. If you move or copy an entire row or column, however, other rows or columns will shift over or down to make room. The row or column that you paste does not replace the one where you paste or drop it, so copying an entire row, for instance, actually inserts another row into the table.

To move a cell, row, or column by drag and drop, select what you want to move, point to the cells, and then drag the mouse. To copy the selection rather than move it, hold down the CTRL key when you release the mouse button.

You can also move and copy cells, rows, and columns using the Clipboard with the Cut, Copy, and Paste commands. When you select cells and choose Cut or Copy, however, you'll see the dialog box shown here. Select to cut or copy just the selected cells (Selection), or the entire rows or columns of the selected cells. Click on OK, and then move the insertion point to where you want to insert the cells, and select Paste.

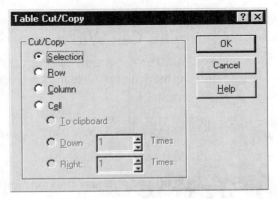

You can also use the Table Cut/Copy dialog box to copy a single selected cell into any number of consecutive cells in the row or column. Click on the Cell option in the Table Cut/Copy dialog box. The default option will be Clipboard, indicating that the cell will be placed into the Clipboard for pasting elsewhere. To copy the cell down to cells in the column, click on the Column option, and then enter the number of cells you want to paste it to in the Times box. To copy the cell across the row, click on the Right option and enter the number of cells.

Working with Tables

Corel WordPerfect provides a number of special ways to work with tables in addition to the Table toolbar. Most of these options in the toolbar, and more, are also in the Table pull-down menu, and you'll find them in the QuickMenu that appears when you right-click in a table.

When you point to a cell in the table, a QuickSpot will appear in the cell's upper-right corner. Click on the QuickSpot to see the Tools dialog box. You can use the Tools dialog box to customize the lines around cells, add a fill pattern, display the Format dialog box, change the numeric format, insert and delete rows and columns, adjust the column width for the widest entry or to make multiple columns the same size, and join and split cells.

Since most table functions are in all of these items, you can perform the function using any techniques. For example, the Size Column to Fit option adjusts the width of a column to the widest entry. You can perform this function using any of these techniques.

- Click on the Size Column to Fit button in the Table toolbar.

- Select Size Column to Fit from the Table menu.

- Right-click and select Size Column to Fit from the QuickMenu.

Changing Cell Width and Height

Corel WordPerfect gives you complete control over the size of rows, columns, and cells. Use the Split option in the Table menu to divide one or more cells into columns, as follows:

1. Select the cells you want to split.

2. Pull down the Table menu.

3. Point to Split, and click on Cell to see the Split Cell dialog box.

4. Select the number of columns you want to create—the default is 2—and then choose OK.

Use the Join command in the Table menu to combine two or more adjacent cells into one. Join is useful when you want to use one column label for two existing columns of data. Select the cells that you want to combine, choose Join from the Table menu, and click on Cell. Any contents in the cells will also be combined, with a tab separating information from side-by-side cells and a carriage return separating cells that were in the same columns.

 OTE: *The Split and Join options are also available in the QuickSpot Tools dialog box and in the QuickMenu.*

You can change the width of a column in several ways. If you point to a vertical grid line in the table, the pointer will appear with a two-headed arrow. Point to and drag a line between two cells to change the width of the cells on either side. As you drag, a QuickStatus dialog box will appear showing the dimensions of the cells. If you drag the leftmost or rightmost grid lines, only the cell next to it will be affected.

You can also adjust columns with the ruler using the markers in the Indentation and Margin area. The down-pointing triangles represent the lines between columns. Drag a triangle to change the width of the cells on both sides. Drag the left or right margin indicator to adjust the width of the end cells. When the insertion point is in a table, dragging the margin indicators does not change the page margins, just the column width.

You will also see left- and right-pointing triangles in the ruler. These represent the indentation of text within the column in which the insertion point is placed. Drag these markers to change the indentation of text within the cell.

Adjusting Column Width Automatically

Rather than dragging column indicators to change column width, you can have Corel WordPerfect automatically adjust the column for you. To adjust the column so it is as wide as the widest entry in it, click in any cell in the column and then click on the Size Column to Fit button in the Table Toolbar.

To make a column just wide enough for a specific entry, select the cell containing that entry first and then click on the Size Column to Fit button. If any cells contain wider entries, however, their text will be wrapped onto two or more lines, making the row higher.

You can also display the Tools dialog box by clicking on a table QuickSpot and choosing the Adjust Columns option. You can select Size Column to Fit, or if you have more than one column selected, you can choose Make Column Widths Equal.

Changing Grid Lines

The grid lines in a table help to separate cells, and they make it easier to keep track of rows and columns. You can customize grid lines, and even add color backgrounds and patterns to the cells, to give your table a more polished look. Of course, grid lines and background fills are for more than just good looks; they can call attention to parts of the table and make it easier to read.

You can add grid lines and fills using either the Table Tools dialog box that appears when you click on a table QuickSpot, or by displaying the Lines/Fill dialog box.

To customize the lines or fill of a single cell, point to it and click on the QuickSpot that appears. To format several cells, select them first, and then point to any in the group and click on its QuickSpot.

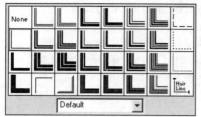

The top six lists in the Tools dialog box all offer the same options. Each list, however, affects a different line around the cell, or a group of lines. Selecting an option from the Left list, for example, will affect the line on the left border of the cell, just as the Right, Top, and Bottom lists affect those lines. Choosing an option from the Outside list adds the selected pattern to all four lines. If you selected a block of cells, however, the Outside option only affects the border around the selected area. If you selected a group of cells, you can also choose an Inside line pattern to appear on the grid lines between the cells, without affecting the border.

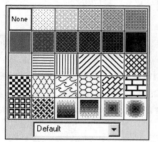

Use the Fill list to add a pattern or shading to the cell, or to the selected cells. You can either click one of the displayed options, shown on the left, or pull down the list and select one by name.

For even more line and fill options, use the Properties for Table Lines/Fill dialog box. Display the dialog box by clicking on the Lines/Fill button in the Table Toolbar, or by choosing Lines/Fill from the Table menu or QuickMenu. The dialog box has two pages, Cell and Table.

Use the Cell page to set the lines and fill pattern for the selected cells. It has all of the same options as the individual lists in the Tools dialog box, but in addition you can choose a foreground and background color for the fill patterns. If you choose a fill pattern, you can also select foreground and background colors. The Table page of the dialog box is shown in Figure 9-2. These options affect the grid lines on the outside border of the table, and the default line between cells. You can also add a fill pattern and alternate patterns in rows and columns.

Changing Table Size

You may create a table, only to realize later that you did not make it the correct size. When this happens, you'll need to insert or delete rows or columns.

Inserting Rows and Columns

If you only need to insert an additional row at the end of the table, place the insertion point in the last cell of the last row and press TAB. Corel WordPerfect will insert a blank row and place the insertion point in the first cell of the new row.

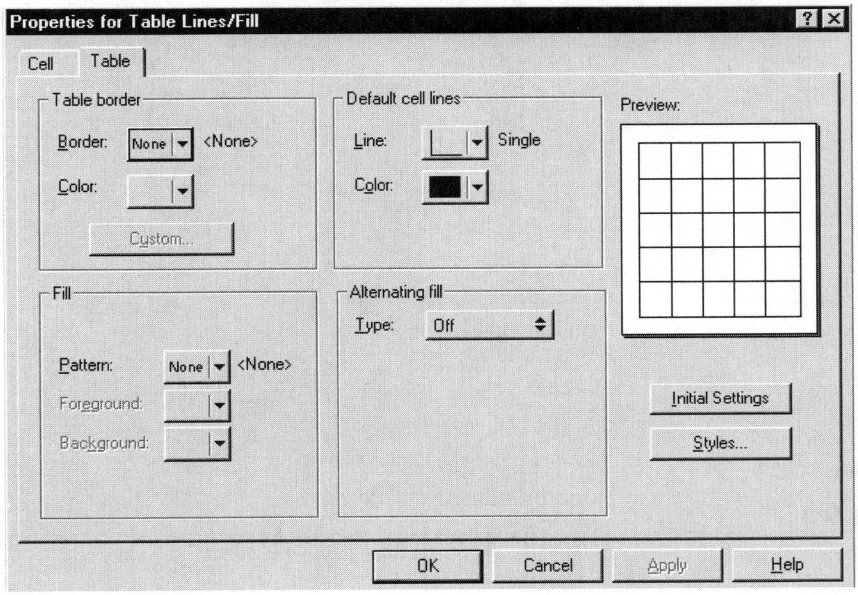

Setting
Border/Fill
options for
the entire
table

FIGURE 9-2

You can also insert a row using shortcut key combinations. Press ALT+INS to insert a row above the insertion point, or press ALT+SHIFT+INS to insert a row below the insertion point.

To insert several rows at one time or to insert new columns, use the Insert command. Start by placing the insertion point in the row or column that you want to insert a new row or column before or after. Then select Insert from the Table menu, or right-click on the row and select Insert from the QuickMenu, to see the dialog box in Figure 9-3. Here's how to use the dialog box.

1. Click on either Column or Row to choose what you want to insert.

2. Enter the number of rows or columns desired.

3. Choose either Before or After the row or column.

4. If you are inserting columns, choose Keep Column Widths Same if you want to insert the columns in the same width as existing ones.

5. Click on OK.

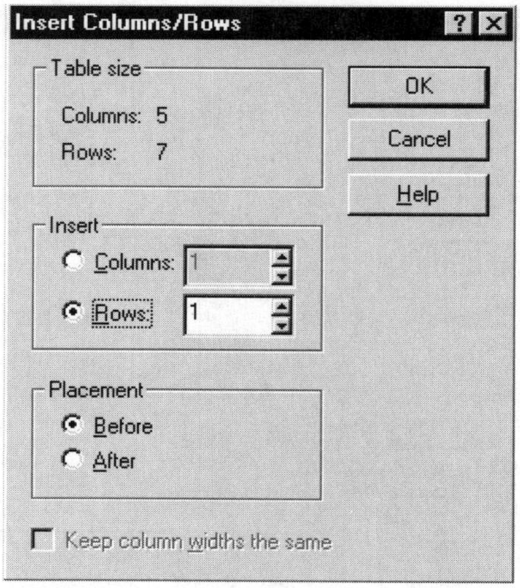

Inserting
columns
and rows

FIGURE 9-3

Deleting Rows, Columns, and Cells

It's as easy to delete rows, columns, and cells as it is to insert them. To delete the current row, press ALT+DEL. This deletes the row at the insertion point. To delete any number of rows or columns, place the insertion point in the first row or column you want to delete, and then choose Delete from the Table menu to see the dialog box in Figure 9-4. Delete rows or columns using these steps.

1. Click on either Column or Row to choose what you want to delete.

2. Enter the number of rows or columns you want to delete.

3. Choose if you want to delete Cell Contents or Formulas Only. Choosing Formulas Only will delete any formulas in the cell by leaving the results of the formulas as text.

4. Click on OK.

Splitting and Joining Tables

One other way to change table size is to split a table into two, or join two tables together. You can only split and join tables at rows, not columns.

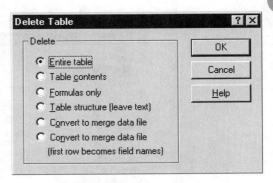

Deleting
columns
and rows

FIGURE 9-4

To split a table into two, start by placing the insertion point in the row that you want to start the new table, and then choose Split from the Table menu and click on Table.

To combine tables, click on the bottom row of the first table, choose Join from the Table menu, and then click on Tables. In order to join tables, they must have the same number of columns, and there must be no blank lines between the tables.

Deleting Tables

You can delete a table by selecting the entire thing and then pressing DEL. If you reveal the codes and delete the table code itself, however, Corel WordPerfect will display the dialog box shown here. Make your choice from the dialog box and click on OK.

Selecting a Table Format

Rather than use a variety of means to format the parts of a table, you can choose a complete set of formats to apply to the entire table at one time using the SpeedFormat command. With the insertion point in any cell of the table, click on the Table

SpeedFormat button in the toolbar, or select SpeedFormat from the Table menu or the QuickMenu to see the dialog box in Figure 9-5.

The Available Styles list contains a series of complete table formats. Click on each of the formats and see how it affects the sample table in the preview panel area. Choosing the Fancy Fills format, for instance, will change our sample table to this:

Chesin	67856	56435	34678	74130
Schneider	56786	67865	45126	78090
Wilson	43456	54367	76578	75432
Randolph	67544	67543	86467	56788
Total				
Average				

Now take a look at some of the options in the dialog box:

- *Apply Style on a Cell by Cell Basis* will automatically apply the same formats to rows or columns that you later add to the table. Deselect this check box if you want to add unformatted rows or columns.

- *Clear Current Table Settings Before Applying* will remove all of the table's original formats so none of them will be retained when you apply a selected style.

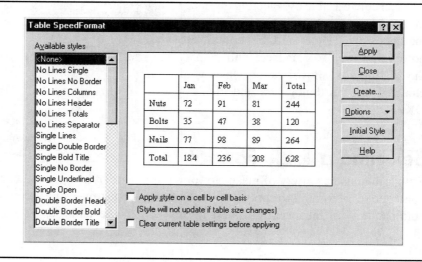

Selecting a
table format

FIGURE 9-5

- *Initial Style* will apply the selected formats to all new tables that you create. Select the style, click on Initial Style, and then click on Yes in the message box that appears.

When you find a format that you want for your table, click on Apply.

Creating Your Own Styles

If you don't like any of the built-in table styles, you can create your own. This way you can quickly reapply the same formats to another table. First, use all of Corel WordPerfect's formatting features to format the table the way you want to. You'll learn more about formatting tables soon. Then follow these steps:

1. Place the insertion point in any cell of the table, and then click on the Table SpeedFormat button to display the dialog box.

2. Next, decide where you want to save your styles. Pull down the Options button and click on Setup to see the Table Style Settings dialog box.

3. You can save your styles in the current document or in the default template. Click on your choice and then on OK.

4. Click on the Create button.

5. In the dialog box that appears, type a name for the style and then click on OK. Your style will now be listed in the Available Styles list and shown on the top of the list, as well as the most recently used style.

You can also save your styles in a separate file on the disk, as follows:

1. Pull down the Options menu.

2. Click on Save.

3. Type a name for the file in the box that appears.

4. Click on OK.

When you want to apply a table style, you have to select the style from the Available Styles list. To display styles that you saved in a separate file, follows these steps:

9

1. Pull down the Options menu.

2. Select Retrieve.

3. Type the name of the file.

4. Click on OK.

To list styles in either the document or the default template, pull down options, click on Setup, and make your choice from the dialog box.

You can also use the Options menu to delete or rename one of your custom styles. You cannot delete or rename Corel WordPerfect's built-in styles.

Applying Table Formats

You can always format the text in cells using the options in the power bar, toolbar, and format menus. Selecting text in a cell and clicking on the Bold button, for example, will format the text in boldface. To adjust the width of columns, you can always use the mouse to drag the column border or the column indicator in the ruler.

You have greater control over formats, however, if you use the Format command to display the dialog box shown in Figure 9-6. Display the dialog box using any of these techniques:

- Click on the Table Format button in the Table toolbar.

- Select Format from the Table menu.

- Right-click and select Format from the QuickMenu.

- Click on the Table QuickSpot and click on Format in the Table Tools dialog box.

The pages in this dialog box let you format cells, rows, columns, or the entire table. The default page displayed will depend on what is selected in the table. If you select a row before displaying the dialog box, for example, the Row page will be open. Let's look at each of the pages and the options they offer.

Applying Cell Formats

These options affect the current cell or the group of selected cells.

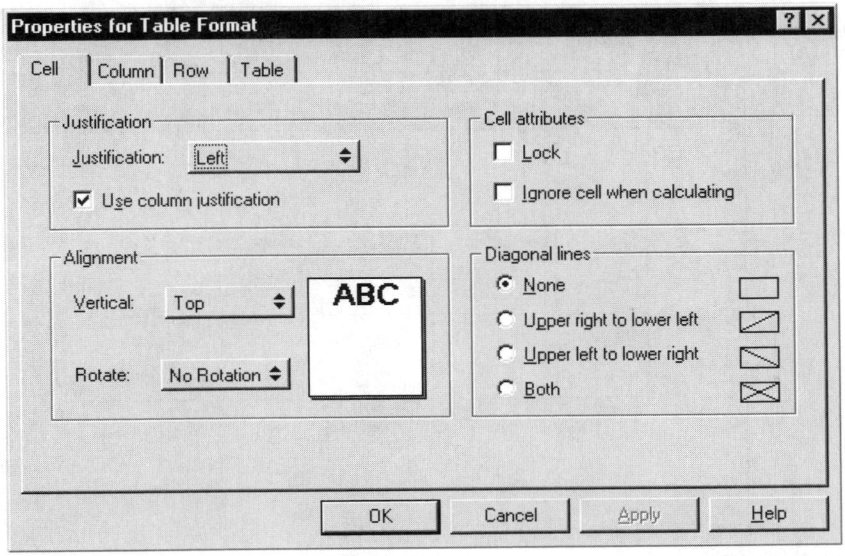

Properties
for Table
Format
dialog box

FIGURE 9-6

Use the Justification list to align the text in the cell on the left, right, center, on the decimal point, or Full or All justification. When you choose an option, the check mark will be cleared from the Use Column Justification box. Select the box if you want the cell to use the default alignment, or the alignment that you've assigned to the entire column.

OTE: *Selecting an alignment is the same as choosing an option from the Justification list in the power bar.*

The options in the Alignment section of the dialog box controls where the text appears vertically in the cell, and its rotation. You can select a vertical position of top, center, or bottom, and you can rotate the text in 90-degree increments—90, 180, and 270 degrees. Figure 9-7 shows some of the effects of these options.

In the Cell Attributes section, decide if you want to lock the cell so it cannot be edited and if you want to ignore the value in the cell when performing math operations. Ignoring the cell during math is useful when you have a numeric label, such as a year, and you want to ensure that it is not accidentally used to calculate a total or average value.

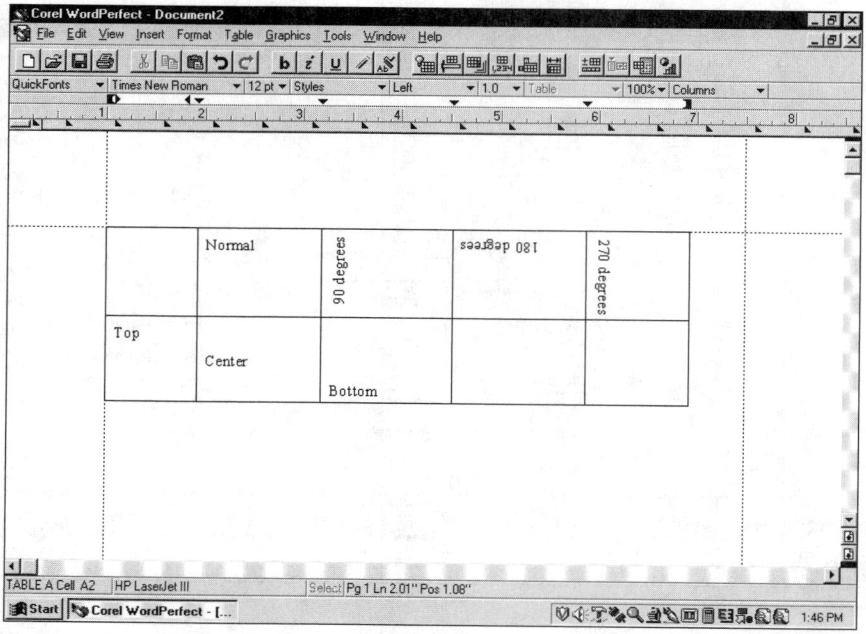

Alignment
options

FIGURE 9-7

The Diagonal Lines section is a nice touch. Diagonal lines are often used to indicate cells that should be ignored because they have no value or significance.

Formatting Columns

The Column page of the Format dialog box is shown in Figure 9-8. Your selections will affect the entire column that the insertion point is in—the column itself does not have to be selected.

Use the Justification section to assign an alignment to every cell in the column. It will not affect any cell that you've already applied an alignment to using the power bar or the Cell page of the dialog box. If you select Decimal Align justification, you should also select one of the options in the Alignment section. These determine the position of the decimal point in the cell, and thus where the numbers align. Choose Digits after Decimal, and enter a number in the corresponding box, to position the decimal point a number of characters from the right. Choose Position From Right, and enter a measurement in the text box, to position the decimal point at set distances.

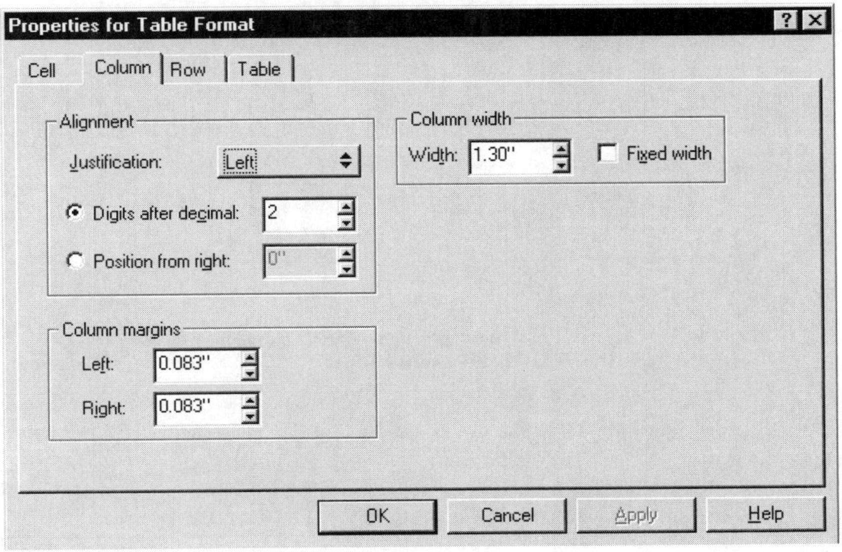

Column
format
options

FIGURE 9-8

The Column Margins are the space Corel WordPerfect leaves on the right and left of text. This determines how much text fits in the cell before Corel WordPerfect wraps the text to the next line.

Use the Column Width box to set the width of the column to a specific measurement. Use this if you have trouble getting the width to an exact amount by dragging. If you select the Fixed Width box, Corel WordPerfect will not change the width of the column as you change the width of others in the table.

You can also apply justification formats using the power bar. Try that now. Select cells B1 through E1, pull down the Justification list in the power bar, and click on Center.

Formatting Rows

The options in the Row page of the dialog box, shown in Figure 9-9, affect the entire row. As with columns, you do not have to select the row first, simply click in any cell in the row.

By default, Corel WordPerfect is set to accept multiple lines in a cell—either lines that are word wrapped or those created when you press ENTER. If you carefully designed a table to fit a certain space, however, wrapped lines will widen the row

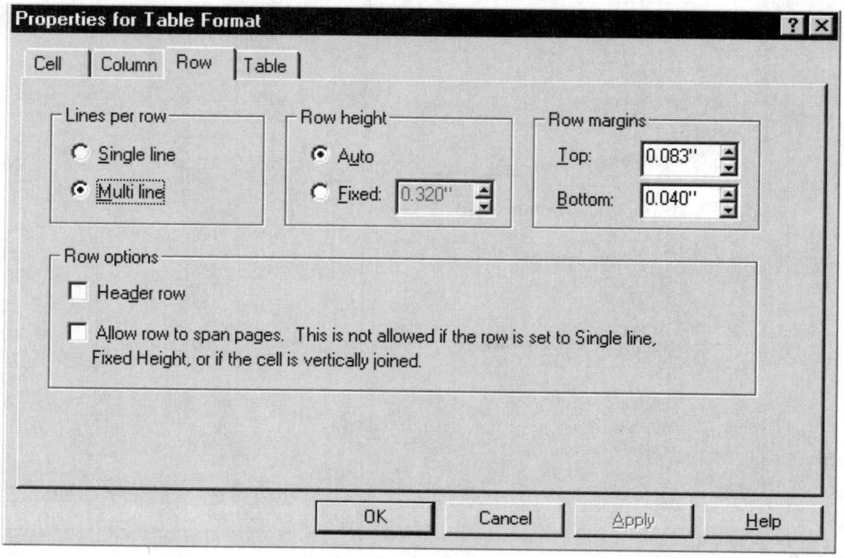

Row format
options

FIGURE 9-9

height and the spacing of the table on the page. If you select Single Line in this dialog box, you can only enter one line of information—Corel WordPerfect will just stop accepting keystrokes when the cell is filled.

Also use this dialog box to create a header row. A *header* is a row or rows that repeat on every page, when your table spans a page break. If you have a row of labels at the start of the table, for example, you might want it to repeat so the reader can identify the columns on the next page. Select the row, display the Row page of the Format dialog box, and click on the Header Row check box.

You can also allow a row to span a page break. If the row contains more than one line of text, this will let the row be divided between pages. Deselect this option to keep the entire row on the same page. The dialog box also lets you set the row height and width to a specific measurement.

Formatting the Table

This last page of the dialog box applies formats to the entire table. Some of these options are the same as those you can set for columns, but they apply to all of the cells. For example, you can select a default justification, set the number of decimal digits and distance from the right cell border, and enter default column margins and width.

In addition, you can determine the position of the entire table between the margins and change the table size by specifying the number of rows and columns.

You can also disable all of the cell locks so you can enter and edit information, and you can control whether or not you can insert rows.

Changing the Numeric Format

As you insert numbers and perform math operations, you may want to customize the way numbers appear. You can, for example, display values as currency, with dollar signs and commas separating thousands, or control the number of decimal places that appear. To change the format of numbers, select the cells that you want to format and then click on the Numeric Format button on the Table toolbar to see the dialog box shown in Figure 9-10. You can also display the box by selecting Numeric Format from the Table menu, the QuickMenu, or the QuickSpot dialog box.

Choose if you want to apply the format to the selected cells, the columns, or to the entire table, and then select one of the numeric formats. An example of this follows.

1. Select cells B2 through E6.

2. Click on the Numeric Format button in the toolbar.

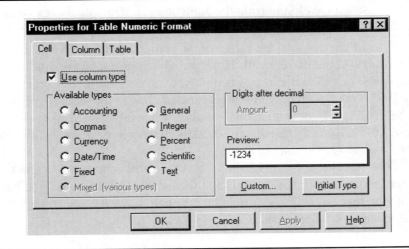

Changing
the numeric
format

FIGURE 9-10

3. Click on the Currency format, and then click on OK. All of the amounts will include dollar signs and two decimal places.

4. Align the cells on the decimal point. The cells should still be selected, so pull down the Justification list in the power bar and click on Decimal.

If you want a special format, create your own. Click on the Custom button and set the options in the Customize Number Type dialog box.

 IP: *You can also assign the type as the default initial style for all tables.*

Performing Calculations in Tables

A Corel WordPerfect table has many of the same characteristics as a spreadsheet. Information is presented in rows and columns, and each cell is referenced by its row and column position. And as with a spreadsheet, you can perform calculations on the numbers in your table. For example, you can display the sum of values in a row or column, compute averages, and insert formulas that reference cells and other values.

The quickest calculation you can make is to total the values in rows or columns using the QuickSum feature. You place the insertion point in the empty cell below the ones you want to total, and then select QuickSum from the Table menu. Do that now:

1. Place the insertion point in cell B6.

2. Select QuickSum from the Table menu or from the QuickMenu.

QuickSum will total the values of the numeric values above the cell, and display the results in the current cell. However, QuickSum totals numbers up to the first blank cell or cell that contains text. If you have a column label that is a year, such as 1997, Quick Sum may mistakenly include that in the total. If you have a column label such as that, or want to total numbers when there are blank cells in the column, select the cells first, including the blank cell where you want to insert the total, and then use the QuickSum command.

You can also use QuickSum to total the value in a row. Click in the blank cell after the last number in the row, and then select QuickSum. If you have values in both the row and column surrounding the cell, however, select the cells containing the values you want to add first.

Using the Formula Bar

QuickSum is useful, but it only totals. When you want to add, subtract, multiply, divide, and perform other types of math operations, you must enter a formula. With Corel WordPerfect, you enter formulas in a special formula bar. Display the bar, shown here, by clicking on the Formula Bar button in the Table toolbar, or by selecting Formula Bar from the table menu or the QuickMenu.

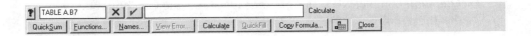

Here's how to use it. Click in the cell where you want to insert a formula, and then click in the formula bar. The cell's coordinates will appear in the text box on the left. Type the formula and then click on the check mark in the formula bar to accept the entry, or click on the X to cancel the formula.

You create a formula with a mathematical operation using the plus sign (+) to perform addition, the hyphen (-) for subtraction, the asterisk (*) for multiplication, and the forward slash (/) for division. Your formula can contain numbers and cell references. For example, to calculate a 6 percent sales tax on the value in cell A6, use the formula A6*.06. When you accept the entry, Corel WordPerfect inserts a plus sign in front of the operation.

Keep in mind the order of precedence that computer programs give to operators. Corel WordPerfect, like other programs, does not necessarily perform the operations from left to right but gives precedence to multiplication and division over addition and subtraction. If you enter 100+100+100/3, Corel WordPerfect will calculate 233.3333 because it first divides 100 by 3 and then adds 100 twice. To perform the calculation correctly, use parentheses to force Corel WordPerfect to follow a different order, such as (100+100+100)/3.

Rather than typing the cell reference into the formula bar, you can insert it by clicking. When you are ready to add the reference to the formula, make sure the insertion point is in the formula bar, and then click on the cell that you want to reference. Drag over cells to insert a reference to their range.

The other options in the formula bar will help you work on tables and perform math:

- *QuickSum* performs the same function as clicking on QuickSum in the Table toolbar.

- *Functions* displays a dialog box of functions that perform operations.

- *Names* lets you name cells and select names to insert in formulas.

- *View Error* displays a description of an error in the cell.

- *Calculate* recalculates the values of formulas and functions.

- *QuickFill* completes a series of entries, just like the QuickFill button in the Table toolbar.

- *Copy Formula* lets you copy a formula from a cell down or across to the cells.

- *Row/Column Indicators* toggles the display of column letters and row numbers.

- *Close* closes the formula bar.

Using Copy Formula

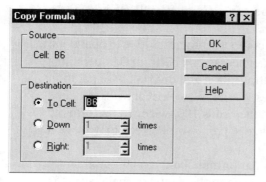

The Copy Formula button lets you copy the contents of a cell down or across cells, in much the same way as copying cells. It displays the dialog box shown on the left.

When you use the button to copy a formula, however, it is copied in a relative way. This means that the cell references in the formula are adjusted for the cell in which the formula appears. To see how this works, follow these steps:

1. Select cells B6 through E6.

2. Click on the Copy Formula button to display the dialog box.

3. Click on Right.

4. Enter **3** in the Cells box.

5. Click on OK.

Corel WordPerfect copies the formulas but adjusts the cell references. Each computes the total of the cells above it in the column.

 IP: *You can also copy formulas using the QuickFill button. Select the formula and the cell you want to copy it to, and click on QuickFill.*

Working with Functions

The QuickSum button actually inserts a function into the cell. A *function* is a shortcut because it performs a math operation that may have taken an entire series of operations, or even a number of formulas. For example, the QuickSum command might insert a formula that looks like SUM(A1:A20). This tells Corel WordPerfect to total the values in the cells from A1 to A20 in a much faster way than the formula A1+A2+A3..., and so on.

Corel WordPerfect comes with over 100 functions that perform all types of operations. To see the functions, and to insert one into the formula bar, click on the Functions button in the formula bar to see the dialog box in Figure 9-11.

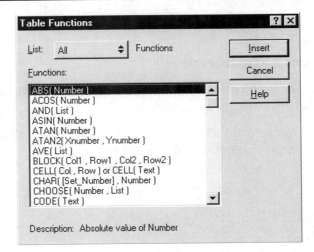

Corel
WordPerfect's
table
functions

FIGURE 9-11

By default, all of the functions will be available in the Functions list. You can also pull down the List Functions list and select to see only functions in these categories:

- Mathematical
- Date
- Financial

- Logical
- Miscellaneous
- String

To insert a function into the formula bar, click on it in the Functions list and then click on the Insert button.

Most functions require one or more arguments. An *argument* is a value or cell reference that follows the name of the function in parentheses. For example, in the @SUM function, the argument is the range of cells that you want to total. This function needs just one argument, the range of cells that contains the values to average. Many other functions require several arguments, separated from each other by commas.

When you insert a function into the formula bar, you'll see its name and a list of its arguments. The first argument will be highlighted, so all you have to do is click on or drag over the range of cells that you want to insert into the argument. After you insert the reference, double-click on the next argument, if it has one, and then click on or drag over the cell references for it. Continue the process until all of the arguments are complete.

Let's use a function now to calculate the average for each quarter in the table.

1. Click in cell B7.

2. Click on the Functions button.

3. Click on AVE[list] and then on Insert. The function will appear in the formula bar with the word list selected.

4. Drag over cells B2 through B5, and then click on the Check Mark in the formula bar to insert the calculated average.

5. Drag over cells B7 through E7, and then click on the QuickFill button to copy the function.

Figure 9-12 shows the table.

Creating Columns

Tables are fine for displaying numbers in columns, but you can also format text in columns just as easily. Newsletters, reports, and other published documents look good in columns where text flows from one column to the next. Corel WordPerfect makes it easy to create columns. In fact, you can type your text first, and then apply the column formats to see how it appears, or you can turn on columns before you type.

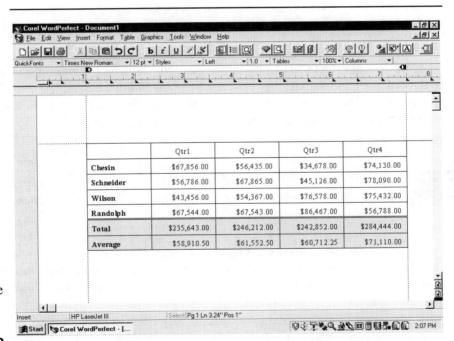

The average added to row 7

FIGURE 9-12

Creating Newspaper Columns

Newspaper columns are just as you see in the newspaper—columns of text flow from one column to the next on the page, from left to right. When you fill the column on the far right of the page, the text moves to the left column on the next page. The text will adjust, moving from column to column, as you insert or delete text above it.

When you create columns, you actually insert a column code into the document. Like a justification code, the column code affects all text from the paragraph in which the insertion point is placed to the end of the document, or until the next column code. This means that you can mix single-column and multiple-column text on the same page, and you can even have a different number of columns on a page.

When you want to format text in columns, follow these steps:

1. Place the insertion point where you want the columns to begin.

2. Pull down the Columns button on the power bar.

3. Select the number of columns desired, from 2 to 5.

Corel WordPerfect will display dotted boxes on the screen representing the width of the columns and the spacing between them, as in Figure 9-13. The word "Col" will appear in the status bar, followed by the number of the column in which the insertion point is placed. If you have the ruler display, it will indicate the width of each column, with the space between the columns.

 IP: *If you do not see the dotted lines, select Guidelines from the View menu, click on Column in the dialog box that appears, and then click on OK.*

If you selected columns in existing text, the text will appear in the column format. Otherwise, type your text starting in the leftmost column. As you type, the text will flow from column to column and from page to page, repeating the column format on each page.

If you want to end a column before the text flows, press CTRL+ENTER. What occurs when you press CTRL+ENTER depends on where the insertion point is placed, and how previous columns were ended. If you press CTRL+ENTER in a column that's not all the way on the right, Corel WordPerfect will end the current column and move the insertion point into the column to its right.

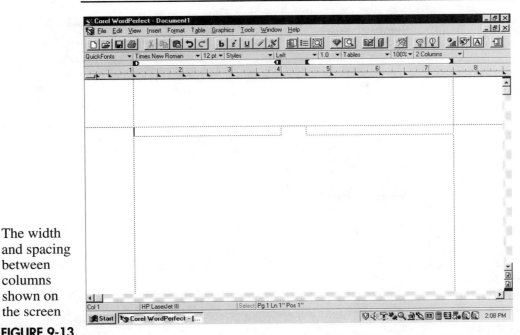

The width
and spacing
between
columns
shown on
the screen

FIGURE 9-13

What about pressing CTRL+ENTER in the rightmost column? If your previous columns were ended by Corel WordPerfect flowing the text, then Corel WordPerfect will insert a page break and begin the left column on the next page. However, if you've ended all of the previous columns by pressing CTRL+ENTER, pressing CTRL+ENTER in the rightmost column ends it and starts a new column group, as shown in Figure 9-14. The group will have the same number of columns and will start under the longest column in the previous group.

You can now continue typing or change the number of columns in the group by selecting another option in the Columns button of the power bar. To type single-column text, for example, pull down the Columns button in the power bar and select Columns Off. You can also select Columns from the Format menu and click on Off. To change the number of columns on the page, simply place the insertion point at the start of the group, and choose an option from the Columns button on the power bar.

OTE: *If you want the columns in a group to be the same length, see "Defining Columns," later in this chapter.*

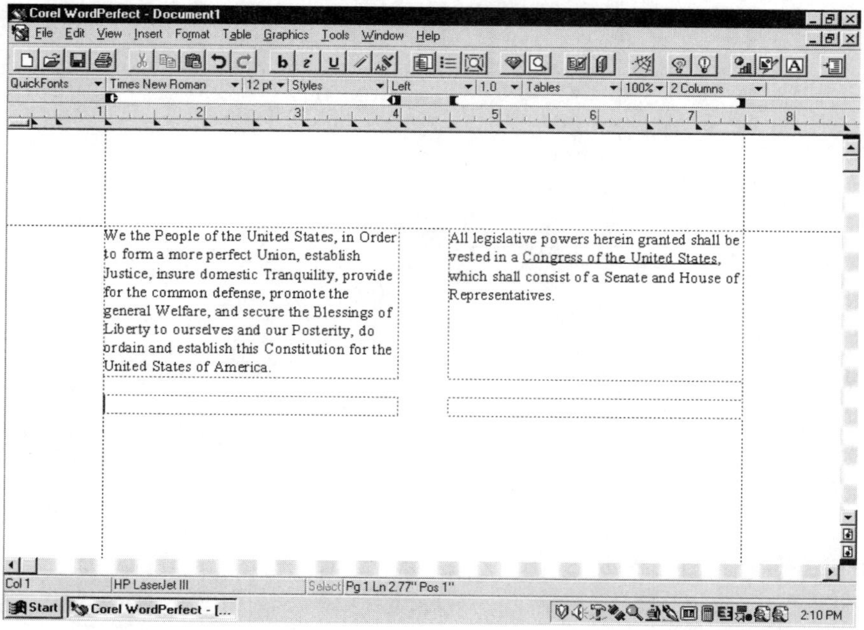

A new
column
group

FIGURE 9-14

Changing the Column Width

Columns that you create using the power bar are always the same width, a half-inch apart, and spaced to fill the page width. You may sometime want to design a newsletter or other document that has uneven columns. To change the column width, use either the column guidelines or the ruler.

The dotted lines on either side of a column are its guidelines. To change the width of a column, drag its guidelines. Dragging the leftmost guidelines on the page really changes the left margin, but the left column adjusts in width accordingly. Dragging the rightmost column guideline changes only the column width, not the right page margin.

When you drag any other column guidelines, you change the width of the column and of the spacing between the columns. As you drag a guideline, a QuickStatus box will appear showing the resulting column and spacing width.

If you want to maintain the same spacing between columns, and just change the column width itself, point in the space between columns and drag. Only the space will move as you drag, changing the columns on both sides if it.

As an alternative to dragging the guidelines, you can change the column or spacing width using the ruler. The ruler will contain individual sections with left and right margin indicators that represent the left and right edges of the column. The section for the column that has the insertion point will also have left and right indentation indicators.

Change column width and the spacing between columns by dragging the right or left column margin indicators. Change only the column width by dragging a gray area that represents the space between two columns.

Placing a Border Between Columns

To insert a vertical line between columns, click anywhere in the columns, select Border/Fill from the Format menu, and click on Column. The Border/Fill dialog box is the same one that you've used to place a border around paragraphs. To add a border between the columns, however, click on the option that the arrow is pointing to in the illustration shown here.

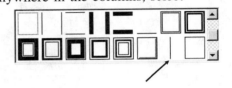

Defining Columns

If you want to create columns of specific sizes without dragging, or a column group in which all of the columns are the same length, then you have to define the columns. Select Define from the Column list in the power bar, or select Columns from the Format menu and click on Define to display the dialog box shown in Figure 9-15.

Enter the number of columns you want to create in the Columns text box. When you move to another section of the dialog box, Corel WordPerfect will calculate the width of the columns and display their measurements in the Column Widths text boxes, along with 0.5 inch spacing between them. To customize the column widths or spacing, enter a measurement, or click the up or down arrows to change the widths. The preview graphic of the page will illustrate the resulting columns.

As you increase or decrease the width of one column, Corel WordPerfect will automatically adjust the width of the other columns to fit the columns between the margins. If you want a column to remain exactly as you set it, regardless of how you change the other columns, select the column's Fixed check box.

You can also change the width of the spaces between columns. To set them all to the same width in one step, enter the spacing in the Spacing Between Columns box.

9

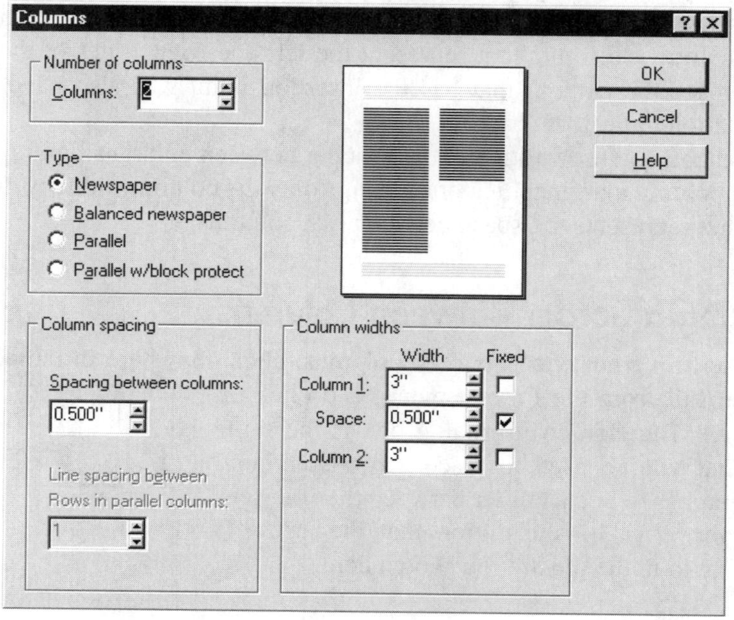

Defining
columns

FIGURE 9-15

Balancing Columns

If you want all of the columns in a group to be the same length, click on the Balanced Newspaper button in the Type section. As you type, Corel WordPerfect will shift text back and forth between the columns to keep them the same length.

You can also apply the Balanced Newspaper format to existing columns. Use this, for example, if you complete a document and the last column on the page is not full. However, if you ended a column other than the one on the right by pressing CTRL+ENTER, Corel WordPerfect will use that position to end the column group. It will divide all of the text above the position of the column break into balanced columns, and start a new column group with the text after the column break position.

Creating Parallel Columns

Parallel columns are ones in which text does not flow from column to column. In this case, you have text on the left that relates to text in the column on the right, as shown in Figure 9-16.

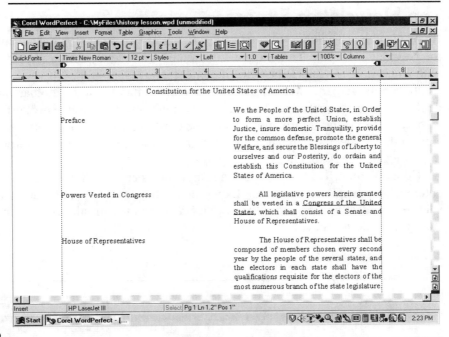

Parallel columns

FIGURE 9-16

To create parallel columns, display the Columns dialog box, enter the number of columns you want to create and click on either Parallel or Parallel w/block protect. Block-protected parallel columns will always be kept next to each other. They will not span a page break, even if it means that Corel WordPerfect must move them all to a new page.

Corel WordPerfect will insert one blank line between each set of parallel columns. To change this setting, enter the number of lines in the Line Spacing Between Rows in Parallel Columns text box.

With parallel columns, you enter text in sets. First, type the text in a column on the left, and then press CTRL+ENTER and type the text in a column to its right. When you press CTRL+ENTER in the rightmost column, Corel WordPerfect starts a new column group. It only inserts a page break when there is not enough room for another set of parallel columns on the page.

The Newsletter Expert

If you want to use columns to create a newsletter, then consider taking advantage of the Newsletter Expert. This Expert will create a completely formatted newsletter, with a masthead, styles, and a table of contents.

To run the Expert, click on the New Document button on the toolbar, and then double-click on <Newsletter Expert> in the main group. Corel WordPerfect will display a Template Information dialog box asking for the newsletter heading, subheading, date, and the headline for the main story. Enter the information requested, and click on OK.

Corel WordPerfect then displays a sample newsletter with the information you entered, along with the Newsletter Expert dialog box, as shown in Figure 9-17. The subtitle and date appear under the newsletter title in the masthead, with the main story title underneath.

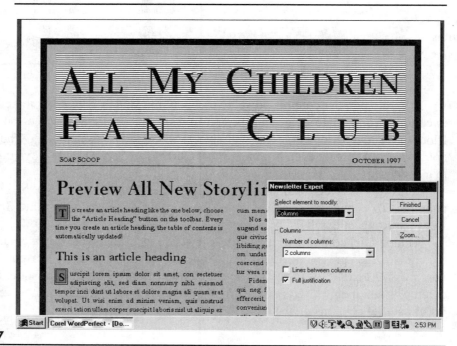

Newsletter
Expert

FIGURE 9-17

Use the options in the Newsletter Expert dialog box to customize the document. Pull down the Select Element to Modify list, and then select from the options that appear. In the Columns options, for example, you enter the number of columns, select to insert a line between columns, and choose if you want the text fully justified.

Title Options determines the type of line around the masthead and the fill pattern in its background. You cannot choose individual line styles and patterns, but you can select from 16 combinations. You can also select to stretch the title so it is justified between the margins, create shadow characters, or use small capitals for lowercase letters.

The Page Border/Fill options let you select the type of line that surrounds the page and a fill pattern. The pattern choices are none, 5%, 10% , 20%, 30%, 40%, and 50%.

The Font options let you select a font and style for the title, subtitle, date, and main headline. The first time you select this option, Corel WordPerfect will take a moment to build and display a font list.

Finally, the Drop Cap options allow you to choose the style of the drop capitals that start each story, including the border line and fill pattern.

When you have finished selecting options, click on Finished to remove the dialog box and display the newsletter. You can now enter text and headlines to complete the newsletter. There will be a sample paragraph explaining how to use the Article Heading feature, which inserts a heading, formats the drop cap, and places the heading in a table of contents at the lower-left corner of the first page.

Drag over and delete the sample text. Position the insertion point under the main heading, and then click on the Article Heading button in the toolbar. In the box that appears, type a headline and then click on OK. The headline and drop cap box will appear. Type the text of the story. The first character you type will appear in the drop cap box. Repeat the process for each story. Because you are working with columns, you can press CTRL+ENTER to end a column, or change column width just as you learned previously.

The styles used by Newsletter Expert will also be available in the Styles list of the power bar. Each style name starts with the underline character. Here are the styles:

- _FirstPara_ inserts the drop capital box.

- _Article_ formats the line as an article heading. When you press ENTER after the heading, Corel WordPerfect applies the _FirstPara style and displays the drop cap box.

- *_BodyText* is the normal text for the second and subsequent paragraphs. Corel WordPerfect automatically uses this style when you press ENTER after the first paragraph of a story.

- *_Headline* is the format for a major headline.

- *_Subtitle* is the style used for the subtitle on the left below the newsletter title.

- *_Title* is the style applied to the newsletter title.

Customizing Corel WordPerfect

10

Y ou probably have personalized your desk and office to make it more comfortable and homey. You've spread out your pictures and handy desk accessories, and arranged things to make it more efficient for the way you like to work. Your office probably looks different than the office next door, because we all have our own personal tastes and ways of working. You can customize Corel WordPerfect the same way, adjusting how things look and work to suit your own work habits.

You already learned in earlier chapters how to change Corel WordPerfect's default document settings. These settings determine how your documents will appear if you don't bother changing any formats.

For example, in Chapter 7, you learned how to change the default template and system styles. In Chapter 6, you learned how to select a new initial font, and in Chapter 9, you found out how to select an initial format for tables.

In this chapter you'll learn how to customize the way Corel WordPerfect works.

Saving Printer Settings

Let's start with something that has everyday use: printer settings. When you display the Print dialog box to print a document, you have to select options, such as the number of copies, printed resolution, and so on. If you find yourself changing the same settings frequently, then consider saving the settings. If you want to use the settings with every new document—as the new default printer settings—then follow these steps:

1. Click on the Print button to display the Print dialog box.

2. Adjust the printer options to the way you want them saved.

3. Click on the Settings button at the bottom of the Print dialog box, and select Save as Application Default from the list.

4. Click on OK in the message box that appears.

The printer settings in the dialog box will be used for every document because they are now Corel WordPerfect's default settings. If you only use the settings occasionally, you may not want to use them as the default. Instead, you can save the settings under a separate name, and then recall them when you need to. To save settings, adjust the Print dialog box options, click on Settings, and then on Named Settings. Corel WordPerfect will display the Edit Named Settings dialog box. Type a name for the settings in the Save Current Settings As box, and then click on Add.

The setting name that you entered will now be included in the Settings drop-down list. To later use the specifications, just click on the Settings button and click on the setting name.

 OTE: *You can also click on its name in the Edit Named Settings dialog box and click on Retrieve.*

If you want to return to Corel WordPerfect's default printer settings, pull down the Settings list and click on Retrieve Application Default Settings.

Making changes to a saved setting is easy. Here's how:

1. Choose the options that you want to save in the Print dialog box.

2. Click on Settings, and select Named Settings.

3. Click on the setting name that you want to change, and then click Replace.

 **IP:** *To delete a setting, click on it in the list and then click on Delete.*

Changing Relative Font Ratios

The percentages that Corel WordPerfect uses to apply relative font sizes are stored as entries in the Windows 95 registry. You can't easily change these settings directly unless you know how to edit registry entries. Because changing the registry can lead to serious problems if you don't do it correctly, it's best not to mess around with it.

However, you can change the font size ratios by using a macro named SIZEATTR.WCM. You'll learn about macros later in this chapter, but if you want to customize the relative font sizes, follow these steps.

1. Select Macro from the Tools menu, and click on Play. Corel WordPerfect will display macro files—those with the WCM extension—in the \Corel\Office7\Macros\WPWin folder.

2. Scroll the list of files and click on SIZEATTR.WCM.

3. Click on Play to display the dialog box shown here:

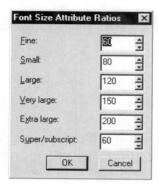

4. Set the ratios that you want to use, and then click on OK.

Setting Corel WordPerfect Preferences

All of the other default ways that Corel WordPerfect works are stored as *preferences*. You edit the preferences, for example, to change the default view and magnification, and even to add your own custom toolbars and menu bars. To set any of the preferences, start by selecting Preferences from the Edit menu to display the dialog box shown here:

The options in the Preferences dialog box represent the categories of default settings. To change preferences, double-click on the icon to display a dialog box, select your options, and then click on OK. Now is a good time to look at the preferences.

Setting Display Preferences

The Display Preferences dialog box, shown in Figure 10-1, controls the default appearance of the Corel WordPerfect document window. The box contains several pages, each dedicated to another classification of options.

Document Page

The Document page of the dialog box controls what Corel WordPerfect elements are displayed on the screen. In the Show section, you can choose to display text and dialog boxes using the Windows 95 color settings rather than Corel WordPerfect's, and you can choose to display or hide these elements:

- Table grid lines

- Comments

- Graphics

- Hidden text

- QuickSpots

In the Scroll bars section you can deselect the Vertical or Horizontal check boxes if you do not want the scrolls bars to appear on the screen. You can also choose to have the horizontal scroll bar only appear when required—when there is text scrolled off the screen. If you choose this option, the scroll bar will appear automatically.

Use the Measurement section to set the units of measurement in dialog boxes and in the status bar and ruler. Use the Units of measure list to determine the default unit accepted in dialog boxes, such as when changing margins and creating a page size. Your choices are inches abbreviated with " or i, centimeters (c), millimeters (mm), points (p), and units of 1200th of inches (w), formerly known as "Corel WordPerfect units." Use the Status/Ruler Bar display list, which offers the same options, to determine the way measurements are displayed on the ruler and in the

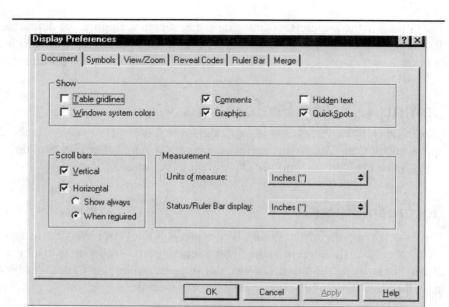

Display
preferences

FIGURE 10-1

position section of the status bar. In this case, for example, the ruler appears marked in points:

Symbols Page

When you click on the Show ¶ command in the View menu, Corel WordPerfect displays symbols for many characters and codes that normally do not appear, such as spaces, tabs, and carriage returns. You can choose which characters appear in this page of the dialog box. Deselect the check box for any items that you do not want to appear.

To turn on the display of codes from within this dialog box, click on the Show Symbols on New and Current Document. When you exit the Preferences dialog boxes, the Show ¶ feature will be turned on, and it will be on for all new documents. You can turn off the feature in a specific document by selecting Show ¶ from the

View menu, but the symbols will still appear for new documents. To turn off the feature, deselect the option in the Symbols page of the Display Preferences dialog box.

View/Zoom Page

Corel WordPerfect starts by default in Page view and 100% magnification. Many users, however, like to work in Draft view so they can see more lines on the screen, so they change to Draft view every time they run Corel WordPerfect.

Use the View/Zoom page to change the default view and magnification. For example, selecting Draft view and Margin width as the default zoom minimizes the amount of scrolling that you'll have to perform.

Reveal Codes Page

The options in this page of the dialog box, shown in Figure 10-2, let you change the appearance of the Reveal Codes window.

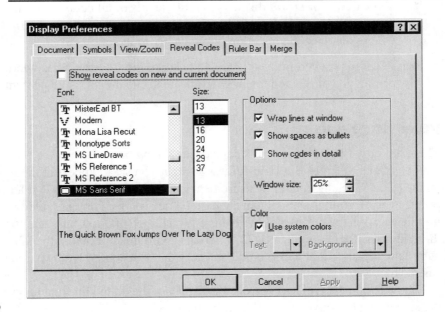

Reveal
Codes
preferences

FIGURE 10-2

Click on the Show Reveal Codes on New and Current Document to have the Reveal Codes window appear automatically. You can always turn off the codes for individual documents by choosing Reveal Codes from the View menu.

Also select the font and size that you want the text to appear in the window—the default is 13 point MS San Serif. Make the font smaller, for example, if you want to see more lines of codes in the Reveal Codes window without taking up additional space on the screen. The options in the Color section let you change the color of the window. You can select to use the default Windows system colors, or you can choose your own color for the text and background.

Your choices in the Options section determine the appearance of the text and the default size of the window:

- *Wrap Lines at Window* will divide codes between lines if they do not fit on the line. With this option deselected, the code may scroll off the right edge of the window.

- *Show Spaces as Bullets* uses bullet characters to represent when you pressed the SPACEBAR in a document. Deselect this option to show spaces with blank spaces.

- *Show Codes in Detail* displays the full details of all codes. With this option off, many codes are shown abbreviated, and only shown in detail when you place the insertion immediately to its left.

- *Window Size* determines the default size of the Reveal Codes window as a percentage of the document window area. The default is 25 percent.

Ruler Bar Page

There are only two options in this page of the dialog box.

Tabs Snap to Ruler Bar Grid forces tabs that you set to appear at the grid point on the ruler. When the unit of measurement is inches, for example, the ruler has grid points every 1/16th of an inch—at each of the tick marks along the ruler, and in the middle between the tick marks. With this option turned off, you can set a tab between the grid lines, for example, at 1/32" intervals. With this option on, the tab stop will automatically appear at a grid point, so every tab is at some 1/16th space along the ruler.

Show Ruler Bar Guides controls the display of the dotted line that appears down the screen as you move tabs and margin markers.

Merge Page

When you create a merge document, as you will learn in Chapter 11, special codes are inserted to indicate where you want information from the database to appear. In this page of the dialog box, you set how the codes will appear—as codes, or graphic markers, or not at all.

Environment Preferences

The environment preferences, shown in Figure 10-3, determine some basic ways that Corel WordPerfect performs.

The Language section determines the interface language—chances are you'll have only one choice.

The User Info for Comments and Summary determines what appears on the summary page and when you create comments. Enter the name you want in the summary page, the initials you want to appear with comments, and the color you want to indicate your comments.

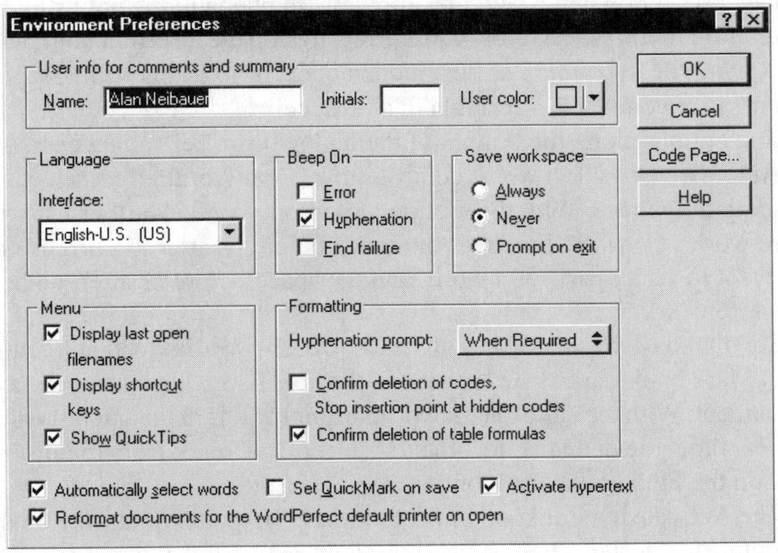

Environment
Preferences
dialog box

FIGURE 10-3

In the Beep On section you tell Corel WordPerfect when to beep at you—when an error occurs, when an automatic hyphenation is suggested, or when a find command cannot locate the text.

The Save workspace section can save you a great deal of time. The Workspace is the arrangement of your document windows on the screen. If you save the workspace, the next time you start Corel WordPerfect, you'll see the same documents, in the same window arrangement, that was displayed when you last exited Corel WordPerfect. You can choose to always save the workspace when you exit Corel WordPerfect, to never save the workspace, or to display a prompt asking if you want to save the workspace when you exit. Prompt on Exit is a good compromise, since it will give you the choice. This way, you can determine if you want to return to the same window arrangement the next time you start.

In the Menu section, choose what you want to appear in menus. You can turn off the display of recently used documents in the File menu, and choose to display the shortcut key combinations in menus or the QuickTips that appear when you point to a menu item, a toolbar button, or other button or screen object.

Use the Formatting section to control when Corel WordPerfect will prompt you to select a hyphenation point and how it operates when you delete codes and table formulas. Pull down the Hyphenation Prompt list and choose if you want Corel WordPerfect to always or never prompt you to select a hyphenation point, or just to display a prompt when a suitable automatic hyphenation is not available. You can also choose if you want Corel WordPerfect to stop the insertion point when pressing BACKSPACE or DEL would erase a hidden code, or to display a message asking you to confirm if you delete a formula in a table cell.

The options along the bottom of the dialog box offer some general features.

Automatically select words controls how Corel WordPerfect selects words when you drag the mouse. With this option turned on, Corel WordPerfect will select the entire work when you drag over the space before or after it. Turn this option off if you want to select parts of a word, and the space before or after, without selecting the entire word.

Set QuickMark on save will have Corel WordPerfect automatically set a QuickMark bookmark at the location of the insertion point when you save and close a document. With the QuickMark, you can quickly return to your last editing position the next time you open the document—select Bookmark from the Insert menu, and click on the Find QuickMark button.

The Activate hypertext option determines if hypertext links are on or off. When this option is selected, clicking on a hypertext or Web link will move to the bookmark or Web page. If you are working in a document with Web page links and don't want to launch your browser accidentally, deselect this option.

Corel WordPerfect documents contain font and other codes that correspond to the features of your printer. If you open a document that was created for another printer, the codes will not match those of yours. To avoid any printing problems, Corel WordPerfect will reformat the document when you open it to match the printer currently being used. You'll know this is happening because you'll see a message on the screen reporting that the process is taking place. Here's the rub. If you save the document and later open it on the computer using the other printer, Corel WordPerfect will have to reformat it again. In some cases, the reformatting back and forth may change spacing or other formats, so you can turn off this feature by deselecting the Reformat documents for the WordPerfect default printer on open check box.

Files Preferences

The Files Preferences dialog box, shown in Figure 10-4, determine where documents, templates, graphics, and other files used by Corel WordPerfect are stored on your disk. Each page of the dialog box sets the location of one type of file.

 IP: *Click on View All for a summary of all file locations.*

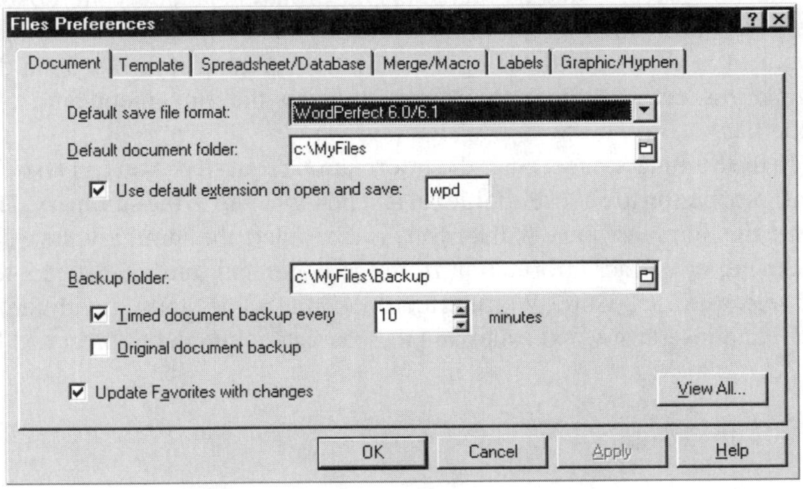

Files
Preferences
dialog box

FIGURE 10-4

Use the options in the Document page of the dialog box, for example, to determine the directory and extension of your documents, and to automatically save documents. In the Default Document Folder text box, enter the folder where you want your documents to be saved. When you display the Open and Save dialog boxes, the files in that directory will automatically appear. You can also designate another default document extension, or choose not to use a default extension at all.

By default, Corel WordPerfect performs a timed backup of your document every ten minutes. As you work, Corel WordPerfect saves the document to a temporary file, so if your computer goes haywire and you have to reboot, you'll have the opportunity to open the temporary file to retrieve your work. This option is turned on when the Timed Document Backup Every check box is selected. The number of minutes between backups is specified in the corresponding text box. The backup files are stored in the location in the Backup Folder box. You can turn off this feature by deselecting the check box, or change the folder or number of minutes between backups.

You can also choose to create Original Document Backups. With this option on, Corel WordPerfect saves a copy of the current version of the document with the same name but using the extension BK!. This file will not contain any of the editing or formatting that you performed since you last saved the document. If you change your mind about all of the last changes you made, open the BK! file.

Summary Preferences

A *summary sheet* contains statistical information about your document, and reference information about who created it, when it was modified, and what the document is all about, including a descriptive name. You can see the document's summary sheet by selecting Document from the File menu and clicking on Properties.

In the Summary page, enter the information requested. You can also click on the Configure button to choose additional text boxes to add to the summary. The Options lists in the Summary page will let you print or delete the summary, save it as its own document, or extract information from the document into the Subject text box. If you select Extract, Corel WordPerfect looks for a line starting with the characters "RE:" and inserts any text following the characters into the Subject text box.

In the Summary Preferences dialog box, you can set Corel WordPerfect to display the Summary page when you save and exit a document, so you can enter information into it. You can also choose these options:

- Show descriptive names in the Open dialog box

- On open, use the descriptive name as the new filename

- When saving a new document, use the long filename as the descriptive name

In addition, you can enter a default descriptive type that will initially appear in all Summary pages, and enter subject search text other than "RE:." For example, if your office uses the phrase "Subject:," enter it in place of "RE:." Then when you click on Extract in the Options list of the Summary box, Corel WordPerfect will insert the text following "Subject:" to the Subject text box.

Convert Preferences

When you open graphic files or documents created by other word processing programs, Corel WordPerfect converts them into a format that it understands. The Convert Preferences option controls how this process is performed.

The Delimiters section of the dialog box controls how ASCII-delimited text files are converted. This is usually a file created by a database or spreadsheet program, in which each row of the spreadsheet or database record is a document line. You use this section of the dialog box to determine the character that separates database fields or spreadsheet cells, and the character or code that separates rows or records.

The Characters section designates any special characters that surround database fields or information from a spreadsheet cell. The default is the quotation mark. You can also designate characters that you want Corel WordPerfect to remove—strip—from the information when it is converted.

The Windows Metafile options control how graphic files are converted. The Metafile format (using the WMF extension) is a common format that Windows applications use for graphic objects. By default, Corel WordPerfect opens a metafile graphic and inserts it into the document but leaves it in its original format. You can also choose to convert the file into Corel WordPerfect's own WPG format, or to save the file in both formats. Choose the WPG option if you want to use the document with earlier versions of Corel WordPerfect.

10

The Options button in the Convert Preferences dialog box lets you set other conversion settings. The options are

- *Code Pages* let you select sets of characters that will be used to convert characters in a document. In most cases, for example, the letter "A" in the original document will be displayed as the letter "A" on the screen. Depending on the system and the font that you used to create the file, there may be some characters in the document that do not have equivalents in Corel WordPerfect. The Code Pages option lets you select character sets to use when converting documents.

- *Document* lets you select the language, units of measurement, underline style, margins, and page size for converted documents.

- *WP 4.2 Fonts* lets you designate the fonts that you used with documents created with Corel WordPerfect 4.2 for DOS so Windows fonts can be substituted for them.

- *DCA/DisplayWrite Fonts* lets you designate the fonts you used for DCA and DisplayWrite formatted documents.

Toolbar Preferences

The Toolbar Preferences let you create and edit toolbars. Use this feature to add buttons for features that you use often, or to create all new toolbars for custom combinations of tools. By adding frequently used functions to a toolbar, you can activate a function with a single click of the mouse. You can create any number of different toolbars, and then recall them to the screen when needed.

You can access the Toolbar Preferences dialog box shown in Figure 10-5 by double-clicking on the Toolbar icon in the Preferences dialog box, or by right-clicking on a toolbar and choosing Preferences from the QuickMenu.

To change the position of a toolbar, as well as the appearance of its tools, click on the toolbar in the list, and then click on Options to see the dialog box shown in Figure 10-6. Choose a Font Face and Font Size to use for the style of text on the button face, and select if you want the tool to show the name of the command, an icon representing the function, or both. Use the Position options to place the toolbar on the top, bottom, or sides of the screen, or to display it as a rectangular pallet. You can also choose to include a scroll bar when there are more buttons than fit across the screen, or to display the buttons in more than one line. Click on OK to return to the Toolbar Preferences dialog box.

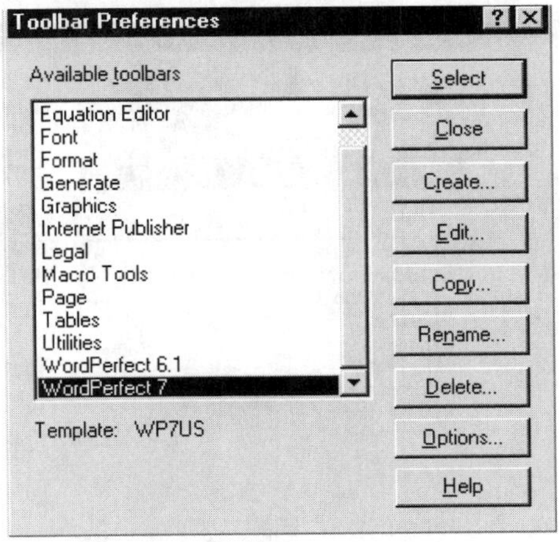

Toolbar
Preferences
dialog box

FIGURE 10-5

To create a new button bar, click on Create, type the name for the bar in the box that appears, and click on OK. The Toolbar Editor will appear with a blank button bar on the screen, as shown in Figure 10-7. The first step is to select the type of item you want to add as a tool. A *feature* is a command that you can perform by selecting an item from a pull-down menu. You select the feature category that corresponds to the menu bar commands and then choose the specific Corel WordPerfect feature.

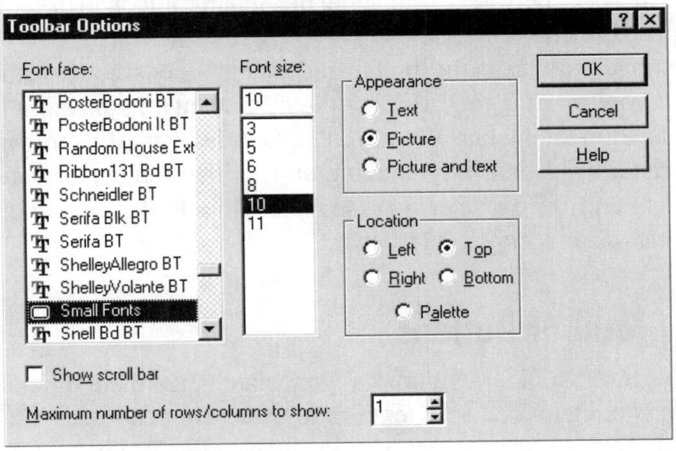

Changing
the position
and
appearance
of the
toolbar

FIGURE 10-6

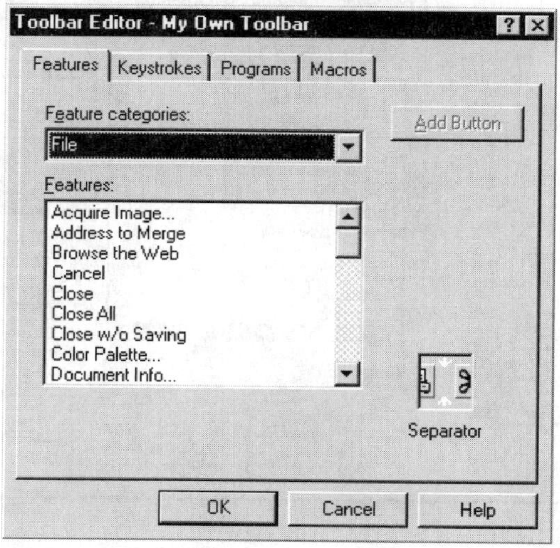

Creating a
new toolbar

■ FIGURE 10-7

The Keystrokes page lets you enter a series of keystrokes that you want the tool to repeat. The Programs page lets you select a program you want the tool to execute, and the Macro page lets you assign a macro to the tool.

To add a feature, double-click on it in the Features list, or click on it and then on Add Button, or drag the item to the blank toolbar—Corel WordPerfect will insert a button for the feature in the toolbar. You can organize buttons into related groups by adding extra space between them. Drag the Separator icon to the bar where you want to add space between buttons.

To remove a tool from the toolbar and change its position, use the Toolbar Editor. Remove a tool by dragging it off of the bar; change its position by dragging it to another location on the bar. When you're satisfied with the toolbar, click on OK.

You can always edit it by clicking on it in the Toolbar Preferences dialog box and clicking on Edit. You can also use the Toolbar Preferences dialog box to delete, rename, and make a copy of a toolbar.

Editing Toolbar Buttons

To customize the toolbar even more, you can change the icon on a tool or the text that appears on it, and edit the text of the QuickTip that appears when you point to the button. To do this, however, you must be in the Toolbar Editor. In the Toolbar

Preferences dialog box, click on the toolbar that contains the tool you want to change, and then click on the Edit button. Next, point to the tool that you want to change in the toolbar, right-click the mouse, and select Customize from the menu that appears. Corel WordPerfect will display the Customize Button dialog box, shown here:

Enter any text that you want to appear on the tool in the Button Text box, and enter the text for the tool's QuickTip. To change the icon on the tool, click on the Edit button to see the Image Editor shown in Figure 10-8. In the box that displays the enlarged icon, click with the left or right mouse button to add one pixel of color. Choose the color by clicking the left or right mouse button on the color in the Color section. Select Draw or Fill to select the action of the click—Draw inserts one pixel, Fill inserts the color in all consecutive cells the color of where you click. You can also

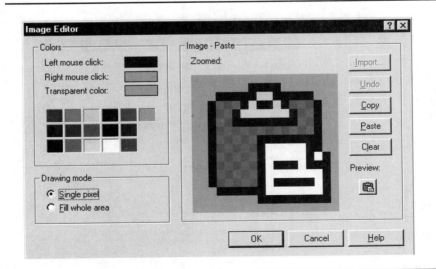

Editing the
button icon

FIGURE 10-8

draw in the small graphic of the button in the lower-left corner. Select Undo to cancel your last change, or click on Clear to erase the entire icon to start from a blank button.

Power Bar Preferences

This preference, which displays the Power Bar Options dialog box, lets you change the appearance of the power bar and edit the power bar by adding new items to it. You can also display this box by right-clicking on the power bar and selecting Options from the QuickMenu.

To add items to the power bar, click on Edit in the Power Bar Options dialog box. Corel WordPerfect will display the Toolbar Editor. Use it the same way as you learned previously for customizing toolbars, but drag items to the power bar instead.

Status Bar Preferences

When you want to change the items that appear on the status bar, double-click on this preference item to see the dialog box in Figure 10-9. Click on the check boxes for the items that you want to add or remove from the status bar, or click on Options to change the font and size of status bar text.

 IP: *Click on Default to return to the default Corel WordPerfect status bar.*

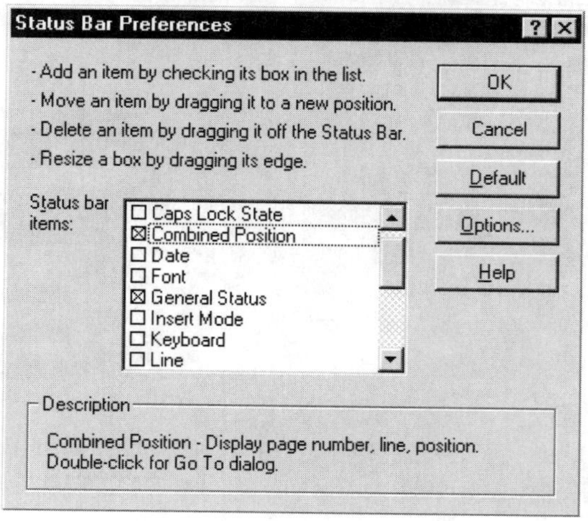

Changing
the items in
the status
bar

FIGURE 10-9

Menu Bar Preferences

Just as you can edit and create toolbars, you can also edit and create menu bars and pull-down menus. Double-click on the Menu Bar icon in the Preferences dialog box to see the options shown here.

You can select to display any of the five built-in menu bars, or to create your own. You cannot edit one of the built-in bars, but you create new menu bars by adding menus and items to an existing one. Start by clicking on the built-in bar that you want to use for the base, and then click on the Create button. Type a name for the bar in the box that appears, and then click on OK.

You'll see the Menu Editor, which is exactly like the Toolbar Editor but with icons labeled "Menu" and "Separator." To add features to the menu that you can perform with a single click, double-click on it. To create a new menu, drag the Menu icon to the menu bar. The item labeled "Menu" will appear; double-click on it to display a dialog box where you give it a name and a description that appears when you point to it. Use an ampersand to designate the underlined selection letter, such as "&Special."

To add an item to a menu, drag the item to the menu you want to insert it in, continue pulling down the menu, and place the item in the desired position. You can also double-click on the program feature to place it in the menu bar, and drag it to the menu. To delete an item, or a menu, drag it off of the menu bar.

Drag the Separator icon to add a separator line between items in the menu.

Keyboard Preferences

If you prefer using keyboard combinations to perform commands, you are in luck. You can use the Keyboard Preferences to create your own shortcut key combinations.

Double-click on Keyboard in the Preferences dialog box to see a list of three built-in keyboard layouts: Equation Editor Keyboard, WPDOS 6.1 Keyboard, and WPWIN 7 Keyboard. To create your own keyboard, select the one that you want to use for the base, click on Create, type a name for the keyboard, and click on OK. Corel WordPerfect will then display the Keyboard Shortcuts dialog box that is shown in Figure 10-10.

Keyboard
Shortcuts
dialog box

FIGURE 10-10

In the list on the left, click on the key combination that you wish to assign to a feature, key combination, program, or macro. To assign the new item to it, select it in the appropriate page in the section on the right of the dialog box and then click on Assign Feature to Key. The item you selected will be assigned to the key combination, replacing any that had already been assigned to it. For each key combination in the list, you can also deselect the Shortcut Key Appears on Menu check box so it will not appear on the related pull-down menu.

If you click on the Allow Assignment of Character Keys, the list on the left will change to contain all of the regular character keystrokes. You can then assign a feature or other keystroke to it.

IP: *To remove a shortcut key function from a key combination, click on it on the list and click on the Remove Assignment button.*

Creating Macros

One other way to customize Corel WordPerfect it to add you own commands through macros. A *macro* is a series of keystrokes, menu, power bar, and toolbar selections that you can store on your disk or in a template. You can then repeat all of the keystrokes and commands by just "playing" the macro at some other time. You can use a macro to insert formatted text, to apply a set of commonly used formats, or to repeat any action that you can save time by repeating.

The easiest way to create a macro is to record it. You just enter the keystrokes, or perform any other function, and Corel WordPerfect records them.

 You can also create a macro using the PerfectScript accessory from the taskbar.

You can record macros in two locations: as a file on your disk or in a template. Storing the macro on the disk means that you can later access it no matter what document or template you are using. You can also copy the macro onto a floppy disk and use it on another computer that's running Corel WordPerfect for Windows. If you store the macro in a template, you still may have two choices. If you are using a template other than the default, you can choose to store the macro with either the default template or the one being used with the document. Saving the macro in the default template will make it available with every document using that template.

To record a macro, pull down the Tools menu and select either Macro or Template Macro, depending on where you want to save it.

Storing Macros on the Disk

To save the macro on the disk, point to Macro and then click on Record in the menu that appears. A dialog box will appear where you select the folder in which to store the macro and enter the macro name. By default, macros are stored in the \Corel\Office7\Macros\WPWin folder and use the WCM extension. It's best to use the default folder so you'll be able to access your macros easily in the default location. Type a name for the macro, and then click on Record.

Saving Macros in a Template

To save your macro in a template, pull down the Tools menu, point to Template Macro, and then click on Record. In the dialog box that appears, type a name for the macro.

Your macro will only be available to documents using the template where it is stored. If you started the document using the default template, then the macro will be available to all new documents that use the default template. If you started the document with another template, the macro will be saved there. To store the macro in the default template, click on Locations to see this dialog box:

Choose the template where you want to store the macro. To use your choice as the default for all template macros, click on the Use As Default check box. Click on OK to return to the Record Template Macro dialog box. Now click on Record to start recording your macro.

Recording Macros

Once you select Record, Corel WordPerfect will display the macro bar shown here and will start recording your keystrokes.

When you are recording a macro, you can only use the mouse to select menu, toolbar, power bar, and dialog box options. You cannot use it to select text and position the insertion point—use keystrokes for that. Perform all of the functions that you want to record, and then click on the Stop button in the macro bar.

Playing Macros

To play a macro, pull down the Tools menu and select either Macro or Template Macro, depending on where the macro is stored. Then click on Play.

If the macro is stored on the disk, the Play Macro dialog box appears listing macros in the default directory. Double-click on the macro name, or type the name and click on Play.

If the macro is stored in a template, the Play Template Macro box appears. Double-click on the macro name, or select it and click on Play. If the macro isn't listed, click on Location and then choose the template where the macro is stored. Click on OK and then select it in the Play box.

Assigning Macros to Menus, Toolbars, or the Power Bar

Earlier in this chapter, you learned how to customize Corel WordPerfect by adding items to the menu bar, toolbar, or power bar. In each case, the Toolbar Editor dialog box used to add items also contained a page called "Macros" (see Figure 10-7 earlier in this chapter).

To add a macro to the bar, select either Add Template Macro or Add Macro, depending on where the macro is stored. Double-click on the macro to insert it into the menu, toolbar, or power bar.

Editing Macros

If you make a mistake when recording a macro, you can record it all over again. You can also edit the macro to change or add commands to it. Editing and writing macros requires knowledge of the command language, and an understanding of the principles of computer programming.

To edit a macro, pull down the Tools menu and select either Macro or Template, depending on where the macro is stored, and then click on Edit. In the dialog box that appears, double-click on the macro you want to edit, or select it and then click on Edit. The macro commands will appear in a separate window along with the macro bar, as shown in Figure 10-11.

All of the commands are listed in Corel WordPerfect's macro language. This is an extensive programming language that can be used to write complete applications built around Corel WordPerfect for Windows.

The first line of the macro identifies the program and default language that it uses. The remainder of the macro performs the reported instructions. For example, the Type command inserts text into the document using the syntax Type(Text: *"insert this text"*). Pressing ENTER when recording the macro inserts the HardReturn( ) command.

If you want to change the text that a macro generates, just edit any of the text within the quotation marks in the Type command. To insert new text, you have to insert a new Type command, following the proper syntax. If you want the macro to perform a carriage return, type the HardReturn( ) command; pressing ENTER in the macro itself will not perform a carriage return when you play the macro. Remember

10

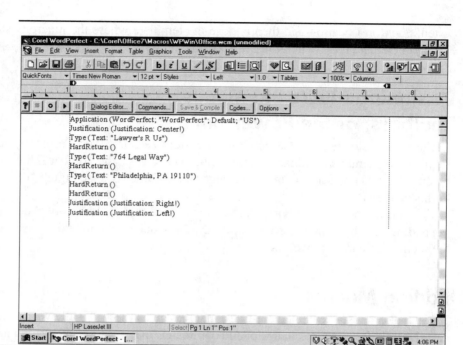

Editing a
macro

FIGURE 10-11

that when you play the macro, Corel WordPerfect will follow the macro commands explicitly. So if you enter commands in an incorrect order, or don't use the proper syntax for a command, your macro will not operate correctly.

Rather than type commands into the macro, it is more efficient to add them by recording. Place the insertion point in the macro where you want the new commands to appear, and then click on the Record button in the macro bar. Corel WordPerfect will open a new blank window with another macro bar. Type the text or perform the functions that you want to add to the macro, and then click on the Stop button. Corel WordPerfect will switch back to the macro window, with your newly recorded commands inserted. Click on the Save&Compile button in the macro bar, and then close the window.

The Command Inserter

Corel WordPerfect's macro language is a sophisticated programming language with hundreds of commands. You can learn about the commands using the online help system and the Reference Center that comes with the Corel WordPerfect Suite CD. You can quickly insert macro commands by clicking on the Commands button in the macro bar to display the dialog box shown in Figure 10-12.

In the Command Type box, select the type of command you want to insert. By default, the box will list all PerfectScript commands. To record a Corel WordPerfect function, pull down the list and select Corel WordPerfect US. Then select the command in the Commands list box. If you select a command that includes parameters, the parameters will appear in the Parameters list box. Select the parameter you want to set. If the parameter has optional items, they will appear in the Enumerators list box, and you can select a value from the list. In the Command Edit text box, you can edit the macro command. When you are ready to insert the command, select Insert.

Other Macro Features

You might find the other options in the macro bar useful. The Dialog Editor displays the PerfectScript dialog box, and the Codes button displays a list of merge codes. Both of these are for advanced macro writers.

The Options button lets you change how the macro is saved. If you are editing a template macro and now want to save it on the disk, for example, click on Options and select Save as Macro. You can also choose Save as Template Macro to store a disk macro on the template. The other options let you remove the macro bar and close the macro.

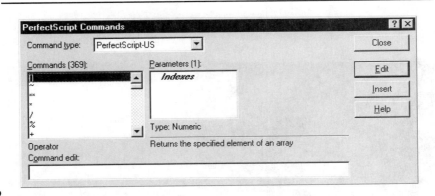

Selecting a macro command

FIGURE 10-12

Creating Form Letters and Labels

11

Although form letters may have a bad reputation, they are one of the best features of Corel WordPerfect. A *form letter* is merely a document that you want to send to more than one person. Each copy of the letter has the same format, and perhaps much of the text, in common. You just need to change some of the text, even if it's only the address and salutation, to customize the letter for each recipient. With Corel WordPerfect you can create form documents of all types—not just form letters. You can merge envelopes and labels, and even create any document that merges information from a database.

Understanding Form Documents

To create a form letter or other document you actually need two things: a *data file* and a *form document*. The file is like an electronic index card file. Every card in the file, called a *record*, contains all the information you need about each object your data file is all about—a person or inventory item, for example. If your database is stored information about people—clients, members, patients, friends, enemies—then it may have their first and last names, address, city, state, and zip code. If your data file is about an inventory item or products, it may contain the product's name, amount you have in inventory, price, and vendor who sells it to you. Each of these items is called a *field*.

The form document contains the standard text that you want to include in each copy of the final merged documents. In every place in the document where you want some item from the data file, you insert a code giving the name of the field that you want inserted at that position. So instead of writing a letter and actually typing the recipient's name, for example, you insert a field code for the last name and first name.

 IP: *You can use the Corel Address Book as the data file, just as it is.*

Once you have these two parts done, you merge them. Corel WordPerfect will automatically insert the information from the data file into the appropriate locations in the letter. For example, Corel WordPerfect inserts the information from the first record in the data file into the appropriate locations in the first copy of the document. It then inserts the information from the second record in the data file into the second copy of the document, repeating the process until all of the records have been used.

You can create the data file and document in any order. For example, you can write the form document and then complete the data file. Before merging the two parts, however, you have to tell Corel WordPerfect what data file to use for the merge operation. You can also create the data file first and then complete the document. This way, you can link the data source with the form document from the start. In fact, once you create the data file, you can use it any time for form documents—letters, envelopes, labels, or any other documents that include the merge codes associated with the data file.

Creating a Data File

With Corel WordPerfect, the data file can take either of two forms. It can appear as a table, with each row in the table a record with the fields in the columns, or as a merge file, with records and fields separated by special codes. Either way, the data file works the same way. Because of the number of steps involved in creating a data source, it would be useful to go through the process together this first time. If you want to use your Address Book as the data file, skip ahead to the section "Associating a Data File."

 You can use a Corel Quattro Pro worksheet or a Paradox database as your data file.

1. Pull down the Tools menu and select Merge to display the dialog box shown in Figure 11-1. The dialog box gives you three choices. Selecting Data File will help you create a data file by prompting for field names, and even displaying a handy form for entering information. Selecting Form lets you create the form document. Choosing Merge lets you combine the data file and the form document.

11

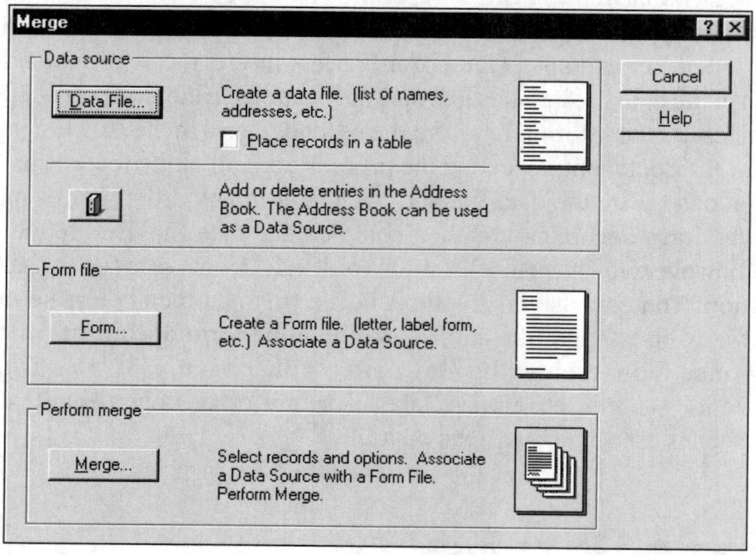

Merge
dialog box

FIGURE 11-1

---

2. Click on Place Records in a Table. This will create a data file in a table format, so you can later work with it using all of Corel WordPerfect's table commands.

3. Click on Data File.

4. If the current document is not blank, you will now be asked if you want to use the file in the currently active window or create a new document window. Click on New Document Window and then click on OK. You should only use the current window if it is empty, or if it contains a table that you want to use for the data file.

5. Corel WordPerfect displays the Create Data File dialog box. You use this dialog box to enter the names of the fields. Type **Last Name** and then press ENTER. Corel WordPerfect adds the field name to the list.

6. Type **First Name** and then press ENTER to insert the next field.

7. Now in the same way, add the fields Address1, Address2, City, State, Zip, Greeting, Last Order Date, Amount Due, and Credit.

8. Select OK to display the Quick Data Entry dialog box shown in Figure 11-2. The Quick Data Entry makes it easy to enter information into the data file, as well as to edit and find records. The insertion point will be in the text box for the first field.

9. Type **Chesin**, and then press ENTER. Corel WordPerfect moves the insertion point to the next field. Now fill in the rest of the fields as shown here, pressing ENTER after each. To enter text that appears on two lines within a field, press CTRL+ENTER.

       Chesin
       Adam
       877 West Avenue
       Suite 302
       Camden
       NJ
       08765
       Adam
       11/1/97
       500
       1000

10. When you press ENTER after typing the entry for the Amount Due field, Corel WordPerfect adds the record to the data file, clears all of the text boxes, and places the insertion point in the first text box to start a new record. Enter the next record using this information, noting that the field Address2 is left blank:

       Schneider
       Josh
       767 Fifth Avenue

       New York
       NY
       20918
       Mr. Schneider
       10/22/97
       467
       1000

11

11. When you have entered the last field, click on the Close button. Corel WordPerfect displays a dialog box asking if you want to save the database.

12. Click on Yes.

13. Type **Clients** and then click on Save. Corel WordPerfect saves the data file with the DAT extension.

Leave the data file onscreen for now.

The Data File Window

The data file will appear onscreen as a table, with the field names in the first row, and the merge feature bar, as in Figure 11-3. The Row and Column buttons let you insert or delete rows and columns. You use the Merge Codes button to display special codes that perform operations with the merge file.

The Merge button will display a dialog box where you can merge the data file with the form document. Click on Go To Form to display the open form document,

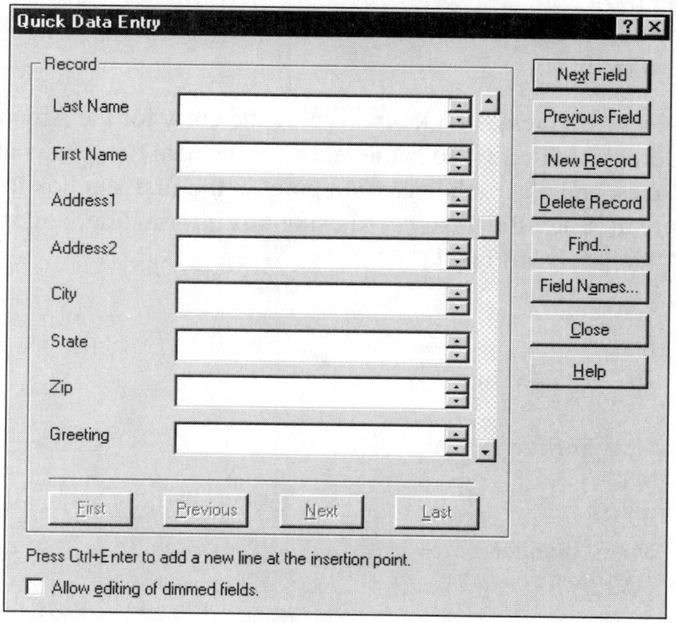

Quick Data Entry dialog box

FIGURE 11-2

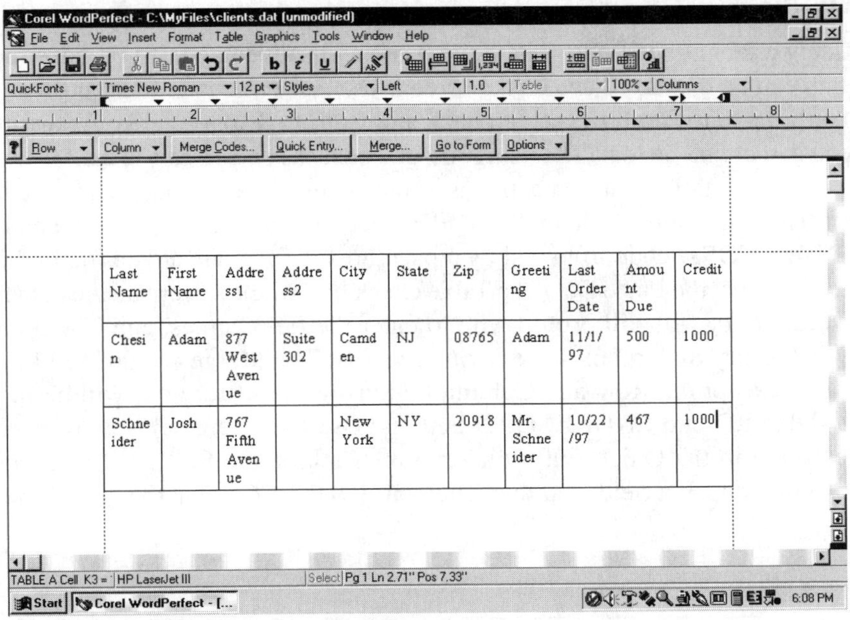

Data file in
Merge
window

FIGURE 11-3

Corel WordPerfect - C:\MyFiles\clients.dat [unmodified]

File Edit View Insert Format Table Graphics Tools Window Help

QuickFonts | Times New Roman | 12 pt | Styles | Left | 1.0 | Table | 100% | Columns

Row | Column | Merge Codes... | Quick Entry... | Merge... | Go to Form | Options

Last Name	First Name	Address1	Address2	City	State	Zip	Greeting	Last Order Date	Amount Due	Credit
Chesin	Adam	877 West Avenue	Suite 302	Camden	NJ	08765	Adam	11/1/97	500	1000
Schneider	Josh	767 Fifth Avenue		New York	NY	20918	Mr. Schneider	10/22/97	467	1000

TABLE A Cell K3 = HP LaserJet III   Select Pg 1 Ln 2.71" Pos 7.33"

Start   Corel WordPerfect - [...   6:08 PM

if any, that is associated with the data file. The options let you sort and print the database, and control how the codes appear onscreen.

Use the Quick Entry button to return to the Quick Entry dialog box for inserting and editing records. The box will appear showing the information from the record in which the insertion point is placed. Here's how to use the Quick Entry dialog box:

■ Edit the information for that record, or click on the New Record button to enter a new record.

■ To display a record in the box, click on the buttons along the bottom of the box—First, Previous, Next, and Last.

■ To search for a specific record, click on Find to display the Find Text dialog box, type the information you are looking for, and then click on Find Next. Corel WordPerfect will display the first record containing that information. Continue clicking on Find Next to locate additional records with that information.

■ To add or edit the field names, click on the Field Names button.

11

Using Merge Files

Using a table to organize a data file has one disadvantage. If you have more fields than can be displayed across the screen, you can't see an entire record at one time. You'll have to scroll the screen back and forth to display fields. As an alternative, you can create the data file using merge codes, as shown in Figure 11-4.

At the start of the data file is a list of the field names. Then each field of information ends with an ENDFIELD code, and each record ends with an ENDRECORD code followed by a page break. To create a data file in this format, do not select the Place Data in a Table check box when you create the data file. Corel WordPerfect will still prompt you to enter the field names, and it will display the Quick Entry dialog box for entering records. The Merge window will also be the same, except the Row and Column buttons in the feature bar will be replaced by ENDFIELD and ENDRECORD buttons. Use these to enter new records without returning to the Quick Entry dialog box. Click on the ENDFIELD after you type information for a field, and then click on ENDRECORD at the end of the record.

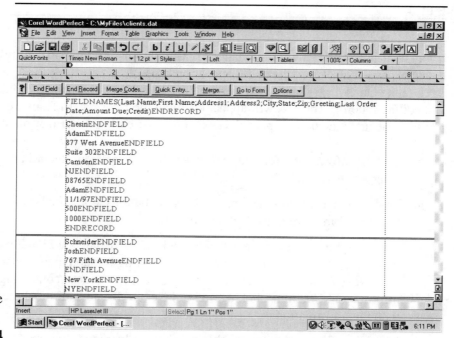

Data file
using merge
codes

FIGURE 11-4

Using Field Numbers Instead of Names

You can create a database where each field is associated with a field number rather than a field name. In our sample database, for example, field 1 is the last name, field 2 is the first name, and so on.

If you do not want to use names, select OK in the Create Data File dialog box without entering any field names. A dialog box will appear asking for the number of fields in each record. Enter the number of fields, and then select OK. The Quick Data Entry dialog box appears with each text box numbered.

Writing the Form Letter

You write, format, and edit a form document using the same techniques you use in any Corel WordPerfect document. However, when you come to a place where you want to insert information from the data source, you enter a field code.

You can use the fields in any order—they do not have to be in the order they are in the data file—and you can use a field as many times as you want to repeat the information in the same document.

Associating a Data File

To access the field names when writing the form document, however, you need to associate the data file with the form document. By creating the association, you can later merge the documents without selecting the data filename. Corel WordPerfect keeps track of the association, so it knows what data file to use during the merge process.

You do not have to associate a form document with a data file when you create it, because you can always associate it later. You can even change the data file associated with a form document—as long as the data file contains the same field names.

You can start a form letter directly from the new data file, or at any time after. Now that the data file is on the screen, here's how:

1. Click on Go To Form in the Merge feature bar. A dialog box will appear reporting that the file is not associated with a form letter.

2. Either click on Create to start a new form letter, or Select to open an existing one.

3. Click on Create.

11

If you closed the data file after you created it, you can start a form letter and associate it with the data file. To do so, select Merge from the Tools menu and click on Form. A dialog box appears where you select the data file that you want to associate with the form document. Select the data file from the box, changing folders and drives if necessary. To associate the form document with the Corel Address Book, click on the Address Book option button, and then select either My Addresses, Frequent Contacts, or another address book. If you want to create the association later, click on No Association.

Corel WordPerfect displays a blank document with a Merge feature bar, as shown here:

| Insert Field... | Date | Merge Codes... | Keyboard... | Merge... | Go to Data | Options ▼ |

Here are the functions of the feature bar buttons:

- *Insert Field* displays a dialog box of fields in the associated data file or address book. Double-click on the field that represents the information you want to insert in the document at the location of the insertion point.

- *Date* inserts the date code.

- *Merge Codes* displays a list of merge codes that you can use in your form document. Use these merge codes to create more sophisticated merge operations.

- *Keyboard* inserts a code that will allow you to type information into the form document as it is merged.

- *Merge* displays the Merge dialog box to begin the merge operation.

- *Go To Data* displays the associated data file or address book so you can add or edit information. To return to the document from the data file, click on the Go To Form button.

- *Options* lets you determine how the merge codes appear onscreen.

Inserting Fields and Text

Now that the letter is associated with the data file, you can access its fields. Follow these steps to create the form document.

1. Click on the Insert Field button to display the Insert Field Name or Number dialog box shown here:

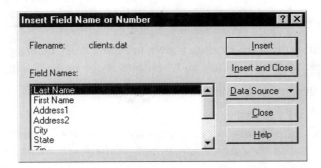

2. Double-click on the First Name field. Corel WordPerfect displays the code FIELD(First Name) in the document, indicating that the contents of that field will be placed into the form letter when it is merged. You'll notice that the dialog box stays on the screen so you can enter other field codes.

3. Press the SPACEBAR to insert a space after the code, and then double-click on the Last Name field. Press ENTER to move to the next line in the document.

4. Double-click on the Address1 field and then press ENTER.

5. Double-click on Address2 and press ENTER to move to the next line. You want to place the next three fields on the same line—City, State, and Zip.

6. Double-click on City.

7. Type a comma, press the SPACEBAR, and insert the State field.

8. Press the SPACEBAR twice, insert the Zip field, and then press ENTER. So far the address looks like this:

11

```
FIELD(First Name) FIELD(Last Name)
FIELD(Address1)
FIELD(Address2)
FIELD(City), FIELD(State) FIELD(Zip)
```

9. Now press ENTER again, type **Dear**, and then press the SPACEBAR.

10. Insert the Greeting field, type a colon, and press ENTER twice.

11. Complete the form letter as shown in Figure 11-5, entering the fields in the appropriate locations, and your own name in the closing.

12. Save the letter with the name **Accounts**.

OTE: *To change or create another association, open the form document and click on the Insert Field button. In the Insert Field or Number dialog box, click on Data Source and choose the data file or address book.*

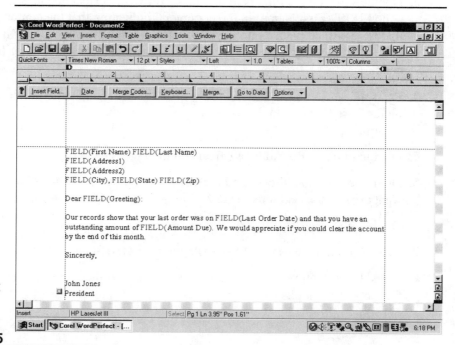

Completing the form letter

FIGURE 11-5

Merging Form Documents

With the form document and data file complete, you can merge them at any time. If you start from a blank screen, start a merge by selecting Merge from the Tools menu and clicking on Merge. You then have to enter the name of the form document and select its associated data file or address book.

It is easier if you open the form letter first. Whenever you open the form document, it will automatically appear with the Merge toolbar, and it will be linked with the associated data file. Once you open the form letter, merge it using these steps:

1. Click on the Merge button in the feature bar to display the Perform Merge dialog box shown in Figure 11-6. Because the document is associated with the data file, the options in the dialog box list the associated data filename.

2. Select where you want to output the letters. The Output setting determines where the merge is performed. When set at New Document, Corel WordPerfect performs the merge, creating one large document containing all of the form letters. Each of the letters will be separated by a page break. You can now edit the documents, print them, or save them together as a new document.

3. To print the form documents as they are merged, select Printer in the Output list. Other Output options let you insert the merged documents into the current document, save them directly to a file on the disk, or e-mail the merged documents.

4. Click on OK to start the merge.

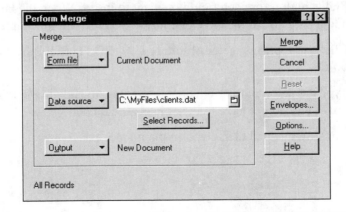

Perform
Merge
dialog box

FIGURE 11-6

Printing Envelopes for Form Letters

When you are merging form letters, you might want to merge their envelopes at the same time. You could use the Envelopes option in the Format menu. This way, each envelope appears after its corresponding letters. If you don't have an envelope feeder, however, you'd have to stand or sit by the printer inserting an envelope into the manual tray after each letter prints.

A better method is to use the Envelopes command from the Perform Merge dialog box. Using this procedure, the envelopes are inserted in a group after all of the letters. This also has the advantage that you can store the arrangement of field codes for various envelopes, and then simply retrieve the arrangement that you want to use for the set of envelopes. Use these steps to create envelopes:

1. Open the form document that contains the letter or other mailing.

2. Click on the Merge button in the feature bar to display the Perform Merge dialog box.

3. Click on the Envelopes button to display the Envelope window shown in Figure 11-7.

4. Design the layout of the fields for the mailing address, just as you did when creating the inside address for the form document. Click on the Fields button to display a list of the fields in the associated data file.

5. Double-click on a field to insert it into the mailing address.

6. Repeat steps 4 and 5 to complete the layout. Because the Fields list does not remain on the screen after you insert a field, you have to click on the Fields button for each field you want to insert. When the layout is done, add a bar code to the envelope just as you learned in Chapter 8.

7. Click on Options, select Include U.S. POSTNET Bar Code, and click on OK.

8. Type the name of the field containing the zip code in the POSTNET text box—you do not have to insert it as a field code.

9. Click on OK and then perform the merge.

Building Address Formats

Because the Fields box does not remain on the screen, it can be time consuming to design the envelope layout. Rather than re-create it for each form letter, you can save the layout of the fields and recall it later.

The Envelope dialog box that appears when you open it from the Perform Merge dialog box contains a mailing address list, as well as the Add and Delete buttons. You use the Add button to save the configuration of the merge fields, and you can later call up that configuration by selecting it in the address list.

After you create the address format, make sure that New Address appears in the list box, and then click on the Add button. You can store any number of configurations the same way. To select one, pull down the address list. Corel WordPerfect will list the first line of each of the stored addresses. Click on the address format that you want to use, scrolling the list if necessary.

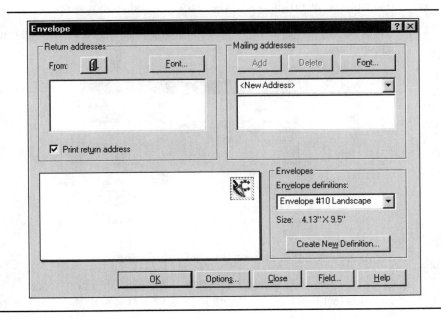

Envelope
dialog box
for merges

FIGURE 11-7

Merging to Labels

You can merge data onto mailing labels as easily as envelopes. You can get started in two ways:

- Create a new form document, as explained above, and then use Labels options from the Format menu to select the label form.

- Starting from a blank document window, select the label form. Choose Merge from the Tools menu, and click on Form. In the dialog box that appears, click on Use File In Active Window, and then click on OK. Enter the name of the data file or select a page from the Corel Address Book.

Use the Insert Field button to add the merge codes for the addresses, just as you created the address for the form document. To print a POSTNET code on the label, however, you need to use merge field codes. Here's how:

1. Position the insertion point where the bar code should appear.

2. Click on the Merge Codes button in the feature bar to see the dialog box shown here:

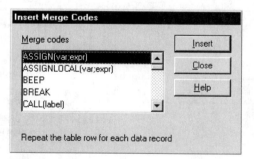

3. Scroll the list and click on the POSTNET(string).

4. Click on Insert and then on Close to close the dialog box. Corel WordPerfect will display the code POSTNET( ), with the insertion point between the parentheses.

5. Click on the Insert Field button, double-click on the field representing the zip code, and then close the dialog box.

The final code will appear as POSTNET(FIELD(ZipCode)).

When you merge this form document, the labels will be filled in with the information from the data file. Perform the merge to a new document, and then insert the label stock into the printer and print the labels.

Merging Lists

When you create letters or envelopes, each record is separated by a page break. Labels print on special label paper. There may be times when you want to use the merge feature to create a list, such as an inventory of your clients or club members. In these cases, you want the records to appear after each other, not on separate pages.

To do this, start by creating a form document, arranging the field codes as you want the list to appear. To create a columnar list, for example, you might arrange the codes like this:

FIELD(First Name) FIELD(Last Name) FIELD(Amount Due)

Before merging the document, however, you have to tell Corel WordPerfect not to insert a page break after each record. To do so, click Merge in the merge feature bar, and then click on Options to see the dialog box shown in Figure 11-8.

The choices in this dialog box let you print more than one copy of each merge document, and control how blank fields are handled. By default, for example, Corel WordPerfect will not print a blank line in an address, if there is no information in

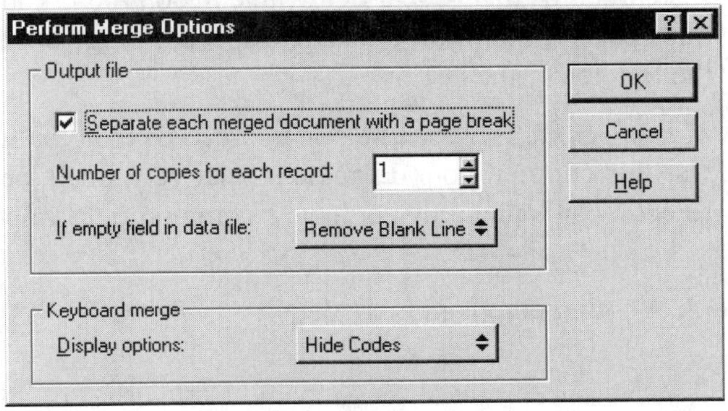

Perform
Merge
Options
dialog box

FIGURE 11-8

Perform Merge Options

Output file

☑ Separate each merged document with a page break

Number of copies for each record: 1

If empty field in data file: Remove Blank Line

Keyboard merge

Display options: Hide Codes

OK

Cancel

Help

11

one of the fields, such as Address 2. If you want, you can pull down the If Empty Field in Data File option and choose to leave the blank line in place. You can also use this dialog box to control how merge codes appear during interactive merges.

To create a list, however, deselect the Separate Each Merge Document With a Page Break check box, and then click on OK. Now when you perform the merge, the records will appear neatly arranged in rows.

Selecting Merge Records

Sometimes you do not want to merge all of the records in a data file with a form document, just selected ones. You might want to send a mailing, for example, to clients who owe you money or who are located in a certain community. Rather than merge all of the records and throw away the letters you do not want, you can select records before performing the merge.

To select records, use this procedure:

1. Open the form document.

2. Click on the Merge button in the feature bar, and then click on the Select Records button in the Perform Merge dialog box. Corel WordPerfect will display the Select Records dialog box shown in Figure 11-9.

3. Select records using either the Specify Conditions or Mark Records option.

   ■ *Specify Conditions* lets you enter search criteria based on the content of the fields. Use this option if you have a large data file and want to select records that have a field value in common. You should also use this option if you want to merge a specific range of records, such as the first ten or the last five.

   ■ *Mark Records* lets you click on the records that you want to merge. Use this option if your database is relatively small, or if you want to select records that may not have a common field value.

Let's look at both methods in more detail.

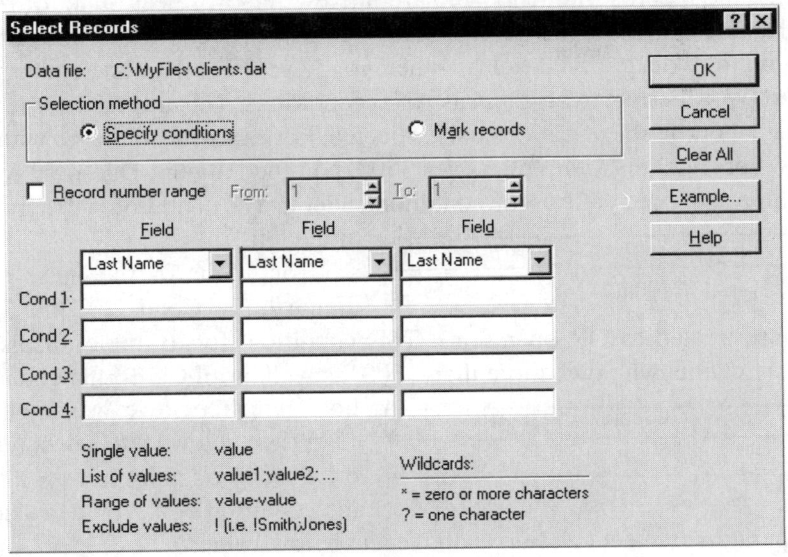

Select Records

Data file: C:\MyFiles\clients.dat

Selection method

● Specify conditions   ○ Mark records

☐ Record number range   From: 1   To: 1

Field	Field	Field
Last Name ▼	Last Name ▼	Last Name ▼

Cond 1:

Cond 2:

Cond 3:

Cond 4:

Single value:	value	Wildcards:
List of values:	value1;value2; ...	* = zero or more characters
Range of values:	value-value	? = one character
Exclude values:	! (i.e. !Smith;Jones)	

OK

Cancel

Clear All

Example...

Help

Selecting
records

FIGURE 11-9

Specifying Conditions

When you want to merge a selected range of records, or records based on a field value—such as all clients in California—use the Specify Condition options.

To merge a range of records, enter the beginning record number in the From box and the ending record number in the End box. The record number corresponds to the table row of the record in the data file.

If you want to limit the records to those meeting a certain condition, then create a filter. A *filter* tells Corel WordPerfect to use only the records that meet certain conditions for the merge operation, ignoring those that do not meet the conditions. The records not used during the merge remain in the data file—they are just ignored, not deleted.

You can select records based on up to three fields. Starting with the column on the left, pull down the list and choose a field that you want to use for a condition.

You can specify up to four selection criteria, each on one to three fields. In the first row, enter the values or conditions that a record has to meet. For example, to

11

merge the records of clients who are in New Jersey, select State for the first field and enter **NJ** in the column under State. To further specify which clients are selected, use up to two additional fields. When you have more than one condition in a row, Corel WordPerfect treats them as AND conditions. This means that the record must meet all of the specifications to be selected. For example, to merge with records for New Jersey clients who owe over $500, add the Amount Due field to the second column, and type **>500** as the condition under it. The condition will appear as shown at the left.

State	Amount Due	Last Name
Cond 1: NJ	>500	

Conditions in the other rows of the dialog box—Cond 2, Cond 3, and Cond 4—are treated as OR operations. This condition, for example, displays all New Jersey clients who owe more than $500, as well as all California clients no matter how much they owe, as shown here.

State	Amount Due	Last Name
Cond 1: NJ	>500	
Cond 2: CA		

When you want to select records based on a specific value, just type the value in the condition box. You can also use > and < operators to meet conditions above and below value.

If you have a list of possible matching values, enter them in the same condition, separated by semicolons, rather than on separate rows in the dialog box. For instance, enter **PA;NJ** under the State field to match clients in either Pennsylvania or New Jersey. You can also choose records in a range of values using a hyphen, as in 200-1000 for clients with a value from 200 to 1000 in the field. To exclude a specific value, precede it with an exclamation point. For example, to list clients in every state but California, enter **!CA** in the state field.

Finally, you can use the * and ? wildcard characters to represent, respectively, any number of characters, and a single character. Entering **N*** in the Last Name field, for example, will select all clients whose last names begin with the letter "N." Entering **8450?** under the Zip Code field will select clients whose zip codes start with the numbers "8450."

Marking Records

To pick the records you want to use, click on the Mark Records option. The dialog box will change as shown in Figure 11-10, listing all of the records in the data file with check boxes. Then follow these steps:

1. In the Display Records boxes, enter the starting and ending numbers of the records you want to pick from. To select from all of the records, leave the boxes with their default values.

2. In the First Field to Display list, select the field that you want to use to select records. For example, if you want to pick records based on the state of residence, pull down the list and click on the State field.

3. Click on the Update Record List. Corel WordPerfect will display the records in the Record List.

4. Click on the check boxes for the records that you want to merge.

5. Click on OK when you have finished, and perform the merge.

Customizing a Merge with Fields

The Merge Codes and Keyboard buttons in the Merge feature bar give you great flexibility in controlling the merge process. You can use the merge codes, for example, to automate operations in much the same way that you can use macros. In fact, you can even run a macro directly from a merge file.

As an example of using merge codes, the next section will illustrate several useful codes, starting with an interactive merge that lets you enter information into the merged document.

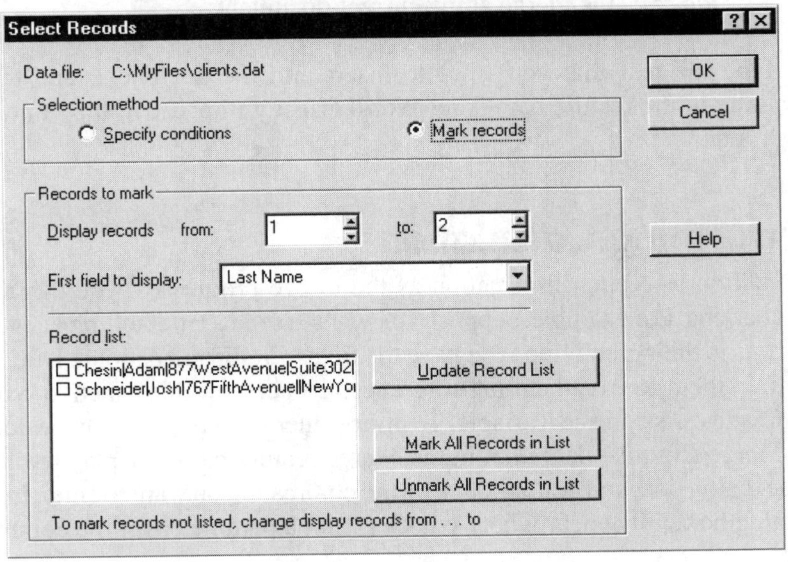

Select Records

Data file: C:\MyFiles\clients.dat

Selection method
- ○ Specify conditions   ● Mark records

Records to mark

Display records   from: [1]   to: [2]

First field to display: [Last Name ▼]

Record list:
☐ Chesin|Adam|877WestAvenue|Suite302|
☐ Schneider|Josh|767FifthAvenue||NewYor

[Update Record List]
[Mark All Records in List]
[Unmark All Records in List]

To mark records not listed, change display records from . . . to

[OK]
[Cancel]
[Help]

Marking records to select

FIGURE 11-10

11

Interactive Merges

In most cases, your data file should have all of the variable information that you need to personalize the form document. But suppose it doesn't? Suppose you want to enter a personal salutation for a letter using a client's first name or nickname. To enter information into the form letter when it is being merged, you need to use the Keyboard code.

Place the insertion point in the form letter where you want to enter the information, and then click on the Keyboard button in the Merge feature bar. In the dialog box that appears, type a prompt that will appear asking for the information you want to enter, and then click on OK.

When you merge the documents, Corel WordPerfect will pause and display the prompt and a special feature bar as shown in Figure 11-11. The bar contains these buttons:

- *Continue* inserts the text you enter into the document and continues the merge.

- *Skip Record* continues the merge without inserting any information in the current documents.

- *Quit* continues the merge but ignores all remaining merge codes.

- *Stop* ends the merge at the current document.

Type the text that you want to insert into the document, and then click on Continue in the feature bar. Corel WordPerfect will pause at the same location for every letter.

Performing Calculations

In addition to typing information as the merge progresses, you can also perform calculations. For example, suppose you want to send a letter telling clients how much remains in their credit line. You have the fields Credit and Amount Due, so you must subtract them to calculate the difference. To perform this function, you need two commands: Assign and Variable. To insert a merge command into the document, use the Merge Commands button in the Merge feature bar to display the Insert Merge Code dialog box, and double-click on the command you want to enter. In some cases, a dialog box will appear where you can enter a parameter for the command.

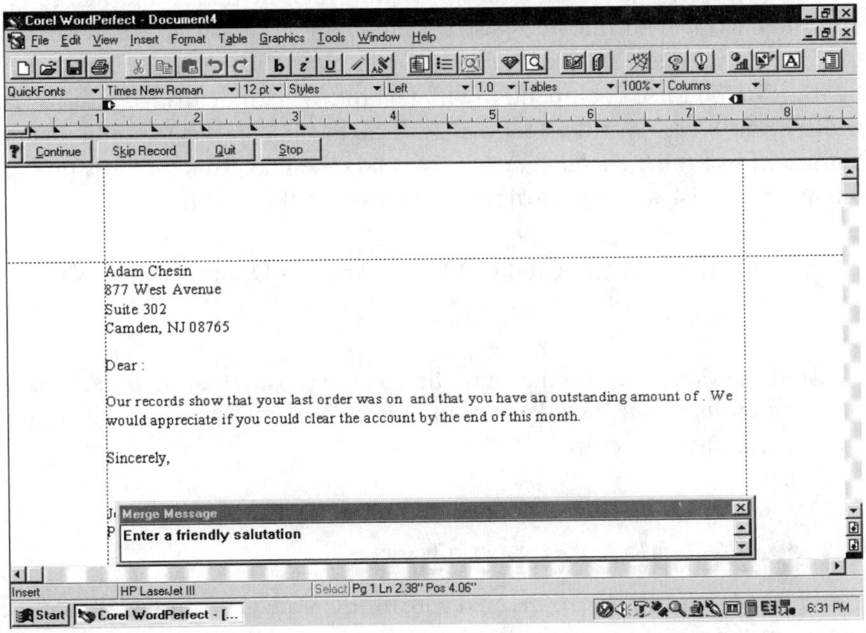

Dialog box
and feature
bar for
keyboard
merge

FIGURE 11-11

The Assign command uses the syntax **ASSIGN**(*variable; value or expression*). Double-click on the command in the Insert Merge Codes box to see this dialog box. Type **Net** in the Variable text box, and then click on OK. Because the expression will use field codes, you have to enter them in using the Insert Field button. The ASSIGN(net;) code will appear in the document. Move the insertion point to the left of the closing parentheses, and then click on Insert Field. Double-click on the Credit field, press the hyphen, and then double-click on the Amount Due field. The final command will appear as ASSIGN(net; FIELD(Credit)–FIELD(Amount Due)).

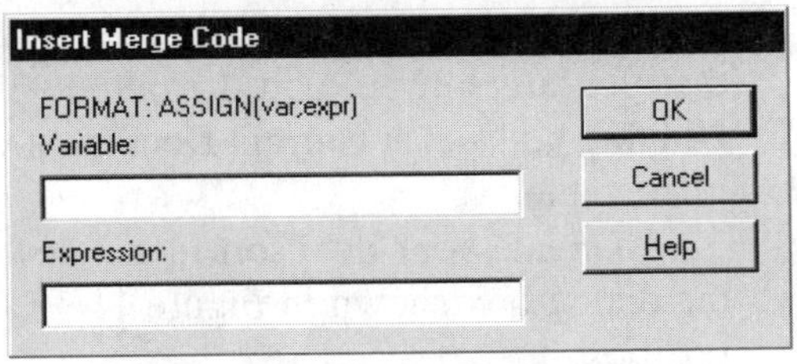

Now when you want to insert the amount in the merged document, use the VARIABLE command. Display the Insert Merge Code box, and double-click on the Variable code near the bottom of the list. Type **Net** in the dialog box that appears, and click on OK. The code will appear as VARIABLE(Net).

There are two unfortunate drawbacks of this method. First, merge commands will only work with integers—whole numbers. That's why whole numbers were used in the sample data file. Second, if you place the ASSIGN command in a line by itself in the form document, it will generate an extra carriage return, resulting in a blank line. Corel WordPerfect will perform the calculation to compute the amount, but it will insert the carriage return that ends the line. To avoid this problem, write the line like this, with the closing parenthesis on the next line:

ASSIGN(net; FIELD(Credit)–FIELD(Amount Due))COMMENT(
)

Start the document on the same line as the closing parenthesis. The Comment command tells Corel WordPerfect to ignore any text or codes that follow it, so it ignores the carriage return.

Sorting Database Records

Your form document will be merged with the data file in the same order as the records appear in the file. In some instances, however, you may want to merge the file in some other order, such as by zip code to take advantage of bulk mail.

To sort a database, click on Sort in the Options menu of the Merge feature bar, or select Sort from the Tools menu. This will display the dialog box shown in Figure 11-12. The box offers a number of predefined sorts, such as the first cell in a table or the first characters in a merge file. It also lets you designate the input file (the data that you are sorting) and the output file where you want to place the document. Leaving both set at Current Document will actually change the order of the records in the table.

To create your own sort to use any other merge field, click on New to display the dialog box shown in Figure 11-13. Type a name for the sort in the Sort Name text box.

You use this dialog box to sort records in a data file, as well as lines, paragraphs, and table rows in a document. Our data file appears in the form of a table, so we want to select the Table Row option in the Sort By section. You would use the Merge Record option button if your data file used merge codes.

Corel WordPerfect will sort the information based on one to nine key fields. A *key* represents a field to sort on, or a word or line within the field. Each key can be sorted in either alphanumeric or numeric order, depending on its contents.

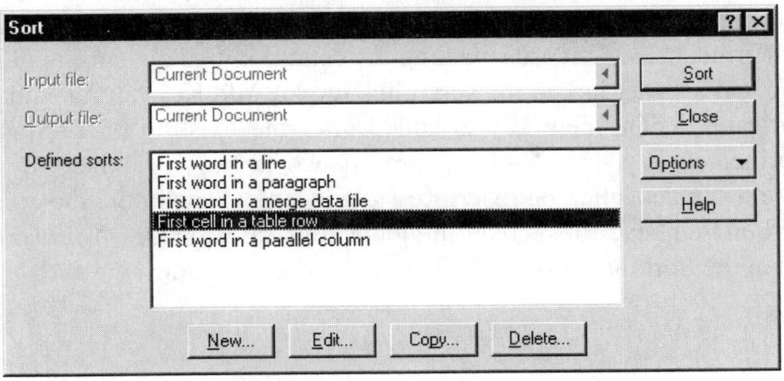

Predefined
sort options

FIGURE 11-12

To sort the table by the Amount Due field, pull down the Type list and select Numeric. Then choose if you want to sort your records in ascending or descending order. Enter **10** in the Column text box because the Amount Due field is in the tenth column. Leave the Line and Word options set at 1.

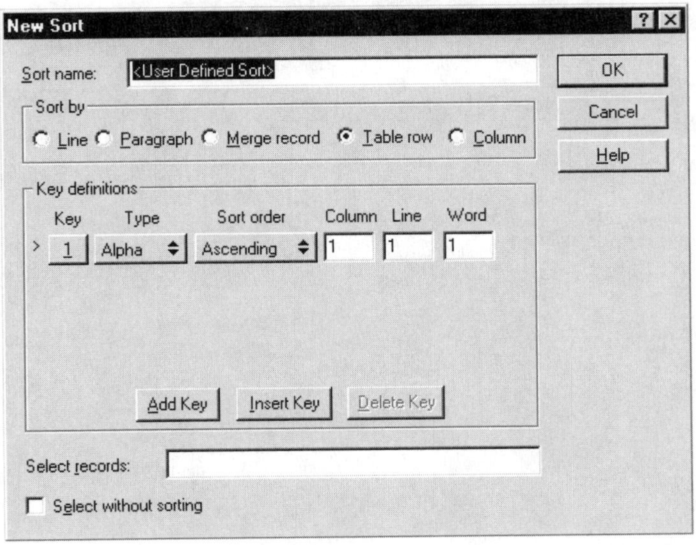

Defining a
sort

FIGURE 11-13

11

You can also enter a criteria to select records, so the function sorts and selects at the same time. If you click on the Select Without Sorting check box, Corel WordPerfect selects records meeting the condition without sorting them.

To add another key to the sort, click on the Add Key button, and then enter its specifications. The new key is added after the existing ones. Since the sort is performed in key order—giving precedence to key one, then key two, and so on—you can also click on Insert Key to add a new key before the current one.

When you have finished defining the keys, click on OK. Your sort will now be listed in the Sort dialog box. Double-click on it to perform the sort.

Working with Graphics

12

All of the formatting techniques that you've learned so far go a long way toward making a professional-looking document. But sometimes nothing does it better than graphics. Corel WordPerfect has a full range of graphics features that let you add clip art, charts, special text effects, horizontal and vertical lines, custom drawings, and even scientific equations to your document.

Picture Basics

Inserting a picture into your document is one of the easiest ways to add pizzazz to a document. To insert a picture, follow these steps.

1. Place the insertion point where you want the graphic to appear.

2. Click on the Insert Image button on the toolbar, or pull down the Graphics menu and select Image to display the Insert Image dialog box. This box lists graphic files in the Corel\Office7\Graphics folder. To access images in some other folder, use the Look In list and the directory/file listing. Open the Advertise, Borders, or Pictures subfolders for even more choices.

3. To see what a graphic looks like before inserting it, click on the Preview button in the dialog box's toolbar.

 OTE: *Many of the graphics are words or phrases, such as "Secret," "Confidential," and "Do Not Duplicate." Others are dividers that you can use between paragraphs, or at the top or bottom of the page.*

4. Double-click on the name of the file you want to insert, or click on it and then on the Insert button.

The graphic will appear in the document with the upper-left corner at the position of the insertion point, as shown in Figure 12-1. The image will be surrounded by small black boxes, called *handles*, showing that it is selected. To unselect the graphic, click elsewhere on the page.

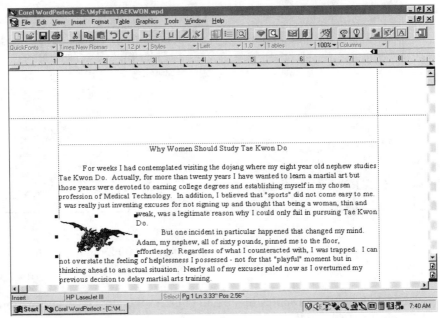

Dragon
graphic
inserted into
a document

FIGURE 12-1

 If you have a graphics-intensive layout, you can create the graphics in Corel Presentations and then import your text from Corel WordPerfect.

Corel WordPerfect Suite comes with more than ten thousand graphic files, many of which are not copied onto your computer but kept on the CD. Table 12-1 summarizes the locations of the files. Substitute the letter of your hard disk where you installed the Suite and the letter of your CD drive.

Using Drag to Create

You can always change the size and position of a graphic after you insert it. As an alternative, you can start by drawing a box the exact size and in the exact position you want the graphic and then inserting the image into the box. This is a good technique if you've already typed and formatted your document and you know exactly where you want the image to appear.

12

Directory	Description
C:\Corel\Office7\Graphics	213 backgrounds, 54 borders, 44 pictures, 189 textures, and 705 general images in STANDARD.QAD
CD:\Corel\Office7\Graphics\QuickArt	5412 images in PREMIUM.QAD
CD:\Corel\Office7\Graphics\ClipArt	4644 images in various folders
CD:\Photos	200 photographs

Where to Find Graphics

TABLE 12-1

To do this, pull down the Graphics menu and click on Drag to Create. Now, when you want to insert a graphic, follow these steps:

1. Pull down the Graphics menu and click on Image. The insertion point will change to a small box.

2. Point to the upper-left corner where you want the box to appear.

3. Drag the mouse to create a rectangle the size of the picture.

4. Release the mouse. Corel WordPerfect displays the Insert Image dialog box.

5. Double-click on the image you want to insert.

Corel WordPerfect will insert the image into the box. To turn off this feature, select Drag To Create from the Graphics menu again.

Linking Graphic Files

Adding graphics to your documents improves their impact, but it also enlarges their size. Graphics can take up a lot of disk space, and when you insert a graphic into a document, you are actually inserting the entire graphic file.

Inserting the graphic has one other drawback. Suppose you used a drawing program to create your company logo and then inserted the logo into your letterhead and in other documents. If you later change the logo with the drawing program, you'd have to reinsert the edited copy into all of the documents.

You can solve both of these problems by selecting the Image on Disk check box when you select the graphic in the Insert Image dialog box.

This creates a link to the graphic on the disk, displaying it onscreen but not inserting the entire file into the document. If you later edit the drawing and save it to a file with the same name, the edited version will be retrieved automatically when you open the document in Corel WordPerfect.

IP: *If you copy your document to a floppy disk to transfer it to another computer, remember to copy the graphic file as well. When you use the Image on Disk option, the graphic file must always be available when you open the document.*

Using Graphics in Headers, Footers, and Watermarks

You can insert a graphic directly into the document. But if you want the graphic to appear on every page, you can insert it into a header, footer, or watermark.

Small graphics and decorative dividers are useful in headers and footers. Create or edit the header or footer, as explained in Chapter 8, and then insert the graphic into the header or footer area.

Some graphics are especially effective when used in a watermark. Displaying "DO NOT COPY" in large letters across a page, for example, certainly gets your point across. It cannot be cut out or ignored, and makes it perfectly clear that duplicated copies are not endorsed.

To insert a graphic in a watermark, create or edit the watermark as you learned in Chapter 8. Click on the Image button in the watermark feature bar, and then select the graphic from the Insert Image dialog box. You can insert several graphics as watermarks to create a special effect. In this chapter you will learn how to edit the graphic in the watermark window.

12

Changing the Position of Graphics

Once you insert a graphic, you can move it to any other position on the page—even to areas below the last text on the page. Use these steps.

1. If the graphic is not selected—that is, the handles do not appear around it—click on it.

2. Point inside the graphic, not on any of the handles, so the pointer appears as a four-pointed arrow.

3. Drag the mouse.

4. As you drag, an outline of the graphic box moves with the pointer. When the box is where you want to place the graphic, release the mouse button.

Changing the Size of Graphics

You use the handles around the graphic to change its size.

- Drag a corner handle to change its height and width at the same time.

- Drag the center handle on the top or bottom to change its height.

- Drag the center handle on the left or right to change its width.

Customizing the Graphic Box

Corel WordPerfect gives you a variety of ways to customize graphic images. First, understand that when you insert a graphic, you are really inserting two elements into the document—a graphic box and the graphic inside of the box. By selecting Image from the Graphics menu, you are telling Corel WordPerfect to insert a box using the Image Box style. You are then telling Corel WordPerfect what graphic to place inside of the box. We'll look at the issue of box styles later; but for now, we'll consider ways to edit the box, as well as the image inside of the box.

When you edit the graphic box, you are changing the container in which the graphic is placed. Dragging the box, or changing its size, for example, does not affect the image itself. These are the other ways you can edit the box:

- Add or change the border line around the box.

- Insert a fill color or pattern.

- Set the way text wraps around the box and the contour of the graphic.

- Set the position of the box in the document.

- Edit the box style.

- Add a caption.

- Modify the position of the contents within the box.

- Change the box size.

You can edit a box using either a QuickSpot dialog box or the QuickMenu.

To use the QuickSpot, point to the graphic and click on the QuickSpot. To display the QuickMenu, right-click on the graphic. Figure 12-2 shows both the QuickSpot dialog box, called *Edit Box,* and the QuickMenu. Clicking on Edit Box in the QuickMenu, by the way, also displays the QuickSpot dialog box.

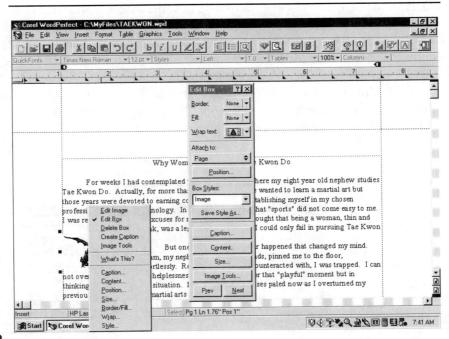

Edit Box and QuickMenu for working with graphic boxes

FIGURE 12-2

Changing the Borders and Fill

Each of Corel WordPerfect's graphic box styles includes a default border and fill style. Image boxes have no border and no fill. Adding a border to the image is similar to adding borders around paragraphs and pages. In fact, the choices are exactly the same. In the Edit Box dialog box, select a style for the box, a fill pattern, or color. To choose options from a separate dialog box rather than a list, select More from either the Border or Fill drop-down list. Corel WordPerfect will display the familiar Border/Fill dialog box with the Border, Fill, and Advanced pages.

Wrapping Text Around Graphics

Wrap refers to the way text flows around a graphic. The default setting for an image box is called *Wrap Square Both Sides.* This means that text will appear on all sides of the image—if there is room for it between the margins—up to the rectangular shape of the image box.

You can select other wrap methods from either the Wrap list in the QuickSpot dialog box or the Wrap dialog box that appears when you select Wrap from the QuickMenu. Figure 12-3 shows the dialog box; the wrap list offers the same options displayed differently.

Choose No Wrap if you want the graphic to be superimposed over the text. Use this option if you want the graphic to appear in the background, or to create special effects by combining text and graphics. Choose Neither Side if you want the graphic to appear with no text on its left or right. The four Square options let text wrap, but stop the text at the box borders. The four Contour options also allow you to wrap text, but only up to the contour of the graphic.

Wrap
options in
the Wrap
Text dialog
box

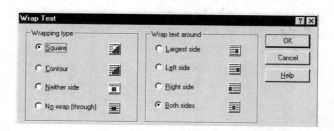

FIGURE 12-3

Setting the Graphic Position

When you insert a graphic, Corel WordPerfect anchors it to the page. This means it inserts it in a specific location on the page, and inserting or deleting text above it will not change its position.

You can also anchor a picture to a paragraph or character. A *paragraph anchor* means that the box will move up or down with the paragraph as you insert or delete text above it. A *character anchor* means that the box is treated just like any other character in the line, and it will move with the line as you insert or delete text before it. Use a paragraph or character anchor when the text refers to the graphic and you want the graphic to be on the same page as its reference. Use a *page anchor* when you want the graphic to remain in the same position on the page regardless of the text. To keep the box on the page, however, you must select Page in the Attach Box To list, and select the Box Stays on Page check box.

To change the type of anchor, pull down the Attach To list in the QuickSpot dialog box and select Page, Paragraph, or Character.

When you select a paragraph or character anchor, the image is anchored at its current location. If you later drag the image to another location, the anchor changes as well. Corel WordPerfect displays a paragraph anchor graphically as you drag, as shown here.

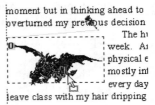

The Push-pin icon shows the paragraph to which the graphic will be linked. Release the mouse when the icon is at the desired paragraph.

For additional position options, click on Position in the Edit Box dialog box or on the QuickMenu to see the Box Position dialog box. Here you can select an anchor type, as well as a horizontal and vertical position relative to the page margins, to the edges of the pages, to the center of the page, or to a column. If you are working with a three-column newsletter, for example, you can choose to center the box across the first two columns. Select Column in the Vertical position list, and then enter 1 and 2 in the column text boxes.

Inserting a Caption

You can also add a caption that numbers the graphic and includes a descriptive word or phrase, just like the captions used with the figures in this book. Numbering graphics makes it easy to refer to them in the text. To caption a graphic, follow these steps:

12

1. Right-click on it and select Create Caption from the QuickMenu. Corel WordPerfect will insert the word "Figure," along with a figure number. Each image that you insert is associated with a number, even if you do not add a caption. The first image box in the document is Figure 1, the second is Figure 2, and so on, based on their positions in the document.

2. Corel WordPerfect leaves the insertion point to the right of the label, so type the descriptive text, as shown here.

Figure 1

3. When you have finished, click elsewhere on the page.

4. To later change the text of the caption, double-click on it and edit the text accordingly.

The position of the caption and its label (such as "Figure") are determined by the graphic box style. The default style for image boxes places the caption on the left below the graphic, outside of the box, and using the label "Figure." To change its position, select Caption in the QuickSpot dialog box to see the Box Caption dialog box.

The Caption Position option determines the position of the caption in relation to the graphic box. You can select the side of the box and whether the caption is inside or outside of it. Pull down the Position list to choose if the caption is at the top, center, or bottom of the selected side. You can also enter a specific location using an absolute measurement, or a percentage offset, such as 25 percent from the left edge.

Use the Rotate Caption option to rotate the text. If you position the caption on the left border, for example, you might want to rotate it 90 degrees so the characters print landscape up the edge, as shown here.

The Auto Width option in the Caption Width section lets Corel WordPerfect wrap the caption as necessary based on the amount of text, the size of the box, and the caption's position. Sometimes, however, this may result in too much blank space around the caption, taking up needless room on the page. As an alternative you can designate a fixed width in inches, but no wider than the box. You can also set the width as a percentage of the box size, between 1 and 100 percent.

Setting Content Options

The graphic box style also affects the position of the graphic within the box and the type of contents in the box. When you select Image from the Graphics menu, Corel WordPerfect assumes you want to insert a graphic image and creates a box the default size for the graphic image. The Content option in the Edit box and QuickMenu give you some control over these default settings. Click on Content to see the Box Content dialog box.

Keep in mind that the graphic and the box in which the graphic appears are two separate objects. This dialog box is designed to let you change what is in the box and its position.

The name of the graphic file you inserted appears in the Filename text box. If you want to replace the graphic with another, enter the new name in the box or use the List button to select the file. The Content list lets you choose the type of content. It is set at Image or Image on Disk, based on how you inserted the graphic. You can also select Empty, Text, or Equation from the Content list. Selecting any of these, however, will delete the graphic from the box because it will no longer be considered an image box. You use the Content list mainly when you are creating a custom box style and you need to specify the type of contents that it will hold.

If you inserted a graphic in a format other than Corel WordPerfect's own WPG format, the Image on Disk option in the Content list has a nice side effect. Remember Image on Disk creates a link to the graphic file. If you select Image on Disk after inserting a graphic, a dialog box appears asking where you want to save the graphic. You can then choose to save the graphic as a WPG file, converting it to Corel WordPerfect's own format.

The Content Position options in the dialog box determine the position of the image within the graphic box. They do not affect the position of the box on the page. The default settings center the image horizontally and vertically, but you can change the vertical position to the left or right, and the horizontal position to the top or bottom.

You won't see the effect of your changes immediately because, by default, the box size is the same as the graphic. This is because the Preserve Image Width/Height Ratio check box is not selected. As you change the size of the graphic box by dragging a handle, the graphic changes as well. If you check this box, however, Corel WordPerfect will always maintain the original proportions of the image inside the box. If you enlarge the box in a different proportion, the box will become larger than the graphic, and you can then adjust the position of the graphic within the larger box.

You can also use the Size option to adjust the size of the graphic box without affecting the image inside it.

12

You can select options from the Rotates Text Counterclockwise section only when you are using a text box.

Setting the Box Size

Trying to adjust a graphic to an exact size by dragging can be difficult, especially if you do not have a steady hand. To use measurements to change the graphic box size, select Size in the QuickSpot dialog box or QuickMenu to open the Box Size dialog box.

Use the Set options in the Width and Height sections to enter a specific size. Use the Full options in the Width section to automatically extend the box fully between the margins or the full width of the columns. Choose Full in the Height section to extend the box to the top and bottom margins and anchor the graphic to the page.

Selecting the Size to Content option will adjust the width and height based on the size of the graphic within the box.

Choose Maintain Proportions in either section to automatically adjust the width or height when you change the other size to maintain the picture's original proportions.

Changing the Image Settings

So far, all of the editing techniques have modified the box in which the graphic is placed. You can also edit the graphic itself. Editing the graphic changes the appearance of the image without affecting the box in which it is placed.

There are actually two ways that you can edit the graphic: you can edit its appearance without changing the actual design, or you can modify the design—the shape and elements that make up the graphic.

To customize the graphic's appearance, click on the Image Tools button in the QuickSpot dialog box or QuickMenu to display the palette of tools shown in Figure 12-4. Now take a quick look at each of these tools. How well you use them will depend on your own design and artistic abilities.

Rotating Graphics

The Rotate tool lets you rotate the image within the box without rotating the box itself. Here's how it works:

1. Click on Rotate to display four corner handles around the graphic.

2. Drag one of the handles to rotate the image.

3. Click on the Rotate tool when you've finished.

Because you are only rotating the image within the box, some of it may now extend beyond the borders of the box and will no longer appear. Don't worry if part of the image seems to be missing, as shown here. The complete image is still in the document so it will be displayed if you rotate the image back or enlarge the box size.

Moving the Image

The Move tool lets you change the position of the image within the box. Follow these steps.

1. Click on the Move tool.

2. Point to the graphic and drag the image.

You can drag the image so some parts of it scroll out of the box, but again, the parts that scroll are not lost—you can later move the image so they appear again.

Image Tools

FIGURE 12-4

12

Mirror Imaging

These buttons let you flip the image vertically from top to bottom and horizontally from left to right. Flipping horizontally is useful for some graphics that appear to be pointing in a certain direction. Flipping vertically is useful for designs that do not contain text or other recognizable people, places, or things. If you use a divider graphic along the top of the page, for example, insert the same graphic along the bottom and flip it horizontally so the two appear to be framing the page. Use the same technique with graphics down the left and right edges of the page, but flip one vertically.

Enlarging the Image

By default, the image box is the same size as the graphic. Changing the size of the box also changes the size of the image within it. You use the Zoom tool to change the size of just the image within the box. Clicking on the Zoom tool displays these three options.

Use the Magnifier icon when you want to enlarge a selected portion of the graphic so it fills the image box. Follow these steps:

1. Click on the Magnifier icon—the pointer will appear as a magnifier lens and a crosshair.

2. Drag the mouse to select a rectangular portion of the graphic.

3. When you release the mouse, that portion is enlarged to fill the image box.

Use the Up and Down arrows to enlarge or reduce the entire image. Here's how.

1. Click on the Arrow icon in the Zoom list. Corel WordPerfect will display a vertical scroll bar next to the graphic.

2. Scroll the bar up to reduce the size of the graphic.

3. Scroll the bar down to enlarge the graphic.

To return the graphic to its original size, click on the 1:1 icon.

Changing the Black-and-White Threshold

You can convert a color graphic or one that contains shades of gray to black and white. This is useful if you want to create some special effect, if you want to print it in black and white on a color printer, or if your monochrome printer does not output gray shades correctly. When you do convert a color to black and white, the color threshold determines which shades of gray are converted to white and which to black. The lower the threshold, the darker the image, since more of the gray shades will be over the threshold and will be converted to black.

If you click on the B/W Threshold button, you'll see a palette representing different threshold levels. Click on the one that you want to use to convert the graphic to black and while using that threshold level.

Changing the Contrast

Contrast is the range of shades between light and dark areas of a color image. To change the contrast, click on the Contrast button and then select a setting from the palette that appears.

Setting the Brightness

Brightness determines the overall saturation of colors in a graphic or the brightness of a black-and-white image. To change the brightness, click on the Brightness button and then select a setting from the palette that appears.

Choosing a Fill Style

The Fill tool controls the transparency of the image. By default, the images are set at the normal fill. This means that areas of the graphic appear in the color or gray shade in which the graphic was designed. The Fill tool offers these options.

- The option on the left is the default normal style.

- The middle option removes the fill displaying the graphic as an outline, so the paper's color or any background text can be seen.

- The option on the right inserts an opaque white as the fill pattern.

12

n **OTE:** *Fill patterns will affect graphics with the WPG extension, but not BMP graphic files.*

Inverting Colors

When you *invert* an image, you change it to its complementary colors. With a noncolor image this will have the effect of displaying it as a photographic negative. To invert the color, click on the Invert Colors button.

Specifying Attributes

Many of the image settings interact with each other, so changing one will have an effect that will require you to change another. You may also want to set the brightness, size, or other attribute to a specific setting. To enter settings, and to change all of the attributes from one location, click on the Edit Attributes button to see the dialog box in Figure 12-5.

When you click on the attribute you want to change in the top section of the dialog box, the settings that you can make or choose from will be shown in the bottom of the box. Select each of the categories that you want to adjust in turn, and

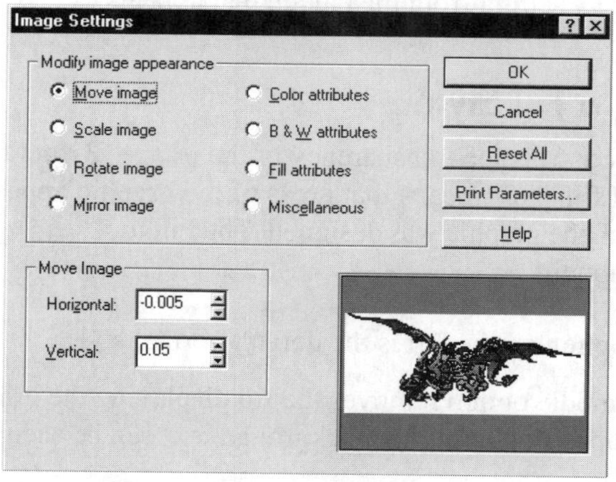

Changing
the image
settings

FIGURE 12-5

then make your choices. The preview of the graphic will show how your choices will affect the picture.

The Print Parameters button displays a dialog box where you can adjust how graphics are printed. The options available in the dialog box will depend on your printer, but you may be able to set a dithering method and source, and a half-tone option.

Dithering is the process of mixing printed dots to simulate colors or shades of gray. You can choose a method to determine how the dot pattern is created, and choose the source—whether dithering is created by your printer or by Corel WordPerfect. The Halftone Options determine the number of lines of dots per inch and their angle.

Resetting the Attributes

Corel WordPerfect always stores the original settings of the graphic with the document. If you want to restore the graphic to these settings, click on the Reset Attributes button. You can also select Reset All in the Image Settings dialog box.

Editing the Graphic

Changing the image settings only affects the way the graphic appears without actually changing the graphic design. To change the graphic itself, you need a set of drawing tools. Corel WordPerfect provides these tools in a special window that accesses the drawing features of Corel Presentations, the graphic presentation segment of the Corel WordPerfect Suite.

To display the graphic in that window, double-click on it or select Edit Contents from the Image Tools box. Figure 12-6 shows one of Corel WordPerfect's graphics in the Corel Presentations window.

Use the tools to draw objects over the graphic and to edit the lines and objects that make up the graphic itself.

Drawing Custom Graphics

You can access the Corel Presentations drawing tools at any time to create your own graphics. Select Draw from the Graphics menu to display the Corel Presentations window with a blank graphic box. Use the drawing tools to create your drawing,

12

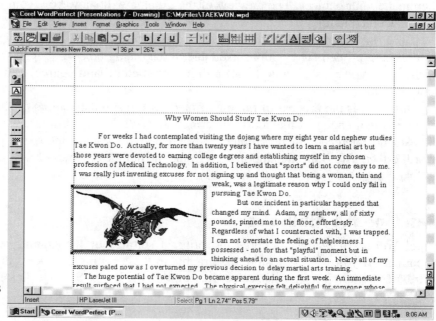

Editing a
graphic
using Corel
Presentations
tools

FIGURE 12-6

and then click outside of the box to return to Corel WordPerfect. Edit the drawing just as you learned in this chapter.

Creating Text Boxes

In Chapter 6 you learned how to insert a border around text. The border isn't a graphic box because you cannot drag it within the document or use any of the image tools, such as rotating the text, to customize it. You can, however, create a graphic text box.

To create a text box, click on the Text Box button in the toolbar, or choose Text from the Graphics menu. Corel WordPerfect inserts a graphic box into the document with a thick top and bottom border, and with the insertion point within the box. The borders are the default styles for a text box. Type and format the text you want in the box, and then click outside of it when you have finished:

The huge potential of Tae Kwon Do became apparent during the first week. An immediate result surfaced that I had not expected. The physical exercise felt delightful for someone whose position involves mostly intense mental activities. Though for six years I have exercised every day, including aerobics, I never realized that on most days I would leave class with my hair dripping wet. I remember those first weeks of lessons vividly. After class I was surprised with the boundless energy that had been created within me. For example, one Autumn

The potential became apparent during the first week...

You can drag a text box within the document, and you can change its size. Even though you cannot use the image tools to customize it, the Size, Position, Wrap, and Border options are available. Double-click on the text box to edit or format its contents, or click on Edit in the Contents box to edit the text in a separate window.

Though you cannot use the image tools to rotate the text, you can rotate it using the Contents box. The Rotate Text Counterclockwise section of that box lets you rotate the text in 90, 180, or 270 degrees.

Using TextArt

Corel WordPerfect's TextArt application lets you create headlines, banners, logos, and other graphics from text. Instead of using plain text in a text box, you can select a shape that you want the text to appear in, choose a fill pattern and shadow, and even rotate or stretch the text for a special effect.

 IP: *If you want to create an effect with text you've already typed, select the text and then choose TextArt from the Graphics menu. To create an effect with text, follow these steps:*

1. Choose TextArt from the Graphics menu to run TextArt.

2. In the Type Here window, type the text that you want to use for the logo, headline, or other effect.

3. Click on one of the options shown in the Shapes box to choose the shape for the text,  or click on More to see all of the available patterns.

4. Use the Font, Style, Justification, and Color buttons to create the effect that you want.

5. Click on the Options tab of the TextArt dialog box to see the page shown in Figure 12-7.

6. Use the Pattern button to choose a pattern and color for the fill.

7. Use the Shadow button to choose a shadow position and color.

8. Use the Outline button to choose a line thickness and color to surround the characters.

9. To rotate the text, click on the Rotation button to display four handles. Drag one of the corner handles to rotate the text as desired, and then click on Rotation again. To use measurements to rotate the text, double-click on the Rotation button and then enter the measurement in the dialog box that appears.

10. Since diagonal lines can sometimes have a jagged or stepped look, select Normal, High, or Very High from the Smoothness list.

11. Use the Insert Character button to add a special character from the font that is not available on the keyboard. The characters available are determined by the current font.

12. Click on Close to insert the graphic into the document.

You can change the size and position of the box, and add borders and fill, just as you learned how to do for graphics. To edit or change the format of the text, double-click on the box to redisplay it in the TextArt window.

  You can also use TextArt in Corel Quattro Pro and Corel Presentations.

Graphic Box Styles

Graphic box styles have been mentioned a number of times in this chapter. When you select Image or Text from the Graphics menu, you are actually selecting a style. The style tells Corel WordPerfect the contents you want to place in the box, its default

TextArt options

border and fill styles, and the caption position and label. There are really 11 different box styles, as shown in Table 12-2.

To change the style applied to an existing box, follow these steps:

1. Click on the QuickSpot to display the Edit Box dialog box.

2. Pull down the Box Styles list and select the style that you want to apply.

These styles can hold three types of information—a graphic image, text, or an equation—and each box style can store any of the types. For example, you can insert text in a figure box or a piece of clip art in a text box. So if you want to insert a graphic in a box with thick top and bottom borders, you can use a text box style. The styles help you organize and coordinate your graphics. The Image, Text, and Equation options in the Graphics menu give you a place to start. But you can create any type of box using the Custom Box option, by following these steps.

12

Style	Description
Image	No borders, page anchor, top-right corner at the insertion point, 1.5 inches wide, auto height
Text box	Top and bottom thick border, paragraph anchor, at the right border, 3.25 inches wide, auto height
Equation	No borders, paragraph anchor, full size between the margins, auto height
Figure	Thin outside border lines, paragraph anchor, at the right border, 3.25 inches wide, auto height
Table	Top and bottom thick border, paragraph anchor, at the right border, 3.25 inches wide, auto height
User	No border, paragraph anchor, at the right border, 3.25 inches wide, auto height
Button	Borders and fill to appear as a button, character anchor, at the position of the insertion point on the baseline, 1 inch wide, auto height
Watermark	No borders, page anchor, full page size
Inline equation	No borders, character anchor, at the position of the insertion point on the baseline, auto width, auto height
OLE 2.0	No borders, page anchor, top-right corner at the insertion point, 1.5 inches wide, auto height
Inline text	No borders, character anchor, at the position of the insertion point on the baseline, auto width, auto height

Box Styles

TABLE 12-2

1. Select Custom Box from the Graphics menu to see the style options in the Custom Box dialog box.

2. Choose the style of box that you want.

3. Click on OK.

4. Use the Contents dialog box to determine what goes in the box—an image, image on disk, text, or equation.

You can also create a custom box type.

1. Select Custom Box from the Graphics menu.

2. Click on Styles, and then on Create.

3. In the dialog box that appears, enter a name for the type.

4. Specify the borders, fill, contents, and other specifics.

5. Click on OK, and then close the Box Style dialog box.

Your new type will appear on the Custom Box list.

Rather than use the dialog boxes, however, you can create a style by example, by following these steps:

1. Adjust the borders, fill, anchor, and other specifications of a box.

2. Click on the QuickSpot to display the Edit Box dialog box.

3. Click on Save Style As.

4. Type a new style name.

5. Click on OK.

You can then apply the style to another box using the steps shown previously.

Drawing Lines

If you just want to add a small unobtrusive graphic element to a page, consider using a horizontal or vertical line. The easiest way to draw a horizontal line is using the QuickLines feature:

1. Start a new line by typing three hyphens or three equal signs.

2. Press ENTER.

Corel WordPerfect will replace the characters with a solid line or double line across the page.

12

You can also draw a horizontal line by selecting Horizontal Line from the Graphics menu. To draw a vertical line down the entire page at the horizontal position of the insertion point, select Vertical Line from the Graphics menu.

Because the lines are graphic elements, you can change their sizes and positions just as you can for graphic boxes.

1. Click on the line with the left mouse button to select it, displaying the handles.

2. To move the line, point to the line so the mouse is shaped like a four-directional arrow, and then drag the mouse.

3. To change the size of the line, point to a handle so the mouse is a two-directional arrow. Drag the center handle on top or bottom to change the height of the line, and drag a handle on a corner to change both the width and height at the same time. If the line is thick enough, drag the center handle on the left or right to change the width of the graphic.

Creating Custom Lines

You can create a custom-sized and formatted line by choosing Custom Line from the Graphics menu to display the Create Graphics Line dialog box. Choose to create either a horizontal or vertical line, and then use the Line Style list to choose the line's shape and thickness or to insert multiple lines.

Corel WordPerfect displays the results of your selections in a right-angled sample line, although only a straight line will be inserted. To draw a right angle, you have to coordinate the position of separate vertical and horizontal lines.

You can then use the remaining options in the box to customize the line:

■ Choose from a palette of 256 colors in the Line Color list.

■ Choose a line thickness. The list has eight options ranging from .01 to .12 inches, and you can enter a custom thickness.

■ Set the Space Above Line and Space Below Line to determine the distance of the line from the text above and below it.

■ Enter the Length of the line.

■ Set the line's Horizontal Position in relation to the left and right margins.

■ Set the line's Vertical Position in relation to the top margin. The default Baseline positions the line on the same baseline as the text.

Corel WordPerfect also lets you create your own line style.

1. Select Custom Line from the Graphics menu.

2. Click on Line Styles.

3. Click on Create to open the dialog box in Figure 12-8. (Click on Edit to edit an existing line style.)

4. Give your style a name, so you can later choose it from the Line Style list.

5. Select a color, pattern, and thickness.

6. To create a multiple line style, select a distance between lines in the Spacing Below Line list, and then click on Add. Select options for the new line, and then add and format any others.

7. Once you have multiple lines, you have to choose which one you want to edit or change. The current line will be indicated by an arrow pointing to it in the preview area. Click on the line you want to edit, or click on the Up or Down arrow buttons to select the line.

8. When you've finished, click on OK and then Close.

To use your style, display the Create Graphics Line dialog box. Your style will be listed at the bottom of the Line Style list.

Inserting Charts

Numbers can be very boring and difficult to read in a document even when displayed in a table. When you want to show a trend or make a quick point, nothing is better than a chart. Corel WordPerfect lets you create charts directly from the document window—you don't have to start Corel Quattro Pro or Corel Presentations.

If you already typed the information into a table, you are halfway there.

1. Select the cells that you want to chart.

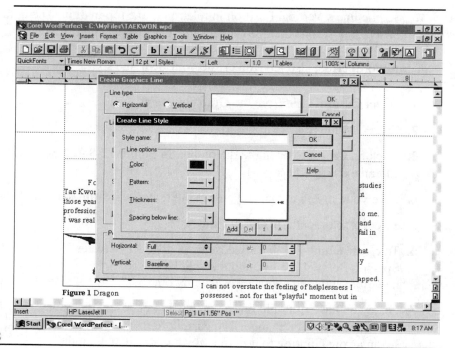

Creating a
custom line
style

FIGURE 12-8

2. Click on the Create a Chart button in the Table toolbar or select Chart from the Graphics menu.

Corel WordPerfect will start the Chart application, displaying your table data and a default bar chart, as shown in Figure 12-9.

 Charting works in about the same way in Corel Word Perfect, Corel Quattro Pro, and Corel Presentations. You can move charts, and the information you need to create them, between applications.

If you did not already create a Corel WordPerfect table, then don't bother. You can enter the information as you create the chart, by following these steps:

1. Select Chart from the Graphics menu to see a sample chart and table of information, as shown in Figure 12-10. Notice that the X-axis labels are listed in the row marked "Labels" and the name for each series in the

column marked "Legend." The color next to each legend entry shows the color that the chart bar or line will appear in.

2. To enter your own information into the chart, delete the sample data by clicking on the empty box above the word "Labels" to select all of the data and then pressing DEL.

3. In the box that appears, click on Both to delete both the data and formats from the chart. Click on OK.

4. Type the information that you want to chart.

Corel Presentations will create the chart as you enter the information. If it doesn't, click on the AutoDraw button in the toolbar.

 IP: *Using the default chart and entering your own data will enable you to quickly update the chart when you change the information.*

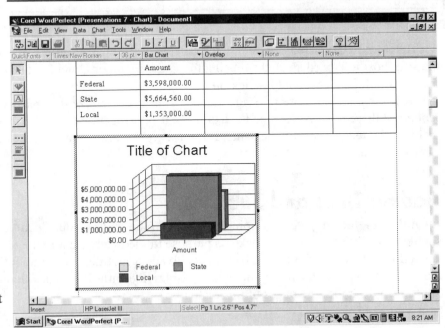

Chart with data from a Corel WordPerfect table

FIGURE 12-9

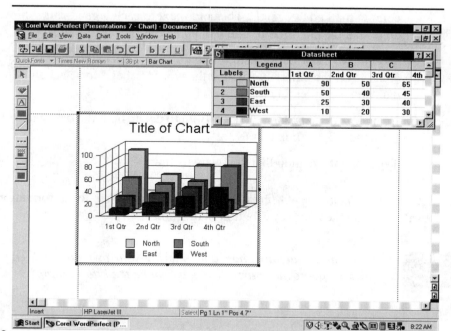

Default
chart and
data when
the table is
not selected

FIGURE 12-10

To return to Corel WordPerfect, click outside of the chart. You can now change the size, position, borders, and fill using the QuickMenu or QuickSpot. To change the design of the chart, double-click on it.

Now there are a lot of options to choose from to customize the chart. We'll be looking at these in more detail in the Corel Quattro Pro section of this book because many of the techniques are the same. For now, we'll summarize some of the most typical options.

Adding Titles and Subtitles

Even though you may be describing the chart in the text of your document, you should add a title or subtitle to make its purpose immediately clear to the reader. To add a title, select Title from the Chart menu. To add a subtitle, choose Subtitle from the Chart menu. Corel Presentations will display the Title Properties dialog box. Table 12-3 describes the pages of this dialog box.

Page	Description
Title Font	Select the font, size, and color of the text.
Text Fill	Select a fill style, pattern, foreground and background colors, and fill method.
Text Outline	Choose the width and line style of the text.
Box Type	Choose the type of the box surrounding the text.
Box Fill	Select a fill style, pattern, foreground and background colors, and fill method for the box.
Position	Position the text on the left, center, or right of the chart.

Setting Options for Text

TABLE 12-3

Enter title or subtitle in the text box. If you deselect the Display Chart Title box, the title or subtitle will not appear—use this option if you want to remove the title but leave the text available.

Customizing the Chart

By default, Corel Presentations creates a bar chart. You can change the type of the chart in two ways, using the Gallery and Layout/Type options from the Chart menu.

The Gallery lists 11 general categories of charts that you can create. When you select a category, two or more different styles of the type will appear in preview boxes. Click on the style that you want to use and then click on OK.

For more control over the chart type, use these steps.

1. Select Layout/Type from the Chart menu to display the dialog box in Figure 12-11.

2. Choose a category from the Chart Type list. Like the Gallery, two or more styles of the type will appear in the preview area.

3. Click on the style you want.

4. Select or deselect the 3D check box to select either a 3-D or 2-D chart.

5. Click on Horizontal for a horizontal chart; clear the box for a vertical chart.

12

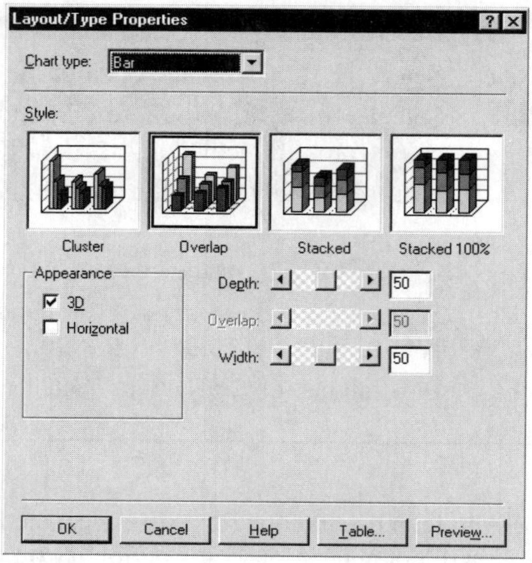

Selecting
a chart
category,
type, and
other
options

■ FIGURE 12-11

The other options that appear in this dialog box will depend on the type of chart you select. Choose from the options and click on Preview to minimize the dialog box so you can see how the chart will appear. In the box that does appear, click on OK if you want to accept the chart as it appears. Click on Back to reopen the dialog box, or on Cancel to return the chart to its previous settings.

If you do create a 3-D chart, you can further customize it by selecting Perspective from the Chart menu to see the dialog box shown in Figure 12-12.

■ Use the Horizontal text box, or the Horizontal scroll bar to rotate the chart around its base. The settings range from 0 to look directly at the chart from its side, to 100 to view the chart from the front.

■ Use the Vertical setting, or the vertical scroll bar, to rotate the chart from top to bottom. The settings range from 0 to view the chart from the top, to 100 to view it from "ground level."

■ Select the Right Angle Axis check box to make the X axis and Y axis perpendicular to each other.

■ Select the Wire Frame View to display the chart as an outline.

■ Click on Reset to return the chart to the default settings.

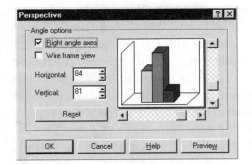

Changing
the 3-D
perspective

FIGURE 12-12

You can change the settings for any part of the chart by double-clicking on it. This opens a dialog box of options for just that part. For example, double-click on the Y-axis lines to see the Primary Y Axis Properties dialog box. In this box you can change the spacing, appearance, and position of axis labels, as well as the scale of the measurements along the axis. Double-click on a series bar to change its shape, color, and spacing from the others. Double-click on a grid line to change its shape and color, and to set the spacing between lines. Double-click on a title or subtitle to change its color, font, size, fill, or the border surrounding it.

Using the Equation Editor

Mathematical and scientific equations require special characters and formats. You can access special characters using the Insert Characters command, and you can create subscripts and superscripts using the Font dialog box and the Advance command from the Typesetting menu. But even with these features, creating complex equations could be difficult.

Corel WordPerfect doesn't want anything to be difficult for you, so they've given you the Equation editor. This is a special set of tools for formatting equations of all types. Through these tools you have easy access to special characters and formats that would be difficult to access any other way.

OTE: *The Equation editor formats equations for you—it does not do the math. That you have to do yourself.*

To start the Equation editor, choose Equation from the Graphics menu to see the window shown in Figure 12-13. You interact with the Equation editor using the menus and the toolbar. The functions of the toolbar are shown in Table 12-4.

Under the toolbar are three panes that you use to create and display your equations. The Editing pane is the large empty box near the top of the window, just under the Equation Editor toolbar. You use this part of the window to type the text and numbers you want in the equation, and to insert formatting commands and codes for special characters. Everything in this pane will appear as plain, unformatted text.

Below the Editing pane is the Display pane. This is where Corel WordPerfect will display the formatted equation, showing the special character and symbols, in the proper spacing and size. The image in the Display pane does not update automatically as you enter the equation in the Editing pane. To see how the equation will appear in the document, click on the Redisplay button in the toolbar. Corel WordPerfect will display an error message if your formatting instructions are not complete.

Along the left of the window is the Equation palette. It is here that you select the commands, codes, functions, and symbols that tell Corel WordPerfect how to format

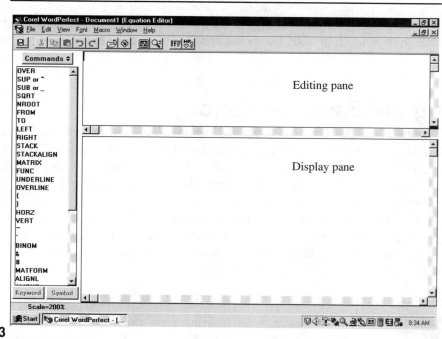

Equation
editor

FIGURE 12-13

Button	Function
Save As	Saves the equation in a separate file from the document
Cut	Places the selected portion of the equation into the Clipboard
Copy	Copies the selected portion of the equation into the Clipboard
Paste	Inserts the contents of the Clipboard at the position of the insertion point in the Editing pane
Undo	Cancels changes
Redo	Cancels an undo
Close	Closes the Equation editor
Insert Equation File	Recalls an equation from disk into the Equation Editor window
Redisplay	Updates the Display pane
Zoom Display	Displays the Zoom dialog box to select a display magnification
Equation Font	Displays a font dialog box for changing the font and point size of the displayed characters
Corel WordPerfect Characters	Displays the Corel WordPerfect Characters dialog box for inserting special characters

Equation
Toolbar

TABLE 12-4

the equation in the Display pane. The Equation palette has eight sections that you access from the pull-down list now labeled Commands. Pull down the list to display a set of characters or commands, and then double-click on the one you want to insert into the Editing pane. Here are the sections and what they do:

- *Commands* lets you select from the most common formats and symbols.
- *Large* displays popular mathematics symbols.
- *Symbols* includes many miscellaneous symbols.
- *Greek* offers Greek characters.

12

- *Arrows* lists various arrows, triangles, squares, and circles.

- *Sets* includes relational operators and set symbols.

- *Other* includes diacritical marks and ellipses.

- *Function* includes symbols for mathematical functions.

Some of your choices can be inserted into the Editing pane as keywords or symbols—they always appear as formatted symbols in the Display pane. To choose how you want Corel WordPerfect to insert items, click on either the Keyword or Symbol buttons under the Equation palette. You can usually also type the commands yourself, such as typing **sub** to create a subscript. You can also enter *variables*—characters or words that represent unknown values.

Here's a simple illustration of using the Equation editor.

1. Select Equation from the Graphics menu.

2. Click in the Editing pane.

3. Type **X~=~** and then click on Redisplay. The tilde character tells Corel WordPerfect to insert a space (the backward accent ['] stands for a quarter space), so the equation will appear as shown here:

$$X =$$

4. If the Command palette is not shown, switch to that set.

5. Double-click on SQRT, the square root command.

6. Type **Y OVER 2 SUB {-Z}**. This means to place the letter Y on a line over 2, and add a subscript –Z to the 2.

7. Click on Redisplay to see the completed equation, as shown here.

8. Click on the Close button in the toolbar and return to the document, inserting the equation into a graphic box using the equation box style.

$$X = \frac{\sqrt{Y}}{2_{-Z}}$$

9. You can now change the size and position of the box, add a caption, or customize the border and fill. Double-click on the equation if you want to edit it in the Equation editor.

Sharing Information

13

Corel WordPerfect lets you share information between it and other parts of the Corel WordPerfect Suite, and even with other Windows applications. Sharing information lets you create compound documents without having to retype information. A *compound document* is one that includes information from more than one application. For example, suppose you created a spreadsheet in Corel Quattro Pro, an organization chart in Corel Presentations, and a drawing in Windows Paint. You can add all of these items to your Corel WordPerfect document to create a professional-looking document. For instance, you don't need to retype the spreadsheet into a Corel WordPerfect table—you can just cut and paste it into Corel WordPerfect, or even open it directly in a document as a table.

Sharing information will also let you send a Corel WordPerfect form document, or name and address information in a Corel Quattro Pro or other spreadsheet, to a mailing list that you've created in Paradox. In fact, you can even link the database or spreadsheet with Corel WordPerfect so your document always has the most up-to-date information.

In Chapter 20 you will learn how to use cells from a Corel Quattro Pro spreadsheet in a Corel WordPerfect document. In this chapter, you will learn how to use Corel WordPerfect information with other applications, and how to import and link database and spreadsheet information. You will also learn how to open documents into Corel WordPerfect that have been created with other programs, and how to save your Corel WordPerfect documents in other formats.

Saving Files

While it is difficult to imagine why, not everyone uses Corel WordPerfect as their word processing program. If you have to share your files with one of these unfortunates, you can make it easier on them by saving your files in a format their program understands.

You should first save your document normally, in Corel WordPerfect's own format. Then follow these steps:

1. Select Save As from the File menu.

2. Pull down the As Type list. You'll see a list of formats that Corel WordPerfect can save your documents in.

3. Scroll the list and click on the format that you want to use.

4. Enter a filename, and then click on Save.

In addition to all previous Corel WordPerfect formats, you can select from the formats shown in Table 13-1. Notice that you can also save your document in a spreadsheet format, such as Corel Quattro Pro, Excel, and Lotus 1-2-3. When you choose Corel Quattro Pro, however, only tables in your document will be saved. Each table will become another page in the Corel Quattro Pro workbook, labeled Table A, Table B, and so on.

The next time you save the document, Corel WordPerfect will display a Save Format dialog box, asking you to confirm the format. You can select to save it in Corel WordPerfect format, in the original type, or click on Other to display the Save As dialog box.

 You can save your Corel WordPerfect documents, Corel Quattro Pro worksheets, and Corel Presentations slide shows as Envoy documents. See Chapter 24 for more information.

Opening Documents

In Corel WordPerfect, one of the quickest ways to use a file that you created with another program is simply to open it. You can open documents created in all of the formats that you can save them in, as well as these additional ones:

- Borland Sprint
- IA5
- QuickFinder Log
- Corel WordPerfect for the Macintosh
- WP Works

13

Application	Version
AmiPro	1.2 to 3.0
ANSI Windows	Text, generic word processing, and delimited text
ASCII DOS	Text, generic word processing, and delimited text
DisplayWrite	4.0 to 5.0
EDGAR	
Excel	3.0 to 4.0
HTML	
IBM DCA	RTF and FFT
Kermit 7-Bit Transfer	
Lotus 1-2-3	1.0 to 4.0
MS Word	5.4 and 5.5
MS Word For Windows	2 to 7
MultiMate	3.3 to 4.0, and Advantage 1.0 and 1.1
Navy DIF	Standard
OfficeWriter	6.0 to 6.2
Professional Write	1.0 to 2.2
Corel Quattro Pro for Windows	1.0, 5.0, and 6.0
RTF	
Spreadsheet DIF	
Volkswriter	4.0
Windows Write	
XyWrite III Plus	3.55 to 4.0
WordStar	3.3 to 7.0, and 2000 1 to 3

File Formats

■ **TABLE 13-1**

While the Open dialog box has a For Type list, it only contains the All Files (*.*) option and the default formats used by Corel WordPerfect. You don't see the other formats because in most cases you don't have to select a format when you open a file. Corel WordPerfect will automatically determine the type of file and do what it must to open it and display it on the screen. If it can't determine the file type, one of two boxes will appear. If you try to open a binary file, such as one with a COM, EXE, or DLL extension, the message "Unknown File Format" will appear. Click on OK to remove the message.

All Files (*.*)
WP Documents (*.wpd)
WP Templates (*.wpt)
WP Merge Data (*.dat)
WP Merge Forms (*.frm)
WP Macros (*.wcm)
Text Files (*.txt)
All Files (*.*)

If you try to open a text file, the Convert File Format dialog box will appear. You can then scroll through the Convert File Format From list and select the format.

ASCII and ANSI text files, by the way, can be opened using two methods. These text files have a carriage return and line feed code at the end of each line. These are the codes, abbreviated CR/LF, that tell the computer to move the insertion point to the start of the next line. You can select to open the document normally, which converts each CR/LF code to a hard carriage return, HRt; or you can select to convert each CR/LF to a soft carriage return, the SRt code. Selecting the SRt option will let you format the document as a series of paragraphs, but you will lose the original line breaks.

When you open a spreadsheet or database file, Corel WordPerfect will display a special dialog box. Refer to "Using Databases and Spreadsheets," later in this chapter.

Sharing Problem Documents

If may be possible that you have a document in a format that Corel WordPerfect cannot open, or you may be using a program whose format Corel WordPerfect cannot save in. All is not lost. Try to find an intermediate format that both programs can accept. Most programs, for example, have the option to save in ASCII text format. While you will lose your formatting by saving as ASCII text, at least you won't have to retype everything.

Sharing Information Through the Clipboard

If you do not want to use an entire document file from or in another application, you can cut/copy and paste information from one program to the other.

For example, suppose you want to copy some information from a Microsoft Word for Windows document to Corel WordPerfect. Follow these steps:

13

1. Open Corel WordPerfect and the document you want to insert the information into.

2. Open Word for Windows and the document containing the information.

3. Cut or copy the information in the Word for Windows document.

4. Switch to Corel WordPerfect.

5. Click on Paste.

You can also paste information from a DOS application. When you run a DOS program in Windows, it will appear in a DOS window with this toolbar:

To copy information from the DOS-application window, follow these steps:

1. Click on the Mark button in the DOS window toolbar.

2. Drag the mouse over the text you want to copy.

3. Click on the Copy button on the DOS window toolbar.

4. Switch to Corel WordPerfect and place the insertion point where you want to insert the text.

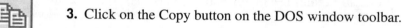

5. Click on the Paste button in the Corel WordPerfect toolbar.

You can also use the Clipboard to copy information within the DOS application itself. Mark and copy the text in the DOS window, place the cursor where you want the text to appear, and then click on the Paste button in the DOS window toolbar.

Creating Organization Charts

You can easily create organization charts in CorelFLOW and in Corel Presentations. Both programs are easy to use, but you still have to enter the information and create the structure showing the chain of command. A quicker way to create an organization chart in Corel Presentations is to type the chain of command as a Corel WordPerfect outline.

1. Start Corel WordPerfect.

2. Select Bullets&Numbers from the Insert menu.

3. Click on Paragraph Numbers in the Styles list, and then click on OK.

4. Enter the name of the top executive as paragraph number 1, and the immediate subordinate as paragraphs 2, 3, and so on.

5. Enter other levels as indented paragraphs, using TAB to move down a level and SHIFT+TAB to move up.

```
1.John Smith
2.William Watson
        a.Kate Jackson
        b.F. F. Majors
3.Steve Austin
4.William Kildair
        a.Ben Casey
        b.Horace Rumpole
```

6. Save the document.

7. Open or switch to Corel Presentations.

8. Insert an organization chart, as you will learn in Chapter 21.

9. Double-click on the chart.

10. Choose Import Outline from the Chart menu.

11. Select the file containing the organization, and then click on Insert.

Corel Presentations will form the organization chart using the text and structure of the outline, as shown in Figure 13-1.

 You can also save an organization chart as a Corel WordPerfect outline. See Chapter 21.

Embedding and Linking Information

Windows lets you insert information from other applications using two general techniques, *embedding* and *linking*.

13

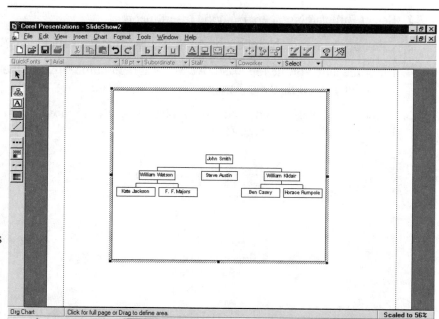

Corel
Presentations
organization
chart using
a Corel
WordPerfect
outline

FIGURE 13-1

When you embed information into an application, such as Corel WordPerfect, you are actually placing a complete copy of it in the document. You won't be able to edit or format the information using Corel WordPerfect commands because it is treated as one solid object. If you double-click on the object, however, Corel WordPerfect will perform these steps:

1. Start the application that you used to create the object.

2. Transfer a copy of the information from Corel WordPerfect to the application so you can edit the object in that application.

When you edit and close the application, the edited version will appear in Corel WordPerfect. However, there is no actual connection between the object's file on the disk and the copy of the object in the document. If you edit the object separately by opening it directly into the application, the copy of it in Corel WordPerfect will not be affected.

When you insert information using a link, however, there is a connection. When you double-click on the object in Corel WordPerfect, it will do this:

1. Start the application.

2. Open the original file on the disk in which the object is stored.

When you save the edited copy of the object, it will be updated in Corel WordPerfect as well. But because there is a link, you can also open the object directly with the application to edit it. The updated version will automatically appear in Corel WordPerfect.

There are several ways that you can embed and link information. One method is to use the Paste Special dialog box from the Corel WordPerfect Edit menu. You'll learn how to do that when we discuss using a Corel Quattro Pro spreadsheet in Corel WordPerfect in Chapter 20.

You can also embed and link information using the Object command from the Insert menu. To create and insert an embedded object, select Object from the Insert menu and click on Create New to see the options in Figure 13-2. The Object Type list contains all of the applications that are registered in Windows as usable as the source of an embedded object.

Select the application that you want to create the object, and then click on OK. Windows will start that application so that you can create the object.

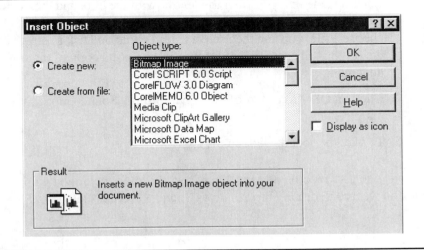

Embedding
a new object

FIGURE 13-2

13

If you already created the object, such as a drawing in Paint, click on the Create From File option in the Insert Object dialog box. Enter the path and name of the file, or use the Browse button to select it. To embed the object into the document, click on OK. To link the object, click on the Link check box and then on OK.

Multimedia Documents

By adding sound and video to a document, you can create an onscreen presentation, a document that comes alive to the reader. While sound and video clips can create very large document files, they can be effective. We'll look at some of the techniques that you can use.

Inserting a Sound Clip

You can insert or record a sound clip for either special effects or just as an annotation that can be played back at some later time. Corel WordPerfect can use sound files in either the WAV or MIDI formats, and you can even record WAV sound directly into the document.

To insert an existing sound file, follow these steps:

1. Select Sound from the Insert menu to see the Sound Clips dialog box.

2. Click on Insert to see the Insert Sound Clip into Document dialog box.

3. Enter a name that you want to identify with the clip, and then enter the path and name of the file, or use the Browse button to locate it. Once you choose a file, you can then select Link To File on Disk to create a link to the original file, or Store in Document to place a copy of the sound in the document.

4. Click on OK. Corel WordPerfect will insert a Sound Clip icon in the left margin.

5. To play the sound, click on the icon.

You can also record and save a new sound file. In the Sound Clips dialog box, click on Record to display the Windows Sound Recorder dialog box:

Click on the Record button, and then speak or sing into the microphone or play the sound you want to record. Choose Save from the File menu, and then Exit the Sound Recorder. Finally, insert the sound file as you just learned.

To play or delete any sound clip in the document, or edit its description, select Sound from the Insert menu to display the Sound Clips dialog box. Figure 13-3 shows the dialog box with several inserted files. To play a sound, click on its name in the list box and then click on the Play button. There are also buttons to stop, rewind, and fast forward the clip. The Length indicator shows how long the clip is; the Position indicator shows how far into the clip is the sound you are hearing.

If you want to access these same features later without redisplaying the dialog box, click on the Transcribe button. The dialog box will close, and you'll see a feature bar (shown in the following illustration) under the ruler. Click on the Sound Clip icon to hear the sound, and then use the feature bar buttons to replay, rewind, or fast forward it. Click on Close to remove the feature bar.

Select and
play sound
clips

FIGURE 13-3

13

Other Multimedia Files

To insert a sound, video, or other multimedia object into the document, select Object from the Insert menu, and then double-click on the Media Clip option. Corel WordPerfect will display the options shown in Figure 13-4. Click on Insert Clip to see the options shown here. Click on Video for Windows to insert a video clip, Sound or MIDI Sequencer to insert a sound clip, or CD Audio to insert a track from an audio CD in your CD drive. An icon or window for the inserted object will appear in the document. Click outside of the icon to return to the standard Corel WordPerfect window. To play the sound or view the video, double-click on the icon for the object in the document.

Using Databases and Spreadsheets

So far you've learned several ways to insert spreadsheet information into a document—you can cut and paste it through the Clipboard, or you can embed or link it using the Object command from the Insert menu.

 In Chapter 20 you will learn even more about using Corel Quattro Pro information in a Corel WordPerfect document.

You can also use information from a spreadsheet or database by importing it, or by creating a link through a process known as *Dynamic Data Exchange (DDE)*. When you import the information, you are placing a copy of it into the Corel WordPerfect document. When you create a DDE link, the information appears in your document, and you can format and edit it, but it is also linked with the original

Media Clip
feature bar

FIGURE 13-4

file on the disk. Changing the file will change the information in Corel WordPerfect as well. This differs from the link you learned about previously, which is called an *OLE link.* With an OLE link you cannot edit or format the information in Corel WordPerfect.

Using the import or DDE link technique, you have the choice of how you want to insert the spreadsheet or database information—as a Corel WordPerfect table, into tabular columns, or as a Corel WordPerfect merge file with merge codes. Inserting the information into either a table or merge file will let you then use the information as a data file for a merge operation. So, for example, you can send form letters to clients listed in a Paradox database or a Corel Quattro Pro worksheet.

IP: *Import or link a spreadsheet or database to use it as a data file for a merge.*

Follow these steps to import or link a spreadsheet or database file.

1. Select Spreadsheet/Database from the Insert menu.

2. Click on Import to import the information, or click on Create Link to link it. Corel WordPerfect will display either the Import or Create Data Link dialog box. Figure 13-5 shows the Create Data Link dialog box. The Import box is identical except for the name in the title bar, and the text box label Link As is replaced by Import As.

OTE: *Corel WordPerfect will display this same dialog box when you use the Open command to open a spreadsheet or database file.*

3. Pull down the Data Type list and choose Spreadsheet, if you want to use a spreadsheet file, or one of these database options: Clipper, dBase, FoxPro, Paradox, ODBC, ODBC (SQL), ASCII Delimited Text, and ANSI Delimited Text.

4. Pull down the Import As or Link As list, and choose how you want to insert the information: Table, Text (as tabular column), or as a Merge Data File.

5. Enter the path and name of the spreadsheet or database file in the Filename text box, or use the Browse icon to search for the file on your disk.

13

Create Data Link   [?] [X]

Data type: Spreadsheet ▲▼   OK

Link As: Table ▲▼   Cancel

Help

Filename: [   ] ☐

Named ranges:

[   ]

Range: [   ]

Create Link
dialog box

■ **FIGURE 13-5**

The procedure now differs if you are inserting spreadsheet or database information.

Using a Spreadsheet

If you are inserting information from a spreadsheet file, follow these steps:

1. Click in the Named Ranges box. Corel WordPerfect will display all of the named worksheet ranges, as well as the notation <spreadsheet> that represents the entire worksheet. The Range box will show the range of cells that contain data. If you named a spreadsheet that has information on more than one worksheet page in the file, you'll see a notation for each page:

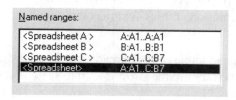

2. Click on the page you want to insert, or select <spreadsheet> to insert the entire worksheet file, or enter a specific range of cells in the Range text box.

3. Click on OK.

If you insert a workbook with multiple pages as tables, each will appear in a separate table. If you insert the workbook as a merge file, the pages will be combined into one large merge file.

Using a Database

When you insert a database file, the options in the Named Ranges list will be replaced by the Fields list. After you specify the database file and click in the Fields box, Corel WordPerfect will list all of the database field names:

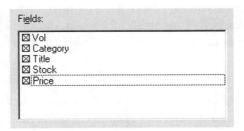

Deselect the check boxes for the fields that you do not want to insert, and select Use Field Names as Heading to place the field names as the row in the table. Click on OK to insert the information.

Updating Links

When you import the information, it appears just as any other Corel WordPerfect text. When you link it, however, Corel WordPerfect will indicate that it is indeed linked. This is an important reminder that you should update the information to retrieve the most current version of the data.

When you insert the information as a merge file, you'll see a link code at the file's beginning and end. When you insert the information in a table or as tabular columns, Corel WordPerfect will display the Start Link icon and the End Link icon at the beginning and end of the table:

13

Vol	Category	Title	Stock	Price
E11	Entertainment	Great Classical Composers	122	23.9
H32	History	Austrian Arms and Armor	450	35.95
T24	Travel	Great European Cathedrals	3	110.9
T35	Travel	Tibetan Adventures	4	35.75

To see the name of the file being linked, and the type of file, click on one of the icons. If you do not want the icons displayed, select Spreadsheet/Database from the Insert menu, click on Options, and deselect the Show Icons check box.

When you want to ensure that the document contains the most up-to-date information, select Spreadsheet/Database from the Insert menu, and click on Update. A dialog box will appear asking you to confirm that you want to update all of the linked objects in the document—select Yes or No. If you edited or formatted the information in Corel WordPerfect, however, your changes will be replaced by the data and formats in the linked file, just as if you were linking the information for the first time. To have all of your linked files update automatically when you open the document, select Spreadsheet/Database from the Insert menu, click on Options, and select the Update on Retrieve check box.

OTE: *To change the name of the file being linked and its format, select Edit Link from the Spreadsheet/Database submenu.*

PART

III

Corel Quattro Pro

Introducing
Corel Quattro Pro

14

Corel Quattro Pro lets you work with information in table format—neatly arranged rows and columns of numbers or text. Formatting capabilities let you design professional-looking tables, combining grid lines, colors, shadings, and special effects for maximum impact. Because the table is computerized, however, you can also perform mathematical and even complex statistical analysis quickly and easily. Don't let the words "mathematical" and "statistical" scare you off. You don't have to know anything about statistics or even much about mathematics to take advantage of the powers of Corel Quattro Pro.

How difficult is using Corel Quattro Pro? Not difficult at all. In most cases, all you need are one or more basic formulas that perform math using values in the table. You have to know when to add, subtract, multiply, and divide, not do the math yourself—Corel Quattro Pro does the actual math for you. In fact, in many cases, you can just click on a button, or select options from a list, and Corel Quattro Pro builds the formula for you.

What's It Used For?

Since you can easily create a table in Corel WordPerfect, you may be wondering why you need a separate program such as Corel Quattro Pro. Corel WordPerfect gives you just some basic capabilities to perform math and organize information in table format. Corel Quattro Pro specializes in it, as you'll see.

Financial Records

Use Corel Quattro Pro to create financial records and documents of all types. Produce budgets, reports, income statements, balance sheets, sales forecasts, projections, and most of the records that you need to maintain your business, household, or organization. Corel Quattro Pro makes it easy to create professional-looking printouts that will impress your stockholders, bankers, and accountant—perhaps even the IRS.

But Corel Quattro Pro is more than for good looks. It can help ensure that your numbers are accurate, even if you have to make last-minute changes. Suppose that after creating the quarterly budget, you realize that you've entered the wrong numbers in certain areas. If you created the budget on paper, you'd have to change the numbers and then recalculate and change all of the gross and net profit figures. Not so with Corel Quattro Pro. Just change the figures that you have to, and Corel Quattro Pro will use the simple formulas that you've entered to make the recalculations for you.

Business Forms

Use Corel Quattro Pro to create business forms of all types, such as invoices, statements, schedules, planners, and professional time and billing logs. Forms are often difficult to create in word processing programs but a snap in Corel Quattro Pro.

And don't imagine that we are talking about only blank forms. By adding simple formulas, ones that Corel Quattro Pro can even create for you, you can complete the forms on the screen. For example, how about an invoice that automatically computes the extended price of each item ordered, calculates the total, and adds tax and shipping charges, as shown in Figure 14-1? All you have to do is fill in a few items and then fax, e-mail, or print and mail it to your customer.

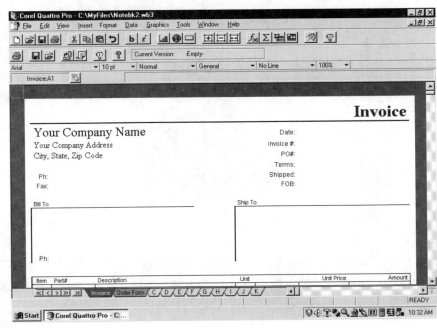

Using Corel Quattro Pro to create business forms of all types

FIGURE 14-1

14

Charts and Maps

Use Corel Quattro Pro to create eye-catching charts and maps directly from information that you've already entered. There is no need to retype the numbers. Just tell Corel Quattro Pro which part of your table contains the numbers you want to chart and where the chart should appear, and the program does the rest. If you want, you can choose the chart type and customize its design; otherwise, just sit back and let Corel Quattro Pro do the work. The chart in Figure 14-2, for instance, was created with a few clicks of the mouse from a quarterly budget table.

When your worksheet contains geographic information, such as sales per state or country, then create a map. You'll see at a glance where your strong sales areas are and where you need to concentrate your efforts. You can even overlay maps with major highways, major cities, and capitals.

For even greater impact, you can combine charts and graphs into slide Corel Presentations. Hook up your PC—even a laptop—to a projector, and you have a complete onscreen presentation for board or sales meetings.

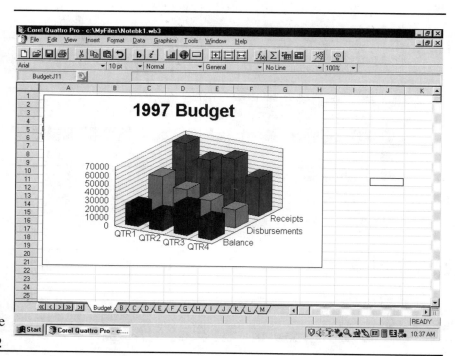

Creating graphs and charts with a few clicks of the mouse

FIGURE 14-2

You can share all of your worksheets, graphs, and maps with Corel WordPerfect to create compound documents.

Databases

Use Corel Quattro Pro to create databases for recording, finding, and analyzing information. Keep records of clients, employees, products, members, or any other item that you need to track and report.

A database is like an electronic version of an index card file or folders in your filing cabinet. With Corel Quattro Pro, you create the database in table format, each row of the table representing another item in the database, as shown in Figure 14-3. You can print reports, locate specific information when you want it, perform statistical analysis on your information, and even print graphs.

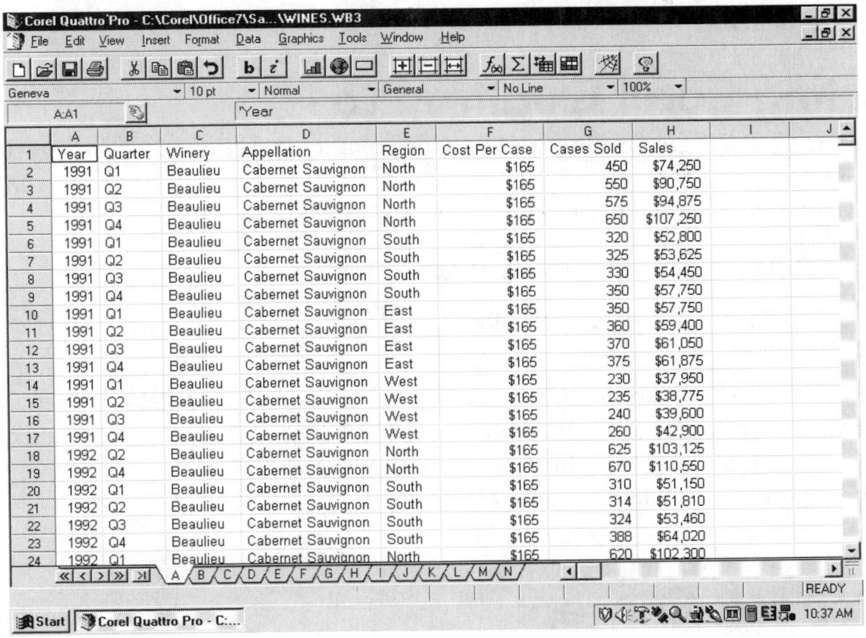

Using Corel Quattro Pro to record and analyze data

FIGURE 14-3

	Year	Quarter	Winery	Appellation	Region	Cost Per Case	Cases Sold	Sales
1	Year	Quarter	Winery	Appellation	Region	Cost Per Case	Cases Sold	Sales
2	1991	Q1	Beaulieu	Cabernet Sauvignon	North	$165	450	$74,250
3	1991	Q2	Beaulieu	Cabernet Sauvignon	North	$165	550	$90,750
4	1991	Q3	Beaulieu	Cabernet Sauvignon	North	$165	575	$94,875
5	1991	Q4	Beaulieu	Cabernet Sauvignon	North	$165	650	$107,250
6	1991	Q1	Beaulieu	Cabernet Sauvignon	South	$165	320	$52,800
7	1991	Q2	Beaulieu	Cabernet Sauvignon	South	$165	325	$53,625
8	1991	Q3	Beaulieu	Cabernet Sauvignon	South	$165	330	$54,450
9	1991	Q4	Beaulieu	Cabernet Sauvignon	South	$165	350	$57,750
10	1991	Q1	Beaulieu	Cabernet Sauvignon	East	$165	350	$57,750
11	1991	Q2	Beaulieu	Cabernet Sauvignon	East	$165	360	$59,400
12	1991	Q3	Beaulieu	Cabernet Sauvignon	East	$165	370	$61,050
13	1991	Q4	Beaulieu	Cabernet Sauvignon	East	$165	375	$61,875
14	1991	Q1	Beaulieu	Cabernet Sauvignon	West	$165	230	$37,950
15	1991	Q2	Beaulieu	Cabernet Sauvignon	West	$165	235	$38,775
16	1991	Q3	Beaulieu	Cabernet Sauvignon	West	$165	240	$39,600
17	1991	Q4	Beaulieu	Cabernet Sauvignon	West	$165	260	$42,900
18	1992	Q2	Beaulieu	Cabernet Sauvignon	North	$165	625	$103,125
19	1992	Q4	Beaulieu	Cabernet Sauvignon	North	$165	670	$110,550
20	1992	Q1	Beaulieu	Cabernet Sauvignon	South	$165	310	$51,150
21	1992	Q2	Beaulieu	Cabernet Sauvignon	South	$165	314	$51,810
22	1992	Q3	Beaulieu	Cabernet Sauvignon	South	$165	324	$53,460
23	1992	Q4	Beaulieu	Cabernet Sauvignon	South	$165	388	$64,020
24	1992	Q1	Beaulieu	Cabernet Sauvignon	North	$165	620	$102,300

14

Integrate IT! *You can use your Corel Quattro Pro database to create form letters in Corel WordPerfect, or transfer it to a database program such as Paradox or Microsoft Access. You can also move data in the other direction, importing information from a database program into Corel Quattro Pro to analyze or chart it.*

Solving Problems

The real jewel in the crown of Corel Quattro Pro, however, is its ability to solve what's known as "What if?" problems. What if costs increase by 5 percent? What if employees are given a raise? What if sales go down? What if inventory is increased?

Since Corel Quattro Pro can automatically recalculate the values in an entire table when you change even a single number, you can see the effects of that change in every place that it affects. Just change a value or two and then analyze the results.

Corel Quattro Pro even has special features for those tougher problems. You can have it solve a problem by automatically changing values itself—for example, to find the optimum combination of factors that give you the results you want. A feature called Scenario Manager even saves different combinations of results so you can switch back and forth between them as you attempt to make a decision.

Starting Corel Quattro Pro

Starting Corel Quattro Pro is as easy as pointing and clicking:

1. Click on the Start button in the Windows 95 taskbar.

2. Point to Corel Corel WordPerfect Suite 7.

3. Click on Corel Quattro Pro 7.

You can also start Corel Quattro Pro by double-clicking on its name in the Windows Explorer, or while surfing through folders from the My Computer icon on the desktop.

In a few moments the Corel Quattro Pro screen will appear with a blank notebook, as shown in Figure 14-4.

Notebook Concept

Before looking at the details of the Corel Quattro Pro screen, you should understand the concept of the *notebook*.

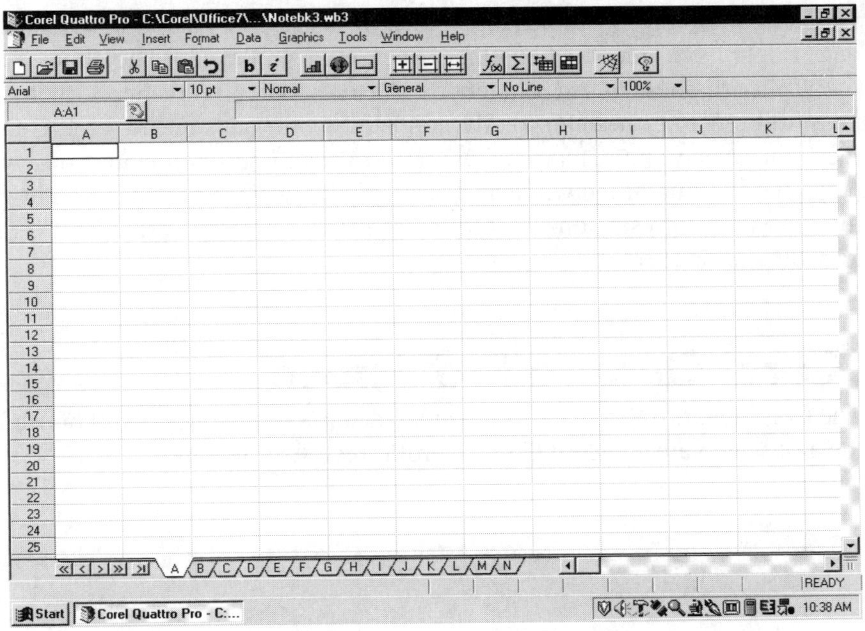

The Corel Quattro Pro screen

FIGURE 14-4

A notebook is a collection of pages, just like a notebook you'd carry to class or to a meeting. Most of these pages will contain worksheets—numbers, text, and formulas that make up the forms, financial reports, or databases that you create. Worksheets can also contain charts and graphs that illustrate the values elsewhere on the page. At the very end of the notebook is a special page called the *objects page*. This page stores copies of all of the charts and graphs in the notebook, as well as slide shows and maps. There are 256 worksheet pages plus the objects page.

What's the benefit of a notebook? With a notebook, you don't need a separate file for every worksheet you want to create. Your budget, for example, may include several related worksheets. Rather than store each one separately on your disk, create them on different pages in the same notebook. When you save the notebook, Corel Quattro Pro saves all of its worksheets, charts, and slide shows in one file on your disk. Then you can simply open one file to access all of the worksheets. If you need to transport the worksheet from the office to home, just copy the one file to a floppy disk or to a Windows 95 briefcase to synchronize the notebook between your home and office.

14

In addition, all of the pages in a notebook can share information in common. A worksheet can refer to values in another worksheet, so changing a number on one page might have an impact on other pages, even on the entire notebook.

While it is best to use a notebook to store related worksheets, there are other possibilities. You can enter totally unrelated worksheets in the same notebook. In fact, you can have more than one report, form, database, or other item on a worksheet page. If you think of the worksheet as a very large piece of paper, you can imagine dividing it up into sections to store more than one table. Corel Quattro Pro won't know the difference.

The Corel Quattro Pro Screen

The Corel Quattro Pro screen, shown labeled in Figure 14-5, is full of useful items, most of which are standard Corel WordPerfect Suite features.

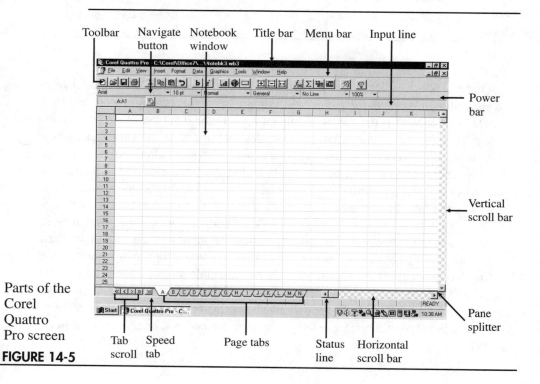

Parts of the Corel Quattro Pro screen

FIGURE 14-5

At the very top of the screen are the title bar, the menu bar, the Notebook toolbar, and the power bar. As expected, pointing to a button or bar area displays a QuickTip, so you can be sure you are choosing the correct command for the job you want to perform. Figure 14-6 shows the buttons in the Notebook toolbar, and Figure 14-7 shows the parts of the power bar. You'll learn more about these buttons later.

Below the power bar is the input line. Here is where you can edit the information that you add to the spreadsheet. On the left side of the input line is a box that shows your location in the worksheet. Next to that is the Navigate button, which will list block names that you can give to sections of the worksheet.

Under the input line is the Notebook window where the pages of the notebook will appear. If necessary, you can open more than one notebook at a time, as you'll learn in Chapter 17.

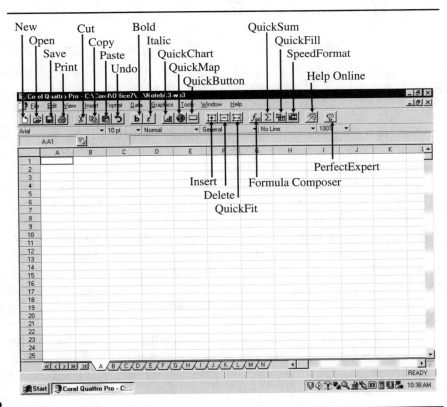

Notebook toolbar

FIGURE 14-6

14

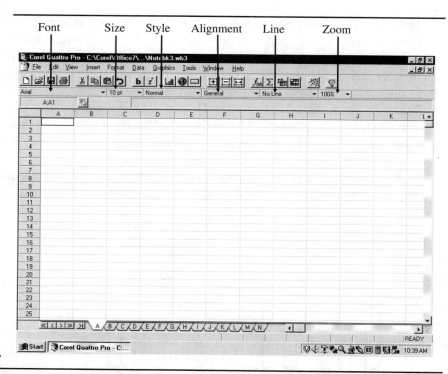

FIGURE 14-7

The first notebook you open during a Corel Quattro Pro session is called NOTEBK1.WB3, the second NOTEBK2.WB3, and so on. Of course, you can give the notebook your own name when you save it.

A worksheet is a series of numbered rows and lettered columns. The intersection of a row and a column is called a *cell*. For example, the cell in the top left corner is called cell A1 because it is in column A and row 1—the column letter always precedes the row number. The cell to its right is cell B1, and the cell below A1 is A2.

Even though you can't see much of the worksheet on the screen, worksheets are very large. There are 256 columns, numbered A through Z, then AA through AZ, BA through BZ, and so on up to column IV. There are 8192 rows. So each worksheet has a total of 2,097,152 cells, and the entire notebook—all 256 pages—has 536,870,912 cells!

The cell selected at the current time is called the *active* cell. This is the cell that will be affected by what you type or by the commands that you select. You can always tell the active cell because it is surrounded by the selector, a dark rectangle, and you'll see its cell reference—the row and column number it represents, as well as its page in the notebook—on the left side of the input line.

Below the Notebook window is the *status line*. This is where Corel Quattro Pro displays information about the notebook and certain indicators, such as when CAPS LOCK and NUM LOCK are turned on. The word "Ready" on the right of the line means that you are in Ready mode—Corel Quattro Pro is prepared to accept your commands. Most menu, toolbar, and power bar commands cannot be selected unless you are in Ready mode.

The *page tabs* let you change pages of the notebook. The 256 notebook pages are numbered like columns from A to IV, followed by the objects page. Just click on the tab for the worksheet that you want to display. After completing a table on the first worksheet page, for example, click on the next page tab—B—to start another worksheet. If necessary, you can delete pages and change their order.

OTE: *Use the tab number when you want to reference a cell on another page. For example, F:A1 represents cell A1 on page F of the notebook. The syntax is always* Page:Coordinates.

The *tab scroll* lets you scroll through the pages. This is useful when you're not sure which page you want to view, and it works like a scroll bar. Click on > to move to the next page, < to move to the previous, >> to move 13 pages forward, and << to move 13 pages backward.

Use the *speed tab* to quickly move from the page you are looking at to the end of the notebook, and vice versa. Click on the speed tab to see the objects page; click on it again to move back to the previous page you were viewing.

IP: *You can also move back and forth between the objects page and worksheet by choosing Spreadsheet or Objects Page from the View menu.*

The *scroll bars,* standard Windows controls, move you around the worksheet. Use the vertical scroll bar to move up and down, the horizontal scroll bar to move side to side. Remember, the Notebook window is a virtual window of the worksheet. While you see only a few rows and columns, the Corel Quattro Pro worksheet is really very large, so use the scroll bars to display other sections of the worksheet page.

14

As you drag the scroll box within the bar, Corel Quattro Pro will display a row or column indicator. When you drag the horizontal scroll box, it will show the letter of the column that will be at the far left when you release the mouse. When you drag the vertical scroll box, it will show the number of the row that will be at the top of the page.

At the lower-right corner of the worksheet—right where the scroll bars meet—is the *pane splitter.* This lets you divide the worksheet into two or more separate panes, or sections. You can view different parts of the worksheet in each page, or even different tables or charts that share the same worksheet page.

Changing Toolbars

Like other Corel Corel WordPerfect suite applications, Corel Quattro Pro includes a number of toolbars that you can use to perform common functions. To choose one, right-click on the displayed toolbar to see a QuickMenu of other available toolbars. Click on the bar that you want to replace the current one.

To display more than one toolbar, choose Preferences from the QuickMenu or select Toolbars from the View menu to see the dialog box shown in Figure 14-8. Click on the check boxes for the toolbars that you want to display—they will appear onscreen immediately—and then click on Close.

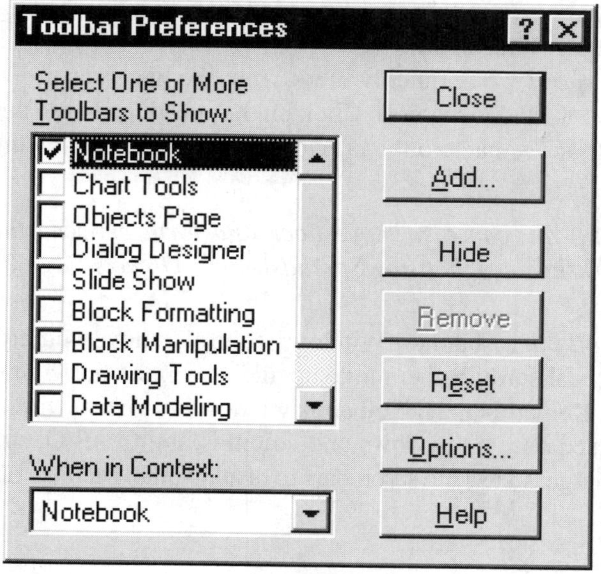

Selecting
the toolbars
to display

FIGURE 14-8

Moving Around the Worksheet

To create a worksheet, you'll have to move from cell to cell to enter or edit information or to see the results of your actions. Using the mouse, click in the cell that you want to enter information into, edit, or format. Use the scroll bars if necessary to bring the cell into view.

Using the keyboard, move around the worksheet using the keystrokes shown in Table 14-1. Pressing ENTER does not move from cell to cell, as you will soon learn.

To move to a specific cell, pull down the Edit menu and select Go To to see the dialog box shown in Figure 14-9. Type the cell reference, including the page letter if it is not on the current page, and click on OK.

Keystroke	Direction
LEFT ARROW	One cell left
RIGHT ARROW	One cell right
UP ARROW	One row up
DOWN ARROW	One row down
CTRL+PGDN	Next page
CTRL+PGUP	Previous page
PGUP	One screen up
PGDN	One screen down
HOME	To cell A1
CTRL+HOME	Cell A1 of the first page
END+HOME	To the lower-right nonblank corner
END+CTRL+HOME	To the last nonblank cell in the notebook
END+arrow key	To the next nonblank cell in the direction of the arrow
TAB	One cell right
SHIFT+TAB	One cell left
CTRL+LEFT ARROW	One screen left
CTRL+RIGHT ARROW	One screen right

Keystrokes for Moving in a Worksheet

TABLE 14-1

14

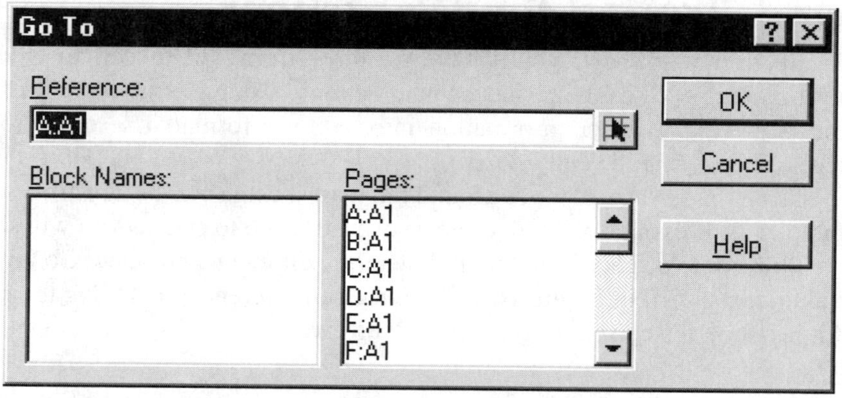

Go To   ? ✕

Reference:
A:A1

OK

Cancel

Block Names: Pages:

A:A1
B:A1
C:A1
D:A1
E:A1
F:A1

Help

Using the
Go To
command
to move to a
specific cell

FIGURE 14-9

Selecting Cells

To perform an action on a cell, you must select it. To select a single cell, just click on it. This makes it the active cell and selects it at the same time. When you make a cell active, whatever is in the cell will also appear in the input line.

There are many actions that you'll want to perform on more than one cell. Groups of selected cells are called *blocks*. To select a block of cells, point to a cell in one corner of the block, hold down the mouse button, and drag to the opposite corner. As you drag the mouse, the cells in the block will become highlighted, with a black background. The first cell you selected, however, will just be surrounded by a border, called the *selector,* letting you know that it was the starting point of the block.

OTE: *If the mouse pointer changes to a hand, and the selected cell becomes bordered with yellow, then you've held down the mouse button too long before dragging. This means Corel Quattro Pro has shifted into Drag-and-Drop mode for moving cells. Just release the mouse button and start over. See Chapter 16, for more details on drag-and-drop.*

To select an entire row, point to the row letter so the mouse pointer appears as a right-pointing arrow and then click. To select an entire column, point to the column letter so the mouse pointer appears as a down-pointing arrow and then click. Drag over row letters with the right-pointing arrow, or over column numbers with the down pointing arrow, to select adjacent rows or columns.

Notice that there is an empty shaded cell in the very upper-left corner of the worksheet. This is the Select All button—click on it to select the entire worksheet page.

Using basic Windows techniques, you can also select cells, rows, and columns that are not adjacent to each other. Hold down the CTRL key and click on the cells, rows, or columns that you want to select. With the CTRL key down, Corel Quattro Pro will not deselect sections already highlighted when you click elsewhere.

Many Corel Quattro Pro functions refer to a block even though they also act upon a single selected cell. So throughout this part of the book, we'll use the term "block" to refer to any number of selected cells, rows, and columns. When an instruction says to select a block, it means select any number of cells that you want to work with, even if it's only a single cell.

Designating Block References

You reference a single cell by its row and column coordinates. To refer to a block, you designate the starting and ending cell references of the group. If the cells are all in one row or column, just use the two end cells in the format A1..A8. In this example, the block includes eight cells—A1, A2, A3, A4, A5, A6, A7, and A8.

If the cells are in more than one row or column, reference any two cells in opposite corners. For example, the reference A1..B5 includes the ten cells A1 through A5, and B1 through B5 as shown here:

	A	B	C
1			
2			
3			
4			
5			
6			

When you type a block reference, you can type a single period between the cells. Corel Quattro Pro will insert the second period when you accept the entry. In addition, you can use any opposite cells. Traditionally, block references use the cell in the upper-left and lower-right corners, or the first and last cells if they are all in a row or column. You can actually enter the cells in any order, such as the lower-left and upper-right corners of a block, as in A5.C1. When you accept the entry, Corel Quattro Pro will rewrite the reference in the traditional way for you.

A block reference can also include noncontiguous cells, that is, cells that are not next to each other. Reference single cells by separating them with commas, as in A2,B4,C10. Include both types of references using the format A1.A10,C3,D5. This refers to the cells in the range A1 through A10, as well as cells C3 and D5.

Pointing to Cells in Dialog Boxes

Many dialog boxes perform a function on a block of cells. In some cases you can select the block of cells before opening the dialog box and the block reference will appear automatically. If the block is incorrect, or you did not select it beforehand, you can change the reference by typing the block coordinates.

In most cases there will also be a Point Mode button, as shown here:

You use Point mode to temporarily leave the dialog box to select the block of cells, rather than type in their references. Here's how:

1. Click in the text box where you want to insert a range of cells.

2. Click on the Point Mode button. Corel Quattro Pro will reduce the dialog box to two lines—the title bar and a line showing the range the box will act upon—and move it up so you can see the worksheet cells.

3. Drag over the cells that you want to reference or click on a single cell to reference it. To point to a block on another page, click on the page tab and then drag over the cells. As you select the cell, the block reference will appear in the range indicator.

4. When the range is correct, release the mouse button, then click on the Maximize button in the dialog box's title bar to redisplay it.

If the cells you want to reference are not contiguous, enter a comma after clicking or dragging on one cell or block, then click or drag on the next cell or block. The reference cells will be separated by commas in the dialog box.

IP: *If you can see the start of the block in the background of the dialog box, just point to it and hold down the mouse button. Corel Quattro Pro will automatically minimize the dialog box and then redisplay it when you release the mouse button.*

Selecting 3-D Blocks

A 3-D block is a block of cells selected on more than one consecutive notebook page. For example, suppose you have the budgets for the last four years on separate pages of the notebook, one year per page occupying the same area on each page. You can apply the same formats to every page at one time by selecting them as one block—a 3-D block.

To select a 3-D block, start by selecting the cell or cells on the first page you want to include. Then hold down the SHIFT key while you click on the tab for the last page you want to include. Corel Quattro Pro will display a black line under the tabs indicating that the 3-D block extends across those pages. While the line appears under the tabs, perform the function that you want to apply to the selected group.

 **OTE:** *You cannot use this type of 3-D block to enter text into all of the cells, although you can use it with QuickFill. See Chapter 15 for more information.*

The 3-D block is temporary; it remains in force only until you click on another cell. You can create a more permanent 3-D block by using a group, as you'll learn in Chapter 17.

Object Inspector

Everything in Corel Quattro Pro is called an *object*. To change an object's properties (one or more of its characteristics), point to it, click the right mouse button, and choose the Properties option at the bottom of the QuickMenu. You'll see a dialog box with several pages, each representing a classification of properties that you can change.

Click on the tab for the properties you want to set, and make your selections. Corel Quattro Pro will change the color of the tab title to remind you that you've already used that tab. When you close the dialog box, your selections will be applied.

14

- To set the properties for the selected block, even if it is a single cell, right-click on the block and choose Block Properties from the QuickMenu.

- To set the properties of the entire page, just right-click on the page tab. This will display the dialog box without first displaying a QuickMenu.

- To set properties for the entire notebook, restore the notebook so it appears in its own window, right-click on the title bar, and choose Active Notebook Properties from the QuickMenu.

- To customize Corel Quattro Pro itself, right-click on the Corel Quattro Pro title bar and choose Application Properties, or choose Preferences from the Edit menu.

You'll learn about properties later in Chapter 16.

Changing the Magnification

If your worksheet is large, then you may spend a lot of time scrolling to see certain sections. One way to avoid scrolling is to reduce the displayed magnification. You'll be able to see more cells on the screen, although they will be smaller and may be difficult to read. You can also enlarge the magnification to make cells appear larger—although you will see less of them.

To quickly change magnification, pull down the Zoom list in the power bar to see the options 25%, 50%, 75%, 80%, 90%, 100%, 125%, 150%, 200%, and Selection. Click on the desired setting, or choose Selection to have a selected block fill the screen. The setting applies only to the current page, not to other pages in the notebook.

You have more control over changing magnification using the Zoom dialog box. Select Zoom from the View menu to see the dialog box shown in Figure 14-10. Click on the desired magnification, or click on Custom and enter another setting. Click on Notebook to set the view for every page in the notebook.

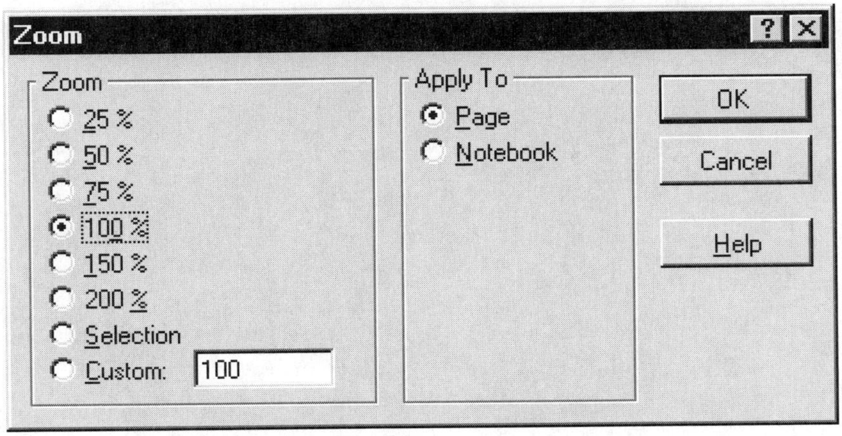

Using
Zoom to
enlarge or
reduce the
display

FIGURE 14-10

Getting Help

The Help system in Corel Quattro Pro works just about the same as it does in Corel WordPerfect. The Help Topics dialog box contains the Contents, Index, and Find tabs. You can also use Ask PerfectExpert to answer your questions and Help Online to go directly to Corel over the Internet or CompuServe.

14

Creating a Worksheet

15

Creating a worksheet is easy if you follow a few basic steps. Most worksheets contain titles, labels, and values. The titles, normally at the top of the worksheet page, explain the purpose of the worksheet, just like a title on a report. Labels are text that explain what the numbers in the other cells represent. These are usually column and row headings, but text can appear anywhere in a worksheet. Values are numbers, formulas, or functions that display information or calculate results.

Basic Principles

To enter information into a cell, make the cell active by clicking on it or moving to it using the keyboard, and then type. When you start typing, the insertion point will appear in the cell, whatever you type will appear in the input line, and you'll see four additional boxes, as shown here:

Clicking on the box with the @ symbol will list Corel Quattro Pro's built-in functions; clicking on the box with the braces will list macros.

The box with the X is called the Cancel box. Click on this box, or press the ESC key, if you change your mind and want to start all over again. The box with the check mark is called the Enter box. Click on this box or press the ENTER key to accept your entry and enter it into the cell. You can also accept your entry and move to another cell at the same time by pressing an arrow key, TAB, or SHIFT+TAB. Pressing ENTER accepts the entry but does not move to another cell.

Before you cancel or accept the entry, you can edit it by pressing the BACKSPACE or DELETE keys, or by moving the insertion point with the arrow keys. Edit the contents as you would using a word processing program. The basic procedure for entering information into a cell is as follows:

1. Click in the cell to make it active.

2. Type the information you want in the cell.

3. Click on the Enter box—the box with the check mark—or press ENTER.

When you are entering or editing information in a cell, the power bar will be dimmed and most of the toolbar and menu commands will be inactive. The word "Ready" in the status bar will be replaced by the word "Label," "Value," or "Edit," depending on the kind of information you are typing or if you are editing the contents of the cell. In order to use the features of the menu, tool, and power bars again, you must accept or cancel the entry to return to Ready mode.

Entering Text

Corel Quattro Pro treats text differently from numbers and distinguishes the two by the first character that you type. This difference is important because Corel Quattro Pro can perform math operations only on numbers, and it aligns text and numbers differently in the cells.

If you start a cell entry with a letter, Corel Quattro Pro assumes you are typing text and displays the word "Label" on the right end of the status line. When you click on the ENTER key, or press ENTER, the text starts on the left side of the cell, the default format for text.

To fill a cell with repeating characters, start with the backslash. Typing *, for example, will fill the cell with asterisks; entering \12 will repeat the characters "12" across the cell.

Aligning Text in Cells

You can change the alignment of information in a cell by using the power bar or by starting your entry with a special formatting character.

The power bar is quick and convenient, but because it is dimmed while you are entering data in a cell, you need to select the alignment before you start typing or after you accept the entry. To choose or change alignment, follow these steps:

1. Click in the cell that you want to format.

2. Pull down the Align section of the power bar.

3. Select General (for the default setting), Left, Center, or Right.

 **EMEMBER:**   *When you click in a cell, the power bar will display the alignment and other formats applied to it.*

You can also change alignment using a special formatting character as the first character of the entry. To center a label in the cell, start it with the caret (^) symbol, as in ^Net. When you accept the entry, the caret in the cell will disappear, and Corel Quattro Pro will center the text. To align text on the right of the cell, start with a quotation mark (").

If you actually want to start the label with a caret or quotation mark, as in "Swifty" Lazar, enter it as '"Swifty" Lazar. Corel Quattro Pro uses the apostrophe to align the entry on the left, inserting the opening quotation mark rather than using it as an alignment command.

The apostrophe is also useful when you want to insert labels that contain all numeric characters, such as years like 1997. It tells Corel Quattro Pro that you are entering a label, to align it on the left, and not to use it in a formula if you accidentally include it as a reference.

You do not have to use the apostrophe, however, when entering social security and phone numbers. If you just type a phone number, such as 555-1234, Corel Quattro Pro will display the word "Value" in the status bar, as it does when you enter numbers, but it will display the entry exactly as you enter it. It will not subtract 1234 from 555, as it would if this were a math operation.

Remember that the apostrophe, quotation mark, and caret characters will not appear in the cell unless you are editing it, but they will appear when on the input line when the cell is active. This is an important concept to understand. What you see in the cell is the displayed results of what is in the input line. The input line shows the actual contents stored in the worksheet. If the worksheet contains ^Title, the cell displays the word "Title" centered. This concept is even more important when you are working with formulas and functions.

Centering Across Cells

A title often looks better centered across the page, and it is no different with Corel Quattro Pro. Rather than trying to center a title by placing it in a column, use the Block Center function. This automatically centers text across the group of cells that you select.

Start by entering the text in the leftmost cell of the block. For example, if you want to center a title across the page, use the following steps:

1. Enter the title in cell A1.

2. Drag it from cell A1 to the end of the page. Using the default column width and orientation, cell H1 will be last on the page.

3. Pull down the Alignment button on the power bar and select Center Across Block.

	A	B	C	D	E	F	G	H	I	J	K	L
1					My Company							
2												
3												
4												
5												
6												
7												

IP: *It is best to wait until you have finished adjusting the width of columns before centering text across a block. If you center first and then change column width, the text may no longer appear centered.*

Wide Text Entries

If you type more characters than will fit in the cell, Corel Quattro Pro will run them into adjacent blank cells. If an adjacent cell has an entry of its own, however, Corel Quattro Pro will display only as many characters as will fit. Don't worry; the full entry is actually stored in the worksheet, and it will appear in the input line when the cell is active. Again, the input line shows the real contents of the worksheet; the cell shows only what can be displayed.

IP: *To display the full entry, you have to widen the cell or reduce the font size.*

Entering Numbers

To enter a number into a cell, start the entry with a number, a plus sign, or a minus sign. Corel Quattro Pro displays the word "Value" on the status line to indicate it recognizes your entry as numeric. When you accept the entry, Corel Quattro Pro will align it on the right side of the cell. You can later change its alignment using the power bar.

OTE: *Do not use commas when entering numbers. If you start with a dollar sign ($), Corel Quattro Pro assumes you are typing a value.*

By default, numbers appear without *trailing zeros,* zeros that come at the end of a number following the decimal point. If you enter 12.10, for example, Corel Quattro Pro will display 12.1. If you enter 12.00, Corel Quattro Pro will display 12.

If you type more characters than will fit in the cell, Corel Quattro Pro will display the number in exponential format or as a series of asterisks in their place. It does not run long numbers into adjacent cells as it does text. To display the number, you have to widen the column width, reduce the font being used, or change its format.

Editing Cell Contents

Once you accept an entry, typing something else in the same cell erases its current contents. This is convenient if you enter the wrong number, for example, and want to quickly correct your mistake. Just move back to the same cell and type the new entry. This is not convenient, however, if you don't want to erase the entire entry, only to edit a long line of text or a complex formula.

You can edit the contents of a cell either in the input line or the cell itself. To edit in the input line, make the cell active and then click on the input line. The insertion point will appear where you click. To edit in the cell, double-click on it or make it active and then press F2.

In either case, the word "Edit" appears in the status bar, and you may now delete and insert text and numbers, just as you would in a word processing program. Once in Edit mode, you can switch between the input line and the cell by clicking where you want to work.

In Edit mode, by the way, the TAB, DOWN ARROW, and RIGHT ARROW keys will not work. Press F2 to exit Edit mode, or accept or cancel your entry as usual. If you change your mind about editing the entry, just press ESC or click on the Cancel box to retain the cell's original contents.

Entering Formulas

The real power of a worksheet comes from its ability to recalculate values as you change the contents of cells. This is achieved by using formulas whenever possible. A *formula* is a mathematical operation that uses any combination of cell references and actual values. You can use a formula to simply perform math, such as entering

+106/3 to display the result of the calculation, but the most important use of formulas is to reference other cells.

You must start every formula with a plus or equal sign even if it does not contain cell references. This tells Corel Quattro Pro that you want it to calculate and display results. Corel Quattro Pro will change the starting equal sign to a plus sign when you accept the entry.

When you want to refer to the value in some other cell, just enter its cell reference. For example, the formula to subtract whatever is in cell A1 from what is in cell A2 is +A2–A1. When you enter the formula, Corel Quattro Pro will calculate the math and display the result in the cell. If you later change the value in either cell A1 or A2, Corel Quattro Pro will recalculate the value and display the new result.

OTE: *Corel Quattro Pro does not perform the calculation until you accept the change in the cell.*

IP: *It is a common beginner's mistake to forget the plus sign. If you type a formula and the formula rather than the results appears in the cell, you forgot the plus sign.*

Even though you see the *results* of the formula in the cell, the worksheet actually contains the formula. When you make the cell active, you'll see the results of the calculation in the cell but the formula itself in the input line.

As a general rule of thumb, use cell references wherever you can in a worksheet—wherever you are performing math using the contents of other cells. For example, suppose you have the worksheet shown in Figure 15-1. The gross pay could have been calculated using the values themselves, as in +40*15.65. But if you have to change either the pay rate or the number of hours worked, you'd need to reenter the value itself and retype the formula with the new value. If you used cell references, +D5*D4, you'd only need to change the value; Corel Quattro Pro would recalculate the formula for you.

IP: *If you need to use the same value in more than one cell, enter it once and reference its cell number elsewhere, as in +B2.*

You can also reference a cell on another page of the worksheet using the format *Tab:ColumnRow*, as illustrated by the cell reference on the left of the input line. For

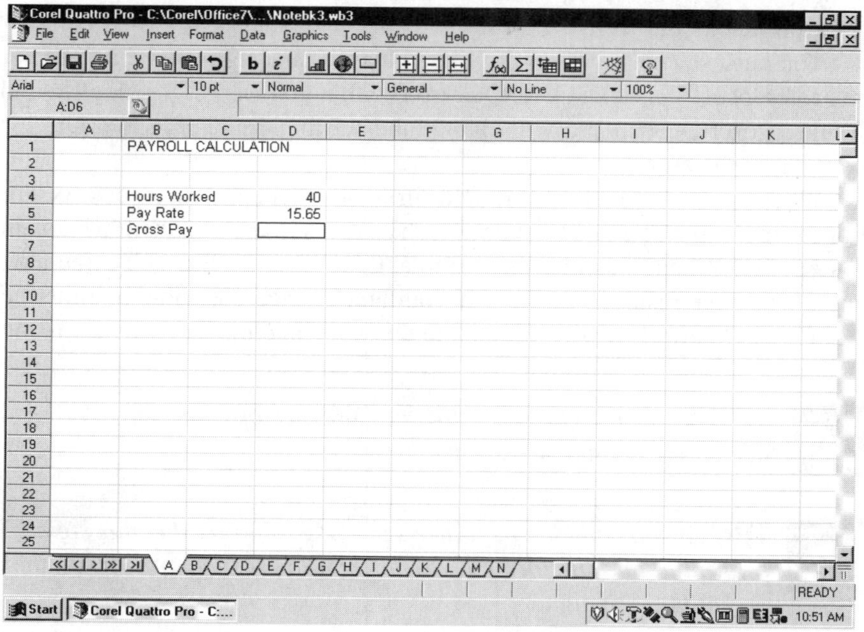

Corel Quattro Pro - C:\Corel\Office7\...\Notebk3.wb3

File Edit View Insert Format Data Graphics Tools Window Help

Arial — 10 pt — Normal — General — No Line — 100% —

A:D6

	A	B	C	D	E	F	G	H	I	J	K	L
1		PAYROLL CALCULATION										
2												
3												
4		Hours Worked		40								
5		Pay Rate		15.65								
6		Gross Pay										
7												
8												
9												
10												
11												
12												
13												
14												
15												
16												
17												
18												
19												
20												
21												
22												
23												
24												
25												

A / B / C / D / E / F / G / H / I / J / K / L / M / N /

READY

Start   Corel Quattro Pro - C:...   10:51 AM

Worksheet for calculating gross pay

FIGURE 15-1

example, B:A1 refers to cell A1 on page B of the notebook. To refer to a cell in another notebook, use the syntax [*Notebook_name*]*Cell*.

Integrate IT! *You can add your Corel Quattro Pro worksheet to a Corel WordPerfect document with a link. Using a link ensures that the Corel WordPerfect document is updated whenever the Corel Quattro Pro worksheet is recalculated.*

Precedence of Operators

When typing formulas, remember "My Dear Aunt Sally," a memory helper for Multiplication-Division-Addition-Subtraction. Corel Quattro Pro, and almost every similar program, does not perform math in the exact order of operators from left to right. Instead, it scans the entire formula, giving precedence to certain operators over others. "My Dear Aunt Sally" means that multiplication and division are performed first (whatever order they are in) and then addition and subtraction.

The most common example of this is computing an average. If you enter the formula +100+100+100/3 (using the values or their cells references), Corel Quattro Pro will display the result as 233.3333. It first divides 100 by 3 and then adds 100 twice.

To perform the calculation correctly, use parentheses to force Corel Quattro Pro to follow a different order, such as (100+100+100)/3. Notice that you can start a formula with an opening parenthesis without using a plus sign. Corel Quattro Pro assumes that entries starting with the "(" character are values.

Automatic Parentheses Matching

You can use more than one level of parentheses, if needed, with complex formulas. You must however, have a closing parenthesis for every opening parenthesis. To help you out, Corel Quattro Pro has a parenthesis matching feature. As you enter a formula, parentheses will appear in black when they are unmatched. When you type a closing parentheses, the pair will change color.

Before accepting complex formulas, scan for black, unmatched parentheses. If you find any, check your formula carefully. You either need to add or delete a parenthesis to have matching pairs, while still performing the math in the order desired. Table 15-1 lists the operators by their order of precedence.

Operator	Function
^	Power of
−, +	Used to denote negative or positive
*, /	Multiplication and division
+, −	Addition and subtraction
>=	Greater than or equal to
<=	Less than or equal to
<, >	Less than, and greater than
=, <>	Equal, and not equal
#NOT#	Logical NOT operation
#AND#, #OR#	Logical AND, and logical OR operations
&	String concatenation

Operators by Their Order of Precedence

TABLE 15-1

Pointing to Reference Cells

Making sure you have the correct cell reference is important, so rather than type the entry into a formula, you can point to it. This places the reference to the cell in the input line. To point to a cell, just click in it. To point to a block, drag over the cells.

For example, create the simple worksheet shown in Figure 15-1. To calculate the employee's gross pay, you need to multiply the number of hours in cell D4 times the pay rate in cell D5. You could do this by typing the formula +D4*D5. Instead of typing the cell references, however, point to them using these steps:

1. Click on cell D6 to make it active.

2. Press the = key to enter the Value mode.

3. Click on cell D4. Corel Quattro Pro inserts the cell reference into the active cell so it appears as = D4.

4. Press the * key to enter the multiplication operator.

5. Click in cell D5 to enter its reference into the formula.

6. Press ENTER to accept the entry.

You can also use this technique to reference a cell or block of cells in another page of the notebook. When you want to point to the cell, click on the tab of the page where it is located, and then select the block. As soon as you enter the next operator, or accept or cancel the entry, Corel Quattro Pro will switch back to the original page.

 OTE: *To point to noncontiguous blocks, separate each with a comma in the input line.*

Formatting Numbers

The default format displays numbers without trailing zeros. You can easily change the format of numbers by pulling down the Style list in the power bar to see the options shown here:

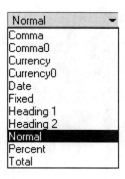

Select from the style list either before you start typing in the cell or after you've accepted the entry. Once you start typing, the power bar will be dimmed. The date and heading styles are not used for numbers, but here's how the number 1234.50 will appear in each of the numeric styles:

1		
2	Normal	1234.5
3	Comma	1,235.50
4	Comma0	1,237
5	Currency0	$1,237.50
6	Fixed	$1,239
7	Percent	123950.00%
8	Total	1240.5
9		

The total style does not change how the numbers appear but inserts a double line on the top of the cell. Choose a number format first, and then click on the total style to add a line to it.

Both Comma0 and Currency0 display no decimal places. The Fixed style uses a set number of decimals that you can designate using the Block Properties.

Entering Dates

In addition to text and values, a cell can contain a date or a time. Dates and times are treated as values because Corel Quattro Pro can perform calculations on them, such as figuring the number of days between two dates. To be used in calculations, the date or time must be entered in one of the formats that Corel Quattro Pro recognizes.

Enter the date in any of these formats:

DD-MMM-YY	11-Nov-97
DD-MMM	11-Nov
MMM-YY	Nov-97
MM/DD/YY	11/16/97
MM/DD	11/16

The last two formats are accepted as the default Long International and Short International date formats of Corel Quattro Pro. You can change these settings to accept other formats by changing the Application Properties.

Enter times in either of these formats:

HH:MM:SS AM/PM	04:12:30 AM
HH:MM AM/PM	04:30 AM

You can also select a Long International and Short International time format using the Application Properties.

When you accept a date or time, Corel Quattro Pro does two things. First, it adds leading zeros to single-digit months, days, hours, and minutes, for example, changing 1/1/97 to 01/01/97. If you do not enter PM, or enter time in 24-hour format, Corel Quattro Pro assumes times are AM.

Corel Quattro Pro also displays in the input line a serial number that represents the date or time. The serial numbers for dates range from –109,571 for January 1, 1600, to 474,816 for December 31, 3199. December 30, 1899, is represented by serial number 0. The serial number for a time is a decimal between 0.000 for the stroke of midnight and 0.99999 for one second before midnight the next day.

Corel Quattro Pro uses the serial numbers to perform math operations. To calculate the number of days between two dates, for example, just subtract the cell reference of the first date from the last date, such as +B6–B3. The number that appears is the difference between their serial numbers.

 IP: *You can use the Block Properties to force a cell to only accept date formats.*

Totaling Numbers Using QuickSum

One of the most typical uses for a formula is to total a series of numbers in a column or row. This is such a common task that Corel Quattro Pro gives it its own button on the toolbar, the QuickSum button.

If the values in a column are contiguous—that is, there are no blank cells between them—click in the blank cell below the last value and then on the QuickSum button. If the values are a row, with no blank cells below them, click on the blank cell after the last value and then on QuickSum. Corel Quattro Pro will calculate and display the total of the cells above (or to the left) of the active cell.

When the cells are not contiguous, select the cells first, including the blank cell below or to the right of the series, and then click on QuickSum. The total will appear in the blank cell. To create the total, Corel Quattro Pro uses the built-in function @SUM that you'll see in the input line. The function uses a range reference, citing the first and last cells in the group to be added, such as @SUM(A1..A12).

OTE: *All functions begin with the @ symbol.*

Always check the range reference, especially when you did not select the cells first, to confirm that the correct cells have been included. If the range is incorrect, edit it or point to the range using these steps:

1. Make the cell containing the function active.

2. Click in the input line.

3. Delete the range reference, leaving the insertion point between the two parentheses.

4. Drag over the range in the worksheet.

5. Accept the entry.

If Corel Quattro Pro displays the message "No Values To Sum" when you click on QuickSum, then it cannot determine the range you want to add, the cells are blank, or they contain labels instead of values. Check your work and try again.

You can calculate totals for several rows and columns of numbers at one time. The selection in Figure 15-2, for instance, will calculate totals for the rows and for the columns, as well as a grand total in cell F10.

Entering Data with QuickFill

In many instances, row and column labels are a series of sequential entries, such as the months of the year or incrementing numbers. These types of entries are so common that Corel Quattro Pro gives you QuickFill, a way of entering a sequence without typing the entire series yourself. This works as follows:

1. Enter the first one or two of the series. These are called the *seed values.*

2. Select the seed values, and the remaining cells in the row, column, or block that you want to fill with the remaining sequence.

3. Click on the QuickFill button, and Corel Quattro Pro will complete the range for you.

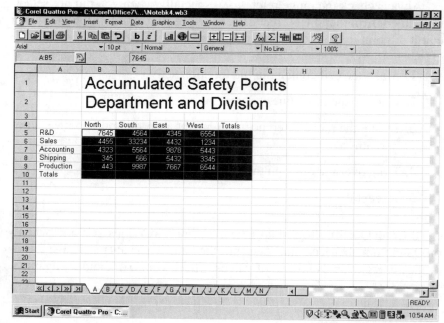

Selecting cells to total rows and columns and create a grand total in one step

FIGURE 15-2

OTE: *You can also right-click and select QuickFill from the QuickMenu.*

Let's try it out now.

1. Type **Jan** in cell A1.

2. Click on the Enter button.

3. Drag over cells A1 to L1 and then click on QuickFill. Corel Quattro Pro automatically completes the series, inserting the month labels Feb to Dec.

Table 15-2 shows the single seed values that Corel Quattro Pro recognizes.

If Corel Quattro Pro does not recognize the entry as a seed value, it will simply copy the entry to each of the highlighted cells. Use this feature when you need to enter the same value in a series of consecutive cells.

When the values you want are not consecutive, enter the first two or three of the series. For example, to number rows with even numbers, enter 2 in one row and enter 4 in the other row. QuickFill will complete the sequence of even numbers across the selected cells.

Seed Values	Sequence
1st	2nd, 3rd, 4th, 5th . . .
Qtr 1	Qtr 2, Qtr 3, Qtr 4, Qtr 1 . . .
1st Quarter	2nd Quarter, 3rd Quarter . . .
Jan	Feb, Mar . . .
January	February, March . . .
Mon	Tue, Wed, Thu . . .
Monday	Tuesday, Wednesday . . .
Week 1	Week 2, Week 3 . . .
Jan 97	Feb 97, Mar 97, Apr 97 . . .
100 Days	101 Days, 102 Days, 103 Days . . .
1, 3, 5	7, 9, 11, 13 . . .
11/16/97	11/17/97, 11/18/97 . . .

Seed Values
for
QuickFill

TABLE 15-2

When QuickFill does not complete the series, or when you don't want to drag across a large number of cells, use the Fill option in the Data menu. Here's how:

1. Click in the cells that you want to fill.

2. Choose Fill from the Data menu. The dialog box shown in Figure 15-3 appears.

3. The reference for the current active cell or selected range of cells will be in the Blocks box. If the range is incorrect, enter a new range, or use Point mode to select it, and click on the Maximize button in the Data File title bar.

4. Once the range is set to the block you want to fill, enter the starting value that you want to place in the first cell. The starting value can be a number, a date, or a time.

5. Enter a step value that you want to increment the series by. A step value of 2, for example, would display every other number, date, or time, depending on the series.

6. Enter a stop value. Corel Quattro Pro will stop the series when it reaches the last cell in the range or the stop value, whichever is reached first. If you enter a date as the start value, enter a stop value of at least 50,000.

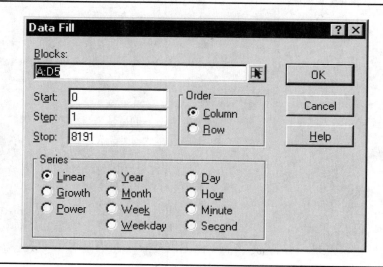

Data Fill
dialog box

FIGURE 15-3

Remember that Corel Quattro Pro converts dates to serial numbers, so you need an ending serial number certain to be larger than the last date in the series.

7. If you selected a rectangular block of cells, also choose if you want them to be filled by column or by row. Filling by column, for example, will add the series down the cells, filling out the first column and then continuing in the column to the right until the range is filled. Using row fill will complete the series in the cells across the first row, then the second row, and so forth.

8. Choose the type of series that you want to complete. If the values are numbers, linear increases it by the step value, growth multiplies the step value by the previous value, and power uses the step value as an exponent.

9. If the start value is a date or time, choose one of the date series options. QuickFill will use your starting date to determine the initial value and increment by the series. For example, if you enter 11/16/97 and choose a Month series, QuickFill will insert only the months starting with November. If you choose Day, QuickFill will insert a series of days.

10. Click on OK.

If none of the series options suit your needs, you can create and save your own custom QuickFill lists. A list is a series of values that you can have QuickFill insert for you. For example, suppose your company uses two-letter state abbreviations for column headings. You can create a QuickFill list to access the abbreviations when you need them. To create a list, use these steps:

1. Click on any empty cell.

2. Click on the QuickFill button. You can also right-click on the cell and choose QuickFill from the QuickMenu, or choose Define Fill Series from the Data menu. The box that appears contains two lists. The Series list contains several built-in series that Corel Quattro Pro uses for QuickFill. The Series Elements box shows the items that are in the displayed list.

3. Click on the Create button to display the dialog box shown in Figure 15-4.

4. Type a series name that you will later use to select the series for a QuickFill operation.

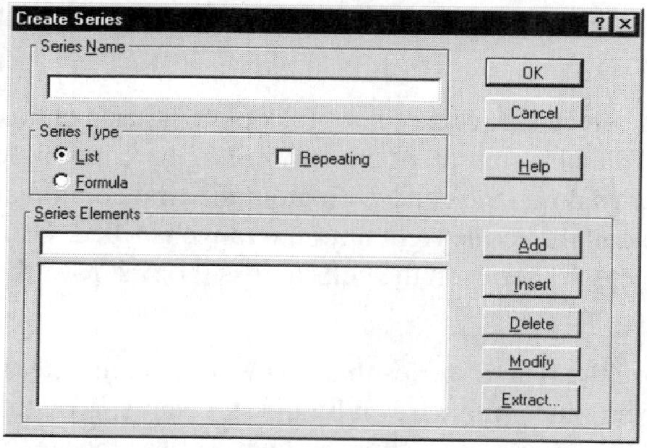

Dialog box
for creating
your own
QuickFill
series

FIGURE 15-4

5. In the Series Type section, choose List. Choosing Formula lets you enter formulas as the series elements. Choosing the Repeating option will cause the list to start over again each time every element has been inserted once.

6. In the Series Elements text box, type the first item in the series and then click on Add.

7. Insert the other items in the list the same way. Each item will be added to the bottom of the list. If you want to insert an item elsewhere in the list, click on the list where you want to add it, type the new item, and then click on Insert. Use the Delete button to remove an item from the list, and use Modify to change an element.

8. If you've already typed the values in a worksheet, you do not have to type them again. Click on Extract. Then in the dialog box that appears, enter or point to the range that contains the value. If you want the extracted range to replace those in the list, click on Override Existing Values. When you click on OK, the items from the worksheet will be inserted into the list. Extract is useful because you can enter the values in a worksheet and then sort them before adding them to the list.

9. Click on OK to close the Create Series dialog box. Then click on OK to close the QuickFill dialog box.

Now when you want to use your list for a QuickFill operation, use these steps:

1. Select the cells you want to fill.

2. Choose QuickFill from the QuickMenu, or choose Define Fill Series from the Data menu.

3. Pull down the Series list and click on the name of your custom list.

4. Click on OK.

Changing Column Width

If your entry is too wide for the cell, widen the column so you can see the full text or number. You can also reduce column width to display more columns on the screen and on the printed page. Reducing column width is useful for columns that have short entries—just a character or two—where space is being wasted.

 To quickly change the width of a column so it is as wide as the widest entry, click on the column letter to select the entire column, and then click on the QuickFit button in the toolbar. Corel Quattro Pro will widen or reduce the column as necessary.

If you want to make the column as wide as a specific entry, click on the cell and then on QuickFit. Corel Quattro Pro will adjust the column around the entry in the cell, so longer entries elsewhere in the column will not show entirely.

You can also change the width of a column by dragging. Point to the line to the right of the column letter—the line between the column and the column to its right. The mouse pointer will change to a double-pointed arrow. Hold down the left mouse button and drag the pointer until the column is the size you want.

To resize several columns to the same width, select the columns by dragging over their column letters, and then change the size of any of the selected columns. When you release the mouse, all of the selected columns will be the same size.

 OTE: *You can also set column width and row height using properties, as explained in Chapter 16.*

Changing Row Height

You can also adjust the height of rows by dragging. Point to the line under the row letter so the mouse appears like a double-pointed arrow and then drag. Resize several rows by selecting them first.

Printing Worksheets

You'll probably want a hard copy of your worksheet for reference or distribution. To print the worksheet, follow these steps:

1. Click on the Print button on the toolbar to see the dialog box shown in Figure 15-5.

2. Make sure that the Print Area setting is set at Current Page.

3. Click on the Print button. This will print the entire contents of the worksheet.

You'll learn about the other options in the Spreadsheet Print dialog in Chapter 17.

The first time you display the Print dialog box, whether you actually print the worksheet or not, Corel Quattro Pro designates what's known as the *print block*. This is the range of cells that contain information. To see which cells are included, look at the box under the Block Selection option in the Print dialog box.

Now when you display the dialog box again, the same group of cells is included in the print block, even if you've added more information to the worksheet. Thus, if you click on the Block Selection and don't change the print block, information that you recently inserted outside of that block will not print. To make sure everything prints, click on the Current Page or Notebook options, or change the print block in either of the following ways:

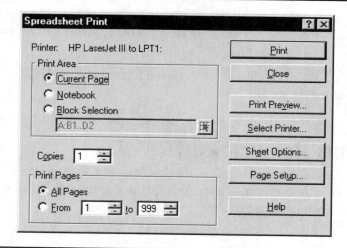

Print dialog box

FIGURE 15-5

■ Select the block before displaying the Print dialog box.

■ Display the Print Dialog box, click on the Block Selection button, and then enter the print range or use Point mode.

When Corel Quattro Pro selects the print block, it will not include columns that contain text that has spilled over from long entries in the column before. If you have such entries, select the print block yourself.

Previewing Before Printing

You can always tell which cells will print by looking at the Block Selection text box. If you want to see how the block will print, click on the Print Preview button to see a screen, as in Figure 15-6. Corel Quattro Pro reduces the image so you can see an entire printed page at one time.

To enlarge the image so it is easier to read, move the mouse pointer over the representation of the page so it appears like a magnifying lens. Now each time you click the left mouse button, the magnification will be doubled—from 100% to 200%, then to 400%, up to 1600%.

Each time you click the right mouse button, the image will be reduced to the previous magnification back down to 100%.

Use the Print Preview toolbar to also adjust the image and select options, as shown in Figure 15-6. When you are satisfied with the print preview, click on the Print button to print the worksheet as it is displayed, or close the Print Preview window to change the print range or to return to the worksheet.

Saving Your Worksheet

Soon after you begin entering information into your worksheet, you should save the worksheet on your disk. You wouldn't want to lose any of your work if your computer suddenly acts up. When you are ready to save your worksheet, follow these steps:

1. Click on the Save button. If this is the first time you've saved the notebook, you'll see the Save File dialog box.

2. Type a document name in the Name text box.

3. Click on Save.

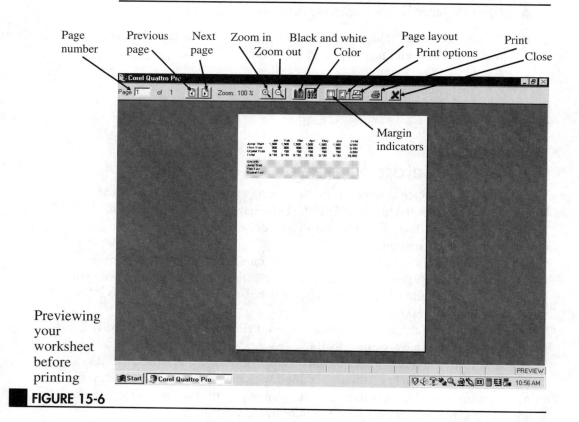

Previewing your worksheet before printing

FIGURE 15-6

OTE: *Corel Quattro Pro saves documents with the WB3 extension in the Quattro7 subfolder.*

Once you save a notebook the first time, you'll need to save it again if you make changes to it. When you click on Save, Corel Quattro Pro saves it immediately under the same name without displaying a dialog box. If you want to save the edited copy under a new name, select Save As from the File menu and then save the file as if it was being saved for the first time.

15

Closing Notebooks

To close the notebook, click on the notebook's Close button or select Close from the File menu. If you did not save the notebook since you last changed it, a dialog box will appear, giving you the chance to do so. Closing the notebook does not exit Corel Quattro Pro, so you can start a new notebook or open one on your disk.

Opening a Notebook

There are several ways that you can open an existing notebook. To quickly open one of the last notebooks you worked with, pull down the File menu, and click on the notebook's name in the list. To open a notebook not listed on the File menu, use these steps:

1. Click on the Open button or choose Open from the File menu to display the Open File dialog box.

2. Select the file, changing folders or drives if necessary. If worksheets are not listed, pull down the List Files of Type list and choose QPW V7 (*.WB3).

3. Click on Open.

File Formats

Corel Quattro Pro lets you save worksheets in formats other than its own, and it allows you to open files created by other spreadsheet and database programs. This means that you can share files with others who do not have Corel Quattro Pro, and that you can use other programs to analyze and work with your Corel Quattro Pro information.

Use the Open command to retrieve data from a Paradox database to analyze it using Corel Quattro Pro or to open an HTML document created with Corel WordPerfect's Internet Publisher.

To open a file in some other format, pull down the List Files of Type list in the Open dialog box, and choose the type of file you wish to open. Then, locate and select the file using the File Name, Folders, and Drives boxes. To save a file in another format, pull down the Save As Type list in the Save As dialog box, and click on the file type. Corel Quattro Pro can open and save files in these formats:

Corel Quattro Pro for Windows and DOS	Text
Microsoft Excel	DIF
Lotus 1-2-3	SYLK
Paradox	HTML (Web documents)
dBase	

Starting a New Notebook

To start a new notebook, click on the New button to display a new blank notebook onscreen.

You can also use the New command from the File menu to start a new workbook or to load a completely formatted notebook already designed for a specific purpose, such as tracking accounts receivable, computing your net worth, or printing a purchase order. Follow these steps:

1. Select New from the File menu. You'll see the dialog box shown in Figure 15-7.

2. To start a new blank notebook, click on OK.

3. To load a formatted notebook, scroll the list of Quick Templates and click on the template for the task you want to perform. When you click on a template in the list, Corel Quattro Pro will automatically select the From Quick Template option button.

4. Click on OK.

If the New File dialog box does not appear when you select New from the File menu, then you have to set the Corel Quattro Pro properties so it does. You'll learn about properties in Chapter 16, but to access the template, select Preference from the Edit menu and click on the File Options tab. Select the Enable QuickTemplates check box and, if necessary, enter **Corel\Office7\Template** in the Quick Templates text box.

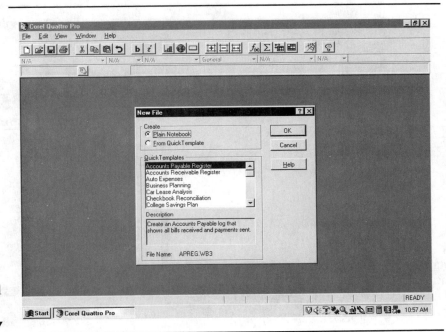

Using a
template to
create a
professional
worksheet

FIGURE 15-7

When the template opens, add the information required and then save and print it. The Quick Template for a sales order is shown in Figure 15-8, along with the template toolbar.

Certain cells are designed for data entry, where you need to enter your own information without replacing built-in formulas and functions. To highlight the cells, making them easy to identify, click on the Highlight button. Click on the Sample Data button to fill the data entry cells with sample information so you can see how the template is used. When you are ready to enter your own information, click on the Clear button.

Using Budget Expert

An Expert is a series of dialog boxes that lead you step by step through a complete task. The Budget Expert will help you create a formatted budget document—all you have to enter are the numbers. To start the Expert, follow these steps:

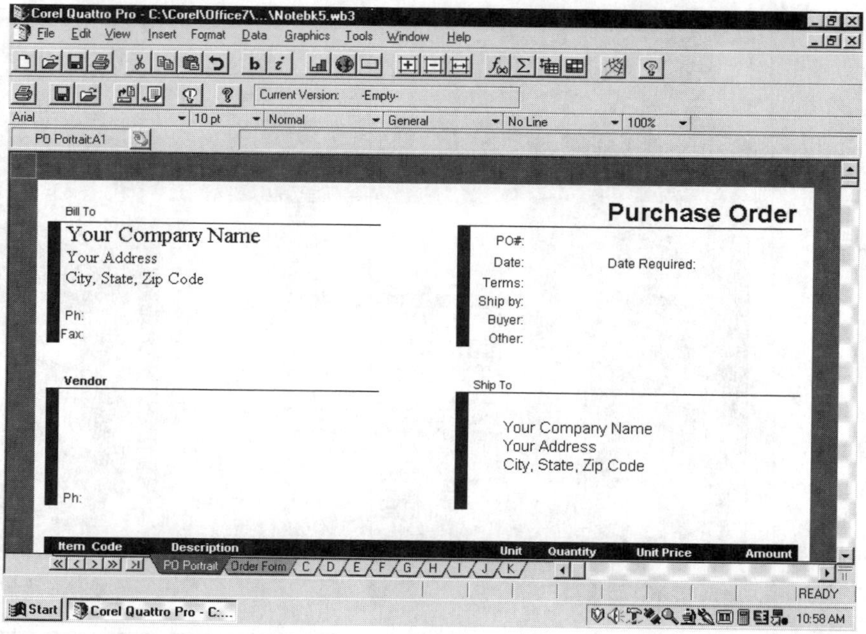

Quick Template and the template toolbar

FIGURE 15-8

[Figure: Corel Quattro Pro screen showing a Purchase Order template with "Bill To," "Your Company Name," "Your Address," "City, State, Zip Code," "Ph:," "Fax:," "Vendor," "Ph:" sections on the left, and "Purchase Order," "PO#:," "Date:," "Date Required:," "Terms:," "Ship by:," "Buyer:," "Other:," "Ship To," "Your Company Name," "Your Address," "City, State, Zip Code" sections on the right. Bottom row shows column headers: Item Code, Description, Unit, Quantity, Unit Price, Amount.]

1. Pull down the Tools menu, point to Experts and click on Budget. Now select options in a series of dialog boxes, clicking on the button labeled Next Step after each. In the first box, select the type of budget you want to create. Your choices are

   - Home—Actual

   - Home—Actual vs Plan

   - Business—Actual

   - Business—Actual vs Plan

   - Business Income Statement

2. Select the type of budget you want to create and then click on Next Step. The second box lists several sample sources of funds. You can delete sources that are not appropriate and add your own.

3. To add a source, type it in the New item text box and then click on Add.

15

4. To delete a source, click on it in the list and then click on Delete.

5. When you are satisfied with the list, click on Next Step. The next box lists sample items where your money goes. Add or delete items and then click on Next Step.

6. You now need to select the period for the budget, the starting date, and the duration. Click on the desired period: Monthly, Quarterly, or Yearly.

7. Select a starting date. The options that appear depend on the period. If you selected Monthly, you can choose a starting month and year. If you selected Quarterly, you can choose a starting quarter and year. If you selected Yearly, you can select only a starting year.

8. Select the duration of the budget: the number of months, quarters, or years.

9. Click on Next Step.

10. Select summation options: Quarter-to-date or Year-to-date.

11. Click on Next Step.

12. In the next box, enter a worksheet title and subtitle. Then click on Next Step.

13. Choose whether to insert the budget in a new notebook or the current one. Then click on Next Step.

14. Depending on the selected period, you can now choose to change pages each month, quarter, or year. You can also choose to display the worksheet in color or in monochrome for output to a laser printer.

15. Click on Build Budget, and Corel Quattro Pro does the rest.

 OTE: *In Chapter 19, you'll learn how to use other Experts to save time.*

Editing and Formatting Worksheets

16

It is as easy to edit and change your worksheet, even make major changes in it, as it is to create it. You can insert and delete information, change its appearance and format, and move and copy information until the worksheet is perfect.

Erasing Information from Cells

Sometimes you'll want to erase all of the information from a cell rather than just edit it. You have two choices: clearing and deleting. Although these have similar effects, they are in some ways quite different. Clearing removes the contents from a cell, row, or column but leaves the cells in the worksheet. Deleting actually removes the cells from the worksheet, moving any remaining cells up or over to take the deleted cells' place. If you clear row 5, for example, the row itself remains empty in the worksheet. If you delete row 5, then row 6 moves up to take its place, and it becomes the new row 5.

Clearing Cells

Choose clearing when you do not want to change the position of other information in the worksheet. You can clear everything from a cell, just the characters, or just the format. Here's how:

1. Select the block you want to clear.

2. Pull down the Edit menu, and select one of these options:

   - *Clear*—Clears all characters and formats from a cell, returning all of the default properties.

   - *Clear Values*—Clears just the displayed contents, leaving formats such as alignment and shading. If you later enter information in the cell, it will automatically take on the formats stored there.

   - *Clear Formats*—Leaves the contents in the cell but returns it to the default formats.

 **OTE:**   *Pressing DEL also clears the contents.*

3. To erase the contents of the entire page, click on the Select All button (or choose Select All from the Edit menu) and then press DEL.

Deleting Blocks

When you delete a block, you are actually removing it from the worksheet. If you delete rows or columns, the remaining ones are renumbered. If you just delete a block of cells, other cells in the row or column shift into their position.

To delete a block, select it and then use any of these techniques:

■ Click the Delete button in the toolbar.

■ Choose Delete from the Edit menu.

■ Right-click on the selection and choose Delete from the QuickMenu.

To delete entire rows or columns, select the ones you want to remove by clicking on their headers. When you choose Delete, Corel Quattro Pro will remove them immediately. When you delete a cell or block of cells, Corel Quattro Pro will first display the dialog box shown in Figure 16-1, which asks how much you want to delete. When this box is displayed, use these steps to ensure that the correct cells are deleted:

1. If the block reference is incorrect, enter or point to the proper reference.

2. Select the Dimension that you want to delete: Columns, Rows, or Pages.

3. Select a Span option: Entire or Partial.

4. Click on OK.

When Entire is selected in Span, Corel Quattro Pro will delete the entire column, row, or page (based on the Dimension setting) in which the selected cells are located, depending on your choice in the Dimension section. So, if you select cell C5 and choose Entire and Row, all of row 5 will be deleted, not just the single cell.

To remove just the selected cells, not their entire row or column, click on Partial. Your choice in the Dimension section determines what cells take the place of the deleted ones. If you choose Rows, for example, the cells below the deleted cells will move up. If you select Columns, the cells next to the deleted cells will move over. Perhaps the best way to visualize this is to look at Figure 16-2. On the left of the figure is the original block of cells showing the ones to be deleted. In the center is

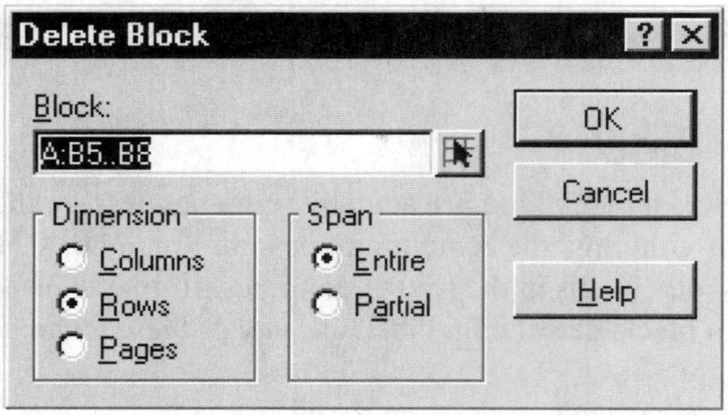

Selecting what you want to delete

FIGURE 16-1

the same block of cells after Columns was chosen in the Delete dialog box. On the right is the same block after Rows was chosen.

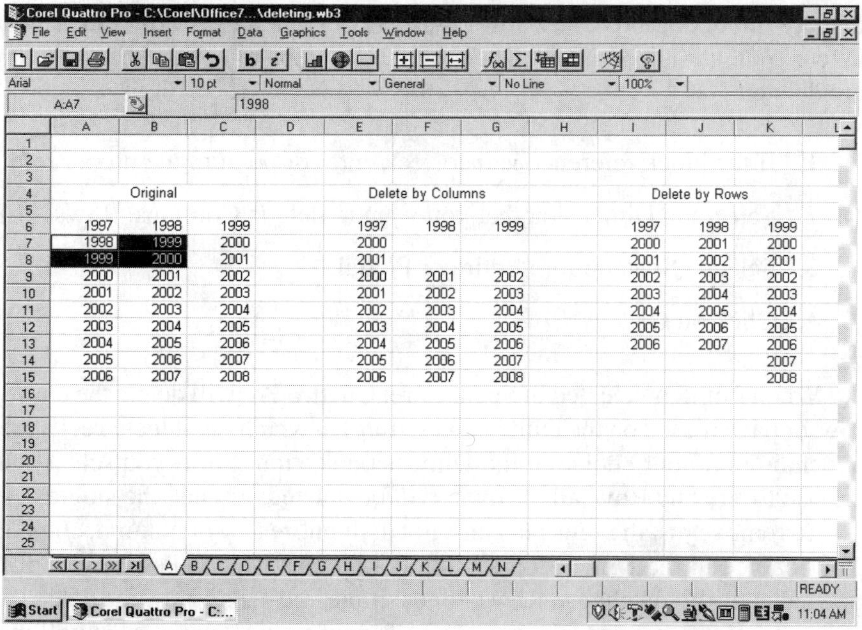

The different effects of deleting by rows and columns

FIGURE 16-2

EMEMBER: *When you select Partial, only the cells selected will be deleted. Existing cells will move up or over, and they will no longer appear in the same row or column as they were originally. If the contents relate to a label, then the label may no longer be in the same row or column. Thus, make certain that that is the effect you want to achieve.*

 OTE: *To delete the entire page, click on Page in the Dimension section and Entire in the Span section.*

Inserting Blocks

No matter how well you plan, it is possible that you'll have to insert cells into the worksheet. When you insert cells, existing ones shift down or over to make room. You insert using either the Insert button in the toolbar or the Insert option from the QuickMenu.

To insert an entire row, use these steps:

1. Click on the number of the row that you want to shift down. For example, to insert a new row number 5, click on the row 5 header.

2. Click on the Insert button in the toolbar. A new row will be inserted, causing the remaining ones to be renumbered.

3. To insert an entire column, click on the letter of the column that you want to shift over and then click on the Insert button.

4. To insert several rows or columns at one time, select the same number of rows and columns before clicking on Insert. To insert two rows, for instance, drag to select two entire rows. To insert four columns, drag to select four columns.

You can also insert a cell or block of cells into the worksheet, rather than entire rows or columns. As with deleting, you can choose to perform the operation by row or column. If you insert cells by row, then cells below will move down to make room. If you insert by column, cells to the right will move over. Here's how to insert a block of cells:

1. Select the cells that currently occupy the space where you want the inserted cells to appear. These will be the cells that will move to make room for the inserted block. For example, if you want to insert cells in positions A1 and B1, select cells A1 and B1.

2. Click on the Insert button in the toolbar to display the Insert dialog box.

3. Click on Partial in the Span section. (Selecting Entire will insert entire rows or columns.)

4. Choose Rows or Columns in the Dimension section. Choose Columns if you want the existing cells to move to the right to make room, or choose Rows if you want the existing cells to move down.

5. Click on OK.

To insert an entire blank worksheet page, display the page you want to follow the new one and then click on the Insert button. Select Pages in the Dimension section and Entire in the Span section and then click on OK.

Moving and Copying Information

The capability to move and copy information from one location to another is as useful in Corel Quattro Pro as it is in Corel WordPerfect. You may need to move information when you've entered it in the wrong location or copy it to avoid having to reenter it elsewhere. Copying information is especially useful when you need similar formulas in several locations, even when the cell references are not exactly the same.

Before moving or copying information, however, you need to decide how you are going to do it because Corel Quattro Pro gives you three choices: drag and drop, the Clipboard, and the Block Move/Copy command.

Using Drag and Drop

Drag and drop works about the same as in all Corel Suite applications. You can drag and drop a single cell, or a block of selected cells as long as they are contiguous—that is, the cells must be next to each other and selected as one group. The advantage of drag and drop over other methods is that you can see where you are placing the information. Here is how it works:

1. Start by selecting the block of cells that you want to move.

2. Point to the selected block and then hold down the mouse button until the pointer appears like a hand and the selection is surrounded by a colored outline.

3. Drag the mouse; a colored outline will move along with it.

4. When the outline is in the desired location, release the mouse button. Corel Quattro Pro moves both the contents and format of the cell, so the original cell will be returned to its default format.

 OTE: *Depending on the speed of your system, it may take a little time for the colored outline to appear as you drag.*

To copy a block using drag and drop, hold down the CTRL key when you drag and drop. A small plus sign will appear with the mouse pointer to indicate a copy operation. Technically, you have to hold down the CTRL key only when you release the mouse button, not the entire time. Just make sure that the plus sign appears before you release the button. If it does not, move the mouse slightly but make sure the colored outline remains where you want it.

To drag and drop an entire page, drag the page tab. As you drag, an outline of the tab with a plus sign in it will move with the mouse. Release the mouse when the tab is where you want the page. Hold down the CTRL key to copy the page rather than move it.

You can also move a page with the Move Pages option from the Edit menu. In the dialog box that appears, enter the number of the page you want to move and the number of the page you want to move it before and then click on OK.

Using the Clipboard

Moving and copying blocks with the Clipboard are straight Windows techniques, using any of these options:

- Cut, Copy, and Paste buttons in the toolbar
- Cut, Copy, and Paste options from the Edit menu

- Cut, Copy, and Paste from the QuickMenu

- CTRL+X (Cut), CTRL+C (Copy), and CTRL+V (Paste) key combinations

The Clipboard gives you several advantages over drag and drop. Once the information is in the Clipboard, for example, you can paste it as many times as you want. You can paste the same information in several locations after cutting or copying it just once. With drag and drop, you'd have to select the information each time.

You can also select and cut or copy noncontiguous cells. Hold down the CTRL key while you select the cells, and paste them in a new location. Drag and drop won't allow that. Use the following steps for this operation:

1. Select the block you want to move.

2. Choose Cut using any of the methods described.

3. Click where you want to place the block. If you are moving a block of cells, click where you want the upper-left corner of the block to begin.

4. Choose Paste.

Copy information the same way but using the Copy command.

Using Paste Special

When you copy using drag and drop or the Clipboard, Corel Quattro Pro copies everything in the block, including the contents and formats, called *properties*. You have more control over what gets pasted using the Paste Special command. When you are ready to paste your copied cells, use the following steps:

1. Select Paste Special from the Edit menu to see the dialog box shown in Figure 16-3.

2. In the Paste section, select what types of cells in the Clipboard you want to paste.

3. Deselect the appropriate check boxes if you do not want to paste formulas, labels, or numbers. Deselect the Properties box if you do not want to include the formats with the pasted cells.

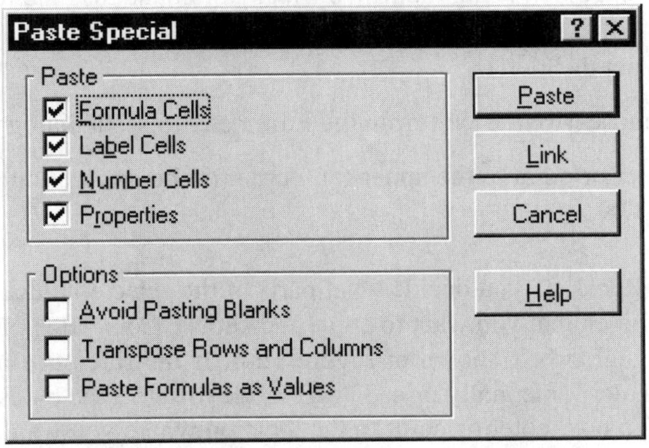

Paste
Special
dialog box

FIGURE 16-3

The following settings in the Options section determine how objects are pasted:

■ Avoid Pasting Blanks will not overwrite the existing contents of a cell by pasting a blank cell into it.

■ Transpose Rows and Columns rearranges the pasted cells, placing copied rows into columns and columns into rows.

■ Paste Formulas as Values pastes the *results* of formulas, not the formulas themselves.

When you've selected your options from the box, click on Paste. If you copied cells into the Clipboard rather than cut them, you can also select Link. Link inserts a reference to the original cells, so if you change a value in the original cells, it will change in the linked position as well.

Using Move Block and Copy Block

The Move Block and Copy Block commands are yet another way to move or copy cells. However, these let you move blocks using their names, and you can control what properties of a block are copied.

 OTE: *You'll learn about naming blocks in Chapter 17.*

To move a block using the Move Block command, use the following steps:

1. Select the block.

2. Choose Move Block from the Edit menu to see a dialog box.

3. Enter or point to the upper-left corner of the destination and then click on OK.

Copy Block lets you decide what parts of the selected block you want to copy. Select the block that you want to copy, and choose Copy Block from the Edit menu to see the dialog box shown in Figure 16-4. If the reference in the From box is incorrect, enter it manually or use Point mode to select the block.

In the To box, enter or point to the location where you want to copy the block. You only need to select the upper-left corner.

The Model Copy option lets you select what elements of the block you want to copy. When the option is not selected, Corel Quattro Pro copies everything —contents, formats, formulas, properties, objects, and the row and column sizes. If you want to copy only certain elements, click on the Model Copy option, then remove the checks from the elements you do not want to move. For example, deselecting Formulas will not copy any cells that contain formulas.

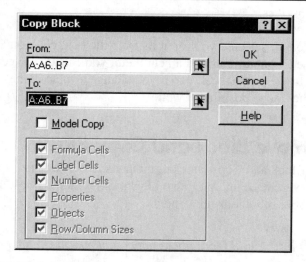

Copy Block
dialog box

FIGURE 16-4

OTE: *When Model Copy is turned on, absolute references are also adjusted.*

Moving and Copying Formulas

You can use any of the techniques described to move formulas from one cell to another. When you move a cell containing a formula, the exact same formula is placed in the pasted cell. When you copy a formula, however, it is copied using a relative reference. This means that the cell references in the formula are adjusted to use corresponding cells in the new location.

As an example, look at the worksheet in Figure 16-5. This worksheet needs a number of formulas. The income and expenses in each column must be totaled, and then expenses subtracted from income to calculate the net in the quarter columns. Because of the way Corel Quattro Pro copies formulas, you only need to enter them once—in the first column—and then copy them across the rows.

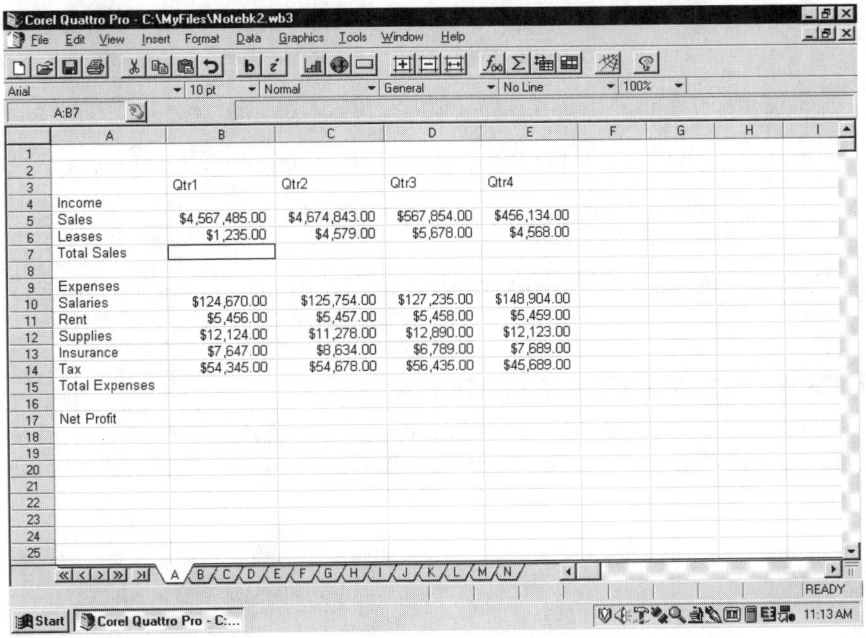

16

	A	B	C	D	E
1					
2					
3		Qtr1	Qtr2	Qtr3	Qtr4
4	Income				
5	Sales	$4,567,485.00	$4,674,843.00	$567,854.00	$456,134.00
6	Leases	$1,235.00	$4,579.00	$5,678.00	$4,568.00
7	Total Sales				
8					
9	Expenses				
10	Salaries	$124,670.00	$125,754.00	$127,235.00	$148,904.00
11	Rent	$5,456.00	$5,457.00	$5,458.00	$5,459.00
12	Supplies	$12,124.00	$11,278.00	$12,890.00	$12,123.00
13	Insurance	$7,647.00	$8,634.00	$6,789.00	$7,689.00
14	Tax	$54,345.00	$54,678.00	$56,435.00	$45,689.00
15	Total Expenses				
16					
17	Net Profit				

Worksheet with copied formulas

FIGURE 16-5

Create the worksheet that you see in the figure, using the following steps. (Use QuickFill to repeat the rent and insurance figures across the row in the Expense sections.)

1. In cell B7, click on the QuickSum button to add the total. Notice that the input line shows @SUM(B5..B6). Now use QuickFill to quickly copy the formula across the rows. Dragging and dropping, the Clipboard, and Copy Block would work the same—QuickFill is just faster.

2. Click on cell B7 and drag over to select up to cell E7.

3. Point to the selection, press the right mouse button, and click on QuickFill from the QuickMenu. (You could also click on the QuickFill button in the toolbar.) Corel Quattro Pro copies the formula across the selected cells.

4. Click on cell C7 and look at the formula in the input line: @Sum(C5..C6). Corel Quattro Pro did not copy the exact formula, which totals values in column B, but adjusted it to total the values in the cells above it. The formulas in the remaining cells have also been adjusted as well.

In a sense, Corel Quattro Pro sees the formula in cell B7 as saying, "Total the values in the two cells above." So when it copies the formula, the cell references automatically change to reflect the two cells above the formula. Each formula really says the same thing. Continue this process.

5. Enter the total in cell B15 and copy it across the row to cell E15.

6. In cell B17, enter the formula +B7–B16 to compute net income.

7. Copy the formula across the row to cell E17.

You've completed the worksheet with 12 formulas, but entered only 3.

Copying Values of Formulas

In most cases, you enter a formula in such a way that it will recalculate if referenced cells change. Sometimes, however, you may want to copy the results of the formula to another cell without changing the values in the new location. To do this, follow these steps:

1. Select the block that contains the formulas, pull down the Data menu, and click on Values. A dialog box will appear with two boxes, From and To.

2. In the To box, enter or point to the destination where you want to copy the values.

3. Click on OK.

 AUTION: *By default, the From and To boxes will contain the coordinates of the selected block. If you leave the To block unchanged, the formulas will be replaced by their values.*

Absolute References

In most cases, you want Corel Quattro Pro to adjust cell references when you copy a formula, but not always. There are times when you'll want to copy a cell reference exactly as it appears. This is called an *absolute reference*.

For example, look at the worksheet in Figure 16-6. The worksheet will calculate costs based on the labor charges in cell B3. In several cells, we need a formula that multiplies the hours in row seven times the labor cost to calculate the labor charges. We can do this easily by entering a formula such as +B7*B3 in cell B8. But if we copy the formula across the row, Corel Quattro Pro will use a relative reference. Only the original formula will reference cell B3. Here's why. The formula in B8 means "multiply the value one cell above times the value in the cell five rows up." This same connotation will be applied where the formula is copied. So when it is copied to cell C8, for example, it will be copied as +C7*C3—multiplying the labor amount (one cell up) times the value in cell C3—which is not correct.

When you want a reference to a cell to remain constant, no matter where it is copied, use an absolute reference. To create an absolute reference, place a dollar sign ($) in front of each part of the reference that you want to remain constant. In this case, enter the formula as +B7*B3. This tells Corel Quattro Pro not to change the reference to column B and row 3.

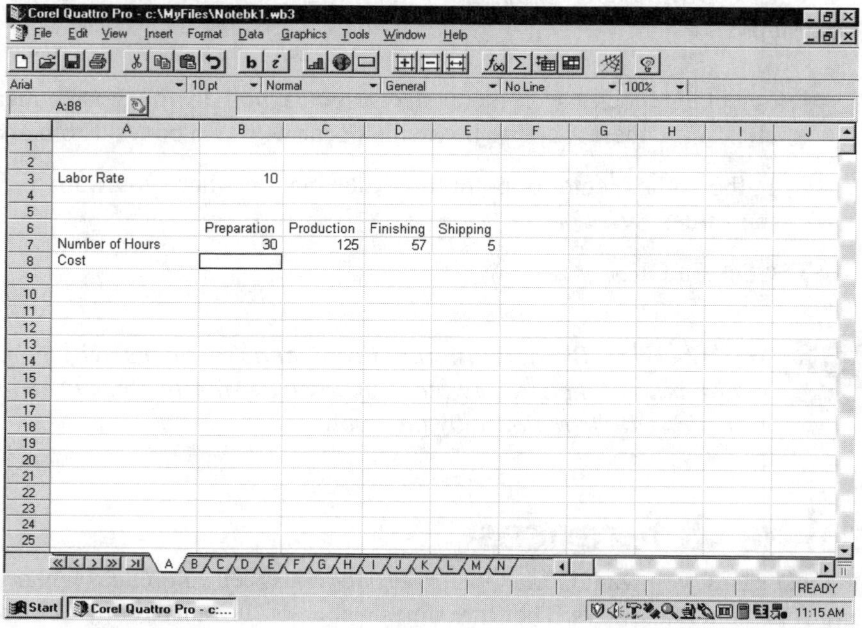

Copying formulas without a relative reference

FIGURE 16-6

Create the worksheet and enter the absolute reference now, and then use QuickFill to copy the formula across the row. The reference to cell B7 will be adjusted because it is not absolute, but the reference to cell B3 will remain constant.

Depending on your worksheet, the $ symbol is not always needed before both parts of the reference. For example, $C5 tells Corel Quattro Pro to always reference a cell in column C, but change the row number relative to the location.

Using Model Copy to Adjust Absolute References

There is one problem, however, with absolute references. Suppose you want to copy the entire block of cells illustrated above to another location on the worksheet so you can use two different labor charges. If you copy cells A3 to E8, the formulas in the new location will still reference cell B3, because of the absolute reference. This is not what you want. You really want the formulas to reference the new location, but again using an absolute reference to it.

To perform this copy, use the Copy Block option but select Model Copy. Corel Quattro Pro will copy the block of cells, modifying the absolute reference but leaving it absolute to its new location.

Formatting Long Text Entries

When you type a long text entry, characters run over into blank cells on the right. When there aren't enough blank cells to display the entire entry, some of it won't show onscreen or print with the worksheet. The Reformat command divides a long entry into more than one row, as in the following steps:

1. Select the cell that contains the long entry—only that cell, not the ones that it spreads into.

2. Choose Text Reformat from the Format menu. A dialog box will appear asking for the block where you want to place the text.

3. Enter the block, or use Point mode to select it.

4. Click on OK.

The block must start with the active cell as the upper-left corner, and it must be large enough to hold all of the text. Pick sufficient cells, in as many rows and column as needed. For instance, suppose you have a note that spans three columns. Your block can be three or four rows and one column wide, or two rows and two columns wide. Both blocks would be sufficient to hold the text.

Keep in mind, however, that Corel Quattro Pro reserves a little space before the first character in a cell and after the last. Some long entries may require a slightly larger block than you imagine. An entry that completely fills three columns, for example, would require a block four cells high.

 OTE: *Using Block Properties, you can also wrap a long entry so it fits entirely within a cell.*

Transposing Columns and Rows

Once you set up your worksheet, you may find it more convenient if your rows and columns were switched, or transposed. For instance, you may find that you have more columns than rows, and that the worksheet would look better if the row labels were used for the columns instead. That way, perhaps, you could fit the entire worksheet on one page, rather than have some columns print on a second sheet.

Before transposing rows and columns, however, find an empty place in the notebook large enough to store the transposed block. If you select a block that contains information, it will be overwritten with the transposed cells. Remember that the rows and columns will be reversed, so make sure there are enough empty rows to store the original columns and enough empty columns to store the original rows. Here's how:

1. Select the block that you want to transpose.

2. Pull down the Tools menu.

3. Point to Numeric Tools, and click on Transpose.

 AUTION: *Cell references are not adjusted when you transpose cells, so avoid transposing cells with formulas or functions.*

Formatting Your Worksheet

Not only must your worksheet be accurate, but it should look good. It should be easy and pleasant to read, formatted to enhance the material, not distract from it. By formatting a worksheet, you can change the typeface and size of characters, add lines and shading to cells, and change the way and position that text appears in the cell.

You can format cells after you enter contents into them or before. In fact, you can apply formats to cells and later add information to them. Your entries will automatically assume the applied formats. One word of caution: formatting blank cells that you never use, such as entire rows or columns, will needlessly increase the size of your files.

There are three ways to format cells—using the toolbar or the power bar, or setting block properties. Block properties may take a little longer than the other methods, but it gives you the most options and lets you set multiple formats at one time.

Remember, you must be in Ready mode to format blocks. You cannot format while you are entering or editing information in a cell. Character formats, such as typeface and size, bold and italic, are applied to all of the characters in a cell. You cannot select and format just part of an entry.

Formatting with the Toolbar

The toolbar has three buttons for formatting—Bold, Italic, and Speed Formatting. To have the characters appear in boldface or italic, or both, click on the appropriate buttons in the toolbar. When you make a cell active, by the way, the buttons will appear pressed down to indicate the formats that have been applied.

Speed Formats

As you will soon learn, you can apply a number of different formats to an entry, such as the font and size, grid lines, and cell shading. Assigning each of the formats individually yourself develops your creativity but can be time consuming. The SpeedFormat command lets you completely format an entire block of cells, even the entire worksheet, by choosing from a list of designs. You can even create and save your own custom SpeedFormat so you can apply it again later with a few clicks of the mouse. Here's how:

1. Select the block that you want to format.

2. Click on the SpeedFormat button in the toolbar to display the dialog box shown in Figure 16-7. The list box on the left contains the names of all of Corel Quattro Pro's built-in designs. When you click on a design in the list, a sample worksheet using that style appears in the Example box.

3. Choose what aspects of the design will be applied to the cells. In the Include section, deselect the items that you do not want applied. For example, to accept all of the formats except the shading, click on the Shading option to deselect its check box. The items on the right of the Include section determine if special styles are applied to those parts of the worksheet.

4. Deselect any element that you do not want formatted. If you deselect Column heading, for example, the column headings will not be formatted differently from the body of the cells. As you choose options in the Include section, the example will illustrate the results.

5. Click on OK to apply the format to the selected cells.

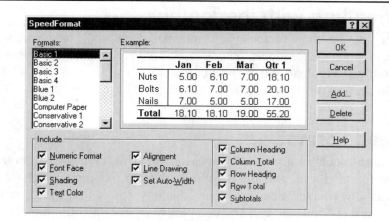

Applying an
entire
design to
the
worksheet
with
SpeedFormat

FIGURE 16-7

Creating Custom Formats

If you've designed a worksheet yourself, you can add the design to the SpeedFormat
list. The next time you want to apply the combination of formats, you can select it
from the list just as easily as you can select those built in by Corel Quattro Pro. Use
the following steps:

1. Start by selecting the block of cells that contain the design.

2. Click on the SpeedFormat button and then on Add.

3. In the dialog box that appears, type a name for the format and then
confirm—or reenter or point to—the block of cells.

4. Click on OK. Your new format will be added to the list.

Formatting with the Power Bar

The power bar has four sections for formatting cells—Font, Size, Style, and Line Draw.

Use the Font list to change the typeface of the characters in the selected block.
The fonts available will depend on your system and what other programs you have
installed. The Standard version of Corel Suite comes with 200 of its own fonts, the
professional edition with 1000.

Use the Size list to change the size of the characters. Corel Quattro Pro will automatically increase the row height when you select a larger font. Just remember: the larger the font, the fewer rows will print on each sheet of paper.

Use the Style list to select a style. A style is one or more formats that are applied at one time. The two built-in text styles are Heading 1 and Heading 2. Heading 1 is 18-point Arial bold; Heading 2 is 12-point Arial bold. You can create your own styles and add them to the list.

You use the Line Draw list to change the grid lines around the cells. Let's look into grid lines in more detail now.

Grid Lines

The grid lines that appear onscreen are there for your convenience—they make it easy to identify rows and columns. The lines will not print with your worksheet, however, unless you select to print them in the Sheet Options dialog box.

If you want custom lines to print out and appear onscreen, you must use the Line Draw feature. With Line Draw you really do not draw the lines, you just indicate where around the cell you want Corel Quattro Pro to insert a line and the type of line you want to use.

 OTE: *You can use the page properties to remove the default grid lines from the screen to make it easier to see your custom lines.*

The Line list in the power bar is useful but very limited because it will only insert a line at the bottom of the selected cell, not on top or on either side. To add a line below a cell, select the cell, pull down the Line list in the power bar, and choose Thin Line, Double Line, or Thick Line. Choose No Line if you later want to remove the line.

To add a line on top of the cell, you must add it to the bottom of the cell above it. If you select a row of cells, it will add the line to the bottom of each. If you select a column of cells, it will only add a line to the last cell in the selection.

For more control over lines, use the Block Properties dialog box instead of the power bar.

Formatting with Properties

Every format and style that you can apply is a property. Instead of using a variety of bars and menus to apply formats one at a time, you can select multiple formats in the Block Properties dialog box. You can also set the properties for a page or for the entire notebook, and even to customize Corel Quattro Pro itself.

To display the Properties dialog box, select what you want to format, click the right mouse button, and choose the Properties option from the bottom of the QuickMenu.

Block Properties for Cells

The Block Properties dialog box, shown in Figure 16-8, is used for formatting cells, rows, and columns. Right-click on the selected block and choose Block Properties from the QuickMenu. The coordinates of the block that will be affected will be shown on the title bar. If that is not the block you want to format, close the dialog box and start over by selecting the block. You cannot change the reference while the dialog box is open.

When you select an option from a page in the dialog boxes, its title on the tab will change color. This is Corel Quattro Pro's way of reminding you which pages you've already used.

Let's take a look at the properties that you can set.

NUMERIC FORMAT   As you can see in Figure 16-8, the Numeric Format tab gives you more choices than the Style list in the power bar. When you choose some items in the list, additional choices will appear to the right. For example, clicking on Currency will give you the option to select the number of decimal places and the country so Corel Quattro Pro can use the correct currency format.

The Hidden format will prevent the contents from appearing in the cell, onscreen, and when printed. Values in the cell will still be used in formulas that reference it, and you can still edit the cell to change its contents. The information in the cell will reappear when you are in Edit mode, but disappear again when you accept the entry.

FONT   Use the Font tab to select the typeface, size, and style of the characters. The styles are bold, italic, underline, and strikeout. Use strikeout to indicate information that you want to delete.

SHADING   One way to really make a block of cells stand out is to add shading. Shading is a color, shade of gray, or pattern that fills the selected block. You can choose two colors for each block and then a specific blend of them, ranging between a solid color fill of each.

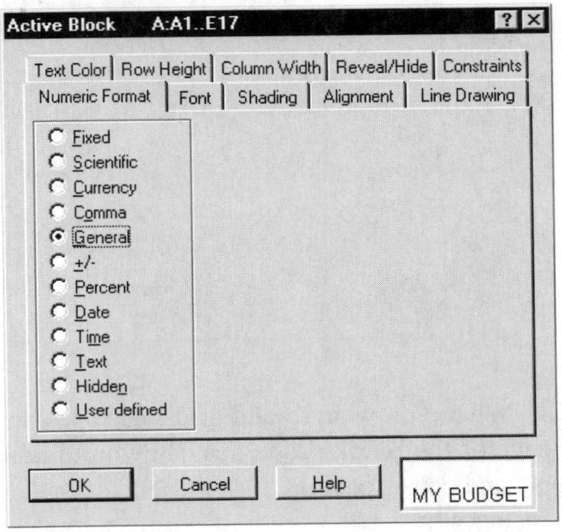

Active Block A:A1..E17

Text Color | Row Height | Column Width | Reveal/Hide | Constraints
Numeric Format | Font | Shading | Alignment | Line Drawing

- ○ Fixed
- ○ Scientific
- ○ Currency
- ○ Comma
- ⊙ General
- ○ +/-
- ○ Percent
- ○ Date
- ○ Time
- ○ Text
- ○ Hidden
- ○ User defined

[OK] [Cancel] [Help] MY BUDGET

Using
Block
Properties
to format
cells

FIGURE 16-8

To fill a block, click on the Shading tab, and choose the colors and the blend. For shades of gray, select black and white as the two colors.

ALIGNMENT The alignment section on the power bar gives you choices for horizontal alignment—the position of text in relation to the right and left sides of the cell. Using the Alignment page in the Block Properties dialog box, you can also choose vertical alignment and orientation, and wrapping a wide text entry so it fits within the cell borders.

The default vertical alignment is bottom. If you increase the row height or use a smaller font, you'll see that the characters appear nearer the bottom of the cell. Vertical Alignment lets you place the text in the center or near the top of the cell as well.

Long text entries run over into blank cells on the right. The Wrap Text option widens the row height and divides the long entry so it fits entirely within the cell. This differs from Reformatting Text, which divides the entry into more than one cell.

Orientation determines if the characters appear across the cell, the default setting, or up and down, expanding the row height if needed as shown here:

LINE DRAWING   When you want to add grid lines to your worksheet, display the Line Drawing page of the Block properties, shown in Figure 16-9. You can select the location, type, and colors of lines.

Start by choosing where you want to place lines by clicking on the diagram of a block or in the preset buttons. The quickest way to add grid lines is to use the preset buttons. All inserts lines around every cell in the selected block. Outline inserts lines only around the outside of the block. Inside inserts lines only on the inside. To specify the individual segments, click on the location in the illustration in the Line Segments section that represents where you want to place the lines. Clicking on a line will

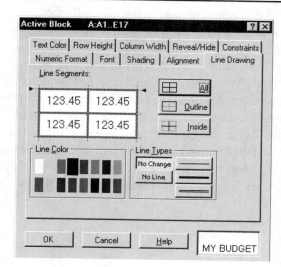

Creating custom lines using Block Properties

FIGURE 16-9

16

place small arrows on its sides that indicate where the line will be placed. Clicking at the intersection of two lines will add the line to both of them. For example, if you click on the lower-right corner of the drawing, Corel Quattro Pro will insert a line on the bottom and right of the block.

Next, choose the line type and color. Choose No Line to remove lines from the cell; choose No Change to cancel your selections.

You can choose a color and line type for each individual line, if you want. To give the block a shadow box look, for example, add a thin line to the top and left side and add a thick line to the bottom and right.

TEXT COLOR   By default, all characters appear black. To choose another color, display the Text Color tab and select from the palette that appears. For a reversed look, select a black background and a white or other light text color.

Choose text colors wisely and coordinate them with the shading color and pattern. Some color combinations may be difficult to read.

ROW HEIGHT   This property lets you set row height to an exact measurement in points, inches, or centimeters. It is more exact than dragging the row with the mouse, but you may have to experiment to get the height correct for your text.

COLUMN WIDTH   Use this property to set the column width to an exact measurement in characters, inches, or centimeters. You can choose Auto Width, which works the same as AutoFit but also lets you specify a number of extra character spaces to insert. The default is 1. For instance, if the longest entry in the column is 6 characters, the column will be 7 characters wide. You can specify as little as no extra spaces, and as many as 40.

 EMEMBER: *If you have a cell selected, Auto Width, like AutoFit, will make the column as wide as the text in that cell. To adjust the column to the widest entry in it, select the column before displaying the Block Properties.*

REVEAL/HIDE   You can temporarily hide rows or columns that you do not want to appear onscreen or print with the worksheet. This feature is useful when you've added some information for limited distribution or notes and messages to yourself. This format is similar to the hidden numeric format, except that it affects entire rows and columns, not individual cells or blocks of cells. When hidden, values in the cells will still be used to calculate formulas, but you cannot edit the contents until you reveal them.

To hide a row or column, click in any cell within it and then display the Reveal/Hide page of the Block Properties dialog box. Select either Rows or Columns, and then click on Hide. When you close the dialog box, the rows or columns will no longer appear, but the remaining rows and columns will retain their original numbers and letters. If you hide row 5, for example, your rows will be numbered 1, 2, 3, 4, 6, 7, 8, and so on.

You can reveal hidden rows and columns with the mouse or using Block Properties. Using the mouse, point just to the right of the border before where the column should appear. To reveal hidden column C, for example, point just to the right of column B's right border. The mouse pointer will appear as if you are changing the width of the column, but when you drag, the hidden column will appear. Use the same technique to reveal rows—just point below the border line.

With the mouse you can only reveal one row or column at a time, and you have to resize the row or column as needed. To reveal more than one row or column, and to have it appear in its original width, use the Block Properties. Select a block that contains the hidden area. To redisplay row 5, for instance, select cells in rows 4 and 6. Display the Reveal/Hide page, click on the appropriate dimension and then click on Reveal.

CONSTRAINTS   The Constraints tab lets you protect a cell from being changed and allows you to specify the type of entry that will be accepted.

By default, all cells are set to be protected. To implement the protection, you need to turn it on using the Active Page Properties that you'll learn about later. In the Constraints tab, however, you designate if you want the cells to be protected or not when page protection is turned on.

You can also specify if you will allow any type of information to be inserted into the cell, or if you just want labels or dates. If you select labels, whatever you type in the cell will be treated as text. Numbers, formulas, dates, and functions will appear just as you type them, aligned on the left, and treated as text. If you select Dates Only, Corel Quattro Pro will display an error message if you do not enter a valid date into the cell.

Page Properties

The Page Properties control the overall look of the page, rather than selected blocks. To display the Active Page dialog box, just right-click on the page tab. The dialog box, shown in Figure 16-10, will appear immediately, rather than a QuickMenu. Here's a recap of the Page Properties:

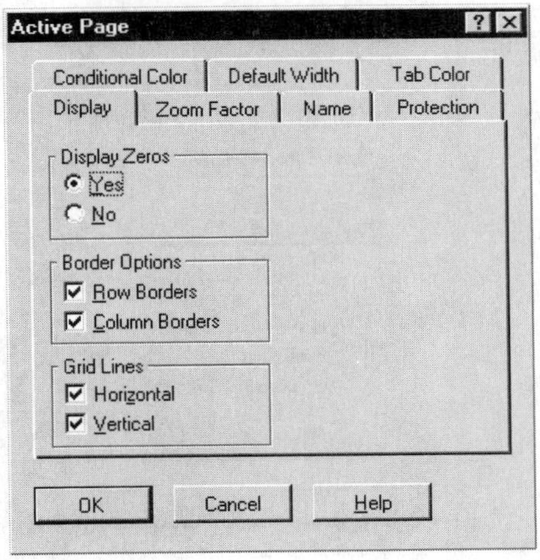

Using Page
Properties
to format
the entire
worksheet

FIGURE 16-10

■ *Display*—Display or hide zeros when entered or when the result of a calculation; display or hide row and column borders; display or hide the nonprintable grid lines without affecting those added by Line Draw.

■ *Zoom Factor*—Select a default magnification for the entire page, without affecting other pages.

■ *Name*—This is one of the most useful of the properties. Rather than stick with tabs A, B, C, and so on, you can name them for the type of worksheet that appears on the page—such as Budget or Amortization.

■ *Protection*—Turn on cell and object locking. Only cells with the Block Property set for locking in the Constraints tab will be affected. By default, all of the cells are set for protection, so if you turn this on, you will not be able to enter or edit information until you turn it off again.

■ *Conditional Color*—Choose to automatically color the contents of a cell based on its value or error condition. The options are shown in Figure 16-11. Enter a minimum and maximum value, and what color will appear when an entry is below the minimum, within the range, above the maximum, or when an error occurs. Click on each option you want and choose a color. To turn on the coloring, you must click on the Enable box. This is useful for displaying negative numbers in a special color.

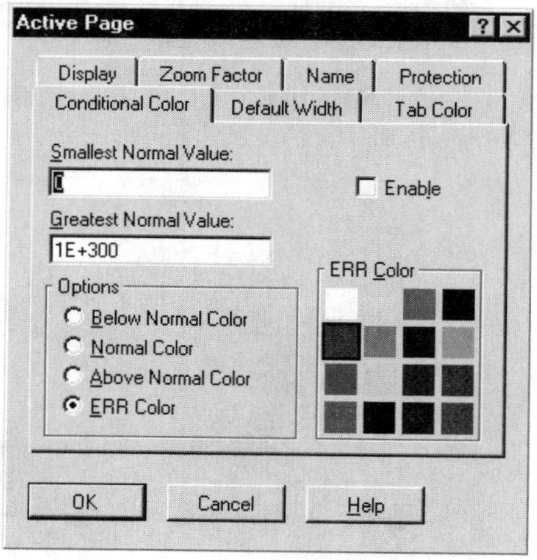

Using Conditional Color to color cells based on their contents

FIGURE 16-11

- *Default Width*—Set the width of every column in characters, inches, or centimeters.

- *Tab Color*—Select the color for the page tab. To choose a color, deselect the Use System Color option in the dialog box, and then pick a color from the list.

Notebook Properties

The Notebook properties affect every page in the notebook. To set these properties, however, you must right-click on the Notebook title bar, which does not appear when the Notebook window is maximized. If necessary, click on the restore button on the right of the menu bar, and then right-click on the Notebook title bar and select Active Notebook Properties from the QuickMenu.

Here are the Notebook properties:

- *Display*—Choose whether or not to display the scroll bars and page tabs, and to display or hide objects or just to show their outline.

- *Zoom Factor*—Select the default magnification for every page.

- *Recalc Settings*—This setting determines how and when Corel Quattro Pro will recalculate your worksheet. The Mode section has three options.

Background recalculates as you work, Automatic waits until you stop working, and Manual lets you recalculate by pressing F9. You can also select a calculation order. Natural first calculates formulas that are referenced by other formulas; Column-wise calculates all formulas in column A, then column B, and so on; Row-Wise calculates all formulas in row 1, then row 2, and so on.

If you have a lot of formulas and functions in your worksheet—and a slow computer—Background and Automatic recalculation may slow down your system's response. If you select Manual, however, remember to recalculate the worksheet before relying on any of its numbers.

■ *# of Iterations*—This determines the number of times Corel Quattro Pro recalculates your worksheet when circular references are used. A circular reference occurs when formulas refer to each other. You can choose a number of iterations between 1 and 255. The Audit Error option will display the cell reference where a calculation problem first started.

■ *Palette*—Determines the palette of colors that you can select from when setting other properties that relate to color, such as text color.

■ *Macro Library*—You can store macros in a special file, called the macro library, rather than in your notebook. The library will be available for every notebook. Select Yes and Corel Quattro Pro will automatically search the macro library when a macro you are running is not in the active notebook.

■ *Password Level*—You can use a password to protect your notebook. Refer to "Protecting Your Worksheet," later in this chapter.

■ *System*—A system notebook is a special notebook that you can hide but have remain open even when all other notebooks are closed. The system notebook becomes a convenient location to store macros and other objects that you want to be available at all times. To convert a notebook into a system notebook, choose Yes for this property, and then hide the notebook with the Window Hide command.

■ *Summary*—Use this page to store a title, subject, the author's name, keywords, and comments about the notebook for later reference.

■ *Statistics*—This page displays the notebook's name and path, when it was created and last saved, who saved it, and the revision number.

Application Properties

When you want to customize the way Corel Quattro Pro works, set Application Properties. Right-click on the Corel Quattro Pro title bar and choose Application Properties from the QuickMenu, or pull down the Edit menu and choose Preferences. Here's a review.

- *Display*—Choose to show a standard or international clock on the left side of the status bar; to display the toolbar, power bar, status line, input line, scroll indicators, and QuickTips; and choose the syntax of 3-D block references. The syntax choices are A..B:A1..B2 or A:A1..B:B2.

- *International*—Select the format of currency, punctuation, dates, times, country, and if negative values are displayed with a minus sign or in parentheses.

- *Macro*—Choose what elements of the screen appear as a macro runs. By default, all menus, dialog boxes, and other elements used to record the macro are suppressed so they do not appear as the macro performs its steps. You can choose to suppress just panels (menus and dialog boxes) or windows. Suppressing everything allows macros to run faster and without distracting elements appearing onscreen. You also use this tab to choose what element of the screen is made active when you press the slash key, and what macro runs automatically when you start Corel Quattro Pro.

- *File*—Select the default directory and file extension used for the save and open dialog boxes, and a worksheet that will open each time you open Corel Quattro Pro. You can also choose to automatically save your work at a specified interval, to display the complete path with the filename in the title bar, and to list templates that you can choose from when you select New from the File menu.

- *General*—Use this tab to customize some ways that Corel Quattro Pro operates. You can turn off the Undo feature, use the key combinations from Corel Quattro Pro for DOS, and move the cell selector down when you press ENTER. The Compatible Formula Entry option lets you start formulas without first entering the plus sign. If you choose this option, however, entering a phone number or social security number will be seen as a formula. The number 555–1234, for example, will appear as –679.

The Cell Drag And Drop Delay Time option sets the interval at which drag-and-drop mode is activated when pointing at cells with the mouse.

Protecting Your Worksheet

The Password level setting in the Active Notebook Properties dialog box lets you determine the extent to which your notebook is protected. When you choose a setting other than None, you will be prompted to enter and then to confirm the password when you exit the dialog box.

- *None*—Requires no password.

- *Low*—Requires a password to edit and view formulas. With the password, only asterisks appear in the input line.

- *Medium*—Automatically hides the notebook once it is saved and closed.

- *High*—You must have a password to open the notebook and to perform any actions on the notebook.

Opening Password-Protected Notebooks

When you open a notebook protected at the High level, a dialog box will appear asking for the password. A notebook protected at the low and medium settings, however, must be opened with a special command line from the Run menu. Click on Start, click on Run, and then enter the command line in this format:

C:COREL\OFFICE7\Corel Quattro7 C:\OFFICE7\Corel
Quattro7*filename*.WK3 /S*password*

Substitute the path where Corel Quattro Pro and your notebooks are stored. Be sure to enter the /S command at the end of the line, followed by your password. If your password is Aardvark, for example, type /SAardvark.

If the Medium-level protected notebook doesn't appear after you open it with the password, pull down the Window menu, click on Show, and then double-click on the notebook's name in the dialog box that appears. The Hide and Show commands in the Windows menu let you temporarily hide your notebook from prying eyes.

Formatting with Style

The SpeedFormat dialog box is handy when you want to create a style for an entire spreadsheet. Often, however, you want a style for a section or element of a worksheet, such as a heading, grand total, or note. A style is merely a collection of properties saved under one name. You can apply all of the properties in the collection by selecting the style name.

Corel Quattro Pro already comes with the Heading 1 and Heading 2 styles. You can modify these styles and create any number of your own so they are available in the Style list of the power bar.

The easiest way to create a style is to first apply all of the formats to a cell and use the cell as a pattern. The following steps show this process:

1. Click in the cell, and then choose Styles from the Format menu to see the dialog box shown in Figure 16-12.

2. Type a name for the style, and then click on the Merge button.

3. In the dialog box that appears, click on Cell, and then point to or type the cell reference.

4. Click on OK.

The formats applied to the cell will be used to create the new style.

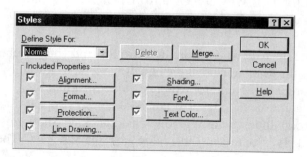

Creating your own styles

FIGURE 16-12

To create a style from scratch, type a name for it in the Styles dialog box, and then select options from the dialog boxes that appear when you click on the Alignment, Format, Protection, Line Drawing, Shading, Font, or Text Color buttons. To apply the selected options, make sure the check box next to the button is selected.

You can delete any style except the Normal style. You can also copy styles to other notebooks. To delete a style, select Styles from the Format menu, click on the style name in the list, and then click on Delete.

To apply your style, pull down the Style list on the power bar and click on the style name.

Creating Numeric Formats

Corel Quattro Pro offers a variety of numeric formats, but you still might have your own special requirements. You can create your own custom formats for numbers, dates, and times, so they are easily selected from the list. To create a format, follow these steps.

1. Select the cells that you want to format.

2. Right-click on the cells and choose Block Properties from the QuickMenu.

3. Click on the Numeric Format tab, if necessary.

4. Click on the User Defined option button. A list box appears labeled Formats Defined.

5. Delete the text in the box, or choose one of the formats in the list to use as a basis for your own.

6. Enter a format using the codes shown in Table 16-1. Start a numeric format with an "n" or "N" and start a date or time format with a "t" or "T."

7. Click on OK.

Your custom format will be added to the Formats Defined list and will be available for all notebooks. To apply a custom format, display the Block Properties dialog box, click on User Defined in the Numeric Format tab, and then choose the format from the Formats Defined list.

Symbol	Action
N or n	Designates a number format
T or t	Designates a date or time format
0	Placeholder for any digit, displaying a 0 if empty
9	Displays a digit in that location
%	Displays the number as a percentage
,	Uses a thousands separator
.	Decimal point separator
;	Delineates different formats for positive and negative values, as in positive_format;negative_format
E – or e–	Uses scientific notation, with minus sign before negative exponents
E+ or e+	Uses scientific notation, with minus or plus sign
d or D	Shows the day of the month in one- or two-digit number
dd or DD	Shows the day of the month in two digits, as in 05
wday, Wday, WDAY	Shows the day of the week as a three-character abbreviation lowercase, initial capitalized, or all uppercase
weekday, Weekday,WEEKDAY	Shows the complete day of the week all lowercase, initial capitalized, or all uppercase
m, M, or Mo	Shows the month in one or two digits (1–12)
mm, MM, or Mmo	Shows the month in two digits
mon, Mon, MON	Shows the month as a three-character abbreviation, all lowercase, initial capitalized, or all uppercase

Characters Used to Create Your Own Numeric Format

TABLE 16-1

Symbol	Action
month, Month, MONTH	Shows the complete name of the month all lowercase, initial capitalized, or all uppercase
yy or YY	Shows the year in two digits
yyyy or YYYY	Shows the year in four digits
h or H	Shows the hour in one or two digits using 24-hour format. Follow by ampm or AMPM for 12-hour format
hh or HH	Shows the hour in two digits; include ampm or AMPM for 12-hour format
Mi	Shows the minutes in one or two digits
Mmi	Shows the minutes in two digits
s or S	Shows the seconds in one or two digits
ss or SS	Shows the minutes in two digits
AMPM	Uses 12-hour format displaying either AM or PM
*	When the entry is shorter than the column width, fills the remainder of the cell to the right of the last character with asterisks
' '	Displays the characters enclosed in single quotation marks; use when you want to display a character that is also used as a format code (quotation marks are not needed for characters not used as codes)
\	Performs the same function as quotation marks but only for the single character following the backslash

Characters Used to Create Your Own Numeric Format (*continued*)

TABLE 16-1

Working with Blocks, Windows, and Notebooks

17

Sometimes you need to make sweeping changes to a worksheet or take actions that affect entire blocks, multiple worksheets, or the entire notebook. With Corel Quattro Pro you don't have to repeat your work on individual cells or pages. In this chapter, you will learn how to use block names to quickly refer to sections of your worksheet, set up your pages for printing, create groups of pages, and use other timesaving techniques.

Block Names

Point mode makes referring to cells and ranges of cells easier than typing coordinates, but it can be inconvenient when you need to scroll to a distant area of the worksheet or refer to the same cell or range frequently. You can try to remember the references of cells that you use often, but who can keep all of those numbers in their head?

The solution to this common problem is using *named blocks*—giving an easy-to-remember name to a cell or block of cells. When you need to refer to the cells in a formula or dialog box, just use the name. You can even display a list of your block names to make them easier to remember.

Not only are names easier to remember than coordinates, they make more sense. After creating a large worksheet, you may forget what the formula +G4–H5 means, but not the formula +Gross–Expenses. The names show you what your formula represents and make it easier to track down worksheet errors. Corel Quattro Pro won't necessarily know, for example, if you enter the wrong coordinates in a formula, but it will warn you if you use a name that hasn't been defined.

To name a block of cells, follow these steps:

1. Select the block you want to name. Remember that a block can even be a single selected cell.

2. Choose Block Names from the Insert menu to see the Block Names dialog box listing any existing block names.

3. In the Name text box, type a name for the block that is not already assigned.

4. Click on OK.

A block name can be up to 63 characters long, including numbers, letters, spaces, and most punctuation marks. You can't use the operator characters (+, –, *, /, ^, =, <, >, #, or &) because they are reserved for formulas; you also cannot use the dollar sign and the opening and closing parentheses. Don't use all numbers or names that are cell coordinates, such as A1. Block names are not case sensitive, but they always appear uppercase in the input line. Click on Add and then close the dialog box.

You can have as many block names as you need in a worksheet, and their ranges can overlap. The same cells can be in more than one named block. In fact, the same set of cells can have more than one name.

 OTE: *When you click in a cell that has its own block name, the name will appear in place of the coordinates in the input line.*

Using Block Names

When you want to use a block name in a formula or dialog box, just enter its name where you would otherwise type coordinates or use Point mode.

To see a list of block names when you are in the input line, press the F3 key or click on the Navigate button in the input line. This procedure works, however, only when you are ready to enter a cell coordinate, such as after a plus sign, an operator, or an opening parenthesis. Otherwise, the Navigate button will be dimmed, and pressing F3 selects the File menu command. If you are in a dialog box, press F3 to see the block name list when you are in a text box that accepts cell coordinates. Click on the block name in the list to insert it into the formula or dialog box.

 **OTE:**   *When you are not entering or editing information into a cell, use the Navigate button to quickly select a block. Click on the button and then on the name of the block you want to select.*

Changing a Block Name

To rename a block, you must first delete the name and then start over by redefining the same block. Delete a name by selecting it in the Block Names dialog box and clicking on Delete. (Click on Delete All to remove all of the names from the worksheet.)

Deleting a block name will not affect formulas. Corel Quattro Pro will automatically replace the names with their references wherever the name appears in a formula. However, it will not automatically replace the coordinates when you give a name to a referenced cell or block.

It is easier to change the block that a name references. Display the Block Names dialog box and click on the name you want to reassign. Enter the cell coordinates and then click on Add. The name now refers to the new block.

The block name, by the way, is linked with the cells in the upper-left and lower-right corners. If you change the contents of these cells with the Move Block command, the block name will no longer be valid.

Creating Block Names from Labels

It is common to have a number of cells that correspond to a series of labels, as shown in Figure 17-1. You can automatically assign the labels as the block names for their corresponding values. In our example, each label in column B would become the block name for the value to its right in column C.

Here's how to use labels as block names.

1. Select the labels that you want to use as the block names. They must be labels, not values.

2. Choose Block Names from the Insert menu.

3. Click the Labels button to display the dialog box shown here:

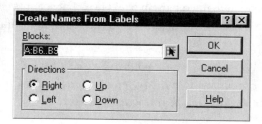

4. Select the position of the cells you want to name in relation to the labels. In our example, you'd select Right.

5. Click OK. Each of the labels will now be listed as block names.

6. Close the Block Names dialog box.

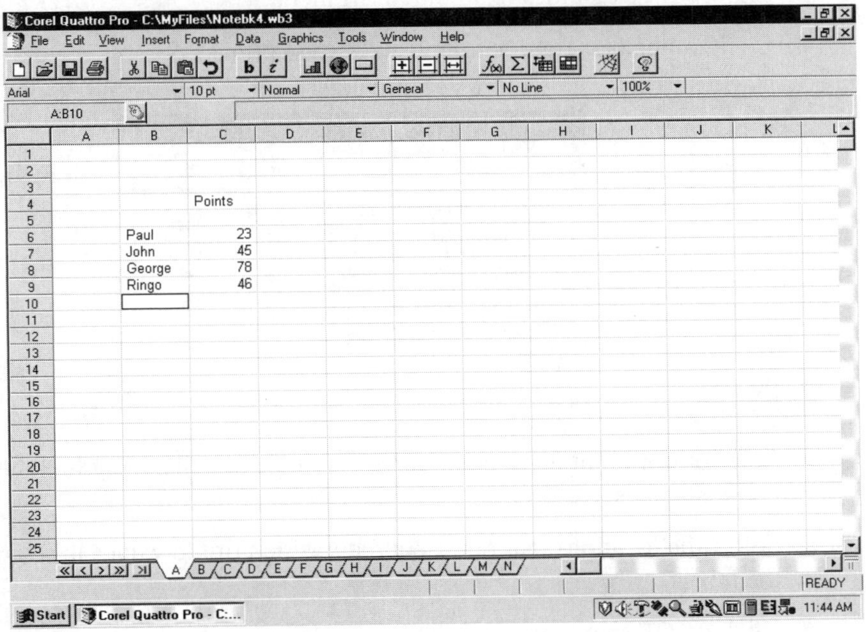

Assigning
labels as
block names

FIGURE 17-1

If you later change the text of a label, the block name does not change automatically. You must still use the old label as the name. To change the name, you must delete it and assign a new one.

If error messages appear when you use one of the names, check the label carefully for extra spaces before or after your label text. For instance, you may accidentally enter a blank space after a label when you're typing it in the cell. You may not notice the space in the cell, but Corel Quattro Pro will include the space in the block name. If you later leave out the space when typing the block name, Corel Quattro Pro will display a message indicating that the block name does not exist.

Using Labels for Multiple Cell Blocks

The Labels button can be used only when naming single cells immediately next to the label. You can also assign label names to a range of cells, or to combine a row and column label into one block name. Follow these steps:

1. Select the labels that you want to use as the block names. They must be labels, not values.

2. Choose Block Names from the Insert menu.

3. Click on the Generate button to see these options:

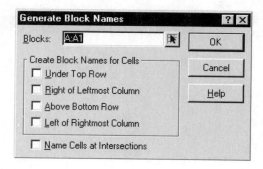

4. Enter or use Point mode to indicate the range of cells, including the labels and the values.

5. Select the locations that represent the position of the values in relation to the labels.

6. Click on OK and then close the Block Names dialog box.

The most important step in this procedure is selecting the correct location options. For example, to use a label as the name for a block of cells in the row to its right, click on Right of Leftmost Column. To use a column header as a label for cells below it, click on Under Top Row.

You can select more than one option to use a label for a block that spans rows or columns. To use a label for values next to it and in the following row, for example, choose both Under Top Row and Right of Leftmost Column.

You can also combine a row and column heading together to reference a single cell. For example, suppose you have a value in the row labeled Wages and in the Column labeled Qtr 1. Select the range, choose both Under Top Row and Right of Leftmost Column, and click on Name Cells At Intersections. The value at the intersection of those labels will now be named Qtr1_Wages.

Displaying a Block Name Table

The Navigate button and F3 key make it easy to list your block names. As a more visual reminder, you can display a table directly on your worksheet listing the block names and their coordinates. To do so, follow these steps:

1. Display the Block Names dialog box and click on the Output button.

2. Select the top-left cell where you want the name table to appear on your worksheet. Corel Quattro Pro will overwrite existing information when it displays the table, so make sure there are enough blank cells below and in the column to the right to display all of the names and their references.

3. Click on OK, and then close the dialog box to display the table. The block names will be in the first column sorted alphabetically.

If you add, rename, or delete block names, Corel Quattro Pro will not update the table automatically. Create the table again in the same location to replace it.

Customizing Printouts

Even though we're on the verge of a revolution in electronic communications, printed copies of your worksheets are still important. Your printouts, or published Envoy documents, should be easy to read and support your information. You use the options in the Print dialog box to control the way your document is printed. There are also two separate dialog boxes that you access through the Print command that let you format and control the appearance of your printout.

Print Options

Use the Print dialog box to choose the print range and which pages of your worksheet to print. By default, the options are set to print one copy of every page in the current worksheet. The Current Page setting actually means the current worksheet, no matter how many pages it fills.

You can choose to print multiple copies or specific pages of the worksheet.

Sheet Options

Sheet Options determine what parts of your worksheet get printed. In the Print dialog box, click on Sheet Options to display the dialog box shown in Figure 17-2.

Headings are rows or columns that will print on every page. If you have a long worksheet, labels in the top row will not print on the top of every page, so readers may have difficulty relating information in the columns. To repeat a row on each page, enter the coordinates of at least one cell in the row in the Top Heading box.

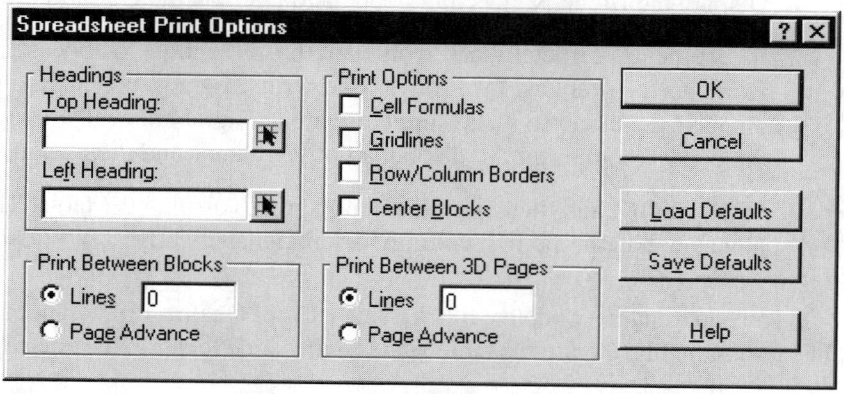

Spreadsheet Print Options   ? ✕

Headings
Top Heading:

Left Heading:

Print Options
☐ Cell Formulas
☐ Gridlines
☐ Row/Column Borders
☐ Center Blocks

OK

Cancel

Load Defaults

Save Defaults

Print Between Blocks
◉ Lines 0
○ Page Advance

Print Between 3D Pages
◉ Lines 0
○ Page Advance

Help

Using Sheet Options to determine what is printed

FIGURE 17-2

To print several rows as a heading, select cells in all of the rows. To repeat a column, enter cells in the columns you want to repeat in the Left Heading box. When you specify the print range, do not include the heading rows or columns. If you do, they will print twice.

The choices in the Print Options group determine what elements of the worksheet appear on paper.

- *Gridlines* prints the normally nonprinted grid lines. Don't use this option if you've already added your own grid lines using line drawing.

- *Row/Column* prints the row letters and column numbers. This is a good choice if you're printing a reference or backup copy.

- *Cell Formulas* prints the actual formulas in the cells, not their calculated results. This is handy for a backup copy of your worksheet; however, headings, grid lines, and row and column borders will not print at the same time, and blocks will not be centered.

- *Center Blocks* centers your printout between the left and right margins. Normally, the first column prints at the left margin.

If your print range includes two or more noncontiguous blocks, you can determine how they are spaced on the page. The Lines setting in Print Between Blocks determines the number of blank lines to place between groups. The Lines setting in the Print Between 3D Pages group determines the number of lines to print between groups on each page. To start each block on a new page, click on Page Advance.

Page Setup

To customize the layout of your page, click on Page Setup to see the Spreadsheet Page Setup dialog box with five pages, as shown in Figure 17-3. In the Paper Type page, select the paper size and orientation. Your choices depend on the printer you have installed in Windows 95. Use landscape orientation when you want to print more columns on a page.

Headers and Footers

A header is a line of text that prints on the top of each page; a footer prints on the bottom of each page. You can enter your own text and choose built-in elements such as the date, page number, or filename. To add a header or footer, click on the Header/Footer tab. In the Header or Footer text box, enter the text that you want to appear on your printout. Use the Font button to change the font and size of the text.

You can also use the special codes shown in Table 17-1. For example, enter Page #p of #P to display Page 1 of 4, or File #f printed on #d for the notebook name and date it was printed. You can use any combination of the codes in the header, footer, or both.

The vertical bar (usually entered with the SHIFT and backslash keys) works like a tab. Enter one to center text, two to align text on the right. To center the notebook name and its full path, for instance, enter |#F.

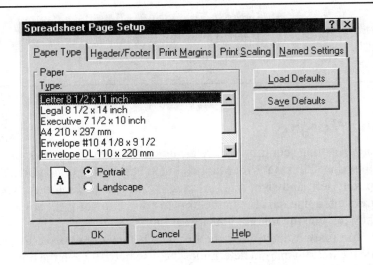

Spreadsheet
Page Setup
dialog box

FIGURE 17-3

Code	Function
|	Centers or right-aligns text
#d	Inserts the current date in the Short International format as set in the Application Properties
#D	Inserts the current date in the Long International format as set in the Application Properties
#ds	Inserts the current date in the Windows Short Date format
#Ds	Inserts the current date in Windows Long Date format
#t	Inserts the current time in the Short International format as set in the Application Properties
#T	Inserts the current time in the Long International format as set in the Application Properties
#ts	Inserts the current time in Windows Short Time format
#Ts	Inserts the current time in Windows Long Time format
#p	Inserts the page number
#p+n	Inserts the current page number plus the number n
#P	Inserts the number of pages being printed
#P+n	Inserts the number of pages plus the number n
#f	Inserts the name of the notebook
#F	Inserts the name and path of the notebook
#n	Prints the remainder of the header or footer on a second line

Codes for Creating Headers and Footers

TABLE 17-1

Setting Margins

The margin settings contribute to determining the number of rows and columns that fit on the page. Click on Print Margins in the Page Setup dialog box, then enter the top, bottom, left, and right margins, and the header or footer. As you highlight a measurement, a line darkens in the drawing at the lower-right corner of the dialog box, showing you the margin you are setting.

The top margin determines the distance between the top of the paper and the headers; the bottom margin determines the distance between the bottom of the page and the footer. Use the Header and Footer settings to control the distance between the header and the first row, and between the footer and the last row. The exact position of the first row, then, is the sum of the top margin and header settings. Enter your settings in the same unit that is displayed, inches or centimeters.

Many laser printers cannot print very close to the edge of the page and need at least a quarter-inch margin. If you get a printer error, or some text does not print properly, widen the margins.

 OTE: *You can also set margins by dragging margin lines in Print Preview mode.*

When your worksheet is more than one page long, Corel Quattro Pro inserts soft page breaks to divide it into pages. If you are using continuous paper or want to fill up as much of the page as possible and let your printer change pages, deselect Break Pages in the Margins tab. This will also turn off all headers and footers.

Printing Large Worksheets

Corel Quattro Pro prints a large worksheet by printing as many columns that can fit on the first page, and all of the rows in those columns on consecutive pages. It then goes back to the first row and begins printing the next series of columns.

If you want your pages divided differently, add hard page breaks where you want one page to end and another to begin. To insert a hard page break, choose Page Break from the Insert menu, or type |:: in a cell in the first column of a print block.

 OTE: *Don't put any other information in the row with the page break because the row does not print.*

Changing the Print Scale

By adjusting the font size, margins, column width, and row height, you can determine how much of a worksheet prints on a page. You can also reduce or enlarge the entire printout without changing any other formats. Reducing the print size fits more cells on each page but makes it more difficult to read. If you've already adjusted margins and other settings and still need to fit an extra row or column on the page, try reducing the scale slightly.

To change the scale, use the Print Scaling option in the Page Setup dialog box. Enter a setting less than 100 to reduce the printout, more than 100 to enlarge it. You can enter a setting between 1 and 1000. Click on Fit To Print to have Corel Quattro Pro automatically reduce the scale to print the worksheet on as few pages as possible.

Scaling affects the size of all characters and graphics, as well as the header and footer margin settings. Other page margins will not be affected.

Saving and Restoring Print Settings

If you change your mind about Sheet Options or Page Setup settings, you can quickly return to Corel Quattro Pro's default values by selecting the Load Defaults button in either dialog box.

Your sheet and page setup settings only affect the current worksheet. If you want to use the same settings with every notebook, make them the new default values. To do so, click on the Save Defaults button in either dialog box. Keep in mind that your own settings will now be used when you click on the Load Defaults button.

To return to Corel Quattro Pro's original settings, use the Windows 95 Notepad accessory to delete the Print Settings section in the file QPW.INI in Windows.

Saving Named Group Settings

If you use a variety of setups, you can save each as a group and then load the group by name when you need to. The group includes the settings in the Print, Print Options, and Page Setup dialog boxes. Save your settings under a name using these steps:

1. Display the Page Setup dialog box.

2. Click on Named Settings.

3. In the New Set text box, type a group name and then click on Add. Click on Update if you want to change an existing group.

4. Click on OK.

5. Save the notebook. Unlike default settings, which are globally available to all notebooks, named groups are stored with the notebook itself.

When you want to use a group, click on the Named Settings tab, select the group you want to use, and then click on Use.

Preventing Titles from Scrolling

As you scroll around a worksheet, the row and column labels will scroll out of view. So if you scroll down the page, for example, you will no longer see the labels that identify the purpose of each column. Likewise, as you scroll to the right, you will no longer see the labels that identify the rows. By locking titles into place, you prevent rows or columns from scrolling out of view, making it easier to enter information into large worksheets.

To lock rows, use these steps:

1. Select the uppermost row that you do not want to be locked. For example, to lock rows 1 and 2, select row 3. To lock columns, select the leftmost column that you do not want to lock—choose column B, for example, to lock column A. If you want to lock both rows and columns, click in the first cell in the top-left portion of the worksheet that you do not want locked. In order to lock row 1 and column A, click on cell B2.

2. Pull down the View menu, point to Locked Titles, and choose Horizontal to lock rows, Vertical to lock columns, or Both to lock rows and columns. If you want to unlock the titles at any time, select Locked Titles from the View menu and choose Clear.

3. Click on OK.

Locking titles prevents them from scrolling, but it does not affect your printout. The locked titles will not print on every page even though they always appear onscreen. To repeat the titles on each page, set the Top Heading and Left Heading sheet options.

You cannot click in a cell in a locked title. So if you want to edit the text in the locked title, unlock it first, or use the Go To command from the Edit menu to go to the cell you want to edit. The Go To command, however, makes a duplicate copy of the locked area that you can edit. Remove the duplicated row or column by scrolling the window.

Creating Groups

In Chapter 14 you learned how to select a 3-D group of cells by clicking on the page tabs while holding down the SHIFT key. These groups are temporary because they only remain in effect until you take some action on the group, such as applying a format or using AutoFill. If you want to use a group periodically, or add or delete information to multiple pages at one time, then name the group of pages and turn on Group mode.

For example, suppose you want to enter the same label in a cell in the first ten pages of the notebook. Or perhaps you want to use Point mode to quickly select the same block on several pages. Rather than repeat your actions on each page every time, you create a group so Corel Quattro Pro will duplicate your actions on every page for you.

You create a group by selecting the pages that you want to include, and then giving the group a name. Here's how:

1. Hold down the SHIFT key and click on the tabs of the pages you want to include in the group.

2. Select Group Names from the Insert menu to display the Define/Modify Group dialog box shown in Figure 17-4.

3. Type a name for the group using the same rules as block names.

4. Confirm that the correct pages are shown in the First Page and Last Page boxes—correct them if necessary.

5. Click on OK to close the dialog box.

When you want to perform an action on a 3-D block of cells in the group, you must first turn on Group mode. Pull down the View menu and click on Group mode,

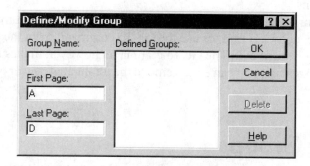

Creating a
group name

FIGURE 17-4

or press ALT+F5. Corel Quattro Pro will display a blue line below the tabs in the group to indicate that Group mode is turned on.

Now formatting and other changes to one cell or block on a page (except entering and deleting) are duplicated on every page. When you no longer want to act on the 3-D block, turn off Group mode—deselect Group mode on the View menu or press ALT+F5 again. The line under the tabs will disappear, showing that the group function is turned off.

To avoid unwanted effects, text that you type directly in a cell when Group mode is turned on will not be duplicated across the pages. When you want to enter text on every page, turn on Group mode, type the text on any of the pages in the group, hold down the CTRL key, and press ENTER. This is called "drilling down." You must press ENTER; clicking the Enter box in the input line will not drill down the text.

 OTE: *Use the Clear command or CTRL+DEL to delete information from every page.*

When Group mode is turned on, most actions affect every page of the group. You have to be careful not to accidentally change something on one page that you do not intend. For example, if you select a group of cells and choose Clear or Delete from the Edit menu, all of the cells on every page of the group will be cleared. The Delete command from the Edit or QuickMenu work the same way. To erase information from just one page, use the DEL key or turn off Group mode first.

The same warning applies to pointing to cells for formulas, functions, and in dialog boxes. With Group mode turned on, you'll get a 3-D reference, using the syntax *group-name:range*. So if you point to a range on one sheet to average a row of cells, you will actually calculate the average of the cells from all of the pages in the group. Before pointing to cells, turn Group mode off.

If you want to copy information from one page to all of the pages, you'll also need to turn off Group mode; otherwise, you'll copy a 3-D group rather than just cells from one page. Turn off Group mode, copy the cells, turn on Group mode, and then paste them. The same two-dimensional block will be pasted to all of the pages.

You can have more than one group in the same notebook, although a page cannot be in more than one group. To delete a group, select Group Name from the Insert menu, click on the group, and then on Delete. To change the pages included in the group, choose its name, and then edit the entries in the First Page and/or Last Page edit fields in the Define/Modify Group dialog box.

Using Window Panes

When you need to refer to a section on a large worksheet, you can always scroll or use the Go To command. But then you'd have to scroll back to your original location to continue working. Instead of scrolling back and forth, you can divide your screen into two panes, either vertically or horizontally, and view two parts of the same worksheet at the same time. You create panes using the Pane Splitter at the lower-right corner of the window, where the horizontal and vertical scroll bars meet, or by using the Split Window command from the View menu.

To split the screen into two horizontal panes, point to the top portion of the Pane Splitter so the arrows points left and right. To split into two vertical panes, point to the lower portion so the arrows point up and down. Now drag the mouse into the window. As you drag, a line appears showing the position of the pane. Release the mouse when the line is where you want the panes to appear. As shown in Figure 17-5, both panes have page tabs, tab scrolls, and scroll bars to move about the notebook. The Pane Splitter will appear where the two panes meet.

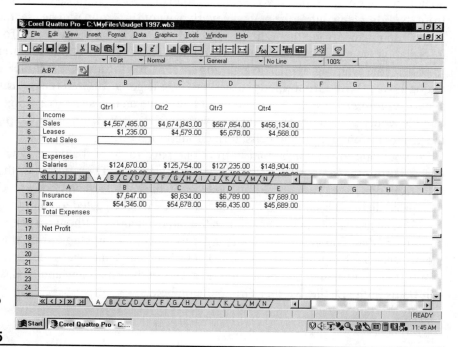

Worksheet divided into panes

FIGURE 17-5

17

Changes you make in one pane will be duplicated on the other. By default, the two panes are synchronized. This means that scrolling one pane in the direction of the split will scroll the other as well. For example, scrolling horizontal panes in a horizontal direction and vertical panes in a vertical direction will be synchronized.

If you unsynchronize the panes, you can scroll them independently to reveal different parts of the same worksheet. To unsynchronize panes, choose Split Window from the View menu, and deselect Synchronized. Click on the same option if you later want to synchronize the panes again.

To move from one pane to another, click in the pane with the mouse or press the F6 key to move from pane to pane.

To change the size of the panes, drag the Pane Splitter. Dragging it all the way off the window will remove a pane, displaying one view of the worksheet.

Duplicating Windows

You use panes to look at different parts of the same worksheet, but both panes will be in the same magnification, and you cannot drag and drop cells from one pane to the other. When you want to use different magnifications and drag and drop between sections of the worksheet, create a second view window for the same worksheet.

Choose New View from the Window menu. Another window appears, displaying the same worksheet. In the title bar, the name of the notebook will be followed by a colon and the window number. Changes that you make to cell contents and format will be duplicated in both windows. However, changes to the locked titles, panes, or magnification are not. To remove the duplicate window, click on its Close button.

Multiple windows are most effective when you can see them at the same time. Arranging multiple windows on the Corel Quattro Pro screen is a straight Windows 95 technique, performed as follows:

1. Choose Cascade from the Window menu to displays the windows overlapped or choose Tile to divide the screen so all of the windows appear.

2. Change the size and move windows as you would normally.

To select a window when more than one is displayed, click anywhere in the window, or select Window from the menu bar and then click on the window name. Use the Window menu to change windows when they are not arranged on the screen, when one window is in the background and cannot be seen. Copy and move cells between windows the same as you would within a window, using drag and drop, or cut and copy.

All of these techniques apply as well to windows from more than one notebook. To work with several notebooks at one time, open each of them and then arrange the screens as desired, cascading or tiling them with the Window menu.

Charts, Maps, and Graphics

18

When you want your data to have maximum impact, try presenting the information as a graph or map, or emphasizing points with another graphic. You can insert clip art and TextArt into a Corel Quattro Pro worksheet just as you can with a Corel WordPerfect document. Charts and maps, however, are ideally suited to Corel Quattro Pro because they can visually convey trends and patterns in numeric data. The techniques for charts and maps are similar—if not almost identical—so once you learn how to create one, you can easily create the other. There are some important differences, so read over each section in this chapter carefully. You can also combine charts, maps, and slides that contain text into an onscreen slide show for an impressive presentation.

 Add TextArt to a worksheet by choosing TextArt from the Insert Object dialog box. Use the TextArt window just as you learned to do in Chapter 12.

Creating Charts

Before creating a graph for the first time, you should understand a few things that go into one. A graph must have at least one data series. A data series is a set of numbers representing the values of something you are measuring or reporting. For example, the graph shown in Figure 18-1 has two series, both of which show dollar amounts in each of four quarters. The first series, represented by the lighter color bars, shows expenses in the four quarters. The second series, in the darker bars, shows revenue. The chart also contains X- and Y-axis labels. The X-axis labels explain what each set of numbers represents, in this case the four quarters of the year. The Y-axis label shows the values being represented.

 OTE: *When you have more than one series, you can have a legend that explains what each series represents.*

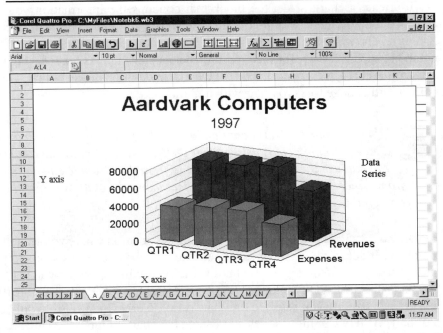

The parts of
a chart

FIGURE 18-1

You can create a graph either as a floating object or in a separate window. A floating object appears on the worksheet page, so you can print it on the same sheet as the data that it represents and change its position on the page. When you create a chart in its own windows, you must print it separately from the worksheet.

 You can insert charts and maps that you create with Corel Quattro Pro into your Corel WordPerfect documents.

Floating Objects

You can create a floating chart in two ways—using the QuickChart button in the toolbar or the Chart Expert. The Expert lets you choose the chart type and other options as you create the chart. You don't get those options with the QuickChart tool, although you can edit any chart to change its properties after you create it.

To create a chart, select the block that contains the information you want to chart—including the row and column labels. The column labels will become the X-axis labels, while the row labels will identify each series in the legend. If you use numbers, such as years, for the column labels, enter them as text starting with the apostrophe character. Then click on the QuickChart button in the toolbar. The mouse pointer will change to a crosshair with a miniature chart.

IP: *You must select a contiguous block of cells, without empty rows, to create a floating chart using either the QuickChart button or Chart Expert. You can use the New Chart command from the Graphics menu to create a chart from noncontiguous cells that you select using the CTRL key, but check your results carefully.*

Drag a rectangle in the worksheet the size and position where you want the chart to appear. It doesn't have to be exact because you can change its size and position later. When you release the mouse button, the chart will appear. (If you just click on the worksheet instead of dragging the mouse, Corel Quattro Pro will create the chart in a default size.) If you selected only one series, Corel Quattro Pro would create a pie chart. With two or more series, it creates a bar chart. Figure 18-2 shows a sample chart and the data that was used to create it. Enter the worksheet yourself, and then create a chart next to it as shown in the figure. Be sure to select the range of cells A4..D7, click on the QuickChart button, and then drag the mouse around blocks E1 to K22.

The small boxes around the border of the graph are called *handles*. You use the handles to change the size of the graph, and they indicate that the chart is selected. If you click outside of the chart area, the handles will disappear and the chart will no longer be selected. To change the chart's size or position, or other properties, click on the chart to select it first.

The chart is linked to the worksheet cells that you selected to create it. So if you change any of the data used to create the graph, Corel Quattro Pro will adjust the chart automatically. One advantage of the floating chart is that you can place the chart and the worksheet side by side on the screen to instantly see the effects of changing values on the chart.

To delete a floating chart, select it and then press DEL. A dialog box will appear asking if you want to also delete the associated worksheet cells. Click on No, unless you want to delete both the chart and the worksheet associated with it. Normally, you would delete only the chart.

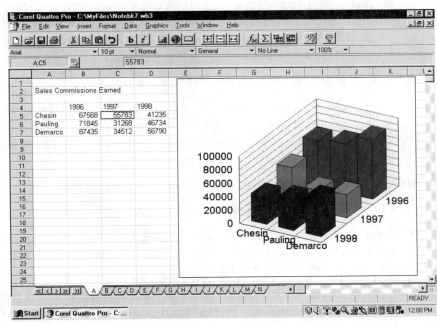

Sample
chart and
worksheet

FIGURE 18-2

Using Chart Expert

You can also create a chart using the Chart Expert. It takes a few extra steps, but you get to select chart options in the process. You can also choose to create a floating chart or to place the chart in its own window. Here's how to use Chart Expert:

1. Select the range of cells that you want to chart.

2. Pull down the Tools menu, point to Experts, and click on Chart. The first Chart Expert box appears, showing the coordinates of the selected block.

3. If you did not select the range first, or if it is incorrect, enter the range or use Point mode. The box has two other options:

   ■ *Swap rows/columns* plots columns as the series, and places the X-axis series labels in the legend.

- *Reverse series* plots last series first. Use this option if you are creating a 3-D chart, for example, and the first series would have larger bars that obscure the others. Reversing the plot would place the smaller bars in the foreground.

4. Select the general category of chart you want to create.

5. Click on Next Step to display a dialog box showing several specific types of chart in the category you selected, as shown in Figure 18-3. If you select a bar chart as the general category, for instance, the dialog box includes several different types of bar charts.

6. Click on the type of chart you want and then click on Next Step.

7. Choose an overall color scheme and then click on Next Step.

8. Enter a chart title and subtitle and labels for the X axis and Y axis. You can also choose if you want to place the chart on the notebook page (floating) or in its own window.

9. Click on Create Chart. If you choose to place it on the notebook page, drag the mouse to indicate the position and size. When you release the mouse button, the chart will appear.

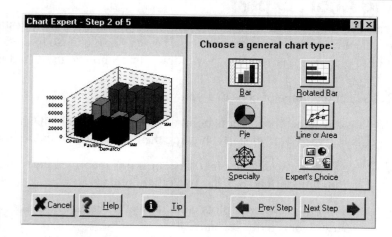

Selecting a chart type in the Chart Expert dialog box

FIGURE 18-3

Changing Graph Size

You can easily change the size and position of a chart, using the same techniques as editing a graphic in Corel WordPerfect. To change the size of a floating chart, point to one of the graph handles and drag.

- Drag a handle on the top or bottom border to change the height.

- Drag a handle on the right or left to change the width.

- Drag a handle on a corner to change the height and width at the same time.

To move a graph, use the following steps:

1. Place the mouse pointer inside the graph and hold down the mouse button so the pointer appears as a hand.

2. Drag the mouse to change the location. The screen will scroll as you drag the mouse, and an outline of the graph will move with the pointer.

3. Position the outline where you want the graph to appear, and then release the mouse button.

Creating a Chart in a Window

When you create a chart in its own window, the chart is not on the worksheet page and Corel Quattro Pro determines its size. This is a good choice if you don't want the chart and worksheet to appear together, and you don't want to use worksheet space for the chart.

To create a chart in a window, use Chart Expert or the New Chart command from the Graphics menu. With Chart Expert, just select the window option in the last Chart Expert dialog box.

To use the New Chart command, select the cells that you want to chart, pull down the Graphics menu, and click on New Chart to see the dialog box in Figure 18-4. The pages in the dialog box give you the same options as Chart Expert. Use the following steps:

1. In the Series page, designate the blocks to use for the X axis, legend, and data series. Corel Quattro Pro will try to identify the blocks from the type of data in them.

2. In the Type page, select the general and specific chart type.

3. In the Titles page, enter the title and subtitle, and axis labels.

4. In the Name page, give the chart a name.

When you close the dialog box, the completed chart will appear in its own window and with its own Chart menu and toolbar, as shown in Figure 18-5.

As with a floating chart, the chart in the window is also linked to the worksheet data, and it will change if you edit the values in the associated cells. To see both the chart and worksheet onscreen at the same time, however, you must tile the windows and adjust their sizes.

The Chart window appears in the foreground, with the worksheet behind. When you want to return to the worksheet, you can either minimize the Chart window or pull down the Window menu and click on the worksheet name in the list of windows. To redisplay the chart, select its name from the Window menu, or if you can see it minimized, click on its Restore button.

If you close the Chart window by clicking on its Close button, you can open it again only from the Objects page. Icons for every chart and map—floating or in their own windows—are placed on the Objects page that you'll learn about later.

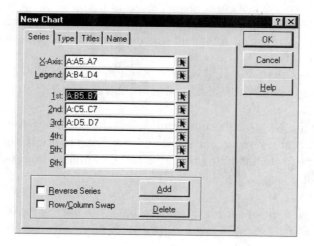

New Chart
dialog box

FIGURE 18-4

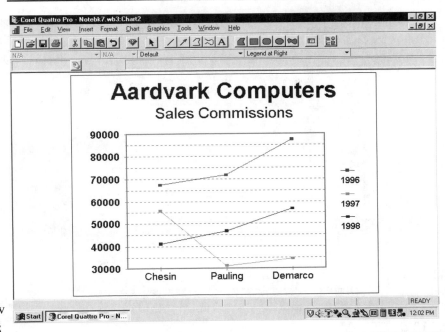

Chart in its
own window

 FIGURE 18-5

Editing Charts

You can modify a chart at any time, changing its type, titles, appearance, and other properties. If you created a chart in its own window, all of the menu and toolbar tools for editing will appear when its window is active.

The quick way to change some properties of a floating chart, however, is to right-click on it to see the QuickMenu shown in Figure 18-6. Here you can change the type, series, and titles. Choose View to display the chart full screen—click the mouse when you have finished.

OTE: *Chart Properties include the border color and type, the object name, protection status, and source.*

To access a full range of editing tools to customize a floating chart, you need to display the Chart menu and toolbar that appear when a chart is in a window. You can do this two ways with a floating chart. If you double-click on the chart, you can

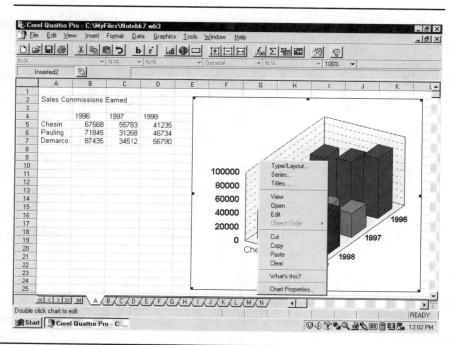

QuickMenu
for editing a
chart

FIGURE 18-6

edit it in place. This means that the Chart menu and toolbar will appear onscreen, but that you can see the chart along with the worksheet. You can also edit the chart in place by selecting Edit from the chart's QuickMenu.

To edit the chart in a separate window, even though it was created as a floating chart, right-click on the chart and choose Open from the QuickMenu. When you close this Chart window, however, you will still see the chart on the worksheet page.

 IP: *The Edit and Open options will only appear in the QuickMenu when the chart is not already in the Edit mode. If you are already editing the chart, click outside of it, and then right-click on the chart to show the QuickMenu.*

Use the Chart menu bar and the toolbar to edit the chart and add other elements to it. The Chart menu offers these features:

■ *View* lets you change the aspect ratio the chart is shown in. Options include Floating Chart, Screen Slide, 35mm Slide, Print Preview, and Full

Extent. Experiment with the options to find the most pleasing appearance onscreen and when printed.

■ *Insert* lets you add other elements to the chart, such as clip art from your disk, a drawing object, or another object from other Windows applications. You can also choose Link to Cells to add a live picture of the charted cells right in the chart box. That way, you'll see your worksheet data when you print the chart.

■ *Format* arranges the relationship of the graphics to the page and to other graphics, with options Align, Position, Space, Group, Ungroup, and Object Order.

■ *Chart* lets you change the appearance and type of the chart. Options are Gallery, Type/Layout, Series, Titles, Legend, Axis, Perspective (for 3-D charts), Background, and Export to File.

■ *Graphics* lets you insert, edit, and delete charts; create, edit, and play slide shows.

Let's take a look at some of the ways you can customize a chart.

Selecting Color Schemes

When you are editing a chart, most of the sections in the power bar will be dimmed. You can pull down the Style list in the power bar, however, to choose an overall color scheme:

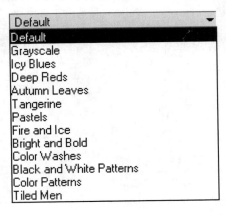

The style determines the background colors and patterns. Select each of the options in turn to see their effects on a chart, and then settle for the one that you like best. Some styles are more appropriate for onscreen display than for printing.

Changing the Chart Type

After you create your chart, you may find that the type you selected does not adequately portray what you want to get across. You may also want to experiment by selecting other chart types, and subtypes, until you find the most effective design. To change the chart type, use these steps:

1. Pull down the Chart menu.

2. Click on Gallery or on Type/Layout.

3. Choose the category and style from the dialog box that appears.

4. Click on OK.

The Gallery dialog box also offers an Advisor button. Click on Advisor to let Corel Quattro Pro help you choose the best type for your data, as shown in Figure 18-7. Start by specifying qualifications called *constraints*. Use the sliders in the Constraints section to indicate your preferences between stressing individual or

Using the Chart Advisor to help select the best chart for your data

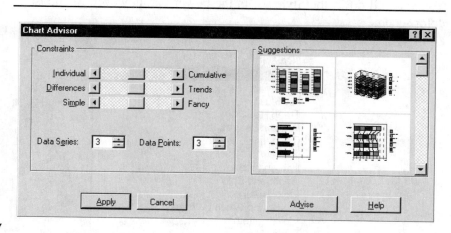

FIGURE 18-7

cumulative results, showing differences or trends, or using a simple or fancy layout. Also, set the number of series and data points. When you click on Advise, Corel Quattro Pro will suggest the chart style for you. To change the chart to that style, click on Apply.

Changing the Chart Background

By default, charts appear in a box with a single border and clear background. To select other settings, choose Background from the Chart menu. The dialog box that appears has three pages:

- *Box settings* determine the shape and color of the box surrounding the chart.

- *Fill color* sets the background color and pattern.

- *Chart button* lets you use the chart as a live button during a slide show. You can determine what happens when you click on the chart.

Select options from the three pages, and then close the dialog box. You can always reopen the box and change your settings if the overall effect is not what you had in mind.

Changing 3-D Perspective

Three-dimensional charts can be quite effective and eye-catching. To customize their appearance, choose Perspective from the Chart menu to see the dialog box shown in Figure 18-8.

In the 3-D View page, adjust the rotation and elevation. Changing rotation would change the perspective as if you were walking around the chart on a plane even with the X axis. It would be like walking around a house. If you rotate in one direction, you'd be looking at the chart more from the right; in the other direction, from the left.

Elevation is the view from top to bottom, as if you could float above the chart at various angles. Elevate in one direction to look "down" at the top of the chart; the other direction to look up at it.

The depth setting affects the distance from the front of the chart to its back wall, the rectangle behind the charted data. Height is the size of the chart from the bottom to the top—the distance from the X axis to the top of the chart.

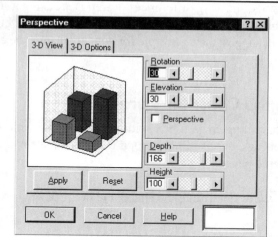

Setting
options for
3-D charts

FIGURE 18-8

 IP: *Click on the Perspective check box to maintain the current ratio as you change settings.*

The 3-D Options page determines if the left and back walls, and the base appear. You can also choose between thick or default walls.

Inserting a Legend

When you create a 2-D chart with at least two series, Corel Quattro Pro will normally also include a legend. If not, you can add a legend yourself. You may have to do this, for example, if you add a series to an existing chart, or if you delete the legend by mistake. Here's how to insert a legend:

1. Select Legend from the Chart window to display a dialog box of legend options.

2. Choose a position for the legend.

3. Select a font for the text.

4. Choose a text color and background.

5. Choose the shape of the legend box and the background color.

6. Click on OK.

You can later move the legend and change its properties.

OTE: *You can only add a legend to charts that do not already have labels identifying the series.*

When you are editing a chart with more than one series, you can also create a legend using the Legend list in the Chart power bar. The options are No Legend, Legend at Bottom, and Legend at Right.

Editing Chart Sections

In addition to editing the overall chart, you can customize each of its individual elements, such as an axis, series bar, or section of the pie. The trick is to first select only that portion of the chart. You'll know the part is selected when the handles appear just around it—not around the entire chart or some other section. You have to start by selecting the entire chart and then clicking again on the section you want to edit. Before right-clicking to display the QuickMenu, or choosing options from the menu bar, make certain that only the desired portion is selected—sometimes it takes a few tries.

Once you've selected the correct area, right-click on it to display the QuickMenu and then change its properties. The options that appear will depend on the object you selected. Properties for wall and background areas, for example, are usually limited to the fill color and pattern, and the shape and size of the border line. The properties for series and axis are more extensive.

Customizing a Series

Setting the properties for a data series controls how the bar, line, area, pie slice, or data points appear on the chart. To change a series, right-click on any of the bars or lines that represent one of its values. Changing the color of one bar in the series, for example, will affect all of the bars in the series.

The exact options that you can set depend on the type of chart, and whether it is 2-D or 3-D. With 2-D bar charts, for instance, you can change the width of the bars, the spacing between them, and the extent that they overlap. In some cases, you can also change the type of just the selected series, so you can show one series with bars and another with lines, for example. For Pie charts, you can explode a section and choose the distance it appears from the center. Properties for 3-D bar charts also let you change the shape of the bars, called *risers,* as shown here:

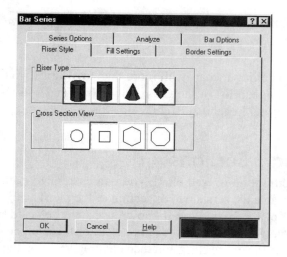

 **IP:** *When you print a chart on a noncolor printer, Corel Quattro Pro colors will be converted to shades of gray. To control how the chart prints, set the series properties to use patterns of black and white instead.*

Axis Settings

Select and customize the properties for the Y axis to change the scale, tick marks, and appearance of the line.

The *scale* determines the values that appear along the axis. When Corel Quattro Pro creates a chart, it automatically assigns values to the axis. The uppermost value, at the very top of the Y-axis line, corresponds to the largest value being plotted. The bottom of the scale will usually be set at the lowest number, with negative values below the zero line. You may want the scale to rise above the highest value.

For example, suppose you are charting student grades and want the scale to reach 100, even though no student had a perfect score. To change the scale, click on the Y axis so only it is selected, and then right-click on it to see the QuickMenu. The last item on the menu should be Y-Axis Properties. If it is anything else, then you probably moved the mouse slightly before clicking and selected another part of the chart. Try again.

Click on Y-Axis Properties and then on the Scale tab to see the dialog box shown in Figure 18-9. Enter the highest and lowest values that you want to appear on the axis, and the steps in between. The Number of Minors represents grid lines between the numbered points.

If your values are in the thousands, click on Show Units. This abbreviates large values and displays their units, such as thousands, next to the axis.

Printing Charts

When you print your worksheet, Corel Quattro Pro will also print any floating charts or maps on the page or in the print block.

IP: *Before printing a chart, select the most pleasing aspect ratio of the chart by using the View menu.*

If you have a chart selected, or a Chart window is active, Corel Quattro Pro will print only the chart itself. When you select Print, you'll see an abbreviated version of the Print dialog box without the options to select a print range or number of pages.

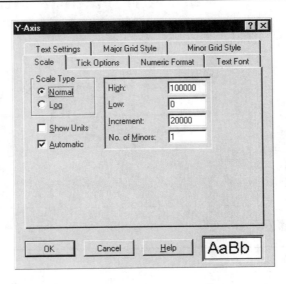

Customizing
the Y axis

FIGURE 18-9

OTE: *These same techniques apply also to printing maps.*

Creating Maps

When your data is organized by geographic areas, such as states or countries, you can chart it on a map. The map will use colors and patterns to represent the values, and it is quite useful in revealing trends and patterns. The map in Figure 18-10, for example, shows membership by state in the United States. By studying the map, you can see where the sales need improvement.

 IP: *To use mapping, you must perform a custom installation of the Corel WordPerfect Suite.*

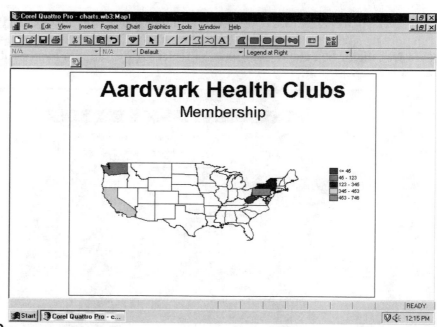

Corel
Quattro Pro
map

FIGURE 18-10

Before creating a map, make sure that your worksheet is set up using state or country names as the row labels. You can use the state name or the standard postal abbreviations for states. Then create the map using techniques similar to creating a chart:

- Use the QuickMap button to create a floating map.

- Use Map Expert to create either a floating map or a map in its own window.

- Use the New Map command from the Graphics menu to create a map in its own window.

18

Floating Maps

To create a floating map, select the range of cells that you want to map, click on the QuickMap button, and then click or drag a map area on the screen. Corel Quattro Pro will choose a map appropriate for your data and assign color and patterns representing the values.

Map Expert lets you create the map by selecting options in a series of boxes. Here's how to use it:

1. Select the cells containing the information you want to use for the map.

2. Pull down the Tools menu, point to Experts, and click on Map to display the first Expert box, shown in Figure 18-11.

3. Select a map to use. Corel Quattro Pro will suggest a map based on your data and illustrate it on the pane on the left.

4. Click on Next Step.

5. Accept or enter the cells representing the region names, and color and pattern ranges. You can chart two different sets of data on a map, using colors for one set and patterns for the other. The color and pattern ranges would correspond to two series on a chart.

6. Click on Next Step.

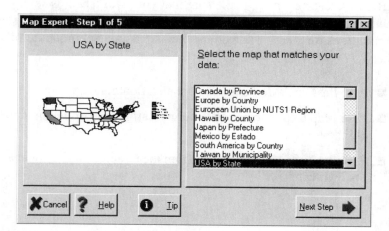

Map Expert

FIGURE 18-11

AUTION: *Corel Quattro Pro will warn you if you've entered a region that it does not understand and let you choose a new label. The warning will appear, for example, if you used England as a label. In this case, scroll the list of choices, choose Britain, and then click on Replace.*

7. Choose a color scheme and the number of colors and patterns you want to apply. More colors and patterns give you greater distinction. For example, suppose your state data ranges in values from 1 to 1000. If you choose two colors, then the map will show only two groups—states with values up to 500, and states with values above 500. If you choose four colors, you will have four groupings.

8. Click on Next Step.

9. Choose an optional overlap map or have Corel Quattro Pro mark the locations with pin numbers or labels.

10. Click on Next Step.

11. Enter a title and subtitle, choose to insert a legend, and choose if you want to place the map in the notebook as a floating object or in a separate window.

12. Click on Create Map and then drag to draw the map areas.

Map Overlays

An overlay is an additional map that appears superimposed over the map that you've charted. You can overlay a world map on the United States or Europe, for example, to get a broader view. You can also overlay U.S. highways on maps of the United States, and add major cities or state capitals.

To add an overlay, right-click on the map and choose Data from the QuickMenu. In the dialog box that appears, click on Add Overlay to see the dialog box shown in Figure 18-12.

Choose the type of overlay you want to add:

- *Region*—Select another map.

- *Static*—Add U.S. highways or a World Grid.

- *Pin*—Add names or coordinates of major cities or state or national capitals.

Click on OK to return to the Map Data dialog box. To later delete an overlay, select it in the list in the Map Data dialog box and click on the Delete Overlay button.

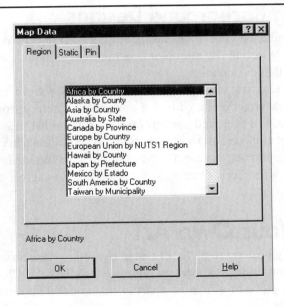

Adding overlays to enhance a map

FIGURE 18-12

Zooming Maps

Corel Quattro Pro inserts an overlay map in a position in relation to its actual coordinates on the globe. If you overlay a map that does not share a common area with the charted map—for example, overlaying Japan on Europe—you may not see it onscreen. To display the overlay, you have to Zoom Out the display to see a larger section of our planet. Right-click on the map and select Zoom Out from the QuickMenu to reduce the magnification to view a larger area.

Other Zoom options available in the QuickMenu, and from the Zoom command in the Edit menu, are

- *Zoom to Normal*—Returns the map to its default size.

- *Zoom In*—Enlarges a section so it fills the window. The mouse pointer changes to a magnifying glass, then you drag over the section of the map you want to enlarge.

- *Center*—Displays the area of your choice in the center of the window. The mouse pointer changes to a crosshair, and you click on the location you want to be centered.

Selecting Background Designs

One way to enhance your maps during editing is to select from the Style list in the power bar to select an overall color scheme. It will include the same choices that you have available for charts.

You can also use the Chart Gallery to choose from completely formatted background patterns. While editing a map, select Gallery from the Chart menu to see a dialog box of prepared backgrounds. Scroll the list to select a background of your choice, or click on Advisor to see the dialog box shown in Figure 18-13. Indicate the constraints you want to use, the types of presentation medium, and then click on Advise to see what Corel Quattro Pro suggests. If you agree, click on Apply.

Creating Your Own Art

You can really customize a chart or map by adding text boxes, arrows, and other objects that you draw, as shown in Figure 18-14. Use the Chart Tools toolbar that appears when you edit a floating chart or map, or that appears in the chart or map

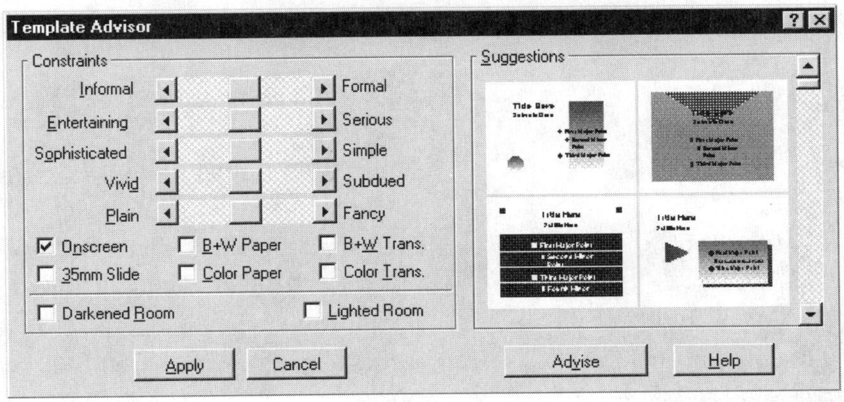

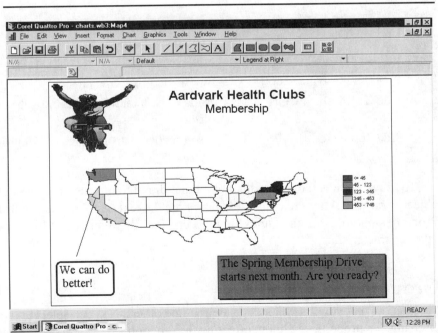

Selecting a background with the help of the Template Advisor

FIGURE 18-13

Customizing a chart or map

FIGURE 18-14

window. In addition to the usual toolbar buttons, the Chart Tools toolbar includes these features:

Clip Art	Adds a clip art or graphic image from your disk
Selection Tool	Selects objects after performing some other function
Line Tool	Draws lines. Hold down the SHIFT key for a straight horizontal or vertical line
Arrow Tool	Draws arrows
Polyline Tool	Draws a series of connected lines
Freehand Polyline Tool	Doodles
Text Box	Inserts a box where you enter text
Polygon Tool	Creates a filled box of freehand lines
Rectangle Tool	Draws a rectangle. Hold down SHIFT key for a square
Rounded Rectangle Tool	Creates rectangles and squares with rounded corners
Ellipse Tool	Draws ovals and circles (with SHIFT key)
Freehand Polygon Tool	Draws filled freehand shapes
Add Spreadsheet Cells	Inserts corresponding data cells into the objects
Add Template	Lets you choose from gallery background patterns

To draw an object, click on the button and drag the mouse where you want the object to appear. After creating a text box, type the text that you want in it. Use the Properties option from the QuickMenu to change fill patterns and line colors and other characteristics.

Grouping Objects

Each object that you draw is independent of the others. You can select and move it, or change its properties, without affecting the other objects on the page. Sometimes you want to apply the same formats to several objects at the same time, or combine objects to treat them as one unit for moving or copying. This is called *grouping*.

To group objects, follow these steps:

1. Click on the first object to select it.

2. Hold down the SHIFT key and click on the others.

3. Right-click on the objects and select Group from the QuickMenu. You can also pull down the Format menu and click on Group. There will now be one set of handles around the entire group rather than around the individual objects. When you now select a format, it will be applied the entire group.

To ungroup the objects so you can work with them individually, right-click on the group and choose Ungroup from the QuickMenu.

Working with Layers

Each new object you draw appears overlaid on top of existing ones, so one object may obscure, or partially obscure, another. You can rearrange the relative position of objects if you picture the screen as consisting of many layers of clear plastic, and you can change the layer that an object is on.

To change the layer of an object, right-click on it and point to Object Order in the QuickMenu (or choose Object Order from the Format menu). Your choices are

- *Bring Forward* moves the object one layer closer to the top layer.

- *Send Backward* moves the object one layer closer to the bottom layer.

- *Bring To Front* moves the object to the foreground, the top layer.

- *Send To Back* moves the object to the background, the bottom layer.

Bullet Charts

You can combine your charts and maps into a slide show for a formal presentation. However, you will also probably want to have one or more title slides, or slides that contain explanatory text. You can use title slides directly from your worksheet using the QuickChart button or New Chart options in the Graphics menu. Corel Quattro Pro calls them bullet charts because they can contain a title and subtitles, as well as up to two levels of bulleted items. By adding drawing objects and gallery background, you can enhance bullet charts so they match the design of your charts and maps.

IP: *To create a totally custom slide from a blank background, see "Creating a Slide Show," later in this chapter.*

You create a bullet chart just as you do a graphic chart: as a floating chart using the QuickChart button, or in its own window using the New Chart command from the Graphics menu. You can also create one or more bullet charts in one step using the Slide Show Expert.

Before creating the chart, however, you must prepare the worksheet. Follow these steps. Just remember that you do not have to type the bullet character yourself because Corel Quattro Pro will inset it for you in the bullet chart.

1. Type the title of the chart in any cell.

2. Optionally enter a subtitle in the cell directly below the title.

3. Enter the first major bulleted item in the cell under and to the right of the title or subtitle. If you enter a title in cell A1 with no subtitle, for example, enter the first major bulleted item in cell B2. If you want any minor bulleted items under it, enter them in the cells under and to the right.

4. Add any additional major and minor bulleted items. Make sure that the major items are in the column to the right of the title and subtitles. The minor items must be in the column to the right of the major items.

To create a floating bullet chart, use the following steps:

1. Select the block of items.

2. Click on the QuickChart button.

3. Click or drag in the notebook to create the chart.

OTE: *To create multiple slides at one time, see Slide Show Expert later in this chapter.*

To create the chart in a window, use the following steps:

1. Select the block of items.

2. Choose New Chart from the Graphics menu.

3. Click in the Name tab of the dialog box and enter a chart name.

4. Click on OK.

Figure 18-15 shows a bullet chart along with the worksheet cells used to create it.

Formatting Bullet Charts

You can customize a bullet chart by adding clip art and your own drawings, and by choosing a color scheme from the power bar, just as you can to a chart or map. Double-click on the chart to edit it in place, or right-click on it and select Open to display it in a separate window.

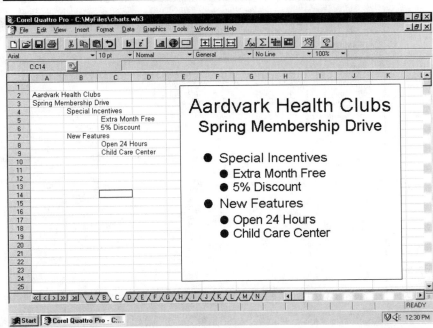

Worksheet
cells and
bullet chart

FIGURE 18-15

To change the font or size of text, click on it and then use the Font and Size sections of the power bar. To format text and change the shape and size of the bullets, you need to set properties. Setting the properties of one item affects all of the other items at that level. If you change the font of a major bulleted item, for example, all of the other major bulleted items in that chart will change as well. Right-click on a chart element, and choose the Properties command from the QuickMenu. You can change the font, size, and color of text, and the size and shape of the bullets.

To change the text on the chart, edit the corresponding cells in the notebook.

The Objects Page

The Objects page at the end of the notebook will display an icon for every chart, map, and slide show that you create. Figure 18-16, for example, shows the Objects page with several charts and maps. You use the Objects page to organize your charts and maps in slide shows.

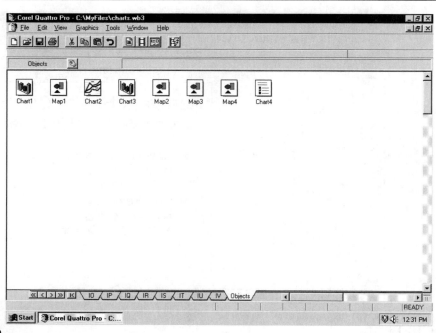

Objects page

FIGURE 18-16

When you display the Objects page, the toolbar will contain several of the standard toolbar buttons, as well as these features:

- *New Chart*—Lets you create a new chart without returning to the worksheet

- *Create Slide Show*—Creates a slide show

- *New Dialog*—Creates a dialog box

- *Play Slide Show*—Lets you run a slide show

To edit an object, double-click on its icon. Corel Quattro Pro will open it in a separate window, even though you might have created it as a floating chart or map. Double-click on a slide show icon to display it in the Light Table, which you will soon learn about.

Slide Shows

A slide show is exactly what it says—a group of charts and maps displayed in a series full screen. With Corel Quattro Pro, you can even add special transition effects that appear when one slide ends and the other begins. You don't have all of the options that are available in a program such as Corel Presentations, but you can still create some rather sophisticated and effective presentations.

Creating a Slide Show

To create a slide show, go to the Objects page and then select the icons of the charts and maps that you want to include. Use these steps:

1. On the Objects page, click on the icon of an item you want to include in the slide show.

2. Hold down the CTRL key and click on the others. Don't worry if you miss some; you can always add slides later on.

3. Click on the Create Slide Show button or choose New Slide Show from the Graphics menu.

4. In the dialog box that appears, enter a name for the show and then click on OK. The selected items will appear in the Light Table view, shown in Figure 18-17.

To add additional slides in the Light Table view, use the following steps:

1. Pull down the Slides menu.

2. Point to New Slide.

3. Click on From Existing Slide. A list of the items in the Objects page will appear.

4. Double-click on the item you want to add to the show.

To add a blank slide that you edit as you want, use these steps:

1. Pull down the Slide menu and point to New Slide.

2. Click on From New Chart to display the New Chart dialog box.

3. Instead of entering cell ranges to create a chart from the contents of a worksheet, leave the dialog box empty and click on OK. A blank slide will be added to the Light Table.

4. Double-click on the blank slide to open it in an edit window, and then add text boxes, clip art, or drawing objects.

5. Close the Edit window to return to the Light Table.

 IP: *To change the order of slides in the show, click on a slide and drag it to its new location.*

Customizing Slide Shows

You can set the properties for individual slides, or for the entire presentation. Properties include items such as the transition from one slide to the next, and how long slides remain on the screen.

To set the default properties for the entire slide show, right-click on the Light Table, but not on a slide, and select the Light Table Properties option from the QuickMenu. The Default Effect pages of the dialog box that appears are shown in Figure 18-18.

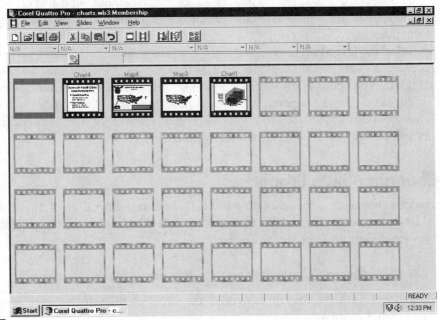

Slides in the
Light Table
view

FIGURE 18-17

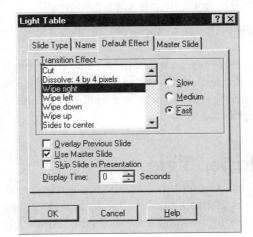

Setting the
defaults for
the entire
slide show

FIGURE 18-18

Choose the transition effect and its speed, and the amount of time you want each slide to appear. You can always change slides with the mouse or keyboard regardless of the timing.

Select the Use Master Slide property when you want all the slides to have the same general color scheme and background. Use the Overlay Previous Slide and Skip Slide in Presentation options only when changing the properties of a particular slide.

The Slide Type property lets you choose the size of the slide in the Light Table—options are Small, Medium, Large, and Name Only. The Master Slide page lets you choose one of your own slides as the master.

Changing Slide Properties

You can change the properties of individual slides using the Light Table feature bar or the Properties command. To customize a slide, click on it in the Light Table, and then select options from the power bar:

- *Use Master*—Choose to apply the master slide to the slide or not.

- *No Overlay*—Choose to overlay the previous slide. If you overlay a slide, you cannot apply the master to it.

- *Transition*—Pick a transition to use when displaying the slide.

- *Speed*—Choose the speed of the transition.

- *Time*—Select the time that the slide remains onscreen. Your options are from 0 to 60 minutes in half-minute intervals.

- *Show Slide*—Choose to show or skip the slide.

You can choose from the same options using the Properties box—right-click on Slide and choose Properties from the QuickMenu. The Properties dialog box also gives you the chance to enter a specific number of seconds to show the slide, and to add a brief description of it.

Using a Master Slide

A master slide serves as a template for the background and color scheme for every slide in the slide show. Use a master slide to include your company name or logo, or some other repeating message on every slide. In the Light Table, the first slide position is reserved for the master. You can choose a master slide that you've created for that purpose, or one of the built-in designs from the Chart Gallery.

 IP: *Slides will only use the master when their properties are set to Use Master.*

To design your own master slide, follow these steps:

1. First create it as a bullet chart or from a blank slide, adding any standard text and graphic objects.

2. In the Light Table, right-click outside of any slide.

3. Select the Light Table Properties option.

4. Choose the slide from the Master Slide page of the Properties dialog box. When you close the dialog box, your slide will appear in the first position in the Light Table, and applied as a background to all of the others.

You can also create the master slide directly in the Light Table by selecting New Master Slide from the Slides menu. Corel Quattro Pro will display a bullet chart in an Edit window showing generic formats for the title, subtitles, and bulleted items. The text shown in the chart will not appear onscreen, it just illustrates formats. Add graphics, drawing objects, and text using the Text Box tool, and then close the window.

For the greatest impact, select one of the professionally designed templates in the Master Slide Gallery. You cannot choose from the gallery, however, until you have a master slide in the show. Start by creating your own master slide with any text that you want to appear, or use the New Master Slide command to create a blank master slide. Next, pull down the Slides menu, and click on Master Slide Gallery. Select one of the templates, using the Advisor if desired, and then click on OK. The template will be applied to every slide whose property is set to use the master, as shown in Figure 18-19.

Showing Slide Shows

When you are ready to show your slide, display the Objects page, click on the Slide Show icon, and then click on the Run Slide Show button in the toolbar. (You can also run the slide from the Light Table in the same way.) If you assigned times to

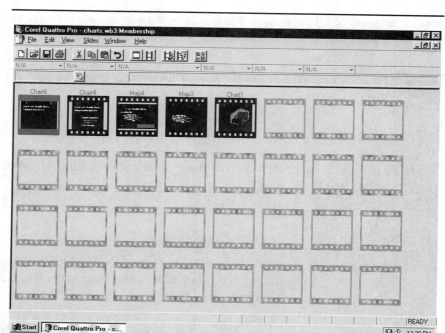

A
background
applied to
all slides

FIGURE 18-19

your slides, Corel Quattro Pro will display each for the time selected. To change slides yourself, even when you did assign times, use these techniques:

- Click the left mouse button to show the next slide.

- Click the right mouse button to show the previous slide.

- Press any key to show the next slide.

- Press BACKSPACE to show the previous slide.

- Press ESC to stop the slide show.

Slide Show Expert

You can create any number of bullet charts and create a slide show of them at one time using the Slide Show Expert from a worksheet window. You can then add other charts and maps to the show later on. Here's how to create a slide show using the Slide Show Expert:

1. To prepare the worksheet, type the text for each of the slides consecutively, with no blank lines between them. Make sure that all of the titles are in the same column. Figure 18-20, for example, shows a worksheet that will become three slides. Slide Show Expert can create only bullet slides.

2. Select the entire block of cells that you want to use for slides.

3. Pull down the Tools menu, point to Experts, and click on Slide Show. The first Expert box will display the block coordinates and the number of slides that will be created.

4. If the coordinates are incorrect, enter or point to them and then click on Next Step. The second Expert box shows all of the background templates available in the Chart Gallery.

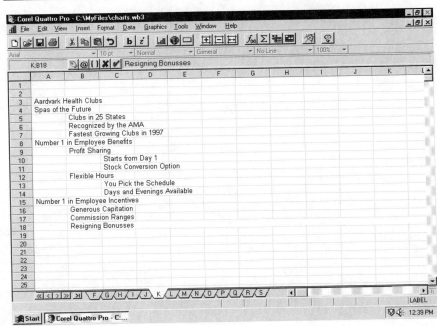

Worksheet for three slides in Slide Show Expert

FIGURE 18-20

5. Choose the template you want to use as the master slide, or click on User Defined and select one of your own. You can also choose to use no master slide.

6. Click on Next Step.

7. Enter a name for your slide show and select either random transitions or a choice from the list.

8. Click on Create Show. Corel Quattro Pro creates the slides and displays them in Light Table view.

Analyzing Data

19

While charts and maps can help you see trends, sometimes you have to analyze data the old-fashioned way. You have to draw conclusions by examining the values in cells and performing statistical operations on them. By analyzing your data, you can make wiser business decisions, and prepare plans and projections. There are literally hundreds of ways to analyze information and perform statistical analysis with Corel Quattro Pro. You can work with information as a database, sort rows to group records, and apply some rather sophisticated analytical techniques. This chapter will survey some of the techniques that you can use.

Working with Databases

A *database* is a place where you store information, an electronic version of a box of 3 × 5 index cards, or even a filing cabinet full of folders and papers. In Corel Quattro Pro you store a database as a series of rows and columns. Each row holds a record, which is a collection of information about one object in the database, such as a client, inventory item, or sales record.

The columns represent the fields, each piece of information that make up a record. The fields for a client record, for example, can include first and last names, address, and phone number. The fields for an inventory record might include the item name and stock number, quantity on hand, and price. Each column is another field, and all of the columns in a row represent the complete record for that item.

Corel Quattro Pro has one other element in a database, the *criteria table*. This lets you find information quickly based on its content, and allows you to create a subset of your database so you see only the information that you are interested in.

 You can import or link the database into Corel WordPerfect for use as a data file for merging.

Creating a Database

Your first task is to enter the information into the table. A database must be one contiguous block and fit on one page. It can be no more than 8191 rows and up to 256 columns. It must have labels in the first row that represent the names of the fields, and each label must be unique. Field names can contain up to 16 characters. They can have spaces between words, but not before or after.

IP: *If you are entering zip codes into a database, enter them as text using the apostrophe. Otherwise, leading zeros will not appear with zip codes that have them.*

Next, assign a block name to the entire database. This isn't mandatory, but it will save time when you need to refer to the database in dialog boxes and functions. Use these steps to assign a block name to the database:

1. Select the database, including the column headings.

2. Pull down the Insert menu, and click on Block Names.

3. Type **Database** as the name, so it will be easy to remember.

4. Click on Add and then Close. Whenever you need to insert the database block, just use the name "database."

If you later insert additional rows within the database, Corel Quattro Pro will automatically adjust the block definition. However, if you add information to the blank row following the database, you have to reassign the block name to include the new row as well. It doesn't matter where you add new rows because you can sort them at another time. You'll learn how to later.

Next, make each of the column labels a field name. Again, this isn't necessary, but it will make it easier to enter criteria to locate specific records. Select the entire database block, pull down the Data menu, and click on Notebook Query to see the Notebook Data Query dialog box. Click on the Field Names button and then on Close. This assigns a block name to each of the labels.

Creating Criteria Tables

Corel Quattro Pro lets you search for information in the database using a method called *query by example.* This means that you type the information you are looking for, as well as any logical conditions, and Corel Quattro Pro searches the database for you.

You have to start by creating a criteria table—a worksheet of at least two rows. Create the table anywhere in the notebook, even on the same page as the database if there is room for it on the page. The first row of the criteria table must contain the names of the fields that you want to search in the database. As a shortcut, copy the field names from the first row of the database and paste them into the first row of the criteria table. This ensures that the field names in the criteria table exactly match those in the database.

You use the other rows in the criteria table to enter the information that you want to search for. For example, Figure 19-1 shows a criteria table to find a record in a database that has the name "Adam" in the First Name column, and "Chesin" in the Last Name column. Searching for values in more than one column of a row is treated as an "and" operation. This means that a record must match all of the information

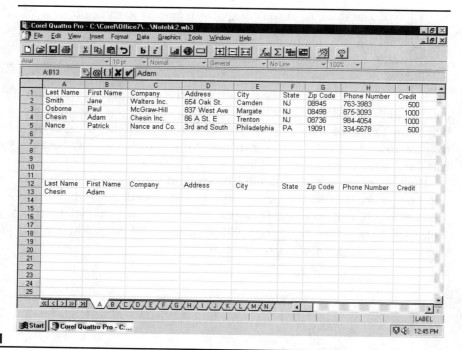

Using a criteria table to locate a name

FIGURE 19-1

in the criteria table row. So, for example, the same search will not locate the record for Adam Smith because only the first name field matches.

To create an "or" operation, enter search information in more than one row. The following criteria table will locate records for Adam Chesin, as well as records for everyone with the last name of Smith, matching one row or the other in the criteria table:

	Last Name	First Name	Company	Address	City	State	Zip Code	Phone Number	Credit
12									
13	Chesin	Adam							
14	Smith								

Searching for Information

Once you define the database and labels, and create a criteria table, you're ready to search. Here's how:

1. Pull down the Data menu and click on Notebook Query to display the Data Query dialog box. You'll notice that the coordinates you used to define the field names are still shown in the Database Block text box. Corel Quattro Pro maintains the last settings you used in this box as default values for the notebook. If you wish, you can replace the coordinates with the name "Database," but the results will not change. If you ever want to clear the defaults, click on Reset and then Close.

2. In the Criteria Table text box, enter the coordinates of the criteria table, or use Point mode to insert them. Just make certain that you do not include any blank rows under the last row of the table that contains search information. If you do, Corel Quattro Pro will use the blank rows to perform an "or" operation and locate every record in the database. That's why it usually does not save time to select and assign the criteria table a block name. You'd only have to redefine the block if you later add rows to the criteria table.

3. Click on Locate. Corel Quattro Pro will highlight the first record in the database that meets the criteria and enter Find mode. In Find mode you use the UP ARROW or DOWN ARROW keys to move from record to record that matches the criteria, automatically skipping over any records that do not. Press the DOWN ARROW once, for example, to move to the second matching record. With the mouse, you can only click on rows that meet the criteria—you'll hear a beep if you click on any other row. Use the

LEFT ARROW or RIGHT ARROW keys to move from field to field within a record so you can edit and format cell contents as you need.

4. To exit Find mode and return to the Notebook Data Query dialog box, press ESC or ENTER.

 IP: *Press F7 to repeat the last Data Query operation.*

Deleting Records

The Delete button in the Notebook Data Query dialog box clears the contents of records that meet the criteria. You will be asked to confirm the deletion, and you can immediately undo it with the Undo button.

As a safeguard, however, perform a Locate first to confirm the records that will be deleted, using these steps:

1. Click on Locate.

2. Press the DOWN ARROW to scroll through the database looking at the selected records.

3. The DOWN ARROW key should select only records that you want to delete. If that's the case, open the Notebook Data Query dialog box again, and then delete the records.

If pressing the DOWN ARROW locates a record that you do not want to delete, then try refining the search criteria.

Using Criteria

Searching for specific values is useful, but it has limitations. If you misspell a person's name in the criteria table, for example, it will not be located in the database. By using wildcards and logical operations in the criteria table, however, you can design searches that pinpoint the exact information you are looking for.

Using Wildcards

Wildcards are special characters that represent one or more characters in text that you are searching for:

?	Represents a single character
*	Represents any number of characters
~	Excludes text from the search, locating records that do not match the value

If you want to find all persons whose last names begin with the letter "N," for example, type **N*** in the Last Name column of the criteria row. This tells Corel Quattro Pro to locate records that start with the letter "N" and have any number of characters following it in that field.

The phrase "c*r" would locate all words that start with "c" and end with "r"—no matter how many characters are between them. On the other hand, entering "c?r" would only locate labels that have one letter between them—"car" but not "caviar."

To locate all clients except those in California, enter **~CA** in the State field. The tilde character must be the first character of the search text.

Logical Conditions

To locate records that fall within a certain range, enter a logical condition in the form of a formula as the search criteria. The condition +Amount Due > 400, for instance, would locate records with a value greater than 400 in the Amount Due field. You can use any of the usual operators:

=	Equal to
<>	Not equal to
>=	Greater than or equal to
>	Greater than
<=	Less than or equal to
<	Less than

 IP: *If you did not assign the column labels as field names, use the cell reference of the column label instead.*

You can enter a logical statement in any cell of the criteria table. It does not have to be in the column that it represents. The Amount Due condition, for instance, can be in any column and still locate the proper records.

When you type the formula in the criteria table, however, Corel Quattro Pro will evaluate it and display its results rather than the formula itself. So all you'll see in the cell is a 1 (for true) or 0 (for false). To make criteria tables easier to work with, format the cells by setting their Numeric Format to Text in the Block Properties dialog box. This way you'll see the formulas in the table, as under the Credit label in the criteria table shown here:

	Last Name	First Name	Company	Address	City	State	Zip Code	Phone Number	Credit
12									
13						NJ			+Credit>500

Output Blocks

The problem with locating records is that you have to scroll down the database with the DOWN ARROW key to see which records have been located. If you have a large database, you won't get an overall view of the selected records because they are spread out over the entire table.

As an alternative, you can copy all of the located records to an output table. This is a separate table that will contain just the located records. You can then view the selected records as a set, without being distracted by the other rows in the database.

To create an output table, follow these steps:

1. Copy the field names to the location where you want the table to appear. If you leave out any fields, they will not be copied along with the record. So, if you only want to see selected fields in the output table, copy only those field names.

2. Pull down the Data menu and click on Notebook Query to display the Data Query dialog box.

3. Enter the coordinates of the row of field names for the output table in the Output Table text box, or use Point mode or an assigned block name.

4. Click on Extract to copy all of the matching records to the output table, or click on Extract Unique to remove any duplicate records when the output table is created.

When you designate the output table coordinates, only include the cells containing labels. If you select blank rows under the cells, Corel Quattro Pro will only copy as many records as there are selected rows.

When you want to merge a form document with selected records from a Corel Quattro Pro database, extract them to a separate block. Then import the block into Corel WordPerfect.

Using Database Functions

As you learned in Chapter 17, database functions help you locate and analyze information in a database. All database functions have the same three arguments: Block, Column, and Criteria.

■ *Block* is the range of cells that contains the database. Use the block name or coordinates.

■ *Column* is where the data is located that you want to analyze, counting from 0. The first column is 0, the second is 1, and so on.

■ *Criteria* is the coordinates of the criteria table. If you use the @DAVG function, for instance, only the values in rows meeting the criteria will be averaged. To include all of the rows, create a criteria table using the field names and one blank row under them.

 OTE: *You can still use standard functions to calculate sums, averages, and other operations on rows and columns.*

Sorting Information

The order of records in a database, or any other worksheet, may not be important. But sometimes placing the records in a certain order will help you draw conclusions about the data and locate records. If you have a database of student information, for instance, it might be useful to sort the rows by attendance or grade point average. Then you can see at a glance which students have the best—or worst—grades or attendance.

To sort a table, select the block that you want to sort. If you are sorting a database or other worksheet that has column labels, do not include the row of labels. If you do, they will be sorted along with the other information and may end up in some other row than the first.

Next, pull down the Data menu and click on Sort to see the dialog box shown in Figure 19-2. The block that you selected will appear in the Block text box. If not, enter or point to the coordinates.

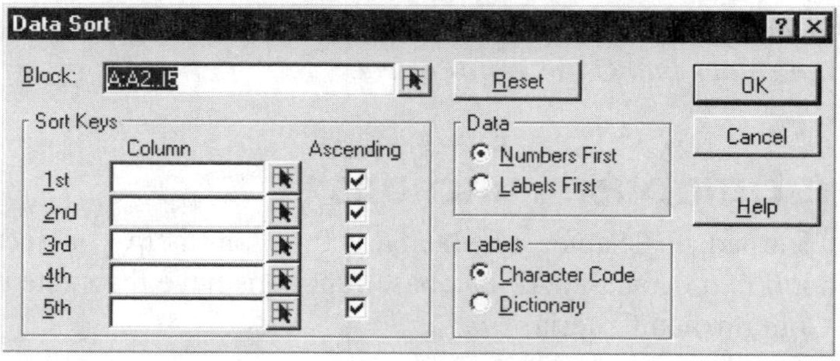

Data Sort dialog box

FIGURE 19-2

You now must specify up to five keys. A *key* is a column that you want to sort by. If you want the records for clients in their name order, for example, enter **Last Name** as the first key, and **First Name** as the second key. If you are sorting a database, enter the field names; otherwise, enter or point to any cell in the column. Corel Quattro Pro will sort all of the records by the first key, then by the second, and so on.

By default, records are sorted in ascending order. Uncheck the Ascending check box to sort in descending order.

Also by default, numbers are placed before labels, so a cell containing "1" will appear before a cell containing "A." To change the order, click on the Labels First button. Labels are sorted by their ASCII character code. Uppercase letters come before lowercase ones; words starting with special characters are at the end. Select Dictionary in the Labels section to disregard case.

You can always revert back to the previous order by using the Undo command. If you want to be able to revert back to the rows' original order, then include an extra column in the table. Number the rows consecutively using AutoFill, or use some other identifying number in consecutive order such as a client or stock number. You can then quickly return to the original order by sorting on that field.

OTE: *Avoid sorting cells that contain relative references to outside of the block. The references will be changed. Use absolute references before sorting.*

Analyzing Data

Corel Quattro Pro offers a number of features to help you analyze your worksheet and solve real-life problems. While many of these features perform sophisticated statistical analysis, others are easy to use and can help you make important business decisions.

The Analysis Expert from the Tools menu, for example, includes the financial, statistical, and engineering tools listed below. In this chapter, we'll explain several especially useful features that do not require an MBA or Ph.D.

- Advanced Regression
- Amortization Schedule
- One-Way ANOVA
- Two-Way ANOVA
- Correlation
- Covariance
- Descriptive Statistics
- Exponential Smoothing
- Fourier Transformation

- F-Test
- Histogram
- Mortgage Refinancing
- Moving Average
- Random Number
- Rank and Percentile
- Sampling
- t-Test
- z-Test

Using Solve For

In most cases, you use a formula or function to calculate and display results from the values you already know. Sometimes you have to work in reverse. You know the result you would like to achieve, but not the combination of arguments that will get those results. The mortgage payment function is a good example. If you know the loan rate, number of periods, and amount of principal, then you can calculate the amount of your monthly mortgage payment.

But suppose you already know how much you can afford to spend each month, and you'd like to determine how much of a dream home those monthly payments can obtain. You now have to work backward, a perfect use for the Solve For feature.

To use Solve For, you need a formula that contains a reference to the unknown value. In the @PAYMT function, you would reference a cell that will contain the principal amount. Solve For automatically changes the value in the referenced cell until the results of a formula reach a value that you specify.

Suppose you know the rate for a 25-year mortgage is 6 percent. You want to find out how much you can borrow to maintain a maximum monthly payment of $1000. Enter the function **@PAYMT(.06/12,25*12,–A1)**, where A1 is a blank cell.

Pull down the Tools menu, point to Numeric Tools, and click on Solve For to see the dialog box shown here:

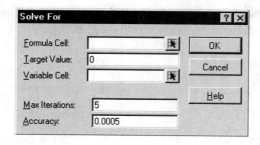

1. In the Formula Cell box, enter or point to the coordinates of the formula you want to solve, the @PAYMT function.

2. In the Target Value box, enter **1000**, the result that you want to achieve.

3. In the Variable Cell, enter the cell that Corel Quattro Pro can vary to achieve the results, cell A1.

4. Adjust the other options as desired. The Max Iterations option determines how many times Solve For will run through its steps to solve the problem. Accuracy determines how close the result has to be to the target value.

5. Click on OK.

Solve For will perform its calculations and display the result in cell A1.

OPTIMIZER

Solve For is limited because it can only adjust one variable cell. When you have more variables to consider, or have constraints placed on their values, use Optimizer. The worksheet shown in Figure 19-3 is a good example. It is our friend the @PAYMT function but with three cells that can vary: mortgage rate, number of years, and amount of principal. Use Optimizer to find a combination of values that results in a target payment.

In real life, however, we'd have to place some constraints on the values that Corel Quattro Pro can use. We know that a realistic mortgage rate might be between 6 and 8 percent, and that we need a loan for at least 20 years to minimize our payments. We're also going to add another constraint: our monthly mortgage

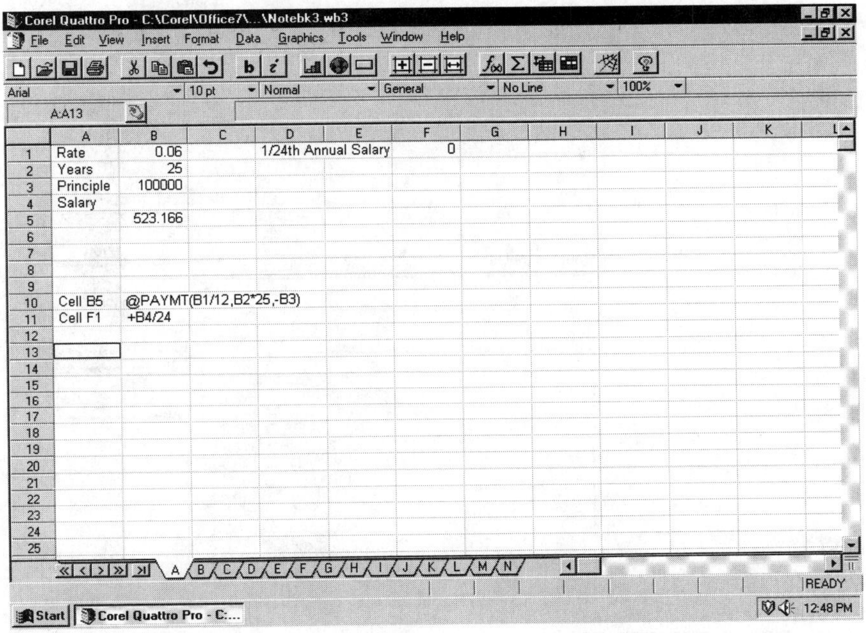

Worksheet to solve a formula based on three variables

FIGURE 19-3

payment cannot be more than 1/24th of our salary. That is, we don't want to spend more than half of our monthly income on the mortgage. When we tell Corel Quattro Pro our constraints, we cannot include a formula, but we can reference a formula in a cell. So create the worksheet shown in the figure, using these steps:

1. In cell B5 enter the function @**PAYMT(B1/12,B2*25,–B3)**.

2. In cell F1, enter the formula +**B4/24** that we'll use to limit the mortgage payment based on salary.

3. Type your annual salary in cell B4.

4. Pull down the Tools menu, point to Numeric Tools, and click on Optimizer to display the Optimizer dialog box shown in Figure 19-4.

5. In the solution cell, enter the coordinates of the formula that will be calculating the result, cell B5.

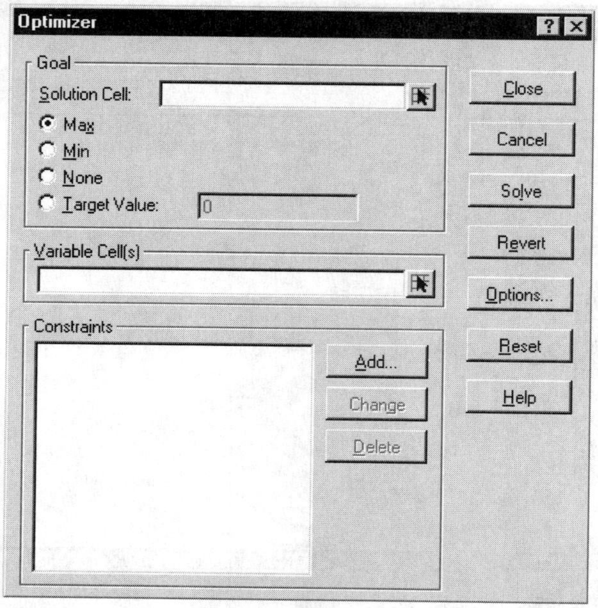

Optimizer dialog box

FIGURE 19-4

6. Click on the Max button, if it is not selected already, so Corel Quattro Pro calculates the maximum payment that we can afford. If you wanted to find a specific value, click on Target Value and enter the amount.

7. Next, specify the variable cells, the ones that Corel Quattro Pro can change. In this case, enter cells B1..B3.

We now have to enter the constraints. Each constraint will be a logical expression referencing a changing cell and the limitations that we want Optimizer to consider. Click on Add to see the dialog box in Figure 19-5.

The first constraint is that the rate must be less than 8 percent. Enter **B1** in the Cell column, leave the operator set at <=, and enter **.08** in the Constant box. The expression B1<=.08 means that the values entered in the cell by Optimizer must be less than 8 percent. Click on Add Another Constraint.

The second constraint is that the rate must be more than 6 percent. Enter **B1** in the Cell column, click on >=, and enter **.06** in the Constant box. With these two constraints, Corel Quattro Pro will only test rates between 6 and 8 percent. Click on Add Another Constraint.

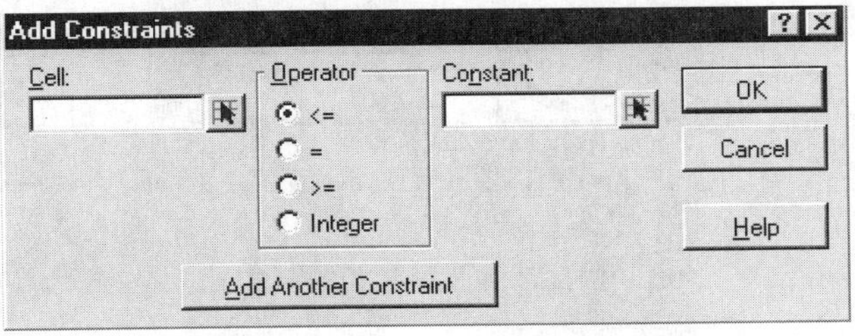

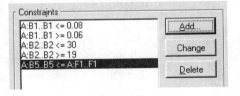

Adding a
constraint to
Optimizer

FIGURE 19-5

Now complete the remainder of the constraints, clicking on OK after you complete the last:

Constraint	Cell	Operator	Constant
Number of years less than 30	B2	<=	30
Number of years greater than 19	B2	>=	19
Mortgage payments no more than 1/24 of your salary	B5	<=	F1

When you have finished entering the last constraint, click on Close. The constraints will appear in your Optimizer dialog box, as shown here. If they do not, select the constraint that is incorrect and click on Change. Use Delete to remove a constraint. Now click on Solve. Corel Quattro Pro will calculate the maximum value for cell B5 using the constraints specified. If you do not want to change the worksheet to these values, select Undo, or display the Optimizer dialog box and click on Revert.

Optimizer Options

You can customize Optimizer for your specific problem by clicking on Options in the Optimizer dialog box to see the options shown in Figure 19-6. Most of these options perform rather sophisticated operations, and they require an equally sophisticated understanding of data analysis. We'll look at options that are more frequently used.

Optimizer
options

REPORTING   The Optimizer solves your problem, but it does not automatically show you how it arrived at its conclusion. The Reporting option lets you create two types of detailed reports explaining how Optimizer works:

■   The *Answer Report* lists the coordinates of the solution and variable cells, along with the starting and final values that Optimizer calculated. It also lists the variable gradient, increment, and decrement values.

■   The *Detail Report* lists values from the solution and variable cells at each iteration, so you can see how they changed during the process.

To create one or both of the reports, click on Reporting. In the dialog box that appears, enter or point to the range of cells where you want to place one or both of the reports. You can designate an entire block, or just the upper-left corner.

Because the report overwrites any existing contents, make sure there are enough blank cells. The Answer Report needs 6 columns and at least 10 more rows than the total number of solution cells and constraints. The Detail Report uses as many rows as iterations, plus three headings.

When you solve the problem, the reports will appear in the designated blocks.

SAVING OPTIMIZER SETTINGS   When you save your worksheet, Corel Quattro Pro saves the Optimizer settings along with it. If you use Optimizer to solve several problems, you should save each set so you can quickly retrieve it. You save the set in a blank area of the worksheet.

Once you have the settings the way you want them, click on Options in the Optimizer dialog box, and then click on Save model. In the dialog box that appears, enter or point to a location in the worksheet at least three columns wide and six rows deep, and then click on OK. Saved settings appear like this:

Solution Cell		
+B5	Maximize	0
Variable Cells		
@COUNT(B1..B3)		
Constraints		
@COUNT(B1..B1)	<=	0.08
@COUNT(B1..B1)	>=	0.06
@COUNT(B2..B2)	<=	30
@COUNT(B2..B2)	>=	19
@COUNT(B5..B5)	<=	+F1..F1

When you want to use the settings, choose Load model from the Optimizer Options dialog box, and enter the upper-left-corner cell where you saved the settings.

Saving Scenarios

Using formulas and functions makes it easy to solve What-If problems. Each time you change a value, you can see the results throughout the worksheet. But once you change them again, the previous results are gone. Certainly you can use Undo to revert back to the last values. But what if you want to see the results of values that you entered before that, or even on another day?

A *scenario* is a set of values that you've used to generate results—a snapshot of the worksheet with one set of values. By saving a scenario, you can quickly return to it when you want to see its effects. By saving a number of scenarios, you can quickly compare results to help make informed decisions.

For example, suppose you create a presentation for an important client. The worksheet contains a series of cost projections based on varying expenses. You can use scenarios to switch between the sets of data, so the client gets a feel for the pros and cons of each plan.

Start by making three decisions:

- The range of cells that you want to include in the scenario

- The cells that will change in value for each scenario, called the *changing cells*

- The formulas that reference the changing cells, called the *result cells*

Using Scenario Expert

The fastest way to create a series of scenarios is to use the Scenario Expert. Start by preparing the worksheet so it contains the first set of the values and results that you want to save. This is called the *baseline scenario*. Then pull down the Tools menu, point to Experts, and click on Scenario. A series of dialog boxes will appear for you to select options.

In the first dialog box, enter or point to the changing cells, the cells whose values will change with each scenario.

The second dialog box contains text boxes for each of the changing cells, showing the baseline settings currently in the worksheet (Figure 19-7). To create another scenario, change the values in the text boxes, type a name for the scenario, and then click on Add Scenario. Repeat this for each set of values and then click on Next Step.

The next Expert dialog box lists all of the scenarios. To see the values in the worksheet, click on a scenario name and then on Show Scenario. If you want to remove one of the scenarios, click on it and then on Delete.

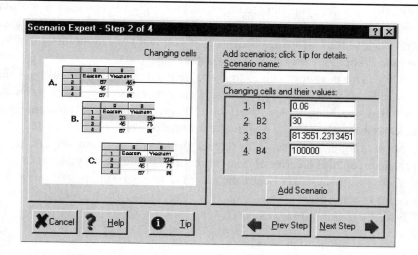

Using baseline settings and adding scenarios in Scenario Expert

FIGURE 19-7

In the last Expert dialog box, you can create an optional report or just exit. If you create a report, Corel Quattro Pro will create a Scenarios page after the worksheet. Display the page to see the changing and result cells and their values in each scenario.

Scenario Manager

Scenario Expert saves the scenarios in the Scenario Manager, a dialog box where you select which scenarios to display, and where you can add, delete, and modify scenarios.

Pull down the Tools menu, and click on Scenario Manager to display the dialog box shown in Figure 19-8. You will see a list of scenarios that you created with the Expert—the Baseline and other scenarios. To see a scenario, just click on it in the list. The values from the scenario will be applied to the worksheet.

 OTE: *Use the Highlight button to select a color for the formulas and changing cells for each scenario.*

To add a new scenario, exit Scenario Manager, and edit the values in the changing cells. Then display Scenario Manager and click on Capture. Type a name for the scenario, and then click on Close. A scenario, by the way, can also include a change in a result cell formula.

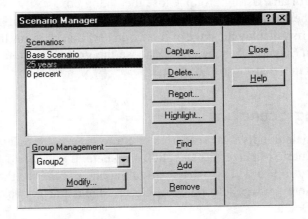

Scenario
Manager

FIGURE 19-8

Creating Scenarios Manually

It is just as easy to create scenarios without using the Expert. Prepare the worksheet with the baseline values and then display Scenario Manager. By default, the scenario will include the entire page of the worksheet, keeping track of cells with changing values and formulas that reference them. If you want to track just a specific block of the page, or the entire notebook, then click on the Modify button. In the dialog box that appears, enter or point to the range of cells, or click on Notebook to change the capture area. Then, close the dialog box to return to Scenario Manager.

Now click on Capture and enter a name for the baseline scenario—the default is Baseline—and then click on OK and close Scenario Manager.

You can now edit the changing cells and capture each of the scenarios. When you capture the first scenario after the baseline, Corel Quattro Pro will automatically identify the changing and the result cells and show them highlighted. The changing cells will be those that have different values than in the baseline. The result cells are formulas that reference the changing cells. If the cells are not identified correctly, click on the Find button in Scenario Manager. If this still doesn't identify the cells, do it manually—select the cells and then click on Add.

Scenario Groups

You can have more than one group of scenarios in a notebook. Each set can track a different set of cells or page, and each can have its own baseline. To create a new group, prepare the worksheet the way you want the baseline scenario to appear. Open Scenario Manager and click on Modify to display the dialog box shown in Figure 19-9.

Click on New, and enter a name for the group. Use the Rename button to change the name of an existing group. Close the dialog box.

Use the Group Management list at the bottom of Scenario Manager to change groups. First, display the page of the worksheet that contains the captured cells, and then open Scenario Manager and choose the group that you want to display. The scenarios in the group will be listed.

Deleting Scenarios

You can delete individual scenarios or entire groups. To delete a scenario, select it in the Scenario Manager list and click on Delete. If you delete the baseline scenario, Corel Quattro Pro will also delete all of the other scenarios that are based on it.

To delete a group, select it in the Group Management, click on Modify, and then click on Delete.

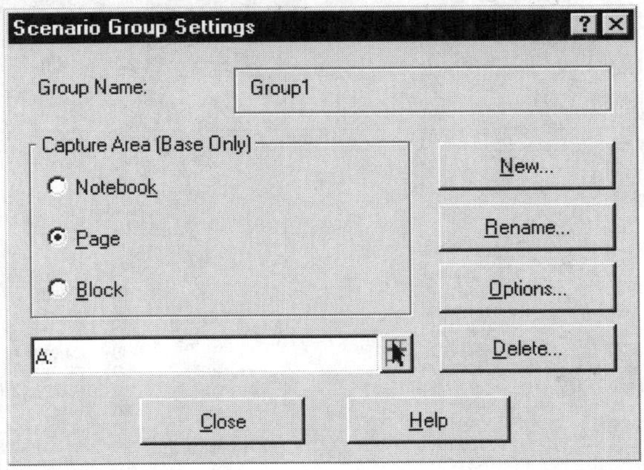

Adding a group

FIGURE 19-9

Creating What-If Tables

One problem with Scenario Manager is that you must choose a scenario each time you want to see the results of changing cells. Wouldn't it be easier if you could just create a table showing the various values in the changing cells and each effect on the result cell? You can do this by creating a What-If table.

There are two types of What-If tables. A one-variable table displays the results of changing one cell on one or two formulas. A two-variable table shows the results of changing two variables on a single formula. As an example, look at Figure 19-10. Both of the tables use the @FVAL function to determine how much an annual investment is worth after a number of years. On the left is a one-variable table that compares the results of saving different annual amounts. The amounts are shown in column B, and the total savings after ten years for each amount is shown in column C. The table on the right compares different amounts and interest rates. The formulas for a one-variable table must only reference one cell, while two-variable formulas reference only two cells.

You can create What-If tables manually, or by using the What-If Expert. Let's use What-If Expert to create the one-variable table shown in the figure. Enter **200** in cell A1, and the formula **@FVAL(6%,10,–A1)** in cell A2. Pull down the Tools menu, point to Experts, and click on What-If.

1. In the first Expert, leave the option set at Vary One Cell Against One or More Formulas, and then click on Next Step.

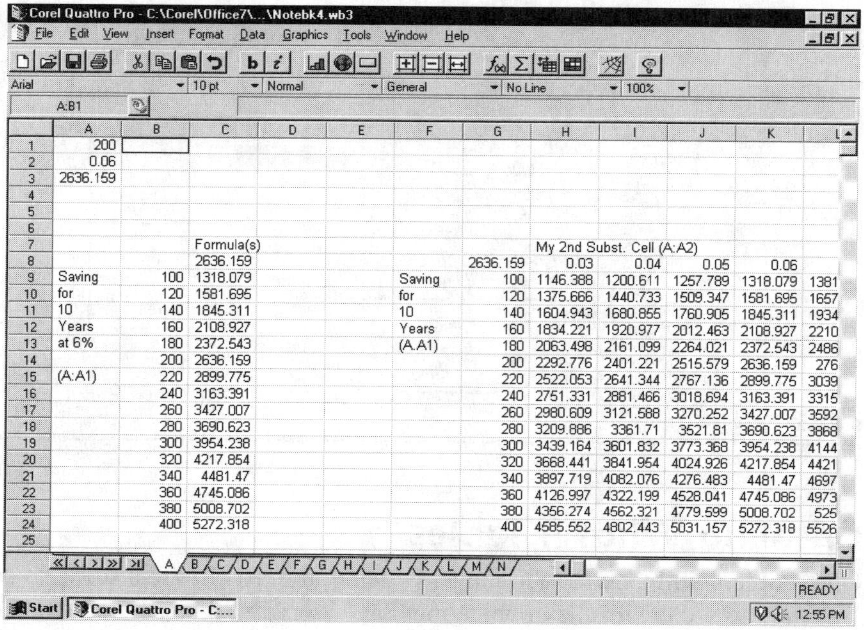

What-If tables

FIGURE 19-10

2. Now you specify the cell containing the formulas. Enter or point to cell A2, and then click on Next Step.

3. You can now designate a second formula to track. This example only uses one, so click on Next Step.

4. In this box, you designate the input cell that is referenced in the formula, and a name for it that will appear on the table. Enter **A1** as the input cell, and type **Annual Investment** as the name, and then click on Next Step. The input cell must contain a value.

5. This box lets you select the values that will be used in the input cell. As you can see in Figure 19-11, Corel Quattro Pro suggested some values for you. For this example, increase the savings.

6. Click on Calculate Different Values. Text boxes will appear so you can enter the starting and stopping values, as well as the steps between.

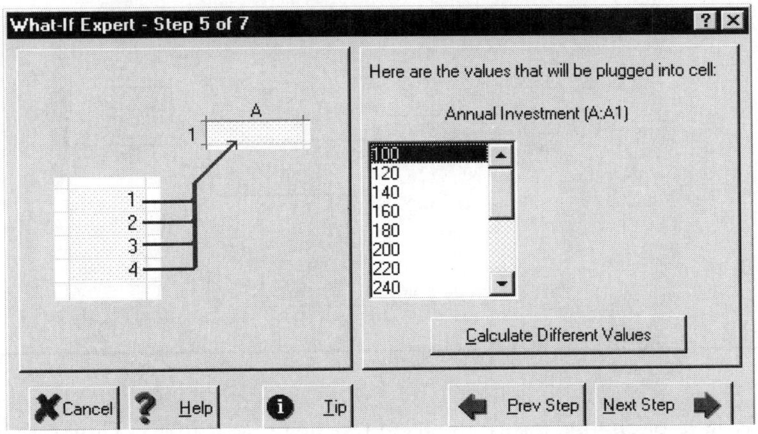

Corel
Quattro
Pro's
suggested
values
based on
the content
of the
changing
cell

FIGURE 19-11

> **7.** Enter **1000** as the Start value, **100** as the Step value, and **2000** as the Stop value, and then click on Next Step.

> **8.** In the last box, enter or point to the block where you want the table to appear, and then click on Make Table.

OTE: *The two-variable Expert is the same, except you designate two input cells.*

To create a What-If table manually, you have to start the table by entering the column of values that you want to substitute in a formula. In the cell above and to the right of the first substitution value, enter the formula that you want to calculate, including a reference to a blank input cell. Pull down the Tools menu, point to Numeric Tools, and click on What-If to see the dialog box shown in Figure 19-12. In the Data Table box, enter or point to the block of cells that contains the substitution values and formula. In the Input Cell box, enter the cell referenced in the formula. Click on Generate to create the table.

To create a two-variable table, you need to add a row of substitution values starting above and to the right of the substitution column. Enter the formula into the top-left cell of the table, making sure that it refers to two blank input cells. In the What-If dialog box, click on Two Free Variables. Indicate the Data Table and the Column Input and Row Input cells, and then click on Generate.

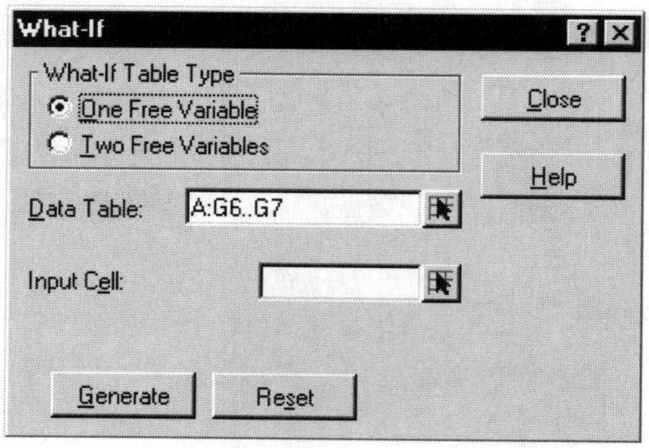

What-If
Table dialog
box

FIGURE 19-12

If you later change a formula used for the table, click on Generate to recalculate the results.

Streamlining Your Work

20

You have a wide range of tools and Experts to make your work easier with Corel Quattro Pro. But there is still more. By recording macros, you can quickly repeat a series of keystrokes and menu selections whenever you need to. You can build libraries of macros to carry out common tasks, and you can write macros that perform sophisticated functions. By linking macros with the keyboard, you run them without using a menu or dialog box, and you can even create a button to run a macro with a single click.

One other way to increase your productivity it to share your Corel Quattro Pro worksheets, charts, and maps with Corel WordPerfect and Corel Presentations. Use the formatting capabilities of these programs to display or publish your data and graphics with maximum impact.

Macros

A *macro* serves the same function in Corel Quattro Pro as it does in Corel WordPerfect and any computer application. It lets you save a series of keystrokes and commands, and then replay the entire series at any time. Recording a macro in Corel Quattro Pro, however, is a little different than on Corel WordPerfect because of the nature of the program.

 Use PerfectScript from the Corel WordPerfect Accessories menu to create a macro so you can run it from the taskbar.

You can record and play two types of macros in Corel Quattro Pro. PerfectScript macros are compatible with the macro language used by other Corel Office applications, and by the PerfectScript accessory. The macros are stored on your disk as individual files, and you can edit them using an editor of your choice, even Corel WordPerfect. Corel Quattro Pro macros are compatible with previous versions of Quattro Pro for Windows. They are stored directly in a worksheet, and you can edit them as you would any labels in the worksheet. These are the easiest macros to create and troubleshoot because it's all done in one application. You can even take advantage of macros that you or others have written for previous versions of Quattro Pro.

Recording a Macro

You don't have to do any preparation before recording a PerfectScript macro because it is stored on your disk. But before creating a Corel Quattro Pro macro, locate a blank area in the worksheet to store the macro. It should be one column wide, with at least as many blank cells as steps that you want to record. To play it safe, make sure that the remainder of the column is empty, and that you won't need any of those cells for the task you'll be recording. You might consider recording all of the macros you want to use for the notebook on page IV, which you probably won't be using for anything else, and which you can reach with the QuickTab button. Using one column for each macro allows you to record 256 macros before you have to worry about space.

To record a macro, follow these steps:

1. Pull down the Tools menu, point to Macro, and click on Record to display the dialog box in Figure 20-1. Your first choice it to select to record either a Corel Quattro Pro or PerfectScript macro. If you choose a PerfectScript macro, the box will change so you can indicate the macro name and location where you want to save it.

2. To record a Corel Quattro Pro macro, designate in the Location text box where in your notebook you want the macro recorded. Enter the coordinates or use Point mode to indicate the first empty cell that you've identified for the macro location. If you gave a block name to the cell, select the name from the Block name list. Only designate a single cell. If you designate a block of cells, then Corel Quattro Pro will only record commands until the block is filled. By specifying a single cell, it will continue recording commands until the end of the column or you stop recording the macro.

3. Click on OK to close the dialog box. Corel Quattro Pro displays the characters "REC" in the status bar as a reminder that you are recording a macro.

4. Perform the tasks that you want to record in the macro. You'll even see the commands appear if the macro block is onscreen.

5. When you have finished recording the macro, pull down the Tools menu, point to Macro, and click on Record again.

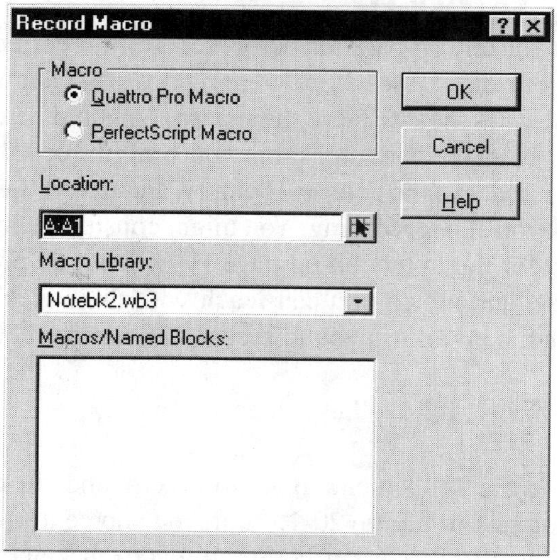

Selecting
the type of
macro you
want to
record

FIGURE 20-1

6. Give your macro a name so you can replay it easily. Click in the first cell in which the macro is stored, and use the Block Names command to give that cell a name.

To play a macro, just follow these steps:

1. Select Macro from the Tools menu, and click on Play.

2. In the dialog box that appears, double-click on the macro name.

If you need to stop a macro while it is running, press CTRL+BREAK and then click on OK in the message box that appears. Corel Quattro Pro will sound a beep and display an error message if it cannot follow the macro instruction. You usually will get errors not with recorded macros, but from ones that you edit or write.

_n_   **OTE:**   _You can play a macro even if you did not give it a name. In the Play Macro dialog box, simply enter the coordinates of the first instruction in the macro and then click on OK._

Relative and Absolute Addresses

By default, macros are recorded using *absolute addresses.* This means that if you click on cell A:A1 when recording the macro, the macro will always select cell A:A1 when you run it. There's nothing wrong with that if that's what you want. But suppose you want to record a macro that will insert a series of labels at a different location each time you play the macro?

To accomplish that, you must change to *relative addresses.* Here's how:

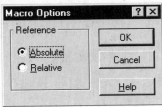

1. Pull down the Tools menu, point to Macro, and click on Options to see this dialog box.

2. Click on Relative and then on OK.

Now each cell selection command you record will select a cell relative to whatever is the active cell at that time. So suppose you start recording when you're in cell A1, and your first action is to click in cell B2. When you run the macro, it will start by selecting the cell one column over and one row down from the current active cell.

This all means that you have to plan your macro well, and think about what you want it to do and where. Consider starting by selecting the cell you will first want to use when you record the macro. Then as your first recorded step, click on that same cell, even though it is already active. This ensures that your macro will start at some known location.

If you are using an absolute address, the macro will start in that cell no matter what cell is active when you begin. If you use relative addresses, the macro will always begin in whatever cell is active at the time—just select it before running the macro.

 OTE: *If you select a cell at the start of the macro but perform any action on it except selecting another cell, the command to select the first cell will not be recorded in the macro.*

Let's record a small macro so you get the feel for it. The macro will enter a series of row and column labels starting in the cell next to the active cell, and insert a row of formulas. Follow these steps:

1. Click in A1.

2. Select Options from the Tools Macro menu, click on Relative, and then on OK.

3. Pull down the Tools menu, point to Macro, and then click on Record to display the Record Macro dialog box.

4. In the Location box, enter **B:A1** to save the macro in the first column of worksheet page B.

5. Click on OK. You can now record the macro.

6. Click in cell B1, and type **Qtr 1** and press ENTER.

7. Drag over cells B1 to E1, and then click on the QuickFill button to complete the series.

8. Click in Cell A2, and type **Income**.

9. Click in Cell A3, and type **Expenses**.

10. Click in cell B4, type **+B2--B3**, and press ENTER.

11. Drag over cells B4 to E4, and click on QuickFill to copy the formulas.

12. To stop recording, pull down the Tools menu, point to Macro, and click on Record.

 OTE: *The Absolute and Relative macro record options do not affect the way Corel Quattro Pro copies formulas.*

Naming Your Macro

To name the macro, you assign a block name to the first cell of the macro instructions. Let's name the macro we just recorded.

1. Go to page B to see the instructions of the macro, as shown in Figure 20-2. The instructions of the macro are listed in the block you selected in the Corel Quattro Pro macro language.

2. Click on cell A1.

3. Pull down the Insert menu, and click on Block Names.

4. Type **Budget** as the block name.

5. Click on Add.

6. Click on Close.

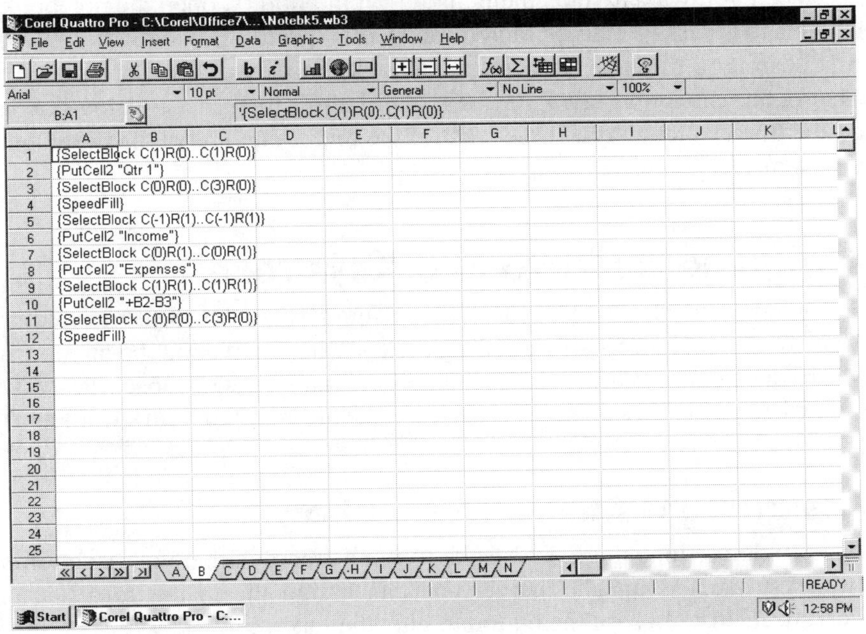

Recorded
macro
instructions

FIGURE 20-2

Running Your Macro

Now run the macro. Click on any cell in worksheet A, pull down the Tools menu, and click on Play. Double-click on Budget in the macro list. The labels and formulas will be inserted starting in the cell next to the active cell on the page.

Creating a Macro Library

A *macro library* is a notebook in which you can store macros. You open the notebook and leave it in the background as you work with other notebooks. When you play a macro, Corel Quattro Pro will first search for it in the current notebook. If it is not there, it will look for the macro in the macro library. You can also tell Corel Quattro Pro to find it there when you play the macro to save time.

To create a macro library, record the macros in a worksheet. Right-click on the notebook's title bar and choose Active Notebook Properties from the QuickMenu. Click on the Macro Library tab, and then click on Yes. Close the Properties dialog box and save the notebook.

When you want to access the macros in the library, open the notebook. It must be open to access its macros. If you want Corel Quattro Pro to run the macro without first searching through the active notebook, pull down the Tools menu, point to Macro, and click on Play. Pull down the Macro Library List dialog box, and click on the library name. You'll see a list of the macros and block names. Double-click on the macro you want to run.

Assigning a Macro to a Keystroke

If you have a macro that you run often, assign it to a CTRL+SHIFT key combination. That way, you can run it by pressing the combination without having to display the Macro dialog box. When you name the macro, name it with a backslash (\) followed by one letter (A to Z), such as \c. Then to run the macro, press CTRL+SHIFT and the letter.

Assigning a Macro to a Button

One problem with using a keystroke to run a macro is that you have to remember the keystroke. As an alternative, you can assign the macro to a button on the worksheet. Just click on the button to play the macro.

First, create the button.

1. Display the worksheet where you want the button to appear.

2. Click on the QuickButton tool on the toolbar.

3. Either click where you want a default-sized button to appear, or drag to create a button any size. When you release the mouse, the button appears selected with handles.

You can always change the size of the button later by dragging the handles. To move a button, use drag and drop.

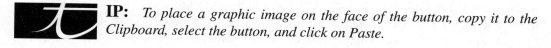

IP: *To place a graphic image on the face of the button, copy it to the Clipboard, select the button, and click on Paste.*

If you click elsewhere in the worksheet, the handles will disappear. To select a button so the handles appear, right-click on it. If you click the left mouse button, Corel Quattro Pro performs whatever function the button has been assigned.

Once you create the button, you must associate the macro with it, using these steps.

1. Right-click on the button and choose Button Properties from the QuickMenu to see the dialog box shown in Figure 20-3.

2. In the Enter Macro text box, type the command {BRANCH *macroname*}, substituting the name of your macro for *macroname*. You must enclose the command in braces.

3. Click on the Label Text page of the Properties dialog box and enter what you want to appear on the button's face.

You can also link the button to a URL address on the Web. Select Link to URL, and enter the URL address. To browse the Web to select a site, click on the Web Browse button in the toolbar.

The other button properties let you change the border color and button box style, protect the button from change, and give it an object name so you can refer to the button itself in macros.

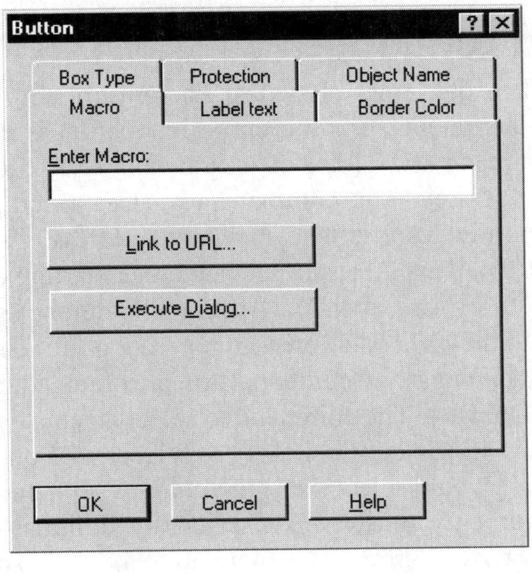

20

Button
Properties

FIGURE 20-3

Running Macros Automatically

Sometimes you want to run a macro every time you start Corel Quattro Pro, or when you open or close a specific notebook. You may want to open your Macro Library file, for example, or insert a standard heading on the initial worksheet. You can designate both an *autoload file* and a *startup macro*. An autoload file will be opened whenever you start Corel Quattro Pro. A startup macro will be played when you start Corel Quattro Pro.

You create both features in the Application Properties dialog box. Right-click on the Corel Quattro Pro title bar and select Application Properties from the QuickMenu. Click on the Macro tab, and enter the macro's block name in the Startup Macro text box. Also use this dialog box to determine what elements are suppressed as the macro runs.

You may also have a macro that you want to run whenever you open or close a specific notebook. Perhaps you want to display a certain area of the worksheet or page when you open the notebook, or print the worksheet when you close the notebook. These are called startup macros and exit macros.

To create a notebook startup macro, just give it the name _NBSTARTMACRO. Name an exit macro _NBEXITMACRO. When Corel Quattro Pro starts, it will look for a macro named _NBSTARTMACRO. If it finds it in the worksheet, it plays the macro. When you exit Corel Quattro Pro, it runs the macro called _NBEXITMACRO.

The Macro Language

Macros follow their own rules of syntax. Each macro command may be followed by one or more arguments, and the entire instruction is enclosed in braces. For example, the command {ESC} has no arguments because it simply equals the task of pressing the ESC key. The command to select a cell, SelectBlock, has one argument: the coordinates to select. A relative address is shown as {SelectBlock C(1)R(0)..C(1)R(0)}. This means to select a block starting one column to the right of the current cell in the same row. The 0 in the cell reference means to use the current row. Movement to the right and down is shown in positive numbers; movement to the left and up in negative numbers. An absolute address would appear as {SelectBlock A:D6..D6}. The command to select an entire row uses only the page and row number, as in {SelectBlock A:1} to select row 1 on page A. The command {SelectBlock C:H} would select the entire column H on page C.

Multiple arguments must be separated by commas, as in the command {BlockInsert.Rows A:1,Entire}. The first argument (A:1) specifies where to insert the row; the second argument indicates an entire, not a partial, row. Notice that the command name itself includes a period. The BlockInsert command is used generically to insert many different objects. The syntax is {BlockInsert.Object block, entire|partial}, using commands such as BlockInsert.Columns and BlockInsert.Pages.

Macro commands do not simply mimic keystrokes. If you use the arrow keys to select a cell, for example, you won't see instructions for each arrow that you press. Corel Quattro Pro records the results of your keystrokes, not individual actions. If you press the UP ARROW and RIGHT ARROW keys to select cell B3 using absolute addressing, the command will simply appear as {SelectBlock A:B3..B3}.

Dialog Boxes Commands

It is likely that you'll be recording macros that select options from dialog boxes, such as opening or printing a file. The command to open a file is simply {FileOpen *filename*}, as in {FileOpen C:\Corel\Office7\Corel Quattro7\Notebk1.wb3}.

When a dialog box contains multiple options, there is usually a different command for each option, often starting with the name of the dialog box. All Print macros, for example, begin with the word "Print," followed by a period and then the command that it performs. Use {Print.DoPrint}, for example, to print the current worksheet using all of the default values.

Other commands are used to set the print options before actually printing. This macro, for example, prints three copies of a block:

```
{Print.Block "A:A1..H4"}
{Print.Copies "3"}
{Print.DoPrint}
```

The first command sets the print block. The name shows that it involves the Print function and the Block option. The second command designates three copies using the Print function and the Copies option. The final command initiates printing.

Writing Macros

Macro instructions are stored as text in the worksheet, so you can edit a macro by changing, deleting, or inserting commands just as you edit worksheet labels. You can also copy instructions from one macro to another, even if they are on different pages or in different notebooks.

One way to insert additional commands into a macro is to record them as a new macro in another location in the worksheet, and then cut and paste them where you want them inserted. Do not try to record additional instructions directly into the macro—new instructions could overwrite existing ones—unless you record them in the first blank cell after the macro's last command.

You can also edit and write macros by typing the macro commands yourself. In order to write macro commands, however, you need to know the Corel Quattro Pro macro language, and a little about the way computer programs work.

To write a macro, just start in any blank cell in an area of a worksheet that you won't need for anything else. Type the commands, making sure to enclose them in braces. At the end of the macro, make sure there is a blank cell, or enter the commands {QUIT} or {RETURN}. If there is anything else immediately after the macro, Corel Quattro Pro will try to run it as a macro command and will generate an error.

When you've finished, give a block name to the first instruction, and then save the worksheet.

If you need help writing the command or using its arguments, refer to the help system. You'll find detailed examples on each macro command, as shown in Figure 20-4. Click on Help Topics in the Help menu, and then double-click on the Macro Command Reference option. You can choose macros by category, or see an alphabetical listing.

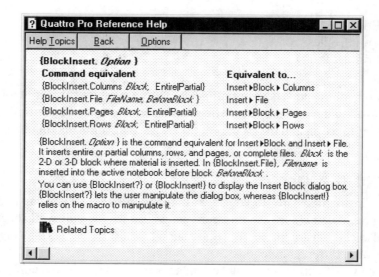

Using the Help system for detailed information on macro commands

FIGURE 20-4

You can test a macro quickly by clicking on the first cell, selecting Macro from the Tools menu, clicking on Play, and then on OK. The coordinates of the active cell will be in the Location text box of the Play Macro dialog box.

Copying Commands

If you are not certain of a command's syntax, you can paste the command in the macro rather than writing it. To paste a command, press SHIFT+F3 to see a dialog box listing the categories of macro commands.

The categories are as follows:

- Keyboard
- Screen
- Interactive
- Program flow
- Cell
- File
- / commands

- Command Equivalents
- OLE and DDE
- UI Building
- Object
- Analysis tools
- Miscellaneous

Select the category of the command you want to use, and then click on OK. If you see a further listing of categories, choose one from the list, and click on OK again. You'll see a list of commands in the category. Click on the command you want to insert and then on OK. The command will appear in the cell and input line.

 IP: *Click on Cancel to move back to the previous dialog box list.*

Use the following steps to write a macro that inserts your name on the top of the current worksheet page.

1. Click on page tab C and then in cell A1.

2. Type **{SelectBlock A1..A1}** and then press the DOWN ARROW to select cell A2. Notice that the page name has been left off the range reference in order to make the macro move to cell A1 of the current page. In a sense, this command is absolute to the cell reference but relative to the page.

3. Type **{BlockInsert.Rows A1..A1,Entire}** and then press the DOWN ARROW. This command inserts a row into the rows of the worksheet.

4. Type **{PutCell *Your Name*}** and press the DOWN ARROW key.

5. Type **{SelectBlock A1..H1}** and press the DOWN ARROW key.

6. Type **{SetProperty "Alignment.Horizontal",Center across block}**. This command centers the label in the active cell across the selected block.

7. Type **{QUIT}** and then press ENTER. The completed macro is shown in Figure 20-5.

8. Select cell A1, the first cell of the macro.

9. Select Block Names from the Insert menu.

10. Type **\n** as the block name, and then click on Add, and then on Close.

To run the macro, just press CTRL+SHIFT+N. Try it now. Click on page tab D and type something in cell A1. Press CTRL+SHIFT+N to run the macro. You can also select Macro from the Tools menu, click on Play, and then double-click on the macro name.

 IP: *To quickly go to your macro, click on the Navigate button in the input line and click on the macro name.*

Fundamental Macro Commands

There are hundreds of macros. As with functions, many of them are for rather sophisticated purposes. In this chapter, however, we will review a basic set of commands that also illustrate some principles of programming.

Entering Information into Cells

There are several commands for inserting information into cells. The simplest is PUTCELL, which uses the syntax {PUTCELL *Data,[Date(0|1)]*}. To insert a

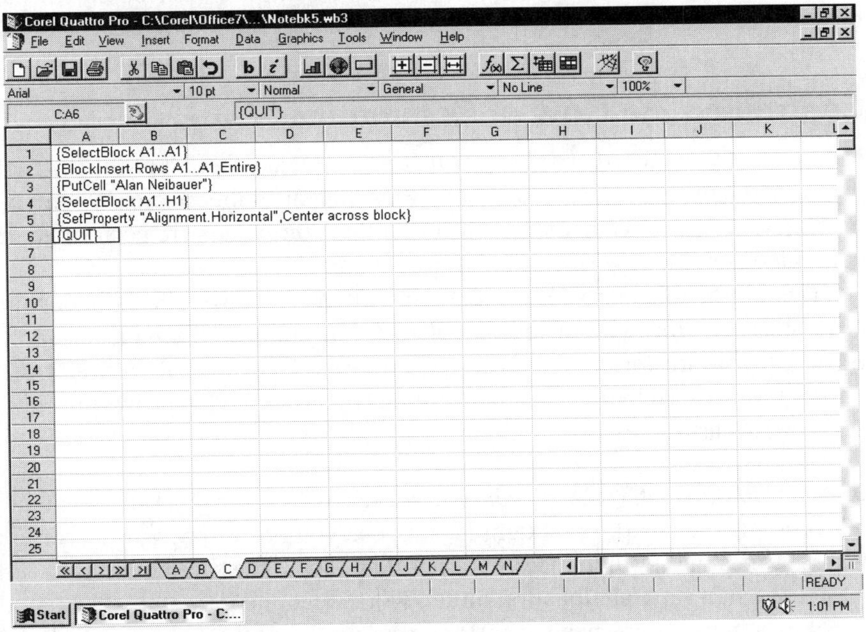

Completed
macro

FIGURE 20-5

numeric value in a cell, enter the value as the argument, as in {PUTCELL 764.76}. Enclose labels, formulas, functions, and dates in quotation marks.

The optional argument is only needed when you insert a date. Use 1 to store the value as a date, or 0 to insert it as a label. The command {PUTCELL "11/16/45",1}, for example, inserts the date into the active cell as a date.

You can also use a related command, {PUTCELL2 *Data*}, which has only one argument. You must start all numeric values with a plus sign, as in {PUTCELL2 +345}, and dates are always inserted as dates, not labels.

To enter the same information in multiple cells, use the PUTBLOCK and PUTBLOCK2 commands, using the syntax

   {PUTBLOCK *Data*,[*Block*],[*Date*(0|1)]}

and

   {PUTBLOCK2 *Data*,[*Block*]}

If you do not specify the optional block, the contents are inserted into the active cell or selected block. Designate noncontiguous blocks in parentheses.

Controlling the Flow of Commands

Macros that you record are always *linear.* This means that all of the instructions are performed, and in the exact order that they appear in the macro. When you write a macro, however, you can control the order that commands are performed, repeating commands or skipping over them as you want.

These type of macros, more than any others, require a basic understanding of program logic, the type of logic applied to programming languages such as C or Basic. If you are familiar with a programming language, then you will find the concepts discussed in this chapter familiar. If you are new to programming, you will get a good starting lesson.

USING SUBROUTINES   A *subroutine* is a series of macro instructions that you can perform when needed. For example, suppose you need to perform a series of tasks several times in the same macro. Rather than repeat the same lines each time, write them once in a separate location on the worksheet and give it its own name.

Now whenever you need to perform those tasks, you call the routine by enclosing the name in braces, as in {Do_This_Routine}. The macro performs the commands in the subroutine until it reaches a blank cell, a value, or the command {RETURN}, after which it goes back and follows the instructions where it left off in the original macro.

By creating a library of subroutines, you can write complex macros more easily and quickly. In fact, some macros may contain little more than subroutine calls to other macros.

MOVING TO OTHER INSTRUCTIONS   One other way to perform another macro, or set of commands in the running macro itself, is to use the Branch command. Unlike a subroutine, however, the Branch command does not return to the original location when the command ends.

You use the Branch command to leave one macro and perform another, or to move to another location in the same macro that you've given a block name. The syntax is {BRANCH *macro*}. The command is most commonly used in conjunction with the IF command.

MAKING DECISIONS   One advantage of writing a macro is that you can have it make decisions for you—for example, skipping over some instructions that you may not want it to perform, or moving to other instructions only under certain conditions.

For example, suppose you only want to print your worksheet if the value in a cell reaches a certain level. Use the IF command to test the value in the cell and print the worksheet based on that value. The syntax is {IF *Condition*}{DoWhenTrue}{DoWhenFalse}. *Condition* is a logical expression. Look at this example:

> {IF due>500}{BRANCH Overdue_Notice}
> {BRANCH GoodClient}

When the value in the cell named "due" is over 500, the macro branches to the macro named "Overdue_Notice" and performs its instructions. When the amount is not over 500, the macro branches to the GoodClient subroutine.

In a strict sense, the IF macro command does not work like an If..Else statement in most programming languages. In these languages, the false command is only performed when the condition is false. With Corel Quattro Pro, if you do not use the Branch or Quit commands, the macro will perform both statements when the condition is true. Look at this example:

> {IF due>500}{PUTCELL "Deadbeat"}
> {PUTCELL "Good Client"}

If the condition is true, Corel Quattro Pro will perform the command and insert "Deadbeat" into the cell. However, it will then continue with the macro, immediately placing "Good Client" in the same cell. It will not skip over the command just because the condition is true.

If this is the last command in the macro, you can always write it like this:

> {IF due>500}{PUTCELL "Deadbeat"}{Quit}
> {PUTCELL "Good Client"}

Then the macro will not run the last statement when the condition is true.

Keep in mind that you can use multiple Branch statements to perform multiple tests. For example, suppose you are checking student grades to determine what values to enter in a cell. Use a macro such as this:

> {IF grade>=90}{BRANCH a_student}
> {IF grade>=80}{BRANCH b_student}

```
{IF grade>=70}{BRANCH c_student}
{BRANCH Failing}
```

The macro now tests for three conditions, and if none of them are true, it performs the macro named Failing.

Even though you are branching elsewhere to the macro, or to another macro, you can still return to the statement following the false statement. Give a block name to the command after the false statement, and then branch back to that when you are ready. For example, look at this logic:

```
{IF grade>=90}{BRANCH a_student}
{IF grade>=80}{BRANCH b_student}
{IF grade>=70}{BRANCH c_student}
{PUTCELL2 "You are failing, sorry"}
{PUTCELL "The End"}
```

Now assume that you've assigned the block name Continue to the cell with the command {PUTCELL "The End"}. When a student has a grade of 90 or more, the macro branches to this macro named a_student:

```
{SELECTBLOCK A1}
{PUTCELL2 "You are very smart. You got an A."}
{SELECTBLOCK A2}
{BRANCH CONTINUE}
```

The last command branches back to the original macro, and continues after the final test of the IF command.

REPEATING COMMANDS   In addition to making decisions with the IF command, let's say you want a macro to repeat a series of instructions with the FOR macro. The syntax is

{FOR *CounterLoc,Start#,Stop#,Step#,StartLoc*}

Here's the purpose of each argument:

■   *CounterLoc* is a cell that Corel Quattro Pro will use to keep track of the number of repetitions. The value in the cell will change with each repetition of the loop so Corel Quattro Pro will know when the maximum value has been reached.

■ *Start#* is the initial value that Corel Quattro Pro places in the CounterLoc cell.

■ *Stop#* sets the maximum value of CounterLoc. When the number in CounterLoc exceeds this value, the repetition ends.

■ *Step#* determines how Corel Quattro Pro increments the value in CounterLoc. When set at 1, for example, the value in CounterLoc is incremented by 1 with each repetition.

For example, the following command runs the subroutine Repeat_This ten times:

{FOR A1,1,10,1,Repeat_This}

It places the value 1 in cell A1, and then performs the subroutine starting at the cell named Repeat_This. It then increments the value in cell A1 by 1—the Step value—and runs the macro again. It repeats this process until the value in cell A1 is greater than 10.

INTERACTIVE MACROS While Corel Quattro Pro has hundreds of macro commands, sometimes you just don't know exactly what you want the macro to do. You might want to insert different text each time the macro runs, or set a dialog box in some specific way. In these instances you want an interactive macro—one that pauses to give you a chance to enter text or select options from a dialog box.

When you want a macro to open a dialog box and then pause so you can select options form the box, use a command in the form {DialogBox}. The command {Print}, for example, displays the dialog box on the screen. Once you choose an option from the box and select Print or Close, the macro continues at the next instruction.

To pause a macro so you can enter text, use the GETLABEL command with this syntax:

{GETLABEL Prompt,Location}

The Prompt argument is a string up to 70 characters long that will appear telling you what type of information to enter. It can be text, such as "Enter your telephone number," or a reference to a cell containing the text you want to appear as the prompt. To reference a cell, enter it as a formula, such as +D3. The Location argument is the cell where the information should be placed.

When Corel Quattro Pro encounters the GETLABEL command, it pauses the macro and displays your prompt in the Enter a Label dialog box. Type the text you want to enter, up to 160 characters, and then click on OK or press ENTER.

For example, the following command displays a message on the screen and accepts an entry into cell A1:

{GETLABEL "Enter your name", +A1}

The GETNUMBER command works the same way, but accepts a numeric value. The syntax is {GETNUMBER *Prompt,Location*}. You can enter a number or a formula that returns a numeric value.

Sharing Corel Quattro Pro Information

Corel Quattro Pro has a wide range of formatting capabilities, and you can enter text into cells, but it is far from a word processing program. When you need more than a few lines of explanatory text with your worksheet, consider sharing it with Corel WordPerfect.

 Share a worksheet with Corel WordPerfect so you do not have to retype the information into a Corel WordPerfect table.

The quickest way to use a worksheet with Corel WordPerfect is to cut and paste. Select the range of cells in Corel Quattro Pro, switch to your Corel WordPerfect document, and then click on Paste. The worksheet will be inserted into the document as a Corel WordPerfect table. So you can now use Corel WordPerfect's table commands to format the information and work with rows and columns.

When selecting cells in Corel Quattro Pro, keep in mind the page margins and width of your document. In Corel Quattro Pro, worksheets wider than a page will just run over into additional columns. If you paste a wide table into Corel WordPerfect, however, the columns will scroll off the edge of the page, as shown in Figure 20-6. Before printing the document, reduce the column size or font so the worksheet fits on the page. The information is there, it just doesn't fit on the page.

Using Paste Special

For more choices in sharing a worksheet, select Paste Special from the Edit menu. You'll have several options, shown in Figure 20-7, including buttons to Paste and Paste Link. Let's look at the Paste options first.

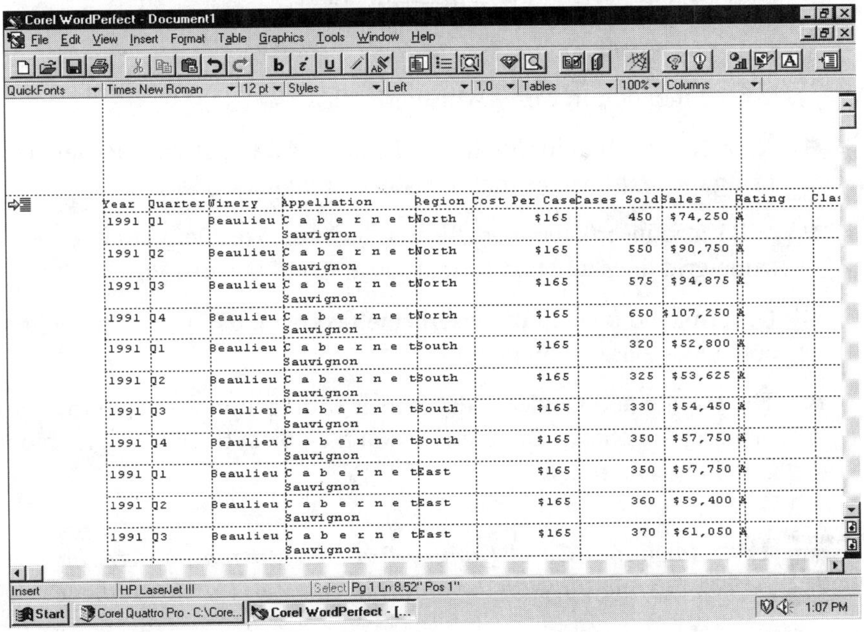

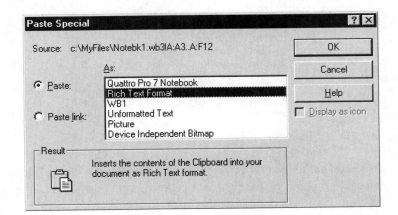

Wide
worksheets
scrolling off
the screen
when
pasted into
Corel
WordPerfect

FIGURE 20-6

20

Paste
Special
dialog box

FIGURE 20-7

You have a number of ways to paste the table:

- Corel Quattro Pro 7 Notebook inserts the worksheet as one object that you cannot edit in Corel WordPerfect.

- Rich Text Format inserts the worksheet as a Corel WordPerfect table, but using the text formats that it has in Corel Quattro Pro.

- WB1 also inserts the worksheet as a Corel WordPerfect table, but with the same grid lines and text formats as in Corel Quattro Pro.

- Unformatted text simply inserts the text from the worksheet, with cell contents separated by tabs.

- The Picture and Device Independent Bitmap options insert the cells as a graphic object. Double-click on the object to edit the graphic in Corel Presentations.

 IP: *Pasting a Corel Quattro Pro chart or map always inserts it as an object. Double-click on the object to edit it in Corel Quattro Pro.*

If you select to paste the worksheet as a Corel Quattro Pro 7 Notebook, the cells will be inserted as one object, surrounded by handles:

Quarter	Winery	Appellation	Region	Cost	Cases Sold
Q1	Beaulieu	Cabernet Sauvignon	North	$165	450
Q2	Beaulieu	Cabernet Sauvignon	North	$165	550
Q3	Beaulieu	Cabernet Sauvignon	North	$165	575
Q4	Beaulieu	Cabernet Sauvignon	North	$165	650
Q1	Beaulieu	Cabernet Sauvignon	South	$165	320
Q2	Beaulieu	Cabernet Sauvignon	South	$165	325
Q3	Beaulieu	Cabernet Sauvignon	South	$165	330
Q4	Beaulieu	Cabernet Sauvignon	South	$165	350
Q1	Beaulieu	Cabernet Sauvignon	East	$165	350

This is an *embedded object*. This means that along with the object, Windows 95 also stores the name of the program used to create it—Corel Quattro Pro. As an object, you can't edit or format the information in Corel WordPerfect, but if you double-click on Object, Windows 95 opens Corel Quattro Pro and transmits the data from the object to it.

Corel Quattro Pro is opened, however, for in-place editing. You'll see a miniature version of the Corel Quattro Pro worksheet right on the Corel WordPerfect window. However, Corel WordPerfect's menus and toolbars are replaced by those of Corel Quattro Pro, as shown in Figure 20-8. This way, you can edit the worksheet data while seeing the document in which it will be printed. If you pull down a menu item, you'll see the Corel Quattro Pro menu options, not Corel WordPerfect's. Nevertheless, the worksheet window appears within the Corel WordPerfect document window.

Keep in mind that there is no link between the object in Corel WordPerfect and the actual Corel Quattro Pro file from which the data was copied. What's in Corel WordPerfect is a copy of the data linked to Corel Quattro Pro as its program of origination. If you change the information in the original disk file, the data in Corel WordPerfect will not change.

If you click on the Paste Link option in the Paste Special dialog box, you have one option—Quattro Pro 7 Notebook. Pasting the worksheet in this way inserts it as an object with an OLE (Object Linking and Embedding) link. Now there is a link between the object in Corel WordPerfect and the Corel Quattro Pro file from which it was

20

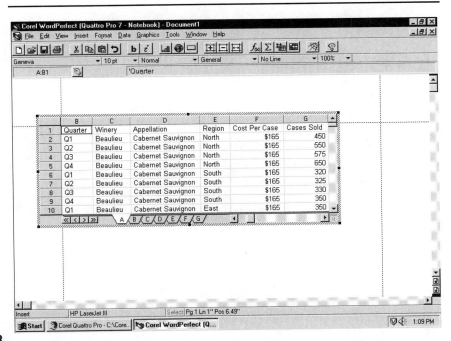

Editing an embedded object in place

FIGURE 20-8

obtained. If you change the information in the file, it will change in Corel WordPerfect as well.

When you double-click on the object, Windows 95 opens Corel Quattro Pro and the associated file, not in place but in a Corel Quattro Pro window. When you edit and save the worksheet, the changes are also shown in the Corel WordPerfect document.

 OTE: *If you want to copy the Corel WordPerfect document to another computer, however, you must also copy the original source file.*

PART IV

Corel Presentations

Using Corel Presentations

21

Corel Presentations 7 is a remarkable program that lets you create anything from a simple cover page for a report to a complete multimedia slide presentation. What makes it even more remarkable is that it is easy—you don't need a background in art or design, and you don't have to spend hours in front of your computer screen to create special effects.

Certainly the program gets its name because you can use it to create a presentation. You can design a series of slides to show on a monitor, to display on a large screen using a projector, or to convert to actual 33mm photographic slides or overhead transparencies. If you design the presentation for computer display, you can also add sound effects and create special effects with the transition from one slide to the next.

But you can use Corel Presentations even when your goals are not that grand. You can create one or more slides to use for report covers, handouts for meetings, even for organization or data charts.

Corel Presentations Basics

Before starting Corel Presentations, let's review some basic concepts that will help you along the way. Corel Presentations lets you create one or more slides. They are called *slides* even if you do not plan to convert them to photographic slides or show them on the screen. So if you use Corel Presentations to design a report cover, for example, you are still creating a "slide."

 OTE: *You can also create pictures that are not slides and that do not have layers.*

Every slide consists of three separate layers. The bottom layer is appropriately called the background. The background contains designs and colors that make up the general appearance of the slide. Imagine going to the store and purchasing colored paper to draw on—the color on the paper is the background. With Corel Presentations, you can select from a list of professionally designed background designs, modify them, or create your own.

Over the background is the *layout layer*. This determines the general position and type of contents for each slide. The contents are represented by placeholders, boxes that appear onscreen suggesting the type of items that should be on the slide. If you do not add any text to a placeholder, it will not appear onscreen when you show the presentation, and it will not print with the slide. Corel Presentations comes with templates for six general layouts, listed in Table 21-1.

You can also create a slide using no template (starting with a totally white background) or just using the background. Both of these types contain no placeholders.

 OTE: *You can change the position and size of the placeholders, delete them, or add your own elements to a slide.*

The top layer is called the *slide layer*. This is where you enter the text, drawings, clip art, or other items that you want to appear on the slide.

With Corel Presentations you can work on your slides in four views:

■ *Slide Editor view* lets you create or edit the slide contents or background, one slide at a time.

■ *Outliner view* displays the organization of a presentation as a text outline, using titles, subtitles, and bullet lists as the outline levels.

■ *Slide Sorter view* displays thumbnails of the slides so you can add and delete slides and change their order.

■ *Slide List view* displays a list of the slide number, title, transition, and advance used with slide presentations.

Slide Template	Placeholders
Title	Title, subtitle
Bullet Chart	Title, subtitle, bullet list
Text	Title, subtitle, text box
Organization Chart	Title, subtitle, organization chart box
Data Chart	Title, subtitle, chart box
Combination	Title, subtitle, bullet list, and chart box

Default Slide Layouts

TABLE 21-1

One of the first choices you have to make when creating a presentation is the category: 35mm, Color, or Printout. The category determines basic design elements, such as the color choices and aspect ratio, for the type of media. You would use Color, for example, if you plan to display the presentation on a color monitor, or if you have a color printer. You might also select Color if you have a black-and-white printer but are using a background design that will translate well into shades of gray. Select the Printout category for simple backgrounds that will print well on a monochrome printer, or choose 35mm if you plan to convert the slides to photographic slides.

Starting a Presentation

You start a new presentation by making two choices—the background that you want to apply to the slides and the template for the first slide. You can later change the order of slides if you want the presentation to begin with a different slide type.

Follow these steps to create a presentation.

1. Click on Start in the taskbar, point to Corel WordPerfect Suite 7, and click on Corel Presentations 7. You'll see the Document Selection dialog box. Once you create a presentation, you can select to open it using either of two options in this dialog box: Work on an Existing File, or Work on the Last File.

2. Click on Create a New Slide show and then on OK. The New Slide show dialog box appears, as shown in Figure 21-1. You should first select a slide background from the Gallery, although you can later change the master background.

3. Click on Gallery to see the Master Gallery box shown in Figure 21-2. The box lists the background formats provided by Corel Presentations.

4. Choose Color in the Category list, if it is not already selected.

5. Scroll the list to see all of the background designs.

6. Click on the design you want, and then click on Apply to redisplay the New Slide Show dialog box.

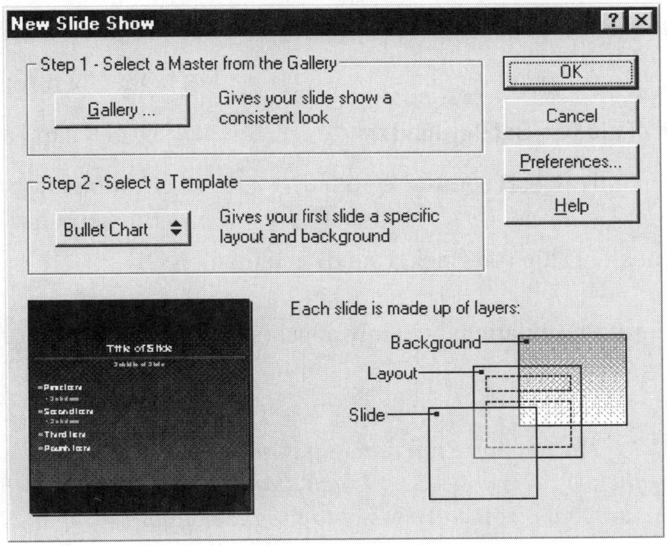

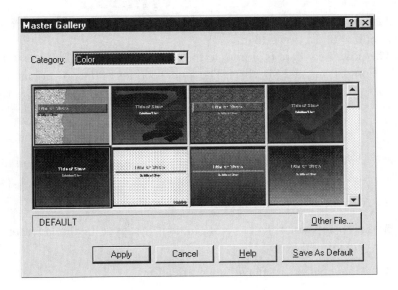

Choosing a
background
and a
starting slide

FIGURE 21-1

21

Available
slide
backgrounds

FIGURE 21-2

7. Pull down the Select a Template list to see these options:

- None
- Background
- Title (on Background)
- Bullet Chart (on Background)

- Text (on Background)
- Org Chart (on Background)
- Data Chart (on Background)
- Combination (on Background)

8. Click on Title (on Background) and then on OK.

The Corel Presentations window appears with the template for a title slide (see Figure 21-3).

IP: *The Startup Preferences button in the Document Selection dialog box, by the way, lets you select which dialog box will appear when you first start the program. You can choose to use the default Document Selection box, or to automatically display the Drawing or Slide Show window.*

The Corel Presentations Window

Look at the Corel Presentations window shown in Figure 21-3. Under the menu bar are a toolbar and a power bar.

The power bar here is similar to the one in Corel WordPerfect, starting with the QuickFonts, Font, and Size lists. The other sections of the power bar are as follows.

- *Style List* lets you change the slide's template.

- *Previous Slide* displays the previous slide in the presentation.

- *Slide List* shows the number of the slide you are viewing and the total number of slides, and lets you pull down the list to display a specific slide.

- *Next Slide* displays the next slide in the presentation.

- *Layer* lets you select to work in the slide layer, layout layer, or background layer.

- *Zoom* changes displayed magnification.

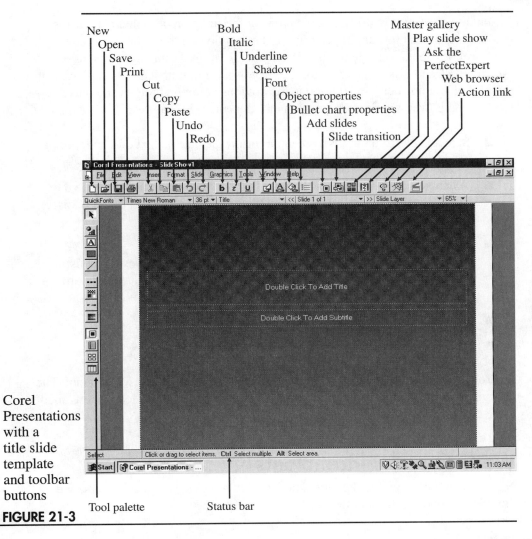

New
Open
Save
Print
Cut
Copy
Paste
Undo
Redo

Bold
Italic
Underline
Shadow
Font
Object properties
Bullet chart properties
Add slides
Slide transition

Master gallery
Play slide show
Ask the
PerfectExpert
Web browser
Action link

Corel
Presentations
with a
title slide
template
and toolbar
buttons

Tool palette   Status bar

FIGURE 21-3

 IP: *The Previous and Next Slide lists will wrap around to the beginning or end.*

You use the Tool palette on the left side of the window to draw and format your own elements to the slide, or to change views.

Finally, the status bar displays the name of the function or tool you are using on the left, and gives hints about performing the function on the right.

Corel Presentations generally offers many of the same features as Corel WordPerfect and other applications. So, if you are familiar with one application, you'll feel at home here. In addition to the obvious common buttons and lists in the toolbar and power bar, here are just some of the common features:

- Select Date from the Insert menu to insert the date as text or a code, or to select or create a date format.

- When you are editing a placeholder that contains text, choose to use the Spell Checker, Thesaurus, Grammatik, or QuickCorrect from the Tools menu.

- Select Preferences from the Edit menu to customize the way Corel Presentations works. The Preferences dialog box offers these options: Display, Environment, Files, Language, Toolbar, Menu Bar, Keyboard, Backup, and Slide Show.

- Use the File menu to access file management options.

- Play and record macros using the Tools menu.

You can also customize the appearance of the screen using the View menu. The options in the View menu are summarized in Table 21-2. You'll learn more about these options in Chapter 22.

Working with Placeholders

Now look at the template. The Title template contains just two placeholders, one for the title and one for the subtitle.

 You can use the Clipboard to paste text from other applications into slides.

To use a placeholder, double-click on it to insert contents into it. For example, double-click on the Title placeholder to enter and format text into the title.

Option	Function
Zoom	Changes the magnification of the display
Toolbar	Displays or hides the toolbar
Ruler	Displays or hides horizontal or vertical rulers
Reveal Codes	Displays codes in the status bar
Show Pointer Position	Displays the horizontal and vertical coordinates of the mouse pointer in the right side of the status bar
Selected Object Viewer	Displays a separate window containing a copy of the selected object in the slide
Slide Editor	Changes to the Slide Editor to work on an individual slide
Outliner	Displays the Outliner to see the organization of text on all slides
Slide Sorter	Displays thumbnail sketches of all of the slides
Slide List	Shows the number, title, transition, and advance time for all slides
Draft Mode	Temporarily removes colors and background graphics so you can concentrate on slide contents
Crosshair	Displays horizontal and vertical lines, with the intersection following the movement of the mouse pointer
Grid/Snap	Displays or hides a dotted grid pattern, controls the snap-to-grid placement of objects, lets you change the grid pattern, and clears guidelines
AutoSelect	Allows Corel Presentations to automatically select an object after you create it

21

View Menu
Options

TABLE 21-2

Every placeholder is similar to a graphic box in Corel WordPerfect. Click on the placeholder to display handles around it, and then perform any of these functions:

- Drag the box to change its position.

- Drag a handle to change it size.

- Press DEL to delete the box.

- Cut, copy, and paste the box.

While a placeholder will not appear with the slide if you do not use it, you may want to delete unused placeholders from the slide. This will make it easier to select other objects that you add, without accidentally selecting the empty placeholder. To delete the placeholder, click on it and press DEL. If you later want to restore the original placeholders, select Slide Re-Apply Layout from the Slide menu. However, this procedure will also return anything you've moved or resized to their default settings, so use this option with caution.

 IP: *To change the layout of a slide, pull down the Layout List in the power bar and click on the layout you want to apply to the slide.*

Now let's create our first slide.

1. Double-click on the title placeholder. The box will be surrounded by heavy lines and the insertion point will appear in the middle, the default justification for titles and subtitles.

2. Type the text of the title: **Educational Technology**. Do not press ENTER, unless you want to add a second line to the title.

3. Double-click on the Subtitle placeholder.

4. Type **Planning for the Future** as the subtitle text.

Formatting Text

You can edit the text using the power bar, toolbar, or Format menus. To edit the text, double-click on the placeholder, then add, delete, or change the text as needed. To format text, use the options in the toolbar or power bar.

For even more formatting options, select from the Format menu or from the QuickMenu that appears when you right-click on the text. You can select line, paragraph, and justification formats similar to those for text in Corel WordPerfect.

To change the appearance of text, select Font from the Format menu or QuickMenu to see the Font Properties dialog box. Use the Font, Fill Attributes, and Outline pages in this dialog box to change the style, color, and size of text, add a fill pattern or color, and select the type and color of the outline around the characters.

Adding Graphics to Slides

The placeholders represent the items that Corel Presentations suggests should be included. You can use the drawing tools to add other elements, and you can add graphics from your disk. Inserting graphics into a slide is similar to adding a graphic to a Corel WordPerfect document.

In Chapter 22, you'll learn how to work with graphics of all types. In this chapter, however, we'll introduce QuickArt. This is a special format of graphic that is accessible from Corel Presentations. The images are not stored in WPG format but a format of their own, although you can convert a graphic to WPG if you want to later use it in Corel WordPerfect.

Follow these steps to add QuickArt:

1. Pull down the Insert menu and click on QuickArt. The mouse will appear with a small square. You can also insert a graphic from the Tool palette, as you will learn later.

2. Drag in the slide to create a box the size you want the graphic, or click anywhere to create a box the default size. When you release the mouse or click, the QuickArt Browser dialog box will appear showing a folder labeled STANDARD.QAD.

3. Double-click on the STANDARD.QAD folder to see a series of folders, each containing a category of art, such as Banners, Computers, and People.

4. Double-click on a folder for the type of image you want to insert. If you see more folders of subcategories, double-click on the one you want. Eventually, you'll see thumbnail sketches of the graphics in the selected folder, as shown in Figure 21-4.

5. Double-click on the image you want to insert, or click on it and then on the Insert button.

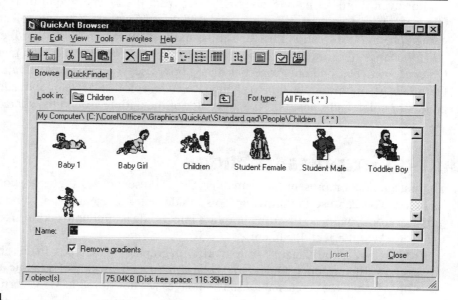

Selecting
the
thumbnail
for the
graphic

FIGURE 21-4

The graphic will appear in the slide surrounded by eight handles. Change the position and size of the graphic by dragging it or its handles. When you drag a handle to change its size, an outline of the graphic appears so you can see the resulting size. You can also drag a handle all of the way to the other side to flip the image vertically or horizontally. Later you'll learn other ways to edit and change graphics. Figure 21-5 shows the title slide with two QuickArt graphics inserted.

IP: *You can use similar techniques to insert graphics other than QuickArt. When the QuickArt browser dialog box appears, enter the path and name of the graphic file in the Name box, and then click on Insert.*

Adding a Slide

You are now ready to add another slide. You can add any number of slides at one time and select the template that you want to use for them. Next, enter a *bullet slide*.

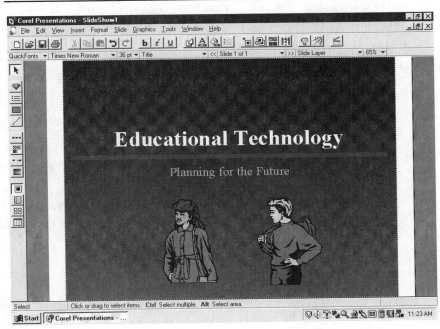

Title slide with two QuickArt graphics

FIGURE 21-5

A bullet slide is just like a bullet list in Corel WordPerfect, with major bullet items and minor ones indented underneath.

 You can create a bullet chart directly from a Corel WordPerfect outline.

1. Click on the Add Slides button in the toolbar to display the Add Slides dialog box.

2. Leave the Number of Slides set at 1. If you want to enter several slides that use the same template, enter the number.

3. Pull down the Template list and select Bullet Chart.

4. Click on OK. Corel Presentations displays the new slide with the Bullet Chart layout, including a title, subtitle, and bullet chart placeholder.

5. Double-click on the Title placeholder, and type **Benefits of Technology**.

6. Double-click on the subtitle placeholder, and type **Academic Achievement**.

7. Double-click on the Bullet list box. The first bullet appears at the left margin of the box, followed by the insertion point.

8. Type **Improved Test Scores**, and then press ENTER to insert the next bullet.

9. Press TAB to indent the insertion point and to insert a second-level bullet.

10. Type **National achievement tests, such as SAT**, and then press ENTER. The program will insert another bullet at the same level. You use TAB to enter entries at subordinate levels and SHIFT+TAB to move back to a higher level.

11. Complete the bullet chart as shown in Figure 21-6.

If you need to edit a bullet chart, double-click on it. You can also click on it and choose Edit Chart from the Edit menu or QuickMenu. To add a new bullet item at the end of the chart, place the insertion point at the end of the last line and press ENTER. Use TAB or SHIFT+TAB to change the position of the item.

To insert an item within the chart, place the insertion point at the start of a line, following the bullet, and press ENTER. Use this technique, for example, to insert a new item at the top of the list.

You can add a bullet chart to a slide even if it does not have a bullet chart placeholder. Suppose, for example, that you created a title slide and then decide that you want it to have a bullet list. Follow these steps.

1. Pull down the Insert menu and click on Bullet Chart.

2. Drag to create a rectangle the size you want the chart, or just click to create one that fills the slide.

The Bullet Chart placeholder will appear when you release the mouse.

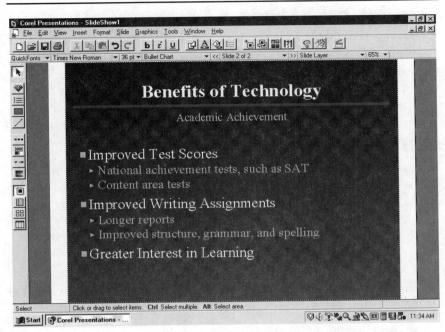

Completed
bullet chart

FIGURE 21-6

21

Importing a Corel WordPerfect Outline

If you've already typed an outline in Corel WordPerfect using the Paragraph Numbers feature, you can import it into a bullet chart. The bullet levels will correspond to the document's indentation levels. Here's how.

1. Create a bullet chart. If you already created the chart, double-click on the chart placeholder.

2. Pull down the File menu and click on Insert.

3. Select the file that you want to use for the chart.

4. Click on Insert.

Creating a Text Slide

A *text slide* is similar to a bullet slide in that it has three placeholders. The Bullet Chart placeholder, however, is replaced with a text box. Double-click on the box to place the insertion point there, and then type and format the text. When you press ENTER, Corel Presentations inserts a carriage return to start a new line.

Creating an Organization Chart

An *organization chart* shows the chain of command within an organization. Creating one manually means drawing boxes and lines, and trying to keep everything in the proper order. Instead, let Corel Presentations do it for you.

1. Click on the Add Slides button in the toolbar.

2. Pull down the Template list and select Org Chart.

3. Click on OK. Corel Presentations displays the new slide with three placeholders: title, subtitle, and the organization chart.

4. Add the title and subtitle, and then double-click on the Organization Chart placeholder to display a default chart, as shown in Figure 21-7.

5. Double-click the Name placeholder in the top box.

6. Type the name of the person for that top position.

7. Press TAB to move to the Title placeholder.

8. Type the title.

9. Continue entering names and titles and in the same way.

10. Delete the boxes you do not need by clicking on a box and pressing the DEL key.

The default organization chart includes a basic set of positions. You can add other positions as required by your organization's structure. Here are the positions that you can insert:

■ A staff position comes directly off of another position, as the assistant position in the following example. The position is not on the chain of command.

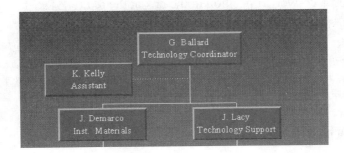

■ A *subordinate* is under another position in the chain of command.

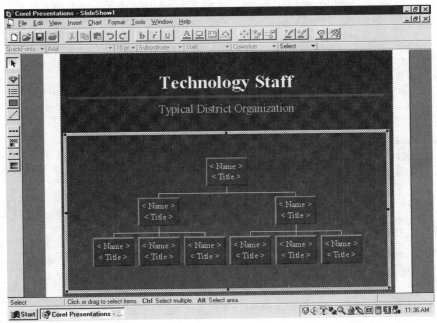

Organization chart

FIGURE 21-7

■ A *manager* is above another position.

■ A *co-worker* is a position of equal authority, neither under nor below the next box in the chain of command. The only limitation is that you cannot insert a co-worker position in the box at the top.

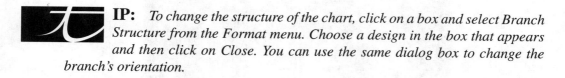 **IP:** *To change the structure of the chart, click on a box and select Branch Structure from the Format menu. Choose a design in the box that appears and then click on Close. You can use the same dialog box to change the branch's orientation.*

To add a position, use these steps:

1. Click the box that you want to add the position to.

2. Pull down the Insert menu and click on the position you want to add. The dialog box that appears will depend on the position.

3. Enter the number of positions you want to add. When you add a co-worker, you can also choose to insert the box to the left or right of the current box.

4. Click OK.

5. Double-click the Name and Title placeholders and type the names and titles.

 IP: *Use the lists in the power bar that appears when you are editing an organization chart to insert any number of subordinates, staff members, and co-workers.*

Inserting Organization Charts

You can add an organization chart to any slide, even one that does not have a placeholder for it.

1. Pull down the Insert menu and click on Organization Chart.

2. Drag to create a rectangle the size you want the chart, or just click to create one that fills the slide. A box appears showing formats of organization charts, as in Figure 21-8.

3. Click on the type of chart you want to insert.

4. Click on OK.

 You can use a Corel WordPerfect outline to add titles and positions to an organization chart. Refer to Chapter 13.

Creating Data Charts

A data chart is a chart or graph, exactly like the charts and graphs you can add to Corel WordPerfect and Corel Quattro Pro. In fact, you use almost the same techniques for working with charts—changing their type, customizing chart elements, adding legends, and so on.

 Use the Clipboard to insert Corel Presentations charts into Corel WordPerfect or Corel Quattro Pro.

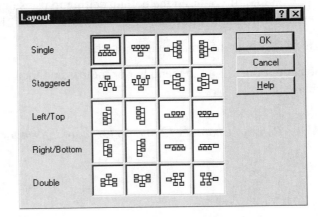

Selecting
the type of
chart to
insert

FIGURE 21-8

To create a data chart, either select the Data Chart template or choose Data Chart from the Insert menu to place a placeholder for it on another slide. To use the template, follow these steps:

1. Click on the Add Slides button in the toolbar.

2. Pull down the Template list and select Data Chart.

**OTE:** *A Combination template has four placeholders: title, subtitle, bullet chart on the left, and data chart on the right.*

3. Click on OK. Corel Presentations displays the new slide with the data chart slide template. It has three placeholders: title, subtitle, and data chart.

4. Add the title and subtitle, and then double-click on the Data Chart placeholder to see the Chart Gallery. The gallery includes a list box of chart types, and preview areas showing styles of the selected type. There are two check boxes: Use Sample Data and 3D. Select Use Sample Data when you want a default chart and datasheet to appear. This feature is useful when you are not sure about the chart design, because you can change the data in the sample chart to see the effect on the chart itself. Use the 3D box to determine if the chart is 2- or 3-D.

5. Click on the type of chart you want to create.

6. Click on the style of the chart.

7. Click on OK. If you used the default setting to use sample data, you'll see a chart with sample information, as shown in Figure 21-9.

8. Enter your own information into the chart.

9. Select options from the menu bar or toolbar and then click outside of the chart area.

IP: *Refer to Chapters 12 and 18 for more information on charts.*

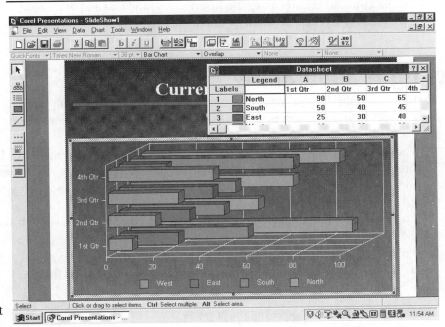

Default
sample chart

FIGURE 21-9

To add a chart to a slide that does not have a chart placeholder, choose Data Chart from the Insert menu, and then click on the slide or drag to create a rectangle that will be the chart area.

Inserting Blank Slides

As you've seen, you can insert bullet, data, and organization charts into a slide even when it does not have placeholders for the objects. So if you want, you can start with a blank slide and then add all of your own elements.

To add a blank slide, choose None or Background in the template list. The None option displays a slide without any background or placeholders—just a blank white slide. The Background option displays a slide using the master background but with no placeholders.

You can then add charts using the Insert menu, and text and other elements using the Tool palette, as you will learn in Chapter 22.

Playing a Slide Show

To display a slide show of your work, with each slide displayed full screen, click on the Play Slide Show button in the toolbar, or pull down the Slide menu and click on Play Slide Show, to see the dialog box in Figure 21-10.

The Starting Slide box will be set at the number of the current slide. Use the Starting Slide scroll bar to change the starting slide number, or type the number of the slide in the text box, and then click on Play. You'll learn all about playing slide shows in Chapter 23.

The first slide in your presentation will appear. To move from slide to slide, use these techniques:

■ Click the left mouse button, press the SPACEBAR, or press the RIGHT ARROW key to display the next slide.

■ Click the right mouse button or press the LEFT ARROW key to display the previous side.

■ Press ESC to stop the slide show.

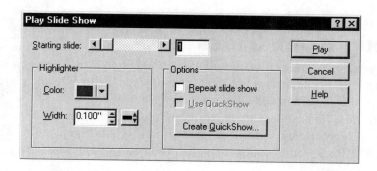

Play a slide show

FIGURE 21-10

Saving a Slide Show

Before doing too much work on your slides, you should save them to your disk. Corel Presentations uses the same file management dialog boxes as other Corel WordPerfect Suite applications. To save your slides, use these steps:

1. Click on the Save button in the toolbar, or pull down the File menu and select Save.

2. In the Name box, type a name for your presentation.

3. Click on OK. Corel Presentations saves your work with the default extension SHW.

You can also save an individual object, such as an organization or data chart. It will be saved as a WPG graphic image that you can then import into other Corel WordPerfect Suite applications. Here's how:

1. Click on the object to select it.

2. Pull down the File menu and select Save As.

3. If Selected Items is not already selected in the dialog box that appears, click on it.

4. Click on OK to display the Save As dialog box. The options in the box will be set to save the object as a WPG file.

5. Type a name for the file and then click on OK.

Printing a Presentation

You need to print copies of your slides if you created them to be included in a report or as handouts. To print your slides, click on the Print button in the toolbar or select Print from the File menu to see the dialog box with all of your printing options. To print the entire presentation, just click on the Print button.

The dialog box offers a number of options that should be familiar to you from working with other Corel WordPerfect Suite applications, such as the number of

21

copies and collating choices, and the Printer and Two-Sided Printing pages of the dialog box. There are some new options that are only in Corel Presentations.

The Adjust Image to Print Blank and White option, for example, will print color slides in black and white. Deselect this option if you have a color printer and you want color copies. When you print a color slide on a noncolor printer, the colors will be converted to shades of gray. If your printer can reproduce the shades so they appear clear and the text and graphics are readable, then you may want to deselect this option as well. Leave this option selected, however, if you want to speed the printing process, if your printer does not handle shades well, or if you want to copy the pages on a copy machine that does not adequately reproduce shades or colors.

The Print background option determines if the slide background prints. Again, print the background only when your printer is color-capable, or can adequately print shades of gray.

Click on Print Preview to see how the slides will appear on paper. Click on Close in the Print Preview toolbar to return to the Print dialog box.

You use the Print list in the dialog box to determine what gets printed. When set at the default Full Document, all of the slides will be printed. You can also choose from these options:

- Current view
- Slides
- Slide list

- Handouts
- Speaker notes
- Audience notes

You use these options, along with those in the other pages of the dialog box, to control the print process even more. The Print Options page lets you determine the number of slides to print on each page, choose to print text as graphics, and print the slide title and number along with the slide.

Printing Notes and Handouts

In addition to printing the slides themselves, you can print handouts, speaker notes, and audience notes.

Handouts have several slides on each page, as shown in the Print Preview in Figure 21-11. The audience can refer to them during your presentation, and take them home as a reference. To print handouts, follow these steps:

1. Click on the Print button in the toolbar, or select Print from the File menu.

2. Pull down the print list and click on Handouts.

3. In the Number of slides box, specify the number of slides you want printed on each page.

4. Click on Print.

OTE: *The Audience Notes option is similar to handouts, but it prints a series of lines below each slide so the audience can take notes as you talk.*

Speaker Notes

It would be nice if you could memorize an entire presentation, but it is all too easy to lose track. To help you, you can print speaker notes. These are thumbnail sketches of each slide along with your own script, reminders, or notes. Before printing speaker notes, however, you must create them.

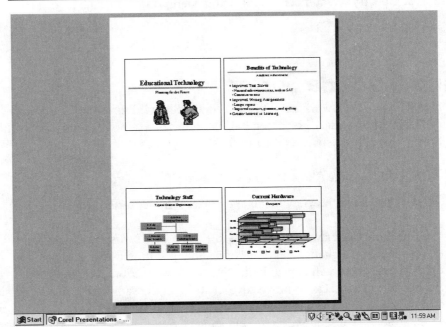

Handouts, four slides on each page

FIGURE 21-11

Use these steps to add speaker notes to your slides.

1. From any view, pull down the Slides menu and click on Speaker Notes to see the Speaker Notes dialog box.

2. Click on the arrow keys at the top of the dialog box to see the number and title of the slide you want to add a note to.

3. In the large text box, type the note that you want to appear with the slide.

4. Repeat steps 2 and 3 for all of the slides.

5. Close the dialog box.

When you are ready to print the notes, follow these steps:

1. Click on the Print button in the toolbar, or select Print from the File menu.

2. Pull down the Print list and click on Speaker Notes.

3. Specify the number of slides you want printed on each page.

4. Click on Print.

Using the Slide Sorter

So far, we've been working with slides in the Slide Editor, which lets you create and edit individual slides. For a general overview of your slides, change to the Slide Sorter view. To do so, use either of these techniques:

■ Click on the Slide Sorter button in the Tool palette.

■ Pull down the view menu and click on Slide Sorter.

The Slide Sorter window, shown in Figure 21-12, displays thumbnail sketches of your slides. To change the order of a slide, just drag it to a new position. As you drag, a vertical bar will appear indicating the new position. Release the mouse when the position is correct. To move several slides at the same time, select them all. To choose slides that are not consecutive, hold down the CTRL key and click on each slide. To select consecutive slides, click on the first in the series, and then hold down the SHIFT key and click on the last in the series.

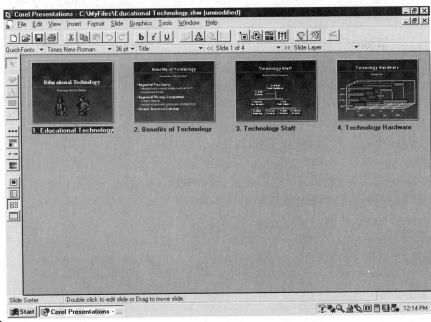

Slide Sorter

FIGURE 21-12

Using the Outliner

While the Slide Sorter is useful for viewing your slides graphically, you cannot read much of the information on the slides. When you want to look at the contents of the presentation, change to the Outliner. The Outliner displays the titles, subtitles, and other text from each slide, in outline format. This makes it easy to see the structure of your presentation without being distracted by graphics and backgrounds.

You can also use the Outliner to add slides to the presentation, even to create an entire presentation by typing an outline. The Outliner will be converted into a series of slides when you change views.

To change to the Outliner view, either click on the Outliner button in the Tool palette, or pull down the View menu and click on Outliner.

A typical Outliner window is shown in Figure 21-13. Each slide in the chart will be marked by the Slide icon. The name of the text placeholders will be shown on the left, with the text in the outline on the right.

To add a slide to the presentation in Outliner view, use these steps.

1. Place the insertion point at the end of the slide above where you want the new slide to appear.

2. Press CTRL+ENTER.

3. Pull down the Slide menu and click on Apply Template.

4. Select a template from the list that appears.

5. Click on OK.

6. Type the title for the slide and press ENTER.

7. Type an optional subtitle.

8. Press ENTER and add other text that you want on the slide.

 Use a Corel WordPerfect outline to create a slide presentation. Pull down the File menu and click on Insert, select the file that you want to use for the chart, and click on Insert.

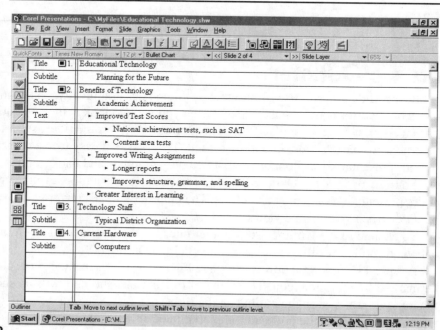

Typical
Outliner
window

FIGURE 21-13

Editing Slides

You have complete control over the appearance and format of your slides. In addition to the toolbar and power bar formatting options, you can edit and format slides by setting properties and by changing the master background.

Changing the Master Background

After you create your slide show, it is not too late to select a different master background. Just click on the Master Gallery button in the toolbar and select another master. Your selection will be applied to all of the slides in the presentation.

You can also add your own elements to the master background. For example, suppose you want your company logo to appear on every slide. Choose a master that you like and that has room for the logo. Then follow these steps.

1. Pull down the Layer list in the power bar or click on the Slides menu, and then click on Background Layer.

2. A slide will appear with only the background.

3. Insert your logo using the QuickArt option from the Insert menu, or add any other elements that you want in every slide.

4. Select Slide Layer from the Layer list in the power bar, or from the Backgrounds menu.

Customizing Template Layouts

You know that each template has two or more placeholders in specific positions on the slide. The text in the title and subtitle placeholders uses a default format, font, and font size. While you can change the position of a placeholder and format the text within it, you can also change the default values for all slides using the template. This presents a consistent look throughout your presentation, so you don't have to worry about making the same changes to each slide individually.

1. Display a slide using the template that you want to change. For example, if you want to change the position of the subtitle in a bullet slide, display any slide using the Bullet template.

2. Select Layout Layer from either the Layer list in the power bar, or from the Slides menu. A slide will appear showing the placeholders.

3. Change the size or position, or format the font in the placeholder.

4. Select Slide Layer from either the Layer list in the power bar or from the Layouts menu.

Your changes will automatically be applied to all existing and new slides that use the template.

Customizing Bullet Charts

Bullet charts contain several elements that you can modify—the appearance and spacing of the text and the bullets, and the box around the chart. While you can format selected text using the toolbar and power bar, it is best to be consistent. By setting Bullet Chart Properties, you ensure that the style of the levels is consistent throughout the entire presentation.

To set properties, click on any bullet chart and then on the Bullet Chart Properties button in the toolbar, or pull down the Format menu and click on Bullet Chart Properties, to see the dialog box in Figure 21-14.

Use the Fonts page to format the text at each level. The Format list on that page contains a number of styles that set the format of all of the levels. When you select a format from the list, for example, a style will be applied to all of the bullet levels. Select each of the options to see its effect on the sample bullet list in the Preview pane. If you find one you like, click on OK.

You can also customize each of the levels separately. Here's how:

1. Click on the level that you want to change.

2. Select a font, style, size, and appearance from the dialog box.

3. Click on the Font Properties button to see a dialog box for setting the fill pattern and outline of text.

4. Select options from that dialog box, and then click on OK.

5. Repeat the steps for each bullet level that you want to edit.

6. To apply the changes just to the current slide, click on Apply. To apply the styles to every bullet chart in the presentation, click on Apply to All.

Setting
bullet chart
text
properties

█ FIGURE 21-14

2 1

Changing Bullet Style and Justification

Use the Bullets tab in the dialog box to customize the type of bullet used for each
level. The Bullet Set list option contains several choices that apply styles to every
bullet level. To change the style of individual levels, use these steps:

1. Click on the level that you want to change.

2. Pull down the Justification list (it says Auto) and select a
   justification—Left, Center, Right, or Auto.

3. Pull down the Bullet list, and choose the character to use for the bullet. To
   choose a special character from the Corel WordPerfect Characters box,
   select More Options from the Bullet list. In the Characters dialog box,
   choose the character set and the character, and then click on the Insert and
   Close button. This box works just as it does in Corel WordPerfect.

4. Choose a size for the bullet. By default, the bullets are the same size as the
   text. You can choose a relative size from 50 to 150 percent of the text size.

5. Select a color for the bullet.

6. Repeat the steps for each level bullet you want to customize.

7. Click on Apply or Apply to All.

To remove a bullet from a level, click on the level and then choose None from the Bullet list.

 IP: *Use the Save Style and Load Style buttons to save your custom bullet formats. You are actually creating a style as you do in Corel WordPerfect.*

Adjusting Bullet Spacing

The options on the Bullet Spacing page of the dialog box controls the spacing between items. You can set the spacing between main and subordinate items, between consecutive subordinate items, and between all lines.

Setting Box Attributes

The Box Attributes page of the dialog box lets you add a box around the bullet chart, with a custom shape, color, pattern, or color fill. Click on the Box Attributes tab, and then deselect the Display Box check box. Choose Options from the dialog box, and then click on the Object Properties button to set the fill attributes, line width and style, and line joints and ends styles.

Using the Format Menu

The Format menu provides a number of other ways to customize your slides. Many of these options are similar to those found in Corel WordPerfect. For example, you can choose Font from the menu to select character formats, Line to adjust the positions of lines, Paragraph to add indentations, and Justification to align text.

If you select Page Setup from the menu, you'll see the Page Setup dialog box. Use the pages of the dialog box to select these options:

Page Size	Select the page size and orientation.
Page Color	Select a color and background other than that of the master. You can also choose to use a picture, texture, pattern, or gradient fill. If you choose a picture, you can select the way it is repeated on the slide.
Margins	Set the left, right, top, and bottom margins.
Save Options	Select the size of graphics and the amount of white space around them.

Creating a Presentation with PerfectExpert

So far, we've been concentrating on the format of slides, letting you decide on the contents. While you want your slides to look good, the messages within them are really the most important part of your presentation.

If you need help organizing your thoughts, start a presentation using PerfectExpert. PerfectExpert will create an outline for you, showing you the type of information that should be included in 11 common types of presentations. Here's how to use it:

1. Start Corel Presentations, click on the New button in the toolbar, or close all of your open presentations.

2. In the dialog box that appears, click on Create a Slide Show using PerfectExpert and then on OK. The New Slide Show dialog box appears.

3. Click on Gallery to display the Gallery box.

4. Select a background and click on Apply.

5. Click on OK to see the dialog box that briefly describes PerfectExpert.

6. Click on Next to see the dialog box shown in Figure 21-15. The box includes four tabs for general categories, or purposes of presentations. The Special tab, by the way, includes options to create a presentation for giving an award or for an introduction.

21

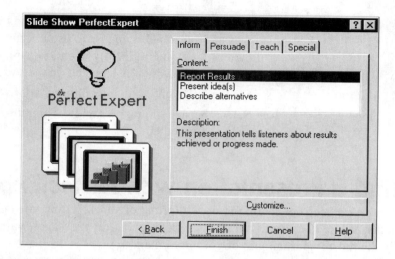

Select a
presentation
type

FIGURE 21-15

7. Click on the tab representing the type of presentation you want to create. Each box displays several general topics.

8. Click on the topic that you want to use for a presentation, and then click on Finish. The Outliner view appears listing several slides, along with the Slide Show PerfectExpert box, as in Figure 21-16.

9. Replace the text in the outline with your own. Use the Slide Show PerfectExpert box to change views, and for hints on how to work on the current view.

10. Edit and format the presentation as desired, adding your own slides where needed.

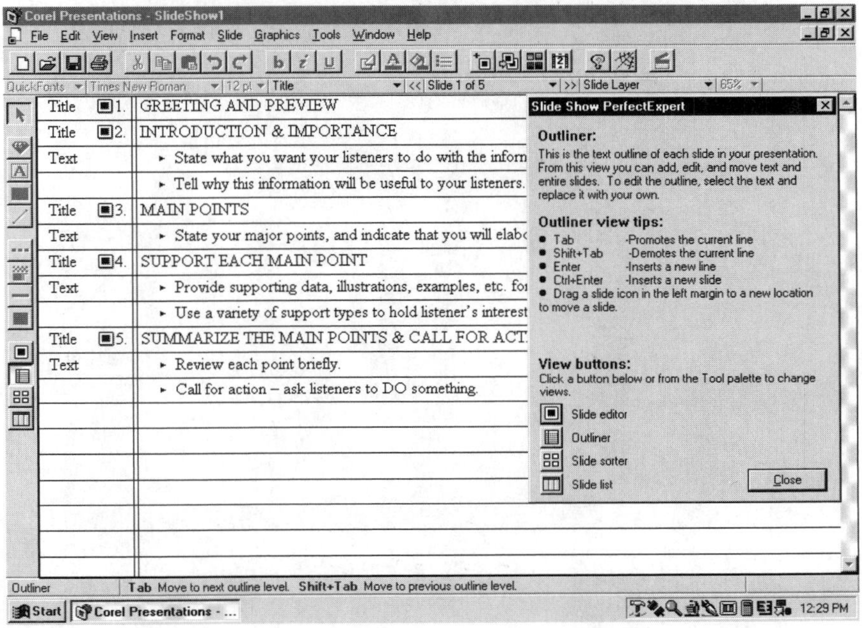

Presentation
created by
PerfectExpert

FIGURE 21-16

Working with Corel Presentations Graphics

22

In Chapter 21, you learned how to insert QuickArt and other graphic images into a presentation. Part of the power of Corel Presentations, however, is that you can customize QuickArt and other graphics, and even create your own drawings. In this chapter, you will learn how to work with and customize two types of graphics: vector and bitmap.

Corel Clip Art

QuickArt graphics are just one type of clip art that Corel WordPerfect Suite provides. There are over ten thousand graphics supplied with the suite, and you can use any of them in your slides. To add any graphic, follow these steps:

1. Pull down the Insert menu and click on QuickArt.

2. Drag within the slide to create a box the size you want the graphic to be, or click anywhere to create a box with the default size. When you release the mouse or click, the QuickArt Browser dialog box, which is similar to a File Open dialog box, appears.

3. Go to the folder containing the graphic. For example, click on the Up One Level button to display the contents of the Graphics folder, shown in Figure 22-1. The files with the WPG extension are general-purpose clip art in Corel WordPerfect's own format.

IP: *You'll also find thousands of graphics on the Corel WordPerfect CD in the \Corel\Office7\Graphics\QuickArt, \Corel\Office7\Graphics\ClipArt, and \Photos folders.*

4. Double-click on the graphic to insert it into the slide.

The other folders in the Graphics folder contain various other categories of clip art, all but the Borders folder containing other subfolders within them. Look through

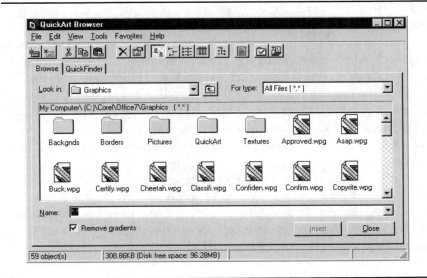

Corel
clip art

FIGURE 22-1

the folders to find a piece of art that you want to use in your slide, and then double-click on it to insert it. Here are the categories and what they contain:

- *Backgrounds* contains WPG graphics that you can use for the background of bullet charts or an entire slide. Most have a border line and one or two images around the border, with a large empty area inside.

- *Borders* contains WPG graphics that can be used for slide borders.

- *Pictures* contains bitmap graphics of various subjects, divided into these categories: business, commodities, finance, food products, government, and nature.

- *Textures* contains bitmap graphics of background designs in these categories: fabrics, paper, stone, and wood.

Working with QuickArt

QuickArt images are *vector* graphics. This means that they are made up of a series of individual lines and curves. Putting three lines together, for example, creates a triangle; four lines, a rectangle. You can make changes to the entire graphic, such as altering its size or rotating it, and you can edit the individual lines and curves within it.

There are two ways to work with a graphic. You can click or right-click on the graphic to select it and to apply certain formats, such as changing its size and rotation. You can also double-click on it or select Edit group from the QuickMenu to access the individual segments that comprise the graphic. If you want to rotate the entire graphic, for example, you right-click on it and choose Rotate from the QuickMenu. If you want to rotate one of the objects within the graphic, you have to double-click on the graphic to enter the Edit mode, and then right-click on the segment you want to rotate.

QuickArt images have a transparent background. This means that you'll be able to see the background of the slide under portions of the graphic that do have any fill or color themselves. To select a graphic, click on a filled portion of it or a line, not on the background of the slide that shows through. If you want to display the QuickMenu, right-click on a filled portion.

Setting View Options

Before learning how to work with graphics, however, consider four options on the View menu that can be very useful: Auto Select, Ruler, Crosshair, and Grid/Snap.

The *Auto Select* option in the View menu is selected by default. This means that after you create an object, it will appear selected with handles so you can immediately work with it. If you turn off this option, you have to select the object after you create it.

By selecting *Ruler* from the View menu, you will display a horizontal ruler along the top of the window and a vertical ruler down the left side. Use the rulers to position objects in precise locations. You can also use the rulers to position guidelines. A *guideline* is a horizontal line across the screen or a vertical line down the screen that you can place at a position along the ruler. Set and use the guidelines for aligning objects. To create a guideline, use these steps:

1. Select the Ruler option from the View menu to display the rules.

2. To create a horizontal guideline, click anywhere in the horizontal ruler, and then drag the mouse down into the window.

3. As you drag, a horizontal line appears across the screen at the mouse pointer.

4. Using the measurements on the vertical ruler as a guide, drag until the line is in the position you want it, and then release the mouse.

Create a vertical guideline the same way, but click and drag from the vertical ruler. If you select *Crosshair* from the View menu, horizontal and vertical lines will appear with the intersection following the movement of the mouse pointer. As you drag the mouse, the crosshairs move with it. The crosshairs are useful for judging the position of objects in relation to others on the screen, and in relation to guidelines.

A *grid* is a pattern of evenly spaced dots superimposed on the screen. By displaying the grid, you can use the pattern to align objects. The *Grid/Snap* option has four choices:

- *Grid* displays the grid pattern.

- *Snap-to-grid* forces all objects that you move or draw to align on a grid line.

- *Grid/Snap options* lets you change the spacing of the grid pattern.

- *Clear guidelines* removes all of the guidelines from the screen.

Changing the Graphic's Size and Position

22

You already know how to use the mouse to change the size and position of the image by dragging. You can also change its size and position using dialog boxes. The boxes let you change the size by entering a specific ratio, such as 50 percent, and aligning the box with a side or the exact center.

To change the size, use these steps:

1. Click on the graphic to select it and display the handles.

2. Point to a handle so the mouse pointer appears as a two-headed arrow and then right-click to see the Size dialog box.

3. In the Multiplier box, enter the amount to reduce or enlarge the box. For example, enter **1.2** to enlarge it 20 percent, or **0.8** to reduce it 20 percent.

4. Select the Around Center option to change the size of the box while leaving its center position in the same location. Without this checked, the upper-right corner of the graphic is the anchor position.

5. Select Copy Object(s) when you want to create a copy of the graphic in the new size, leaving the original as it is.

6. Click on OK.

To adjust the position of the graphic, use these steps:

1. Right-click on a part of the graphic to display the QuickMenu.

2. Point to Align and select from these options:

   - *Left* moves the graphic to the left of the slide in its current vertical position.

   - *Right* moves the graphic to the right of the slide in its current vertical position.

   - *Top* moves the graphic to the top of the slide in its current horizontal position.

   - *Bottom* moves the graphic to the bottom of the slide in its current horizontal position.

   - *Center Left/Right* centers the graphic between the left and right.

   - *Center Top/Bottom* centers the graphic between the top and bottom.

   - *Center Both* places the slide in the exact center of the slide.

Rotating a Graphic

Another way to customize a graphic is to rotate it. Sometimes you can rotate a graphic that doesn't seem to fit so that it no longer interferes with text. But most often, you rotate a graphic to add a special effect, or to have it appear as if it is pointing in another direction. With Corel Presentations, you can both rotate a graphic and skew it. *Skewing* changes just one axis of the image, while keeping the other stationary. Let's see how this works.

1. Right-click on Graphic to display the QuickMenu.

2. Click on Rotate. The graphic will be surrounded by eight special handles that control rotation:

3. Drag a handle in the corner to rotate the entire image.

4. Drag one of the center handles on the top, bottom, left, or right to skew the graphic. When you drag, only that side of the image moves with the mouse:

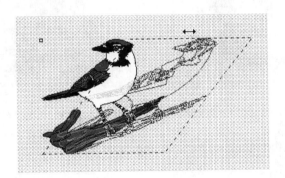

5. Click the mouse when you have finished.

Editing Graphic Objects

While a vector graphic is composed of individual lines, groups of lines are collected into objects, such as a rectangle or other shape. You can customize the objects themselves, as well as the entire drawing. For example, the graphic shown here contains a computer monitor that is made up of several different objects. By selecting just the object that is the face of the monitor, you can change its fill pattern without affecting the rest of the graphic.

22

You can edit an object in two ways: by using Edit mode, or by separating the picture into a series of separate objects. Edit mode also lets you change the individual lines that make up each object, so let's look at it first.

To enter Edit mode, either double-click on the image, or right-click on it and select Edit Group from the QuickMenu. You'll know you are in Edit mode when the graphic is surrounded by a thick line without handles. You can now select and edit the individual objects that make up the image. Click on the part of the graphic that you want to edit, to display handles around just it. You can then move, resize, or delete that part of the artwork. For example, here is the graphic with one of its objects moved to another position:

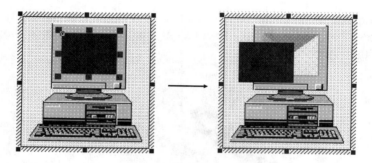

To change the object's appearance, for example, use these steps:

1. Click on the object so handles appear on it.

2. To change its color, click on the Fill Colors button in the toolbar, and then select a foreground and background color from the palette.

3. To change the color of the line around it, click on the Line Colors tool and choose a color from the palette.

4. To change its pattern, click on the Fill Attributes button and select an option.

5. To change the width and style of line around it, click on the Line Attributes button and select an option.

To make even more changes, use the Object Properties dialog box. Select the object that you want to edit, and then click on the Object Properties button on the toolbar, or right-click and choose Object Properties from the QuickMenu. In addition to the Fill Attributes and Line Width/Style pages, the dialog box contains options for the line joints and ends, as shown in Figure 22-2.

The other choices in the QuickMenu also affect just the selected objects. For example, choose Rotate from the QuickMenu to see rotation handles only appear around the selected object, or choose an Align option to change its position.

OTE: *The Graphics menu offers a number of choices for further customizing a graphic element. Refer to "Customizing Objects," later in this chapter, to learn more.*

Separating Graphic Segments

While you can edit the individual parts of the graphic in Edit mode, the entire graphic is still treated as one object outside of that mode. As long as you do not double-click on it and select a specific object segment, for example, you can rotate and drag the entire graphic as one unit.

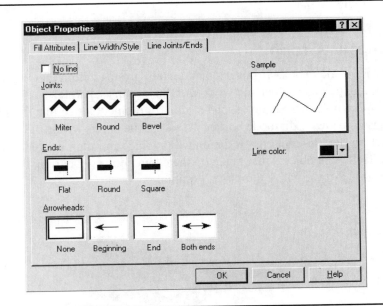

Object
Properties
dialog box

FIGURE 22-2

If you wish, however, you can separate the graphic into its objects so each one is a separate entity on the slide. Follow these steps:

1. Make sure you are not in Edit mode—click outside of the graphic so it is not selected.

2. Right-click on the graphic, and choose Separate from the QuickMenu.

3. Click away from the object to deselect it.

4. You can now select the individual objects to change size, position, color, or rotation. As far as Corel Presentations is concerned, each object is a separate graphic.

If you later want to work with the entire graphic again as a unit, you have to regroup it. Here's how.

1. Select all of the individual objects. Either drag the mouse to draw a selection box around them, or hold down the CTRL key and click on them.

2. Right-click on the selected objects and choose Group from the QuickMenu.

Groups in Graphic

There are some QuickArt images that contain groups within them. Once you enter Edit mode, you can select and work with the groups separately.

For example, here is one such QuickArt graphic. Notice that the picture of the cabin is in its own Edit mode border. To access the points within the cabin, you have to start by double-clicking on the entire graphic, and then double-clicking on the cabin itself. The objects that make up the cabin comprise a group that is within the larger group of the entire QuickArt graphic.

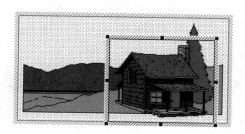

Working with Layers

Just as a slide is composed of several layers, so is a graphic. Two or more objects can overlap, with one in the foreground partially (or totally) obscuring the others in the background. You can also change the position of an object in relation to others, moving an object from the foreground to the background, even moving in several steps through multiple overlapping objects.

To change the position of one object in relation to another, use these steps.

1. Double-click on the graphic to enter Edit mode.

2. Right-click on the object.

3. Click on Back in the QuickMenu to move the object to the background, or click on Front to move it to the foreground.

IP: *You can use the Back and Front commands to layer separated graphic objects as well.*

Moving Segment Points

You already know that each object in a vector graphic consists of a series of lines. The intersection of two lines is called a *point*. If you drag the point, then you change the size and position of the lines on either side.

1. In Edit mode, right-click on the object and select Edit Points from the QuickMenu. The points that make up the object will appear as shown here.

2. Drag one of the points to a new position; when you point to a point, the mouse will appear as a crosshair. To create the effect you want, you may have to drag a series of points.

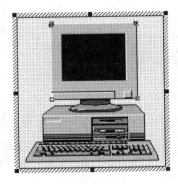

If you right-click on a point, a QuickMenu will appear with these options

■ *Delete* deletes the selected point.

■ *Add* inserts a new point after the selected one.

- *Open* removes the line between the points, removing its color.
- *To Curve* creates a Bézier curve at the selected point.

Creating Your Own Drawing

The Tool palette on the left of the Corel Presentations window offers a number of tools to add some of your own custom artwork to a slide. You can use the tools to draw objects directly on the slide, such as adding a text box, or to supplement a bullet chart, QuickArt graphic, data chart, or organization chart.

Each object that you draw is treated independently, and you can apply all of the same techniques to them as you learned previously—choosing colors and patterns, setting Object properties, rotating objects, and editing points. If you create a picture by drawing and positioning several objects, however, you may want to combine them so you can move and resize them as one unit. You can also add an object to a QuickArt or other graphic, and combine them. To combine graphic objects, select them using the CTRL key, right-click on them, and choose Group from the QuickMenu.

You can also create a new drawing outside of a slide presentation, and then save it in any of 16 popular graphic formats, such as WPG, PCX, JPEG, and GIF. This will enable you to use the graphic in another Windows program. To create a new drawing, select the Create a New Drawing option when starting Corel Presentations or after selecting New from the File menu. The Drawing window will appear as in Figure 22-3.

 IP: *Use the View options to help position graphic objects on the slide.*

Using the Tool Palette

The empty slide is like a blank canvas with the drawing tools along the left. The tools in the Tool palette work exactly the same as they do when you use them to draw directly on the slide.

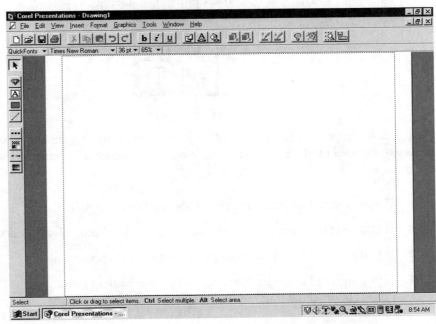

Drawing
window

FIGURE 22-3

22

You already know how the Attribute and View buttons in the palette work. In this section you'll learn about the Select, Chart or Graphic, Text Object, Closed Object, and Line Object tools.

The Select Tool

You use the Select tool to return to Select mode after drawing an object. *Select mode* means that clicking on an object selects it. This cancels the function of the previously used tool.

Inserting a Graphic

In addition to using the drawing tools to create your own drawing, you can insert a QuickArt image, organization chart, or data chart, and then modify it. Click on the Chart or Graphic Tools button to see these options:

Data Chart   Organization Chart

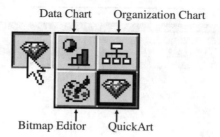

Bitmap Editor   QuickArt

Select the type of item you want to insert, and then drag in the window to designate the area to place it. When you release the mouse, the appropriate options will appear.

- If you selected a data chart, you'll see the Data Chart Gallery.

- If you selected an organization chart, the Layout dialog box appears.

- If you selected QuickArt, the QuickArt browser appears.

- If you selected to create a bitmap image, the Bitmap Editor appears (you'll learn about that later in this chapter).

Select the appropriate option or create the chart as you've already learned.

Text Object Tools

Use the Text Object Tools option to insert text into the drawing. Point the mouse on the tool and hold down the button to see these options:

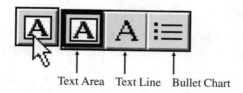

Text Area   Text Line   Bullet Chart

Use the Bullet Chart tool to create a bullet list—click on the tool, and then drag to where you want the bullet chart to appear. Use the Text Area tool to enter multiple lines of text, and use the Text Line tools to enter just a single line.

For example, to add lines of text to the drawing, use these steps:

1. Click on the Text Area tool, and then drag in the window to create a box the width you want the text. When you release the mouse, a box will appear with the insertion point inside.

2. Type the text. When the insertion point reaches the right side of the box, it will wrap to the next line.

3. Click outside of the box when you have finished.

 OTE: *If you use the Text Line tool, just click where you want the line of text to begin, and then type.*

You can edit the text and the box just as you can the graphic box:

- Drag the box to change its position.

- Drag a handle to change its size.

- Rotate the text in the box by choosing Rotate from the QuickMenu.

- Change the position using the Align option in the QuickMenu.

- Change the size ratio by right-clicking on the handle.

You can also create special effects by clicking on the Shadow Properties button on the toolbar to see the Shadow Properties dialog box. Deselect the No Shadow button to access the other options.

- Click on Transparency to lighten or darken the color.

- Select the color of the shadow from the Color list.

- Set the position of the shadow by setting the amount in the X offset and Y offset text boxes, or by dragging the scroll bars in the preview area.

Drawing Closed Objects

The Closed Objects tool lets you create rectangles, circles, arrows, and other objects. Click on the tool to select from the following options:

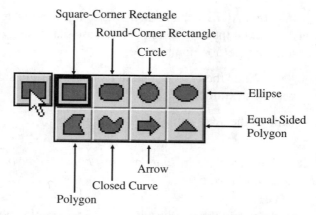

Square-Corner Rectangle

Round-Corner Rectangle

Circle

Ellipse

Equal-Sided Polygon

Arrow

Closed Curve

Polygon

Click on the tool you want, and then drag to draw the object. When you've finished, you can change its size, position, or color; add a shadow; or edit it like other graphic boxes.

If you select the Arrow tool from the Closed Object Tool menu, drag away from the object you want to point to. After you release the mouse, move it to the left or right to create a curved arrow, and then click when you've finished:

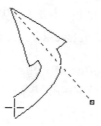

 IP: *If you create an object without a full pattern, you must select it by clicking on a border line. If you have trouble moving an unfilled object, drag it by the small white handle near the upper-left handle.*

Drawing Lines

The Line Object tool offers these choices:

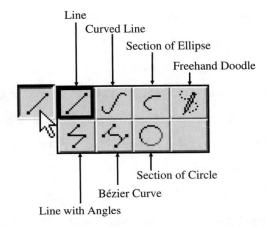

Select the object you want to create, and then drag to draw it. Simple.

Customizing Objects

The Graphics menu on the toolbar gives you a number of ways to customize your object even further. Experiment with the options by selecting one or more objects and see the effects that each option applies. For example, the QuickWrap option lets you create special text effects similar to TextArt, and Quick3D creates 3-D objects. Here's a review of the Graphics menu options.

- *Order* lets you move an object to the front, back, forward one, or backward one.

- *Flip* flips objects left/right or top/bottom.

- *Align* gives you the same choices as in the Align option in the QuickMenu.

- *Evenly Spaced* spreads out selected objects so they are spaced evenly between the left and right, or top and bottom of the slide.

- *Combine* integrates selected objects into one figure. If different fill patterns are used, they will all take on the pattern in the leftmost object.

- *Group* combines selected objects without changing their attributes.

- *Separate* creates separate objects from a group.

- *Contour Text* forms text around a graphic object.

- *Trace Bitmap* converts a bitmap drawing to a vector image.

- *Trace Text* converts each character in selected text into a vector drawing.

- *Convert to Bitmap* converts the selected vector image to a bitmap.

- *Blend* creates a blended object.

- *Quick3D* creates 3-D characters from a selected text box.

- *QuickWrap* forms selected text into a shape, similar to TextArt.

Most of these options are rather intuitive and easy to use. If an option in the menu is dimmed, then you have not selected any objects. You'll know how each of these options work when you first try them. However, contoured text and blending may need some explanation.

While the QuickWrap command forms the text into a preset format, the Contour Text option forms it around any shape you can create with drawing tools as shown here. Here is how to use it:

1. Drag the text so it is next to the object.

2. Select both the object and the text.

3. Choose Contour Text from the Graphics menu to see the Contour Text dialog box.

4. Pull down the Position list and choose where you want the text to appear around the graphic.

5. The Display Text Only option will make the object transparent. Leave this selected if you just used the object to create the shape for the text, and you really do not want it shown. Deselect the check box if you want both the object and the text to appear.

6. Click on OK.

The Blend command will create a series of smaller objects. Select two or more objects, and then choose Blend from the Graphics menu. In the dialog box that appears, select the number of objects to create, and then click on OK. You can then delete duplicates that you do not want. The following illustration shows two examples of blending. On the left is the arrow and text object immediately after they were blended. On the right, the duplicate copies of the text were deleted.

Saving Your Drawing

When you have finished with your creation, click on the Save button or choose Save from the File menu to display the Save dialog box. By default, the As Type box will be set at WPG 7, so you can save the drawing as a Corel WordPerfect graphic file. You can also select from other graphic formats. For example, if you want to share the drawing with a friend who has a Macintosh computer, select Macintosh PICT.

Enter a filename and then click on OK.

Creating Bitmaps

Corel Presentations also lets you create a bitmap graphic. Unlike a vector drawing that consists of lines, a bitmap graphic is a series of individual pixels, or picture elements. When you create a bitmap image, you can add, delete, and modify each of the individual pixels.

To start a bitmap image, use these steps:

1. Pull down the Insert menu and click on Bitmap, or click on the Chart or Graph Tools button and click on the Create a Bitmap icon.

2. Click in the window to create a full-page bitmap area, or drag to create a bitmap a selected size. Corel Presentations will display the Bitmap Editor window with its own toolbars (see Figure 22-4).

You can now create the bitmap drawing as you will learn next in the section "Using the Bitmap Editor." When you have finished, pull down the File menu and select Close Bitmap Editor, or click on the Close Bitmap button on the toolbar.

22

The bitmap will appear in the slide in a graphic box, just like vector images, so you can use the handles and other tools to change the size and position of the graphic, or to rotate or skew it. If you want to edit the graphic itself, however, double-click on it to display the Bitmap editor.

Using the Bitmap Editor

The Bitmap Editor has three sets of tools in addition to the menu bar that you can use to create bitmap graphics. The options in the toolbar and those in the power bar are shown in Figure 22-4. You will learn how to use these tools and the Tool palette throughout this chapter.

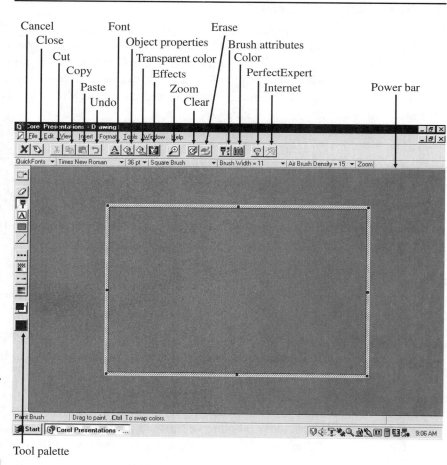

Bitmap Editor window with toolbar buttons, power bar, and Tool palette

FIGURE 22-4

IP: *If you do not like working with pixels, create the drawing as a vector graphic and then convert it to a bitmap drawing.*

 OTE: *Click on the Color tool to select and create custom color palettes.*

Before you start drawing the picture, however, you can change the size of the drawing area by dragging one of the handles. After you start drawing, however, dragging the handles to make the box smaller crops the area—cutting out the part of the drawing no longer in the box. As long as you do not leave the Bitmap editor, you can restore the deleted area by making the box larger. If you close and then return to the editor, however, the cropped area will be deleted.

Many of the tools in the Bitmap Editor Tool palette are the same that are available for vector graphics. The toolbar has the Text Object Tools button, Closed Object Tools, and Line Object Tools, along with the four Attribute buttons: Line, Fill, Line Color, and Fill Color.

The Select Area tool is similar to that found in the Vector editor, but you have to draw a selection box around the items you want to select.

The two boxes at the bottom of the toolbar show the current colors and pattern:

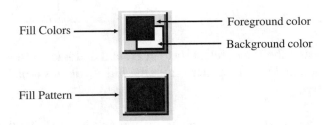

Fill Colors ⟶ Foreground color

Background color

Fill Pattern ⟶

Here's a review of the different tools.

Using the Eraser

You use the Eraser tool to delete (erase) pixels. When you select either of the two options from the Eraser tool, the mouse changes to a small square. Drag the mouse over the area that you want to erase. There are two tools available:

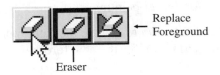

Replace Foreground

Eraser

Use the Eraser tool to completely remove pixels that you drag over. Use Replace Foreground tool to erase just the foreground color, replacing the pixels with the background color.

 IP: *Click on the Clear button on the toolbar to erase the entire contents of the image. Click on the Erase button to delete the selected object.*

Using the Paint Tools

The Paint tool button offers four ways to add pixels to the drawing:

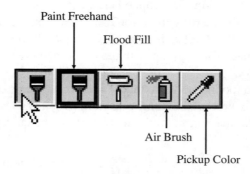

Before using the tools, select the foreground and background colors from the Fill Color tool, and select a pattern from the Fill Attributes tool. Then select a tool and be creative.

- Use the *Paint Freehand tool* to draw pixels by dragging the mouse.

- Use the *Flood Fill tool* to fill in an area. The tool looks like a small paint roller with a small triangle of paint. Place the tip of the triangle in the area that you want to fill in, and then click. The tool adds the color to all of the consecutive pixels in that area that have the same color.

- The *Air Brush tool* acts just like a can of spray paint. Hold down the mouse button and drag the can to spray the pixels onto the drawing. Drag the tool slowly for denser painting.

- Use the *Pickup Color tool* to change the foreground color. Point it to the color that you want to use for the new foreground and then click.

You can change the size and shape of the Freehand Brush and Spray tools using either the power bar or a dialog box. By default, the brush shape is square, 11 pixels wide. The airbrush has a density of 15 pixels. Change the size and shape, for example, if you don't like how your artwork appears. To do this with the power bar, follow these steps:

1. Pull down the Brush Shape list and choose a shape for the brush. The options are Circle, Square, Diamond, Horizontal Line, Vertical Line, Forward Slash, and Backward Slash.

2. Pull down the Brush Width list and select a width.

3. Pull down the Air Brush Density list and choose the density of the spray.

You can also change all three settings from a dialog box using these steps:

1. Click on the Brush Properties in the toolbar, or select Brush from the QuickMenu or Format menu, to see the Brush Attributes dialog box.

2. Pull down the Shape list and choose a new shape.

3. Set the brush width in pixels.

4. Set the density of the air brush.

5. Click on OK.

IP: *You can also display the dialog box by choosing Other from the Brush Width or Air Brush Density list in the power bar.*

Editing Pixels

Because a bitmap is pixel oriented, Corel Presentations gives you a way to work on each individual pixel itself. This means you can edit the graphic at its smallest level, each dot that makes up a line or other shape.

You work with pixels in a special Zoom mode with three panes, as shown in Figure 22-5. In the upper left of the window is a pane containing a picture of the entire bitmap drawing area. The small rectangle within the pane represents the area that is enlarged on the right so you can see and work with the individual pixels. The pane in the lower left shows that area full size. That pane also has a rectangle indicating the enlarged area.

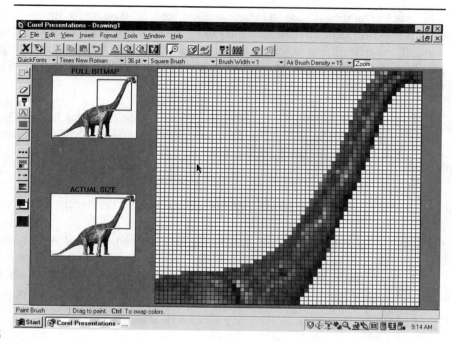

Zoom
display of
bitmap

FIGURE 22-5

You can display the Zoom panes using any of these techniques:

- Click on the Zoom button in the toolbar.
- Click on the Zoom button in the power bar.
- Select Zoom from the View menu.
- Right-click and select Zoom from the QuickMenu.

Here is how to work with pixels.

1. Enter Zoom mode using either of the techniques described.

2. To change the area of the drawing that is enlarged, drag one of the rectangles in the two smaller panes. Drag the rectangle to the area of the picture that you want to edit, and then release the mouse.

3. Select the pattern and foreground and background colors that you want to apply.

4. Click the mouse or drag it to change the color of the pixels.

5. When you have finished, select Zoom again.

Creating Special Effects with Bitmaps

You can apply a special effect to the entire bitmap drawing to create some unusual and appealing designs. The effects either apply a pattern, adjust the colors, or modify the appearance of pixels. When you are satisfied with the content of your drawing, save it first before applying an effect. After selecting an effect, you may not be able to restore your original design after choosing several effects. If you save the design first, you can always insert the original bitmap into a slide and double-click on it to edit it.

When you are ready to add a special effect, use these steps.

1. If you want to apply the effect to a specific area, choose the Select tool and then drag on the drawing. You can drag over an area that you want to apply the effect to, or drag over an area that you want to protect from the effect.

2. Click on the Effects button on the toolbar, or select Special Effects from the Tools menu or QuickMenu to see the dialog box shown in Figure 22-6.

3. Pull down the Effects list and choose the effect that you want.

4. If you selected an area prior to displaying the dialog box, select an option in the Apply To area—the Full Image, Inside Area, or Outside area.

5. Some effects will offer additional choices in the Options section. Set or select options as desired.

6. Click on the Apply button to see the effect of your choice in the After preview area. Compare it with the Before preview. If you change your mind, click on Reset, or click on Cancel.

7. When you are satisfied with your choice, click on OK.

22

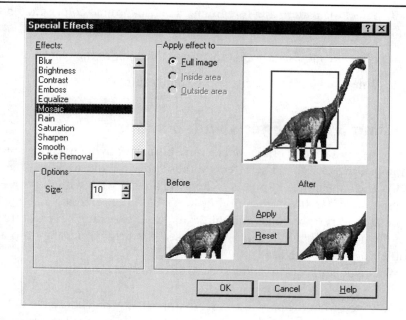

Special
Effects
dialog box

FIGURE 22-6

Here is a list of the effects:

- *Blur* blurs the borders between color and objects.

- *Brightness* darkens or lightens the drawing.

- *Contrast* changes the contrast between colors.

- *Emboss* adds a 3-D effect to pixels.

- *Equalize* evens the contrast between objects.

- *Mosaic* creates a pattern of squares of different colors, like mosaic tiles.

- *Rain* makes colors appear to be running down the page.

- *Saturation* makes colors more or less vivid.

- *Sharpen* sharpens the borders between colors and objects.

- *Smooth* smoothes the borders between colors and objects.

- *Spike Removal* removes horizontal and vertical lines in patterns, leaving pixels at the intersection.

- *Stereogram* converts the image to a random black-and-white stereogram that can display 3-D images when stared at.

- *Trace Contours* removes all colors by the contour lines.

- *Wind* makes the colors appear to run across the page.

 IP: *For information on a feature in the dialog box, click on the Help icon (the question mark at the right of the title bar) and then click on the feature.*

22

Creating Slide Shows

23

Oe of the most effective ways to display Corel Presentations slides is as a slide show. Using a large monitor or a video projection system, your slides become an instant multimedia presentation. You can add special effects, such as animation and transitions between slides, and sound and music. You can even link a slide to the Internet to jump to a Web page.

By publishing your entire presentation to the Internet, you make it accessible to the world. Web surfers can download your presentation to their own computer with a click of the mouse, and they can use a page frame to select slides from a table of contents.

In this chapter, you will learn how to create a slide show, adding effects and features that create professional presentations.

Slide Transitions

When you display a slide show, you click the mouse or press the SPACEBAR to move from slide to slide. The next slide immediately replaces the previous one, just as if you changed slides in a slide projector. By adding a transition, you create a special effect that takes place as one slide replaces the other.

You've probably seen a television show or movie in which one scene slowly fades out as the next fades in. A fade is just one of over 50 transitions that you can select for your slides. Other transitions make it appear as if a slide flies in from the side or appears slowly from a mosaic or other pattern. Because most transitions let you select what direction the slide appears from, there are over 150 different combinations. Just don't overdo it. Adding too many different transition effects can make the presentation difficult on the eye, and can distract from the content of your slides.

You can add a transition to a slide in any view. To add a transition effect, use these steps.

1. Click on the Slide Transition button in the toolbar, or pull down the Slide menu and click on Slide Transition to see the Slide Transition and Sound Properties dialog box, shown in Figure 23-1.

2. To use a transition for every slide in the show, click on the Apply to All Sides check box. Otherwise, use the left or right arrows to see the number and title of the slide you want to add a transition to. Click on the right arrow to move to the next slide; click on the left arrow to choose the previous slide.

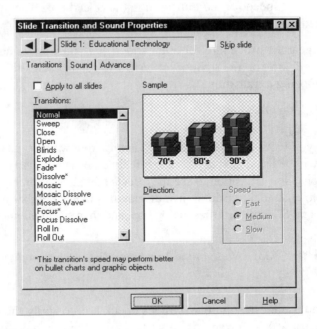

Slide
transition
options

FIGURE 23-1

IP: *Click on the Skip Slide check box when you do not want to show the current slide during playback.*

3. Pull down the Transition list and choose the transition. The program will demonstrate the transition in the Sample panel.

4. If direction options appear in the box, click on a direction of your choice. The choices are determined by the transition style. For example, if you select the Sweep transition, your choices are Top to Bottom, Bottom to Top, Left to Right, and Right to Left. Other transitions include these sets of choices:

■ Clockwise or Counter Clockwise

■ Right & Down, Left & Down, Left & Up, or Right & Up

■ Horizontal or Vertical

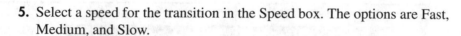
5. Select a speed for the transition in the Speed box. The options are Fast, Medium, and Slow.

6. Repeat the procedure for other slides that you want to add a transition to, clicking on the right or left arrow to select each slide, and then choosing a transition.

7. Click on OK.

When you view your slide show in Slide List view, the type of transition and its direction will be listed next to the slide title. In other views, pull down the Slide menu and click on Slide Transition to see the effects that have been applied to the slides. If you want to change a transition, just display the slide's number and title in the Slide Transition and Sound Properties dialog box, and then select another transition.

IP: *Choose None in the Transition list to remove the effect from a slide.*

You can use the Apply to All Slides check box to apply the transition to every slide in the show. If you want to apply a transition to just a few selected slides, select them first in the Slide Sorter view. Here's how:

1. Change to Slide Sorter view.

2. Hold down the CTRL key and click on the slides that you want to format.

3. Pull down the Slide menu and click on Slide Transition. The notation Multiple Slides Selected will appear in place of the right and left arrows.

4. Choose the transition, direction, and speed, and then click on OK.

OTE: *Clicking on Skip slide will skip all of the selected slides.*

Advancing Slides

The default setting leaves a slide on the screen until you advance it manually by clicking the mouse or pressing the SPACEBAR. Rather than manually advancing slides, however, you can set a time delay—how long each appears in seconds. By using a time delay, you can leave your slide show playing as you do other things.

You set advance options in the Advance page of the Slide Transition and Sound Properties dialog box. Use the left and right arrows at the top of the dialog box to display the number and title of the slide for which you want to set an advance. To set an advance, just follow these steps.

1. Pull down the Slide menu and click on Slide Transition.

2. Click on Advance.

3. To apply the advance to every slide in the show, click on the Apply to All Slides check box. Otherwise, click on the arrows to see the number and title of the slide.

4. Click on Time Delay and enter the number of seconds that you want the slide displayed. You can later click on Manually to remove the time delay.

5. Repeat the procedure for other slides.

6. Click on OK.

 IP: *To apply an advance to selected slides, select them in Slide Sorter view first.*

23

Animating Bullets

A slide transition determines how a slide appears on the screen. You can also create some very effective techniques by adding a special effect to determine how a bullet chart appears. There are two types of effects that you can apply to bullet charts: a transition and an animation. The transition options are the same as for the slide itself, including the direction and speed options. An animation is similar to a transition, but the choices include items for adding a bounce or curve to the movement.

After the title and subtitle appear, the bullet chart list is added to the display using the transition or animation effect. By using one transition for the slide itself, and another for the bullet chart list, you can add a lot of movement to the slide display.

You can also choose to cascade the individual items in the bullet chart. With a cascade, each item appears by itself, rather than the entire list at one time. This is quite effective when you want to explain or describe each item separately. In fact, you can even have the program dim the bulleted items already shown to highlight just the current point.

You apply all of these techniques using the Bullet Chart Animation Properties dialog box, shown in Figure 23-2. Here's how to use it:

1. Display the slide in the Slide Editor view.

2. Click on the bulleted list to select it.

3. Pull down the Slide menu and click on Object Animation to display the Bullet Chart Animation Properties dialog box.

4. Deselect the No Effect check box to make the other options accessible.

5. To apply the effect to every bulleted list in the show, click on the Apply to All Bullet Charts box.

6. Pull down the Effects list and choose either Transition or Animation. A list of available choices will appear in the large list box.

7. Select the transition or animation you want to apply.

8. Select a direction and a speed.

9. To cascade the items, click on the Display One at a Time check box.

10. To dim each previously displayed bullet item, click on the Highlight check box.

11. Click on Reverse Order to show the items from the bottom of the list to the top.

12. Click on OK.

When you are using manual advance, click the mouse when you are ready for the bulleted list to appear. If you are using a time delay, however, Corel Presentations will begin the transition automatically before the next slide is displayed.

Animating Objects

You can also add a transition or animation to one or more graphic objects in the slide, such as a QuickArt graphic or drawing, so you can have a graphic bounce onto the

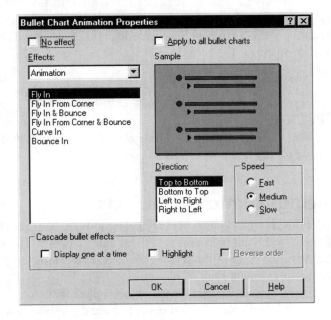

Animating
bullets

FIGURE 23-2

screen or fade into view. You can select a transition or animation for every object, so when combined with the slide transition and cascading bullets, the entire presentation can appear animated.

Follow these steps to animate a graphic object:

1. Display the slide in Slide Editor view.

2. Click on the object that you want to animate.

3. Select Object Animation from the Slides menu to see the Object Animation dialog box.

4. Deselect the No Effect check box.

5. Choose either Transition or Animation from the Effects list.

6. Select the transition or animation that you want to apply.

7. Choose a direction and a speed.

8. If you already have an effect assigned to an object on the screen, you can choose the sequence that the current slide appears in. Pull down the Object Display Sequence list and click on the number for the current object.

9. Click on OK.

 **IP:**   *You cannot animate a title or subtitle in a slide placeholder. To create the same effect, however, replace the placeholder with a graphic text box and apply a transition or animation to it.*

Advancing Animated Objects

Using the default settings, you have to click the mouse to begin each object transition or animation. If you want the items to appear automatically, choose options for the slide in the Advance page of the Slide Transition and Sound Properties dialog box, which you saw previously in this chapter.

You can, for example, have all of the objects appear automatically in sequence, or only after you click to display the first one. Here are the options you can select from:

- *Immediately after Slide Transition* starts to display the first object as soon as the slide appears—you do not have to click the mouse.

- *In an Automated Sequence after First Object Is Displayed* shows the second and subsequent objects after the first appears—regardless of the setting for the first slide.

- *In an Interrupted Sequence after First Object Is Displayed* requires you to click the mouse to display the second and subsequent objects.

- *Before Bullet Chart* displays the objects before any bullet chart on the slide.

- *After Bullet Chart* displays the objects after the bullet chart.

Enhancing Slides with Sounds

Recorded music, sound effects, and narration make a slide show more entertaining and effective, adding another dimension to a purely visual presentation. You can insert a sound clip, a track from an audio CD, and your own narration into a slide.

There are two ways to insert sounds into a slide. You can add the sound as an object that plays automatically when the slide appears, or as an ActionLink that you have to click on or press a keystroke to play. You can insert three types of sound objects on a slide: Wave, MIDI, and tracks from an audio CD. You can add as many sounds as you want associated with ActionLinks, and, if your system supports it, up to three sound objects that play simultaneously.

 OTE: *Corel WordPerfect Suite comes with a wide selection of sound files that you can insert. They are in the Wave and MIDI formats in the Sounds subdirectory. Most of the filenames are self-explanatory.*

To insert an existing sound clip or CD track, follow these steps:

1. Pull down the Slide menu and click on Sound to see the dialog box in Figure 23-3. You can also click on the Sound tab any time the Slide Transition and Sound Properties dialog box is displayed.

2. Click on the arrows to display the number and title of the slide that you want to add a sound to.

3. In the Sound files section, click on the check box for the type of object you want to insert: Wave, MIDI, or CD.

4. If you select Wave or MIDI, enter the path and name of the sound file in the corresponding text box. You can also click on the Browse button (the folder icon on the right of the text box) and choose the sound file from the Open file management dialog box that appears.

5. If you selected CD, insert the CD into your player, and then click on the CD icon to see the Slide CD-Audio dialog box. Choose the track number or the starting and ending time, and then click on OK.

6. Repeat the steps, if desired, to add one or more of the other types of sound files to the slide.

7. For each type of sound, drag the sliders in the Sound Controls section to set their volume levels.

8. Click on Play to hear how the file sounds.

9. Repeat the procedure to add sounds to other slides.

10. Click on OK.

23

Slide
Transition
and Sound
Properties
dialog box

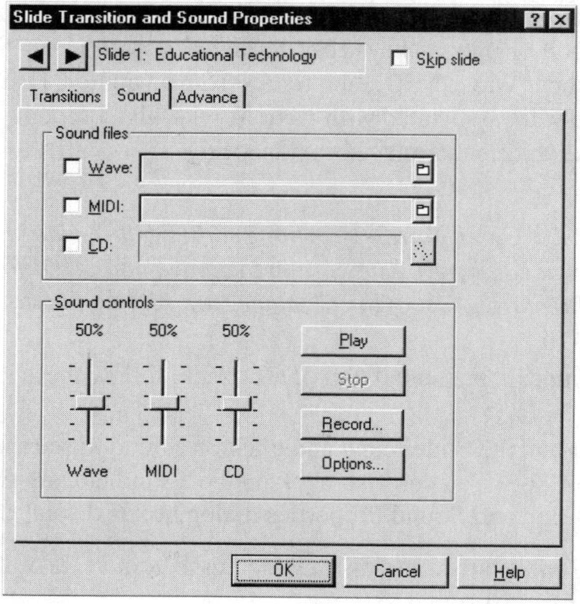

FIGURE 23-3

The sounds will play when the slide appears.

You can record your own narration or sounds, and add them to the slide. Click on Record from the Sound dialog box to display the Sound Recorder application. Record and then save the file, and then add it to the slide as just described.

Use the Options button in the Sound box to select to loop each type of sound so it plays continuously as long as the slide is displayed. You can also select to embed the sound into the slide rather than retrieve it from the disk each time it is played. Leave the option set to the disk when you want to access the same sound from more than one slide.

Creating ActionLinks

An *ActionLink* is an object on the slide that you click on to perform an action. Use an ActionLink to play a sound file, launch your Web browser and jump to a Web site, open another application, or move to another slide in the show.

For example, suppose you have one or more slides in the show that you might not want to display, depending on the audience. You can add an ActionLink to the slide before these. When you choose not to display the slides, just click on the link to skip over them.

You can add an ActionLink to any graphic object in the slide layer. When you point to a link, the mouse appears as a hand—just click to perform the action. There are two general categories of functions a link can perform, a Go To event or an Action. A *Go To event* lets you display a slide. It can be linked to a specific slide number or to any of these options:

- Next Slide
- Previous Slide
- First Slide
- Last Slide

For example, you can click on an ActionLink to display a specific slide or to return to the start of the presentation.

The Action options are

- Play Sound
- Stop Sound
- Quit Show
- Launch Program
- Internet Browser

 You can use an ActionLink to launch another Corel WordPerfect Suite application.

23

To add an ActionLink, follow these steps:

1. Display the slide in Slide Editor view.

2. Click on the object that you want to use for the link.

3. Click on the ActionLink button in the toolbar, or pull down the Slide menu and click on ActionLink to see the dialog box in Figure 23-4.

4. Deselect the None check box.

5. Select either the Go To or Action option button, and then choose the specific event or action.

6. If you choose to play a sound, click on the Sound check box to display the Sound dialog box, and then select any combination of Wave, Midi, or CD

tracks just as you previously learned. If you choose to launch a program, select the program file. For the Internet Browser action, enter the URL of the Web site.

7. In the ActionLink name text box, type a name for the link.

8. If you do not want the object to appear onscreen during the presentation, select the Invisible While Playing Slides check box. Use this when you want to perform an action but not take up screen space with the link. To find the link when showing the slides, move the mouse until the pointer changes to a hand.

9. If you want to activate the link by pressing a keystroke, click on Keystroke, and then pull down the list and select the keystroke.

10. Click on OK.

Editing and Viewing Links

After you create ActionLinks, you can edit or delete them, or just display a list of the links in your presentation. Pull down the Slide menu and click on ActionLink List to see the Action Link List dialog box. Use the arrow keys to display the slide that has the link you are interested in. To change a link, or to delete it, click on the link name and then on Edit to display the ActionLink dialog box. To delete a link, click on the None check box. To change the link, just choose other options from the box, and then click on OK.

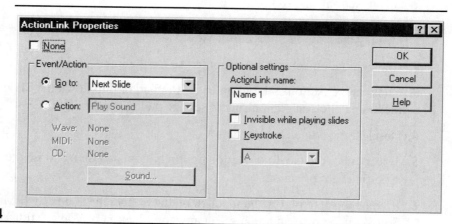

Creating an
ActionLink

FIGURE 23-4

Creating 3-D Buttons

One very effective way to use an ActionLink is to associate it with a 3-D button, as shown here.

By adding several buttons to a slide, you can give yourself, or the viewer, a menu of choices. In fact, you can create a table of contents slide at the start of the presentation that lets the viewer start the slide show at a specific section.

You create a 3-D button by using a Corel Presentations macro. Here's how:

1. Select Macros from the Tools menu and click on Play.

2. Click on Textbttn.wcm in the list of macros that appears.

3. Click on Play to display a dialog box that prompts you to enter the text for the face of the button.

4. Type the text that you want to appear in the button, and then click on OK to display the 3-D button.

5. The button will appear selected, with handles. Use the handles to change the button's size, or drag the button to another location on the slide.

6. To edit the text on the button, double-click on it to place the insertion point in the text.

7. Next, assign an ActionLink to the button. Right-click on the button and choose ActionLink from the QuickMenu, and then assign the function to the link.

23

Using ActionKeys

While an ActionLink is associated with an object, an ActionKey is associated with the slide or even the entire slide show. You can assign an ActionKey, for example, to play a sound or move to another slide at any time during the presentation. As with ActionLinks, you can assign an ActionKey to a Go To or an Action event. Here's how:

1. Open the slide show.

2. Pull down the Slide menu and click on ActionKeys to see the ActionKey Management dialog box.

3. To associate the keystroke with the entire presentation, so you can use it on any slide, deselect the Active on Current Slide Only check box. Otherwise, click on the arrows to see the number and title of the slide you want to associate with the link.

4. Click on New to see the dialog box in Figure 23-5.

5. Pull down the Keystroke list and select the keystrokes that you want to press.

6. Select either Go To or Action, and then choose the function that you want the link to perform.

7. Click on OK.

 OTE: *To remove an ActionKey, choose the keystroke in the ActionKey Management dialog box, and then click on the Delete button in the dialog box. Use the Edit button to change the ActionKey.*

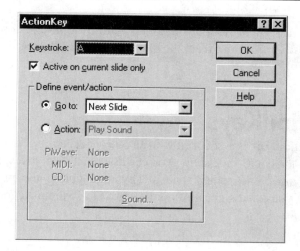

Creating an
ActionKey

FIGURE 23-5

Playing a Slide Show

You can run your slide show in two ways—from within Corel Presentations or directly from the Windows desktop.

- Run the slide show from Corel Presentations when you are still working on it, and may want to make changes as you go along.

- Run the show from Windows on machines that do not have Corel Presentations installed, or when you want a stand-alone application.

Keep in mind that the quality of your presentation will depend to some extent on your hardware. Watching a slide show on a small laptop monitor, or a low-resolution desktop monitor, is not the best way to view your work. For greater impact, hook up your computer to a large-screen television or, better yet, to a projection device for even a larger screen.

In addition to the transition, animation, and sound effects that you've added to the slides, you can use the mouse as a pointing and highlighting tool. By dragging the mouse, you can draw directly on the screen, emphasizing major points.

Playing a Show from Corel Presentations

To play the show from within Corel Presentations, you must start the program and then open the slide show. There will be some delay between slides as Corel Presentations displays them, but you can select to create a QuickShow file. This is a separate disk file containing the slides. It runs a little faster than otherwise, but it can take up large amounts of disk space. If you edit the slides, you also have to generate a new QuickShow file.

1. Start Corel Presentations and open the slide show that you want to play.

2. Click on the Play Slide Show button in the toolbar, or pull down the Slide menu and click on Play Slide Show to see the dialog box in Figure 23-6.

3. The presentation will be set to start with whatever slide is selected in the current view. To start with some other slide, enter the slide number in the Starting Slide text box.

23

4. Choose a color and width of the highlighter. Choose a color that can be seen over the slide background, and a width that will support the type of highlighting you want to do. Use a thinner width, for example, if you want to write on the screen without taking up a great deal of space. Use a thicker width to highlight an area with a line or circle.

5. To save a QuickShow version of the presentation, click on the Create QuickShow button.

6. To run the show continuously, click on the Repeat Slide Show check box.

7. To use the QuickShow file, click on Use QuickShow.

8. Click on Play.

9. If you are using manual advance, click on the left mouse button or press the SPACEBAR to move from slide to slide, to display animated bullets and objects, or to click on ActionLinks.

10. Drag the mouse to draw in the screen with the highlighter. Your highlighting will disappear when you change slides.

11. Press ESC if you want to end the presentation before the last slide.

 OTE: *If you edit the slides, you have to re-create the QuickShow file.*

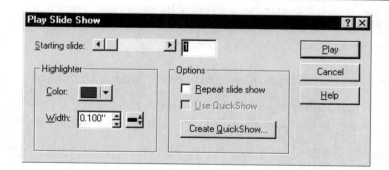

Playing a
slide show

FIGURE 23-6

Running the Show from Windows

Once you perfect your slide show, why go through the trouble of starting Corel Presentations just to show it? By creating a "runtime" version of the show, you can display it on a computer that doesn't have the Corel Presentations program. This is ideal if you are on the road.

 OTE: *The Professional version of Corel WordPerfect Suite includes the Runtime Expert that lets you copy a large slide show to multiple disks.*

The runtime version will consist of a special version of your presentation, and other files that will be required to run it. Those files depend on the configuration option you select. For example, you can choose to create a runtime that only works with Windows 95, or that works on Windows 3.1 as well. You can also choose to create a runtime that can run with any Windows display, or with one having the same resolution and color options as on your machine.

To create a runtime version of your presentation, follow these steps.

1. Open the presentation that you want to play.

2. Pull down the Slide menu and click on Make Runtime to see the Make Runtime dialog box.

3. Enter the name for the slide show file in the Name text box.

4. In the Copy Runtime Files To box, enter the path where you want the runtime files.

5. Select configuration options.

6. Click on OK.

Make sure you have all of the files you need to run the presentation. If you selected the Windows 95 only configuration, you'll need these files:

- POOLE70.DLL
- SHOW70.EXE
- The runtime version of the slide show with the PQF extension

23

When you choose the Windows 95 and Windows 3.1 runtime, you need these files:

- BOLE1.DLL
- PRSHOW30.DLL
- SHOW31.EXE
- Files with the slide show name and the PQW and SHW extensions

Publishing Your Show on the Web

Corel WordPerfect's Internet Publisher lets you create one or more linked Web pages. It's a great time-saver over learning and writing HTML documents, but it pales when compared to the Web capabilities of Corel Presentations.

When you publish a Corel Presentations show to the Web, each slide can become a separate Web page. Web surfers can view your slide show even if they do not have Corel Presentations on their computer, regardless of their computer's platform. In addition, you can

- Create a separate table of contents slide with hyperlinks.
- Create a page frame table of contents with hyperlinks, using either text or thumbnails of each slide.
- Add a Go To Slide Bar so the viewer can change slides.
- Insert a Download button for users to download the entire slide show.
- Include page numbers.
- Display your speaker's notes.

OTE: *Transition and animation effects will not appear when the slides are shown on the Web, but ActionLinks are active.*

There are four Web page organizations that you can create, shown in Table 23-1. The other options available are determined by the organization that you choose. However, all offer these two options: Include Slide Show File for Downloading, and Update HTML File(s) Only. The first option lets the viewer download your entire presentation to his or her computer, launch Corel Presentations, and view the show,

Page Arrangement	Description
Frame-Enhanced Pages	Creates a Web page with two frames. The frame on the left contains a table of contents listing links to your slide and a link to Corel Corporation. The frame on the right contains your slides—each slide on another page. There will be arrows under the slide to move to the next and previous pages.
Multiple Pages	Creates one Web page for each slide. You can create a separate slide with a table of contents using the slide titles as links.
Single Page	Creates one long Web page containing all of the slides. You can include page numbers, but not a table of contents.
Web Page Organization	Single Gallery Style Page	Creates one Web page containing thumbnail sketches of the slides.

TABLE 23-1

complete with transitions, animation, and sounds. The Update option lets you change existing Web pages if you've modified the organization of your slide show.

Here are some of the other options available:

- *Page Numbers* displays "Slide X of Y" at the top of each slide.

- *Page Titles* inserts the title above each slide.

- *Speaker Notes* displays speaker notes under each slide.

- *Go To Slide Bar* inserts a bar under each slide for changing slides.

- *Table of Contents* creates a separate slide with links to each slide.

- *Generate Table of Contents with Text* creates a table of contents using the slide title.

- *Generate Table of Contents with Pictures* creates a table of contents using a thumbnail sketch of each slide.

To publish your presentation to the Web, just follow these steps.

23

1. Open the presentation that you want to publish.

2. Pull down the File menu and click on Publish to see the options Envoy and Internet.

3. Click on Internet to see the dialog box in Figure 23-7. The dialog box includes a list of page arrangements. (The options are shown in Table 23-1.)

4. Click on the arrangement that you want. The dialog box that appears will depend on the page arrangement that you selected. The boxes for all of the arrangements will have at least the Title Name and Save File(s) to Text Boxes, and the two check boxes under them.

5. In the Title name text box, type a title for the presentation that you want to appear on the viewer's Web browser title bar area.

6. In the Save file(s) to box, enter the drive and path where you want to save the Web page files.

7. If the dialog box has an Advance button, you can create a self-running slide show. Click on Advance. In the box that appears, select the Self-Running Slide Show option, enter the number of seconds for each slide, and then click on OK.

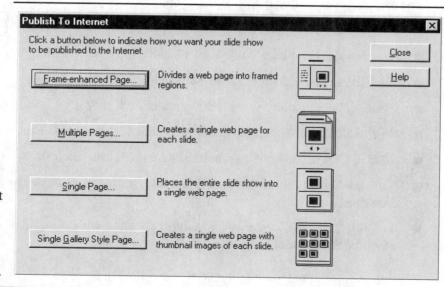

Options for page arrangement when publishing to the Internet

FIGURE 23-7

8. Use the Color Options button to change the color of links and background, just as you learned in Chapter 7.

9. Select other options from the dialog box, and then click on Finish. You'll see an animation appear as your slides are converted into .GIF-formatted graphics, and the Slide List view in the background highlighting each slide as it is converted.

10. A dialog box appears asking if you want to launch your Web browser to view the presentations. Click on Launch Web Browser with Slide Show to see the show, or click on OK to return to Corel Presentations.

Figure 23-8 shows Corel Presentations slide show on a frame-based Web page. If you select the Include Slide Show File for Downloading option, there will be a link for downloading on the slide. When clicked, the slide show is downloaded to the viewer's computer, the viewer's copy of Corel Presentations is launched, and the slide show is started.

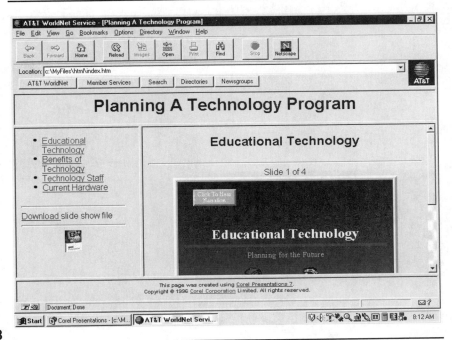

Published Web page

FIGURE 23-8

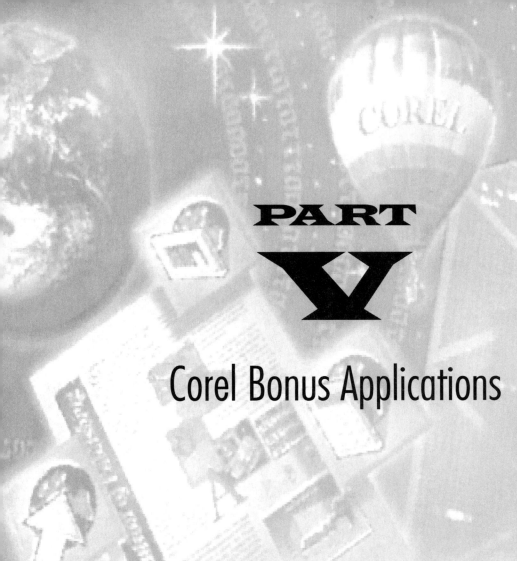

PART

V

Corel Bonus Applications

Publishing with Envoy

24

Envoy is a program that lets you share your Corel WordPerfect Suite documents with other users, even if they do not have the Suite. This means that they can read your document, worksheet, and presentation fully formatted, just as if they had the application that you used to create it. They can even print pages, add annotations and bookmarks, and use links to move to other parts of the document, or to sites on the World Wide Web.

This is all accomplished by using Envoy to create a runtime version of your document, much like Corel Presentations can create a runtime of a slide show.

Running Envoy

When you install Corel WordPerfect Suite on your computer, Envoy is installed as well and integrated directly into the other applications. So you can start Envoy from the Windows 95 desktop as you can start any application, or from directly within Corel WordPerfect, Corel Quattro Pro, or Corel Presentations. Starting Envoy from one of these programs automatically inserts the current document—whether a letter, worksheet, or slide show—into the Envoy window. It is easy to use because you'll find it as an option under the File menu.

When you launch Envoy from an application, your program will actually generate an electronically "printed" copy of the document. The copy has been converted into a format that Envoy understands so it can be displayed in the Envoy window.

Here's how to use Envoy directly from a Corel application.

1. Prepare your document, worksheet, or slide show just as you want to print or display it.

2. Pull down the application's File menu.

3. In Corel WordPerfect and Corel Quattro Pro, click on Publish to Envoy.
   In Corel Presentations, point to the Publish To option in the File menu and click on Envoy.

Since the application must create a special printed version of the document for Envoy, it will behave similarly to when you are actually printing a document. From Corel WordPerfect, for example, you'll see a box reporting that the program is preparing the document for printing. From within Corel Quattro Pro, the Print dialog box appears—click on the Print button in the dialog box to continue. From within Corel Presentations, you'll also see a dialog box reporting that the slide show is being printed.

Don't worry. In all of these cases, the program is preparing the document to be displayed in Envoy, and in a moment or so, the Envoy application will open with your document displayed as in Figure 24-1.

Use the menu bar and toolbar to customize the way the document appears onscreen and to add bookmarks, annotations, and hyperlinks. The buttons on the toolbar are shown in Table 24-1.

The status bar shows a hint or tip about the function you are performing on the left, followed by the page number and total pages, and the current magnification.

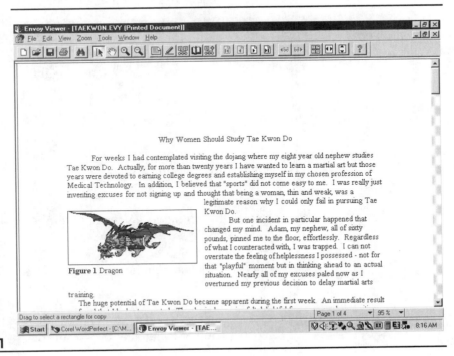

Document in Envoy

FIGURE 24-1

Button	Name	Function
	New	Opens a blank Envoy window
	Open	Retrieves an existing Envoy file
	Save	Stores the current document onto the disk
	Print	Prints the current document on paper
	Find	Searches the document for text, a QuickNote, highlight, OLE-embedded object, hypertext link, or bookmark.
	Select	Selects text, notes, or other objects
	Scroll	Moves the document by dragging
	Zoom In	Enlarges the display
	Zoom Out	Reduces the display
	QuickNote	Inserts a QuickNote
	Highlight	Lets you highlight text or graphics
	Hypertext	Creates a hypertext link to move to another location in the document

Envoy
Toolbar

TABLE 24-1

Button	Name	Function
	Bookmark	Inserts a bookmark
	Web Links	Creates a link to Web site or to another document
	First Page	Displays the first document page
	Previous Page	Displays the previous page
	Next Page	Displays the next page
	Last Page	Displays the last page in the document
	Previous View	Returns to the previous view, such as the magnification or page
	Next View	Returns to the next view
	Thumbnails	Displays or hides the thumbnail views
	Fit Width	Adjusts the magnification so the page fills the screen width
	Fit Height	Adjusts the magnification so you can see the full height of the page
	Help	Displays the Envoy Help system

Envoy
Toolbar
(*continued*)

24

■ **TABLE 24-1**

Click on the page number to display a dialog box to move to a specific page. Click on the magnification indicator to select another magnification. If you set bookmarks, there will be a bookmark button at the right of the status bar. Click on the button to select a bookmark to go to.

Opening and Importing Envoy Documents

While it is easy to start Envoy from within a Corel application, you can also start it as a separate program from the Windows desktop. Click on the Start button in the taskbar, point to Corel WordPerfect Suite 7, and then click on Envoy 7. A blank Envoy window will appear.

You can now open an existing Envoy document to read or annotate it, or you can import a file. Importing a file, such as a Corel WordPerfect document, converts it into Envoy format and displays it on the screen. To import a file, use these steps:

1. Pull down the File menu and point to Import.

2. Click on File.

3. In the dialog box that appears, select the file, and then click on OK.

 OTE: *Envoy does not use the same file management boxes as the major Corel applications.*

Saving Files in Envoy

The reason why you publish a document to Envoy is so you can save it in a format that others can view and annotate. From Envoy, you can save your document in three formats:

- *Envoy format* requires that the user have Envoy itself or a program called the Envoy Distributable Viewer. The Viewer is a special program that lets the user read but not create an Envoy document.

- *Runtime format* is an executable program file with the .EXE extension. Like the Viewer, this lets the user read the file, but it does not require the special Viewer file.

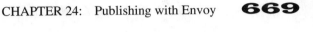

■ *Text format* saves just the text of the document without any of its formats.

 AUTION: *An Envoy and Envoy Runtime file created in Windows 95 cannot be used in Windows 3.1.*

Follow these steps when you are ready to save the file.

1. Select Save from the File menu to see the Save As dialog box.

2. Pull down the Save As Type list and choose a format.

■ Select *Envoy Files (*.EVY)* if the person you are sharing the file with also has Envoy or you will provide the Distributable Viewer.

■ Select *Envoy Runtime Files (*.EXE)*.

■ Select *Text Files (*.TXT)* to save the document as plain text without any formatting.

3. Enter a name for the Envoy document in the File Name box. Make sure the name ends with .EXE if you are saving it as a runtime file, or in *.EVY if you are saving it as an Envoy file.

4. Click on Save.

Using Security

The Security option in the Save As dialog box lets you assign the document password protection and a security level. Click on the Security button in the Save As dialog box to see the Security Settings dialog box.

To require a password to open the document, click on the Password check box and then type the password in the text box—the password appears as asterisks as you type. Next, select the type of access you want to provide:

■ *Unrestricted* allows the user to view, print, and annotate the document.

■ *View and print only* does not allow the user to annotate the document.

■ *View only* does not let the user print or annotate the document.

Click on OK. A box will appear asking you to reenter the password. Type the password again and click on OK.

Using Envoy Files

If you saved the file as a runtime, anyone can display the file by running it from the Run option in the Start menu, or by double-clicking on it in Windows Explorer. The document will appear in an Envoy window.

A Macintosh user, by the way, will not be able to run an Envoy runtime file. Sharing documents with a Macintosh user requires that the user have the Envoy 7 Viewer for Macintosh, available from Corel. Save your files in the Envoy format with a .EVY extension.

If you save the file in Envoy format, either the user must have Envoy, or you must supply the user with a copy of the Distributable Viewer. To do so, copy the file DVSETUP7.EXE from the folder in which Envoy is stored onto the destination drive, such as a shared folder on a network.

 OTE: *The file DVSETUP7.EXE is too large to fit on a single 1.44 MB floppy disk.*

Annotating Documents

While the document is in the Envoy window, you cannot edit or format text, but you can annotate it in a number of ways. An annotation is a way to give the reader more information than is in the actual document. There are five ways that you can annotate text:

- Highlight text with a Highlighter tool.

- Insert a sticky note.

- Insert a bookmark.

- Create a hypertext link to somewhere else in the document.

- Create a link to the World Wide Web or to another local file.

 OTE: *Use the Insert Object command from the Edit menu to insert a graphic or other OLE object into the document.*

Highlighting Text

Highlighting text calls attention to it on the screen. You already learned how to use the Highlighter tool in Corel WordPerfect. Its works just the same way in Envoy.

1. Click on the Highlight tool on the toolbar, or select Highlight from the Tools menu.

2. Point to one end of the text that you want to highlight.

3. Hold down the mouse button, drag to the other end of the text, and release the mouse.

4. Drag over any other text that you want to highlight.

5. Click on the Highlight tool or press ESC to turn it off.

To remove the highlighting from text, click on the Highlight tool, right-click on the highlighted text, and select Clear from the menu that appears. Press ESC or click on the Highlight tool again to turn it off.

 IP: *Use the Annotations option from the File Import menu to copy the annotations from one Envoy document to another. The annotations will be copied to the same page number as they are in the source file.*

Changing the Highlight Properties

The default setting displays the highlight as a solid color over the text. You can change the color used for the highlighter, and you can set it to strikeout the text with a single line. Use a strikeout highlighter, for example, when you want to indicate text that you feel should be deleted.

Follow these steps:

1. Click on the Highlight tool.

2. Right-click on any highlighted text.

3. Select Highlight Properties to see this dialog box:

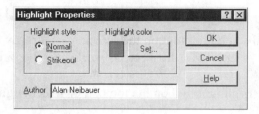

4. To change the color, click on Set, choose a color from the palette that appears, and then click on OK.

5. To highlight text with a color line, rather than a solid block of color, click on Strikeout.

6. Click on OK.

Adding a QuickNote

Although you cannot edit the text of the document in Envoy, you can add your own messages. Certainly you've seen those yellow stick-on notes that you can attach to a printed document. A QuickNote works the same way, but on the screen:

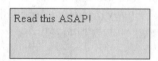

1. Click on the QuickNote icon on the Toolbar, or select QuickNote from the Tools menu.

2. Click in the Envoy document window to insert a standard-size note about 2" by 3", or drag the mouse to create a note any size you want it. You'll see an insertion point inside the note.

3. Type the text of the note.

4. Click outside of the note when you're done.

To later edit the text of the note, double-click on it to position the insertion point within it. You can also copy text from the document into a note. Here's how to create a new note with text from the document:

1. Drag over the text in the document.

2. Choose Copy from the Edit menu.

3. Choose Paste from the Edit menu to turn on the QuickNote feature.

4. Click or drag in the document to create a note containing the text from the document.

5. Edit or add to the text as desired.

6. Click outside of the note.

To add text from the document to an existing note, select the text and choose Copy from the Edit menu. Double-click on the note and choose Paste from the Edit menu.

To delete a note, click on it so it appears surrounded by eight handles, and then press DEL. To change the position of a note, click on it, point inside of it so the mouse appears as a four-pointed arrow, and then drag the mouse. Change the size of a note by dragging one of the handles.

Customizing QuickNotes

You can reduce the note to a smaller icon, and you can even change its color and the way text appears inside of it. These functions are chosen from the QuickMenu that appears when you right-click on a QuickNote.

 To change the note to a small icon, right-click on the note and choose Close QuickNote from the menu that appears. The note will now appear as shown at left.

To open the closed note so you can read it, double-click on it, or right-click on it and choose Open QuickNote from the menu.

 IP: *You can also toggle the note on and off by selecting it or the icon and pressing F2.*

To change the appearance of a note, right-click on it and choose QuickNote Properties from the QuickMenu to see the dialog box shown in Figure 24-2. In this dialog box, you can change:

■ The alignment of text in the note—on the left, centered, on the right, or fully justified

24

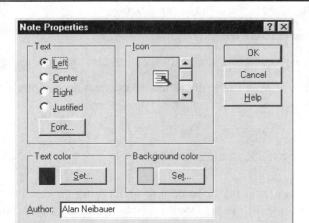

Changing
QuickNote
properties

FIGURE 24-2

- The font and font size of the text in the note
- The icon that appears when you close the note
- The text color
- The note background color

Creating a Bookmark

You've already learned how to use bookmarks in Corel WordPerfect documents and in Netscape. A *bookmark* is simply a way to hold a place in a document. Set a bookmark at a location that you may want to quickly return to at some other time.

   To set a bookmark, follow these steps.

1. Click on the Bookmark tool in the toolbar, or choose Bookmark from the Tools menu.

2. Click on the text where you want the bookmark to appear, or drag over selected text. Envoy will display the Bookmark Properties dialog box.

3. Type a name for the bookmark in the Bookmark Name text box.

4. If you selected text in step 2, you can also choose the Select Bookmark content after jump box. This will highlight the same text when you move to the bookmark.

5. Choose a bookmark style. This determines how the bookmark appears when you move to it.

   ■ Select *Center Bookmark in Window* to show the bookmark in the center of the window.

   ■ Select *Fit Bookmark to Window* to enlarge the bookmark so it fills the screen.

6. Click on OK.

Now when you want to move to a bookmark, pull down the Bookmarks list in the lower-right corner of the Envoy window. You'll see a list of your bookmarks, so click on the one you want to see.

Creating a Hypertext Link

A *hypertext link* is like a bookmark, but you just click on it to move to a specific location. For example, suppose you have a reference in your document such as "See page 3 for more information." You can create a hypertext link so the user can click on the reference to jump directly to the third page.

To create a hypertext link, follow these steps.

1. Click on the Hypertext tool on the toolbar, or select Hypertext from the Tools menu.

2. Drag over the text that you want the user to click on to move to another location. The text will be highlighted in the default color.

3. Move to the location where you want to appear when the link is used, and then drag over the area that you want the link to display.

4. Click on the Hypertext tool or press ESC to turn the feature off.

To go to a hypertext link, point to the text so the pointer appears as a small hand, and then click.

Changing Hypertext Properties

Envoy displays the link in the default color, and when you click on it, the linked area is displayed centered on the screen. You can change the appearance of the link and the linked area by changing the Hypertext Properties. Here's how.

1. Click on the Hypertext tool on the toolbar.

2. Right-click on the link and select Hypertext Properties from the QuickMenu to see the dialog box in Figure 24-3.

3. Choose an option in the Source text style section to select how the hypertext text appears.

4. To change the color, click on Set and select a color from the palette that appears.

5. Choose an option from the Link style section to select how the linked area appears when displayed.

6. Click on OK.

7. Click on the Hypertext tool or press ESC to turn the feature off.

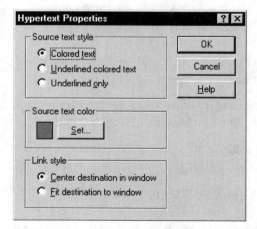

Changing
Hypertext
Properties

FIGURE 24-3

Creating a Hypertext Button

To add a little sparkle to your hypertext links, create a Link button rather than just selecting text. The button can be a plain rectangle with or without a fill color, or it can contain a graphic image, as shown to the left.

Follow these steps to create the button:

1. Click on the Hypertext tool on the toolbar.

2. Drag in the document to create a rectangle that you want to click on.

3. Move to the location in the document where you want the link to move.

4. Drag to set the location.

5. Click on the Hypertext tool or press ESC to turn the feature off.

The default rectangle is just an empty box. To add a fill pattern or graphic to the button, use these steps:

1. Click on the Hypertext tool on the toolbar.

2. Right-click on the box and select Hypertext Properties from the QuickMenu to see the dialog box in Figure 24-4.

3. To add a color to the box, click on Set and choose a color from the palette that appears.

4. To add a graphic to the box, click on the Button option. Scroll the list and choose one of the graphics provided by Envoy.

5. Click on OK.

6. Click on the Hypertext tool or press ESC to turn the feature off.

Linking to the Internet

While the Hypertext tool creates a link within the document, the Web Links tool creates a link to a site on the Internet or to another document. Click on the Web Links tool in the toolbar, and then drag over the area you want to use for the link. When you release the mouse, you'll see the Create Web Link dialog box.

24

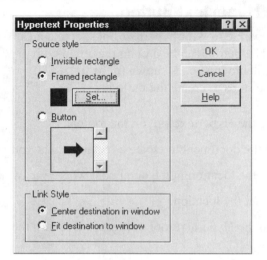

Hypertext
button
properties

■ FIGURE 24-4

To link to the Internet, type in the Destination text box the Web address or URL that you want to jump to. You can also click on the Browse Web button to launch your Web browser to locate the address. To jump to another document, enter its path and filename in the Destination box. If you want to move to a specific bookmark in the document, enter the bookmark name in the Bookmark text box.

 IP: *You can also drag to create a Web Link rectangle and add a color fill or graphic as you learned to do for hypertext links.*

Using Thumbnail Mode

While you cannot edit the text of a document in Envoy, you can add, delete, and rearrange pages. You work with pages using *thumbnails,* miniature versions of every page in the document.

 AUTION: *If you want to add, delete, or change pages, do so before you set any bookmarks or links.*

To create thumbnails, click on the Thumbnail button on the toolbar. Click on the button once to see the thumbnails on the top of the window, as shown in Figure 24-5. Click on it a second time to place the thumbnails on the left, and a third time to remove the thumbnails. You can select the same options by choosing Thumbnails from the View menu.

To change the arrangement of pages, drag the thumbnail of the page to the position where you want it in the document. To delete a page, click on its thumbnail and press DEL. This only deletes the page from the Envoy document, not from the original file.

 AUTION: *Delete with care–you cannot undelete the page!*

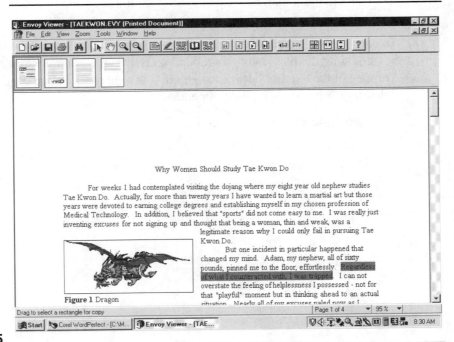

Thumbnail view

FIGURE 24-5

You can also add a page from another document. To do this, you need to open the other document at the same time into a second Envoy window. With one of the documents already open, follow these steps:

1. Click on the Open tool on the Toolbar, or select Open from the File menu.

2. Enter the path and name of the other Envoy file, or select it from the list boxes.

3. Click on Open.

4. Select Tile Top to Bottom, or Tile Side by Side, from the Window menu. This displays both documents on the screen at the same time, in two separate windows.

5. Display the thumbnails on the top if you tiled the documents Top to Bottom. If you tiled them Side by Side, display the thumbnails on the left.

6. Click on the thumbnail of the page you want to insert into the other document.

7. To copy the page from one document to the other, hold down the CTRL key and drag the page to the thumbnail section of the other document. You do not have to hold down the key if you want to move the page, deleting it from its original document.

8. Save and close each of the windows.

Diagramming with CorelFLOW 7

25

There was a time when no self-respecting computer programmer or engineer would imagine starting a project before drawing a flowchart. A *flowchart* is a diagram that shows the logical sequence of events. Each action or event appears in a box, with lines, arrows, or other symbols from box to box indicating the sequence or direction of activity. The shape of the box helps to indicate the type of action being performed, so it is easy to look at a flowchart and get an idea of the processes being described by it.

Flowcharts are not as fashionable as they used to be, but they are still invaluable in planning and organizing projects of all types, and in drawing timelines and custom organization charts and other diagrams, as the two in Figure 25-1 illustrate. In this

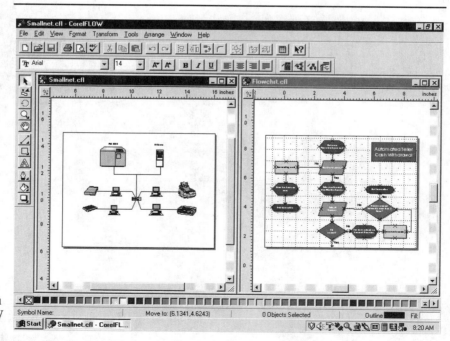

Network diagram and flowchart created with CorelFLOW

FIGURE 25-1

chapter, you will learn the fundamentals of CorelFLOW 7, an invaluable tool for creating flowcharts.

Some Common Elements

CorelFLOW has elements in common with the other Corel WordPerfect Suite applications, but with slight differences. For example, you use the Tools menu to access the Spelling and Thesaurus features, but their dialog boxes are different.

 OTE: *The Tools menu also offers the Type Assist option, which is the program's equivalent to QuickCorrect.*

There is no Preference option in the Edit menu, but you can customize CorelFLOW by choosing Customize from the Tools menu. In the dialog box that appears you can change keyboard assignments, menus, toolbars, and the color palette. There is also an Options command in the Tools menu that lets you change several CorelFLOW default settings.

The Open, Save, and Print dialog boxes work about the same as in most Windows applications, but they are not the same as those in Corel WordPerfect. You cannot access QuickFinder or search for a file based on its name or contents from the file management boxes, for instance.

 You can use the Clipboard to copy your CorelFLOW diagram to Corel WordPerfect and other applications.

The Print dialog box has just one page. You can select the printer to use, the number of copies, if you want to print to a file, display a print preview, or to print the entire page or just the selected objects. There are no Two-Sided Printing or Collate options. CorelFLOW diagrams are just one page.

CorelFLOW doesn't have macros, but it has their equivalent, called *scripts*. These are plain text files comprised of commands in the CorelScript language. To create a script, select Start Recording from the Tools menu, perform the actions that you want to record, and then select Stop Recording from the Tools menu. To save the script on the disk, select Save Recording, type the name of the script in the box that appears, and then click on Save. You can later run the script by choosing Run Wizard/Script from the Tools menu and selecting the script from the dialog box that appears.

CorelFLOW also offers hyperlinks. To set a hyperlink, right-click on an object and choose Define Hyperlink from the QuickMenu. In the dialog box that appears, you can choose to link the objects to a new diagram, an existing diagram, or to some other application or file. You cannot create a link directly to a Web page.

 IP: *To insert an object into a CorelFLOW diagram, select Insert New Object from the Edit menu.*

Starting CorelFLOW

When you start CorelFLOW, you can select from a choice of options, just as you can when you start Corel Presentations. To start the program, use these steps:

1. Click on the Start button in the taskbar.

2. Point to Corel WordPerfect Suite 7.

3. Click on CorelFLOW 7.

You'll see the Welcome to CorelFLOW dialog box with five options. From this menu you can

- Start a new CorelFLOW diagram from a blank drawing screen

- Open an existing diagram for printing or editing

- Open the last diagram you worked on for editing or printing

- Start a diagram using a sample template

- Run a tutorial explaining how to use CorelFLOW

How to use the templates will be discussed later in this chapter. For now, start a new diagram by clicking on the first option in the dialog box to show the CorelFLOW window in Figure 25-2.

The window has a menu bar and these elements:

- *Standard toolbar* for performing common functions

- *Text toolbar* for formatting text

- *Wizards toolbar* for creating complete diagrams using interactive dialog boxes

- *Horizontal and vertical rules*

- *Ruler/Grid button* for controlling display of the rulers and grid lines

- *Toolbox* for creating and formatting objects

- *Smart Library palette* of predrawn symbols

- *Color palette* for changing colors

- *Status bar* displaying the current symbol name, the number of objects selected, and the outline and fill colors

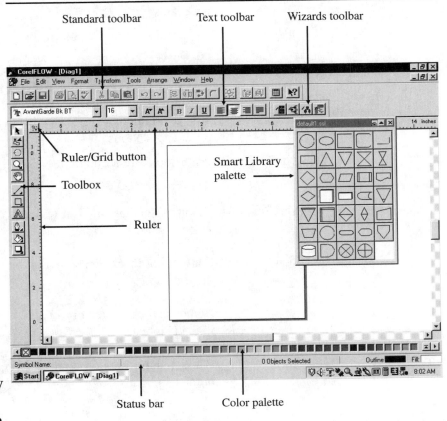

CorelFLOW screen

FIGURE 25-2

25

The functions of the buttons in the Standard toolbar and toolbox are shown in Tables 25-1 and 25-2. The buttons on the Text toolbar are similar to those found in other applications for selecting the font and size, increasing and decreasing the font size, and selecting font attributes and alignment.

Button	Name	Function
	New	Starts a new diagram from a blank diagram. Use the New command from the File menu to start a diagram using a template.
	Open	Opens an existing CorelFlow diagram.
	Save	Saves the current diagram. CorelFlow does not use the File Management dialog box found in other Corel WordPerfect Suite applications.
	Print	Prints the current diagram.
	Print Preview	Displays the diagram as it will appear when printed.
	Spell Check	Starts spell-checking the text in the diagram.
	Cut	Removes the selected object and places it in the Clipboard.
	Copy	Places a duplicate of the selected object in the Clipboard.

Standard
Toolbar
Tools

TABLE 25-1

Button	Name	Function
	Paste	Inserts the contents of the Clipboard into the diagram.
	Undo	Cancels the previous action.
	Redo	Cancels the previous undo action.
	Align	Positions the selected objects in relation to each other.
	Distribute	Evenly spaces selected objects.
	Connect	Draws connection lines between selected objects.
	Rounded Corners	Rounds the corners of selected objects.
	Group	Combines the selected objects into a single group.
	Move to Front	Moves the selected objects to the foreground.
	Move to Back	Moves the selected objects to the background.
	SMARTLIB Open	Displays library files of symbols.
	Help	Displays context-sensitive help on a selected command.

Standard
Toolbar
Tools
(*continued*)

TABLE 25-1

25

Button	Name	Function
	Select	Lets you select objects by clicking or dragging. Use SHIFT plus the mouse to select multiple objects.
	Connector Tool	Inserts a connector pin on an object for later addition of a connections line.
	Rotate Tool	Lets you rotate a selected object.
	Zoom Flyout	Displays options for changing the displayed magnification.
	Panning Tool	Lets you move the displayed page in the window.
	Line Tool	Draws lines.
	Rectangle Tool	Draws rectangles and squares.
	Text Tool	Enters text into the drawing.
	Outline	Adjusts the type of line around selected objects. When no object is selected, Outline changes the default outline for all new objects.
	Fill	Adjusts the fill color and pattern of selected objects. When no object is selected, Fill changes the default fill for all new objects.
	Shadow	Adjusts the shadow style of selected objects. When no object is selected, changes the default shadow for all new objects.

Toolbox
Tools

TABLE 25-2

Drawing Symbols

You could create the boxes and lines and other objects of the diagram using the tools in the toolbox. For example, to draw a rectangle, use these steps:

1. Click on the Rectangle tool.

2. Drag within the page. Hold down the CTRL key while you drag to draw a square.

3. Release the mouse.

4. Draw another object, or click on the Select tool.

When you release the mouse, the object will be surrounded by eight handles, with an extra handle in the center. Use the handles to change the size of the object, or to drag the object to change its position. Use the open box in the center of the object to align the exact center of the object at another position. You'll learn how later.

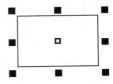

IP: *To add text, click on the Text tool, click where you want the text to appear, and then type. Use the Text toolbar to change the font, size, style, and alignment of the text.*

The Line tool works about the same way, except that you can use it to create a series of connecting lines. Here's how:

1. Click on the Line tool.

2. Click in the drawing where you want the line to start.

3. Move the mouse—you do not have to hold down the mouse button. Hold down the SHIFT key while you drag to draw a straight horizontal or vertical line.

4. If you do not want to immediately draw another line connecting to the current one, double-click.

5. To begin another connecting line from the end point of the one you just drew, click the mouse and then drag to draw the line. Double-click when you have finished.

25

Using the Smart Libraries

The Smart Library palette that appears on the screen contains shapes commonly used to create flowcharts. You can use any of these objects simply by dragging them into the drawing area:

1. Point to an object in the palette. If you hold the mouse still for a moment on the object, a box will appear showing the actual size:

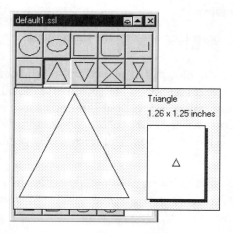

2. Drag the mouse to the drawing area.

3. Release the mouse. The object will appear with handles, but also with connection pins—the small "X" symbols—that are used to draw connecting lines between objects, as shown here.

If you want to insert several of the same symbols, you could insert the first, and then drag and drop using the CTRL key to make copies. You can also "rubber-stamp" multiple copies from the library. Here's how.

1. Click on the symbol that you want to insert.

2. Click in the drawing to place the symbol. The mouse pointer appears like a rubber stamp.

3. Continue clicking where you want to insert the symbol.

4. Click on Select Tool when you have finished.

Opening Other Libraries

CorelFLOW includes more than 6000 different symbols that you can include in your drawings. The symbols are collected in library files around common themes, such as business symbols, local area networks, wide area and other networking diagrams, organization charts, arrows, and patterns. You can have more than one Smart Library open at a time, making it easy to add a variety of shapes and symbols to the diagram.

To open another library, follow these steps:

1. Click on the SMARTLIB Open button in the Standard toolbar. A dialog box appears listing files with the SSL extension.

2. Double-click on the library you want to open. A palette with the library symbols will appear on the screen.

To print a copy of the tools in the library for your reference, right-click on the palette and choose Create Diagram for Printing from the QuickMenu. CorelFLOW will start a new diagram and add all of the symbols to the page along with their names.

You can also change the size in which the symbols are displayed. Right-click on the palette, point to the Tool Size option in the QuickMenu, and select Small, Medium, or Large. This only changes the size of the palette, not of the actual objects themselves in the drawing.

25

Zooming the Display

The default display shows the entire page on the screen. You use the Zoom Flyout tool in the toolbox to enlarge or reduce the display as needed. Click on the tool to see these options:

From left to right, the options are

- *Zoom In* enlarges the display and lets you drag the mouse over an area of the diagram to enlarge that portion.

- *Zoom Out* reduces the display.

- *Zoom Actual Size* adjusts the display so the objects appear their actual size.

- *Zoom to Selected* enlarges the display so the selected object fills the window. If no object is selected, this displays the entire page.

- *Zoom to All Objects* enlarges the display so all of the objects in the page can be seen.

- *Zoom to Page* displays the entire page.

Adding Connecting Pins

Once you draw or insert your objects, you have to connect them to show the relationship between them. You create lines between objects by using the connection pins—the "X" characters on objects from the libraries. You can add pins to your own objects, and insert additional pins on library objects.

To add a pin, use these steps:

1. Click on the Connector tool on the toolbox. The pointer appears like a small arrowhead.

2. Click on a line around an object where you want to connect a line, and the connection pin will appear.

IP: *To remove a pin, click on the Connector tool, click on the pin to select it, and press DEL. Move a pin by dragging it to another location.*

Connecting Objects

Once you have connection pins, it's easy to connect two objects. You can connect them by dragging a line between two pins, or by letting CorelFLOW do it for you.

CorelFLOW will automatically align a line to the nearest connection pin, so you don't have to worry how steady your hand is. To drag a line between pins, use the following steps:

1. Click on the Line tool in the toolbox. The mouse pointer will appear as a crosshair.

2. Click on one of the pins that you want to connect.

3. Move the mouse to the other pin. As the mouse gets close, the pointer will change to a four-directional arrow with a symbol indicating that it is snapped to the nearest pin:

4. Double-click to draw the line.

If you move an object after it is connected, the line will automatically move to maintain the connection with the object.

You can also connect objects using the Connect tool in the Standard toolbar. Here's how.

1. Click on the first object you want to connect.

2. Hold down the SHIFT key and click on the other objects you want to connect.

3. Click on the Connect tool.

CorelFLOW will draw connection lines. The lines may not connect at pin locations if there is no straight path between pins on the objects.

Aligning Objects

To get your diagram just right, you'll have to align objects on the screen. CorelFLOW gives you several ways to align objects.

The easiest way to align objects is to drag them with the mouse. Just make sure you're using the Select tool—the mouse pointer will appear like an arrow. If the Line or Rectangle tool is still active, you'll draw when you drag.

The center handle inside of each object will let you automatically position the object's center. As you drag the object, the normally open handle will become filled when it is over a pin, or center handle, of another object. You'll know the center is on the pin when it becomes filled; at that point, release the mouse.

To help you position objects, you can display guidelines and work with a grid pattern. Set a guideline as you learned how to do in Corel Presentations, by dragging down from the horizontal ruler or over from the vertical ruler.

To work with both grid lines and guidelines, right-click on the Ruler/Grid button at the intersection of the rulers. Select Guidelines Setup from the QuickMenu to display a dialog box where you can set, move, delete, or hide the guidelines. To display or adjust the grid lines, select Grid and Ruler Setup from the QuickMenu. You'll see the Grid & Ruler Setup dialog box with two tabs—Ruler and Grid.

Use the Ruler page to set the units of measurement along the rulers and the starting measurement. Use the Grid page to turn Show Grid and Snap-to-Grid off and on, and to set the distance between the grid lines. If you select Show Grid, the pattern will appear on the page like this:

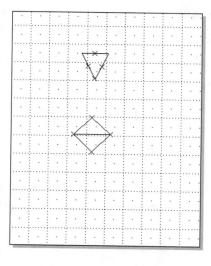

If you do not like to drag objects to align them, you can select them and use the Align or Distribute buttons in the Standard toolbar. The buttons show different pages in the Align and Distribute dialog box. The dialog box in Figure 25-3, for example, displays the Align page of the dialog box showing three objects that are selected in the drawing.

The drawings next to the check boxes illustrate the effect the boxes will have. For example, use the options along the left side of the box to align the objects so their top, center, or bottom is aligned across the page. Selecting the Center option on the left would align the three objects like this:

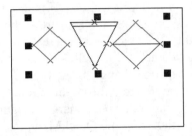

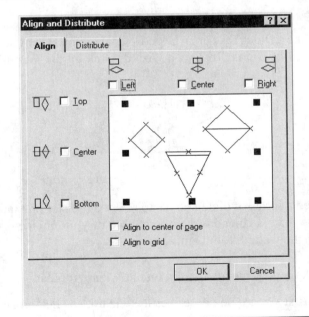

Align
options

FIGURE 25-3

NOTE: *You use the Distribute option similarly, but to control the spacing between objects.*

Setting Object Properties

You can format the appearance of an object by selecting it, and then choosing options from the Outline, Fill, and Shadow tools in the toolbox. But as in Corel Presentations, you can also change the appearance of an object in CorelFLOW by setting its properties.

Right-click on the object that you want to format, and then choose Properties from the QuickMenu to display the Shape Properties dialog box. The options that appear will be determined by the object—a line, text, or symbol.

The options displayed when you right-click on a connection line, for example, are shown in Figure 25-4. You can change the color, type, and thickness of the line, and you can add arrows to the line to indicate direction.

To change the size, orientation, or page margins, right-click on a blank part of the page and choose Properties from the QuickMenu, or select Page and Diagram Setup from the File menu. Select options from the Properties box and then select OK.

Using the Wizards

A *wizard* is like a QuickTask or an Expert—it takes you step by step through creating common types of charts. To start a wizard, click on the Wizard tool for it on the toolbar:

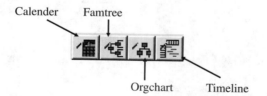

You'll see a series of dialog boxes to select options. For example, the Calendar Wizard will create a calendar, with a graphic of your choice, as shown in Figure 25-5. To use the wizard, follow these steps.

1. Click on the Calendar button on the Wizard toolbar.

2. The first Wizard box describes the wizard, so click on Next.

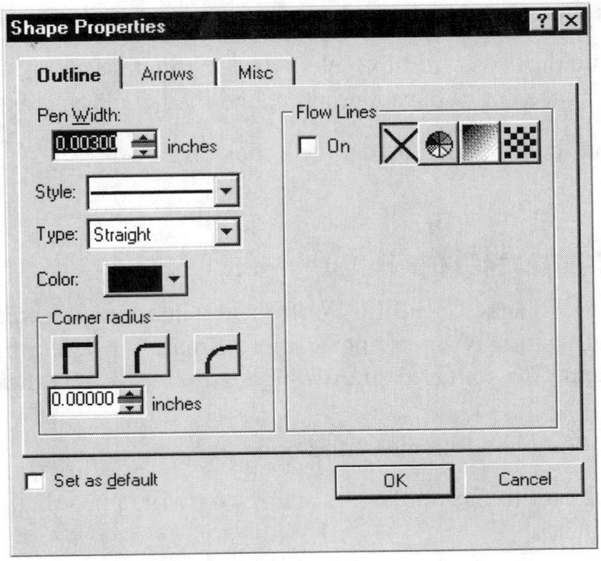

Setting
properties
for lines

FIGURE 25-4

Calendar
created by
the Wizard

FIGURE 25-5

25

3. In the second Wizard box, choose the month and year for the calendar, and the colors for the text, boxes, and page, and then click on Next.

4. In the third Wizard box, select the graphic that you want on the calendar, or choose not to have a graphic, and then click on Next.

5. Read the last Wizard, and then click on Finish.

Using a Template

In addition to wizards, CorelFLOW offers less interactive *templates*. These are files that will automatically open one or more Smart Libraries that revolve around a common theme. To start a diagram with a template, follow these steps:

1. Pull down the File menu and point to New.

2. Click on From Template. A dialog box will appear listing the available templates.

3. Double-click on the template you want to use.

CorelFLOW will start a new diagram, opening the symbol libraries that you'll need for the type of template selected.

 OTE: *You can also create a document from a template by selecting the option when you start CorelFLOW.*

Using Layers

While every diagram is only one page, the page can contain up to 99 layers. Picture each layer as a sheet of clear plastic. When the sheets are on top of each other, the drawing appears as one entity. But you can separate the layers to work with each individually. If you are creating a family tree, for example, you can draw each generation on a separate layer. You can then print out the entire tree or just selected generations.

To work with layers, select Layers from the Arrange menu, and then click on the Options >> button to display all of the dialog box, as in Figure 25-6.

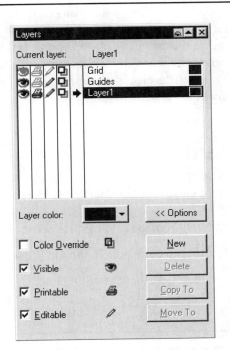

Layers
dialog box

FIGURE 25-6

Each diagram has at least three layers—grid, guidelines, and layer 1. The icons next to each layer indicate how objects on the layer are treated. The icons are

- Color Override
- Visible
- Printable
- Editable

A dimmed icon means that the feature is off. So if the Visible icon is dimmed, no objects will appear on that layer. If the Printable icon is dimmed, the objects will not print. The Color Override feature, when selected, displays all objects on the layer in the layer color—the color indicated in the box to the right of the layer. Change the color by clicking on the layer, and then choose from the Layout Color list. The color does not affect the printed color, but only helps to distinguish layers on the screen. You change a setting by clicking on the icon. You can also click on the Layer In list to highlight it, and then select or deselect the check boxes.

To add a layer to the diagram, click on New.

To make a layer active—so objects that you insert are on that layer—click in the column just to the left of the layer number. An arrow will appear indicating it is the active layer. While new objects will be placed on that layer, you can still select, edit, and move all other visible and editable objects, regardless of the layer they are on.

To print a specific layer, deselect the printable icons for all other layers. To view just one layer, deselect the viewable icon.

Inserting a Memo

You can insert a "sticky note" into a diagram, similarly to a QuickNote in Envoy. CorelFLOW calls them *memos* rather than *notes*. Here's how to insert one:

1. Select Insert Memo from the Edit menu to see the dialog box in Figure 25-7.

2. Type a header (title) for the note in the top section.

3. Press TAB, and then type the text of the note.

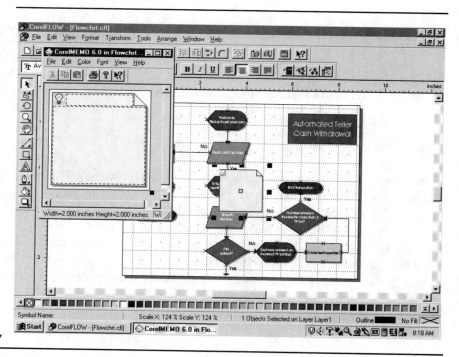

Inserting
a memo

FIGURE 25-7

4. To change the color, pull down the Color menu and choose to change the Header Text, Body Text, or Paper. Select a color in the palette that appears and click on OK.

5. To change the font, pull down the Font menu and choose to change the Header Text or Body Text. Select a font, size, and style in the box that appears, and then click on OK.

6. To change the icon in the header, select CorelMEMO Picture in the Edit menu to see the following options. Select an icon and then click on OK.

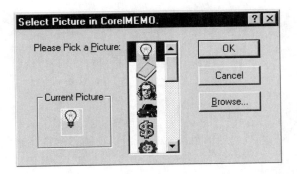

7. When you have finished, select the Exit and Return option from the File menu.

8. In the dialog box that appears, click on Yes.

9. The memo will appear like a sticky note on the diagram. Double-click on the note to edit it.

25

Using Sidekick 95

26

A sidekick is a friend, a companion, an amigo that you can always count on in a pinch. Sidekick 95 is a set of tools that is always handy, always ready to help. Some of the tools have equivalents in the Windows accessories menu, but they also have additional features and are integrated into one convenient package.

In this chapter, you'll learn the basics of using Sidekick. To learn all about it, select the Sidekick option from the Corel WordPerfect Reference Center.

IP: *Sidekick is not installed automatically with the other Corel WordPerfect Suite CD applications. To install it, click on the Bonus Applications button in the Corel opening window.*

Introducing Sidekick

Sidekick 95 is a complete set of desktop utilities—the same type of resources that you'd keep handy on your actual desk. It includes

- A *calendar* for keeping track of appointments, calls, and things you have to do—with daily, weekly, monthly, or yearly views. There is even a Reminder view that summarizes your activities. You can also print your calendar in formats compatible with popular planners, such as DayRunner, Day-Timers, and Franklin Planner.

- A *cardfile* for recording names and addresses like an address book, or for use as a simple database.

- A *word processing program* for writing memos or letters, or just notes to yourself. There are QuickLetters, sample letters that you can select from, and you can mail merge information from the cardfile.

- An *expense recording and reporting system.*

- A *phone dialer.*

- *EarthTime*, a program that shows you the time around the world in eight locations and gives information about each city. You can choose from 350 cities and learn the time difference between them.

- A *goal list* for recording and tracking priorities.

- A *calculator.*

- A *contact manager* to review activities with a contact.

- A *report writer* for printing information from the database.

- A *launch bar* for running other programs.

You can drag and drop information from one feature of the program to another. For example, need to make a call? Drag the card from the cardfile to the phone dialer.

OTE: *In Sidekick, when you point to an area that requires a mouse action, such as a double-click, the pointer will appear as a small mouse.*

The best way to learn the features of Sidekick is to start the program and look at its window. To start Sidekick, click on the Start button in the toolbar, and click on Sidekick 95 on the menu. If Sidekick is not on the menu, point to Corel WordPerfect Suite 7, and then click on Sidekick 95 in the menu that appears.

Now look at the Sidekick 95 window in Figure 26-1. The initial screen shows the Calendar view with your schedule for the current day, complete with a To Do list and a list of calls. The current time will be selected in the appointment book on the right. The toolbar buttons will be determined by the Sidekick feature you are using (Figure 26-1 shows the toolbar buttons for the Calendar feature).

IP: *Use the Daily, Weekly, Monthly, and Yearly tabs to select how you want to look at your appointments.*

Down the right side of the window are the deskpad buttons that change the view—the feature of Sidekick that you are using. To record or report expenses, for example, click on the Expense deskpad icon.

IP: *Click on the Daily Information button to see the sunrise and sunset times, the moon phase, next moon phase, astrological sign, and the day of the year.*

At the bottom of the appointment book are the viewport buttons. A *viewport* is an area that you can display that shows information from another Sidekick feature.

26

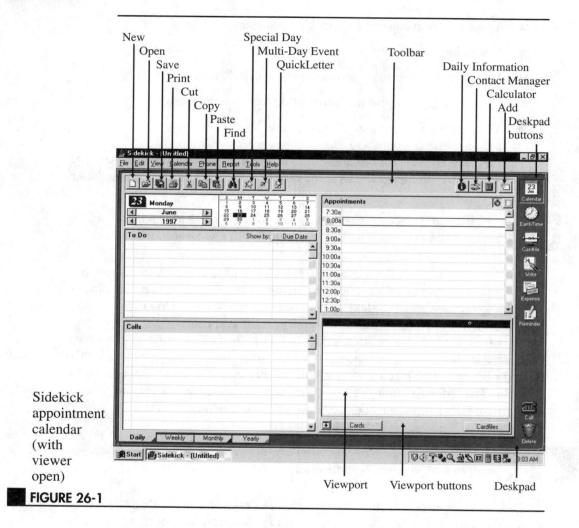

New
Open
Save
Print
Cut
Copy
Paste
Find
Special Day
Multi-Day Event
QuickLetter
Toolbar
Daily Information
Contact Manager
Calculator
Add
Deskpad
buttons

Sidekick
appointment
calendar
(with
viewer
open)

Viewport   Viewport buttons   Deskpad

FIGURE 26-1

For example, when working with the calendar, you can display a viewport listing information from cardfiles, a contact log for the current card, or your list of goals. To open the viewport, click on the Up Arrow viewport button. (The button changes to a down-pointing arrow when the viewport is open.) To select what appears in the viewport, click on the button next to the arrow and select from the list that appears. When you choose to display Cards, you can also choose the cardfile to use. When you display your goal list, you can select to sort them by various means. Choose the cardfile to use or the sort order by clicking on the button on the right and selecting from the list.

 IP: *You can use the viewport to drag information between features, such as a name from a card to an appointment.*

Using the Calendar

You can enter information into the appointment book, add a To Do item, or record a call. To see your appointments for another day, just click on the date in the monthly calendar. Scroll the month and year bars to change months.

To add an appointment, follow these steps:

1. Select the month and year of the appointment.

2. Click on the day in the monthly calendar.

3. Click on the time in the appointment book, scrolling the times if you have to.

4. Type information about the appointment.

An icon of an alarm clock will appear next to the appointment. Each appointment can be associated with additional information. Double-click on the appointment to see the dialog box in Figure 26-2.

You can enter more information about the appointment, change its day and time, and set an alarm to sound when the time occurs. To set an alarm, use these steps:

1. Click on the Alarm check box.

2. Enter any lead time that you want. Lead time is how long before the time of the appointment the alarm will sound.

3. Pull down the Tone list and select the alarm sound you want, if any options other than the default sound are listed. You can click on Play to hear what the alarm sounds like.

4. Select from the three buttons in the bottom of the box:

26

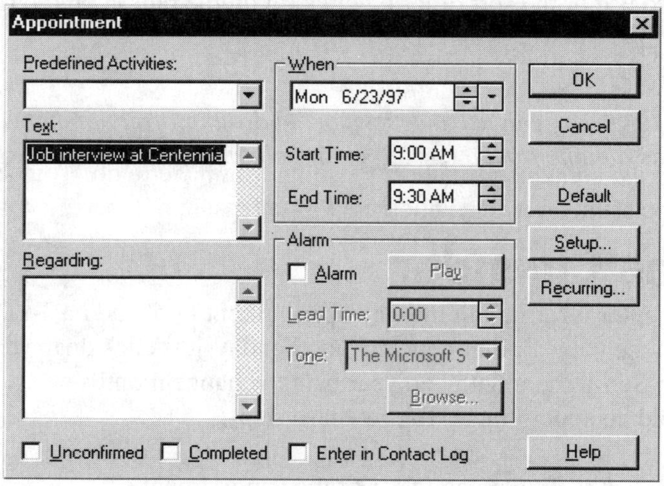

Entering
appointment
information

FIGURE 26-2

- *Unconfirmed* displays a question mark next to the appointment.

- *Completed* places a strikeout over the appointment.

- *Enter in Contact Log* makes an entry for the appointment in the Contact Log.

When you return to the calendar, a Bell icon will appear next to the appointment, indicating that an alarm for it has been set.

OTE: *The Setup button lets you create a list of predefined activities that you can select from to categorize your appointments. Click on the Default button to use the current settings for all new appointments.*

Special Events

A *multi-day event* is one that extends over several days, such as a conference. A *special day* can be a birthday, anniversary, or other event that you want to be reminded of. You use the Special Day and Multi-Day Event buttons on the toolbar to display a dialog box for entering information about these events.

After selecting options from the dialog box that appears when you choose these options, special days appear in the top-left corner in Daily view, while multi-day events appear at the top of the Appointments list.

Using the To Do List

A *To Do list* contains reminders of things you have to do. You add items to the list and associate them with additional information, similar to appointments. Here's how.

1. Click on an empty line in the To Do list.

2. Type a reminder or message. A small Page icon appears next to the item.

3. Double-click on the column to the right of the text to see the dialog box in Figure 26-3.

4. Select a predefined activity, change the text, or enter a note in the Regarding box.

5. Select a priority. If you select Advanced, you can click on the Advanced button and choose from additional settings.

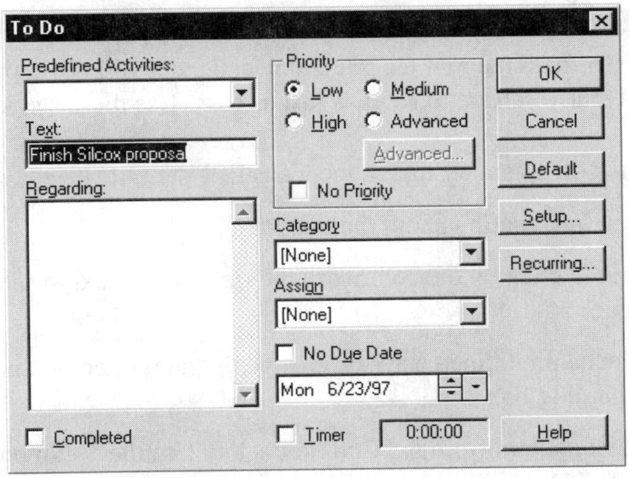

Entering
To Do
information

FIGURE 26-3

6. Select a category.

7. Select an item from the Assign list.

8. Select the due date, or click on the No Due Date button if there isn't any.

9. Click on Timer if you want Sidekick to begin timing in seconds how long it takes for you to complete the task.

10. Click on Completed when the task is done.

11. Click on OK.

OTE: *Use the Setup button to add to the Predefined Activities, Category, and Assign lists.*

You can mark your actions as completed when they are done, and choose how you want them sorted in the To Do list. When you complete an activity, click on the empty box to the left of the item in the To Do list. Sidekick will place a check mark in the box and strike out the item. If a timer is set, it will stop—double-click on the column after the item to see the amount of time.

To sort the lists of items, pull down the Show By list and select from these options: Assign, Category, Due Date, Enter Date, Priority, and Timer.

Entering Calls

Entering information about the telephone calls that you have to make, or the faxes and e-mail that you have to send, is just as easy. Use these steps:

1. Click on an empty line in the Calls list.

2. Type information about the call.

3. Double-click on the column to the right of the text to see the dialog box in Figure 26-4.

4. Select a predefined activity, change the text, or enter a note in the Regarding box.

5. Select an item from the Call Status list. Use the Setup button to add Predefined Activities and Call Status items.

6. If the call is already completed, click on the Completed check box.

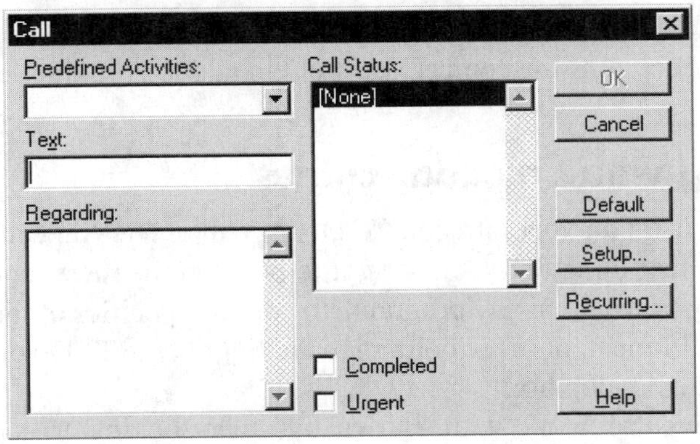

Entering
call
information

FIGURE 26-4

7. Click on the Urgent check box to mark the call with an exclamation point in the third column.

8. Click on OK.

When you complete the call, click in the empty column next to it to mark it as completed.

Scheduling an Activity for a Contact

Later in this chapter you will learn how to use the cardfile view to record address book entries and other information. You can use the cardfile to add a person's name directly into an appointment, To Do, or Call. This not only saves you typing, but it will let Sidekick keep track of activities for that person in the contact manager. You add a person's name by dragging it from the viewport. Here's how:

1. Click on the Viewport arrow to open the viewport. By default, you'll see a list of index items in the cardfile.

2. Drag the person's listing from the viewport into the Appointment, To Do, or Call block.

If the names from the cardfile do not appear, follow these steps:

26

1. Click on the button next to the arrow and choose Cards from the list.

2. Click on the Cardfiles button under the viewport and select the cardfile that contains the contact you want to add to Appointment, To Do, or Call.

Working with Calendar Entries

After you insert an appointment, To Do, or call entry, you can edit or delete it. To change the text of an entry, click on it to position the insertion point, and then edit the text as you would in any program. To edit the specifics of the entry, double-click on the appointment, or in the column to the right of the To Do or Call text, to display the associated dialog box.

You can also work with entries by right-clicking to display the QuickMenu shown here. In addition to the usual QuickMenu options found in Windows applications (such as Cut, Copy, Paste, and Delete), you can select these options:

Can't Undo	Ctrl+Z
Cut	Ctrl+X
Copy	Ctrl+C
Paste	Ctrl+V
Insert	
Delete	
Check As Complete	
Edit	
Reschedule Activity	
Recurring	

- *Check as Complete* adds strikeout to the entry to indicate you have completed it. The option will then appear as Check as Incomplete.

- *Edit* displays the dialog box to change the specifics of the entry.

- *Reschedule Activity* lets you change the date and time of the activity.

- *Recurring* lets you add the entry to later dates or times at periodic intervals.

For example, if your schedule changes, you can reschedule an appointment, a call, or a To Do item. Right-click on the item and select Reschedule Activity from the QuickMenu. The Reschedule Activity dialog box appears with options to change the time and date. Make the changes and then click on OK.

Entering Recurring Items

Many appointments, calls, and tasks you have to perform are recurring—they occur at regular intervals, such as every week or the first day of the month.

Each of the dialog boxes you just saw had a button marked Recurring, and the option appears on the QuickMenu that lets you enter the interval so Sidekick can automatically add the item to future days in your calendar. Use either of those options if you've already scheduled the event and you want to add it to the calendar periodically.

You can also create a new recurring activity using the Calendar menu. Follow these steps:

1. Change to Daily View, if you are not already in it.

2. Pull down the Calendar menu and point to the type of activity—Appointment, To Do, or Call.

3. Click on Recurring. The options in the dialog box that appears will be determined by the type of activity. Figure 26-5 shows the options for a recurring appointment.

4. Enter the text of the activity and any Regarding notes.

5. Select other options from the box.

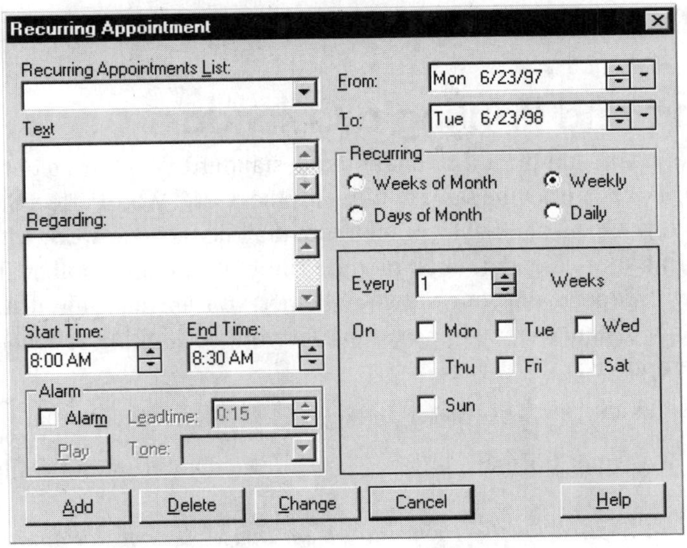

Setting a
recurring
appointment

FIGURE 26-5

6. Select an option in the Recurring section, whether the event repeats by weeks of the month, weekly, days of the month, or daily. The Weeks of the Month option lets you repeat the activity on the same day of the week in monthly intervals, such as the first Monday of every month or every other month.

7. Set a number in the Every list. The value will be Every *n* Months, Every *n* Weeks, or Every *n* Days, depending on the Recurring option.

8. Specify or select from the other options that appear to indicate the period.

9. Click on Add, and then on OK.

The event will automatically be inserted into the appropriate pages and locations on the calendar.

To delete a recurring activity, pull down the Calendar menu and choose Recurring from the type of item. Select the item you want to delete in the pull-down list, click on the Delete button, and then select from these options:

- All Occurrences
- Future Occurrences
- Past Occurrences

Saving and Printing a Calendar

You save, open, and print a calendar using standard Windows techniques, although the dialog boxes are not the same as those in other Corel WordPerfect Suite applications. Use the New, Open, and Save options from the File menu to work with files.

To print your calendar, click on the Print button in the toolbar. The options that appear will depend on your view—whether you are looking at a Daily, Weekly, Monthly, or Annual view. For example, if you are looking at a Daily view, you'll see these options:

- Sidekick Daily Format
- Franklin Format
- Day-Timer Format
- Day Running Daily Format

 IP: *Click on the Print button on the toolbar to automatically select the Sidekick format option.*

Your selection will determine the options in the dialog box that appears. The options for the Sidekick Daily Format are shown in Figure 26-6. If not all of the choices appear on your screen, click on the Options button in the dialog box. You can select the range of appointments to print, the style, what to include, and the Paper Type, which determines the margins—click on Edit to see or change them.

Next, select other options from the dialog box.

- *Include Mini Calendar* prints miniature monthly calendars on the page.

- *Skip Empty* does not print empty time blocks.

- *Include Regarding* prints the Regarding note for each appointment.

- *Text Wrap* prints up to 500 characters in each field, wrapping the text on multiple lines if needed.

- *Include Completed Item* prints completed items.

- *One Page* prints only what will fit on a single page.

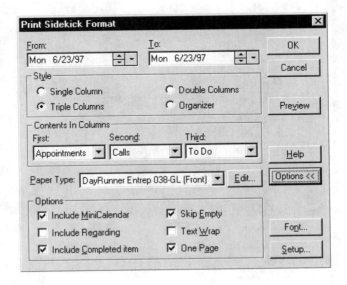

Printing
calendar
information

FIGURE 26-6

26

OTE: *Use the Font button to select the font, size, and style for each element on the page, and use the Setup button to select a printer, paper size, orientation, and source.*

Using EarthTime

The *EarthTime* feature displays a world map with eight locations around the world, as shown in Figure 26-7. To display the map, click on the EarthTime icon in the deskpad. The light areas of the map represent daylight, the dark areas nighttime. Above and below the map are panels showing the dates and times in other cities, which you can change.

To change the cities, use these steps:

1. Right-click the city panel that you want to change to display the QuickMenu.

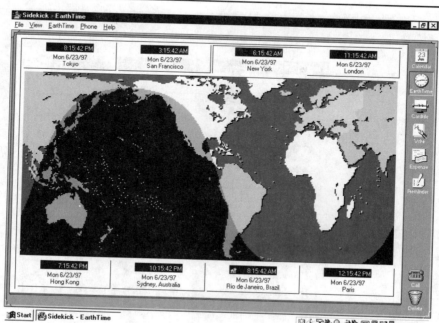

The EarthTime view

FIGURE 26-7

2. Click on Change City to display a dialog box listing countries and cities.

3. To list cities in a specific country, select the country in the pull-down list.

4. Scroll the City list and select the city. If your city is not listed, select one that is closest to you in the same time zone.

5. Click on OK.

To make the display more useful, you should select the city where you are located as the Home Clock. This lets you match your time with the time in other cities. If you travel with a laptop computer, you can also set a Local Time to that in whatever city you are in.

1. Choose the panel that has your city.

2. Right-click on the panel and select Choose As Home Clock from the QuickMenu.

To designate the local clock, select Choose as Local Clock from the QuickMenu. The program will display a dialog box for you to confirm the city. The box also contains a check box labeled "Adjust your system time when click OK." If you select this option, the program will change your computer's system clock to the time shown in the panel, so remember to set the time back when you get home.

Here are some other ways to use EarthTime:

■ Select *Facts about City* from the QuickMenu or the Change City box to display this information:

26

- Select *Time Difference* from the QuickMenu to display a dialog box showing the time differences between any two locations that you can select.

- Select *Clock Setup* from the QuickMenu to change the colors used and to enter an alternative name for the city in the current panel. For example, if you live in a small community outside of Chicago, select Chicago as the city but enter your own community name so it appears on the panel.

Using the Cardfile

The *cardfile* is a mini database manager. You can use it as an address book, or to record almost any type of information. To display the cardfile, click the Cardfile icon in the deskpad, or pull down the View menu and click on Cardfile. The Cardfile view is shown in Figure 26-8.

In addition to the standard first seven toolbar buttons, the Cardfile toolbar contains these options:

- *Sort* lets you select the fields to use for the index.

- *Find* locates information in the cardfile.

- *QuickLetter* inserts information from the card into a complete form letter and starts Write view.

- *Edit view* toggles the display between the card full screen and with the index. The button changes to Indexes View when the index does not appear.

- *Contact Manager* lets you organize events based on a person or organization in the cardfile.

- *Calculator* displays a calculator with a "paper tape" showing your entries and calculated results.

- *Add Cards* inserts a new card into the file.

The cardfile can store up to 20,000 cards, and they can be sorted on up to three fields. The sort information appears on the Index line of the card and in the Index section of the window. You have to design a card by specifying up to 100 fields, but rather than enter your own fields, you can create a cardfile using a template provided by Sidekick.

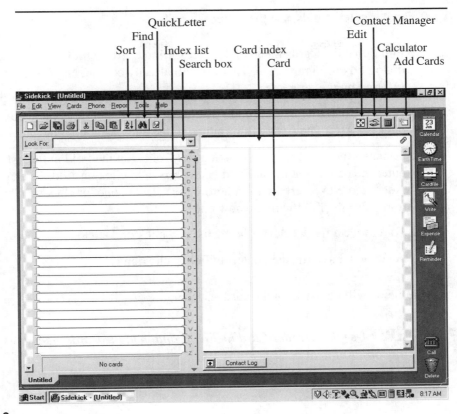

Sidekick's
Cardfile
view

FIGURE 26-8

IP: *If an existing Cardfile is on the screen, select New Cardfile from the File menu. A Tab will appear at the bottom of the window showing the name of the open cardfiles. Click on a tab to select a file.*

1. Pull down the Cards menu and select Define Cardfile Fields.

2. Pull down the Cardfile Template list and select one of the predefined templates, or choose None if you want to name all of your own fields.

3. Click on OK.

4. If you selected a template, the fields in that template will appear on the card. If you chose None, the Define Cardfile Fields dialog box will appear.

26

To add or delete fields, use these steps:

1. Pull down the Cards menu and select Define Cardfile Fields to see the dialog box in Figure 26-9. The box will already contain any fields inserted by the template.

2. Enter the name of a field (up to 39 characters) in the Field Name box and click on Add. The field will be added to the end of the list.

3. To insert the name after an existing field, click on the field in the list, enter the new name in the Field Name box, and click on Add. Click on Add Before to insert the field before the selected one, or click on Change to replace the field with the new one.

4. To remove a field, select it in the list and click on Delete.

5. When you have finished entering fields, click on OK.

The fields will be listed on the card, as in Figure 26-10.

 IP: *Use the Reorder Cardfile Fields option in the Cards menu to change the order of fields.*

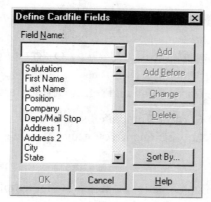

Designating
fields

FIGURE 26-9

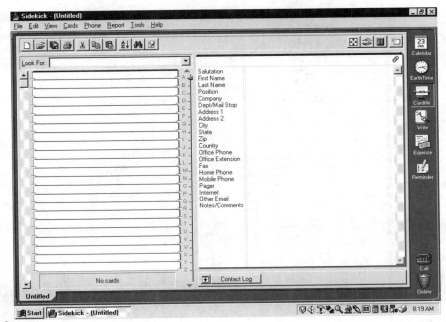

Card with
fields

FIGURE 26-10

Adding Cards

To add a card, click on the Add Cards button on the toolbar, or select Add Cards
from the Cards menu. A dialog box will appear listing the fields. Enter the
information (up to 98 characters) into the text boxes, pressing TAB to move from
field to field, and then click on Add when you have finished. Click on Close when
you have no more cards to enter. The fields making up the index will appear on the
index line and in the card index, as shown in Figure 26-11.

Edit a card by clicking the line you want and then editing the text. You cannot
click on a blank line and type. To enter information into a field, you must press
ENTER from a field that already has information to move to the blank fields.

Changing the Index

The cards are sorted by the three fields that make up the index. The fields are
normally the first three on the card, but you can change the fields and their order to
control how the cardfile cards are sorted.

26

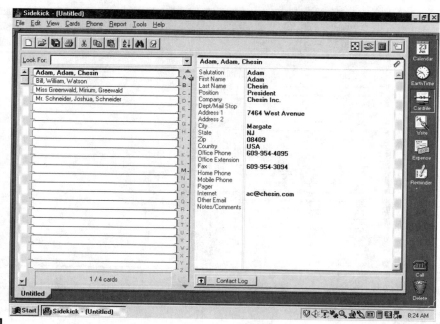

Index entries inserted from the cardfile fields

FIGURE 26-11

Click on the Sort button in the toolbar or pull down the Cards menu and choose Sort Cardfile, to see the Sort Cardfile dialog box shown in Figure 26-12. To add a field to the index, click on it in Field Name list and click on >> to add it to the Sort By list. If you already have three fields, it will replace an existing field. To remove a field from the index, click on it in the Sort By list and click on the << button. To change the order of fields in the index, click on it in the Sort By list and click on Up or Down. Finally, select to sort in ascending (alphabetical) or descending (reverse alphabetical) order.

Working with Cards

To display a card, click on its entry in the Index list. You can also use the scroll bar to scroll through the index, or click on an alphabetical index tab to go to the cards starting with a specific letter.

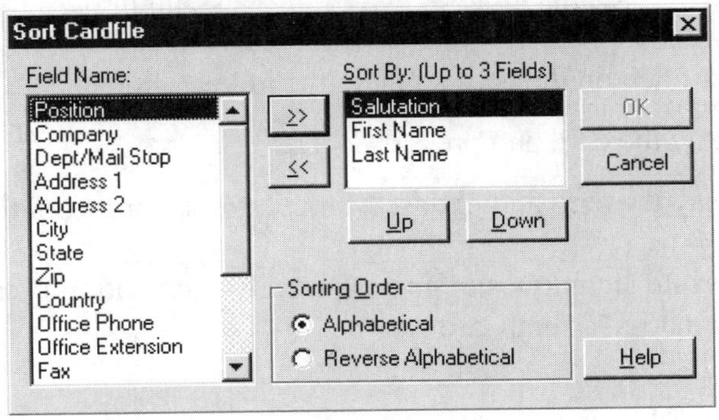

Changing
the sort on
your cardfile

FIGURE 26-12

IP: *To delete a card, drag it to the Delete icon on the bottom of the deskpad.*

If you have a lot of cards, however, you may find it better to search for indexed information.

In the Look For box, start to type text that you are looking for. As you type, the program locates the cards with an index entry matching what you've entered. It highlights the entry in the index and displays it in the Card window. If the displayed card is not the one you are looking for, continue typing more characters to look for.

An alternative way to search for information is by clicking on the Find button to display the Find Text dialog box. Enter the text you are looking for, select where you want to search within (for example, index, cards, contact log), and then click on OK.

CARDFILE VIEWS   The default view that appears when you open a cardfile is called the Index view—the index is on the left and the card on the right. In that view, you can drag the border between the card and index to change the size of the two areas. You can also click on the Edit View button to remove the index from the screen and show just the card. Click on the Edit View button again to display the index.

MARKING CARDS   While you normally work with one card at a time, you may want to mark a group of cards to print them all at one time or perform some other action.

When you mark a card, a red triangle appears next to its index showing that it is part of the group. To mark a card, use any of these techniques:

- Right-click on the card's line in the index.

- Display the card and press CTRL+L.

- Display the card and choose Mark Current Card from the Cards menu.

Use the same techniques to unmark a card—the option in the Cards menu will appear as Unmark Current Card.

IP: *Choose Unmark All Cards from the Cards menu to remove the mark from every card in the file.*

To make a copy of a card, select it and then choose Duplicate Card from the Cards menu. In the box that appears, select the number of copies to make and click on OK.

Saving and Printing a Cardfile

Use the options on the File menu, as expected, to save, open, and print a cardfile. To print cards, select Print from the File menu to see these options:

- Print Cards

- Print Labels

- Print Address Book

- Print Envelope

The dialog box that appears with the Print Cards option is shown in Figure 26-13. The boxes for other options are similar but let you choose a layout to use for labels, address book entries, or envelopes. Select options from the dialog box and click on OK.

Using Write

The Write view offers a basic word processing program. It doesn't have the capabilities of Corel WordPerfect, but it does offer these features:

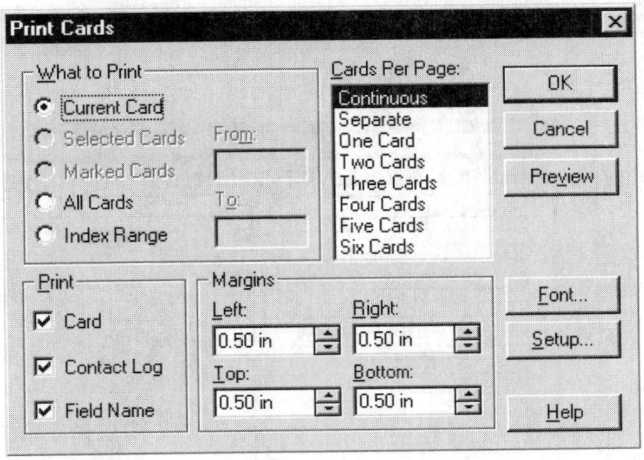

Printing
cards

FIGURE 26-13

■ Format the font, size, and style of characters

■ Set tabs along a ruler

■ Format paragraph alignment

■ Spell check your document using the Spelling Check option in the Tools menu

■ Insert bullets

■ Merge information from a cardfile

■ Select a QuickLetter

■ Drag the ruler to change indentations

■ Use Page Setup from the File menu to change page size

26

If you are already familiar with Corel WordPerfect, you'll find the options in the Write view intuitive. This chapter reviews some of its features.

To change to Write view, click on the Write icon in the deskpad. The view appears with a blank document, as shown in Figure 26-14.

Write is similar to the cardfile in many respects. Each Write file can contain many different documents, so you can have multiple Write files, each with multiple

QuickLetter   Contact Manager
        Edit View
                    Calculator
                    Add Document

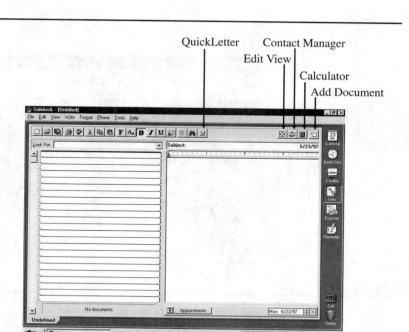

Write view

FIGURE 26-14

documents. Each document (at the right of the window) has a subject line that will be used to sort the documents, and this line is displayed in the index at the left. The date is automatically inserted to the right of the subject.

 IP: *Use the Edit View button to display the document full screen without the index.*

To type a document, use these steps:

1. Enter the subject that will be used for the index.

2. Click on the document window and type the document.

3. Use the toolbar and Format menu to format the text.

4. To start a new document, click on the Add Document button in the toolbar, or select Add Document from the Write menu.

You can also select a QuickLetter, a form document with standard text that you add information into. To select a QuickLetter, use these steps:

1. Pull down the Tools menu and click on QuickLetter to see a list of templates.

2. Click on the template and then on OK.

When the QuickLetter appears, the program will automatically change to Edit view. You can now enter information into the letter, or you can merge it from the cardfile.

Merging Letters and Cards

By merging a cardfile with a letter, you can create form documents of all types. The concept behind merging is identical to that in Corel WordPerfect; only the implementation is different.

You will notice that the templates contain codes, such as {#Name of position#}, that indicate where merge information is required. If you have a cardfile open when you select a QuickLetter, the information from the current card will automatically appear in the appropriate locations, even if you do not have a viewport open in the Write window. To merge the letter with the cardfile cards, use these steps:

1. Pull down the Tools menu and select Mail Merge to display this dialog box:

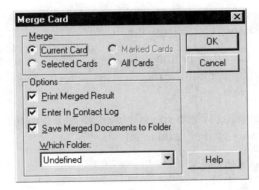

2. Select what you want to merge.

3. Choose from the options in the box.

4. Click on OK. The Print Merged Documents dialog box appears, asking if you want to include the subject.

5. Choose if you want to include the subject, and then click on OK.

6. If there are any merge codes that do not have a matching field in the cardfile, the code is highlighted in the text, and a dialog box such as this one appears.

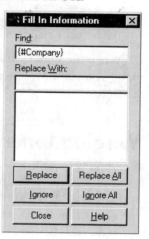

7. Type the text you want to insert in the Replace With box.

8. Select a replace or ignore option to continue the merge.

9. When all of the merge information has been added, the letters will be printed and each added to the index.

If you want to merge the letter with a specific card, or change cardfiles, then you should open the viewport and drag the card into the letter. Here's how:

1. If the Index view is not displayed, click on the Indexed View button.

2. Click on the Viewport arrow to open the viewport.

3. If Cards does not appear in the button next to the arrow, click on the button and choose Cards from the list.

4. Click on the Cardfiles button under the viewport, and select the cardfile that you want to use for the merge. The index entries for the file will appear in the viewport.

5. To merge the letter with a specific card, drag it into the letter. Drag any card if you want to merge them all.

6. Perform the merge as explained previously.

Creating Custom Merges

You do not have to use a QuickLetter to create a merge document—you can write your own document and add field codes to it. Here's how:

1. Click on Add Document to start a new document.

2. Select Create Merge Template from the Tools menu. You'll see a dialog box with a list of fields in the open cardfile.

3. Type the form letter.

4. Where you want to insert a field code, click on the field in the dialog box and then on Insert.

5. To merge the files, pull down the Tools menu and select Mail Merge.

6. Select what you want to print, select options, and then click on OK.

Using Expense View

The *Expense view,* shown in Figure 26-15, is really a special cardfile that helps you collect, track, and report expense information. Display the view by clicking on the Expense icon in the deskpad. The index on the left will list each of your expenses—the expense type, the account, amount, and date.

Before you enter receipts, however, you should customize a few Expense options. When you enter a receipt, for example, you'll be able to enter an account. Rather than type the account name into a text box, you can create and select from a Pick List. Each expense has a number of fields you have to insert. Many of these contain pick lists, such as the airline you used, the hotel you stayed in, and the gas station where you filled up. Use these steps:

1. Pull down the Expenses menu and select Receipt Setup to see the dialog box in Figure 26-16.

2. Enter the rate you want for mileage.

3. The default currency symbol is the dollar sign. You can add other characters and select them from a pick list. To do so, click in the Currency field, type the character to use, and click on Add.

26

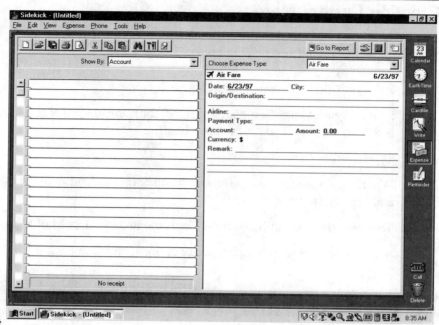

Expense
view

FIGURE 26-15

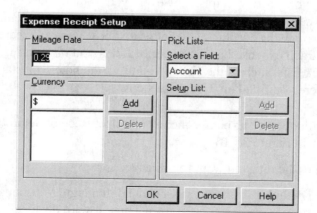

Setting up
the Expense
view

FIGURE 26-16

4. Pull down the Select a Field list and choose the field you want to add a pick list item to.

5. Type the item in the Setup List text box and click on Add.

6. Enter other pick list items for that field.

7. Repeat the process, selecting each field and adding pick list items.

8. Click on OK.

You are now ready to enter a receipt.

1. If you've already entered an expense, click on the Add Receipt button.

2. Pull down the Choose Expense Type list and choose the expense category.

3. Move from field to field—they are determined by the category—and enter information.

4. If a pick list arrow appears to the right of the item, pull down the list and select an item. You can also type an entry into the box. As you enter the information, the appropriate fields will be added to the index on the left.

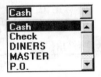

5. To insert another expense, click on the Add Receipt button. To make it easy to enter recurring expenses, the program copies the information from the current record to the new one.

 IP: *To sort the index, pull down the Show By list and select Account, Amount, Type, or Expense Date.*

Printing an Expense Report

You can print a single expense item by selecting Print Receipt from the File menu. But when you want to see or print all of your weekly expenses, click on the Go To Report button on the top of the Expense View window. Sidekick will display a weekly report, as shown in Figure 26-17. The full report also includes an explanation of business meals and entertainment, and a list and description of miscellaneous expenses. Click on the Print button, or select Print Report from the File menu to print the report.

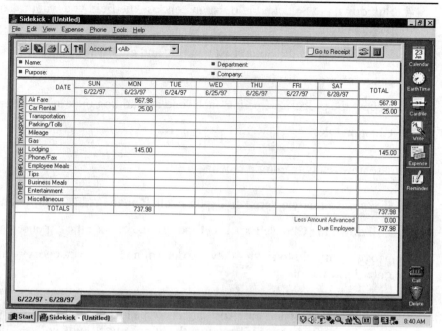

Expense
report

FIGURE 26-17

 IP: *Click on Preview to see how the report will appear when printed.*

The LaunchBar

You can create a *LaunchBar* to start Windows applications directly from Sidekick. The bar will contain icons for the applications you select—just click on the icon to run the program. Here's how to create the LaunchBar.

1. Pull down the Tools menu and select LaunchBar Setup to see the dialog box in Figure 26-18.

2. Use the File List to display the name of the application you want to add to the LaunchBar.

3. Click on the program name and then click on Add to add the program to the Your Selections list.

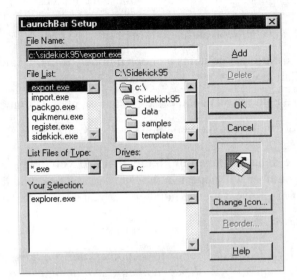

Creating a
LaunchBar

FIGURE 26-18

4. To delete a program from the LaunchBar, click on it in the Your Selections list and then click on Delete.

5. Add other desired items to the list and then click on OK.

6. If the LaunchBar does not appear on your screen, pull down the View menu and click on LaunchBar.

The LaunchBar will appear on the left side of your screen with icons for each of the applications. If you want, you can drag it to another location.

Using the Phone Dialer

Use the *phone dialer* feature to dial your telephone. You can enter the number you want to call or use a number that you've entered into a cardfile. The program can even record information about the call into your Contact Log.

 OTE: *You must have a modem installed to use the phone dialer.*

To start the phone dialer, use any of these techniques:

■ Click the Call icon at the bottom of the deskpad.

■ Drag a card that contains a phone number from the cardfile or viewport to the Call icon.

■ Drag a call or To Do entry that contains a phone number to the Call icon.

■ Pull down the Phone menu and click on Call.

The phone dialer is shown in Figure 26-19. If you dragged a phone number to the icon, the number will appear in the Number text box, and the program will dial the number. Otherwise, type the number that you want to dial and then click on the Dial button.

 OTE: *If you did not drag a number and you have an open cardfile, the phone number from the current card will appear in the dialer.*

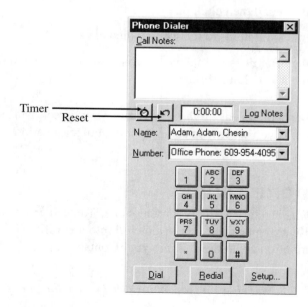

Phone
Dialer

FIGURE 26-19

IP: *If you drag a card that contains more than one number, pull down the Number list and select the one to dial.*

If there is no answer or a busy signal, click on Hangup. Use the Redial button on phone dialer to dial the last number again.

Pick up your telephone and talk. To time the call, click on the Timer button—use the Reset button to reset the timer to 0. When the call is done, click on the Timer button to stop the time, and then click on Log Notes to insert the note and time into the card. The program will insert the word "CALLED" and time and date information in the Contact Log, followed by your call notes.

IP: *Use the Setup button in the phone dialer to configure your modem.*

Reminder View

The *Reminder view* is easy to use and extremely useful. It displays a report listing the Date, Activity, Description, and Details of all appointments, To Do items, and calls. It will list the items for the current date, but you can choose to display items for tomorrow, this week, next week, this month, and next month.

Using the Contact Manager

Organizing your activities by date and type is useful, but most businesses also want to keep track of activities by client or company. It is easier to prepare invoices and review the progress of a project if you organize activities by contact. That's the job of the *contact manager.*

When you think about it, information about a contact may be spread out over the various Sidekick views. You may have appointments with an individual, several phone calls, and a To Do item regarding the project. The contact manager collects all of the information about a contact into one source.

You access the contact manager by clicking on the contact manager button on the right side of the toolbar in all Sidekick views, except EarthTime and Reminder, or from the Tools menu in all views except EarthTime.

Here is how to use it.

26

1. Click on a listing for the contact you want to see activities about. It can be in either view.

2. Pull down the Tools menu and click on Contact Manager. If you have an open cardfile, the contact information for the current card in the file will appear in the Contact Manager window, as shown in Figure 26-20.

3. Click on Search Setup to see the Search Setup dialog box.

4. Select the check boxes for the items (Appointments, Calls, To Do items, Contact Log) that you want to search.

5. Click on OK to return to the Contact Manager dialog box.

6. Pull down the Date Range list and select today, tomorrow, this week, next week, this month, and next month. A list of items for the person will appear.

7. To go to a view that contains details for the activity, click on it in the list and then click on the Go To button. The item will appear in the background, so you can move or close the contact manager to see it.

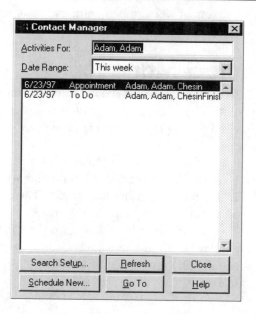

Contact
Manager

FIGURE 26-20

8. To schedule a new activity for the person, click on the Schedule New button to see a dialog box asking if you want to schedule an appointment, call, or enter a To Do item, and asking for the date. Select the item you want to schedule and then Date, and then click on OK. The appropriate dialog box will appear where you enter the details of the activity.

 OTE: *Use the Refresh option to update the list of items in the Contact Manager window.*

Printing Reports

You have already learned how to print calendars, cardfiles, and appointments using the Print command from the File menu. For even more reporting options, use the Report command from the Calendar or Cardfile views. You'll be able to generate reports with titles and headers, select the appearance of the report, create reports on contacts or free time, and summarize activities, phone calls, and the time you spend on specific tasks. The report is generated onscreen, much like the expense report, so you can then save and print it.

The Report menu offers these options: Cardfile, Calendar, Free Time, To Do List, Contact Log, and Open Report. The dialog box that appears when you select an option is determined by the report type. The Free Time report, by the way, will list all time periods in a select range of dates, marking scheduled periods with an X character. Blocks of time with the X are free.

 AUTION: *You can only have one report open at a time. If you do not save a report, a dialog box will appear, asking if you want to save it when you start a second report.*

Once the report is generated and displayed, save or print it using the options in the File menu. To change views, just click on the icon of the view in the deskpad. Return to the report by selecting Go To Current Report from the Reports menu.

You can also customize its appearance, and even save the settings as a report style that you can later recall. A report appears like a worksheet, with column headings and row numbers. To customize the report, pull down the Layout menu and choose from these options:

■ *Choose Report Style* lets you retrieve a style that you have saved.

- *Save Report Style* lets you save the current style.

- *Update Current* updates the current style to reflect changes that you've made to the report.

- *Font* lets you select the font, size, and style of text.

- *Header* lets you enter a report title and subtitle.

- *Change Column Width* lets you change the width of individual columns, to fit the longest entry in the column, or change the widths of every column to the same amount.

- *Hide Row Title* removes the row numbers.

- *Hide Column Title* removes the column headings.

Using Dashboard 95

27

If Sidekick 95 can be compared to your desktop, Dashboard 95 is like the dashboard of your car. Your car's dashboard contains all of the gauges and controls that you need to operate your car. Dashboard 95 does the same for your computer.

Dashboard is designed to replace the functionality of the Windows 95 Start menu. In one graphic interface, you can access all of your programs, organized both by the group in which they belong and by their type of function. If you have a money management program such as Quicken or Microsoft Money installed on your computer, for example, you can access it in Dashboard from either the group it was originally installed under or from a new area, called a *panel,* labeled Finance. Likewise, you can access Corel WordPerfect and other word processing programs from a panel called *Publishing,* and all of your online services in a panel called *Internet.*

You can even save the overall layout of Windows 95—the arrangement of windows and open applications—and then recall the same layout at any time with the click of a mouse.

 OTE: *Dashboard offers extensive capabilities. Use the Corel Reference Center to learn more about them.*

Starting Dashboard

Dashboard, like Sidekick, is not installed automatically with the other Corel WordPerfect Suite CD applications. To install it, click on the Bonus Applications button in the Corel opening window, and then follow the instructions on the screen.

To start Dashboard, use these steps:

1. Click on the Start button in the taskbar.

2. Point to Corel WordPerfect Suite 7.

3. Point to Accessories, and then click on Dashboard 95.

Dashboard may take a few minutes to organize all of your programs and other files into categories, and collect some information about your computer system. Then the Dashboard window appears.

CAUTION: *Windows 95 does not require program extensions with shortcuts on the desktop, but Dashboard 95 does. If Dashboard will not start on your system, check the properties for all of the shortcuts on the desktop. Shortcuts without extensions may be preventing the program from starting.*

The exact contents of everyone's Dashboard screen will appear different because it is determined by the programs that you have installed on your computer. One typical Dashboard window is shown in Figure 27-1. Your own Dashboard will look similar, although the number and names on the tabs on the top and bottom of the window and some items inside the window will differ. Still, it is easy to get around Dashboard once you learn how it is organized and understand that virtually everything in Dashboard can be customized.

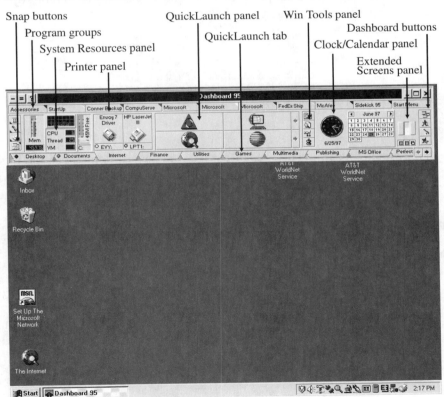

Sample
Dashboard
95 window

FIGURE 27-1

Program Group Tabs

The tabs on top of the window correspond to the groups you have installed on Windows 95 and Windows 3.1. To access a program by its group, just click on the group tab. A drop-down menu appears, listing the programs in the group—click on the program you want to run.

If your system has more groups than can be displayed, there will be Left and Right Arrow icons on the right side of the tabs. Click on the arrows to scroll additional groups into view.

 IP: *Whenever you see the arrows in Dashboard, it means that there are more options that you can choose. Click on the arrows to display them.*

The small colored triangle at the top right of each tab is a color key. You can assign each a color to categorize groups:

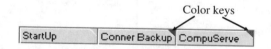

Panels

In the window itself are a series of buttons and panels. Remember, the Dashboard in Figure 27-1 will serve as an example, and the content and position of the panels may be different on your screen.

 **OTE:**   *You will learn later how to add two more panels: Corel WordPerfect Suite and Games.*

QuickLaunch Panel

The tabs on the bottom of the window are called the *QuickLaunch tabs* because they determine what appears in the QuickLaunch panel. Each tab represents a category of programs installed on your computer:

The first two tabs—Desktop and Documents—are added by Dashboard on all systems, and they are called *system panels*. You will learn later how to add a third system panel called *Layouts*. The other tabs will be determined by the software you have installed.

When you click on a tab, icons for the programs in the category are shown in the QuickLaunch Panel. To run a program, click on the icon.

 IP: *You can change the size of the QuickLaunch and Printers panels by holding down the SHIFT key and pointing to the border of the panel so the mouse appears as a two-directional arrow, and then dragging.*

Printers Panel

This panel displays each of the printers installed on your system. Below each icon is a Radio button with the port or driver used by the printer. The button on the current default printer is selected.

Click on a Radio button to change printers. Point to a printer for a list of current print jobs. Click on a printer to set its properties.

 IP: *To print a document, click on the Documents QuickLaunch tab and drag the icon of the document to the printer icon.*

The Win Tools Panel

This panel is a series of buttons to access Windows 95 features. The panel in the figure includes the following:

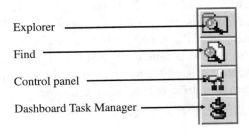

Explorer

Find

Control panel

Dashboard Task Manager

27

Click on the tool for the feature you want to run. The Dashboard Task Manager, by the way, displays a list of all open and minimized applications, along with buttons to arrange windows on the screen, as well as to switch to or close applications.

Clock/Calendar Panel

This panel shows a running clock and monthly calendar. The current date is in color. Use the arrows above the calendar, on either side of the month, to change the month that is displayed.

You can change the way they are displayed and set alarms.

Extended Screens Panel

You can use this very powerful panel to indicate all running programs, arrange windows on the screen, and create layouts. You'll learn about these features later.

System Resources Panel

This is the System Resources panel:

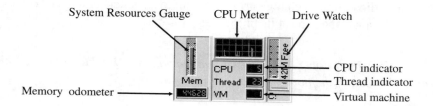

The Memory Odometer shows you in kilobytes how much free memory you have, and the System Resources Gauge graphically illustrates the current use of the system resources that Windows sets aside for its own operation, including user and Graphic Device Interface (GDI) memory.

The CPU Meter graphically shows how much of your computer's resources are being used. Like an EKG of the heart, the meter shows a plot of the CPU usage. The higher the green area, the more your CPU is being used. If you have no programs running and are not using the mouse, you should see just a thin green line moving across the meter. Rolling the mouse around the screen will add some small "blips" to the meter—starting a program will drive the meter up the scale.

Below the meter are three indicators of your system usage.

■ The *CPU indicator* shows how busy your system is, and it will correspond to the meter. The higher the number, the more resources your CPU is using.

■ The *Thread indicator* shows the number of concurrent execution threads, or simultaneous activities, that are operating.

■ The *VM indicator* shows the number of "virtual machines" that are running. Your Windows 95 system is one virtual machine; each DOS window that you open will be another.

The Drive Watch shows you how much space is available on your disk drives.

Dashboard Buttons

There are two other sets of buttons in addition to those in the Win Tools panel.

Snap Buttons

The buttons along the left side of the screen are the Snap buttons. Use these to turn a tab or panel off and on, or to convert the tabs or panels into a separate window:

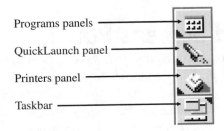

Programs panels

QuickLaunch panel

Printers panel

Taskbar

Clicking on the Snap Programs button, for example, will remove the program group tabs and display them in a window as shown here:

To restore the tabs, click on the Snap Programs button again.

The Dashboard taskbar works about the same as the Windows 95 taskbar. To display the bar, click on the Snap Taskbar button.

 **IP:** *Right-click the panel and choose Snap On or Snap Off from the Shortcut menu.*

Dashboard Buttons

Buttons on the right perform Dashboard tasks:

 ■ *Layouts* lets you save and manage arrangements of windows in the Extended Screens panel.

 ■ *Dashboard Run* displays a dialog box from which you can perform DOS commands and start programs.

 ■ *Customize* displays a dialog box from which you can customize most features of Dashboard.

 ■ *About Dashboard 95* tells you how to contact Starfish Software, the distributor of Dashboard and Sidekick, and shows a nice photograph of the Starfish development team.

Using the Extended Screens Panel

The Extended Screens panel contains miniature views of your entire monitor. Each view can display one or more program windows in their relative position on the screen. By adding programs to extended screens, you can switch back and forth between them, and you can see at a glance their arrangement. If you move a window in the extended screen, the actual program window moves as well.

When you first start Dashboard, the Extended Screen panel is in "compact size" so the miniature screens are minimized. The three gray bars in the panel represent three screens, and the buttons under the bars let you change the arrangement of windows:

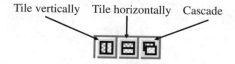

If you open an application, it will be assigned to the extended screen in the center. If you switch to Dashboard, you can then minimize the program by clicking on one of the other bars. Each program you open is added to that same screen. Clicking on another extended screen bar minimizes all of the currently open applications. Clicking on the bar for the extended screen containing the applications redisplays them all.

You can also open programs into other extended screens. By default, Dashboard starts with three but you can change that number. When you open a program into another extended screen, it's like having a second or a third monitor connected to your computer.

For example, you can open Corel WordPerfect and the Windows Paint accessory in one extended screen, Corel Quattro Pro and the Calculator in another, and some other combination of programs in the third. Clicking on an Extended Screen button will then display the programs in that screen, keeping the others minimized.

You can then save the layout of each screen, so you can quickly open the same combination of programs, and place them in the same window arrangement.

In order to open programs into an extended screen, you have to display the screens full size.

1. Right-click on the Extended Screen panel.

2. Click on Full Size in the QuickMenu.

Full-size extended screens appear like this:

 IP: *Choose Compact Size from the QuickMenu to display each screen as a button.*

To open a program into an extended screen, drag its icon from the QuickLaunch panel or a group listing to the extended screen. The program will open. If you moved the program into a screen that is not selected, it will open but not appear because it is not on the "monitor" that is being displayed. The relative size and position of the program window will then appear in the extended screen. For example, look at the following layout:

27

The Paint program is open on the first extended screen in the upper right corner. Corel WordPerfect is in the second screen. Corel Quattro Pro and Calculator are open on the third screen, with their windows arranged as shown.

The miniature representations of program windows in the extended screens are called *miniwindows*. If you move a miniwindow in the extended screens, the program that it represents will also move on the full screen. If you move or change the size of a program on the full screen, its miniwindow moves and resizes as well. The miniwindows of programs not selected will appear dimmed in the Extended Screen window.

  OTE: *You can drag a miniwindow from one extended screen to another.*

To display the programs in a screen, click on the button below the screen. This will display the programs—at least those in the foreground—but not switch to them. For example, clicking on the third extended screen in our illustration would result in the screen shown in Figure 27-2. Click on the program window to use it—it will then appear bright in the Extended Screen window if Dashboard is still in the foreground.

You can display and switch to a program by double-clicking on its window in the extended screen. Double-click on a background in the screen to switch to the window but not the program.

Saving and Using Layouts

When you save a layout, you are saving the arrangement of the open programs in the extended screens. Once you arrange a group of programs just the way you want to work with them, you can save their layout so you can automatically open the windows in the same arrangement at some later time.

To save the layout, use these steps:

1. Click on the Layout button in the Dashboard tools panel.

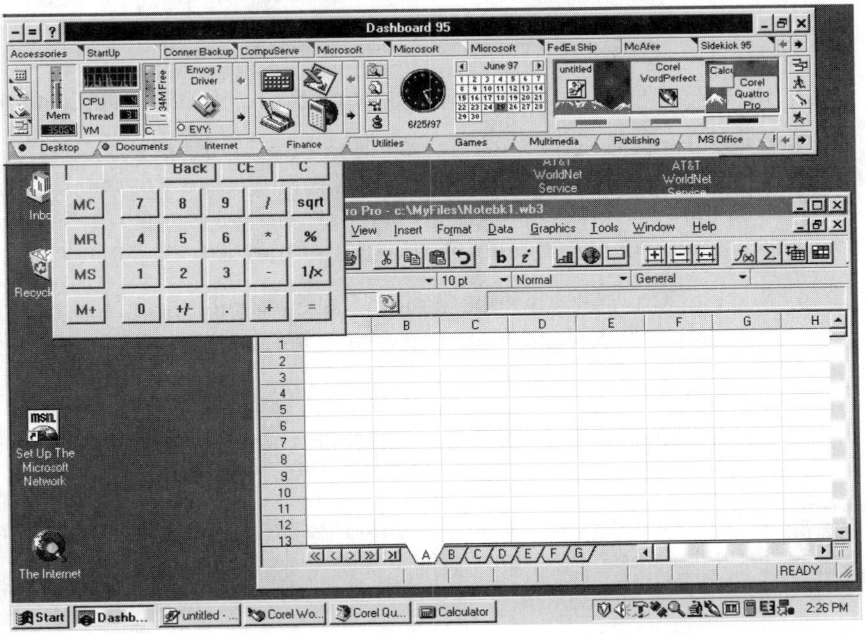

An extended screen with programs in the background

FIGURE 27-2

2. Select Save Layout to see the Save Layout dialog box. The dialog box will contain a list of all of the open and minimized programs.

3. Type a name for the layout.

4. To load the layout automatically when you start Dashboard, select the Load layout on startup check box. To prevent Dashboard from loading the layout, hold down the SHIFT key while Dashboard starts up.

5. To not include a program in the layout, click on it in the list and then click on the Delete button. This only removes the program from the layout; it does not close it.

Dashboard will save the name and position of application windows, but not the names of documents within the programs. You may want to include the documents with the layout, however, so the same documents, worksheets, or other files open

27

when you recall the layout. To do this, you need to edit the application item from the Save Layout dialog box. Here's how.

1. In the Save Layout dialog box, click on the name of the application.

2. Click on the Edit button to see the Edit Layout dialog box.

3. Click on the Parameters text box.

4. Type the path and name of the document file.

5. You can also pull down the Window Size list and select Normal (the current window size), Maximized, or Minimized.

6. Click on OK.

7. Finally, click on OK in the Save Layout dialog box to save the layout.

 IP: *In some cases, you can add a parameter, file, or startup macro after the name of the program in the Command Line text box.*

Opening a Layout

To open a layout, click on the Layout button. A list of your saved layouts appears, along with the choice Sample, which contains Calculator, MS Paint, and WordPad. Click on the layout that you want to open.

Managing Layouts

After you have created layouts, you can delete or edit them as necessary. Just follow these steps:

1. Click on the Layout button.

2. Click on Manage Layouts to see the dialog box in Figure 27-3.

3. To see the programs in the layout, click on the name in the Layout list.

4. Use the buttons in the Layout section to delete and rename a layout. Use the Icon button to select the icon that appears when you add the layouts to the QuickLaunch panel.

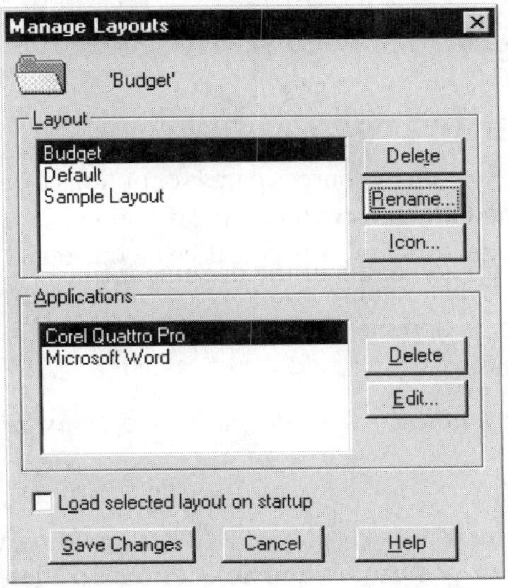

Manage Layouts

'Budget'

Layout

Budget
Default
Sample Layout

Delete
Rename...
Icon...

Applications

Corel Quattro Pro
Microsoft Word

Delete
Edit...

☐ Load selected layout on startup

Save Changes   Cancel   Help

Managing
layouts

FIGURE 27-3

5. Use the buttons in the Applications section to delete and edit applications within the layout.

6. Use the Load Selected Layout On Startup button to assign the default layout used when you start Dashboard.

7. Click on Save Changes to record your changes to the layout.

Using Dashboard QuickMenus

You can change almost everything about the dashboard window using either the QuickMenus or a Customize dialog box.

When you right-click on a part of Dashboard, for example, a QuickMenu appears with options for that section. All of the QuickMenus have the Customize option that lets you display a dialog box for making extensive changes to Dashboard and its panels. The other options on the menu depend on the objects. For example, the Printers Panel QuickMenu lets you hide or set up a printer, or snap off the panel. The QuickLaunch Panel QuickMenu lets you snap off the panel or remove the button that you clicked on.

27

Some of the other QuickMenus have more extensive options, so a review of them is in order now.

System Resources

Right-click on the System Resources panel for options to hide the memory odometer, the gauge, all of the CPU information, and drive watch. Once you hide an item, the menu options changes to Show. You can also select Details, which displays the dialog box in Figure 27-4. This dialog box gives detailed information on the system and lets you change some options.

 OTE: *Double-click on the panel to display the details.*

The system information displayed is determined by the part of the panel you clicked on; however, you can use the Select Item To View list to display details for the five system areas listed. Each of the areas gives information and options, as follows:

■ The *Memory Resources* section reports on the amount of memory, and lets you choose when to sound a low-memory alarm and whether to display the odometer, gauges, and CPU indicators. You can also select the shape of the memory gauge—the options are bar, fuel gauge, and resources with bars for types of memory.

■ The *System Environment* section lists information about our computer system, such as the type of processor, display, and output devices.

■ The *Drive Usage* section lists all of your drives and their specifications. You can use the dialog box to add or remove drives displayed in the Drive Watch window. To add a floppy disk, for example, click on the A: item in the window, and then click on the Add button on the Drive Watch window. The Drive Watch window is updated periodically to display current information on the drives. Use the Update Interval setting to determine the number of seconds between updates.

■ *Environmental Variables* lists DOS environment variables that your system is using.

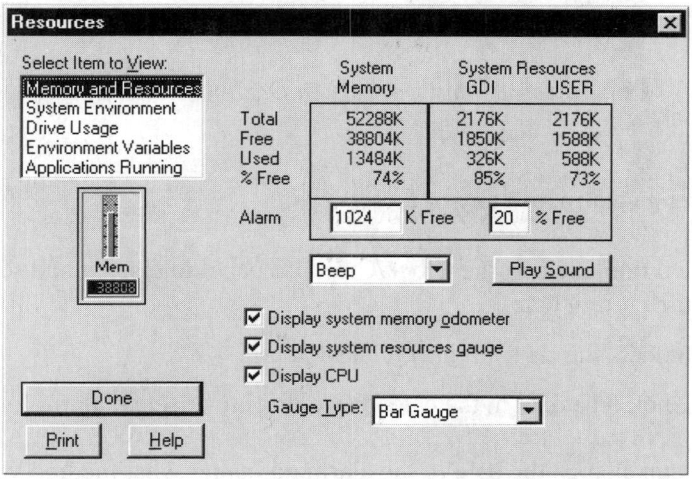

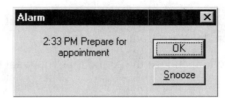

Details of
system
resources

FIGURE 27-4

■ *Applications Running* shows the names of all running programs and their
memory size.

Clock/Calendar Panel

Right-click on the Clock/Calendar panel to set an alarm, choose the type of clock,
hide or show various parts of the panel, and set the date and time.

You set an alarm in Sidekick to remind you of a scheduled appointment.
Dashboard alarms are similar, but you can also use them to launch an application or
set a recurring alarm. When the alarm goes off, a sound plays and this dialog box
appears:

27

Click on the Snooze button to clear the dialog box but have it repeat in a few minutes.

 OTE: *Alarms only work when Dashboard is running.*

To set an alarm, use any of these steps:

■ Double-click on the Clock/Calendar panel to display and set alarms for the current date.

■ Select Alarms from the QuickMenu.

■ Click on a date in the calendar to display or set an alarm for that date.

You can change the date of the alarm no matter what method you use to start. The program will display the Clock Alarms dialog box. The box will list any alarms already set for the current date or the date you clicked on in the calendar. Use the choices in the Options section to disable the alarms, or to change the snooze setting.

 OTE: *Use the Edit or Delete buttons to change or delete alarms already set.*

1. To set an alarm, click on the Add button to see the dialog box in Figure 27-5.

2. In the Alarm Text box, type the message that you want to appear when the alarm sounds.

3. Specify the time to sound the alarm.

4. In the Alarm Date section, choose to have the alarm repeat every day or a specific day of the week, or set the date for the alarm.

5. In the Application section, enter the path and name of a program that you want to run when the alarm sounds.

6. In the Chime section, choose the sound that you want to play when the alarm goes off.

7. Click on OK.

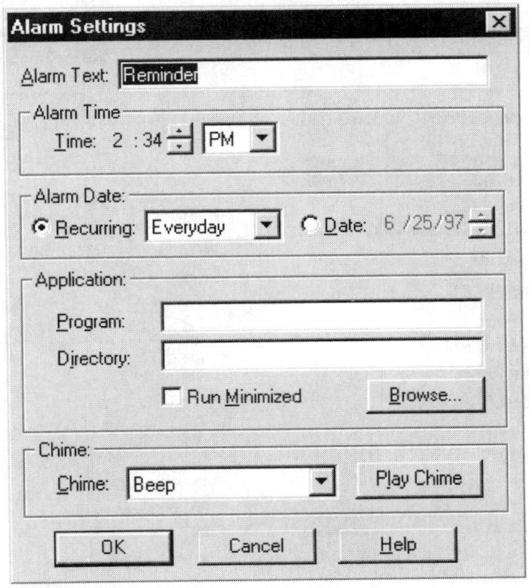

Specifying
an alarm

FIGURE 27-5

Dates with an alarm set will appear in a color other than that used for the current date.

Customizing Dashboard

The Customize button, and the Customize option on the QuickMenus, let you make more extensive changes to Dashboard through a dialog box.

The options that appear in the Customize dialog box depend on how you displayed it, but you can access all of the customization options from within the box at any time. Figure 27-6 shows the dialog box as it appears when you click on the Customize button. The list on the left contains the items that you can customize—Dashboard itself, the program groups, and the panels. When you select an item from the list, one or more tabs appear in the section to the right. Click on the tab for the options that you want to change, and then make your choices.

IP: *To change the position of a panel, drag it within the list.*

27

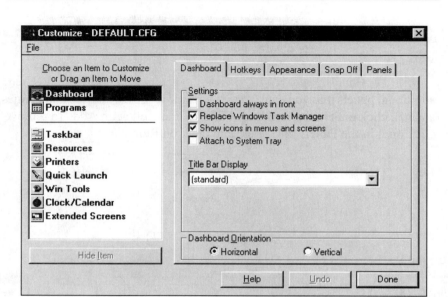

FIGURE 27-6

Dashboard

You use the Dashboard page to customize the look and operation of Dashboard itself. The section has five pages, as follows.

The *Dashboard page* lets you keep the program in the foreground, replace the Windows Task Manager, show icons in menus and screens, or appear next to the date in the taskbar (called the *system tray*) when minimized. You can also choose to display the time and date, or the amount of free memory and disk space in the Dashboard title bar, and to display Dashboard horizontally or vertically.

The *Hotkeys page* assigns key combinations to Dashboard, the Windows 95 Explorer, and for the Dashboard Run dialog box. You can also assign a mouse hotkey to activate Dashboard—a combination of the ALT, SHIFT, or CTRL keys and a mouse button.

Use the *Appearance page* to set the font, style, and size of text in the Dashboard window, and to select a color scheme. Click on the Reset Defaults button to return to the default settings.

Use the *Snap Off page* to snap on or off panels as you can with the Snap buttons, and to control the action of snapped panels:

- *Panels minimize with Dashboard* will minimize snapped-off panels when you minimize Dashboard.

- *Enable ToolTips* displays the ToolTip when you point to an object.

Use the *Panels page* to add or remove panels from Dashboard. There are two additional panels that you can add to the window—Corel Office and Games. To add a panel, click on it in the Available Panels list and click on Add. To remove a panel, click on it in the Panels in Use list and click on Remove.

 IP: *If a panel does not appear, there is not enough room for it. Remove another panel.*

The Corel Office panel includes a button for Corel WordPerfect Office applications. It is not displayed by default because the same options are available from the DAD bar.

The Games Panel offers three games to help relieve stress or just for fun. By default, the slot machine appears:

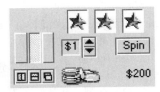

Click on the Spin button to spin the wheels, and on the Bet button to place your bet. Dashboard keeps track of your winnings.

Right-click on the panel to choose the Poker game or a slide puzzle. Once you add the Games panel, you can select it in the Customize dialog box. You can then customize each of the three games.

Programs

There are two pages of options for the Programs panel—Program Groups and Options.

Use the Programs Group page, shown in Figure 27-7, to add, delete, change the order, hide, or open a group. For example, to change the order of a group, drag its name to another position in the list. The Modify option on the page lets you assign

27

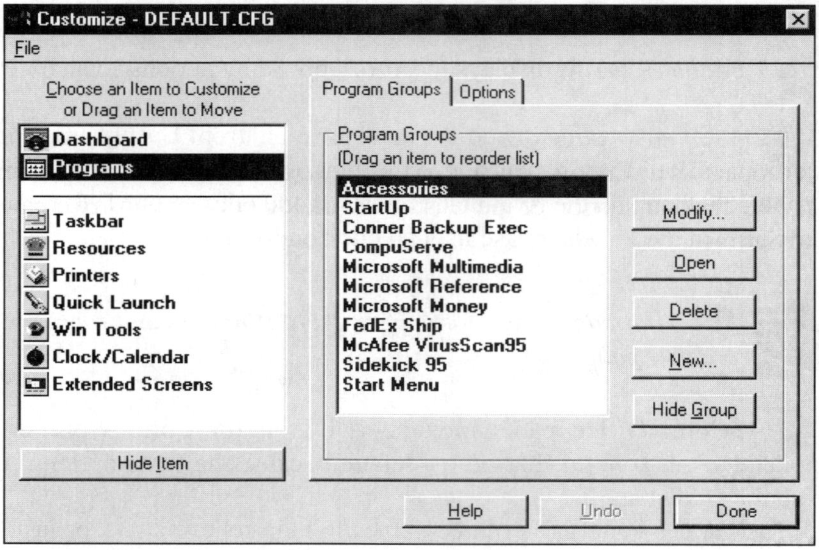

Working
with groups

FIGURE 27-7

a color key to each group. The color keys appear as triangular notches on the upper-right of the tab, and can be used to categorize groups.

Use the Options page of the dialog box to select these options:

- *Tall Buttons* displays two lines of text on each tab. Use this if the tab does not show the entire group name.

- *Show Color Keys* turns the color keys on the tabs off or on.

- *Sort Alphabetically* places the tabs in alphabetical order.

- *Sort by Color* groups the tabs by their color keys.

- *Reread Groups from System* updates the tabs to changes in your Windows 95 setup.

The Taskbar

The Dashboard taskbar is similar to the Windows 95 taskbar, but it appears at the bottom of the Dashboard window:

To display the taskbar, click on the Snap Taskbar button. By default, the taskbar is floating. So if you click on the Snap Taskbar button when the bar is displayed, it will appear as a window that you can move to any position on the screen.

The Taskbar section of the Customize dialog box contains two pages: Taskbar and Settings.

Use the Position page to control if and where the bar is displayed. You can choose the Floating option, or to have it snap to the top, bottom, left, or right edge of the screen. You can also choose to hide the taskbar until you move the mouse pointer over it, or to always keep the taskbar in front of other windows.

The Settings page has two options: Button Style and Button Options. In the Button Style section, choose whether you want to display the names of the programs and open files in the bar. In the Button Options section, you can select Hide Iconized Applications to display minimized applications, and Show Icons in Buttons.

Resources Options

The Resources part of the dialog box offers the Memory and Drive Watch options that you can change in the Resources Details dialog box. It contains two pages:

- The *Memory page* displays your system's memory usage and lets you change the alarm and beep sound, and the appearance of the odometer and gauge.

- The *Drives page* lets you setup the Drive Watch section of the panel.

Printers

The Printers section also has two pages:

- Use the *Printers page* to hide a printer in the panel, change the order, set the default printers, change its icon, or give it a descriptive name.

- The *Options page* lets you select to show the paper orientation in the panel.

27

Clock/Calendars

The Clock/Calendar section has three pages:

- Use the *Clock page* to select an analog or digital clock, to change the face and color of the clock, and to show a second hand on the analog clock.

- Use the *Calendar page* to turn the calendar on or off, to set the colors used to show the current day and days with alarms, or to change your computer's time and date.

- Use the *Alarms page* to set and work with alarms.

Win Tools

The Win Tools page lets you choose what Windows 95 functions to assign to each of the four tool buttons. For each button you want to change, pull down the list shown with the tool number and select a function.

Extended Screens

The Extended Screens section has three pages:

- *Screens* sets the number and appearance of the extended screens.

- *Hotkeys* sets keystroke combinations to use when switching between extended screens without displaying Dashboard.

- *Sticky Apps* assigns an application to every extended screen.

On the Screens page, for example, you can select the number of screens to display (three, five, seven, or nine), the size of the screens (full or compact), and the background graphic.

The Hotkeys page displays text boxes labeled 1 through 9. Click on the box for the screen you want to assign a hotkey, and then press the key combination.

If you have a program that you want to appear on all of the extended screens, assign it as a Sticky App. This is perfect for utility programs, such as the calculator, that you use all of the time. To create a Sticky App, use these steps:

1. Open the program before displaying the Customize menu.

2. Click on the Customize button.

3. Click on the Extended Screens option, and on the Sticky Apps tab.

4. Click on Add to see a list of open applications.

5. Click on the application you want to make a Sticky App and then on OK.

QuickLaunch

The Customize dialog box for the QuickLaunch panel has four pages: Applications, Groups, Launch Bar, and Options.

Use the *Applications page,* shown in Figure 27-8, to add, delete, change the order of programs in a panel, edit the application's settings, and assign it a hotkey. To select a program to edit or delete, click on the group name in the Groups panel, and then click on the program name on the Applications panel. Click on the Delete button to

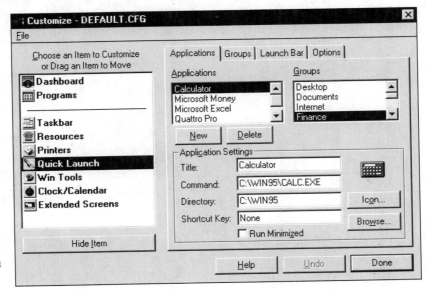

Setting
QuickLaunch
applications

FIGURE 27-8

remove the application from the panel, or change its specifications for the Application Settings section. To add a new application, click on the New button. An item called "untitled" will appear in the Applications list and on the Title box of the Applications Settings. Enter the program's name and other specifications and then click on Done.

The *Groups page* lets you add and delete groups, and to hide or display the Desktop Tab, Documents Tab, and Layouts Tab. Select to show the Layouts Tab if you've created Extended Screen layouts and want to access them from the QuickLaunch panel.

The *Launch Bar page* lets you select the position of the launch bar. The options will be dimmed if the Launch Bar is not already displayed.

The *Options page* lets you select the type of buttons in the QuickLaunch panel.

- *Button Style* lets you choose labeled, unlabeled, or mini buttons.

- *Sort Groups* lets you sort the QuickLaunch groups alphabetically or by personal preference with the most recently used groups at the start of the list following Desktop, Documents, and Layouts.

- *Re-Synchronize* updates the Desktop, Documents, and Layouts groups to reflect any changes to your system.

NOTE: *Italic* page numbers refer to graphs, charts, or illustrations.

INDEX

F

merging to form documents, 327-328

logical conditions, searching databases, 531-532

M

macro commands (Corel Quattro Pro), 562-568
    Branch, 564
    FOR, 566-567
    GETLABEL, 567-568
    If, 565-566
    PUTBLOCK, 563-564
    PUTCELL, 562-563
    repeating, 566-567

Macro Library tab, Corel Quattro Pro Notebook properties, 463

Macro tab, Corel Quattro Pro Application properties, 464

macros (Corel Quattro Pro), 550-568
    assigning to buttons, 556-557
    assigning to keystrokes, 556
    autoload files, 558
    Branch command, 564
    commands, 562-568
    copying commands, 561-562
    cut and paste commands, 559-560
    defined, 550
    dialog box commands, 559
    Help system for commands, *560*
    If command, 565-566
    interactive, 567-568
    language, 558-559
    libraries, 555-556
    linear, 564
    linking to URLs, 557
    naming, 554
    recording, 551-552
    relative and absolute addresses, 553-554
    repeating commands, 566-567
    running, 555
    running automatically, 558
    startup, 558
    subroutines, 564
    writing, 559-561

macros (Corel WordPerfect), 304-309
    assigning to menus, toolbars, and Power Bar, 307
    Command Inserter, 308-309
    defined, 304
    editing, 307-308
    Options button, 309
    PerfectScript, 21-23
    playing, 306-307

recording, 306
saving in templates, 305-306
saving to disk, 305

magnification
    Corel Quattro Pro, 408, *409*
    Corel WordPerfect, 110

mail. *See* e-mail

Make It Fit dialog box, Corel WordPerfect, *238*

managing files. *See* file management

maps, 394-395, 506-510
    backgrounds, 510
    EarthTime (Sidekick 95), 716-718
    floating, 507-508
    objects and, 510-513
    Objects page, 397, 516-517
    overlays, 509
    Template Advisor, *511*
    zooming, 510

margin settings, printing worksheets, 480-481

margins
    aligning text between, 158-160
    indenting text with, 217
    page formats, 216-218
    tabs (Corel WordPerfect), 162-167

Mark Records option, merging form documents, 330-331

Master Backgrounds, Corel Presentations, 605

Master Slides, slide shows, 520-521

Match menu, finding and replacing text, 127

mathematics
    See also formulas
    Equation Editor, 367-370

measurements
    Document page, 289-290
    page format, 216

Media Clip option, multimedia documents, 382

Memory Odometer, Dashboard 95, 744

memos, CorelFLOW 7, 700-701

menu bars
    Corel Quattro Pro charts, 498-499
    Corel WordPerfect, 303

Menu section, environment preferences, 294

menus
    assigning macros to, 307
    QuickMenus. *See* QuickMenus

Merge Codes buttons, form documents, 331

Merge dialog box, form documents, *314*

Merge feature bar button functions, form letters, 320

merge files, form documents, 318

Merge page, display preferences, 293

merge records, selecting, 328-331

Merge window, form documents, *317*

merging
    Assign command, 333-334
    calculations and, 332-333
    form documents, 323
    form documents to labels, 326-327
    interactive form document, 332
    letters and cards with Write view (Sidekick 95), 727-729
    lists to form documents, 327-328

messages
    e-mail. *See* e-mail
    newsgroup, 80-81

Metafile options, Windows, 297

mirror imaging, graphics, 350

mistakes, Undo/Redo commands, 102-104

Model Copy, absolute references (Corel Quattro Pro), 450-451

modems, QuickConnect, 11-13

mouse
    building tables with, 250-252
    selecting text with, 100-102

Move Block command, 445-446

moving
    cells in tables, 254-255
    data in worksheets, 442-447
    files, 38
    formulas, 447-449
    graphic images, 349
    tab stops, 165
    text, 114-117
    text between documents, 135
    toolbars (Corel WordPerfect), 111-112

multimedia documents, 380-382
    Media Clip option, 382
    sound clips, 380-382

multiple documents and windows, Corel WordPerfect, 133-135

N

Name tab, Page properties, 461

named blocks. *See* block names

named group settings, saving, 482

naming macros, Corel Quattro Pro, 554

navigating the Internet, defined, 62

Netscape Navigator, 60-64

S

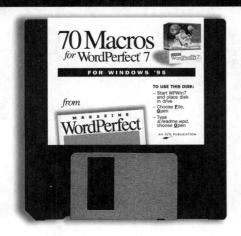